FILM, THEORY AND PHILOSOPHY

FILM, THEORY AND PHILOSOPHY
The key thinkers

Edited by Felicity Colman

ACUMEN

For Nia, who loves *Jaws*

First published in 2009 by Acumen

Acumen Publishing Limited
4 Saddler Street
Durham
DH1 3NP
www.acumenpublishing.co.uk

ISBN: 978-1-84465-184-9 (hardcover)
ISBN: 978-1-84465-185-6 (paperback)

British Library Cataloguing-in-Publication Data
A catalogue record for this book is available from the British Library.

Typeset in Warnock Pro.
Printed and bound in the UK by MPG Books Group.

CONTENTS

III CINEMATIC NATURE

CONTRIBUTORS

Zsuzsa Baross is Associate Professor of Cultural Studies at Trent University, Canada. She is the author of *The Scandal of Disease in Theory and Discourse* (1989), a series of essays entitled "The Ethics of Writing after Bosnia" in the journal *International Studies on Philosophy* and a forthcoming book on the lure of the image.

Fred Botting is Professor in the Department of Media, Film and Cultural Studies at Lancaster University. He is the author of *Gothic* (1996) and *Sex, Machines and Navels* (1999), and co-author with Scott Wilson of *The Tarantinian Ethics* (2001) and *Bataille* (2001).

Louise Burchill is Assistant Professor in Global Communications at the American University of Paris. She is the author of journal articles on Deleuze, Derrida and contemporary French philosophy. She is the translator of Alain Badiou's *Deleuze: The Clamor of Being* (2000), for which she wrote the preface.

Rex Butler is Senior Lecturer in the School of English, Media Studies and Art History at the University of Queensland. He is the author of *An Uncertain Smile* (1996), *Jean Baudrillard: Defence of the Real* (1999), *Slavoj Žižek: Live Theory* (2005) and *A Secret History of Australian Art* (2002).

Claire Colebrook is Professor of English at Pennsylvania State University. Her books include *Gilles Deleuze* (2001), *Irony: The New Critical Idiom* (2003), *Deleuze: A Guide for the Perplexed* (2006) and *Milton, Evil and Literary History* (2008).

Felicity Colman is Senior Lecturer in Film and Media Studies at Manchester Metropolitan University. She is the co-editor of a special issue of *Angelaki: Journal of the Theoretical Humanities* on creativity and philosophy (April 2006), co-editor of *Sensorium: Aesthetics, Art, Life* (2007) and author of *Deleuze and Film* (2010) and *Contemporary Film Theory* (2010).

Tom Conley is Abbott Lawrence Lowell Professor of Romance Languages and Literatures and of Visual and Environmental Studies at Harvard University. He is the author of many books, including *Cartographic Cinema* (2006) and *Film Hieroglyphs: Ruptures in Classical Cinema* (1991).

Catherine Constable is Senior Lecturer in Film Studies at the University of Warwick. She is the author of *Thinking In Images: Film Theory, Feminist Philosophy and Marlene Dietrich* (2006).

Sarah Cooper is Reader in Film Studies at King's College London. She is the author of *Selfless Cinema? Ethics and French Documentary* (2006) and *Relating to Queer Theory: Rereading Sexual Self-Definition with Irigaray, Kristeva, Wittig, and Cixous* (2000).

Sudeep Dasgupta is Senior Lecturer in Media Studies at the University of Amsterdam. He has published a critical introduction to the Dutch translation of Jacques Rancière's *L'Inconscient ésthetique* and *Partage du sensible*, and is the editor of *Constellations of the Transnational: Modernity, Culture, Critique* (2007). He has published on visual culture, postcolonial studies and globalization.

Garin Dowd is Professor of Critical Theory and Film Studies at the London College of Music and Media, Thames Valley University. He is the author of *Abstract Machines: Samuel Beckett and Philosophy after Deleuze and Guattari* (2006) and co-author with Fergus Daly of *Leos Carax* (2003).

Scott Durham is Associate Professor of French at Northwestern University. He is the author of *Phantom Communities: The Simulacrum and the Limits of Postmodernism* (1998) and the editor of a *Yale French Studies* special issue on Jean Genet.

Helen A. Fielding is Associate Professor of Philosophy and Women's Studies at the University of Western Ontario. She is the co-editor with Gabrielle Hiltmann, Dorothea Olkowski and Anne Reichhold of *The Other: Feminist Reflections in Ethics* (2007), and co-editor with Mauro Carbone of *Chiasmi International: Trilingual Studies Concerning Merleau-Ponty's Thought*, "Vie et Individuation", v.7 (2005).

Colin Gardner is Professor of Critical Theory in the Department of Art at the University of California, Santa Barbara. He is the author of a critical study of the black-listed American film director *Joseph Losey* (2004), and a monograph on the Czech-born British film-maker and critic *Karel Reisz* (2006). He is currently researching a book on Deleuze's reading of Samuel Beckett's work for television.

Gary Genosko is Canada Research Chair in Technoculture at Lakehead University, Canada. He is the author and editor of many books, including *Marshall McLuhan: Critical Evaluation in Cultural Theory* (3 vols, 2005), *The Party Without Bosses: Lessons on Anti-Capitalism from Félix Guattari and Lula da Silva* (2003), *Félix Guattari: An Aberrant Introduction* (2002) and *The Uncollected Baudrillard* (2001).

Michael Goddard is a Lecturer in the School of Media, Music and Performance at the University of Salford. His books include *Gombrowicz, Deleuze and the Subversion of Form* (2009) and *Images without Frontiers: The Cinema of Raul Ruiz* (2008).

Julie Kuhlken is Assistant Professor of Philosophy at Misericordia University, Dallas, Pennsylvania. She has published numerous articles on the relation between philosophy and art, and the philosophy of Adorno.

Patricia MacCormack is Reader in English, Communication, Film and Media at Anglia Ruskin University, Cambridge. She has published numerous chapters and articles on viceral horror, body modification, post-human ethics, teratology and perversions. She is the author of *Cinesexuality* (2008) and co-editor with Ian Buchanan of *The Schizoanalysis of Cinema* (2008).

Adrian Martin is Senior Research Fellow in Film in the Department of Film and Television at Monash University, Melbourne. He is the author of many books and articles on film, including *Brian De Palma* (forthcoming), *Raúl Ruiz: Sublimes Obsesiones* (2004) and *Que es el cine moderno?* (2008), and co-editor of *Movie Mutations* (2003) and the film journal *Rouge* (www.rouge.com.au).

Christian McCrea is Lecturer in Games and Interactivity at Swinburne University of Technology, Melbourne. His work describes the material aspects of cinema, games and new media, with foci on media physicality, nostalgia and explosive-body aesthetics.

John Mullarkey is Senior Lecturer in Philosophy at the University of Dundee. He is the author of *Post-Continental Philosophy: An Outline* (2006) and *Bergson and Philosophy* (1999).

Dorothea Olkowski is Professor of Philosophy at the University of Colorado. She is the author of *Gilles Deleuze and the Ruin of Representation* (1999) and co-editor of, among other books, *Gilles Deleuze and the Theatre of Philosophy* (1994).

Patricia Pisters is Professor of Film Studies in the Department of Media Studies, University of Amsterdam. She is the author of *The Matrix of Visual Culture: Working with Deleuze in Film Theory* (2003) and editor of *Micropolitics of Media Culture* (2001).

Anna Powell is Reader in English and Film at Manchester Metropolitan University. She is the author of *Deleuze, Altered States and Film* (2007), *Deleuze and the Horror Film* (2005) and *Psychoanalysis and Sovereignty in Popular Vampire Fictions* (2003), and founding editor of *A/V*, a Deleuze Studies online journal (www.eri.mmu.ac.uk/deleuze).

Drehli Robnik is a film theorist and researcher at the Ludwig Boltzmann-Institute for History and Society, Vienna. He teaches at universities in Vienna, Brno and Frankfurt am Main and is the author of *Geschichtsaesthetik und Affektpolitik. Stauffenberg und der 20. Juli im Film 1948–2008* (2009).

Richard Rushton is a Lecturer in the Department of Media, Film and Cultural Studies at Lancaster University. He has published numerous articles on film and visual culture, and he is co-author with Gary Bettinson of *What is Film Theory?* (forthcoming).

Laurence Simmons is an Associate Professor in the Department of Film, Television and Media Studies at the University of Auckland. He is the author of *The Image Always Has the Last Word: On Contemporary New Zealand Painting and Photography* (2002), *From Z to A: Žižek at the Antipodes* (2005) and *Freud's Italian Journey* (2006), and co-author with Victoria Grace and Heather Worth of *Baudrillard West of the Dateline* (2003).

Robert Sinnerbrink is Lecturer in Philosophy at Macquarie University, Sydney. He is the author of *Understanding Hegelianism* (2007), co-editor of *Critique Today* (2006), and has published widely on the film–philosophy relationship, including articles on Peter Greenaway, David Lynch, Terrence Malick and Lars von Trier.

David Sorfa is Senior Lecturer in Screen Studies at Liverpool John Moores University, and managing editor of the journal *Film-Philosophy*. He has published work on Michael Haneke, Jan Svankmajer, Czech cinema and a wide variety of other film-related subjects.

Lisa Trahair is a Senior Lecturer in the School of English, Media and Performing Arts at the University of New South Wales, Sydney. She is the author of *The Comedy of Philosophy: Sense and Nonsense in Early Cinematic Slapstick* (2007).

Hunter Vaughan is Lecturer in Film and Media Studies at Washington University in St Louis. His research includes film theory and aesthetics, French cinema and problems of race and gender representation, and he is a guest editor of a special issue of the *New Review of Film and Television Studies* on "French Philosophy of Cinema".

Stephen Zepke is Lecturer in Philosophy, Art and Cinema at the Academy of Fine Arts, Vienna. He is author of *Art as Abstract Machine: Ontology and Aesthetics in Deleuze and Guattari* (2005) and co-editor with Simon O'Sullivan of *The Production of the New* (2008).

ACKNOWLEDGEMENTS

This book owes its existence to Tristan Palmer, although any faults herein are entirely mine. I am thankful for Tristan's professional assistance and advice, and extend my sincere gratitude to him and the publishing team at Acumen, and especially Kate Williams. I am also appreciative of the feedback from the anonymous reviewers who commented on various stages of the manuscript.

I am most grateful to all the authors who contributed to this project, for their time in writing and, in correspondence with me, patience and generosity of scholarship. It takes courage to practise film-philosophy. I am also indebted to all my students, the brilliant, the banal and the downright awful, who taught me to seriously consider film and the larger philosophical questions: this book is for you.

I am appreciative of the institutional framework afforded me by the University of Melbourne and am especially grateful to those who helped keep me in/sane during my stint in Melbourne and contributed to the daily dialogue in one way or another: Edwina Bartlem, Barbara Bolt, Lucian Chaffey, Blythe Chandler, Leonie Cooper, Tessa Dwyer, Peter Eckersall, Hélène Frichot, Wendy Haslem, Chloe Johnson, Graham Jones, Keely Macarow, Peta Malins, Christian McCrea, Mehmet Mehmet, Anna Hickey-Moody, Angela Ndalianis, Patrick Porter, Simone Schmidt, Erin Stapleton, Luke Stickels, Veronica Tello, Annie Turner, Saige Walton, Ashley Woodward, KZ.

Thanks also for technical support of all kinds to Jane Brown, Barbara Creed, Larissa Hjorth, Ian Kendrick, Alex Ling, Steve McIntyre, Annie Mulroney and Kate O'Halloran.

I also owe a debt of gratitude to the many friendships extended to me by my larger academic community and their collegial generosity with sharing ideas and providing academic encouragement and support, with special thanks to Adrian Parr and C. J. Stivale.

Thank you to the wonderful Xhrise Zikos and amazing Apollonia Zikos, who supported me through broken bones, long nights, some grim and good times, and who have patiently explained horror films to me.

And a toast: to the boy with green hair.

Felicity Colman

INTRODUCTION: WHAT IS FILM-PHILOSOPHY?

Felicity Colman

What is film-philosophy? Film-philosophy begins with the moving sound-image. Definitions of the topic require more than academic and mechanical experience. The moving image generates screen forms and cinematic conditions for things outside those forms. Screen-based forms provide an everyday medium for information retrieval, communication, distraction and entertainment. Film, television, Web services, data repositories, gaming screens, mobile screens and art-based and non-commercial screen-related forms materialize the issues and ideas of the content provided in their situated medium and in the mediation of the content they produce: global news, sports events, the natural world, imaginative worlds and so on. Whether commercial or alternative, all of these forms pass through mediating distributive networks (communities of all kinds, human and non-human), and produce different kinds of knowledge forms. Further, screen-based content – ideas, histories, empirical data – generate different types of cinematic conditions. Engaging with this screen vernacular in academic terms requires that practitioners of film-philosophy are not just experiencing, speaking and writing about screen forms as passive observers, but are aware of their participation in screen cultures and their mediation through distributive networks. What participants have access to will determine the type of conceptualization they have about a particular issue. Screen forms are thus contentious and complex media that format and challenge the participant's perceptual capacities. In these terms, film-philosophy is a study of dynamic forms and conditions. This book offers examples of thinkers who engage in the processes and conceptualization of cinematic values and discourses, as they relate or develop philosophical and theoretical ideas.

The screen-based form and all of its related products, from mass to experimental media, is not only one of the most powerful communication modes, but has become one of the most significant vehicles for creating organizational conditions and assembling systems for forms of knowledge. Screen technologies are a central currency for all types of scientific and social communication, information and analytic economy. Marketplaces regulate and analyse information that is generated through screen forms. Screen-based entertainment and screen-based art forms, commercially distributed, public and privately displayed, are able to question, dismiss, create and destroy philosophical beliefs concerning perception, memory, the imagination, knowledge,

1

aesthetics and scientific laws. On screen, disasters are structured, emotions are styled, intimate details are given public arenas, abstract things such as time, history and economics are furnished with material forms and fetishized, and social identities and behavioural models are figured.

The current forms of screen mediation find their formal parameters of technology, knowledge and experience redistributed through the scientific discovery and economic perspectives of the *cinematic* twentieth century's invention. Yet the cinematic reality evidenced in this currency is continually subjected to *redirection* through the construction and contingency of events, their interpretation, expression and historicization, and it is on this point of redirection that the practices of film-philosophy find themselves in debate and development. Film theory and film-philosophy seek to account for the constituent parts that determine the ethical and aesthetic values generated through cinematic conditions, but there are various kinds of practices of screen-based analysis, their definition often as contentious as the screen conditions they describe: amateur, philosophical, theoretical and critical. The authors in this book provide examples of the processes of the practice of film-philosophy and film theory as practices that are as vigorous and as contentious as the medium they engage.

Before we can answer what constitutes film-philosophy, a preliminary question arises: *what are screen forms?* Screen forms themselves not only reveal but also *produce* physical and social entities. Things in the world move past us and change: nothing is static until it is made that way (a moment in time as fixed on your screen), and we are accustomed to viewing the world as it moves, while either we are in locomotion or the things around us are. Organized in ways to suit the essential economies of their technological devise, screen forms have a value to convey and they are thus restricted and motivated by the limits of their pre-formatted and/or semi-contingent, mediated content. Cinematic forms, films, television, computer gaming and online communications media all produce different activities and they can be as constructive of new modes of existence and new forms of knowledge as much as they just render existing modes through new platforms. Alternative and commercial film forms (and the broad spectrum therein) are at the service of various stages of the movements of capital and are thus directed to reproduce certain types of consumers. On screen, sex, gender, ethnicity, social roles, the laws of physics and the formation of chemical and biological substances are determined and moulded according to the parochial laws and aesthetic values of the culture of their production. Yet we perceive that individual films and their content can completely ignore or refigure the conditions of their fabrication just as they can take on meanings slightly or significantly in excess of their original forms. Screen forms thus *question and resource* the dimensions, directions and contingencies of life from which they are drawn.

How can it be that at the same time as a form is defining the nature of its existence it is determining what that nature is? One of the great preoccupations of Western and Eastern philosophies has been to devise and critique accounts of how such conditions can be possible, thought or even real. Philosophical debates have always been concerned with questions of ontology, and in the twentieth century's massive redistribution of ontology, questions of metaphysics, of Being and the categorization of experiences became prominent. Screen forms produced questions that film-philosophy and film theory explore: are things always in process, or is it just our imagination, our perception of reality? How could we ever "know" an entity beyond its molecular, genetic, technical, ideological, ethical or awe-inspiring construction; can screen forms "apprehend" the complexities of the various movements of life? How do moving images differ from still images? How does filmic sound affect the content of images? In their attention to certain areas and development of specific content, the divergent practices of film-philosophy have set specific critical agendas for the study of the screen medium. An overriding component of the rhetoric of this discipline concerns itself with the question: *what is the very nature of the cinematic?*

To provide some responses to these questions, I shall now discuss the notion of film-philosophy as a practice. The themes and tendencies of this practice are then discussed in terms of their paradigmatic conditions. Finally, I shall briefly introduce and collate the divergent approaches of film theory and film-philosophy in the chapters in this book.

THE DISCIPLINE AND PRACTICE OF FILM-PHILOSOPHY AND FILM THEORY

There are many differences within the respective discipline fields of philosophy and film and its commonly known subject of film theory. How the two converge to create a new and diverse discipline remains a point of contention among scholars. The question of what constitutes film-philosophy as a discipline is thus bound to the shifting notions of the traditions of the dual disciplines it sources. This double inheritance is additionally qualified when we look at how the disciplines of film-philosophy and film theory are practised. The qualification of how the discipline of film-philosophy has been constituted and in its academic usage is to be found in the hyphen: the cojoining "and" of film and philosophy. The hyphen represents different meaning in different applications: it can be a proposition or a conjunction; it might argue for multiplicity or for singularity; or it might be posed as a presumption for or argument against various aspects of the two disciplines. *How* that conjunctive hyphen is practised becomes indicative of a particular aesthetic and politic of film-philosophy.

Film forms service many of the philosophical categories through their very existence, and some theorists argue that film-philosophy is an illustrative methodology. Others argue that film itself is a philosophical process. The disparate camps of so-called "analytic" philosophical procedures and "continental" philosophical approaches for both fields of enquiry divide opinion. There are disagreements over whether philosophical concepts can be "applied" to the study of a film, or whether they should be a statement of method or engaged as an approach. There remains no one "correct" system for practice, and most theorists would agree that there should not be, although the combination of the two disciplines into film-philosophy has undeniably been intellectually stimulating in its production of different modes of reflection on the constitution of the world, and of subjectivities productive of that world.

The practice of engaging with screen forms thus is as varied as the diversity of the field of production. The workings of the individual practitioner's environment inform the type of screen platform and influence choices for disciplinary technique and critical strategy. I am using the term "practitioner" here to encompass the productive side of the industry, although the creative aspects of distribution are applicable, such as the machinic functions of Google and YouTube information harvesters. In this sense, "practitioner" includes all theorists engaging with screen-based work, the film theorist, film-philosopher, film and screen enthusiast, film director and producer, and the participant in screen-based forms and cinematic conditions. "Practice" is a localized system that gathers and organizes information, tests, systematizes and creates. Practitioners tend to characterize the workings of their system using procedural terms (explicit or unacknowledged) that provide indicators for the type of method or approach. A method implies application and an approach implies testing, and both modes of engagement can be either inventive or normalizing: investigative or prescriptive in their handling of the screen-based form or cinematic condition. Further, discipline indicators for the type of practice are given through language style and epistemic and content specialization. It must be stressed that theorists of any disciplinary persuasion present no homogeneous group. Film theorists might engage in formal issues such as the modes of "realism in the diegesis" or explore sociological and psychological concepts in screen forms, while film-philosophers will talk up the film–mind analogy, the question of rhetoric and the values inherent in scientific knowledge. However, while we can generalize, the terminological differences remain important indicators for determining purpose and direction of content. The history of philosophy has been at pains to separate itself from its disciplinary cousins of mysticism and mythology in its study of the large issues of aesthetics, existence, knowledge, the law, religion, the language, the mind, truth and reality, by devising rational, systematic and reasoned analysis. Will film-philosophy mend that breech? Film theory is certainly not shy of engaging with a mythical moment or two. Theoretically speaking, film theory takes its cues from critical work done across the twentieth century and has thus been concerned with the specificities of the technological medium as well as the cultures of social and historical issues it engages. The number of disparate interdisciplinary approaches required to incorporate all of the things that the study of film-making involves was usefully noted by Gilbert Cohen-Séat as the "methodological enterprise" required of *"filmologie* [filmology]" (1946: 63).[1]

In attempting a summary of the different modes of practice, then, a number of common points can be understood to mobilize both film theory and film-philosophy to write to, from and around film. First, an enthusiasm for the cinema manifests as a form of *amateurism*, which is the practice of connoisseurship that begins as soon as we can discern and articulate what kind of sound-image we prefer. As film theorist Dudley Andrew pointed out, we can defiantly posit a certain degree of "amateurism", in fact as a "matter of pride, particularly when set against dehumanised disciplinarity" (Andrew 2000a: 342–3). Secondly, in a less than ideal world, compromise enforces politically determined quantification of study and the results produce more icons and neologisms to pursue the study of [your love of] cinema. Many deterministic schemas have arisen in the formal study and research of all areas of film, theory and philosophy, and many arguments and value judgements have been made against the potential of the moving image. Thirdly (and the content of this book), divergent disciplinary fields set off on critical trajectories in pursuit of their object of study in a post-industrial age acknowledging that film-making is produced and screen-viewing is enabled only under the conditions of specific political economies. All approaches require making political choices in and out of the marketplace: the heart of all philosophy. How does a film-philosophy account for watching a screening about revolution that concerns a culture other than its own? How does a film-philosophy account for watching a screening of a revolution involving its own current constitution? For answers to these kinds of questions, I suggest that we look to the paradigmatic categories that film-philosophy and film theory frame in their choice of content and approach for analysis.

Film theory and film-philosophy circle similar material: the historical screen and cinematically generated conditions. Both bring together a number of disciplinary academic fields of enquiry. Examples of film theory and film-philosophy draw on various histories of philosophy, film theory, scientific theory, aesthetic theories, artistic practices, the work of specific ancient and contemporary philosophers and, increasingly, the work of thinkers who engaged with the filmic medium.[2] Approaches may engage a "pure" stream of their discipline, or they take an interdisciplinary approach. It is in the practice of framing and the articulation of that framing and the content of screen forms and cinematic conditions that differences of thematic, pedagogic and theoretical opinion arise.

Despite the diversity, in the brief history and broad praxes of the disciplines of film, philosophy and theory, the shared exploration of the questions of what cinema is, the nature of cinema, the historical event of cinema and film forms remains central. Further, regardless of the theoretical position adopted, the discussion, theorization, classification and analysis commonly used in film theory and philosophy provides a purview where film and cinematic conditions are approached in terms of the categories of: (i) *technological epistemology* and (ii) *event epistemology*.

Epistemology is a theory of knowledge that I engage here in a post-twentieth-century philosophical critical sense. Epistemology is a theory that not only asks what knowledge is and what it is possible to know, but, most importantly, "how do we know what we do know?" (Greco & Sosa 1999: 1). It is this third proposition of epistemology – it is not only what we know but *how* we know it that has been a central tenet of philosophical investigation – that leads me to characterize two of the core paradigms of film theory and philosophy in terms of their epistemological pursuits. Under the terms of the aesthetic and political moulding of content, consideration of the philosophical bands of epistemology enables us to distinguish between the forms of history that are produced, modified and examined by the practices of film-philosophy and film theory.

Thinking about the categories of epistemological approaches to screen-worlds seeks to extend and not merely reflect on the production of knowledge and the epistemic concepts applied to the understanding of things. Rather, knowledge in all forms lies at the core of philosophy, theoretical studies and the histories of the people and ideas generated in screen-worlds. Knowledge informs the production of ideas; it is a concept that has been rejected, developed, argued against, replaced, questioned, investigated, radicalized and interrupted by screen-worlds. Every theorist, every filmmaker, every philosopher, every place has a different story to tell, thereby engaging some form of knowledge, whatever the methodological lens used.

Alongside such events as early-twentieth-century discoveries in quantum mechanics, which refigured the principles of all physical systems, and massive changes in patriarchal, fiscal and military economic systems, screen forms and theories about them have completely reshaped what we assumed "knowledge" to be, and the social and political changes of the twentieth century altered understanding of the problematic histories of ethnicity, gender, sexuality and nationality. Since the inception of cinema, cinematic forms have been engaged as platforms for different types of knowledge: illusory, indigenous, utopic, cautionary, scientific, biased, legal, hallucinatory, gendered, historical, dramatic, experimental, materialist and so on. Should we refer to screen forms in terms of the epistemological paradigms of technology and event? Of course, screen forms are not reducible to a sound/image = content formula, and film-philosophy is often at pains to avoid simple ideological categorization. Nevertheless, the practice of forming the staging of knowledge and the acceptance or critical questioning of the concept of knowledge are engaged at every turn, and varied according to societal values, cultural mores and the epistemic community of the film-philosopher or theorist. The diversity of positions on the intentionality of screen-worlds, according to the terms of constructions of events, people, ideas and access to different technological modes of production and consumption, has been at the forefront of film analysis since the redress of colonialist and race histories in the 1960s, re-examination of the determining histories of gender and sexuality in the 1980s and analysis of the histories of perception, phenomenology and cognition, and so on. However, film-philosophy and film theory mutate as new events arise in the world, shifting the technological epistemology of perceptual histories of knowledge. History is a dynamic process, pummelled by technology and event epistemologies. These two are interdependent in mediating the ontology of the screen form. The description of the moving image to a large extent revolves around how to argue the appearance of something – the analysis of its ontological qualities – and how and as what the experience of that something might be classified. Theorists will disagree over identification of representation and issues of "reality" – their structure and/or content – and their subsequent mode of discussion and argument style will take different turns. How they choose to engage and proceed with analysis is what marks out their methodological stakes. If we can identify a thinker's mode of practice, the type and method of analysis they use, then we can name thinker X's practice of film-philosophy. However, what is of interest for theory are the ways in which that thinker participates with and responds to the screen form of their choosing, making evident the qualities of an entity and the substance provided for concepts.

In recuperating the notion of epistemology from its purely philosophical application (negative or positive, depending on a practitioner's disciplinary preference), epistemology understood as a theory of *historical* knowledge provides a useful concept that can be set to work as a way of characterizing the practices of film theory and film-philosophy, whatever their disciplinary impetus. We can further use the resources of epistemological thinking in the feminist senses of enabling ethically productive knowledge (cf. Haraway 1997: 79; Braidotti 2006: 263–78), with which both analytic and continental camps are variously concerned. Engaging a feminist epistemology challenges the political, metaphysical and scientific knowledge, hierarchical and gender-biased values and judgements made by the exclusions to knowledge in the canon of Western epistemology (Harding 1991: 106–10), and the frequent denial of the politics of the social situation of all practices by that canon.

The task for film theory and film-philosophy is to engage a conceptual approach that is ethically situated, empirically appropriate and theoretically adequate to address the diverse and complex concepts presented by screen-worlds. Film-philosophy recognizes and responds to the immanence of screen epistemology – the types of epistemology generated from various screen-worlds. Practitioners describe this immanent world in terms of their reaction and relation to the types of knowledge and history as formations of that screen-world: knowledge as process, practice, and as a series of dynamic and multiple possible conditions, the already classified, and as potential histories (cf. Deleuze 1988: 98–9; Foucault 1972: 86). The question to be asked, then, is not "Is this a 'correct' or 'successful' application of this or that mode of epistemology?", as these are value judgements; rather, the question is, first, one of an understanding what the mode of approach to knowledge is and, secondly, of understanding how that knowledge is engaged. In other words, it is in the analysis of *how* different theorists and philosophers and film-makers choose to practise and/or approach knowledge that we can discern a film theory or film-philosophy. From this, then, we may consider the findings of a film-philosophy in terms of the mode of screen conditions engaged and produced: as a dynamic response or relation to those conditions.

There obviously exists a myriad of methods for theoretical practice to engage with: in a conceptual and historical sense and in an analytic and linguistic sense. To think more broadly about the terms of critical practice in theory and in philosophy – through its paradigmatic address of the screen form, the ontological nature of the cinema and its historical trajectories – proposes a knowledge fold that can pocket the problems of practice-demonstration. Within the two categories of technological epistemology and event epistemological enquiry are divergent transitive and intransitive methods and approaches; however, both types of study are evident in the pages of most examples of film-philosophy and film theory in some form or another. Let me briefly examine these two paradigmatic areas that are drawn together in practice.

Technological epistemology

From the outset film-philosophical and film-theoretical practices have investigated the technological epistemology of film and cinematic conditions. Technological epistemology here refers to the study of the issues relating to the formation and distribution of technical and empirical knowledge relating to screen forms.[3] Issues of technological epistemology occur at the level of the form, style and architecture of different screen platforms (e.g. digital, analogue, mobile, fixed, projection, flat-screen, film, television product, Web, etc.) as well as at the level of shifts in content and the perception of technological changes as they relate to screen and film forms and cinematic conditions. Under this type of study, traditional philosophical categories and methods for analysis of forms are engaged (these tend to treat screen forms as philosophical problems), and contemporary philosophical and twentieth-century theoretical knowledge forms are also applied and tested (these tend to approach screen forms as generative of types of knowledge). The philosophical study of film, in particular, has focused on the generative ontology of screen forms.

What is it that film produces? One of the positions of technological epistemological enquiry is that film itself can engage in "philosophizing" (Mulhall 2005: 67); film can "sometimes do ... screen philosophy" (Wartenberg 2007: 93, 142); and there exists a "filmind" (Frampton 2006: 6). Film-thinking, according to this form of film-philosophy, occurs through its technological epistemologies of narrative, audition, spectacle, experimentation and reification of knowledge and beliefs. Other positions reject the purely phenomenal or aesthetic type of "film mind", arguing that film and cinematic conditions can be understood only as labour-intensive forms produced through industrialized systems that result in the "capitalization of the aesthetic faculties and imaginary practices of viewers" (Beller 2006: 14), an interference "in men's minds" (Adorno & Horkheimer 1997: 127), the eradication of "direct vision" through warfare (Virilio 1989: 11) and the creation of a "machinic subjectivity" (Guattari 1995: 24).

Marking a modal change in perceptual capacity is a common practice at the inception of new technological platforms. For example, the philosopher Henri Bergson explored how cinematic conditions lend themselves to defining human ontology. In 1907 Bergson argued that "the *mechanism of our ordinary knowledge is of a cinematographical kind*" ([1911] 1983: 323). Sergei Eisenstein devised a technology of editing that he terms the "montage of attractions", whereby the editing technique would produce a collision effect between shots because of the images they contain. Eisenstein's hope was that this technological epistemology would incite the spectator to take political action (1949: 37). Siegfried Kracauer noted how the physical mechanics of the movie camera can bring to perceptual attention the "transient", observing: "The motion picture camera seems to be partial to the least permanent components of our environment" (1960: 52). Such practices of technological epistemology not only account for the object (whether it is a talkie film, a 16mm film, a DVD, a computer game, a flight simulator, a mobile phone camera, the Web), but explore definitions of shifts in perception as compared with the essential nature of the singular cinematic possibility or range of possibilities. Film-philosophers have tended to synthesize elements of their theory on film with other technologies such as painting, photography or literature (a comparative method). Many dead-end arguments were had over the "validity" of film as an art form and discipline for study, in a quest for some type of "ontological commitment" (in what analytic philosophers characterize as either a realist or idealist/nominalist position). Through various misapprehensions of the nature of what constitutes an art form, and an eternal quest for definition of modes of aesthetic sensibility, film was variously assimilated to categories of analysis used for literature, the plastic arts, and treated as a language form "to be read" or as an impenetrable transcendental form "to be understood".[4] The introductory pages of a number of books dealing with the issue of film-philosophy display the ambivalence of authors to their medium. This state exists despite the fact that we could observe that cinematic modes have existed ever since people observed the shifts in light through the changes of celestial bodies, and were thrilled with light plays through early entertainment modes akin to the film venues of the twentieth century (cf. Charney & Schwarz 1996).

Whatever the technological medium used for comparison, emphasis or argument type, the screen form has activated a change and prompted a revision/extension of philosophy and of theories of production and consumption of cinematic conditions. Walter Benjamin addressed the fate of the "aura" of an artwork in an essay of 1936, where looking for objective traits for the purposes of definition and classification, then as today, is a politically fraught exercise (Benjamin [1936] 1968). Screen forms and cinematic conditions cause ontological change, as identified by various theorists (further addressed by the chapters in this book), named in terms of ethics, aesthetics and new categories of thinking that are commonly defined in terms of their meta-physical shift: an event. In terms of technological epistemology, theory investigates the question of the technical real: the cinematic ability to record events in time and as time. Further, the apprehension of event time is developed in film theory to look at the various questions of perception theory: different modes of *apprehending* know-ledge. In film-philosophy, and for some theorists, reflection on the ways in which the cinema generates ideas about time has seen philosophy augment its metaphysical knowledge, which we can characterize as event epistemology.

Event epistemology

Event epistemology, as signalled in film, theory and philosophy, is an approach that explores or is representative of change, time, movement or aesthetic positions. An event can be understood as something indicative of shifts in thinking, a critique of the past cycles of history, a new system; these paradigms have caused radical proposals for what the ontology of cinema can mean and produce. Event epistemological approaches may thus also incorporate technology epistemology in certain instances, although the focus on how something works (at the levels of formal analyses of *mise en scène*, nar-rative, genre, prototypologies) can defer the question of content and essences.

When considering an event on screen, film-philosophy will take different approaches. There is, of course, a difference in treatment of an event as an *actuality* (the name given to the genre of news infotainment forms), a physical moment in time, and considera-tion of an event as a point indicative of a paradigmatic or signifying system. The ques-tion of "reality" and "realism" forms a large body of theory in film-philosophy, and these discussions draw from event epistemologies (cf. Žižek 1993; Baudrillard 1994; Daney 2007; Grimonprez 2007).

The paradigm of event epistemology can be characterized through its attention to the types of conditions that are generated through screen forms (for example, tem-poral conditions such as memory forms, imagination and time concepts). Event epis-temologies will take the ideas and the concepts of film as the object for investigation. The core issues for event-epistemological paradigms are concerned with the meta-physical. By metaphysical, I mean that the cinema produces events that engage with thoughts and concepts: things that have no material body but are nonetheless the stuff of existence. This includes abstract notions such as time and space, the dynamics of social situations, political residues, historical concepts translated into emotions (memories, feelings of nostalgia, anticipation, fear, desire, love, etc.), imaginary stimulus by fictive screen-worlds, and screen-situations that engender an embodied state. Theorists describe event epistemologies of this type in terms of their provocation of a dynamic physicality, drawing from phenomenologically informed positions, such as Merleau-Ponty's (1964: 48–94) conception of the "truths" of perceptual experience that the cinema creates, not through a synthesis of events and things, but through, as Vivian Sobchack describes, the cinema's use of *"modes of embodied experience"* (1991: 4). Laura Marks (2000: 183) describes this truth to the cinematic event in terms of the "haptic visuality" of the cinema, and post-phenomenal accounts of event epistemologies are developed by directors Jim Jarmusch (1999), Agnes Varda (2000) and Brian De Palma (2007).

The specific qualities of screen forms are productive of their own technological event and the event is a necessary topic of film-philosophers and film theorists; after all, the nature of film is nothing if not the staging of something. It is on this point of analysis – the ontology of something – that internal disciplines and methods of film theory and film-philosophy will take different pathways for investigation. Concepts including the aura, conflict, *das Ding, différance, dispositif, entre temps,* the fetish, a gesture, libidinal economy, memory, the minor, the parallax, the postmodern, the punctum, a singularity, the *sinthome,* a spectacle, the spectral, a rhizome, realism, the *uncanny,* the vector and a voyeur are all conceptual devices that signal an event epistemology. Technically, theoretically, they all work in different ways, but how they are engaged and organized is what creates a particular practitioner's theory of film. How these devices are put into practice is what enables a theorist or philosopher to engage with the content they signal; that is, the philosophical categories engaged to argue a point or make the filmic phenomena apparent constitute a practice of film theory or film-philosophy. Different practitioners engage alternate terms to address their sense of event epistemology, and it is on this point that their content emerges. Searching for a moment of clarity, a sentimental trigger, a lost love, the moment of disappointment, death or hope and future possibilities, all such events are given careful and considered treatment in film-philosophy.

In the ontological sense, theory and philosophy that engage screen forms produce conditions that enable us to perceive how things have been made, or could be made. And in this sense, the practice of film-philosophy affords a focus on technical details – on the everyday, on functions of things, on processes of producing film and methods of thinking – as much as it provides scope to investigate the larger dimensions of representational forms, as a product of the cinematic. How theorists engage technological and event epistemologies in their work is also a matter of their political aesthetic. They may engage in a practice that describes the notion of a sensibility, or a system that will express both an "immediate" and a "post" (or later) relationship between recognition, cognition and an image or object of that image. Or, the practice may engage an aesthetic that approaches as a mediation between recognition/cognition of an image/object/presence, and the mediation of that knowledge through concepts and judgements relating to that mediated experience. In other words, does a practitioner treat time and space as aesthetic categories, as political ones, or as purely philosophical?

As I have already indicated, one of the issues arising from engaging types of technology and event epistemologies for analysis is that this paradigmatic approach can universalize issues that have arisen from specific, localized practices. Nevertheless, it is through the development of the cinematic that enormous changes have occurred in some levels of human organization, and epistemological analysis assists in locating and defining these often systemic changes.

FILM, THEORY AND PHILOSOPHY

We can thus characterize film-philosophy as being concerned with ontological investigation engaging the sciences of perception, movement and knowledge. The moving image has shown philosophy different things about the nature of the abstractions of space and time and the categories of sex and gender. Like philosophy, film has created new concepts to articulate being and ontology. Hence, this book focuses on the areas that hold a mutual resonance for both disciplines. These areas are by no means exhaustive, but they are representative of some of the key concerns that you will find in any film-philosophy.

What form that screen-based ontology (the question of what kind of filmic entity/ related entities exist) takes, and how, is dependent on the types of methodological approaches employed in order to describe that ontology. There are commonly known terms that we associate with different methodological approaches and strategies: analytic, cognitivist, empirical realist, feminist, formalist, humanist, nominalist, phenomenological, postmodern and so on. Classificatory headings are useful for historicization in their abstraction and useful in their dogmatic provocation for debating technical details, but often prove to be somewhat redundant for experiential discussions. For each of those titles there exists the "anti-" and "post-" classification: anti-metaphysical, post-feminist, and so on. Classical and modern philosophical approaches are combined with classical and contemporary film-theoretical approaches. Some methodologies have cross-disciplinary foundations themselves, such as psychoanalysis. Films present us with a range of what philosophy likes to call "problems". Ready-made social schema, for example, engage questions of actions, ethics, outcomes. In the type of approach that engages traditional philosophical categories and methods for analysis, screen forms and filmic conditions become philosophical *problems* to be rationalized, often naturalizing the thus-framed "problem" to be "solved". Categories might include the philosophy of knowledge, scepticism, questions of truth, the categorization of reality, aesthetics (imitation, sensory impression, imagination), mathematical schema, rhetoric and poetics. Different theorists approach the reconfigured object or condition of cinema and its ontological categorization (in analytic or experiential categorical terms) in different ways and with different methods.

An issue that arises for this approach – and all types of film-philosophy – is that the form of philosophical and theoretical criticism produced is often determined by the approach, which in turn is determined as much by intellectual fashion as by intellectual knowledge. For example, in examining the material dimensions of changes in technological operations of screen forms, theorists become bound into the intellectual impasse of diagnostic analysis where discussion about the content and meanings is limited to technical definitions, of the type of content via "problem". In the creation of all manner of different or new ontologies (different categories of experiences) film and its related screen forms have produced many models for critical thought and their requisite classification for investigation. That the philosophical problems of Plato in ancient Greece are different from the philosophical problems outlined by Alain Badiou in the twenty-first century is something that not all theorists appear to recognize. The continuation of thinking through philosophical categories devised from centuries past to situations arising from contemporaneous cinematically produced situations is not the issue; it is a matter of situating the (changed) metaphysical relations of that use. For example, in a theoretical discussion of genre or gender stylistics, the limitations of categorical analysis are shown where "critique" not only becomes non-definitional through its breadth of stylistic incorporation or dismissal, but conceals content in its quest for cognitive summation. For this book, thinkers have been chosen for their awareness and articulation of the situated conditions of their practice.

I have chosen to group chapters according to three broad subheadings, observing some core paradigmatic theoretical and philosophical approaches for the practices of film, theory and philosophy. The chapters collected here aim to address a serious limitation in much of the discussion of film-philosophy that tends to engage analytic and/or cognitive practices of analysis. The analytic practice of argumentation provides valuable material for film-philosophy, and useful terminology for definitions and critical engagement (cf. Cavell 1979b; Carroll 1988a; Read & Goodenough 2005). In particular, the analytic philosophical tradition of care and interest in linguistics is of great importance for all practices of analysis, as will be obvious in the work of many of the thinkers included in this book, who develop analytic linguistic methods into critical practices. However – as with any practice – tacit and overt biases towards methodology have limits for understanding the breadth of all possible meanings of the study of the complexities of film, its history and all possible cinematic conditions. Film and cinematic conditions cannot be "read"; they are a medium in movement, and they are born of and address real world conditions. This book does not claim any exhaustive overview of the topic but seeks to augment further aspects of the study of film, theory and philosophy.

The intention of the book is to further enable discussions of the divergent ideas of form, life and meaning that the cinema and philosophical thinking through cinematic conditions have created. It is hoped that the variety of essays in this collection might inspire readers to recombine, rethink and revisit their notions of writing film-philosophy. As readers will find, film-philosophy is also the practice of the redirection of cinematic propositions, for rethinking the various criteria engaged for understanding, assessing and relating to the worlds we inhabit, the ways we think and our understanding of the contingencies and dogmatisms of that knowledge.

The book is organized by these thinkers' key ontological interests for ciné-philosophy. Chapters are structured to describe and address the key concepts in each thinker's work as they relate to film, and how and where they use screen forms and/or cinematic concepts in their work. Each chapter provides an overview of what that thinker's film theory or film-philosophy is, or what it might become in the instances where thinkers may have only mentioned cinema or film concepts in passing in their work, but have nevertheless generated critical interest in their ideas.

Part I takes on the ontological and phenomenological question posed by André Bazin: "What is cinema?" Part II presents a selection of philosophers and theorists who have been integral to providing accounts of twentieth-century cultures. Part III presents a selection of film theory and film-philosophy that demonstrates the ways in which different event and technological epistemologies are approached (through structures, methods and conditions of knowledge). In various ways, these three arenas provide an overview of how the two mediums have worked to reshape what we understand the categories of philosophy and film to be.

How different thinkers of film-philosophy practise the fundamental issues of the nature of the cinema – movement, change and the affective constitution of subjectivity – lies at the heart of this book. Film-philosophy is the process of the redirection of propositions. It intervenes in any given screen work and redirects its filmic world, extending or reproducing phenomenal and cinematographic knowledge and screen ontology, practising a particular form of critical epistemology and extending or diminishing a given discourse.

What film-philosophy does in the process of rethinking is to consider propositions given in films in terms of their filmic *and* discursive production. That is, concepts – such as we find in any given film – are given as forms of experience, but this experience is a completely mediated expression of material and transient things that have been selected, named, ordered, and thus signify within specific cultural systems – which can support or reject or extend them. So, for different cultures, the terms and figures of any body (and its attendant arrangement within the whole) have different connotations as they are formed as much by the rhetorical and discursive conditions of their specific culture as they are by their essential forms as given within a film.

Although extremely diverse in their approaches, most of the essays in this book focus on thinkers who are said to belong to a "continental school" of philosophy (such as Merleau-Ponty, Derrida and Agamben), and those film-thinkers who have been influenced by "continental" methodologies (Barthes, Metz, Heath). The continental approach to screen theory is a distinctive one, acknowledging that cinema is a politically divisive medium with a long creative history. Although based on and limited by the sciences of its technological boundaries, its production irregular and economically governed, its creative dimensions are bound only as far as those mediating factors propel or deny possibilities. As a politically creative philosophy, continental thinking is concerned with the analysis of such operational methods, as it is a philosophy concerned with the description of experience, the terms of human agency and interdisciplinary methods of enquiry, and the outcomes of the scale of human endeavours, thus making it arguably a more sympathetic method for the practice of film-philosophy. Hence the theorists, philosophers and film-makers chosen for inclusion here are those whose work has been concerned with the centrality of the Heideggerian questions of "what calls for thinking?" and "what calls on us to think?" in relation to the moving image, as a redirection and a rethinking of the propositions of life as rethought: screen life. Every film has its own "aesthetic", just as every film can be described as "philosophical"; its type, genre or provenance do not matter. From the most obscure art house film you were bored to tears in, to the most memorable scene, to the most vacuous piece of commodity-endorsing vehicle you wasted two hours of your life with, all films impart something. Films set up structures and then generate multiple variations on that structure. If the aesthetics of that structure augment and produce perceptions of your reality, then you are more likely to recognize your film aesthetic: that thing. We all have recollections of such moments when watching a film when we were ourselves redirected in our aesthetic awareness of the critical and qualitative dimensions of the world. The practice of film-philosophy is to be critical of the ways in which films produce their particular aesthetics: particular styles and particular abstractions and/or narrativizations of situations and conditions. Philosophy offers specific methods for film analysis, and the medium of film in turn offers specific models for philosophical reflection. As the range of approaches in this book demonstrates, philosophy has made visible a number of assumptions and theories that are held about the world, the organization of societies, the classification of things and the methods of thinking that are employed. Films have made accessible the dimensions of these methods and critiques through their expression of different attitudes, political positions, representations of genders, of sexuality, of ethnicity.

What both disciplines emphasize is that how we see things does not always depend on vision: on physical sight. Different thinkers question, ignore or develop how the body, or the subject, is conceptualized, addressed and/or formed in diagrammatic relation with the screen: the film image. That image is given as a conglomerate cognitive and perceptual sponge: genetically informed, culturally conditioned, socially manipulated, politically impaired, parasitically dependent on a host of sensorial and aleatory determining factors. Film-philosophy offers a rethinking and redirection of screen images, productive of new theories of cinema. After reading this book we might conclude that film-philosophy is not always about the aesthetics of form; it does not always engage responsible perception, and it does not always produce an ethical perception, but it seeks to engage the moment at hand in order to determine the position of the image and, if possible, redirect ontological formations.

NOTES

1. For an account of the *filmologie* movment and the role of Gilbert Cohen-Séat, see Edward Lowry, *The Filmology Movement and Film Study in France* (Ann Arbor, MI: UMI Research Press 1985).
2. Compare the diversity of approach to screen forms in D. Andrew, *Concepts in Film Theory* (Oxford: Oxford University Press, 1984); W. Dissanayake (ed.), *Colonialism and Nationalism in Asian Cinema* (Bloomington, IN: Indiana University Press, 1994); G. Perez, *The Material Ghost: Films and their Medium* (Baltimore, MD: Johns Hopkins University Press, 1998); H. Naficy, *An Accented Cinema: Exilic and Diasporic Filmmaking* (Princeton, NJ: Princeton University Press, 2001); D. N. Rodowick, *Reading the Figural, or, Philosophy after the New Media* (Durham, NC: Duke University Press, 2001); A. Butler, *Women's Cinema: The Contested Screen* (London: Wallflower, 2002); T. Leighton & P. Büchler (eds), *Saving the Image: Art After Film* (Glasgow: Centre for Contemporary Arts/ Manchester: Manchester Metropolitan University, 2003); S. B. Plate (ed.), *Representing Religion in World Cinema: Filmmaking, Mythmaking, Culturemaking* (Basingstoke: Palgrave Macmillan, 2003); L. Bersani & U. Dutoit, *Forms of Being: Cinema, Aesthetics, Subjectivity* (London: BFI, 2004); J.-L. Godard & Y. Ishaghpour, *Cinema: The Archaeology of Film and the Memory of a Century*, J. Howe (trans.) (Oxford: Berg, [2000] 2005); S. Dennison & S. H. Lim, *Remapping World Cinema: Identity,*

Culture and Politics in Film (London: Wallflower, 2006); L. Williams, *Screening Sex* (Durham, NC: Duke University Press, 2008).

3. Further discussion of what constitutes a technical object and a philosophical history of the differences between technique and epistemology is in Bernard Stiegler's *Techniques and Time, 1: The Fault of Epimetheus*, R. Beardsworth & G. Collins (trans.) (Stanford, CA: Stanford University Press, 1998).

4. "Ontological commitment" is a term described by W. V. Quine ("On What There Is", in *Contemporary Readings in the Foundations of Metaphysics*, S. Laurence & C. Macdonald [eds], 32–45 [Oxford: Blackwell, [1951] 1998), which pupports to "help us decide" whether to argue a case for the so-called conditions of "realism", consisting of "instantiatable entities" or the "concrete particulars" of nominalism (Laurence & Macdonald, *Contemporary Readings*, 5). An application of this type of thinking and a rejection of the "nominalist framework" of film theory is to be found in Allan Casebier's *Film and Phenomenology: Toward a Realist Theory of Cinematic Representation* (Cambridge: Cambridge University Press, 1991), 3, and a useful critical appraisal of the issues in Casebier's method is in David Sullivan's response in the online journal *Film-Philosophy* ("Noemata or No Matter?: Forcing Phenomenology into Film Theory", *Film-Philosophy* **1**[3] [July 1997], www.film-philosophy.com/vol1-1997/n3sullivan.htm). Noël Carroll has described some of the history behind what he terms the "prejudice against cinema" as a new technological expressive form in terms of similar "problems" that had beset nineteenth-century French realist painters with the introduction of photography (*Philosophical Problems of Classical Film Theory* [Princeton, NJ: Princeton University Press, 1988], 20–29). Seen in twenty-first-century terms, the argument articulates an instance where a lawsuit is invoked, purportedly because the copyright of artistic integrity is at stake, but in realist terms the question of determining objective traits involves staving off a potential loss of business.

I   WHAT IS CINEMA?

This section contains ten examples of practitioners from the first half of the twentieth century, whose various systems and approaches are taken to address the question of the cinema as ontology, phenomenology and situated production of a physical ontology.

As articulated by film critic André Bazin, the very form of the question "What is cinema?" is ontological. That is, the question itself asks about the ways in which the cinema can bring together quite disparate parts, expressions, technologies and events and produce a whole unit: a film. Ontology is understood philosophically to be the study of being but, as with any study, different philosophers and theorists hold divergent positions on what ontology means for them, at particular times across history. The cinema can thus be considered a creative medium: a producer of new and different things. What governs, what drives, what produces this being are the issues that many film-theorists and film-philosophers articulate.

Film is also an unstable form. Film forms and products – cinema, television, computer games, online media industries that draw on the cinematic, that is, the film industry in its entirety – have reshaped knowledge of the world through various categorizations, genres, fields of enquiry, different methods of representation, intervention, provocation. Through its various assumptions and different purposes, film represents and questions the ways in which we think about things in the world, including the very nature of thinking as a perceptual activity that is entirely mediated in some form or another. In this sense, the question "What is cinema?" is also a phenomenological (and later post-phenomenological) question, where the cinematically produced explorations of consciousness and being through the perception of experience and movement are situated. Central to these questions of the constitution of the screen form and its theorization is the human subject, and its coded guises as a type of body (revolutionary, rebellious, obedient, sick, multiple).

The ways in which film-philosophy and film theory have been practised have shifted dramatically alongside shifts in the medium itself. As the filmic medium became a more widely distributed product and the industry grew, theorists and philosophers began to account for its impact. From its early development in the hands of theorists including Gilbert Cohen-Séat, Jean Mitry, Rudolph Arnheim, Béla Balázs,

Siegfried Kracauer and Hugo Münsterberg, film theory sought to account for not only the medium of film, but the conditions and ideas that film concealed and revealed. Henri Bergson (Ch. 6) had begun to address cinematic possibilities at the turn of the century, but it was not until the first half of the twentieth century that book-length studies addressing film-philosophy appeared, such as Münsterberg's *The Photoplay: A Psychological Study* (1916). In Chapter 1, Robert Sinnerbrink explores what constitutes the "enduring legacy" of Münsterberg's pioneering work for film-philosophy. This legacy, of appreciation of the aesthetics of everyday perception, is a question also discussed in the respective works of Flusser, Theodor Adorno, Maurice Merleau-Ponty and Roland Barthes, as described in this part. The "techno-imagination" and "passivity"-inducing control exerted by the cinema over its audience is a powerful argument put forward by Vilém Flusser, to which Adrian Martin alludes (Ch. 2). Also transfixed by the medium's capabilities, in his chapter Drehli Robnik describes how Kracauer came to take the position that the cinema exposed "a totalitarian media-machinery's grip on reality" during Hitler's system of Nazi rule (Ch. 3). Robnik explores what constitutes Kracauer's enormously influential aesthetic for other models of film theory.

While there are a plethora of such interlinking connections to make in this book, some of the names who appear to be absent are nevertheless here in spirit, and act as comparative and/or catalysing figures: Rudolf Arnheim, Alexandre Astruc, Jacques Aumont, Balázs, Walter Benjamin, Noël Burch, Jean Epstein, Sergei Eisenstein, Jean Mitry, Thierry Kuntzel, V. F. Perkins, Edgar Morin, Germaine Dulac, Meya Deren – the list goes on. For example, while Benjamin did not make it to Hollywood, his observations on film resonate in the words of his colleagues Adorno and Kracauer, who worked together as journalists in Berlin, and whose journey from Berlin via Paris to Hollywood and New York caused a critical renegotiation of the "pleasures" afforded the masses. Julie Kuhlken's chapter on Adorno (Ch. 4) demonstrates a shift in the thinking of the cinematic form, where the "disillusions" of the cinematic form and its influence over the masses mean that the filmic ontology shifts from the purely perceptual aesthetic that Münsterberg had argued to an overt political designation. The site this label attaches itself to is the body of the user of screen forms, a not always compliant vehicle, as Anna Powell explores in her chapter on Antonin Artaud's theory of film (Ch. 5). Artaud took a phenomenological approach to the cinema and, as Powell describes, Artaud was convinced of the "consciousness-altering" capacity of film. The theme of the capacity for mental as well as physical change is taken up in the subsequent chapters on Bergson, Merleau-Ponty, Emmanuel Levinas, André Bazin and Barthes.

In his chapter, Colin Gardner takes us through how Barthes' thinking about the problematic of the body and its doubling through the visual image cannot rely just on simple identification methodologies, but must be able to account for a different question, as Gardner phrases it in his essay. The question for Barthes, writes Gardner, becomes "lifelong" and "unsolved": "how can an aesthetics of the cinema utilize this *aporia* as a form of transformative, affective intensity instead of locking down the medium as a closed orthodoxy?" (Ch. 10). As Dorothea Olkowski describes in her chapter on philosopher Henri Bergson, the answer to Barthes' conundrum might be found in the movement of the "whole of affective life" itself (Ch. 6). Drawing from Bergson's startlingly prescient claims for the movement of the image that the cinema produced, Olkowski argues how the physics of movement, of mobility, produces cognitive abilities that have dramatically changed the directions of the evolution of certain species. However, when it comes to the cinema, Olkowski argues how this form of mechanistic movement is something, as Bergson and Barthes realized, that is reflective of a non-evolutionary type of "ordinary knowledge": that is, as Olkowski puts it, "not evolutionary, it does not reflect the inner becoming of things" (Ch. 6). In different ways, some of the thinkers in this section and the next (Merleau-Ponty, Gilles Deleuze, Jacques Derrida and Paul Virilio) explore the directions of screen/film movement-evolution. What is this world that the cinema creates? Helen A. Fielding demonstrates that, for Merleau-Ponty, "our perception of movement is intentionally situated within a world" (Ch. 7). Whether or not the subject of this perception is manipulated by cinematic conditions remains a topic for all thinkers in the book. The temporal manipulation of the subject by the conceptual movements made by the cinema is the paradoxical topic under examination by Sarah Cooper on Levinas (Ch. 8). Like many of the other thinkers in this book, Levinas was severely affected by the two world wars and existence becomes a paramount question, bound to the physicality of the body as a conduit for meanings. Finally, Bazin and Barthes offer, in their respective phenomenal positions, critiques of the everyday as material for film-philosophy. As Hunter Vaughan's chapter explains, Bazin's immediate worldly concerns find their voice through the theories of Bergson, eventually constructing a position for his film theory that realizes the immanent nature of the cinema (Ch. 9). Bazin's mandate to let the camera simply record the material nature of "reality" finds resonance in Barthes' concern with his vernacular.

What becomes interesting, as we read even this small selection of thinkers from both ends of the twentieth century, is how, over a hundred years, similar issues of the forms of film ethics seem to engage to direct the aesthetic concerns and rethinking of the writers. We see this in the opening section of the book with chapters on Münsterberg, Flusser, Kracauer, Adorno, Artaud, Bergson, Merleau-Ponty, Levinas, Bazin, Barthes: all legendary thinkers whose ideas find resonance in many screen media and film-philosophers working today (cf. Cubitt 2004; Beller 2006; Frampton 2006).

1 HUGO MÜNSTERBERG

Robert Sinnerbrink

Hugo Münsterberg (1863–1916) was a leading psychologist and philosopher who worked in Germany and the United States. He studied medicine and experimental psychology (with Wilhelm Wundt), and become Professor of Psychology at the University of Freiburg in 1892. His friendship with American psychologist and philosopher William James led to his appointment to the faculty at Harvard University in 1897. While in America, he became a famous academic, publishing numerous books on applied psychology, including *The Principles of Art Education* (1905), *Psychology and Crime* (1908), *Psychotherapy* (1909), *Vocation and Learning* (1912), *Psychology and Industrial Efficiency* (1913), *American Patriotism and other Social Studies* (1913), *Business Psychology* (1915) and *Psychology* (1916). In his final book, *The Photoplay* (1916), Münsterberg argued for the psychological and aesthetic distinctiveness of film as a serious art form. Following the outbreak of the First World War and his increasing criticisms of American life, Münsterberg's work fell out of favour with the public. Despite almost a century of neglect, *The Photoplay* is generally recognized today as the first genuine work of film theory.

How could we not have known him all these years? In 1916 this man understood cinema about as well as anyone ever will.   (Jean Mitry)[1]

Dedicated film enthusiasts might imagine that philosophical interest in film is a relatively recent phenomenon, dating back to Stanley Cavell's work in the 1970s or perhaps to the heyday of French film theory in the 1960s. It might be surprising, then, to learn that philosophical reflection on film was flourishing already in the early part of the twentieth century. In 1916, Hugo Münsterberg, Harvard professor of psychology and philosophy, and close colleague of William James, published *The Photoplay: A Psychological Study*, a book that many regard as the first work of film theory and the first to take seriously the specific potentials of film as an independent art form (Langdale 2002: 2).[2] Sadly, Münsterberg's groundbreaking text went out of print soon after the First World War, and remained so until it was reissued as a Dover reprint in 1970. Although still largely unknown today, Münsterberg was regarded as one of the leading intellectual figures of his day, prominent as one of the founders of applied psychology, and a philosopher who counted James, George Santayana and Josiah Royce among his peers (Andrew 1976: 14–15; Colapietro 2000: 477). He was a tireless proselytizer for the new medium, promoting it as a legitimate art form capable of synthesizing photography, drama, literature and music. Like many early film theorists, Münsterberg attempted to identify the artistic specificities of the new medium, championing the validity of cinema as a novel art form distinct from, and in ways even superior to, theatre and photography. More originally, he also articulated the distinctively *psychological* dimensions of cinematic experience, presenting one of the earliest – and most striking – instances of what Noël Carroll has called the "film/mind analogy": the suggestive parallel between cinematic techniques and perceptual experience (Carroll 1988b; cf. Wicclair 1978).

The fall from favour of thie remarkably prescient and eloquent study – one that Jean Mitry was amazed to discover anticipated his own psychological aesthetics of film – was probably due in large part to Münsterberg's rather abrasive critiques of contemporary American cultural life, coupled with the anti-German sentiment pervading American society during the Great War (Langdale 2002: 5–6). After nearly a century of neglect, however, it is surely time for a proper appropriation of Münsterberg's groundbreaking work, the full impact of which, as J. Dudley Andrew remarks, is perhaps "still to come" (1976: 26).

MÜNSTERBERG ON FILM AS ART

Like many later theorists, Münsterberg was quick to recognize the interplay of technological developments and psychological verisimilitude that made the cinema a unique modern art form. At the same time, he quickly discerned the popular appeal of the new art form and was receptive to both its liberating and "corrupting" potentials.[3] Trained as an experimental psychologist, and regarded as one of the founders of applied psychology, Münsterberg was a relative latecomer to the new art form of film, which he called, in keeping with the theatrical parallel common in his day, "the photoplay" (literally a filmed play, although Münsterberg will argue that cinema cannot be reduced to theatre). Overcoming his professorial disdain for the "vulgar" new art form, he describes the day in 1914 when he and a friend "risked seeing *Neptune's Daughter*", an experience that rapidly converted him to the "marvellous possibilities" that film had to offer (Langdale 2002: 8).[4] This conversion included immersing himself in the history of the new technology, meeting well-known directors and film stars of the day, and writing voluminously on film for newspapers and magazines. Yet he also quickly discerned the psychological power of film, as well as its artistic possibilities, and distilled all of these insights into *The Photoplay*. The latter is both an argument for the artistic validity of film in comparison with the theatre, and an original exploration of the analogy between film compositional devices (close-up, flashback, flash forward and so on) and psychological acts of consciousness (attention, recollection, imagination, emotional states and so on).

MÜNSTERBERG'S PSYCHOLOGY OF FILM

Münsterberg's most original contribution to the philosophy of film involves his fascinating examination of the parallel between cinematic devices and acts of consciousness. We can understand film's aesthetic power, Münsterberg ventures, once we attend to the way it "influences the mind of the spectator", which means analysing "the mental processes which this specific form of artistic endeavour produces in us" (Münsterberg 2002: 65). He commences with the important phenomenological point that while we know that we are watching "flat" two-dimensional images while in the cinema, we nonetheless *experience* the strong impression of depth and movement on the screen.[5] Drawing on numerous psychological experiments (including ones that he conducted himself), Münsterberg's claim endorses the idealist thesis that the experiences of depth and movement are not objectively present in the image as such, but are "added on" by the psychological (or cognitive) operations of our own minds (*ibid.*: 69–71). What is the difference between our perceptions of movement on stage compared with those on film? For Münsterberg, the former is obviously a real movement in space while the latter is an impression of movement generated by the "inner mental activity" uniting separate phases of movement in "the idea of connected action" (*ibid.*: 78). Depth and movement on screen are a mixture of "objective" perception and the subjective investment of this perception, which we do not even notice once we are perceptually and psychologically immersed in the complex visual world of the film.

Depth and movement, however, are only the elementary features of the film image. It is the psychological act of *attention* that Münsterberg emphasizes as the key to understanding the film–mind analogy. "Attention" is broadly taken to refer to the intentional directing of consciousness that selects what is relevant or not in our field of conscious awareness. Such directing can be further distinguished into *voluntary* and *involuntary* acts of attention. Voluntary attention involves our mindful focusing of consciousness through particular ideas or interests that we bring to our impressions or observations, ignoring whatever does not serve our interests or desires (attending to a task at hand, making something, solving a problem). Involuntary attention, by contrast, refers to the way events or objects in our environment can provide the cue for the (unwilled) focusing of our perceptual awareness (an explosion, a flashing neon sign, a cry that commands our notice). Involuntary attention also spans emotional and affective responses to what is happening in ourselves or in our environment: "Everything which appeals to our natural instincts, everything which stirs up hope or fear, enthusiasm or indignation, or any strong emotional excitement, will get control of our attention" (*ibid.*: 80). Clearly, ordinary experience involves a complex interplay of voluntary and involuntary attention (as when I attend to a friend's injury, prompted by my reaction to her cry of pain).

Münsterberg then turns to the question of affective and perceptual involvement in film and theatrical performance, exploring the kinds of psychological and philosophical issues that would later become central to theories of cinematic identification. In theatrical performance, as in film, it is *involuntary* attention that must be elicited in order to ensure aesthetic and psychological involvement. In the case of film, voluntary attention may, of course, come into play in a distanced, reflective way (as when we muse on an actor's attire or how a shot was achieved, or notice an inconsistency in the editing). Genuine aesthetic engagement with the film, however, demands that we open ourselves up to the capturing of our involuntary attention: "we must accept those cues for our attention which the playwright and the producers have prepared for us" (*ibid.*: 82).

As with the theatre, film (and here Münsterberg means *silent* film) relies on the expressiveness of the human face, the gestures of the actors' bodies and the movement and action of the characters to compose the images commanding our involuntary attention. Not only movement but also what later theorists dubbed *mise en scène* (the specific arrangement of objects and figures composing the image) can elicit our rapt attention: "An unusual face, a queer dress, a gorgeous costume or a surprising lack of costume, a quaint piece of decoration, may attract our mind and even hold it spellbound for a while" (*ibid.*: 84). Finally, the power of landscape and setting opens up immensely powerful visual means of capturing audience attention and even of expressing emotional colouring or mood.

To this extent film parallels or extends the possibilities of theatre. But film truly comes into its own through its capacity to emulate the intersecting aspects of acts of attention: intensification of attentive focus to what is most arresting or interesting and the withdrawal of attentive focus from what is not; the adjustment of the body towards that which captures our attention and the clustering of meanings – "ideas and feelings and impulses" (*ibid.*: 86) – around the object of our attention. In the theatre, too, our attention is focused on that which is most relevant (the hand of the actor carrying the gun, the look of terror on his victim's face); but the theatre also has limits as to how vividly it can actually emulate these acts of attention (although my gaze is intent on the killer's hand, I can only see that man's hand from a distance). Film, however, can surpass theatre in this respect, for it can visually elicit and direct our involuntary attention through cinematic devices of composition and montage in ways that theatrical performance would find difficult to match.

The close-up, for example, provides a visual analogue for the intensification of perception that attends attentive focus. Münsterberg is the first of many theorists to highlight the unique possibilities of the cinematic image – particularly the close-up – in drawing our attention to particular objects, gestures or expressions. His originality lies in underlining the strong analogy between perceptual attention and cinematic devices, which cannot be emulated in live theatrical performance: "*The close-up has objectified in our world of perception our mental act of attention and by it has furnished art with a means which far transcends the power of any theatre stage*" (*ibid.*: 87). Not only does the close-up focus our immediate attention, but it quickly becomes part of the familiar grammar of film narrative.

To the close-up we must add the flashback and its rather striking suggestion of the operation of memory. Here again a film–mind parallel can be readily found, which Münsterberg draws out by contrasting film with the theatre. Understanding a theatrical performance, for example, relies on our remembering the sequence of scenes that preceded the one that is before us. A character can draw attention to an earlier scene, stage props, lighting and music can also suggest these to us, but the scene itself cannot be directly "replayed" before our eyes. With film, however, things are different.

The act of remembering can be screened, so to speak, before our very eyes thanks to the use of flashbacks. Here Münsterberg claims that the film literally "screens" memory; whether it is our recollection, the recollection of a character or the film's recollection of an earlier scene or narrative sequence, "*the act which in the ordinary theatre would go on in our mind alone is here in the photography projected into the pictures themselves*" (*ibid.*: 90). The film–mind analogy is thus most strongly drawn in the case of the flashback, which provides "an objectivation of our memory function" that parallels the "mental act of remembering" (*ibid.*). It is as though the outer world (of film images) were now shaped by our fleeting perceptions or imagined recollections, the narrative on screen magically expressing "the inner movements of the mind" (*ibid.*: 128).

So how do we make sense of the flashback? Münsterberg notes that it is not just our own recollection of past scenes that can be re-presented on the screen; more typically, we are given privileged access to a character's recollection of past events (or a redramatization of those events). Münsterberg thus carefully anatomizes the varieties and conventions of the flashback as part of his strong claim for it being an "objectification" of memory (*ibid.*: 90–96). We might question, however, the grounds on which Münsterberg draws such a strong parallel between the flashback and memory. While it is certainly true that flashbacks are often connected with a particular character, it is not clear that we should simply assume that these "belong" to the character in question or, more bizarrely, that they are an "objectification" of his or her mental processes (most flashbacks are *about* rather than *of* a character). Nor is it obvious to what extent an analogy can be plausibly drawn between "mental images" and cinematic images; what "mental images" are remains a vexing question, while attempts to show that film directly screens "mental images" are at best controversial (cf. Frampton 2006: 15–26).

In a famous childhood flashback sequence from Orson Welles's *Citizen Kane* (1941), for example, we see the young Charles Kane's sled, with its Rosebud insignia, shown to us in close-up (and in a long take) as it is slowly covered by snow. This intense focus on the sled suggests that it will be an important clue in unravelling the enigma of Kane's life. While we might loosely describe this as "a scene from Kane's childhood", it is not, strictly speaking, Kane's own recollection of a childhood experience, since it includes elements he could not have experienced (such as the important conversation between his parents occurring while he played outside in the snow). It cannot be wholly attributed to any of the characters in the sequence either, since it includes images that occur, strictly speaking, '"for no one" (apart from us, who remain outside the diegetic world of the film). Such "anonymous" images – the "Rosebud" sled being slowly covered by snow – can often be precisely what a scene or sequence is about. Rather than say that this is a particular character's recollection, we might more accurately say that it is the film's "recollection" of a past that intersects with, although it is not reducible to, those of the various characters in the scene. This move, however, would be to attribute to *the film* (rather than to a character, or even the film-maker) an animating intentionality or consciousness – a "filmind", to use Daniel Frampton's term – whose thoughts animate and compose the image-world we experience as the film (Frampton 2006: 73–102).

What of the other aspects of this analogy? Emotional expression is clearly one of the most important dimensions of our experience of film. Indeed, the central aim of cinematic art, Münsterberg remarks, must be "to picture emotions" (2002: 99). This is an interesting point given the absence of audible verbal dialogue in silent film, which means that actors have to rely on facial expression, physical gestures and bodily comportment in order to communicate emotional meaning. Here again the close-up reveals possibilities of emotional expression that theatre would struggle to convey through strictly visual means. At the same time, silent film also courts the risk of attempting to reproduce stage-like modes of performance, which may not be quite appropriate to the medium and indeed can quickly degenerate into caricature (*ibid.*: 100–101).

In a lucid discussion of distinct forms of emotional identification, Münsterberg notes that it can be divided into identification with a character's emotional state and our more independent emotional responses to a character's behaviour. In Jonathan Demme's *The Silence of the Lambs* (1991), for example, we readily identify with FBI agent Clarice Starling's (Jodie Foster's) terror as she tries to find and shoot notorious serial killer Buffalo Bill in the darkened cellar of his house. To add to the horror of the scenario, we can see Clarice's terrified face and hear her panicky, shallow breathing from the perspective of Buffalo Bill himself, thanks to his unnerving night-vision goggles. We are not (one hopes!) thereby disposed to identify with *his* murderous intent, although we do, disturbingly, see Clarice from his point of view. On the contrary, this disturbing proximity enables us to sympathize with her terrifying plight all the more, while at the same time forcing us to observe her precisely from the killer's viewpoint, Clarice's trembling hand and gun just inches from his face in the darkness. The scene strikingly enacts both forms of emotional response that Münsterberg describes: the direct identification with Clarice's terrifying plight, and the horror we feel in response to Buffalo Bill's hideous night-vision game of cat and mouse – not to mention the satisfaction and relief we experience once Clarice shoots him in the dark. It also masterfully plays with the affect of *suspense* – will she slay the killer or become his victim? – that Münsterberg identifies as essential to successful cinematic drama (Langdale 2002: 21).

Of course, it is not only the emotional expression of characters to which we respond. As Münsterberg points out, film can elicit emotional investment in many different ways: for example, through objects (the "Rosebud" sled in *Citizen Kane*) or via landscape (romantic-sublime in Terrence Malick's *Days of Heaven* [1978]; indigenous dreaming meets Western image-making in Rolf de Heer and Peter Djigirr's *Ten Canoes* [2006]); or through camera movements (Alfred Hitchcock's probing, roving, "thinking" camera in *Rear Window* [1954]; the "reality-effect" of the hand-held camera in Lars von Trier's *Breaking the Waves* [1996]; the extraordinary continuous camera movement across time and history in Alexander Sokurov's *Russkiy kovcheg* [Russian ark, 2002]; or the vertiginous, disorienting hypermobility of the camera in Gaspar Noé's *Irréversible* [2002]). As though anticipating some of these examples, Münsterberg explicitly mentions how a film-maker might wish to "produce the effect of trembling", such as we find in the use of hand-held cameras today, and how mounting the camera on "a slightly rocking support", such that it would trace complex figures of movement with an "uncanny whirling character", would result in "unusual sensations which produce a new shading of the emotional background" (2002: 107). All of these techniques are capable of generating powerful emotional and affective responses in distinctively cinematic ways. Münsterberg's analyses are remarkably prescient in their emphasis on the distinctive possibilities of the film image to generate affect compared with theatre and other visual arts.

MÜNSTERBERG'S AESTHETICS OF FILM

Film aesthetics has sometimes been described as the "poor cousin" of film theory, an awkward amalgam of philosophical analysis and film criticism. Yet in this very early text of film theory we find a rich vein of philosophical aesthetics brought to bear on the new art of the cinema. This is not really surprising, considering that Münsterberg was a philosopher–psychologist who was able to bring classic motifs from neo-Kantian aesthetics into productive relationship with a strongly empiricist commitment to experimental psychology. It is worth remembering that much of the early debate over film concerned the question whether it qualified as a new art form or was merely a clever technical gadget, apt to record reality faithfully but devoid of real artistic merit. Like Rudolph Arnheim, Münsterberg's aesthetic approach to film in *The Photoplay* strongly argued the case for film as art: a medium capable of artistically transfiguring, rather than simply recording, our visual and perceptual experience.

Münsterberg combines, in novel fashion, a Kantian "aesthetic attitude" approach to film with a Schopenhauerian metaphysics of art as enabling us to transcend our immediate spatiotemporal context. He begins with the critical point that the traditional mimetic approach – art as an imitation of nature – is clearly inadequate as an account of art (2002: 113–17). Art cannot simply be imitation since imitation as such is not necessarily aesthetically pleasing (compare duck lures and wax dummies), while many of the most aesthetically striking arts are non-mimetic (architecture and music) or involve decidedly non-imitative aesthetic techniques or devices (such as poetic speech in dramatic performance). Indeed, art is defined precisely by its *transcending* of the mere imitation of reality: "It is artistic just in so far as it does not imitate reality but changes the world, selects from it special features for new purposes, remodels the world, and is, through this, truly creative" (*ibid.*: 114). Art is about the artistic transfiguration of our experience, which will always trump mere imitation or decorative attractiveness.

The second point is that experiencing art aesthetically requires that one adopt the appropriate *aesthetic attitude*: a detached, "disinterested" pleasure in the appearance of the object for its own sake. Echoing Immanuel Kant and Arthur Schopenhauer, Münsterberg points out that the same object can be experienced differently depending on the cognitive and practical interests we bring to bear on it: the same landscape strikes the farmer, the scientist or the photographer in quite different ways (as pasture, as geological stratum or as aesthetic image). What Münsterberg adds to this familiar Kantian point is an interesting Schopenhauerian twist. The theorist (scientist or scholar) seeks to find the causal networks of which the object is a part, to situate it in the physical processes of the universe (*ibid.*: 116). The artist, by contrast, presents the object independent of its causal relations or obedience to general laws; the artist creates an image of the singular object in splendid isolation, like a self-sufficient world that we can nonetheless enjoy (*ibid.*: 116–17). Like Schopenhauer, Münsterberg claims that art presents a part of our experience "liberated from all connection" with the world; the unified, harmonious, perfectly isolated work is what procures genuine aesthetic pleasure. Why? Because it is only in art, to paraphrase Schopenhauer, that we can find temporary solace from the vicissitudes of desire and the sufferings that attend our ceaseless striving. Artworks provide a transfigured image of unity – "complete in itself" – that transcends our involvement in the practical world, thereby satisfying our desires in a way that brings temporary aesthetic delight (*ibid.*: 121).

How does this strongly Kantian and Schopenhauerian aesthetic relate to our experience of film? For one thing, film has its own distinctive aesthetic that cannot be imported from painting, literature or theatre. From both aesthetic and psychological perspectives, narrative film presents a human story *"by overcoming the forms of the outer world, namely, space, time, and causality, and by adjusting the events to the forms of the inner world, namely, attention, memory, imagination, and emotion"* (*ibid.*: 129). In other words, the inherent abstraction of the film image (especially in silent film) takes the screen performance away from the physical realm and brings it closer to the mental dimensions of experience. Cinema emulates subjectivity. Movement can be presented in ways that defy the limits of our natural perception; time can be "left behind" as we revert to the past, jump back to the present, divide along different timelines or imagine the future in different ways. The sheer fluidity of cinematic representation makes possible *the aesthetic transcending* of the ordinary constraints of time and space that order our practical experience of the world. This is what Münsterberg means by contrasting the time- and space-bound character of theatre and theatrical performance with the liberation from time and space constraints opened up by the use of film narrative techniques (most vividly displayed, I suggest, in animation).

What are we to make of this intriguing claim? Carroll suggests (1988b: 489–99) that Münsterberg construes the aesthetic "isolation" of film art to mean that it *quite literally* attempts to "overcome outer forms of space, time and causality" (*ibid.*: 494). More precisely, Münsterberg's idea – derived from Schopenhauer's discussion of art in *The World as Will and Representation*, Vol. I – is that film art can "somehow release us from our ordinary experience of things with respect to space, time and causality" (*ibid.*: 496). Carroll argues, however, that this is incoherent since narrative film (or even experimental film) is necessarily parasitic on these fundamental conditions of cognitive experience in order to represent any kind of meaningful action (or to plot a narrative). Indeed, the only way of experiencing the world independently of space, time and causality, Carroll argues, would be to imagine something like a "sheer bodily existent" living in a perpetual present (*ibid.*: 495–6). And this is, of course, a form of experience that necessarily remains inaccessible to us. Hence Münsterberg's claims about film, Carroll concludes, cannot be sustained, since there is no meaningful contrast to be made between our cognitive experience and something that would allegedly transcend the very conditions of such experience (*ibid.*: 496).

Carroll's critique, however, rests on an overly literal interpretation of Münsterberg's claims concerning the aesthetic possibilities of cinema. It is not a metaphysical or epistemological claim so much as a claim about the kind of *aesthetic experience* that film makes possible in contrast with other art forms such as the theatre. Cinematic performance is not as bound to "space, time, and causality" as is "live" stage perform-ance, since the latter is always necessarily confined to the spatiotemporal present of the performers' speeches and actions. The screen performer's image, on the other hand, can be juxtaposed with any number of other images from disparate spaces, times, even "defying" ordinary causality through the creative use of montage and special effects (especially today with the blurring of cinema and animation thanks to computer-generated imagery [CGI] and digital image technology).

To be sure, Münsterberg perhaps invited this confusion by his rather loose Schopenhauerian talk of "overcoming" space, time and causality. What we should say, rather, is that cinema *manipulates* outer forms of space, time and causality, in order to stress that we are not dealing with outlandishly metaphysical claims. The technical devices and aesthetic techniques of the film medium make possible an *aesthetic manipulation* of space, time and causality in ways that are often simply not available for theatrical performance. Carroll underplays this key hermeneutic point; hence his rather tendentious critique of the idea that, for Münsterberg, film is an art that can "overcome" the very conditions of our cognitive experience of the world.

MÜNSTERBERG'S FILM–MIND ANALOGY

What are we to make, then, of Münsterberg's intriguing analogy between film and the human mind? Mark Wicclair has argued that it is supposed to be a *phenomenological* correlation between film images and perceptual experience (1978). The close-up phe-nomenologically resembles an act of attention; the flashback is a phenomenological analogue of memory; and so on. As Wicclair points out, however, we do not actu-ally perceive objects as a "close-up" image, nor do we recollect our own experiences from a third-person or "objective" point of view. As Wicclair, Carroll and Frampton all observe, a phenomenologically correct "flashback" would show the persistence of my present perception along with the imaginary "superimposition" of my recollected image (seeing my absent partner's face as I stare at waves on the beach). For this rea-son Münsterberg's film–mind analogy fails to show a phenomenological correlation between film image and human perception.

How, then, should this analogy be taken? Wicclair suggests construing it *function-ally* rather than phenomenologically (1978: 43): certain cinematic images or devices serve the same *functional role* as certain acts of perception or recollection. This deftly avoids the difficulties afflicting the phenomenological version of the film–mind ana-logy (after all, we do not actually perceive the world in close-up, with zooms, or via rapid cuts). In drawing a functional analogy between films and minds, we can better understand film's aesthetic power as well as the striking affinity between film and perceptual experience.

Here again, Carroll argues, a serious problem emerges, one that potentially afflicts *all* versions of the film–mind analogy (1988b). The logic of analogy – I compare *A* to *B* in order to illuminate *A* – requires that we know more about the nature of *B* than of *A*, since that is the point of the analogy (to illuminate *A*). In Plato's *Republic*, for example, Socrates compared human beings to prisoners in a cave taking shadow-images for reality, who gradually discover that the real world outside is illuminated by the sun. We know from ordinary experience what that is like, so the cave analogy helps us to understand the meaning of Platonic philosophical education.[6] The problem with film–mind analogies, Carroll argues, is that they fail to follow this logic of analogy; we do not know enough about the mind in order to make the analogy theoretically illuminating. As Carroll notes, I can usefully compare the mind to a computer because we know how computers work, how they are programmed, and so on; hence the cognitive science analogy between consciousness and artificial intelligence can be theoretically illuminating (*ibid.*: 498). But to say that a computer is like the mind is not really illuminating in the right way, since we know very well how computers work but not really how our minds do, which is what the analogy is supposed to show. Hence, Carroll concludes, to say that *film is mind-like*, as Münsterberg does, is similarly unhelpful, because we do not really know enough about consciousness (memory, attention, imagination and so on) to make the analogy theoretically useful.[7]

Does this mean that Münsterberg's attempt to theorize the film–mind analogy, while historically interesting, remains a theoretical dead end? Not at all. As Frampton argues, we can respond to Carroll by making a familiar phenomenological point: "Münsterberg was obviously making a comparison with common 'experience', and Carroll's critique seems better suited to those who propose that film can show mental states" (2006: 22). Carroll assumes that the point of Münsterberg's film–mind analogy is strictly theoretical: *knowledge* of what *film is*, pursued with reference to the mental states, which implies that we need to presuppose adequate knowledge of the mind (which we may not actually have). But what if the analogy is supposed to describe our complex experience of film, of what Cavell more felicitously called "the world viewed"? After all, I do not need a theory of mind in order to perceive the world; likewise, I do not need a theory of mind in order to understand how images can have a functional role similar to ordinary states of consciousness. So, *contra* Carroll, Münsterberg's film–mind analogy *can* be illuminating because it draws on our *ordinary experience* of perception, attention, emotion and imagination, all of which we must presuppose in understanding and enjoying any kind of film.

To this phenomenological remark I shall add an aesthetic pendant. Wicclair and Carroll both assume that Münsterberg is making an epistemological or ontological claim rather than an *aesthetic* one concerning the relative "superiority" of film art over theatrical presentation. Indeed, Münsterberg's film–mind analogy, I would suggest, is an *aesthetic analogy*, more like a poetic figure than a theoretical argument. It is a way of drawing attention to new aspects of our experience of film by way of a powerful metaphor: one that draws on ordinary experience but also refers to our experience of film – its history, culture and aesthetic complexity. It is not so much conceived as a theoretical problem, although this is relevant, but as a way of transforming our own experience of film. That is the enduring legacy of Münsterberg's pioneering work in film-philosophy: can we think philosophically about film in a way that remains true to our aesthetic experience of it?

NOTES

1. Quoted by J. D. Andrew, "Hugo Münsterberg", in his *The Major Film Theories: An Introduction*, 14–26 (Oxford: Oxford University Press, 1976), 26, and attributed to a "private conversation with the author" (*ibid*.: 255). As Vincent Colapietro notes, Mitry's remark carries the authority of one of the great French film theorists; his major work, *The Aesthetics and Psychology of the Cinema*, C. King (trans.) (Bloomington, IN: Indiana University Press, [1963] 2000), is dedicated "to the very topics to which Münsterberg devoted the two main parts of *The Photoplay*" (ibid.: 495).
2. As Allan Langdale notes, Münsterberg's book was preceded by American poet Vachel Lindsay's *The Art of the Moving Picture* (New York: Macmillan, 1915) but is "clearly more compelling"; "S(t)imulation of Mind: The Film Theory of Hugo Münsterberg", in *Hugo Münsterberg On Film: The Photoplay – A Psychological Study and Other Writings*, A. Langdale (ed.), 1–41 (London & New York: Routledge, 2002), 27. It anticipates Rudolf Arnheim's better-known and theoretically quite similar *Film as Art* (London: Faber, 1957), which has had an immense effect on film theory, whereas *The Photoplay* has been all but ignored (Langdale, "S(t)imulation of Mind", 27).
3. See Münsterberg's cautionary essay of 1917 advocating censorship of depictions of immorality, "Peril to Childhood in the Movies", in *Hugo Münsterberg On Film*, 191–200.
4. As Langdale notes, *Neptune's Daughter* (1914) was a fantasy film directed by Herbert Brenon and starring Annette Kellerman, an Australian swimming star who founded synchronized swimming, and pioneered "that rarefied genre of Hollywood films involving aquatic spectacles" ("S(t)imulation of Mind", 7–8).
5. Arnheim's *Film as Art* makes the same point. After noting how depth perception can be emulated by "the stereoscope" (the simultaneous projection of slightly different images for each eye), Arnheim remarks that the "effect of film is neither absolutely two-dimensional nor absolutely three-dimensional, but something between" (*Film as Art*, 20). Münsterberg made the same observations on the stereoscope and the "depth effect" of motion pictures over a decade and a half earlier (2002: 65–71): "*We have reality with all its true dimensions; and yet it keeps the fleeting, passing surface suggestion without true depth and fullness, as different from a mere picture as from a stage performance*" (*ibid*.: 71).
6. This is an analogy, incidentally, with a long history in the philosophy of film: Plato's cave as film theatre.
7. On the other hand, to say that the mind is like film – as philosophers such as Henri Bergson, Edmund Husserl and Bernard Stiegler have done – can be highly illuminating.

2 VILÉM FLUSSER

Adrian Martin

Vilém Flusser was born in Prague on 12 May 1920. He grew up in a family of Jewish intellectuals, and began studying philosophy in 1939. Facing the German Occupation, he and his wife Edith first fled to London, and then settled in Brazil. During the 1940s and 1950s, he worked in industry. In 1959 he became Lecturer in the Philosophy of Science at the University of São Paulo, and began publishing his first academic essays and newspaper articles. His first book, *Língua e realidade* (Language and reality), appeared in 1963. Throughout the 1960s, Flusser's work addresses his formative interests in existentialism, phenomenology and linguistics, but his general concern with communication leads him increasingly towards media and technology, subjects on which his reflections were far-reaching and prescient of radical changes in the organization of human society. In 1972, owing to conflict with Brazil's military dictatorship, the Flussers move to Europe, eventually settling in Robion in the south of France. Throughout the 1970s and 1980s his books, articles, courses and conference interventions multiply, written by him in five languages, and also disseminated through translation. Currently, five books exist in English: *Towards a Philosophy of Photography* (1983; English trans. 2000), *The Shape of Things* (1993; English trans. 1999), *From Subject to Project* (1994; English trans. 1996), *The Freedom of the Migrant* (1994; English trans. 2003) and *Writings* (2002). Flusser died in a car accident on 27 November 1991, shortly after revisiting Prague for the first time in over fifty years.

Of all the great philosophers whose work has brushed against cinema, Vilém Flusser may be the purest in his activity of theorizing. In fact, this is a constant of his work in almost every domain. Whether speaking of film, still photography or the design arts – among the very many fields he addressed in his prolific output – Flusser eschews virtually all reference to specific works, artists, genres or movements. This can disconcert first-time readers of his texts, as it seems so odd in an era of connoisseur–aesthetes such as Gilles Deleuze (1986; 1989), Santos Zunzunegui (1989) or Jacques Rancière (2006a). Flusser's writings on design, for example, rarely even mention designers, famous or otherwise; Flusser prefers to meditate on certain prototypes of "the shape of things" (the title of his collected essays on this topic) – tent, typewriter, wall, wheel, desk. Occasionally, a very broad distinction will be drawn – between, say, family snapshots and artistic photography – but usually in order to be dissolved at a higher level of medium-related generality. In his discussion of cinema, even less particularity comes into play than in his celebrated book *Towards a Philosophy of Photography* (2000). The distinction between, for instance, commercial–mainstream and alternative–experimental cinema does not register as significant for Flusser; indeed, as we shall see, his line of argument about film imperiously opposes any such distinction.

Flusser is, quite simply, a theorist: a pure theorist, as in the distinction in mathematics and science between pure and applied theory. He passes over (for the most part) individual instances of an art or craft medium, because what concerns him is precisely the grounding of the medium itself: what defines it, and what it allows. An unshakeable tenet of his view of things is that, at least since the modern, industrialized, technological age, people (humble citizens or elevated artists) do not *use* media as some means to an expressive end: they are *used by* these media, reduced to mere effects, mere *operators* of a mechanism that they scarcely understand (hence his vision of the camera as an unknowable "black box"). In a typical turn of phrase, he refers to "a human being in possession of a camera (or of a camera in possession of a human being)" (2000: 33).

Such an analysis, coming from Flusser, is not a matter of an anti-humanist philosophy – akin to the poststructuralist maxim of the 1960s and 1970s that "we do not speak, we are spoken" by language – but a simple fact of how he sees, on a grand scale, the so-called progress of civilization. Once rational society has perfected first the camera and then the computer (among its many advanced machines), it abandons rational foundations for an inexorable trip back to the age of magic; "our" images – Flusser calls them *techno-images* – come into being almost without us, or despite us, via intricate technical means that comparatively few of us truly understand. As in a story by Jorge Luis Borges or Philip K. Dick, these images proliferate, connect up and cover the entire surface of the world, whether actual or virtual: they create a New World, one that may not, ultimately, be entirely hospitable or comprehensible to us.

Yet Flusser, when he conjures such a destiny, although he may be circumspect and even droll, is never gloomy. He plays the part of neither the thundering Grand Pessimist (as a media critic such as Neil Postman does) nor the cynical, resigned, nihilistic Man of Philosophy at world's end (as Jean Baudrillard gleefully does). In Flusser's view, we may be running out of time to grasp the New World coming into being around us, but we nonetheless have the chance to seize the day and reboot ourselves into a state of advanced consciousness. "One of my commitments is to teach people, as far as I can, to ask the right questions, not to become victims of the image, but to use the image as a tool for critical analysis" (Flusser 1988). For the world of techno-images is, for Flusser, concrete and therefore usable, and in this he opposes Baudrillard:

> Baudrillard believes that we are living in a world where the simulations hide reality. I think this is a nonsensical proposition. ... Images are just as concrete as is the table on which your machine is standing now. We do not have any ontological tool any longer to distinguish between a simulation and a non-simulation. The critical tool which we have to use is concreticity as opposed to abstractness.
> *(Ibid.)*

And there is no greater testament to this possibility of concrete, practical analysis than Flusser's own writing, much of it produced on a daily or weekly basis for newspapers and magazines, as well as academic journals, arts events, conferences and many sorts of "occasional" utterance. On this level, Flusser must be considered on the same plane as André Bazin, Roland Barthes, or Siegfried Kracauer during his early years in Germany: in other words, at least in part, as a journalist. As Raymond Bellour once said of Serge Daney, they all, in rising to the occasion and delivering on demand, perpetually reconciled the "charming lightness" of regular journalism with the "exacting duties of rationality", and it is "from this tension … that poetry is born" (Bellour 1986: 15).

The poetry of Flusser's prose is born from a very particular variant of this tension inherent to the situation of an intellectual writing popular journalism. On the one hand, he honed his discourse to the point where it was perfectly simple, clear, lucid, and thus, as a side effect, fairly easily translatable from one language to another, a fact borne out by his practice of sometimes stopping the composition of a piece midway and beginning it over in another of the five languages (Czech, German, French, Portuguese and English) in which he was fully fluent as a writer (Pawley 1999: 14). Each of his pieces takes the form of an elegant, step-by-step demonstration of an idea: the terms and premises are defined, the consequences and ramifications are explored, and a sober, limpid conclusion is reached. There is nothing abstruse in his work; everything proceeds concretely, plainly.

At the same time, on the other hand, Flusser would exploit the freedom to range very widely very swiftly, across centuries and epochs, civilizations and historic revolutions, the births and deaths of vast social or cultural formations, in order to place whatever phenomenon was before his immediate attention into his large-scale story of Mankind. It was a style of writing he dubbed "philosophical science-fiction" (*ibid*: 13). This is what gives a reader the impression of a certain sweeping generalization, an overarching abstractness.

Flusser was the consummate Big Picture guy. He gave the impression – obviously a true one – of having processed and mastered thousands of documents of all sorts (written, pictorial, architectural, economic, technological); yet, despite his early schooling (during the late 1930s and 1940s) in Heidegger, existentialism and phenomenology, he scarcely ever provided a single footnote, or bowed to any of his philosophical contemporaries. He preferred to work on the level of identifying broad tendencies, in a dramatic and sometimes deliberately comical style of argumentative rhetoric.

Before delving into Flusser's statements on film and video, it is necessary to outline briefly the rhetorical and argumentative structure of several of his typical, characteristic, short texts. A preliminary step towards this can be supplied from a characteristically succinct statement from the opening lines of *Towards a Philosophy of Photography*:

> This book is based on the hypothesis that two fundamental turning points can be observed in human culture since its inception. The first, around the middle of the second millennium BC, can be summed up under the heading

"the invention of linear writing"; the second, the one we are currently experiencing, could be called "the invention of technical images".

This hypothesis contains the suspicion that the structure of culture – and therefore existence itself – is undergoing a fundamental change.

(Flusser 2000: 7)

In his essay "The Factory", Flusser urges us to pay attention to the development of what he calls "working-floors" throughout history, from the Neolithic pottery centre to the modern factory layout. We will learn, for instance, more about "the roots of Humanism, the Reformation and the Renaissance" by studying a fourteenth-century shoemaker's workshop than by interpreting "works of art and political, philosophical and theological texts" of the time (1999: 43–4). Flusser sees "human history as the history of manufacturing and everything else as mere footnotes" (*ibid*: 44). Our contemporary "information society" is, for him, precisely, the point at which inherited, biological information is replaced by "acquired, cultural information" (*ibid.*). Manufacturing involves – in a rich example of Flusser's linguistic–etymological excavation – the action of *turning*, which is a prime example of "genetically inherited information": "Manufacturing means turning what is available in the environment to one's own advantage, turning it into something manufactured, turning it over to use and thus turning it to account" (*ibid.*).

Thus, Flusser sees four "rough periods" of turning in human history: by hands, tools, machines and robots. And "factories are places in which new kinds of human beings are always being produced: first the hand-man, then the tool-man, then the machine-man, and finally the robot-man" (*ibid.*: 44–5). Each mode of turning generates its own kind of workspace: the primitives could move about and use their hands anywhere, but tools require a space, which alienates us from nature and ensures we are "both protected and imprisoned by culture" (*ibid.*: 45). From the humble potter's studio we then pass, in the Industrial Revolution, to the model of the factory, where the machine is placed at the centre of the workspace (and the entire site is placed at the centre of various sorts of social transportation flows), while human beings become mere operatives; this is the era of the assembly line. The coming robot age, however, promises (at least in its hype) to free human beings from the factory "madhouse" and return us to a condition akin to primitive times: we will be accompanied by or connected to our robot "prostheses" wherever we go (*ibid.*: 46). Flusser's prescience, on this point, is acute: "Everyone will be linked to everyone else everywhere and all the time by reversible cable, and via these cables (as well as the robots) they will turn to use everything available to be turned into something and thus turned to account" (*ibid.*: 48).

A second example: in his breathtakingly brief (two-and-a-half-page) essay "Shelters, Screens and Tents", Flusser muses on the idea of a wall, and on the difference between different types of walls – for him, the convenient key (like so many mundane, everyday phenomena) to understanding our civilization and its discontents. The solid wall marks, for Flusser, a neurotic society: a society of houses and thus dark, Gothic secrets, of properties and possessions; and of folly, too, because the wall will always be razed, in the final instance, by the typhoon, flood or earthquake. But whereas the solid wall gathers and locks people in, what Flusser calls the *screen wall* – incarnated in history variously by the tent, the kite or the boating sail – is "a place where people assemble and disperse, a calming of the wind". It is the site for the "assembly of experience"; it is woven, and thus a *network* (*ibid.*: 57).

It is only a small step for Flusser to move from the physical, material kind of screen to the immaterial kind: the screen that receives projected images, or (increasingly) holds computerized, digital images. From the Persian carpet to the Renaissance oil painting, from cinema to new media art, images (and thus memories) are stored within the surface of this woven wall. A wall that reflects movement, but itself increasingly moves within the everyday world, made portable with the development of the laptop computer and the mobile phone.

In the material so far made available in the languages I can read (English and French), only two of Flusser's pieces tackle cinema – or its later outgrowth, video – directly and at length: the essay "On the Production and Consumption of Films", dating from 1979 (Flusser 2006); and the work on video/conceptual artist Fred Forest, which exists as a (poorly translated) 1975 essay and as a book, *L'Art sociologique et vidéo à travers la demarche de Fred Forest* (Sociological art and video through the work of Fred Forest; 1977). Is this latter effort an exception to the "no-artist" rule in Flusser's researches? In fact, no: as we shall see, his specific interest is in what he construes as the *gesture of videography* practised by Forest.

There may be more to be found on cinema amid the complete archive of Flusser's work (published and unpublished) in all languages, which is today held at the University of Arts Berlin.[1] He did, after all, spend time between 1967 and 1972 as Appointed Professor for Philosophy of Communication at the Escola Dramática and the Escola de Superiore de Cinema in São Paulo.

I shall not dwell long here on Flusser's piece on Fred Forest, an artist with whom he collaborated from the 1970s onwards. It takes its place within Flusser's ongoing work on human gesture, its actuality (as a process of communication), recording and depiction. (The very last work he saw published in his lifetime was the 1991 German text *Gesten: Versuch einer Phänomenologie* [Gestures: towards a phenomenology].) What attracts Flusser to Forest's protean work in many artistic and cultural forms is the latter's capacity to *intervene* in the situation or medium he addresses: to, in some sense, transform it (as in his celebrated project *150cm2 of Newspaper*, involving the hiring of advertising space in *Le Monde* in 1972 to publish small blank squares accompanied by the invitation to readers to fill the space with their own artwork).[2] Related to Flusser's reflections on the physical act or gesture of photographing in *Towards a Philosophy of Photography* (see below), he eagerly observes the feedback loop or "curious dialogue" created by Forest's videographic recording of gestures (including his own gestures of pipe smoking!):

> The camera that Forest held between his hands inevitably followed my gestures, via corresponding "gesture-movements". But his gestures obliged my own gestures, in turn, to alter in response. So a dialogue settled, whose numerous levels were not entirely conscious, neither for Forest nor for me, because they were not entirely deliberate. My hands answered the camera's

gestures, and this modification of my hand movements changed, subtly, my words and my thoughts. And Forest not only moved in response to my movements, but also to the thoughts that I articulated verbally.

(Flusser 1975, trans. modified)

"On the Production and Consumption of Films" is a major essay on the cinematic apparatus.[3] On this point, however, there are two issues for us to deal with. First, we must understand Flusser's own use of the term, since it bears no necessary relation to its better-known uses and definitions within the annals of contemporary theory; and secondly, we must clear up a prevalent misunderstanding about the concept in English-language film cultures.

In the "Lexicon of Basic Concepts" at the back of *Towards a Philosophy of Photography*, Flusser defines apparatus in a two-stroke movement as "a plaything or game that simulates thought" and an "organization or system that enables something to function" (2000: 83). The English translator feels compelled to amplify, after the first stroke, that an apparatus is any "non-human agency", from the camera or computer to the state or market (*ibid.*). These two parts of Flusser's definition in fact correspond fairly well to the two quite different ideas contained in film theory's adoption of the term. It is poorly understood how, in translation, the word apparatus covers two separate concepts in the thought of Jean-Louis Baudry: the basic cinematic apparatus (camera, filmstrip, projector) is the *appareil de base*, while what he called the metapsychological situation of the spectator positioned before the screen image is a *dispositif* – the material set-up or system of elements in a social situation, like traffic lights or a factory layout.[4]

In Flusser's essay, the gestures and processes of film *production* – staging, shooting, editing images – correspond to the game-like side of the apparatus, the use of its basic machinery; while the ritual act of film *consumption* belongs to the more sinister regime of the social system or *dispositif*. Where shooting involves various sorts of turning, whether physical, mechanical or conceptual – the film turns in the camera, the cinematographer moves about in his or her capturing of images, the editor rearranges temporal relations at will – the moment of consumption in a sense forbids, or at least renders meaningless, another kind of turn: the turning of one's head, away from the screen, to take in the surrounding theatre architecture or the materiality of the projection booth with its beam of light.

Since this piece appears to be Flusser's distillation of his theoretical thoughts on cinema, its moves are worth summarizing in some detail. Its first part, on production, reiterates and extends certain meditations in *Towards a Philosophy of Photography*, particularly in relation to the physical gestures of photography and cinematography. A characteristically Flusserian formulation is: "if what is meant by 'ideology' is the fact of always keeping the same viewpoint, the act of photographing is a post-ideological movement" (2006: 77) – and thus the systematic expression or exercise of a *doubt* (in place of ideological certainty). Cinematography, however, changes this situation somewhat, because it involves a new gesture: *gliding* with the movie camera instead of *leaping* (or stalking one's prey) with a still camera (2000: 33–40). The process of doubt is thus no longer so decisive or dramatic: "The man with a movie camera does not jump from one decision to another; on the contrary, lets his decisions dissolve in an indecisive blur" (2006: 77).

But Flusser considers the central aspect of film production to be situated elsewhere: in editing. He waves away aesthetic debates concerning "two-dimensional screen, three-dimensional sound, the linear time of the film's unfolding, the organized time of the story it tells" (*ibid.*: 78), and therefore much of what traditional film criticism addresses under the rubrics of *mise en scène* and storytelling. For him, the true "film producer" is not the person with the money, or the manager of on-set resources, but the one in control of editing: "the man who cuts and splices, 'on top' of the celluloid so as to work it" (*ibid.*), and for whom all the material staged for and captured by the camera (however intricately and artfully) is only raw material (*ibid.*). It is this figure, whom Flusser dubs the producer–editor, who "makes use of a techno-imagination of a completely different order" (*ibid.*). Although Flusser makes no reference here to the work or theories of master Russian film-maker Sergei Eisenstein, he is in accord with him on the central role accorded to processes of montage.

However, montage is not primarily an aesthetic question for Flusser (as it is for Eisenstein). In this essay on film, he returns to his essential, overarching distinction between the historical reign of linear writing and the new age of techno-images. For the producer–editor reveals a new type of social, intellectual and cultural competence, a more cerebral form of "turning to account"':

> Faced with the celluloid, the film's "producer" (its author) finds himself at a point which transcends linearity – writing, linear calculus, linear logic, in short: historical time – for linearity is, from his viewpoint, only the primary material that he proceeds to treat "from the outside". The editor, he who cuts and splices, does not care, unlike the hero inside the story (the line), about modifying it; for him, the story is merely a pre-text that he uses, from without, to fabricate a message. His place is, in certain respects, comparable to that of the Judaeo-Christian God. Like Him, he sees simultaneously the beginning and end of the story (the filmstrip) and can work miracles, i.e., intervene from beyond. But the editor's omnipotence surpasses even God's. He can repeat events, reverse their unfolding, leap over phases as a horse leaps over steeples, go from past to future and return from future to past, accelerate the course of time or slow it down, splice together the beginning and end of linear time and thus form a cyclical story; in short, he can play with linearity.
> (*Ibid.*: 78–9)

Flusser's conclusion, in this first part of his essay, signals a warning: "Most of our films are 'bad' because they spring from a historical consciousness. If we are menaced by technocracy and apparatuses, it is because we are scarcely capable of leaving history in order to hurl ourselves into the techno-imagination" (*ibid.*: 81).

The second section of the essay, on film consumption, is a tour de force of conceptual insight, invention and wit. Flusser especially fixes on the architectural *dispositifs* of what he called the "codified world" (the title of his 1973 book). In a likely nod to Baudry and like-minded theorists of the 1970s, Flusser acknowledges the popular

37

equation of the cinema theatre with a cave: since "the Platonic myth of the cave can probably be considered the very first act of film criticism" (*ibid.*). But neither the cave nor the theatre – associated etymologically with the Greek *theoria* or theory – will do for Flusser. Where live theatre is an "emitter", the cinema theatre is only a "transmitter"; and it is "one of the rare places that allows us to sacrifice theory" – or where, more exactly, theory reigns only at intermission, "in order to program us more completely" (*ibid.*: 82).

Flusser pursues a comparison of the "picture theatre" with the Roman basilica, since this is, for him, the prototype of the modern supermarket, but merged with the function of also serving as a temple or church. And the layout of the supermarket, categorically for Flusser, "hides what such a space, in reality, is: a prison" (*ibid.*: 83).

The essay poses the cinema theatre as the "other face" of the supermarket. With its open doors, free entry and blinking advertising screens everywhere, a supermarket "offers the illusion of a public space", an *agora* (marketplace) for a *polis* (population). But to get out of this phony *agora*, this vast *dispositif* of "lure", one must queue up and forfeit money. The cinema-going situation inverts this: we queue up to pay at the start and leave freely at the end. But – and here Flusser anticipated today's merging of hypermart with multiplex – "the price of entry into the cinema and the price of release from the supermarket are two sides of the same coin"; in the "metabolism" of consumer society, filmgoers are programmed to visit the supermarket, and vice versa (*ibid.*).

This essay takes prime place among Flusser's most pessimistic meditations. The behaviour of the filmgoer, he muses, is "almost unbelievable: how can it be the case that people collaborate to such an extent with an apparatus which they know transforms them into passive receptors, into known units, into a mass?" (*ibid.*: 84). There is a specific reason for this passivity, and it lies in our awareness of the serial diffuseness of the cinematic apparatus, its lack of a central point of emission that could be targeted or attacked (for instance, by the proponents of a radical counter-cinema, which Flusser regards as a vain, ineffectual illusion). Let the final, somber, magisterial word go to Flusser himself:

> We know that this projection apparatus, behind our heads and beyond us, is not the true sender of the message, but only the last link in a chain linking the theatre to this sender. We know that the celluloid which passes through this apparatus is not an original message, but merely the stereotype of an inaccessible prototype, and that there are innumerable identical stereotypes playing out right now in theatres "all over the world". So we know that any "revolution", any turning of the head towards the projection booth, and the message it delivers, would be a desperately vain enterprise. We cannot free ourselves from domination by the apparatus by smashing the projector or burning the celluloid, because the centres of this apparatus-formation will remain intact and entirely inaccessible. The cinema theatre is thus a place which excludes any treacherous revolution – and that is precisely one of the goals it pursues. (*Ibid.*: 84–5)

NOTES

1. See information at the Vilém Flusser Archive, www.flusser-archive.org/archive (accessed July 2009).
2. For details, see Fred Forest Retrospective "Sociologic Art – Aesthetic of Communication", Web Net Museum, www.webnetmuseum.org/html/en/expo-retr-fredforest/actions/02_en.htm (accessed July 2009).
3. All quotations are from my own translation of this text, forthcoming in *Rouge* **16** (December 2009), www.rouge.com.au. The French translation by Claude Maillard, "De la Production et de la consummation des films", is published in *La Civilisation des medias*, C. Maillard (trans.), 75–88 (Belval: Circé, 2006).
4. See Jean-Louis Baudry, *L'Effet cinéma* (Paris: Albatros, 1978); English translations of his key essays can be found in T. H. K. Cha (ed.), *Apparatus, Cinematographic Apparatus: Selected Writings* (New York: Tanam Press, 1981). For an excellent discussion of Baudry's definitions of the apparatus, see Frank Kessler, "The Cinema of Attractions as *Dispositif*", in *The Cinema of Attractions Reloaded*, W. Strauven (ed.), 57–69 (Amsterdam: Amsterdam University Press, 2007).

3   SIEGFRIED KRACAUER

Drehli Robnik

Siegfried Kracauer (1889–1966) studied architecture and engineering in Germany, where he worked as an architect until 1920. He was a film critic for newspapers and magazines from 1920 to 1950, first in Frankfurt and Berlin, then in Paris from 1933, after his forced emigration as a Jewish left-wing intellectual after the Nazis came to power, and finally in New York from 1941. His two major books on film are *From Caligari to Hitler* (1947) and *Theory of Film* (1960).

With Siegfried Kracauer, the relationship of cinema to philosophy is peculiar. From his reviews and essays on modern culture to his books written in America, Kracauer's cinema theory is not primarily about films, film-makers, cultures or media technologies. Rather, cinema is itself something comparable to philosophy; as Kracauer describes, it is "an approach to the world, a mode of human existence" (1960: li). He conceives of cinema as a never entirely normal mode of perception, sensation, thought – and sometimes enlightenment. "All that remains of the 'art with a difference' in late Kracauer is the subjectivity which constitutes it" (Schlüpmann 1987: 107). In the end, Kracauer sees in, or rather through, cinema a mode of experience in rivalry with philosophy and art; he calls it "history".

Long before cinema is history Kracauer equates it to capitalist economy: "The form of free-time busy-ness necessarily corresponds to the form of business" (1995: 325). In his 1926 essay "Cult of Distraction", busy-ness/business – the same word *Betrieb* in the original – designates the fragmented mobility experienced both in film and in factory or office work. This view anticipates Walter Benjamin's "Artwork" essay, which reuses Kracauer's notion of distraction, and Theodor Adorno's condemnation of the "Culture Industry". To Kracauer, however, cinema also offers solutions to the problem it is part of. An example of this view is his interpretation of Buster Keaton's or Charlie Chaplin's burlesque comedies. In a 1926 essay he writes: "One has to hand this to the Americans: with slapstick films they have created a form that offers a counterweight to their reality. If in that reality they subject the world to an often unbearable discipline, the film in turn dismantles this self-imposed order quite forcefully" (quoted in Hansen 2000: 342–3).

According to Miriam Bratu Hansen, Kracauer sees in cinema an "alternative public sphere" that "engages the contradictions of modernity at the level of the senses" (*ibid.*:

343). Slapstick films are emblematic for this alternative public sphere in so far as they not only contain an antidote to industrial rationalization, but also intimate a different order of things. In his 1928 review of *Steamboat Bill, Jr.* (dir. Charles Reisner, 1928), Kracauer reads Keaton's machine-like "grace" as a "promise": "Buster could at last move freely and laugh" only "when the ban is lifted from the world" (2004: vol. 2, 148).[1] This is the grace of mechanized movement as antidote and promise: this logic also guides Kracauer's interpretation in 1927 of the abstract patterns of movement displayed by girl dance troupes and gymnastic crowd spectacles. With reference to the fragmentation of human behaviour by psychotechnical aptitude tests and assembly lines, Kracauer writes: "The mass ornament is the aesthetic reflex of the rationality to which the prevailing economic system aspires" (1995: 79). Again, Kracauer equates culture to industry, but there is a hopeful ambiguity, because in mass culture's reassembly of life, the rationalization process, which capitalism aborts at the stage of disciplined abstraction, still hints at enlightenment. According to Thomas Y. Levin, translator and editor of *The Mass Ornament*, Kracauer's own compilation of his 1920s essays, Kracauer endorses disintegration as a necessary precondition to a breakthrough of reason (Levin 1995: 17). This appears most clearly in cinema: "Here, in pure externality, the audience encounters itself; its own reality is revealed in the fragmented sequence of splendid sense impressions", Kracauer writes; their lack of deep and stable meaning enables films to expose "the *disorder* of society" (Kracauer 1995: 326–7).

Cinema's experiential potentials also become manifest when compared to photography. Like the mass ornament, photographic images are ambivalent. On the one hand, "the flight of images is a flight from revolution and from death" for late-1920s Kracauer (1998: 94). There is a high probability that photography's penetration of the world just endlessly reproduces its appearance and mythically naturalizes its presence. (Today, such criticism is often directed at television.) And yet, there is a chance that all those photographs that make people laugh, even shudder, at the exposure of their own awkward embodiment and, ultimately, mortality, might provide a self-perception in the image of transience. "It is therefore incumbent on consciousness to establish the *provisional status* of all given configurations, and perhaps even to awaken an inkling of the right order of the inventory of nature" (Kracauer 1995: 62). Although Kracauer always thinks of cinema as based on photography, his 1927 essay "Photography" distinguishes between the simply confusing "disarray of the illustrated newspapers" and film's "capacity to stir up" and "play with the pieces of disjointed nature" (*ibid.*: 62–3). Film has the possibility to literally disassemble and re-member the world: "Europe is ready to be seen through, decomposed in its elements and reassembled in montage by him", Kracauer writes on Vsevolod Pudovkin in 1928 (2004: vol. 2, 195). Around 1930, however, the messianic, redemptive orientation running through Kracauer's theory starts to shift (cf. Koch 2000): from revolutionary/messianic intervention into false organizations of reality (which mass culture helps to disorganize) to redemption as the preservation of what is left of reality to experience. His criticism increasingly attacks the "blindness to reality" and "emptiness" especially of German films, from Walter Ruttmann's *Berlin: Die Sinfonie der Großstadt* (Berlin: symphony of a great city; 1927) to *Der Blaue Engel* (The blue angel; dir. Sternberg, 1930); only in dispersed cinematic moments of realism and disobedience – such as in Jean Renoir's *La chienne*

(Isn't life a bitch?; 1931) or Leontine Sagan's *Mädchen in Uniform* (Girls in uniform; 1931) – is an antidote to the "vacuum" provided.

After Hitler came to power in 1933, Kracauer's *horror vacui* motif changes its object: instead of bourgeois rationalization, he now sees Nazi rule as hollowing out reality. His study "Propaganda and the Nazi War Film", undertaken in New York in 1942 and published as a supplement in his *From Caligari to Hitler* (1947), shows how Nazi documentary films celebrating German conquests in Europe treat reality as material to be randomly formed: the invader's "blitz" flashes "through an artificial vacuum", a "never-never land where the Germans rule over time and space" (Kracauer 1947: 279–80). Yet, cinema once again provides an almost homoeopathic antidote to the loss of world, by betraying and exposing a totalitarian media-machinery's grip on reality. Kracauer reads a newsreel of Hitler's 1940 blitz-visit to occupied Paris allegorically so that a resistance of reality to its mistreatment becomes visible: "Paris itself shuts its eyes and withdraws. The touching sight of this deserted ghost city that once pulsed with feverish life mirrors the vacuum at the core of the Nazi system" (*ibid.*: 307).

The ghost city becomes paradigmatic in Kracauer's 1947 book *From Caligari to Hitler* (hereafter *Caligari*). This book is infamous for its central thesis: the frequency of hypnotic tyrants such as Dr Mabuse and fanaticized crowds in the films of Germany's Weimar Republic (1918–1933) anticipated the Nazis' seizure of power. The concluding paragraph is typical: "Since Germany thus carried out what had been anticipated by her cinema from its very beginning, conspicuous screen characters now came true in life itself" (*ibid.*: 272). We could read this idea of reality reenacting images as a precedent to postmodernist "simulation" theories. Thomas Elsaesser suggests an alternative: we should turn Kracauer's argument – which had shifted the blame for the subjugation of perception from bourgeois rationality to a (proto-)Nazi media-machinery – around again, as it were. In this perspective, *Caligari* is not a teleology of cinema leading to Hitler, but an "incisive analysis of bourgeois conceptions of narrative and subject-positions … Kracauer's antipathy to Weimar films was ultimately due more to their gentrification of cinema than to any anticipation of the course of history" (Elsaesser 1987: 84). Since the German comedies and action melodramas once cherished by Kracauer the critic have disappeared from his 1947 retrospection, Weimar cinema now seems to consist of prestige productions and the expressionist canon. This makes *Caligari* look like a dark mirror-image of Kracauer's subsequent book *Theory of Film*. Also begun in the 1940s, *Theory of Film* is a celebration of cinema's potential to redeem reality that excludes large parts of international film production as "uncinematic"; *Caligari* is a condemnation of an uncinematic type of film, yet there is a redeeming subcurrent.

Referring to the "Men at Work" road sign, Kracauer writes that films such as *Das Cabinet des Dr Caligari* (The cabinet of Dr Caligari; dir. Wiene, 1920), which project vexed psyches into a distorted outside world, should be labelled "Soul at Work" (1947: 71–2). But he cautions not to see in his psychological history of German film "the concept of a fixed national character" (*ibid.*: 8). What *Caligari* offers, rather than a nation's "mentality", is cinema as a new epistemology, a way of understanding the social alternative to sociology, economics or politics. In a way, Kracauer suggests that we should have asked the films in order to find out sooner about the "secret history" and "emotional fixations" of white-collar workers living in a "vacuum" outside traditional class definitions (*ibid.*: 11; 1998: 81, 88), or about authoritarian dispositions that leftist voters, hateful of liberalism, shared with the Nazis (Koch 2000: 79). For Kracauer, cinema's insights into mass subjectivities are almost psychoanalytic, because film is "particularly concerned with the unobtrusive, the normally neglected" (1947: 7). Here, Kracauer is halfway between Benjamin's "optical-unconscious" and his own later realism of the ephemeral; his notion of films as "visible hieroglyphs" recalls his Weimar essays deciphering "surface-level expressions", "spatial images" and cinematic "daydreams of society".

"Effects may at any time turn into spontaneous causes", Kracauer writes in the introduction to *Caligari* (1947: 9): "psychological tendencies often assume independent life, and, instead of automatically changing with ever-changing circumstances, become themselves essential springs of historical evolution" (*ibid.*). Are German horror films right after all in showing souls coming to life in the outside world? The important thing is the shift introduced here: from a critique of despotic intentions subsuming reality to a philosophy of history highlighting irregularity and heterogeneity. Elsaesser sees a break with traditional logics of causation here. To Kracauer, cinema is irreducible to determining fact(or)s; it is both effect, cause and effect without cause; its images manifest an event- or phantom-like ontology. Elsaesser traces this back to György Lukács' 1913 aesthetics of cinema, where we confront "life without soul, mere surface", and "'virtuality' no longer functions as opposed to 'reality'" (Elsaesser 1987: 88; 1997: 33–4).

Kracauer's *Theory of Film* appeared in 1960. Reading it, we should neither focus on its moments of systematic grandeur nor follow those who condemn its "naive" realism. "Reality is a construction" (1998: 32), Kracauer had asserted in 1929, and at one point in *Theory of Film*, he qualifies realism in this way: "What accounts for the cinematic quality of films … is not so much their truth to our experience of reality or even to reality in a general sense as their absorption in camera reality – visible physical existence" (1960: 116). So, what is "visible physical existence"? According to Kracauer's "material aesthetic", films have "an affinity … for the continuum of life or the 'flow of life'", for "open-ended life" (*ibid.*: 71). This emphasis on "life as a powerful entity", with passing references to Friedrich Nietzsche and Henri Bergson (*ibid.*: 169), echoes in his posthumous *History: The Last Things Before the Last* (hereafter *History*). Published in 1969, it uses cinema as a model for defining the experiential specificity of history and often repeats or explicitly quotes passages from *Theory of Film*. As a philosopher of history who sets history apart from philosophy's certainties about "last things", Kracauer here equates "historical reality" with "camera-reality" and "life-world": historical reality is "full of intrinsic contingencies", "virtually endless" and "indeterminate as to meaning" (1969: 45). Camera-reality, which structurally parallels historical reality, "has all the earmarks of the *Lebenswelt*. It comprises inanimate objects, faces, crowds, people who intermingle, suffer and hope; its grand theme is life in its fullness" (*ibid.*: 58).

Is it all about life? Does Kracauer's realism turn into vitalism? Two recent approaches to his work by scholars indebted to feminism and critical theory rather emphasize the role of death in *Theory of Film*. Hansen's introduction reconstructs that book's palimpsestic character, beginning with notes Kracauer had taken in Marseille while fleeing from the Nazis in 1940. "The desire for film to 'include the death's head beneath the face' ... had presided over the Marseille project as an epigraph and a never realized final chapter, to be called, variably, 'Kermesse funèbre', 'Danse macabre', or 'The death's head'" (Hansen 1997: xxiv). After many revisions this chapter, renamed "The Redemption of Physical Reality", becomes part of the epilogue to *Theory of Film*, which contains passages like this: "We literally redeem the world from its dormant state, its state of virtual nonexistence, by endeavoring to experience it through the camera. And we are free to experience it because we are fragmentized" (Kracauer 1960: 300). So, instead of a continuum, fragmentation now appears to be a precondition for experience. Kracauer's deviation from his "life-flow" pathos appears less sudden if one reads it in connection with "The Mass Ornament". Here, Kracauer sees the "abstractness" of life under capitalism as "ambivalent", harbouring threats of rationalization becoming mythical, but also chances for emancipated experience (1995: 83). The anticommunist climate in 1950s' America probably contributed to Kracauer's replacing of the terms "mass", "material" and "capitalism" with "life", "physical" and "science": in *Theory of Film*, science appears as ambivalent, "double-edged"; "it alerts us to the world", but also "tends to remove that world from the field of vision" (1960: 299).

Kracauer's emphasis on being fragmentized also recalls the aesthetics of destruction in his Marseille notes: "The material elements that present themselves in film directly stimulate the *material layers* of the human being: his nerves, his senses, his entire *physiological* substance" (quoted in Hansen 1997: xxi). The spectator's "'ego' ... is subject to *permanent dissolution*, is incessantly exploded by material phenomena" (*ibid.*: xxi). Some of this violent reception physiology survives in *Theory of Film* in passages on how films "cause a stir in deep bodily layers", provoke "organic tensions, nameless excitements" – and turn audiences into "dope addicts", "habitués who frequent [cinemas] out of an all but physiological urge" (1960: 158–9).

Gertrud Koch's analysis of Kracauer's work offers a taxonomy of strains of thought in *Theory of Film*: "a *sensualist* aesthetics", "an *existential ontology*", "a redemptive figure based on an *aesthetics of reconciliation*" (2000: 106). Kracauer's sensualism seems to turn existentialist in epiphanies experienced by the self-unconscious spectator: "Images begin to sound, and the sounds are again images. When this indeterminate murmur – the murmur of existence – reaches him, he may be nearest to the unattainable goal" of exhausting what the film presents (1960: 165). Koch quotes this passage and rightly calls it "misplaced enthusing" reminiscent of Heidegger (2000: 103). To her, it is important that the pathway to sheer existence, which Kracauer's sensualist "ethics of enjoyment" might open up to us, is blocked by the "crypto-theological core" of *Theory of Film*. In Koch's view, Kracauer's flow of life sweeps away "things and the dead"; film "arrests" that flow to redeem them in a kind of messianic intervention (*ibid.*: 106–8). In her reconstruction of Kracauer's redemptive realism, Koch emphasizes its aspects of Jewish messianic theology, especially the invocation of "redemption through memory" and "solidarity with the dead". This idea resembles Benjamin's philosophy of history and echoes Kracauer's comment on "fact-oriented" historiographies that insist that "nothing should go lost" as if they "breathed pity with the dead" (1969: 136). But here, Koch sees Kracauer's insistence on the "primacy of the visual" and on sensory concreteness confronting intrinsic theoretical limits (2000: 108–13): *Theory of Film* mentions the Nazi Holocaust only in passing (in the "Head of Medusa" section), because it marginalizes the crisis of representation posed by a mass annihilation that is beyond images and imagination.

A different recent approach is proposed by Heide Schlüpmann. She also (and more explicitly) opposes Kracauer's theory to ethics, but focuses on a proto-political notion of life rather than death and theology. Like Koch a German, critical, feminist film theorist, Schlüpmann has also written a book on Kracauer (of which chapters are available in English translation). Kracauer's concepts appear frequently in her three-part cinema aesthetics. In the third part, Schlüpmann sketches a reversal in the relationship of cinema and philosophy (2007: 15–16, 291–3): for decades, philosophy time and again gave conceptual shelter, sometimes condescendingly so, to cinema in its cultural worthlessness. Today it is increasingly cinema that houses a question peculiar to, but abandoned by, philosophy. The question is how to live, especially how to live inactively. The context for this problem is that today's neo-liberal economy subsumes inactive life; capital's regime of valorization extends into spheres of life not yet subsumed by the former disciplines of factory and office (as the discourse on "post-Fordism" puts it). Schlüpmann uses Kracauer to point out cinema's separation from the success (hi)story of digital mediatization, in which the screens of labour and leisure are now the same. What is lost in this process is a utopian experience: cinema as an "impossible" site for a "morality" of life, alternative to bourgeois ethics of self-preservation and to neo-liberal ethics of universal productivity. As early as 1987, Schlüpmann wrote with respect to Kracauer's concept of cinematic self-encounters: "The moral task of the medium is no longer the symbolization of the ethical, but rather the mirroring of the enslaved, damaged quality of life" (1987: 102).

But maybe there is something ethical in Kracauer's theory – and also in philosophies close to or indebted to his work. The notion of ethics relevant here is, however, quite different from the ethics of individual self-preservation; we find its definition in Giorgio Agamben, whose meta-political philosophy, as we shall see, relates to Kracauer, sometimes explicitly. Agamben calls "ethos" a manner of proper being that does not forget about the improper that engenders it: "the only ethical experience … is the experience of being (one's own) potentiality, of being (one's own) possibility – exposing, that is, in every form one's own amorphousness and in every act one's own inactuality" (1993b: 29, 44).

Embodying what makes us shapeless, inactual, inactive: there are similarities between this concept of Agamben's and Kracauer's realism, which is realism with a difference. While the realism of classical Hollywood film (and the theory celebrating its normalcy) uses reality as the playground of goal-oriented individuals, Kracauer's realism is about losing one's grip on the world. *Theory of Film* is an ethics of acknowledged powerlessness, which – in a manner comparable to contemporary writings of André Bazin – praises Italian neo-realism for its "found" rather than constructed stories. In Kracauer's *History*, there is an ethos close to Agamben's idea of every act exposing the non-act: the subject of historical experience is marked by "active passivity" and "self-effacement" (1969: 84). What this entails becomes clear in one of

Kracauer's comparisons of realist history to film-making: documentary realists such as Joris Ivens practise "deliberate suspension of their ... creative powers" to "produce the effect of impersonal authenticity" (*ibid.*: 90). Central to history and cinema is a surrender to unexpected life forms and improbable incidents encountered in the past and in physical reality. As Schlüpmann writes about *Theory of Film*, "the priority of physical reality has above all a negative meaning, that is, to negate the principle of self-assertion in the subject" (1991: 123).

It is instructive to turn to a review of *Theory of Film* by a German film and art theorist who, like Kracauer, had also emigrated to America. In 1963, Rudolf Arnheim saw in Kracauer an aesthetic of "unshaped matter" and a "melancholy surrender" to "concrete reality" (1963: 296–7). This aesthetic, Arnheim argued, could point the way to new beginnings of thought: after taking us to the "nadir" of "the world before Creation, the attractive infinity and variety of chaos. It is the escape from the duty of man, the final refuge and the final refreshment" (*ibid.*). In this perspective on Kracauer's work, reality is redeemed – from humanity: we (whoever that is) regain the world only by letting cinema help the world to get rid of us. To say it with Kracauer, "the world that is ours" is only found as "something we did not look for" (1960: 296); history and the cinema are both "means of alienation" (1969: 5), but in their affinity to unshaped life, they "virtually make the world our home" (1960: 304).

Such a version of Kracauer matches well with Stanley Cavell's ontology of cinema's projecting the world to us and screening us out of it, or with Vivian Sobchack's neo-phenomenology of "being-in-the-world" sensed through the medium of our "lived-bodies" in cinema. Most of all, *Theory of Film* (or Arnheim's version of it) appears as a precursor to motifs in Gilles Deleuze's philosophy of film, especially the idea of film's reconstitution of the world as prehuman chaos and post-human Outside. For Deleuze, "the luminous plane of immanence, the plane of matter and its cosmic eddying of movement-images" is the matrix, ever present virtually to classical film's rhythmicized sensations (1986: 68). In this way, cinema poses (and partly answers) the "question of attaining once more the world before man, before our own dawn" (*ibid.*). Prehuman movement-in-itself echoes in the post-humanism of modern film's *time-image*: "the point is to discover and restore belief in the world, before or beyond words" (1989: 172). Nothing less than the building of "an ethic or a faith" (*ibid.*: 173) becomes the vocation of cinema, for which, without referring to Kracauer, Deleuze uses the latter's key term: "Redemption, art beyond knowledge, is also creation beyond information" (*ibid.*: 270). This is reminiscent of Kracauer's invocations of film as a pathway to "the murmur of existence" (Kracauer 1960: 165) and as a means to find the world through its alienation from us.

Further, I suggest Jacques Rancière's interpretation of Deleuze's philosophy of film as an approach, because much in it is valid also for Kracauer's film theory. For Rancière, Deleuze's dualism of classical and modern cinema amounts to a "restitution of world-images to themselves. It is a history of redemption" (2006a: 111). It is as if the time-image came to the rescue and undid the appropriation of the movement-image by knowledge, human intention, authorial consciousness. Alternative to this, Rancière conceives of cinema dialectically, as an endless spiral: "Artistic activity must always be turned into passivity, find itself in that passivity, and be thwarted anew" (*ibid.*: 119). This corresponds to the core formula of Rancière's *Film Fables*: "to thwart its servitude, cinema must first thwart its mastery" (*ibid.*: 11). Are we close to an ethical Kracauer here? Are we close to passivity within activity; to cinema's openness to reality thwarting its formative mastery, thus granting us an ethical relationship to the world, mindful of our tenuous link with it? In fact, Rancièrian "self-thwarting" does not restore any cinematic affinities to a Bergsonian immanence of matter, to murmuring existence, to the world before words, redeemed and restituted. It is not the purity but the impurity of cinema that counts. Rancière locates cinema's strength in a kind of self-abuse (which so many cinéphiles deplore as a weakness): cinema submits its unique potential, the material, sensorial, rhythmic chaos of images, to film industries with their representational orders of genre and storytelling; this submission, however, can in its turn be cancelled at any time – and actually is at so many times in film history. This permanent self-thwarting, rather than any Romantic or vitalist utopia of perfect disorder, holds the key to cinema's political dimension. I propose to use Rancière's philosophy, in which the political is inherently aesthetic, as one guideline for tracing political – rather than ethical – aspects of Kracauer's theory of cinema, history and mass culture. The other guideline is Adorno's 1965 intellectual portrait of his long-term friend Kracauer.

> The state of innocence would be the condition of needy objects, shabby, despised objects alienated from their purposes. For Kracauer they alone embody something that would be other than the universal functional complex, and his idea of philosophy would be to lure their indiscernible life from them. (Adorno 1991c: 177)

Adorno sees Kracauer's realism, which focuses the *res*, the *thing*, and lacks "indignation about reification", as "curious" (*ibid.*: 177); the German word for this, "wunderlich", also intimates "wonder" and "miracle". Kracauer's realism shows how we are among other things; it emphasizes how cinema makes actors appear as "object among objects" (Kracauer 1960: 45), and how film resembles history in that they both "help us to think *through* things, not above them" (1969: 192). Also, this realism probes the degree to which the life of things can generate a politics of dissensus. In his 1930 essay on an outdated Berlin shopping arcade, Kracauer bids "Farewell to the Linden Arcade": "What would be the point of an arcade [*Passage*] in a society that is itself only a passageway?" (1995: 342). Kracauer reads the "Lindenpassage" as an allegorical space-image of social exclusion: all kinds of shabby commodified objects exiled from respectable life "like gypsies", "banished to the inner Siberia of the arcade, ... took revenge on the bourgeois idealism that oppressed them by playing off their defiled existence against" it. "By disavowing a form of existence to which it still belonged" the "passageway through the bourgeois world articulated a critique that every true passerby understood" (*ibid.*: 341–2).

Rather than Adorno's "state of innocence", what becomes paradigmatic is reified life's capacity to disavow the order it belongs to. Where do things belong? In *History*, Kracauer criticizes philosophies of teleology or "present interest" because they treat "history as a success story [and] closed system" that "shuts out the lost causes, the unrealized possibilities" (1969: 199). To this he opposes his image of the historian (the subject of historical experience) as someone who is not "the son of his time. Actually he is the son of at least two times – his own and the time he is investigating" (*ibid.*: 93). Double belonging as a ruptured belonging to the present: this makes of Kracauer's historian a critic of the present order, an archeologist of possibilities marginalized in the past – "his present concerns are identical with a compassionate urge to uncover lost causes in history. He not only views the past in the light of the present but turns to the present from a primary involvement in the past" (*ibid.*: 209). Schlüpmann subscribes to Kracauer's notion of historicity as "being exterritorial in relation to the present", because it directs the attention of feminist archaeologies to lost histories of early cinema: a cinema that sheltered the "counter-publicizing" of private existences of women in patriarchy (1994: 84–5). Philosophical to the extent that it is a morality of non-triumphant life, cinema can preserve lost causes and becomes itself a cause lost to media culture's progress of digitization.

A second objection raised by Adorno concerns Kracauer's "antisystematic tendency" (1991c: 161): his thinking "binds itself to something contingent and glorifies it simply in order to avoid glorifying the great universal" (*ibid.*: 165). "The utopian trait, afraid of its own name and concept, sneaks into the figure of the man who does not quite fit in" (*ibid.*: 176). One should not argue against such a charge of cowardly not going all the way; Kracauer freely admits to it. His 1922 essay "Those Who Wait" proposed an attitude of "hesitant openness" towards modernity's ephemera (Kracauer 1995: 138); and in history, a conceptual "anteroom" or "waiting-room" crowded with "last things before the last", "stopping mid-way may be ultimate wisdom" (1969: 213). For David Rodowick, "this acknowledgment constitutes not the problem but the solution", because history and cinema as modes of "knowing" are to be valued exactly for "their resistance to closure and their elusiveness with respect to systematic thought" (2001: 167).

In Kracauer's notion of a "Utopia of the in-between", Utopia is not an idea, but rather an aesthetic of what does not quite fit (in); cinema is its model. Explaining the "nonhomogeneous structure" (1969: 217) of historical experience, he compares the problematic "traffic conditions" between the "micro" level of particular events and the "macro" level of explanatory narratives and generalizations to the relationship of close-up and long shot in cinema (*ibid.*: 125–7). Here, *History* quotes from and refers to passages on D. W. Griffith in *Theory of Film*. Where most film theories would see the normalization of cinematic movement through continuity editing, invented, as it were, by film-makers such as Griffith, Kracauer remarkably observes a "paradoxical relation" and "fissures" (1960: 231). To him, even conventional transitions between part and whole are not smooth; the close-ups Griffith inserts are at the same time part of the narrative flow and independent of it, even arrest it, not unlike Deleuze's "affection-images". The "admirable nonsolution" that Kracauer attributes to Griffith could be another name for his own refusal of conceptual integrity: Griffith "keeps apart what does not belong together" (*ibid.*). Following a similar logic, Kracauer's intermediary area of history places things "side-by-side" rather than in subordinations or "either–or" relations by keeping them apart (1969: 200–206): Particulars are side-by-side with generalities, and Kracauer's anteroom is a zone of separation between the "immediacy" of experience and the "timelessness" of philosophy (Rodowick 2001:

169). Instead of film unalienated by story form, plunging us into a wild microphysics of particulars or an idyll of details, Kracauer ultimately votes for cinematic stories that are found or emergent; he favours togetherness in paratactical separation and provisional configurations to utopian purity.

Another of Adorno's criticisms accuses Kracauer's antisystematics of opportunism: "the enthronement of a form of individual experience, however eccentric, that is comfortable with itself remains socially acceptable. However much it feels itself to be in opposition to society, the *principium individuationis* is society's own" (1991c: 164–5). In this context, Adorno highlights the theoretical importance of Charlie Chaplin: "Kracauer projected his self-understanding of the individual onto Chaplin: Chaplin, he said, is a hole" (Kracauer 2004: vol. 1, 269). The phrase is from Kracauer's 1926 review of *The Gold Rush* (dir. Chaplin, 1925), which under the simple title "Chaplin" contains what is probably Kracauer's shortest sentence: the tramp character "has lost his Ego" – "In pathology, this would be called split of ego, schizophrenia. A hole [*Ein Loch*]. But out of the hole, the purely human radiates in disconnection" (2004: vol. 1, 269). In *Theory of Film*, Kracauer compares "the life force which [Chaplin] embodies" to "films on plant-growth" (1960: 281). Is this the self-assured individualism that Adorno sees in Kracauer? Or is there not in Kracauer a "dividual" ontology in the sense of Deleuze and Félix Guattari, complete with "schizo" and "becoming-plant"? Even stronger, however, is Kracauer's connection with Agamben's messianic ontology.

In *The Coming Community*, Agamben mentions "Siegfried Kracauer's observations on the 'girls'" as one of those texts that in the 1920s read in cinema's commodifications of bodies a "prophecy". "The dances of the 'girls'", anonymous and coordinated in abstraction, announce a "perfectly communicable" body, free from any foundations in identity or theology: "Neither generic nor individual, … the body now became something truly *whatever*" (Agamben 1993a: 47–8). Agamben's reference is to Kracauer's essay "The Mass Ornament", which invokes a disorganized, dividual body: "The human figure enlisted in the mass ornament has begun the *exodus* from lush organic splendor and the constitution of individuality toward the realm of anonymity" (Kracauer 1995: 83). The mass ornament's promise might be to make Chaplins of all of us: "[w]hen the knowledge radiating from the basis of man dissolves the contours of visible natural form", that is the moment, as Kracauer writes in another essay on Chaplin, "when those features which usually turn humans into individual humans are dropped" (2004: vol. 2, 493). In that moment "there remains in Chaplin the human being as such" (*ibid.*).

Is there a political aspect to being neither generic nor individual? In Agamben, the politics of "whatever being" and belonging without preconditions is always yet to come, pointing towards Utopias of perfect peace (1993a: 83–7, 1998: 180, 188). Life is categorically powerless: Agamben's ethics of humility displays "bare life" in every life form, inactivity in every act. With Kracauer it is also the other way around: he emphasizes moments of unexpected empowerment of the impotent – "Chaplin rules the world from below, as one who represents nothing at all" (2004: vol. 2, 493). Carrying on from Kracauer, Schlüpmann criticizes Agamben for leaving no room in his metaphysics of socially excluded life for a perspective in which the excluded might imagine themselves as something other than "bare life" (2007: 219). And she proposes a theory focusing the interruption. For Schlüpmann, cinema is a multiple self-interruption or split, an outside externalized, an inside permeated by the excluded (*ibid.*: 271–4). In cinema, we can perceive our belonging to society as something external, while that which capital excludes as superfluous, unproductive life is subjectivized in its images, spaces, durations. Yes, we hear the "murmur of existence" in cinema: it is the stranger next to us in the theatre whose talking during the film recalls the contingency of our mass existence.

Using Rancière as a perspective, we can frame Kracauer's hole-thinking politically: "There are always holes in the wall for us to evade and the improbable to slip in" (Kracauer 1969: 8). Rather than last things – Utopia to achieve, a world to regain – politics presupposes only equality, which designates the fact that every social order is contingent, every power relation can be changed: subordination can at any time dissolve into the "side-by-side" relation that gives it no secure foundation. The holy is a hole: miracles can always happen. The political act is rare, local, provisional, improbable – but always possible; it is an unmotivated subjectivization of the anonymous and speechless, an interruption in the ethos of identity and belonging. Political being-together is a "being in-between", a "belonging twice over": belonging simultaneously to the world of well-defined social parts and to a world of non-parts that disrupt its order (Rancière 1999: 137–9). Kracauer gives many examples for the logic of "belonging twice over": the subject of historicity as a child of two times; the passageway – society as the hole in itself – which belongs only by disavowing what it belongs to; the song and dance numbers of film musicals, which "form part of the intrigue and at the same time enhance with their glitter its decomposition" (1960: 213).

Adorno is wrong in calling Kracauer's thinking "successful adjustment", but he certainly picks the right quotations. Kracauer, he writes, "smuggled a manifesto for himself into his theory of film: 'All these characters seem to yield to powers that be and yet manage to outlast them'" (1991c: 173). The sentence is from one of Kracauer's comparisons of neo-realist cinema to Chaplin (1960: 281). On neo-realism and its inherent slapstick, Rancière and Kracauer perfectly agree: for Rancière, Roberto Rossellini's "falling bodies" manifest "the incomprehensible power that is the strength of the weak" (2006a: 127); for Kracauer, "[b]ehind many nonsolutions" of neo-realist films and old Chaplin comedies lies "a desire to exalt the power of resistance of the seeming weak" (1960: 270). Read politically rather than ethically, Kracauer's philosophy of nonsolution offers a concept of cinema as a mode of theorizing through self-thwarting and waiting that diagnoses how power emerges where no one expected it.

NOTE

1. All translations in this chapter are my own unless otherwise indicated.

4 THEODOR ADORNO

Julie Kuhlken

Theodor W. Adorno (1903–69) was the Director of the Institute of Social Research in Frankfurt am Main from 1958. He is the author of many books, including *Dialectic of Enlightenment* (with Max Horkheimer, 1947; English trans. 1972), *Composing for the Films* (with Hanns Eisler, 1947; English trans. 1997), *Philosophy of Modern Music* (1949; English trans. 1973), *Minima Moralia* (1951; English trans. 1974), *Against Epistemology: A Metacritique* (1956; English trans. 1982), *Negative Dialectics* (1966; English trans. 1973) and *Aesthetic Theory* (1970; English trans. 1984), and co-editor and co-author of *The Authoritarian Personality* (1950). Adorno's pessimistic view that film is irredeemably popular in the consumerist sense is so well known as to cause a recent critical theorist to entitle his book on popular culture *Roll over Adorno*. Whereas in literature and particularly in music Adorno identifies the promise of a genuinely emancipatory art, in film he largely (although, as will be shown, not entirely) sees all the reasons why we need liberation. In part his attitude is a product of personal experience: he spent his exile from Germany during the Second World War in Los Angeles just next door to Hollywood, the headquarters of what he, along with Max Horkheimer, came to call the "culture industry."

A telling indication of Adorno's relation to film lies in the fact that it is mentioned a mere eight times in the voluminous body of *Aesthetic Theory* (2002), his primary work of philosophical aesthetics. In this dense book of interpretation and philosophical analysis, the only cinematic technique that is deemed worthy of extended consideration is *montage*, and it itself is quickly dispensed with as a "cultural-historical curiosity", whose "assemblage … becomes merely indifferent material" once its initial "shock is neutralized" (Adorno 2002: 156). In fact, it is quite easy to conclude that Adorno's relative silence about cinematic aesthetics is symptomatic of a more general snobbism – or even, ignorance – about film and popular art more generally, a view that finds much fuel in his disdain for jazz. However, this broadbrush approach ignores the reality that, for Adorno, the development of film marks an unequivocal change in the social landscape of art. Like his close friend Walter Benjamin, Adorno recognizes the resounding impact of "the era of mechanical reproduction" on the relation between art and society, particularly in post-Second World War consumerist societies, and consequently the need to account for it philosophically.

Thus, what Adorno's philosophy offers the investigation of film is less an *aesthetics* of cinematic techniques – although he and Hanns Eisler do offer an aesthetics of film *music* in *Composing for the Films* ([1947] 2005) – than a fine-grained analysis of film's relation to society. The two notions that dominate this examination – the culture industry, and the dialectic of serious and light art – are interrelated. What makes for the conditions of the culture industry is precisely the forced suspension of the dialectic between serious and light art. Even though this means that the dialectic precedes the culture industry, we shall start by looking at the latter since it serves as a more straightforward introduction to the relation between cinematic production and its social reception. We shall then turn to the more difficult issues raised by the dialectic of serious and light art. Unlike many theorists of his generation, Adorno's preference for art of the European avant-garde tradition does not lead him to conclude that there is a *qualitative* gulf separating "high" and "low" artistic production. In other words, the term "serious art" does not unequivocally refer to classical music any more than "light art" refers to pulp fiction. Rather, the dialectic of serious and light art is present in all artworks, such that a symphony by Schönberg is as likely to bear traces of light art as is a Disney cartoon. In fact, the paradoxical result of Adorno's dialectical conception of art is that if art were truly and totally serious, it would no longer be art. Film participates in this dialectic to the extent that its products are torn between the desire to be taken seriously and the unadorned joy in being able to entertain.

IN THE SHADOW OF THE HOLLYWOOD HILLS

The theory of the culture industry is one of the most famous products of Adorno's philosophy. Developed in a collaborative effort with Max Horkheimer during their common exile in the US during the Second World War, and first published as a chapter in *Dialectic of Enlightenment* (1997), the theory bears the imprint of Adorno's experience of living in the shadow of the Hollywood hills, both formally and materially. As regards its form, the effect of Hollywood is felt in the very brand-like quality of the notion itself. In a spirit of self-conscious irony – evident even in its exaggerated style of writing – the theory of the culture industry is exactly the kind of all-encompassing model for cultural production that it criticizes. By this irony, Adorno and Horkheimer performatively underscore their awareness that they are just as much a part of the culture industry as John Wayne is, and thus cannot make the "pretentious claim to know better than the others" (Adorno & Horkheimer 1997: 134). Given their paradoxical position, they conceive of their role as cultural critics as that of exemplary participants showing the rules of the game. Moreover, one of the rules that they disclose is that a Roberto Rossellini film is not better than a Frank Capra simply because it is more "serious". Since the culture industry is itself a "synthesis of Beethoven and the *Casino de Paris*",[1] all the debates about the line distinguishing high and low art are so much hot air. Because the culture industry arises precisely when all culture becomes organized, it incorporates everything from Pedro Almodóvar to Benny Hill and back again (*ibid.*: 135).

The consequences of this total cultural organization are particularly evident, writes Adorno, in "film, the central sector of the culture industry" (1991a: 100). Here 1940s'

Hollywood exerts its influence on the content of the theory, informing the four aspects of film identified by Adorno and Horkheimer. First, there is the fact of mass audiences, such as was the cinematic mainstay in the 1940s. Secondly, there is the corresponding phenomenon of mass production, and its reliance on economic rather than aesthetic criteria. Thirdly, there is the need to produce apparent exceptions to the mass model in the form of "stars" and mavericks. Fourthly, there is the inescapability of the culture industry as long as one refuses to see its social and political underpinnings. In what follows, we shall consider these various aspects of film under the culture industry as a way of negatively defining film's social possibilities.

PRODUCTION OF CULTURAL CONSUMERS

Like Benjamin, Adorno recognizes the link between mass audiences and mass reproductive technology; however, unlike his then recently deceased friend, Adorno does not see technology as the determining factor in the culture industry (Benjamin 1999b). Rather, for Adorno and Horkheimer, it is the human element, the organizing and classifying of audiences – what we would today call marketing – that really distinguishes modern culture. It is because "[m]arked differentiations such as those of A and B films … depend not so much on subject matter as on classifying, organizing, and labeling consumers" that Adorno and Horkheimer develop their theory under the bold slogan: "Something is provided for all so that none can escape" (1997: 123). Only if all audiences – from aficionados of the *Three Colors* trilogy (dir. Kieslowski, 1993, 1994a,b) to fans of the *Terminator* series (dir. Cameron, 1984, 1991; dir. Mostow, 2003; dir. McG 2009) – are united in their role as consumers can the culture industry function as a single totalizing unit.

So the critical question becomes: whence (and why) do cultural consumers arise? Adorno and Horkheimer seem to offer two explanations for this essential change in the nature of cultural audiences, one politically sharp-edged but somewhat far-fetched, and the other deeply philosophical. The first holds that all industry – and not just the entertainment industry – is tied together by such a strong sense of shared economic interest that it bands together in great national monopolies, such that "demarcation lines between different firms and technical branches [can] be ignored" (Adorno & Horkheimer 1997: 123). Because it is determined by economic rather than artistic factors, the entertainment industry shares with all other industries the desire to moud its audiences as consumers. To the extent that this explanation says something about Hollywood in the era of the big studios, it contains a grain of truth. But only a grain, which is why it is far-fetched. Very few find convincing their assertion that "there is the agreement … of all executive authorities not to produce anything that in any way differs from their own rules" (*ibid.*: 122). Nevertheless, the political basis for this caricature of monopolistic capitalism lies close to the surface: the description is so redolent of B-movie conspiracies hatched in smoke-filled rooms that one cannot help but react against it. To the extent that one does, the "explanation" succeeds. It breaks us out of the role of passive cultural consumers, which for them links the nationalization of industry found in Western democracies to the advance of "the rule of complete quantification" promulgated by fascism. As exiles from Germany, Adorno and Horkheimer are painfully aware of how Nazism's rise was eased by the refusal of many to take its showy propaganda seriously until it was too late. As such, their denouncement of the "ruthless unity of the culture industry" is only partially an effort to describe facts on the ground, and as much an attempt to issue a warning cry about "what will happen in politics" if people do not sit up and start taking the culture industry seriously (*ibid.*: 123).

In this call, they echo another philosopher, the first to raise the question of the political seriousness of the arts: Plato. However, unlike Plato, for whom the *illusory* character of the arts is so explosive as to require the expulsion of the poets from the Republic, for Adorno and Horkheimer the real problem with the arts is not illusion so much as *dis*illusion. For them, cultural consumers arise, not because they are tricked by cinematic illusions so much as because they become *disillusioned* by them. This other philosophical explanation for the appearance of cultural consumers is easiest to grasp if we think in terms of Plato's allegory of the cave (*Republic* 514a–520a). As they themselves note, the shadow-play of the allegory of the cave makes something very close to motion pictures the model of reality. Like the prisoners in the cave, consumers are the passive recipients of the empty entertainment of a bad political order. Plato's response is to insist on the tutelage of the philosopher-kings, who are charged with enlightening their fellow citizens. But for Adorno and Horkheimer, this "enlightenment" is the worst form of cultural fascism: there is no room for freedom in a Republic that "impedes the development of autonomous independent individuals who judge and decide consciously for themselves" (Adorno 1991a: 106). Most citizens of Plato's Republic will never be allowed to ascend to the Forms, and rather will continue to be fed the same shadowy drivel that they watched before its institution. To make matters worse, now, thanks to the philosopher-kings, these same individuals will *know it is just a show*, just shadows meant to distract and entertain. This political cynicism is what Adorno and Horkheimer also recognize in the culture industry. For them it is like all tyranny. It leaves one free to think only to brand as deviant anyone who thinks differently: "[n]ot to conform is to be rendered powerless, economically and therefore spiritually" (Adorno & Horkheimer 1997: 133). As such, people do not actually have to be convinced of the culture industry's lies and exaggerations for it to function; it is just necessary that they prefer to be entertained than socially excluded. As Adorno puts it later, "if [the culture industry] guarantees them even the most fleeting gratification [cultural consumers] desire a deception which is nonetheless transparent to them" (1991a: 103). In this sense, the culture industry produces its own consumers. It "has molded men as a type unfailingly reproduced in every product" (Adorno & Horkheimer 1997: 127).

Adorno and Horkheimer's difference from Benjamin is starkest on this point. For them, the culture industry marks less an "era of mechanical *reproduction*" than an era in which reproduction is entirely subordinated to the needs of mass production – both of cultural commodities and of the masses that will consume them. As Adorno objects to Benjamin, there is nothing new in reproduction: it is just as much a feature of "auratic" works as technological ones – every "work, insofar as it is intended for many, is already its own reproduction"; rather, what changes in the modern era is the fact that reproduction ceases to reflect a work's creation and becomes simply a fact of its production (Adorno 2002: 33). Rather than being allied to artistic interpretation such as in the case of theatre, reproduction in film is the servant of the technically perfected illusion "that the outside world is the straightforward continuation of that presented on the screen" (Adorno & Horkheimer 1997: 126). Because it blurs the distinction between art and reality, film makes it impossible for its audience to "take the position of a critic" *vis-à-vis* what it sees, as Benjamin suggests (1999b: 222).

SYSTEMS OF STARS AND MAVERICKS

Instead, the position that film viewers take is identification with the "star". Again in direct contrast to Benjamin, who proposes imaginative "identification with the camera" (the mechanism of reproduction), Adorno and Horkheimer focus on the human element and the avatars of administration. For them, stars are the exceptions that prove the rule or, as they put it, the "ideal types of the new dependent average" (1997: 145). The waitress does not really believe she will become a starlet, but the illusion that she could – fostered in the 1940s by the unceasing "search for talent", and continued today in television programmes such as *American Idol* – makes it possible for her to "write off" her lack of luck and "rejoice in the other's success" (*ibid.*). Because fame attaches to circumstances not individuals – there will be a new "teen pop idol" next year – it promises that you or I could have a glamorous life some day, even if *not* today. In other words, for Adorno and Horkheimer, what makes fame so compelling is not that the stars are so different from the rest of us, but rather that they are exactly the same. They have children, get divorced, lose and gain weight. Fame offers a hyper-democratic social hierarchy; however, it is one that implies that everyone "is interchangeable, a copy" (*ibid.*).

Moreover, this rigorous cultural democratization operates on both sides of the camera. The many maverick directors over the decades and the more recent rise of an independent film industry would lead one to believe that the film industry is ripe for substantial change. Nevertheless, the same studios that dominated Hollywood in the 1940s stride the global film stage today. They survive by fostering what Adorno and Horkheimer colourfully call "realistic dissidence". By noting each maverick's "brand of deviation from the norm", the film industry turns resistance to its advantage (Adorno & Horkheimer 1997: 132). Any truly obstinate refusal to fit in will be met by the threat of exclusion, which carries with it the "outsider" status that means one can "easily be accused of incompetence" (*ibid.*: 133). To retain one's right to criticize, one must remain a member of the fraternity. For this reason, "[a]nyone who resists can only survive by fitting in" (*ibid.*: 132).

Taken together, the system of stars and mavericks and the production of cultural consumers are part of the same tyrannical outlook. Like Plato's philosopher-kings, the cinematic elite do not lay claim to special endowments relative to their less privileged fellow citizens – except perhaps the good fortune of fame – and yet the net result is that the minority have the chance to "demonstrate [their] superiority by well-planned originality" (*ibid.*: 132), while the majority idle away their time in a dark room "with their backs to reality" (*ibid.*: 143). This situation gives an ironic truth to the claim that the "viewer is king". The consumer is the supreme product of the culture industry, and his fixed attention on the "magic-lantern show" is its lifeblood. However, like King Midas, these kings will have to "be satisfied with the menu": in spite of all "those brilliant names and images", the film industry "perpetually cheats its consumers of what it perpetually promises" (*ibid.*: 139). For Adorno and Horkheimer, this deception is doubly significant because it is not just a matter of an aesthetic degradation – the "idolization of the cheap" that makes "the average the heroic" (*ibid.*: 156); it is the failure to strive for a different society whose morality is more than a "cheap form of yesterday's children's books" (*ibid.*: 152). Although many will protest that films just mean to entertain, and not to shape society, for Adorno and Horkheimer this protest rings hollow: on the one hand because of the moral role clearly claimed by the film industry, which in their day was summarized by the Motion Picture Production Code, commonly known as the Hays Code (*ibid.*: 140); and on the other because it is the sign that something is seriously wrong that most would expect so little from their culture.

DIALECTICS OF SERIOUS AND LIGHT ART

Nevertheless, there is a paradoxical aspect to Adorno and Horkheimer's views on film under the culture industry. Even though their description reads as a declamation, and thus a call for something better, their own theory bars any fundamental change. Some, such as Frederic Jameson, have taken this as a cue to rethink the political economics underlying their theory (cf. Jameson 1991). However, even if there is some justification for the argument that the monopolistic economic situation Adorno and Horkheimer describe no longer prevails, there may be an equally important philosophical loophole in their theory. As we have noted, according to their theory, the culture industry arises at the moment the dialectic of serious and light art is arrested in favour of unity. However, this dialectic could only be dissolved internally, by its very terms, and such a reconciliation between serious and light art seems distant indeed. The tension between wanting to be *taken seriously* as art – which runs in the veins of even the most inveterate Hollywood insider, think of Tom Cruise in *Eyes Wide Shut* (dir. Kubrick, 1999) – and the desire to be truly lighthearted, and not the alibi for current social conditions – which even Adorno recognizes in Chaplin – lives on.

Moreover, Adorno admits as much to the extent that most of the rest of his philosophical consideration of the arts is focused on tracing the possibilities for serious and light art. As we will recall, these possibilities do not correspond to individual artworks or types of artworks, but rather to animating tendencies within works. All artworks that strive for more than a fleeting smile aspire to both seriousness and lightheartedness, and the truly great ones, in Beckettian fashion, feed avidly off their tensions (cf. Adorno 1991b). Just the same, Adorno's biases mean that he largely considers film under the banner of light art, leaving it mostly to modern music to realize serious art's potential. In the last two sections of this chapter, we shall first say a little more about how Adorno conceives of light art, and then how film typifies it.

THE UNBEARABLE LIGHTHEARTEDNESS OF FILM

For Adorno, the tendency toward lightheartedness traces back to the popular art of circuses and fairs, which has remained nearly unchanged since the time of the Roman mimus. Socially this makes light art a static reflection of its conditions as consolatory stimuli designed by the elites for the masses, which at its worst fixes into the grinning mask of the culture industry. However, artistically it means that light art has remained tied to the delight of pure appearance – what Adorno calls "remnants of that orgiastic intoxication" (1976: 21) – otherwise associated with the experience of nature. Calling on fireworks as models of this phenomenon, he explains that just as they seem "a sign from heaven", but are in fact "artifactual", light art's gaiety is prepared and yet in the moment seems to gush up unbidden as if a natural phenomenon (2002: 81). As Adorno puts it regarding film, "the technological medium par excellence is … intimately related to the beauty of nature" (1991a: 180). The reason for this surprising connection is that the beauty of nature is itself just as much a product of civilization as is light art. It is only as civilization frees man to view nature as appearance – rather than as "an immediate object of action", as in farming or hunting – that natural beauty arises. Nevertheless, the "sloughing off of the aims of self-preservation", at least for the few, that makes nature appear beautiful depends on its transformation into raw material for human ends (2002: 65). By a cruel irony, natural beauty is nature's mute protest against its domination. Similarly, lightheartedness is *art's* protest against the domination of men by men. By its unchanging mode of expression, light art bears witness to the "discontent with civilization" experienced by those excluded from its fruits, but forced to accept its burdens. Its character is particularly evident when placed beside serious art, which panders to the civilizational elites by progressively eliminating traces of "orgiastic intoxication" in favour of greater "logicity" (1976: 21). Acting as "the social bad conscience of serious art", light art protests the principled "injustice" that divides society into the avant-garde and the backward (Adorno & Horkheimer 1997: 135).

In this duality, the dialectic of serious and light art finds its roots. In contrast to serious art's guilt-ridden complicity with progressive enlightenment, which leads to its withdrawal into a brooding autonomy, light art innocently – even naively – seeks to convey an experience of freedom to those denied it. To the extent that it offers this freedom as if already achieved – as in B-movies where conflicts are solved "in a way that they can hardly be solved in … real lives" (Adorno 1991a: 104) – it is the ideology of the culture industry, where freedom is "freedom from thought" (Adorno & Horkheimer 1997: 144). However, to the extent that it underscores the striving itself, light art, like nature, "recollects a world without domination" (Adorno 2002: 66). In this "recollection", light art does not reject civilization outright – it cannot, since just like serious art, it is a product of it – nevertheless, it manages to mock civilization's belief in the liberating effects of rational progress by means of a "Mark Twain absurdity" that allows it to walk sideways with regard to the historical dialectic (Adorno & Horkheimer 1997: 142). Rather than escape into a utopian future in the manner of serious art, light art's "escapism" is an escape into the present and all its rich ambivalence, "associations and happy nonsense" (*ibid.*). Light art rejects serious art's lofty course of originality, autonomy and singularity in favour of a self-denying orgy of reproductive realism, material heterogeneity and irony.

In the concluding section of the chapter, we shall consider these traits in more detail as they appear most characteristically in film. Our aim in this examination is to recognize how these traits allow film to be popular in a way that serious art has rarely succeeded in being, and thus turn popularity itself into an art to rival serious art: a kind of *art of popularity* that does not simply pander to popular tastes, but rather has its own resistive vision of freedom.

ART OF POPULARITY

Adorno's best account of this potential appears in his book *Composing for the Films*, written in collaboration with the composer Hanns Eisler (and first published in 1947). By focusing on the difficulties faced by composers of film music, this work is able to take a concrete look at the situation of film as a whole. One basic part of this situation reflects light art's relation to its origins. Whereas serious art has a negative relation to its roots (as elite entertainment) and turns to feats of originality in order to transcend them, light art revels in its popular origins "in the country fair and the cheap melodrama" (Adorno & Eisler [1947] 2005: 35). Rather than sublimate the reproductive realism of such forms of entertainment, it thrives on sensationalizing otherwise unremarkable stories of the type boy meets girl. Nevertheless, there is still an important difference between film and its country-fair cousins: namely, the element of technique. This is not to say that technique is an end in itself. Like advanced music, film must avoid "modernism in the bad sense of the word, that is to say, the use of advanced media for their own sake" (*ibid.*: 43). Just the same, when used well, film technique can "give everyday life, which it claims to [simply] reproduce ... an appearance of strangeness", revealing "tensions that are 'blacked out' in the conventional concept of 'normal' average existence" (*ibid.*: 36). In other words, by using the most advanced technical means available in order to reproduce reality – something we could presumably experience better by walking outside – film makes us conscious of the sensational tissue of experience itself. Film's sensationalism is in this sense an extension of its realism, rather than a contradiction as some might believe: a way of highlighting the sensations that make reality *seem* real. The political import of this is that by keeping "sensation [as] its life element", film gains "access to collective energies that are inaccessible to sophisticated" art (*ibid.*). Rather than ivory-tower seriousness, film rubs shoulders with the very popular reality that it would like to change.

The most important way in which film pursues this popular approach to art, according to Adorno and Eisler, is through its material heterogeneity: the fact that it is the amalgamation of material – "pictures, words, sound, script, acting, and photography" – from a variety of sources – "drama, psychological novel, dime novel, operetta, symphony concert, and revue" (*ibid.*: lii). Unlike traditional arts, which respond to the risk of being assimilated into the culture industry by withdrawing into *autonomous* material development, film takes the opposite tack and tries to outdo the culture industry at its own game, assimilating the very media that would assimilate it. For instance, the mutual assimilation between news reportage and film is almost as old as film itself; while newspapers were quick to start carrying "news" about films and their stars, early films such as *M* (dir. Fritz Lang, 1931) and *Nosferatu* (dir. F. W. Murnau, 1922) use shots of newspaper articles to give social perspective. Nevertheless, whereas news reportage has only ever been able to relate to film in terms of its contents and methods, such as through film footage in television news, film has been able to make the news visible *as* news, that is, as a particular medium. It is this citational aspect of cinematic amalgamation – that we still see the fissures that link snippets to their original context – that gives it political import. As Adorno and Eisler put it, the "alienation of the media from each other reflects a society alienated from itself" ([1947] 2005: 74).

Additionally, the amalgamation of material is not simply cumulative, but rather modelled on the process of building up immunity. Just as "[m]usic was introduced as a kind of antidote against the picture", new elements are constantly introduced as immunizations against new social and cultural dangers (*ibid.*: 75). Unlike autonomous art, which claims mastery over its material, film alienates itself in its material, gaining immunity against being treated as material in its turn. In this regard, a revealing contrast can be found in Stanley Kubrick's *A Clockwork Orange* (1971). Whereas Alex's (Malcolm McDowell) "ultra-violence" compromises the Romanticism of Beethoven's Fifth Symphony, reminding us of the Nazis' similar manipulation of art, the film's inclusion of "Singin' in the Rain" lends unexpected, if disquieting, depth to both the song and the earlier film of the same name (dir. Stanley Donen & Gene Kelly 1952). Whereas in the 1952 film, the breakthrough of sound pictures is exemplified by Gene Kelly's performance of the title song, Malcolm McDowell's performance in 1971 as "Clockwork Orange", or man as machine, turns the theme of technical mastery on its head. The filmed song "Singin' in the Rain" (both in 1952 and 1971) is revealed as a showcase of technology that treats the human voice as a tool no different from those used to record it. This ambiguity in filmic material between production and reproduction is what allows it to build up immunity against its assimilation into the culture industry. Because the performance of "Singin' in the Rain" was already a cinematic appropriation in 1952, its reappropriation by Kubrick in 1971 is not a copy of an original that is being subordinated to the culture industry, as much as a copy of a copy. At its extreme, this material heterogeneity annuls the priority of original over copy, and the concomitant relation of subordination, so that the earlier *Singin' in the Rain* can be seen as much a product of the later *A Clockwork Orange* as it is an element of it.

This ironic process, by which assimilation is used as an antidote to assimilation, means that complete realization of any given film is effectively deferred in perpetuity. Just as every film awaits its subsequent quotation, the amalgamated elements mock the "the obtrusive unity" of each film as "fraudulent and fragile" (Adorno & Eisler [1947] 2005: 75). In this way, film takes leave of the notion of the unique artwork – the singular product of genius – in favour of a more detached, self-ironic posture. Adorno and Eisler see this tendency even in the relation between the most basic components of sound and image. Even though ostensibly added to increase reproductive realism, sound not only reminds us of images' "ghostly character" (*ibid.*: 75) when projected silently, but also mocks reality by its "impersonal character" (*ibid.*:

77), because it "feigns the 'natural'" (*ibid.*) rather than be it. As a consequence, the filmic reproduction of reality is always part mime, part self-quotation – always "reality", and as such a reminder of how much remains to be done before we can embrace reality without the quotation marks. If, then, Adorno and Eisler (*ibid.*: 17, 36, 66n.) choose to speak about sensational films such as *King Kong* (dir. Merian C. Cooper & Ernest B. Schoedsack, 1933) and cartoons such as Disney's *Silly Symphonies* (1929–39), rather than the usual suspects of film theory, such as *Birth of a Nation* (dir. D. W. Griffith, 1915) and *Battleship Potemkin* (dir. Sergei Eisenstein, 1925), it is because these unabashedly lighthearted films highlight the seriousness of all lightheartedness: the fact that escapism means that we have something that we want to escape. Bringing us to this awareness transforms popularity from being a tool of mass manipulation to an art of collective formation, wresting "[film's] *a priori* collectivity from the mechanisms of … irrational influence … in the service of emancipatory intentions" (Adorno 1991a: 183–4).

As distant as these hopes seem from the theory of the culture industry with which we began, it is important to note in conclusion the continuities. In both cases, Adorno presents film as essential to forging the modern relation between art and society, which is itself understood as involving indissoluble dialectical tensions. From both theoretical perspectives, the reproductive realism of film and its material heterogeneity are presented as giving film a self-ironic character, which in the case of the culture industry means that it disillusions those who identify with it (cf. Adorno & Horkheimer 1997: 145), and in the case of *Composing for the Films* means it offers a wink and a nod against assimilation. This last-named difference is less a question of attitude about film – pessimism versus optimism – than a divergence of perspective on it: spectator versus artist. Given that by teaming up with Eisler Adorno recognizes the liberating perspective of the artist relative to that of the spectator, it is curious that he never formulates any Beuysian notion of a democratization of art-making. Nevertheless, it still leaves the very Adornian conclusion that the best relation of film to society would be that in which the film-maker sets out not to tell us what society *is* but to help us discover what our society could be.

NOTE

1. The Casino de Paris is a music hall on the rue de Clichy, which opened in 1880 during the Haussmannization of Paris. In the 1910s and 1920s – the period in which Adorno probably knew it – it put on elaborate revues with lavish costumes and musical numbers.

5   ANTONIN ARTAUD

Anna Powell

Antonin Artaud (1896–1948) was a French poet, playwright, director and film actor. He was an early member of the French surrealist movement, credited as writing one of the first surrealist films, *La Coquille et le clergyman* (The seashell and the clergyman; dir. Germaine Dulac, 1928). He hoped that the new art form of cinema would induce the shock needed to produce radical thought. From 1926 to 1928, Artaud ran the Alfred Jarry Theatre, along with Roger Vitrac. Disappointed that cinema failed to realize his hopes, he returned to live performance, founding the Theatre of Cruelty in 1935. Spending the war years in asylums, he suffered prolonged electroshock treatment. After his release, he recorded *To be Done with the Judgment of God*, a (banned) radio play/noise performance, and died in 1948. Artaud's books include *The Theatre and Its Double* (1938; English trans. 1958) and *Les Tarahumaras* (1955; published in English as *The Peyote Dance*, 1976), which records his experiences in Mexico. Many of his essays on cinema are collected in an anthology of his works, *Antonin Artaud: Selected Writings* (ed. Susan Sontag, 1976).

> Cinema exalts matter and reveals it to us in its profound spirituality, in its relations with the spirit from which it has emerged.   (Artaud 1976e: 152)

Joan of Arc has condemned herself to burn at the stake. Massieu, a young monk, is sent to prepare her for death. Stone arch, pale robe and black tonsure frame a vivid face with glittering eyes, hollow cheekbones and strongly chiselled lips. Massieu's face is striking in its formal aesthetic beauty, but even more powerful in its mobile affects, as ascetic rigour struggles with passion, spirit with flesh. The angst-ridden face of Antonin Artaud, the actor, is a moving plane of compassion, spiritual hunger and despair. The diagonally skewed close-up of Massieu's face is match-cut with the previous image of Joan (Maria Falconetti) to underline their empathy. The features shift with intensive forces in combat: brows rise, lips part and breathing distends the chest. Yet unity of the image is imposed by purity of purpose, expressed by the static, formal rigidity of Carl-Theodor Dreyer's unrelenting close-ups, which induce a non-localized, durational intensity.

For Artaud, Dreyer was "determined to elucidate one of the most agonising problems that exist" (1976f: 183). Gilles Deleuze, noting the philosophical affinity of actor and director, suggests that "the Passion" appeared in *La Passion de Jeanne d'Arc* (The

61

passion of Joan of Arc; 1928) "in the 'ecstatic' mode and passed through the face, its exhaustion, its turning away, its encounter with the limit" (Deleuze 1986: 108). For Deleuze, the affection-image emphasizes responsive sensation and the struggles of contained passion, expressed by movement on the spot rather than action. Intensified by magnification, the cinematic face epitomizes the "unextended" affection-image and extends its powerful affect to the viewer (*ibid.*: 66). The facial close-up epitomizes the spatially unextended affection-image as it opens up to "a fourth or fifth dimension, Time and Spirit" (*ibid.*: 107). Close-ups magnify modalities, "shadowy and illuminated, dull and shiny, smooth and grainy, jagged and curved" (*ibid.*: 103). An "unextended" affection-image, the cinematic face presents the intensive qualities of "the pure affect, the pure expressed" as a "complex entity" (*ibid.*).

Massieu's intensive struggle with the implications of Joan's martyrdom erupts in a shot of his head leant to one side at an extreme angle. His responses to her simple and profound statements reveal increasing conviction of her sanctity. In a state of "exaltation", he pants heavily and his eyes shine with impending tears as he bends to hear her confession with a beatific smile (Artaud 1976f: 183). In a final extreme close-up of his profile caught in the intensity of "turning away", he prepares her for death. At the foot of the pyre, he will raise his crucifix for Joan's hungry gaze, maintaining his devotional stance amid choking fumes and a rioting crowd.

My clip of Artaud's face opens the issue of faciality in film. Artaud asserts that the human face carries "a kind of perpetual death" from which the artist can "save it/by giving it back its authentic features" (Barber 1999: 75). According to Adrian Gargett, faces are "the only authentic element of the anatomy" for Artaud, whose facial sketches are both animated with "turbulent movement" and disciplined into "hard bones/concentrated eyes" (*ibid.*: 26). Faciality exemplifies the affective potency of Artaud's aesthetics. It conveys the ecstasy and limit of the body *in extremis* through the power of film as a body without organs (BwO). This is a virtual not an actual, physical body (although it might engage the flesh): a body of thought and feeling that lives in the flicker of light and moving images on screen and in the engaged spectator.

La Passion de Jeanne d' Arc is the "affective film par excellence" (Deleuze 1986: 70). This film is a fitting introduction to Artaud's impact on film-philosophy, which stems from his belief that "no matter how deep we dig into the mind, we find at bottom of every emotion, even an intellectual one, an affective sensation of a nervous order" (Artaud 1976e: 150). The shaping force of Artaud's concepts is manifest in his alignment of screen and brain in an anti-authoritarian aesthetics of affect. I shall begin my exploration by outlining Artaud's own fragmented theory and practice of film.

ARTAUD'S CONCEPTS AND FILM

Of Artaud's fifteen film scenarios, only one, *La Coquille et le clergyman*, was ever shot, being directed ("butchered" according to Artaud) by Germaine Dulac in 1928 (Barber 1999: 7).

So what kind of films might Artaud have made? He sought "extraordinary sub-jects, climactic states of mind, an atmosphere of vision" (Artaud 1976f: 181), asserting cinema's power to effect "a total reversal of values, a complete overthrow of optics, perspective and logic" (quoted in Flittermann-Lewis 1996: 117). Emerging from sur-realism, with its radicalization of consciousness by the repressed energies of the id, his scenario sought to express the affective intensities of thought. For Artaud, a dream concretized "the dark truths of the mind", materializing "secrets stirring in the deep-est parts of consciousness" (*ibid.*). He intended dream images to be raw and disjunc-tive, but Dulac instead produced a smoothly linked flow, metaphorically loaded with superimposition and anamorphosis.

Artaud envisaged a form of cinematic cruelty. He wanted to shock the audience into thought, using affect to induce a "scream from the extremities of the mind" (Artaud 1976e: 152). In his scenario "Eighteen Seconds", the protagonist wants "to really possess the full extent of one's mind, to really be the master of one's mind, in short, to think!" (1976c: 116). By 1933, the early promise of cinema had evaporated for him, reduced to "a nourishment that is ready made [and] a world which is fin-ished and sterile" (1976i: 311). By omitting a productive gap for thought, the cinema's vision had become "dead, illusory and fragmented" (*ibid.*: 312). Repudiating cinema, Artaud transferred his appetite for thought to live performance, founding the Theatre of Cruelty in 1935.

Artaud drafted two German expressionist-style scenarios, *The 32* and *The Monk*. In *The Butcher's Revolt* (1935) he envisaged "eroticism, cruelty, the taste for blood, the search for violence, obsession with the horrible, dissolution of moral values, social hypocrisy, lies, false witness, sadism, perversity [given] the maximum read-ability" (Barber 1999: 17). The obsessions of the "madman" protagonist are presented in an image–sound collision, evoking "extremes of sensation from joy to paralysing despair" according to Stephen Barber (*ibid.*: 13). In the scenario, "the texture of meat is aligned with human flesh" and a chase ends up in the slaughterhouse (*ibid.*: 16). Artaud intends to bombard the spectators with a "visual flood of disintegration and disaster" for radical ends, keeping them both "alertly grounded in the tactile world, aware … of what the film is subjecting them to" and "incited to react, in simultaneous physical and revolutionary ways" (*ibid.*: 25).

Artaud aimed to expand space and compress time. He rejects the politically repres-sive aesthetics of representation. Intensive images seek to render bodily immanence immediate and dense. For Barber, Artaud's project of "raw" cinema aimed to "trans-plant" the image "directly into the spectator's ocular nerves and sensations" (*ibid.*: 24). Its cruelty would work by "the simple impact of objects, forms, repulsions, attractions" (*ibid.*: 25). Artaud's ideal film induces "purely visual sensations in which the force would emerge from a collision exacted on the eyes" (*ibid.*: 24). To achieve this effect, the scenarios "project an atmosphere of darkness, blood and shock at the boundary between intention and chance" (*ibid.*: 25).

READING FILM VIA ARTAUD

So how has Artaud been applied to film practice and theory? Both the Lettrists (Isidore Isou and Maurice Lemaître) and the Vienna Action Group (Otto Muehl and Herman Nitsch) made "Artaudian" films of corporeal and stylistic extremity. His concepts of the primacy of thought and the body's affective immanence have recently been applied to *Fight Club* (dir. David Fincher, 1999). For Gargett, Artaud's body in process is a "wild/flexible but flawed instrument" capable of transforming itself and breaking free of social restriction and "terminal incoherence and inexpressivity" (Gargett 2001: 5). In the film, "violence becomes spiritual. *Fight Club* is not so much a competition between individuals as it is a communal experience" (*ibid.*: 5).

An Artaudian *Fight Club* hymns "the explosion of the useless body into a delirious mesmeric new body with an infinite capacity for self-transformation" (*ibid.*). Jack, the protagonist narrator, uses strikingly Artaudian referents to evoke the delirious breakdown of language and the resurrection of the fighting body, which "wasn't about words, the hysterical shouting was in tongues like a Pentecostal Church" (dir. Fincher, 1999). Artaud's poetry likewise breaks language down into component sounds and unnerving glossolalia.

Artaud asserts the body without organs as a virtual double, used to escape his actual body's vulnerability. "Because they were pressing me/to my body/and to the very body/and it was then/that I exploded everything/because my body/can never be touched" (Artaud 1976j: 568). A form of BwO also emerges in Jack's citation of:

> an article written by an organ in the first person:
> "I am Jack's medulla oblongata without me Jack could not regulate his heart rate, blood pressure or breathing" …
> "I am Jack's smirking revenge."
> "I am Jack's cold sweat."
> "I am Jack's broken heart."
> "I am Jack's complete lack of surprise." (dir. Fincher, 1999)

Yet, to produce a true BwO, possessive pronouns must be totally relinquished, by the "distribution of intensive principles of organs" (Deleuze & Guattari 1987: 165). Although Jack "initiates the projection of external states of identity" (Gargett 2001: 1), he does not attain the indefinite article that conducts desire via "'A' stomach, 'an' eye, 'a' mouth: the indefinite article does not lack anything; it is not indeterminate or undifferentiated, but expressed the pure determination of intensity, intensive difference" (Deleuze & Guattari 1987: 164).

My own linkage of Artaud with film-philosophy via Ken Russell's lavishly affective *Altered States* (1980) focuses on drug-induced delirium, the BwO and its radical becomings (Powell 2007). Artaud's account of his initiation into the *Ciguri* ritual of the *Tarahumara* presents peyote as an autopoetic tool of self-creation without the need for God. During his vision, Artaud, acutely aware of corporeal immanence, conceived its virtual extension as the BwO. Divisions between subject and object are undermined by synaesthetic distortions. Russell's cinematography presents the hallucinogenic onset of alterity with fireworks in a flamboyant mix of sound and vision.

The drug's destratification mobilizes radical becomings as "personal consciousness ... expanded in this process of internal separation and distribution" (Artaud 1976k: 24). Artaud details his schizoid dissolution into component elements, as "from what was your spleen, your liver, your heart, or your lungs" organs break away and burst in "this atmosphere which wavers between gas and water" (*ibid.*: 36). One stage in his *Ciguri* trip, when "you no longer feel the body which you have just left and which secured you within its limits, but you feel much happier to belong to the limitless than to yourself" embraces subjective dissolution (*ibid.*). This intensity induces ego loss, as he becomes "an effervescent wave which gives off an incessant crackling in all directions" (*ibid.*). Yet the delirious event does not dissipate force, but deploys its insights to set further thought and action in motion.

THE BRAIN IS THE SCREEN

Artaud, addicted to opiates, conceives of cinema itself as a consciousness-altering drug that "acts directly on the gray matter of the brain" and has "the virtue of an innocuous and direct poison, a subcutaneous injection of morphine" (quoted in Flittermann-Lewis 1996: 116). Its qualities are uniquely suited to stimulate thought via "a sort of physical intoxication which the rotation of images communicates directly to the brain. The mind is affected outside representation. This sort of virtual power of the images finds hitherto unused possibilities in the very depths of the mind" (*ibid.*: 119). One of the most significant film-philosophical concepts pursued by Artaud, then, is the elision of screen and mind, summarized in Deleuze's succinct statement "the brain is the screen" (Flaxman 2000).

Artaud believed that a new era was immanent in which "life – or what we call life – is going to become inseparable from the mind. A profound mental terrain is starting to break through to the surface" (Barber 1999: 39). He hoped that "the cinema, better than any other art form, is capable of tracking the movements of this terrain" (*ibid.*). The use of cinema to tell stories or record external reality deprives it of

> the best of its resources and obstructs its most profound aim ... to express the elements of thought, the interior of the consciousness – not so much by the play of images than by something harder to seize, which directly restores the matter of images to us, without any intermediation, without any representation in "direct and immediate language". (*Ibid.*: 39)

Artaud notes the "essential quality of secret movement and of material images" to induce and extend thought via affective images in motion, by which "a detail appears which you had never imagined, igniting with intense force, and heading off in search of the impression you yourself were searching for" (*ibid.*: 37). Deleuze stresses the originality of Artaud's film-philosophy as "capable of restoring hope in a possibility of thinking in cinema through cinema" (Deleuze 1989: 165). He links

Artaud to Sergei Eisenstein via the figure of collision, "the nerve-wave that gives rise to thought" and also to the surrealists, but for Artaud "the dream is too easy a solution to the 'problem' of thought" (*ibid.*). Rather than the psychological nightmares of expressionism, Artaud "*makes dream pass though a diurnal treatment*" (*ibid.*: 167). He innovatively links cinema, automatic writing and the "spiritual automaton", which "brings together critical and conscious thought and the unconscious in thought" (*ibid.*: 165).

The crux of Artaud's significance for film-philosophy, according to Deleuze, is his "recognition of powerlessness [which] defines the real object-subject of cinema", which does not advance "the power of thought, but its 'impower'" (*ibid.*: 166). It is this "difficulty of being, this powerlessness at the heart of thought" from which Artaud made "the dark glory and profundity of cinema" (*ibid.*). In Artaud's scripts, the protagonist's "'spirit has been stolen' or he 'has become incapable of achieving his thoughts'". Artaud's "central inhibition" is the "internal collapse and fossilization [and] 'theft of thoughts'", but cinema is able to reveal this aporia (Deleuze quoting Artaud, *ibid.*).

As both "agent and victim" of thought, Artaud's "spiritual automaton" has become a "dismantled, paralysed, petrified, frozen instance" (*ibid.*) that must "confront thought as higher 'problem'" or "enter into relation with the undeterminable, the unreferable" (*ibid.*: 167). For Artaud, surrealism's "irreducible core", the dream that stymies thought, has become the "reverse side of thoughts" (*ibid.*).

For Artaud, the innermost reality of the brain is a crack or fissure. Cinema has a "dissociative force" that would introduce a "'figure of nothingness', a hole in appearances" (*ibid.*). Seeking to "uncouple" rather than link images, Artaud overturns "the totality of cinema–thought relations" by his dual realization: montage cannot think the whole and "internal monologue utterable through image" is impossible (*ibid.*).

Artaud despaired at the inherent powerlessness to think. His film aesthetics are, for Barber, "an oblique, tangential theory with an impulse towards self-cancellation" led by the "intractable slippages" of mental images when committed to text, appearing mainly as fragments in letters and articles (Barber 1999: 22). For Deleuze, Artaud's "singular problem" was the search for the ever-elusive concept, the "being of thought which is always to come" (Deleuze 1989: 167). Yet this very elusiveness actually generates new thought and action. Rather than being a shortcoming, powerlessness is an integral hiatus and "we should make our way of thinking from it, without claiming it to be restoring an all-powerful thought. We should rather make us of this powerlessness to believe in life, and to discover the identity of thought and life" (*ibid.*: 170).

Despite its formal adventurousness and literalized images of a brain on screen, *Fight Club* remains an accessible, mainstream narrative of a schizoid split. In order to explore the impower of thought and its regenerative power when confronted by literal death, I shall use *The Act of Seeing with One's Own Eyes* by independent American film-maker Stan Brakhage (1971). The film is both about organs without bodies and itself a BwO. In this remarkably affective piece of cinema, thought encounters the unthought and the unthinkable, the hole at the heart of thought.

BRAKHAGE'S CINEMA OF CRUELTY

[D]eath is not outside the realm of the mind, it is within certain limits knowable and approachable. (Artaud 1976d: 123)

Brakhage's uncompromisingly avant-garde practice encountered Artaud via the Lettrist film *Traité de bave et d'éternité* (Tract of drool and eternity; dir. Isou, 1951) (Barber 1999: 32). Like Artaud, Brakhage repudiates epistemologies of stasis that seek to possess the object and freeze the perpetual flow of matter. To counter this, he seeks an affective eye *in* matter that "does not respond to the name of everything but which must know each object encountered in life through an adventure of perception" (Brakhage 1967: 211).

The Act of Seeing With One's Own Eyes is a thirty-two-minute, silent documentary. The title translates the Greek *autopsia*. The film is "about" official police investigation into the causes of death. A notice at the start warns viewers to expect undiluted "footage of actual autopsies" and the film is notorious for its explicitness. Artaud himself uses images of autopsy to describe the cruelty demanded by autopoesis, to "not be afraid to show the bone/and to lose the meat in the process" (Artaud 1967j: 560). Artaud's drawings, too, show the body "spread out, dissected as in an autopsy session" (Schroeder 2005: 1). His announcement that "man" must be placed "on the autopsy table to remake his anatomy" is literalized here in Brakhage's relentless emptying out of human subjectivity to make a BwO (Artaud 1967j: 570).

For Artaud, sound heralded cinema's decline as "the elucidations of speech arrest the unconscious and spontaneous poetry of images" and focus shifts to narrative and character interaction. Brakhage likewise preferred silent footage to enhance the impact of the visual encounter. To stretch the eye's capacities, silence ensures that the "interference" of soundtrack does not detract from, or even counterpoint, the image dynamic. Preferring poetry to more mundane language, Brakhage refuses dialogue and intertitles. Nevertheless, he asserts that his films are "inspired-by-music", so musical qualities are present, although not actually heard (Brakhage 1982: 49).

Brakhage's film can be aligned with Artaud's cinema of cruelty. The film-maker's initial act of cruelty involved "torturing" the celluloid film stock itself "by deliberately spitting on the lens or wrecking its focal intention [to] over or under expose film filters [or use] unbalanced lights, neons with neurotic colour temperatures" (Brakhage 1967: 215). Brakhage describes the self-enforced cruelty of filming in the morgue. He was "driven", he says, by personal "desperate reasons" into a situation that he "would never choose to enter without a camera" (Brakhage 1982: 195).

"Everything that acts is a cruelty" to Artaud, who promoted "extreme action, pushed beyond all limits" (Artaud 1958: 85). Brakhage, surrounded by murder victims, suicides and people who had died by violent accident, filmed "desperately" and overshot, keeping the camera running to stave off a distress that threatened to overwhelm him (Brakhage 1982: 198). Nevertheless, he was compelled into "the *act* of seeing, something different from just seeing" (*ibid*.: 199). The film-maker's "primary masochism" extends outwards as sadism to a captive audience. Artaud likewise sought a cinema "of purely visual sensations whose dramatic action springs from a shock designed for the eyes, a shock founded ... on the very substance of the gaze" (quoted in Flittermann-Lewis 1996: 114).

The Act of Seeing with One's Own Eyes tests the endurance of eyes and mind under a cinema of cruelty. It makes uncompromising demands on consciousness via a shocking and violent collision of image and eye. Self evaporates and conceptual thought is stymied as pure affect and the unthought prevail. The viewer loses his or her sense of time so that the film feels much longer than its thirty-two minutes. The event unfolds in duration rather than clock time.

The brutal acts of death are marked on rows of bodies, shot, burned, crushed or poisoned, "frozen in postures of act, action" and the mortuary workers' acts strip off the last vestiges of subjectivity (Brakhage 1982: 199). Editing enacts further violence by ellipsis. One second a young woman's body is a recumbent whole, the next, a severed breast sags over one arm. Her trunk is peeled apart to reveal layers of skin, flesh, fat and viscera. Artaud asserts that "it is through the skin that metaphysics will be made to reenter our minds" and the viewer engages in the profoundly terrible act of their own defacement as a new becoming (1976h: 251).

The autopsy worker cuts round the scalp, pulling a face down over the head, peeling it away like a tight garment. The face in process resonates in Artaud's work as "an empty power, a field of death ... one still has the impression / that it hasn't even begun to / say what it is and what it knows" (Barber 1999: 75). Faciality as a *tabula rasa* is developed further by Deleuze and Guattari's "white wall/black hole" relation (Deleuze & Guattari 1987: 169). Here, Brakhage conveys the horror and fascination of physical defacialization. During the autopsy, they "lift the scalp completely over the face, and bend the face almost in half" to make it "so rigid and so rubbery that you can lift it off and clearly wear it" (Brakhage 1982: 199). The face becomes a mask as the marks of subjectivity are unremittingly peeled away. As Deleuze and Guattari remind us, "dismantling the face is also a politics" in the death of the subjective ego (1987: 188).

Affective engagement in cinema occurs through the "tactisign", "a touching which is specific to the gaze" (Deleuze 1989: 12). Not an extensive act of the hand, it is the intensive sensation of touch "on condition that the hand relinquishes its prehensile and motor functions to content itself with a pure touching" (*ibid.*). We haptically experience the virtual sensation of touch in "tactile–optical function", encountering the wet drip or sticky, thickening texture of blood, or the smooth softness of delicate skin (Deleuze 2003: 151).

The first shot plunges into tactisigns with a close-up hand grabbing flabby flesh and wiry curls of body hair. In the "external" autopsy when the body is left intact, the sensation of pinching and poking is "felt" by the viewer as bruises left on dead skin. The agony of tooth extraction is displaced on to an emptied skull. Gloved hands dismantling a head are coated with slimy, shiny, wet fluid. The entire brain is held, a heavy lump between the hands. The bodies are sawed, sliced and drilled by cold, shining steel blades. Glinting scissors, slicing through muscle and fat, unimaginable agony for a sentient body, is haptic cruelty to the viewer. Brief textural relief is offered by crisp cotton sheets and soft woolly blankets on the gurney. In some shots, the flicker of light on steel is distanced by blur that both softens the image and increases its tactile presence beyond functionality.

Artaud's writings do not foreground colour and he may well have repudiated col-our film for its increased realism, yet Brakhage's use of it here intensifies corporeal affect. For Deleuze, colour "immediately renders a force visible" (*ibid.*: 151). Brakhage uses excessively saturated colours to intensify the tactile impact of pallid flesh, dark crimson blood and the purpling of bruises. Solarization produces an iridescent dark blue/green quality. Reddened skin evokes a sensation of soreness, the blue light of refrigeration, chill.

From Alex Cobb's phenomenalist perspective, Brakhage's lens "remains resolutely reticent" (Cobb 2007). He argues that the bodies "are charged with a profound, innate meaning [in this] film about intersubjectivity" (*ibid.*). Yet, for me, only the first part of the film makes the dead recognizably human. The later part is much less subjective in its emotional impact as long and mid-shots are increasingly replaced by close-ups and extreme close-ups. Excised organs become defamiliarized objects and substances. For Deleuze, the affective close-up can also be the *equivalent* of a face, such as the body parts here. As well as its obvious presentation of organs without bodies, the film becomes a true BwO, in which "forms become contingent, organs are no longer anything more than intensities that are produced, flows, thresholds and gradients" (Deleuze & Guattari 1987: 164).

The possessive pronoun is relinquished in a montage of individual parts: a foot, a penis, body cavities. Slices of rib are pulled away after being neatly sawed through. Gleaming rubbery intestines glide out without cavity walls to hold them. The brain is lifted from the severed skull with ease. The spread flesh of an abdomen reveals a thick layer of dense white fat. The originary carcass flayed beyond recognition, these are no longer "organs in the sense of fragments in relation to a lost unity" (*ibid.*).

The more organs are cut up and pulled out, the less recognizable they are *as* organs. Extreme close-up renders amorphous textures, shapes and reflective sur-faces, transformed into qualitative affection-images by soft focus and glinting light. As affect intensifies, rhythm and play of light become more frenetic. The shaky hand-held camera vibrates on the spot. The dripping of blood and the trembling of severed membranes brings a kind of intensive movement to the not-entirely passive bodies themselves. They become a kind of relief map or interior fleshscape, with ravines, pools and chasms. One charred body is pitted with craters. Blood spills down from a severed artery, a lake overflowing into a stream.

The viewer gives up trying to identify body parts and becomes affectively absorbed into the array of unrecognizable yet qualitatively distinct matter. Rhythmic alternation between light and darkness hypnotizes by its pulsing systole and diastole as the film steals the life-force. Close-ups of prying fingers take the eye and the lens as far inside as they can go. Shooting becomes rapid fire and expressionistic in frenetic prying, pulling and cutting open. Jagged intercutting alternates with a smoother swooping glide around the torso and into its cavity. The camera/eye almost gives up its epis-temological ability to process the images. It is in danger of losing control, swooping rapidly in and out, a vertiginous torrent of affect.

Yet speculative thought still operates, as Brakhage's camera moves in close, enter-ing the defamiliarized empty head cavity, membranes, flesh, muscle and bone. As images become even more tactile, the gleam of reflection becomes brighter and more lucent. Spirit or thought floats virtually on the surface of material actualization, spreading wide, not losing itself in the depths. Discussing the "crack-up" of schizoid artists such as F. Scott Fitzgerald and Artaud, Deleuze counsels our aesthetic "identification with a distance" to distinguish the truth of the event from its actualization (Deleuze 1990a: 161). The distancing devices of art thus "give the crack the chance of flying over its own incorporeal surface area, without stopping at the bursting within each body" (*ibid.*).

CONCLUSION

Artaud's project remains contradictory. According to Gargett, although his imagery is "materialistic (the mind is a thing/object)", he also "demands that the mind attain the purest philosophical idealism" (Gargett 2001: 1). Barber, too, suggests that the contradiction between matter and idealism stymied Artaud's own film practice. Artaud was nevertheless a seminal influence on film-philosophy, by the process of "[t]earing the conscious away from the subject in order to make it an exploration, tearing the unconscious away from significance and interpretation in order to make it a veritable production" (Deleuze & Guattari 1987: 160). Artaud's metaphysical insights into cinematic affect are seminal. For Deleuze, he "lived and said something about the brain that concerns us all: that its 'antennae turned towards the invisible', that it has a capacity to 'resume a resurrection from death'" (Deleuze 1989: 212). Film-philosophy turns Artaud's angst into affirmation.

6 HENRI BERGSON

Dorothea Olkowski

Henri Bergson (1859–1941) was appointed Chair of Ancient Philosophy at the prestigious Collège de France in 1900. In 1922 he became president of the International Commission for Intellectual Cooperation (a precursor to UNESCO). His life work includes a paper on observed hypnosis sessions, "De la simulation inconsciente dans l'état d'hypnotisme" (On unconscious simulation in states of hypnosis) (in *Revue Philosophique*, 1886), *Time and Free Will* (1889; English trans. 1910), *Matter and Memory* (1896; English trans. 1911), *Laughter* (1900; English trans. 1901), *Creative Evolution* (1907; English trans. 1910), his reflections after a debate with Albert Einstein in *Duration and Simultaneity* (1922) and *The Creative Mind* (1946; published in French as *La Pensée et le mouvant*, 1934).

THE LOSS OF INNOCENCE

For philosophers and film theorists today, there can be no innocent account of the philosophy of Henri Bergson, and especially no innocent account of Bergson and film. The latter is due in large part to the two books on cinema written by Gilles Deleuze, *Cinema 1* (1983; 1986) and *Cinema 2* (1985; 1989). Both books acknowledge Bergson's rich and inventive notion of the image, but simultaneously seek to circumvent Bergson's own so-called "overhasty critique" of cinema, a critique that apparently arises when he characterizes the medium as a model for the forces of rationality that immobilize and fragment time (Deleuze 1986: xiv). As Amy Herzog has written, "cinema, for Bergson, or rather the cinematic apparatus, corresponds directly to the function of the intellect. ... 'The camera isolates fragments of reality, erasing the nuances of transformation occurring between frames'" (Herzog 2000, quoting Bergson, *Creative Evolution* [1911] 1983: 306). However, according to Deleuze, when Bergson puts forward his three theses on movement and thereby accuses cinema of producing a false movement, a movement distinct from the space covered by that movement, in this Bergson is mistaken and must be corrected. Deleuze implies that Bergson calls this false movement "the cinematographic illusion" (1986: 1) but Bergson himself refers to it as "the contrivance of the cinema" ([1911] 1983: 322). The contrivance of cinema, Bergson is careful to say, "consists in supposing that we can think the unstable

DOROTHEA OLKOWSKI

by means of the stable, the moving by means of the unmoving" (*ibid.*: 273), and it is *this* that constitutes the illusion at work in the production of film (*ibid.*: 307). *The illusion would be to imagine that an understanding of duration can be produced by static means.* Even so, "the cinematographical method is the only practical method", for by this means knowledge conforms to action, since "the mechanism of the faculty of knowing has been constructed on this plan" (*ibid.*: 306–7). In other words, our knowledge is pragmatic; it follows our interest in acting. So using the intellect to think does not yield illusion; rather, it simply yields a pragmatic type of knowledge. If the error of cinema is that it reconstitutes movement from immobile instants or positions, at least, Deleuze argues, this frees it from the privileged instants or poses of antiquity, the Forms or Ideas that refer to intelligibility. At least the error of cinema can be identified with modern science, no longer privileged instants but what are called "any-instants-whatever", which, for Deleuze, are immanent and material, derived from the continuous and mechanical succession of moments of classical science, according to which time is an independent variable.[1]

Thus, according to Deleuze, Bergson demonstrates that cinema belongs to the modern scientific conception of movement. This conception may be traced from the invention of modern astronomy by Johannes Kepler, who sought to determine the relation between the trajectories of orbits and the time a planet takes to circumscribe them, to classical physics, which sought the link between the space covered by a falling body and the time of this fall, to modern geometry, which worked out the equation for determining the position of a point on a moving straight line at any moment in its course, and, finally, by differential and integral calculus, examining sections of space brought infinitely close together.[2] Isaac Newton proposed the idea of absolute space – invisible empty space at rest relative to any motion in the universe – so that motion could be measured relative to this absolute space. Newton also proposed an absolute, mathematical time flowing without relation to anything external (Wheeler 1990: 2–3). The special theory of relativity does away with the absolute reference of space and time, eliminating any privileged point of view and introducing the concepts of time dilation and space contraction: that is, the idea that time passes more slowly for people and objects in motion and distances shrink for people and objects in motion, and that events that are simultaneous from a moving point of view are not simultaneous from a stationary point of view (DeWitt 2004: 209). Thus, time and space exist in relation to one another; they are what Deleuze will call a bloc of becoming.[3] Nevertheless, the speed of light remains an invariant governing motion and the theory of relativity maintains a fundamental role for observation and measurement. "Time is relative in Einstein's special theory of relativity, but this relativity is expressed by equations which are always valid. Time is not, therefore, chaotically relative, but .... relative in an ordered way" (Durie 1999: xvii).[4] In spite of the profound changes in physics' conception of space and time, Bergson still maintains that the scientific conception of time "surreptitiously bring[s] in the idea of space" by successively setting states side by side, whereas the time he calls duration is "succession *without [the] mutual externality*" of temporal states (*ibid.*: vii, emphasis added). So it seems that much depends on how one understands Bergson's complaint, and Deleuze is very cagey here. He quotes Bergson, "Modern science must be defined pre-eminently by its aspiration to take time as an independent variable" (Deleuze 1986: 4).[5] Yet, Bergson goes on to ask, "with what time has it [modern science] to do?" ([1911] 1983: 336). And so it seems that Deleuze ignores what is most important for Bergson, that is, what the attitude of science is, including the theory of relativity, towards change and evolution. Moreover, Deleuze's argument that space and time are a bloc of becoming might well rest on his assertion – an assertion that seems to have been anticipated by Bergson – that the theory of relativity alters Bergson's fundamental critique of cinematographic knowledge. Yet, although Bergson most certainly accepted the special theory of relativity, did he not do so precisely with the hope of freeing it from the restraints imposed by classical physics, restraints that eliminate duration for the sake of impersonal time (Durie 1999: v–vi)?[6]

Herzog (2000) has argued that Bergson's and Deleuze's positions can be reconciled if we do not take film to be a model for perception or an image of reality but, rather, if we study it as simply an image in its own right, with its own duration (Bergson 1983: 272).[7] As agreeable as this solution may be, it leaves open some interesting if not urgent questions, as Herzog also points out. How, we might ask, are our philosophical concepts influenced and formed by, not so much our technological developments, as the dominant scientific structures and concepts arising from the so-called "invention of modern science" (Stengers 2000)? Ilya Prigogine and Isabelle Stengers have argued that there exists "a strong interaction of the issues proper to culture as a whole and the internal conceptual problems of science in particular" (1984: 19).[8] The reorientation from the modern classical to the contemporary view is, for them, equally reflected in the conflict between the natural sciences and the social sciences and humanities, including philosophy.

Like Bergson, Prigogine and Stengers state that if the development of science has been understood to shift away from concrete experience towards mechanical idealization, this is a consequence of the limitations of modern classical science and its inability to give a coherent account of the relationship between human beings and nature. Many important results were repressed or set aside in so far as they failed to conform to the modern classical model. In order to free itself from traditional modes of comprehending nature, science isolated and purified its practices in the effort to achieve greater and greater autonomy, leading it to conceptualize its knowledge as universal and to isolate itself from any social context (ibid.: 19–22). If this is what occurred, it is not surprising that modern classical science was soon faced with a rival knowledge, one that refuted experimental and mathematical knowledge of nature. Immanuel Kant's transcendental philosophy clearly identified phenomenal reality with science, and science with Newtonian science. Thereby, any opposition to classical science was an opposition to science in its entirety. According to Kant, phenomena, as the objects of experience, are the product of the mind's synthetic activity. So the scientist is, in effect, the source of the universal laws discovered in nature, but the philosopher reveals the *limits* of scientific knowledge in so far as it can never know things in themselves. Beyond those limits, *philosophy* engages with ethics and aesthetics, the noumenal realm that belongs to philosophy alone. What Kant refuses, for the scientist, is any notion of activity, of choice or selectivity with respect to the theoretical and experimental situation (ibid.: 88).[9]

Unlike Kant, who at least proposed détente, G. W. F. Hegel systematically denied the principles of Newtonian science, insisting that simple mechanical behaviour is qualitatively distinct from that of complex living beings who can become self-conscious. Although "Hegel's system provides a consistent philosophic response to the crucial problems of time and complexity", it ultimately failed in so far as no science could support it (*ibid.*: 90).[10] Prigogine and Stengers deliver a similar verdict initially with respect to Bergson. Bergson, they argue, wished to create a metaphysics based on intuition, "a concentrated attention, an increasingly difficult attempt to penetrate deeper into the singularity of things" and attributed to science in general limitations that were applicable only to the science of his time (*ibid.*: 91).[11] It was Bergson who, in 1922, attempted to introduce and defend (against Albert Einstein) the possibility of simultaneous "lived" times, but since, for Einstein, intelligibility remained tied to immutability, Bergson's thesis was widely understood to have failed (*ibid.*: 293–4). And yet, if philosophy is to be something more than the mere handmaid of science, its status is, for Stengers and Prigogine, closely associated with an understanding of time that, they claim, can span the spiritual and physical aspects of nature, including human nature. If the mechanistic view and laws of motion put in place by Newton formulated a world that is closed, atomistic, predictable and time-reversible, Prigogine and Stengers reformulate this world as open, complex, probabilistic and temporally irreversible. "In the classical view, the basic processes of nature were considered to be deterministic and reversible ... Today we see everywhere, the role of irreversible processes, of fluctuations" (*ibid.*: xxvii). For this reason they give an account of the conceptual transformation of science from classical science to the present, particularly as it applies to the macroscopic scale, the scale of atoms, molecules and biomolecules, with special attention to the problem of time, a problem that arose out of the realization that new dynamic states of matter may emerge from thermal chaos when a system interacts with its surroundings. These new structures were given the name *dissipative structures* to indicate that dissipation can in fact play a constructive role in the formation of new states (*ibid.*: 12).[12] Prigogine and Stengers thus take us from the static view of classical dynamics to what they take to be an *evolutionary* view arising with non-equilibrium thermodynamics. They conclude that the reversibility of classical dynamics is a characteristic of closed dynamic systems only, and that science must accept a pluralistic world in which reversible and irreversible processes coexist (*ibid.*: 79–290).[13] In place of general, all-embracing schemes that could be expressed in terms of eternal laws, there is time. In place of symmetry, there are symmetry-breaking processes on all levels. And yet, there remains a kind of unity, that is, time irreversibility has become the source of order on all levels.

Bergson himself expresses a similar idea in his introduction to *Creative Evolution*. He says that a theory of knowledge and a theory of life seem to be inseparable, but that life cannot simply accept the concepts that understanding provides for it (1983: xiii).[14] This is an old problem. How can the intellect, created by the processes of evolution, be applied to and understand that evolutionary movement that created it? Certainly, human beings are not pure intellect, for there lingers all around us, around our conceptual and logical thought, "a vague nebulosity, made of their very substance out of which has been formed the luminous nucleus that we call the intellect". Beyond this, he continues, are other forms of consciousness that, although not freed of external constraints as the human intellect is, nevertheless do express something "immanent and essential in the evolutionary movement" (*ibid*.: xii).[15] Thus, in so far as the cinematographic mechanism of thought arises in the evolutionary context, it may be that in order to truly understand it we need to examine this evolutionary context more fully. That is, why does Bergson's critique of cinematographic knowledge appear in the final chapter of *Creative Evolution*? What is the relation between his critique of this concept of rationality and modern classical science and the theory of relativity? Can a bridge be constructed, as Prigogine and Stengers suggest, between the spiritual and physical aspects of life, an evolutionary bridge based on time irreversibility as the source of order on all levels?

EVOLUTION

Nearly three-quarters of a century before Prigogine and Stengers, Bergson begins his account of cinematographic knowledge with the assertion that *duration is irreversible*, but he asserts more than this: not only, he claims, is something new added to our personality, but it is something absolutely new that not even a divine being could predict. This must be contrasted with geometrical deductive reasoning, in which impersonal and universal premises force impersonal and universal conclusions. For conscious life, the reasons of different persons that take place at different moments are not universal, they cannot be understood "from outside" and abstractly; for conscious beings, to exist is to change, meaning, to create oneself and to go on creating oneself (Bergson 1983: 6–7).[16] This is the case, for Bergson, owing to his general idea of the evolutionary process. Life, he argues, does not develop linearly, in accordance with a geometrical, formal model. For life, change is not merely the displacement of parts that themselves do not change except to split into smaller and smaller parts, molecules, atoms, corpuscles, all of which may return to their original position and remain time-reversible. In principle, any state of such a group may be repeated as often as desired; the group has no history, nothing is created, for what it will be is already there in what it is, and what it is includes all the points of the universe with which it is related (*ibid*.).[17]

Without doubt, evolution had first to overcome the resistance of inert matter, which changes only under the influence of external forces, where such change is no more than the displacement of parts (*ibid*.: 8).[18] The difficulty would be not to fall into the path of Hegel, for whose notion of change no mathematical or scientific justification could be found. There is no question that Bergson recognizes this difficulty, but in order to make the transition from inert matter to life, phenomena had first to participate in the *habits* of inert matter, meaning the behaviour of inert matter, in so far as it is influenced causally by external forces (*ibid*.: 99). This behaviour can be said to follow the laws that external forces prescribe and, as thermodynamics had already revealed, those laws produce probabilities not certainties; that is, their patterns can be called habits. From the point of view of contemporary evolutionary biology, life arose as a phenomenon of energy flow; it is inseparable from energy flow, the process of material exchange in a cosmos *bathing* in the energy of the stars. Stars provide the energy for life and the basic operation of life is to trap, store and *convert starlight into energy*. So, for example, carbon, so essential to living matter, was formed out of the lighter elements baked by the nuclear fission of exploding stars following the initial "singularity", the explosion from an immensely hot, infinitely dense point 13.5 billion years ago, and in photosynthesis, photons are incorporated, building up bodies and food (*ibid.*).[19] Thermodynamics developed as the science that studies these energy flows from which life emerges, as living matter internalizes, with ever increasing variation, the cyclicity of its cosmic surroundings. For evolutionary biology, the science of non-equilibrium thermodynamics supports the idea that energy flows through structures and organizes them to be more complex than their surroundings, that organized and structured patterns appear out of seemingly random collisions of atoms (Margulis & Sagan 1997: 28).[20] All the more reason to accept Bergson's conclusion that the simplest forms of life were initially both physical and chemical *and* alive, and that life is simply one tendency, a tendency that diverges over and over, sometimes preserved by nature and sometimes disappearing.

In evolution, adaptation is mechanism in so far as species must adapt to the accidents of the road, but it appears that *these accidents do not cause evolution*: that evolution remains creative and inventive in spite of adaptation. Likewise, evolution is not finalism, the realization of a plan, for this would make it representable prior to its realization, and in any case, rather that reaching a final harmonious stage, evolution often scatters life, producing incompatible and antagonistic species (Bergson 1983: 102–3).[21] Moreover, it is difficult to clearly separate animal and vegetable worlds. At best, we can say that vegetables create organic matter out of mineral elements that they draw from the elements – earth, air and water – while animals cannot do this and so must consume the vegetables that have accomplished this for them. Thus, Bergson's claims seem to be compatible with those of evolutionary biologist Lynn Margulis, when he states that the first living beings must have sought to accumulate energy from the sun so as to expend it in a discontinuous and explosive manner in movement (1983: 115–16).[22] It is crucial, then, that evolution not proceed merely by association, but always by dissociation or divergence; species participate in an original identity from which they diverge, even while retaining something of their origins, the original tendency out of which they evolved. Although animal and vegetable worlds each retain some of the characteristics of the other, animals are characterized by movement (*ibid.*: 108–9).[23] What makes mobility so important is its link to consciousness, "the humblest organism is conscious in proportion to its power to move *freely*" (*ibid.*: 111).[24] So perhaps it should not shock us that recent research involving ravens, creatures that freely move through at least three dimensions, reveals a startling capacity for consciousness and abstract thought (Heinrich & Bugnyar 2007).[25] If this is so, we might conclude that it is not impossible to define animals by their sensibility and consciousness, and vegetables by their insensibility and lack of consciousness, as long as one accepts that these tendencies derive from a common origin, the first living creatures oscillating between animal and vegetable, participating in both (Bergson 1983: 112).

Bergson contrasts this view of evolution as tendencies to an understanding of evolution as a causal mechanism, a theory he associates with cinematographic movement and rejects (*ibid*.: 102).[26] A mechanistic evolutionary theory "means to show us the gradual building up of the machine under the influence of external circumstances [forces] intervening either directly by action on the tissues or indirectly by the selection of better adapted ones" (*ibid*.: 88).[27] Bergson, we noted, also opposes finalism, the idea that evolution takes place and parts of the machine are brought together as a projection of a preconceived plan, realizing an idea or imitating a model. But mechanism and finalism are both constructed in the same manner as cinematographic knowledge; they proceed through *the association and addition* of elements.[28] As the film of the cinematograph unrolls, different immobile photographs of the same scene follow one another so that the film apparatus operates just like the geometrical deduction. *Extracting* or deducing from each individual figure, it produces an impersonal abstract and simple movement in general, a homogeneous movement of externally related entities. The movement particular to each figure, the so-called *inner becoming of things*, is never developed, and we are left with the artificial, abstract, uniform movement connecting the singular, individual attitudes, in place of real, evolutionary change: association and addition rather than dissociation and even dissipation. Unfortunately, Bergson argues, "the mechanism of our *ordinary* knowledge is of a cinematographical kind": perception, intellection and language, the fundamental *human* relations with the material world, proceed in accordance with the rules of this "cinematograph inside us" (*ibid*.: 306). Not surprisingly, then, the cinematographic mechanism, which is a *mechanical* mechanism, operates with precisely the same structure as that of ordinary knowledge. In short, it is mechanical; ordinary knowledge is not evolutionary, it does not reflect the inner becoming of things. It operates through the association and addition of homogeneous units (frames) and always under the influence of external circumstances, the mechanism of the projector in this case. Likewise, it imitates certain aspects of human behaviour, notably those that require association and addition, such as perception, intellection, language and, especially, action. Our acts reflect the insertion of our will into reality whereby we perceive and know only that on which we can act.

Given this state of affairs, what is missing from cinematographic movement, from change as described by cinema, and therefore also from the cinematographic *image*, is precisely the "movement particular to each figure, the inner becoming of things", the evolutionary movement of dissociation and dissipation. But what is the inner becoming of things? "Things" are matter and matter has a tendency; it tends to constitute isolable systems that *can* but need not be treated geometrically. This tendency appears to preclude any notion of inner becoming even though it is only a tendency and not an absolute. Yet recall the glass of water into which Bergson pours sugar. "I must wait, willy nilly, wait until the sugar melts" (*ibid*.: 9).[29] Why not, Deleuze suggests impatiently (1986: 9), simply stir it with a spoon; why wait around for the sugar to melt on its own? One waits, according to Bergson, because even material objects may be observed to unfold as if they occupied a duration like our own. Such waiting does not take place in the time of our ordinary knowledge, the time of the succession of homogeneous instants whereby the past, present and future of material objects and isolated systems can be simultaneously spread out in space as if they are eternal. One waits because the isolation of matter is never complete and only waiting reveals

77

that the system belongs to another, more extensive system: the sugar, the water, the glass, the temperature and humidity of the air, the table, the room and on and on into the solar system transmitting, in this way, a duration immanent to the whole universe including the duration of the observer (1983: 10–11).[30] With respect to cinema, this raises the following question: is the cinema itself only a tool of mechanism and/or finalism? Is it an isolated system, a geometrical abstraction, so that it is not, for this reason, a genuine creative practice, but a manifestation of perception, intellect, language and action in the context of the homogeneous and mechanical material world?

Deleuze attempts to answer these questions with reference to Bergson's conception of duration. He calls the answer to these questions "Bergson's third thesis", which when reduced "to a bare formula would be this: not only is the instant an immobile section of movement, but movement is a mobile section of duration, that is, of the Whole" (Deleuze 1986: 8). Matter moves but does not change, but duration is change, and this is, we are told, the very definition of duration. Moreover, movement expresses this change in duration or in the whole. Movement is a change of quality; the fox moves in the forest, the rabbits scatter, the whole has changed. When water is poured into sugar or sugar into water, the result is a qualitative change of the whole and not merely a succession of homogeneous instants. Deleuze admits that "what Bergson wants to say … is that my waiting, *whatever it be*, expresses a duration as a mental, spiritual reality" (*ibid.*: 9, emphasis added). Whatever it be, it is not the whole since the whole is open, the universe is open to evolution, which is to say, to duration. But again, contrary to Bergson, Deleuze goes on to define the whole as "Relation", which is not a property of objects but is "external to its terms" (*ibid.*: 10).[31] Bergson concurs that there exists a duration immanent to the whole of the universe and that the universe itself endures, but what this means is not movement of a mobile section: what it means is "invention, the creation of new forms, the continual elaboration of the absolutely new" (Bergson 1983: 11). And this is why the time of waiting for the sugar to melt coincides with the impatience of the one who waits; in other words, it coincides with the duration of the one who waits. And as coinciding with the duration of the one who waits, "it is no longer something *thought*, it is something *lived*. It is no longer a relation, it is an absolute" (Bergson 1983: 10).

NOTES

1. Deleuze writes, "the cinema is the system which reproduces movement as a function of any-instant-whatever, that is, as a function of equidistant instants, selected so as to create an impression of continuity" (*Cinema 1: The Movement-Image*, H. Tomlinson & B. Habberjam [trans.] [London: Athlone, 1986], 5).
2. Certainly these are part of Deleuze's general interest as well. In departing from the Greek notions of Form and Substance, and by embracing the concept of the differentiable instant on a plane of immanence, developed by calculus, as well as the notion of time as an independent variable, Deleuze is simply formulating a metaphysics compatible with modern science (Deleuze, *Cinema 1*, 4).
3. For Bergson, every affective image emerging into perception is a point of view on the whole of affective life. As such, when we are not acting merely out of habit, our perceptual life and the choices we make concerning when and how to act come from interpretations informed by virtual memory

images called forth by perceptual consciousness in an interval of attentive reflection; cf. D. Olkowski, "Maurice Merleau-Ponty: Intertwining and Objectification", *Phanex, the Journal for Existential and Phenomenological Theory and Culture* **1**(1) (November 2006), 113–39, and Bergson, *Matter and Memory*, N. M. Paul & W. S. Palmer (trans.) (New York: Zone Books, 1994), 102.

4. Robin Durie cites the physicist Andre Metz's review of Bergson's *Duration and Simultaneity*, first published in *Revue de Philosophie* **1** (1924), and reprinted as "The Time of Einstein and Philosophy, Concerning the New Edition of M. Bergson's Work, *Duration and Simultaneity*", in Henri Bergson, *Duration and Simultaneity*, M. Lewis & R. Durie (trans.) (Manchester: Clinamen Press, 1999), appendix VI, 160–83.

5. The English translation of *Cinema 1* quotes Bergson's *Creative Evolution*, A. Mitchell (trans.) (Boston, MA: University Press of America 1954: 355) at p. 219, n.4.

6. Durie argues that for Bergson, "the acknowledged superiority of Einstein's special theory of relativity is that it demonstrates the fallacy of Newton's hypothesis of an absolute time" ("Introduction", in Bergson, *Duration and Simultaneity*, vi).

7. This is Bergson's title for chapter four of *Creative Evolution*. He does not use the term cinematographic illusion.

8. The French title of this book, *La Nouvelle alliance*, an earlier and slightly less developed version, reflects the "new alliance" between science and culture.

9. "Kant is after the *unique* language that science deciphers in nature, the unique set of apriori principles on which physics is based and that are thus to be identified with the categories of human understanding"; I. Prigogine & I. Stengers, *Order Out of Chaos, Man's New Dialogue with Nature* (New York: Bantam, 1984), 88.

10. The theories Hegel relied on were soon shown to fail. However, Hegel's reliance on logic rather than mathematics was to have long-term ramifications, opening the way eventually to logical positivism.

11. Science and intuition are, for Bergson, two divergent directions of the activity of thought. Science exploits the world and dominates matter. Intuition is engaged with nature as change and the new (Prigogine & Stengers, *Order Out of Chaos*, 91–2). Bergson's frequent engagement with the theory of relativity seems to put into question the conclusion that he "sums up the achievement of *classical science*"; possibly he does more than this (*ibid.*: 93).

12. Equilibrium thermodynamics studies the transformation of energy and the laws of thermodynamics recognize that although "energy is conserved", when "energy is defined as the capacity to do work", nevertheless, nature is fundamentally asymmetrical; that is, although the total quantity of energy remains the same, its distribution changes in a manner that is irreversible. So, for example, although human beings long ago figured out how to convert stored energy and work into heat, the problem has been to convert heat and stored energy into work. Otherwise expressed, how are we able to extract ordered motion from disordered motion? Cf. P. W. Atkins, *The Second Law* (New York: Scientific American Library, 1984), 8–13.

13. These theories and others along with their philosophical implications are discussed at length.

14. "A theory of knowledge which does not replace the intellect in the general evolution of life will teach us neither how the frames of knowledge have been constructed nor how we can enlarge or go beyond them" (Bergson, *Creative Evolution*, xiii).

15. Bergson notes that if these other forms of consciousness were joined with human intellect, this might yield a complete vision of life.

16. This is due to the structure of duration.

17. This corresponds to the static view of classical dynamics set forth by Prigogine and Stengers, *Order Out of Chaos*.

18. It seems to me that Bergson is proposing a new image for science but, as he was a philosopher and not a physicist, he was and remains widely misunderstood.

19. Photons are a quantum of electromagnetic radiation; cf. L. Margulis & D. Sagan, "The Universe in Heat", in their *What is Sex?* (New York: Simon & Schuster, 1997), 8, 24.

20. Lynn Margulis is a well-known evolutionary biologist and Dorion Sagan is a science writer. Life is only one example of a thermodynamic system but, as the authors admit, it is among the most interesting.

21. Evolution sometimes involves devolution, turning back (Bergson, *Creative Evolution*, 104).

22. Bergson cites the chlorophyl-bearing Infusoria.

23. Bergson provides examples of plants that climb and eat bugs and animals, such as parasites, that do not move.
24. Motor activity maintains consciousness but consciousness directs locomotion.
25. Ravens use logic to solve problems and manifest abilities surpassing those of the great apes.
26. Margulis and Sagan seem to evade mechanism as well as finalism altogether.
27. This corresponds to what Deleuze calls "force"; cf. G. Deleuze, *Difference and Repetition*, P. Patton (trans.) (London: Continuum, 1994), 141.
28. For this reason, *Creative Evolution* is a thorough critique of empiricism and empirical principles as well as of Kantianism and Kantian principles.
29. "Common sense, which I occupied with detached objects, and also science, which considers isolated systems, are concerned only with the *ends of the intervals* and not with the intervals themselves" (Bergson, *Creative Evolution*, 9, emphasis added).
30. When science does isolate matter completely, Bergson admits, it is only in order to study it.
31. The difference of viewpoints on this is quite remarkable.

7 MAURICE MERLEAU-PONTY

Helen A. Fielding

Maurice Merleau-Ponty (1908–61) was a key thinker in existential phenomenology of the twentieth century. He was active in the French Resistance during the Second World War. He taught at the École Normale Supérieure, the University of Lyons and the Sorbonne. From 1952 until his death he held the Chair of Philosophy at Collège de France. He was the co-editor (with Jean-Paul Sartre) of the journal *Les Temps Modernes* from 1945 to 1952. Merleau-Ponty wrote a number of books on the philosophy of perception, drawing from the phenomenological method of German philosopher Edmund Husserl. His works include *The Structure of Behavior* (1942; English trans. 1963), *Phenomenology of Perception* (1945; English trans. 1962), *Humanism and Terror* (1947; English trans. 1969), *Sense and Non-Sense* (1948; English trans. 1964), *The Visible and the Invisible* (1964; English trans. 1968) and *The Prose of the World* (1969; English trans. 1973). A number of his essays appear in *The Merleau-Ponty Aesthetics Reader* (1993).

Maurice Merleau-Ponty wrote only one essay on film, yet his phenomenological approach informs problems of perception central to film. Taken up by some theorists as a welcome counterbalance to Marxist and psychoanalytic theories that tend to consider the film as text, a phenomenological approach provides a methodology for thinking through the perceptual experience of viewing (cf. Sobchack 1991: xvi).

In a lecture given in 1945 at l'Institut des Hautes Etudes Cinématographiques, titled "The Film and the New Psychology" (1964), Merleau-Ponty turns to film as evidence that perception is linked to bodily comportment rather than either unmediated sensation or cognition. By interrogating the "historical crisis" encountered by psychology, a crisis initially addressed by Edmund Husserl and Henri Bergson that revolved around a Cartesian split between materialism and idealism, matter and thought, Merleau-Ponty explains that in classical psychology the visual field was considered to "be a sum or mosaic of sensations", each sensation corresponding to "the local retinal stimulus" on which it was dependent. The relationship between the elements of the visual field was accounted for by a cognitive construction, a unity provided by the representative faculty (1964: 48–9). Cinema, which was developing at the time of this crisis, directly challenged such mind–body dualism and thus had to be taken into account.

Elaborating on his corporeal phenomenology as a lifelong project, Merleau-Ponty sought to overcome the dualism of materialism and idealism, mind and body, through the embodied subject's corporeal intentionality, one that allows for encountering a world that is there through the mediation of an individual's horizon, which is shaped by subjective experience. We can encounter the world only as situated and embodied beings. Whereas a critic such as Gilles Deleuze sees phenomenology as ultimately not succeeding in accounting for corporeality since in the end it relies on a constructed, or "prehensive" consciousness rather than material flows, theorists such as Vivian Sobchack understand this return to reflection as precisely what allows us to access the film experience (cf. Sobchack 1991: 3; Deleuze 1986: 57). Ultimately, Merleau-Ponty did not equate the camera eye with the phenomenal body, yet in concluding that film is art when it does not simply refer to established meaning, but rather shows it as it emerges, he reveals the experience of embodying film.[1] In fact, I would suggest, a phenomenal approach reveals how film can contribute to the cultivation of perception.

Merleau-Ponty took film to be an "ambiguous ally" (Deleuze 1986: 57); in the few instances in the *Phenomenology of Perception* (1962) where Merleau-Ponty does address film it is in order to show how film differs from natural perception.[2] Yet, in his essay, Merleau-Ponty wants to elaborate on how film is "peculiarly suited to make manifest the union of mind and body, mind and world, and the expression of one in the other" (1964: 58). This ambiguity is evident in his descriptions of the horizon and the gestalt, both of which provide the contextual field for perceptual understanding. Natural perception does not rely merely on either the empirical registration of sensation by the eye or a calculation or cognitive interpretation of what is perceived. Rather, we see according to gestalts – to see something is to "plunge oneself into it" – and this object appears from within a "system in which one [object] cannot show itself without concealing others". This means that other objects become the horizon against which the specific object appears (1962: 67–8). Hence, we see according to systems sedimented through our participation in a world. We see people and trees against a background, and not the background or interval emerging between figures and objects. Things and people leap out at us, taking shape as we try to make sense of the world that stands before us. This is the logic of perception: "To see is to enter a universe of beings which *display themselves*, and they would not do this if they could not be hidden behind each other or behind me. … to look at an object is to inhabit it, and from this habitation to grasp all things in terms of the aspect which they present to it" (*ibid.*: 68). Film draws on this fundamental aspect of perception. Not only does film rely on the figure against a background – when we watch a film we do not just see colours and movement, we see people, buildings and places – but the film itself has a particular meaning that takes shape through its temporal flow, a meaning that could never be reduced to mere facts or ideas. Providing its own gestalt, a "film is not thought; it is perceived" (1964: 58).

As a temporal gestalt the meaning of one shot depends on the preceding shots. In "normal vision" I look at something and it is disclosed as that thing, the horizon guaranteeing the identity of the object. In a film, however, the camera might move in on an object for a close-up shot. In this case we "*remember* that we are being shown the ashtray or an actor's hand, we do not actually identify it. This is because the screen has no horizons" (1962: 68). Nevertheless, just as a melody, which is also a temporal gestalt, is not a sum of notes but emerges in the temporal flow of the whole piece – a whole that can be transposed into different keys without losing its meaning – so too does a film exist as a whole. Even if only a few notes of a melody are changed, the entire piece is affected. Similarly, one film scene can shed light on how to understand or take meaning from the film in its entirety. If our perception depends not on the sum of parts but rather on our perception of the whole, then the meaning of the film as temporal gestalt depends on the entire film's rhythm.

While film might in some ways parallel human vision, it cannot be equated with it. As Sobchack argues, it is after all not a human body, but rather a technological apparatus with its own intentionality, its own film body (1991: 243). Merleau-Ponty explains that the reduced and flat surface of the film screen does not allow for the experience of depth provided in human perception. We do not objectively calculate that the man in the distance walks away from us because he becomes smaller but, rather, as he moves away, he gradually slips from the hold of our gaze. This experience of depth "is born beneath my gaze because the latter tries to see something" (1962: 260–62); it provides the anchor for the visual field.

If we perceive according to the whole that appeals to our senses in a total way, then clearly, for Merleau-Ponty, a film does provide a system that allows us to distinguish between signs and what they signify, "between what is sensed and what is judged" (1964: 50). Phenomenologically, Merleau-Ponty argues that our perception of movement is intentionally situated within a world. It is not a matter of cognitively assessing a situation, but of being anchored within a field of relations. This is an insight that film can exploit. In Merleau-Ponty's example, sitting in a railway carriage in the station playing cards with his companions, he looks up to see the adjacent train pull away from the station. When, however, his gaze is fixed on someone or some activity taking place in the nearby carriage, then it appears to him that it is his own train that is pulling away from the station. He concludes that it is not that we cognitively assess what is actually happening; rather, the experience is derived from the "way we settle ourselves in the world and the position our bodies assume in it" (*ibid.*: 52). The camera lens can similarly be situated to suggest movement of either its gaze or that which it observes. This corporeal relation to the world is one that precedes and supports our cognitive assessments and makes them possible. It is because we are embodied that we are even able to engage with the world, to perceive it and hence to think about it.

Yet, if we do not make judgements about the sensory data that impinge on our vision, then how are we able to recognize an object from one situation to the next? For Merleau-Ponty, this recognition must depend on the constancy of our perception of that object despite, for example, varying lighting levels. We do not calculate that the dark-blue book hidden in evening shadow must be the same light-blue book I left there in full daylight, which would logically account for the contrasting colours. Instead, I see the book in different lighting levels because I see within a field and against a horizon. I do not need to make judgements because I see the thing itself. The world "organizes itself in front of me" (*ibid.*: 51).

Accordingly, in experiments where one looks through a pinhole at a screen, the field is unanchored. So, for example, a black box well lit and a white box faintly lit can appear as the same grey unless a piece of white paper is introduced into the black box and one of black into the white. In those cases, the fields appear and the differences between the colours with them (1962: 308). When I first enter a darkened cinema, leaving behind the bright lights of the lobby, my body tries to anchor itself in this new lighting level. I am initially aware of the screen as a light that flickers with the montage of shots, often providing inadequate light to search out a seat. But after a moment my eyes begin to adjust to this new lighting level, allowing me to find my way. As my body further adjusts, the screen recedes as light and becomes instead the world I inhabit, the relations among things, and my body reasserts itself according to this new level of the film.[3] In natural vision, "objects and lighting form a system which tends towards a certain constancy and a certain level of stability" (1964: 51). This constancy, as I have discussed elsewhere (Fielding 2006), is the conservative aspect of phenomenological vision that relies on an established logic of perception, without which it would not be possible to make sense of that perceived, and which provides a constancy from one lighting level to the next. Yet film vision, which cannot rely on the horizon and an anchoring in a field, can take advantage of this potential to disrupt the cinematographic syntax and attempt to account for that which is left out, for alternate perceptions, for requiring that we think about that which we perceive. Merleau-Ponty explains how we make sense of the world, but does not fully explore the implications of this phenomenal aspect of the body for disjuncture: for that which does not appear within the logic of a system. For the problem with the organization of a field is that all sense-data form a system, a certain logic that we come to corporeally understand. This logic "assigns to each object its determinate features in virtue of those of the rest, and which 'cancel out' as unreal all stray data; it is entirely sustained by the certainty of the world" (1962: 313). Since perception gives the world to me as a system, I make assumptions about the world according to the systems that have already been given, according to a world that precedes me, that is given by others. Yet this is where film can either confirm constancy, the logic of the dominant perceptive level – the tendency in Hollywood cinema – or it can challenge it, breaking the logic, allowing stray data to come into view. Laura Marks, whose work I shall come back to, takes this up in her discussion of intercultural cinema (2000).

This constancy that belongs to the logic of perception is further supported by sensual synaesthesia. Film relies on vision and sound: only two of the five senses. Yet, since our senses, which cannot be collapsed into one another, nevertheless intertwine, overlap and come together in the synergic system of being in the world, one can see the hardness of ice, and hear the brittleness of glass as it breaks. This makes sense if we understand the senses as opening existentially on the world: to perceive is to grasp the unified structure of the thing, its "unique way of being which speaks to all my senses at once" (1964: 50). Film might generally not provide for the experiences of smell, taste or touch, yet these senses can be evoked and spoken to in the film experience simply in the ways they evoke the smells and tastes of a sumptuous meal in Gabriel Axel's *Babettes gæstebud* (Babette's feast; 1987), or even Julie's "hearing of blue" in Krysztof Kieslowski's *Trois couleurs: Bleu* (Three colours: blue; 1993) (Coates 2002: 48). As Merleau-Ponty writes, "When I say that I see a sound, I mean that I echo the vibration of the sound with my whole sensory being" (1962: 234). Thus, when a film is dubbed, it is not merely "the discrepancy between word and image" that comes to the fore, but one has the impression that a whole other conversation is taking place "over there". The dubbed text does not have an "auditory existence". Similarly, when the sound breaks down, faces become thickened and frozen and lose their lively appearance. In short, "[f]or the spectator, the gestures and words are not subsumed under some ideal significance, the words take up the gesture and the gesture the words, and they inter-communicate through the medium of my body" (*ibid.*: 234–5). For the film to work as a field of relations, then, as a level into which we enter that shapes and adjusts the ways we perceive, the parts of the film cannot add up to its sum; they must provide a total temporal gestalt. There must be a bond between sound and image.

For this reason, there is no sharp divide between our interior emotions or feelings and our outward expression of them. We do not show signs of fear that must then be cognitively interpreted by someone else. Rather, we embody fear and this fear is perceived by others precisely because it is a way of behaving, of comporting ourselves, our gestures; it is visible in our bearing. Importantly for Merleau-Ponty, our emotional world is not one of an interior psyche cut off from the world. Referring to the French philosopher Paul Janet, he understands emotion as a "disorganizing reaction which comes into play whenever we are stuck" (1964: 53). Emotions are responses to our engagement in a world and to our relations with others. They vary the ways we relate to others, the ways we comport ourselves with them. For this reason we cannot understand emotions in terms of signs of love or anger providing an indication of an interior psychic fact; rather, "we have to say that others are directly manifest to us as comportment" (*ibid.*).[4] This is also why we cannot truly understand love from an examination of our own interior feelings since the essence of love emerges in our relations of love, our relations with others. Even as the film moves beyond the "blurs, smudges and superfluous matter" of our everyday reality to provide the precision of a carefully wrought reflection, it is because we are perceiving beings who have learnt through our corporeal experiences to understand the logics of perception – the way shadows fall when the light shines in this way, the way things are lined up one behind the other as they recede in depth – that we are able to perceptually comprehend what the film presents. And what a film presents is anger, and dizziness: an emotional world. We apprehend the inside's relation to the outside through our perception of the ways the characters comport themselves, and this is indeed how we perceive in the world: "A film like a thing appeals to our power tacitly to decipher the world or men and to coexist with them" (*ibid.*: 58).

For Merleau-Ponty, films, like phenomenological and existential philosophy, are an "attempt to make us *see* the bond between subject and world, between subject and others, rather than to *explain* it" (*ibid.*). Merleau-Ponty does not hesitate to establish links between film, artworks and philosophy as showing how meaning emerges, is created, rather than merely explaining or describing already established ideas. The film employs a particular cinematographic language, a syntax that is part of the meaning of the gesture of the film as a whole. Just as I do not read or interpret anger in someone's contorted face – I see and experience an angry person – so too I experience more than representation in a film: through an ensemble of music, dialogue and images it reveals meanings that could be reduced to neither cognitive explanation nor a replication of reality. Film can allow us to feel palpably, as the embodied beings we are, the sentiments it explores. For this reason, all parts of the film – for example dialogue, music and shots – should work not towards translating these emotions but towards giving them an existence in our own bodies. In fact, film as art does not replicate or represent reality; rather, in creating, it brings new meanings into being.

In short, film that is art, like phenomenology, cultivates perception. We learn to see the world differently according, for example, to Kieslowski's cinematographic vision. The colour blue takes on a new vibrancy and reverberates with corporeal meaning in the film of that name; for a colour can only be fully explored and experienced corporeally even as the word "blue" itself becomes saturated with emotions and feelings that accompany and overlap the designating function of the word. Blue takes on an ontological function establishing a level or field of relations as the background of the film (Merleau-Ponty 1968: 217). We enter into the level of blue. As Merleau-Ponty explains in the *Phenomenology of Perception*, our bodies have this enormous capacity to move into new situations and to take them up. Just as we shift into a new lighting situation to which our eyes adjust, so too do we move into the level of a film. Our eyes become accustomed to a certain way of seeing, a certain way of hearing; indeed, our perceptions themselves under the guidance of an expert cinematographer and director are further shaped. Thomas Riedelsheimer's *Touch the Sound* (2006), a documentary about deaf percussionist Evelyn Glennie, rhythms its viewers into a world of sound. One enters into the aural level that it provides and one's hearing actually becomes more acute. While watching this film in class, my students became aware of the ambient sounds in the room: tapping on keyboards; breathing; the rustling of paper. This effect lasts for a while after viewing.

Yet this phenomenological body that Merleau-Ponty so carefully describes as one that moves into and takes up the world is not unproblematic. While film for Merleau-Ponty had the potential to reveal the bond between subject and world, for a thinker such as Deleuze, this is precisely the problem with phenomenology. Deleuze identifies the phenomenological body with the sensory-motor schemata that he associates with clichés. These schemata allow our bodies to respond, to turn away "when it is too unpleasant", to prompt "resignation when it is terrible", and assimilation "when it is too beautiful" (Deleuze 1989: 20). In other words, perception is shaped by a world created by others, and it is tied to interest. Merleau-Ponty recognized that we shut out stray data and perceive according to a gestalt. Nevertheless, for Deleuze, via Bergson, this gestalt is tied to our "economic interests", our "ideological beliefs" and our "psychological demands": in other words, clichés. Since perception is the attempt to make sense of what is there and this making sense is reliant on sedimented perceptual structures, then the trick for film is, as Deleuze puts it, to "jam or break" the schemata allowing for the pure optical-sound-image, an image beyond metaphor, marked by its excess that defies all justification (*ibid.*). In post-war European cinema, Deleuze sees certain directors as shattering these schemata from the inside, severing the ties between perception and action: "Some characters, caught in certain pure optical and sound situations, find themselves condemned to wander about or go off on a trip" (*ibid.*: 41–2).

For Merleau-Ponty, in his challenge to mind–body dualism, the problem is one of mediating between the purely empirical realm of sensation and the representational world of idealism; but the problem, as Deleuze understands it, is "how is it possible to explain that movements, all of a sudden, produce an image – as in perception – or that the image produces a movement – as in voluntary action?" Materialism wished "to reconstitute the order of consciousness with pure material movements", and idealism "the order of the universe with pure images in consciousness" (Deleuze 1986: 56). Cinema provides evidence of a movement-image effectively collapsing any artificial boundary. He comes to this conclusion drawing on Bergson, who sought to move beyond the dualisms established by classical psychology and, drawing critically on the emerging quantum physics, understood the *"movement-image* and *flowing-matter"* to be "strictly the same thing" (*ibid.*: 58–60); in this understanding, "IMAGE = MOVEMENT", which is "entirely made up of light". For Merleau-Ponty, however, light remains that which illuminates, but when light is captured in film, in his account, in the film image of someone descending into a cellar, lamp in hand, the light does not appear as "an immaterial entity exploring the darkness and picking out objects", remaining discreetly in the background so that it can *"lead* our gaze instead of arresting it". Rather, it appears as a solid object on the screen's surface (1962: 309–10). This example of light leading our gaze and illuminating parallels Deleuze's understanding of consciousness for Merleau-Ponty, which is, he argues, still squarely situated within the philosophical tradition that placed "light on the side of spirit and made consciousness a beam of light which drew things out of their native darkness" (Deleuze 1986: 60). The only difference for phenomenology is that the light is not internal but rather external, with consciousness providing a beam of light that illuminates what is there (*ibid.*). Dorothea Olkowski takes this critique even further: Merleau-Ponty ultimately resists a philosophy of difference because he still relies upon a "classical dynamical system" which unifies and does not allow for the excluded middle (2007: 217). It should be noted, however, that in Merleau-Ponty's later writings he comes closer to Deleuze's understanding of sensation and affect as belonging not to subjectivity but rather to a desubjectified field of forces, material flows that are not bound to the intentional subject.

Rather than seeing the conscious and reflexive aspect of phenomenological description as a negative, for Sobchack it is in reflection "that experience is given formal significance, is spoken and written". She finds in phenomenology an approach to film theory that addresses the pre-reflective experience fundamental to film, an experience that is "neither verbal nor literary". In fact, a film is in itself "an expression of experience by experience", in other words, a phenomenological reduction. In reflecting on this experience, what is found in film is this "original power" to signify (1991: 4). Sobchack is interested in the way that film provides a reversibility or chiasmus between perception and expression; it draws on the wild being or corporeal experience that precedes signification, and reflection. Indeed, a film has itself a kind of wild being that precedes its dissection into the language of critical and theoretical analyses. There is, Sobchack notes, a kind of cinematic language, but this language is grounded in the structures of pre-reflective corporeal existence shared by "filmmaker, film and spectator" (*ibid.*: 5). Just as Merleau-Ponty is critical of a philosophical tradition that presupposes the body in its cognitive assessments, Sobchack's concern is that "film theory has pre-supposed the act of viewing", taking the film itself as an object that is viewed rather than as a viewing subject with which we corporeally engage. Moreover, in the visible expression of its perception, film makes visible the intrasubjective exchange "between the perception of the camera and the expression of the projector", both as "viewing subjects and as visible objects" (*ibid.*: 19–23). As Merleau-Ponty puts it: "the world is *what we see* and, … nonetheless, we must learn to see it – first in the sense that we must match this vision with knowledge, take possession of it, *say* what *we* and what *seeing* are, act therefore as if we knew nothing about it, as if we still had everything to learn" (1968: 4). As incarnate beings, human beings can see the world, but it is as human beings that they have the particular ability to see with their "own eyes", as viewing subjects, since it requires a "reflexive and reflective consciousness" (Sobchack 1991: 54). It is this "reflexive and reflective consciousness of vision" with its "reversible structure" that allows for the possibility of the film experience (*ibid.*).

Marks draws on Merleau-Ponty's insights into the mimetic body: the body that moves into its world taking it up through compassionate involvement rather than through abstraction or domination in her analysis of intercultural cinema (2000: 141). Critical both of Merleau-Ponty's desire for contact with "wild-being", the sensual embodied being not yet colonized by cognitive structures, as well as Bergson's dismissal of the habitual, Marks herself is interested in the ways that the sensual body is also the habitual body, the ways in which culture is corporeally inscribed in the very ways we perceive. If perception is, as Bergson argues, subtractive, or, for Merleau-Ponty, has its own logic, then for Marks, perception, which is also shaped by trauma, can be a mine-field of that which is to be avoided as well as a multi-sensory experience that arises out of our personal and collective histories. Drawing on Merleau-Ponty's insights into syn-aesthesia, Marks explores how certain images are thick with other sensual experiences, experiences that will differ depending on the sedimented and habitual body we bring to them. The magnolia flowers filmed in Shani Mootoo's *Her Sweetness Lingers* (1994) remind Marks of "how they feel and how they smell, and the buzzing of insects reminds [her] of the heat of summer", calling up associations from her ancestral Alabama (2000: 148). In intercultural cinema, then, certain objects can be laden with the traces of cor-poreal memories, suddenly evoked through a visual or auditory perception. Smell is perhaps the most elusive to intentional memory and yet is suddenly evoked for Marks by the images of the magnolias. For Merleau-Ponty our perceptions are temporally sedimented; shaped through past perceptions, they gear us towards the world allowing us to grasp what is there, to encounter what is new – we learn how to perceive.

For Marks, haptic vision is particularly important to intercultural cinema since it disallows the dominating aspects of optical vision that rely on a separation of the viewer from that which is viewed. For those living in diaspora, or exile, cut off from a past often both painful and sweet, sensual reminders that belong to the phenom-enal body can also elide the objectification that too often accompanies optical vision. Instead, haptic vision brings vision close to the body by drawing on its multi-sensorial possibilities. Images that are not accessible as such to vision require of the viewer that she rely on other senses such as touch in order to perceive, that is, to make some kind of corporeal sense of the image (*ibid.*: 154). Just as touch needs movement in order to explore its object, so too does haptic vision tend to move over the surfaces of objects, focusing on texture more than form, thereby avoiding focus; it tends "to graze" rather than "to gaze" (*ibid.*: 162). In contrast to the "representational power of the image" privileged by optical perception, haptic vision "privileges the material presence of the image"; hence haptic images are often so "'thin' and unclichéd" that the viewer must draw on her own sensual "memory and imagination to complete them" (*ibid.*: 163). Haptic images demand contemplation rather than a narrative; optical visuality assumes that the image is complete in itself. In this way, haptic cinema encourages the viewer to enter into a bodily relationship with the image (*ibid.*: 162–3). Haptic images invite the viewer to see as if for "the first time" in a process of gradual discovery rather than immediate knowledge (*ibid.*: 178). For this reason they encourage intersubjective relations, demanding of the viewer that she draw closer to the other even as the impossibility of knowing the other is inherently acknowledged.

Merleau-Ponty's insights into the phenomenal body reveal the logic of vision, and thus how embodied subjects experience film. In his challenge to mind–body dualism, he shows how our most abstract thinking is anchored in embodied perception. We think because we are embodied, and because our bodies have their own logic, their own ways of interpreting and moving into the world that are not processed through cognitive representation. Film, as he intuits, shows precisely how ideas are taken up corporeally in the film itself, and in the ways viewers experience and respond corporeally.[5] This is not a world of interiority, but rather one of comportment. Deleuze's critique, while significant, does not dismiss the phenomenal body, only its potential for radical change and creativity; yet I would suggest that the phenomenal body's openness to the cultivation of perception does in fact allow it to be transformed.

NOTES

1. Examples of sources that take up his work that are not further addressed in this chapter include: J. R. Resina, "Historical Discourse and the Propaganda Film: Reporting the Revolution in Barcelona", *New Literary History* **29**(1) (1998), 67–84; E. del Rio, "The Body of Voyeurism: Mapping a Discourse of the Senses in Michael Powell's 'Peeping Tom'", *Camera Obscura* **15**(3) (2000), 115–49, and "Alchemies of Thought in Godard's Cinema: Deleuze and Merleau-Ponty", *SubStance* **34**(3) (2005), 62–78; J. M. Gaines, "Everyday Strangeness: Robert Ripley's International Oddities as Documentary Attractions", *New Literary History* **33**(4) (2002), 781–801; M. Szaloky, "Sounding Images in Silent Film: Visual Acoustics in Murnau's 'Sunrise'", *Cinema Journal* **41**(2) (2002), 109–31; M. Hansen, "The Time of Affect, or Bearing Witness to Life", *Critical Inquiry* **30**(3) (2004), 584–626; and D. Pursley, "Moving in Time: Chantal Akerman's 'Toute une Nuit'", *MLN* **120**(5) (2005), 1192–205.
2. Dorothea Olkowski argues that Merleau-Ponty's philosophical affinity to film goes beyond his own overt claims; D. Olkowski, *The Universal (in the Realm of the Sensible): Beyond Continental Philosophy* (Edinburgh: Edinburgh University Press, 2007), 216–22.
3. In elaborating on levels, Merleau-Ponty, *Phenomenology of Perception*, C. Smith (trans.) (London: Routledge & Kegan Paul, 1962), 253–4, explains that the body is the first level, the seat of our capacities that allows us to be anchored in the world, to move into situations and to take them up – what L. U. Marks, *The Skin of the Film: Intercultural Cinema, Embodiment, and the Senses* (Durham, NC: Duke University Press, 2000) refers to as our mimetic ability.
4. *Comportement* is translated as "behaviour" yet behaviour is a psychological term that cannot be precisely equated with the phenomenological term "comportment", which has more to do with

the way we hold our bodies in relation to the world; M. Merleau-Ponty, "Le Cinéma et la nouvelle psychologie", *Sens et non-sens* (Paris: Nagel, [1948] 1963), 95.

5. In his late lectures on nature, he writes: "My body, as I see the things, is mediator of an isomorphism = structure of the distributions of light (the 'image' of the film) scanned by the perceiving body"; *Nature: Course Notes from the Collège de France*, R. Vallier (trans.) (Evanston, IL: Northwestern University Press, 2003), 278.

8 EMMANUEL LEVINAS

Sarah Cooper

Emmanuel Levinas (1906–95) studied philosophy at Strasbourg University in France. He spent the academic year 1928–9 in Freiburg, Germany, where he took seminars with Husserl and then with Heidegger. He was interned as a prisoner of war in a German labour camp during the Second World War and most of his Jewish family were killed in the Holocaust. After the war he was the Director of the École Normale Israélite Orientale in Paris until 1961. From 1947 to 1949 he studied the Talmud. His first university appointment was in 1964 as Professor of Philosophy at the University of Poitiers and then at the newly established Paris X University Nanterre in 1967. He was appointed Professor of Philosophy at the Sorbonne (Paris IV) in 1973, where he remained until his retirement in 1976, after which he held an honorary professorship. He held a visiting professorship at the University of Fribourg in Switzerland from 1970. His works include *Existence and Existents* (1947; English trans. 2001), *Time and the Other* (1948; English trans. 1987), *Totality and Infinity* (1961; English trans. 1969), *Difficult Freedom* (1963; English trans. 1990), *Quatre lectures talmudiques* (Four Talmudic readings; 1968), *Otherwise than Being or Beyond Essence* (1974; English trans. 1981), *Du sacré au saint* (From the sacred to the saint; 1977), *Ethics and Infinity* (1982; English trans. 1985), *De Dieu qui vient à l'idée* (Of God who comes to the idea; 1982), *Entre Nous* (1982; English trans. 1998) and *God, Death and Time* (1993; English trans. 2000). This chapter outlines the paradox of exploring Levinas's philosophy in relation to film in the light of his early polemical work on aesthetics. In line with recent scholarship, however, the ensuing discussion seeks to establish a more enabling relationship between his philosophy and cinema. Focusing on what Levinas has to say about images, movement and, especially, time, this chapter offers Levinasian reflections on time and mortality, with a view to critically expanding discussion of the ontology of photography and film.

Emmanuel Levinas is among the least obvious of twentieth-century philosophers to feature in a volume devoted to philosophy of film. From a philosophical grounding in the phenomenology of Edmund Husserl and Martin Heidegger that remained an important influence throughout his career, Levinas's work traverses the fields of religion, aesthetics, politics and, most crucially, ethics. Levinas articulates his ethics in dialogue with the Western philosophical tradition principally in his two major works: *Totality and Infinity: An Essay on Exteriority* and *Otherwise than Being or Beyond Essence*. Western philosophy, for Levinas, has for the most part been an ontology, by which he means that otherness has been reduced perpetually to a system of self-sameness in which nothing other than being can appear (Levinas 2007: 43). Although the phenomenological undertakings of Husserl and Heidegger remain a key point of reference for him, Levinas aims to create a space of transcendence from within the realm of light and appearance crucial to phenomenology (*ibid.*: 27). Apparently turning his back in his ethics on the conditions for seeing and being in the visible world, he questions two of the key senses fundamental to the production and reception of film. His main concepts in outlining the possibility of an ethical encounter in *Totality and Infinity* are the *visage* (face) and the *caresse* (caress), both of which are theorized as giving rise to a relation to alterity never fully to be encompassed by any of the senses, least of all sight and touch. These sensory connections are totalizing gestures, for Levinas, which reduce alterity to our experience of it alone and thus shrink otherness to self-sameness, rather than creating a possibility for its emergence in and on its own terms. It is language, for Levinas, that allows such gestures to be transcended. It is for this reason that the *visage* is first and foremost a speaking face. The first words that the face utters are those of the commandment "you shall not commit murder" (*ibid.*: 199). This ethical injunction that the face speaks, and that cuts through the phenomenological world, has long prompted scholars to ask how his ethics comes into being. More recently, literary and film scholars have joined this debate and taken his work into the aesthetic dimension, moving from the being of life to that of art.

Such a Levinasian move within film scholarship is not without its problems. Not only does his thinking bear a persistently interrogative relation to images, but his early work on aesthetics distances all art forms from his conception of ethics. Furthermore, his brief occasional references to film are made to support a philosophical argument rather than constituting a reflection on film *per se*. In two books, for example, Levinas draws on the films of Charlie Chaplin: he refers to *The Gold Rush* (1925) in *Entre Nous* and *City Lights* (1931) in *De l'évasion*, showing how film can furnish philosophy with illustrations of its arguments similarly to the way in which literature does. Yet recent scholarship has begun nonetheless to explore more enabling and complex points of contact between central concepts in his work and film, as well as film theory. Film-makers have also engaged with his work, either by featuring references to his books in their films, or in their writings on their film-making. In Jean-Luc Godard's *Notre musique* (2004), for example, an Israeli journalist leafs through a copy of *Entre Nous*, and this occasions Levinasian-inspired thoughts on the reconstruction of the Mostar Bridge in Bosnia-Herzegovina that will link the Catholic Croats and Muslim Bosnians who live on opposite sides of the River Neretva. And Luc and Jean-Pierre Dardenne indicate their debt to Levinas in their writings, suggesting how their films work through his ethical themes, in terms of both how the films are made and the subjects they treat.[1] My aim in this chapter is to extend scholarly discussion of this particular conjunction of film and philosophy into the broader arena of debate on the ontology of film to reflect on what Levinas says about movement and, especially, time. My point of entry into discussion of Levinas and cinema here will pay attention to his critical comments on aesthetics, which set up a specific relation to movement, time and the image. I turn subsequently, however, to what Levinas says about time in his other philosophical writings, and his debt to

Henri Bergson, in order to assess the possible insights that his philosophy can bring to thinking about cinematic time.

Levinas marks a clear debt to Bergson throughout his career and refers to his work frequently. In the preface to the German edition of his 1961 text *Totality and Infinity* (written in 1987), he signals the importance of Bergson's work to his own. In "L'Autre, Utopie et Justice" (The other, utopia and justice; 1988), he says that he feels close to certain Bergsonian themes (1998: 193). And in "Diachronie et représentation" (Diachrony and representation), a lecture given originally in 1985, Levinas turns to a later text (*Les Deux sources de la morale et de la religion* [The two sources of morality and religion]; Bergson [1932] 1948) in order to show how compatible his ethical thinking is with that of Bergson (Levinas 1998: 153). Although Levinas is critical of Bergson, and he parts company with the earlier philosopher in his positing of ethics as first philosophy, this has not stopped prominent readers of Levinas from seeing his notion of alterity as "an ethical *durée*" (Critchley 1992: 175). Levinas's two texts on time that will be my focal point here are those in which he engages explicitly with Bergson's writings on *durée* (duration): *Time and the Other* and "La Mort et le temps" (Death and time; in Levinas 2000). But first of all, we need to consider what Levinas says about time in relation to the aesthetic dimension.

BETWEEN LIFE AND DEATH

First published in 1948 in the journal *Les Temps Modernes*, Levinas's polemical early essay on aesthetics, "Reality and its Shadow", casts art into a shadow realm, and distinguishes it from the order of revelation or creation. For him, "every artwork is in the end a statue – a stoppage of time, or rather its delay behind itself" (Levinas 1989: 137). Rather than being entirely indifferent to duration, however, Levinas characterizes the life, or death, of the artwork as "the paradox of an instant that endures without a future" (*ibid.*: 138). Imprisoned in time, in what he terms the *entre temps* (the interval), art introduces the paradox of an instant that can stop. Levinas defines this instant against the continuity of time, understood as the essence of duration since Bergson. He writes: "The fact that humanity could have provided itself with art reveals in time the uncertainty of time's continuation and something like a death doubling the impulse of life" (*ibid.*: 140). This notion of art as duration in the interval, which immobilizes even the time-based arts, the fixity of whose images can never be shattered, reinforces the fact that the instant cannot pass. The eternal duration of the interval runs parallel with the duration of the living, but is fixed forever rather than open to change. To extend this in cinematic terms would not necessarily deny that figures within a film move, but reinforces that they are destined to repeat themselves time and again, trapped in the prison of film's myriad forms. Within the *entre temps*, L. B. Jefferies (James Stewart) will always be the largely passive but fully engrossed spectator of his neighbours' activities in *Rear Window* (dir. Alfred Hitchcock, 1954), and James Bond will never die, however many times we re-watch the series of Bond films made to date, and, presumably, however many more Bond films will succeed them in the future.[2]

The artwork for Levinas is eternally immobilized as a moment that can never pass, a semblance of life that can never really be lived but can also never die. In a sophisticated commentary on "La Réalité et son ombre" in relation to F. W. Murnau's *Nosferatu* (1922), Colin Davis argues that Levinas's essay constitutes a brilliant reading of this classic film, even though it is never mentioned. Levinas writes that there is "something inhuman and monstrous" (Levinas 1989: 141) about the eternal duration of the interval, and Davis suggests that this description holds true of the undead vampire in the uncanny, shadowy spaces of his filmic existence (Davis 2007: 42–3). Levinas's reflections on death cut off the artwork from ethical time, founded in a relation to the human other, and therefore contrast with his other writings on death, time and alterity.

At the same time that Levinas was forging his specific conception of temporality in art, he was formulating a very different sense of time in relation to human life. Delivered originally at the Collège de Philosophie in Paris in 1946–7, and published initially in an edited collection in 1948, the four lectures that make up *Time and the Other* were republished in 1979. Levinas's introduction to the republication of the lectures contains the kinds of caveats with which all writers could no doubt identify if looking back at work they completed thirty years previously. Levinas writes that it is as if he is providing the preface for somebody else's work, except that the book's deficiencies are felt all the more painfully when one knows that it is one's own (1987: 29). Many of the ideas in the text are embryonic and are developed or reworked throughout his subsequent texts. The overall aim of the lectures, however, resounds as one of the most sustained lines of his thinking: he sets out to show that time is not the fact of a subject who is isolated and alone but is, rather, founded in the relation that the subject has to others, in death and in life. The question that one might ask of Levinas's philosophy here is how this different thinking about time may enable his conception of the prison house of the *entre temps* in art to be unlocked.

In *Time and the Other*, Levinas thinks time in relation to death, but marks out a difference from Heideggerian philosophy that will be extended further in "La Mort et le temps". Death, for Heidegger, marks the subject's arrival at the final possibility of *Dasein*. For Levinas, in contrast, death marks the limit of what is possible. In this sense, death is a confrontation with the absolutely unknowable and presents us with a unique relation with the future. This relation to something absolutely other breaks the solitude of existence as Levinas conceives it. In his view, the relation to the future is defined through the relation with the other: "It seems to me impossible to speak of time in a subject alone, or to speak of a purely personal duration" (*ibid.*: 77). Commenting on the future as something that cannot be grasped, he distances his understanding of time from the theories of Bergson through to Jean-Paul Sartre, who he suggests speak of the present of the future, rather than the authentic future. Rather than having literally to wait for our death in order for this opening to temporality and others to occur, Levinas locates it less morbidly in the day-to-day existence of our relations with other people:

> The relationship with the Other, the face-to-face with the Other, the encounter with a face that at once gives and conceals the Other, is the situation in which an event happens to a subject who does not assume it, who

is utterly unable in its regard, but where nonetheless in a certain way it is in front of the subject. The other "assumed" is the Other.   (*Ibid.*: 78–9)

Levinas says further that the Bergsonian conception of freedom through duration tends in the same direction: "But it preserves for the present a power over the future: duration is creation" (*ibid.*: 80). What Levinas does is to show that creation itself supposes an opening onto a mystery and that this cannot be the product of an isolated subject. *Time and the Other* culminates with reflections on eros, the other privileged realm of encounter with what cannot be known or possessed. The workings of time are conceived not just as the renewal of creation, which retains a link to the present: "More than the renewal of our moods and qualities, time is essentially a new birth" (*ibid.*: 81). Levinas works in tune here with Bergson's association of time with novelty and invention. Yet he also distinguishes his thinking from Bergson's *élan vital* and its equation with duration, since this forward movement of vitality does not take account of death (*ibid.*: 91–2).

MOVEMENT, TIME AND IMMOBILITY

In film theory, the association between immobility, death and the image appears most frequently in discussions of the photographic, rather than the cinematic, dimension. The difference between photography and cinema is set out on the basis of their contrasting relations to movement and time.[3] Through his interest in the immobility of the artwork in the *entre temps* and his work on time elsewhere, Levinas allows us to rethink the relation between the photographic and the cinematic differently, without returning to a Bazinian conception of the emergence of the latter from the former, or a Deleuzian conception of the ontology of cinema in which the image is always already moving. Levinas's observations on time, both with regard to the artwork and mortal life, provide another way of conceiving the ontology of cinema, and it is the relationship between death and time that is at stake.

As with *Time and the Other*, Levinas's later work on death and time is also a series of lectures, given at the Sorbonne in 1975–6, and published in 1993. "La Mort et le temps" is essentially a course on temporal duration. Levinas enters into detailed dialogue with Heidegger, Kant, Hegel, Aristotle, Bergson and Bloch. Contrary to Heidegger, though, it is not a being-towards-death that concerns him, and it is not the experience of death through which he will address the subject, but the way in which the death of the other concerns me more than my own death. Rather than use this death to think about our relation to time, Levinas reverses the philosophical logic of priority and uses time to think about death. In this, he locates himself closer to Ernst Bloch than any of the other philosophers he discusses (Levinas 2000: 92–106). Yet he also brings out a further relation to Bergson here. Although, as in the earlier work, he distances himself from Bergson's understanding of the *élan vital*, arguing that the equation of duration with this life-force excludes death, he refers to Bergson's later work and glimpses a relation to the other that is closer to his own sense of the bond between time and the other:

But the vital impulse is not the ultimate signification of the time of Bergsonian duration. In *Two Sources of Morality and Religion*, the duration that *Creative Evolution* considered as vital impulse becomes interhuman life. Duration becomes the fact that a man can appeal to the interiority of the other man. (*Ibid.*: 55–6)

This glimpse of an opening to the other in time is excluded from the thinking of time in relation to a single subject. Building on his previous works, Levinas conceives time as a relation to infinity rather than the limitation of being. The relation to death comes to us through our relation to the other, differently from in *Time and the Other*, even though the terminology and thinking are similar. Instead of my encounter with death-the-unknowable being traced in the face-to-face encounters with other people, death enters life through the loss of others and constitutes the self as a responsible survivor. Levinas asks: "Can one understand time as a relationship with the Other, rather than seeing in it the relationship with the end?" (*ibid.*: 106). Rather than characterize his sense of duration as the mobile image of immobile eternity, flux or being-towards-death, duration troubles us, in Levinas's view, by what is still to come, and what has yet to be accomplished (*ibid.*: 114). The relation to time is described ultimately as the responsibility that one mortal has for another (*ibid.*: 117). A connection can be made to both the photographic and the cinematic dimensions through this focus on mortality.

Films repeatedly engage issues of mortality, both thematically and formally. Death is fundamental to Bazin's pioneering essay "Ontologie de l'image photographique" (The ontology of the photographic image; 2002b): the photograph prevents the second spiritual death of its captured subject and film mummifies change. In contrasting ways, Roland Barthes and Susan Sontag also make the association between photography and mortal fragility (Barthes 1980a; Sontag 1979). Locating Levinas's philosophy between a vision of the emergence of cinematic time from the presumed eternal temporal stasis of the photograph, and a desire to read vital forces in relation to any emergence of immobility, a different ontological vision becomes apparent here, fissured by Levinasian ethics. By enabling us to look beyond the Bergsonian equation of the *élan vital* with duration and its connection to cinema, this reading of Levinas suggests a connection between death and cinematic time.

BRINGING THE INTERVAL TO LIFE

Levinas argues that art replaces its object with an image rather than a concept, and both movement and time come to a halt in the process. In this, the image neutralizes the real relationship that we have with objects through action, and as Reni Celeste (2007) suggests, the cinematic screen is "frozen" regardless of how fast-paced the action is that we watch on it. Lacking a future, Levinas's characterization of the artwork, cinema included, resembles Barthes' description of the photograph in *Camera Lucida*, which he deems to be "*sans avenir*" (without a future), unlike cinema, which he compares to the flow of life (Barthes 1980a: 140). Levinas's definition of the artwork contrasts with this description of the photograph, nonetheless, in so far as the artwork keeps its figures suspended between life and death: an eternal limbo, an instant that can stop. The *entre temps*, as we have seen, lies between death and life, and, as also observed, the space between these two extremes in theoretical discourse to date has tended predominantly to be mapped on to the distance between photography and film. In contrast, the levelling gesture of the Levinasian *entre temps* suggests that we might contest the life and mobility of the latter, as well as the fully fledged death of the former, thus bringing the two closer to one another than the varied theoretical distinctions of Bazin, Barthes and Deleuze have hitherto made possible. A Levinasian-inspired intervention in this debate is thus aligned, rather, with more recent discussions in photographic theory, which have sought to question any strict mapping of the binary of cinema–photography onto that of life–death.[4] As the presence of photography in film suggests more insistently than any theory – and the oeuvre of Chris Marker performs this brilliantly, not only through his three photo-films (*La Jetée* [The jetty; 1962]; *Si j'avais quatre dromadaires* [If I had four dromedaries;1966]; *Le Souvenir d'un avenir* [with Y. Bellon, Remembrance of things to come; 2001]), but also in the presence of photographs in almost all of his other films – the life and death of the photographic and the filmic image are intimately interwoven and do not allow the photograph always to signify death, or the film image life. Yet there is still a difference between the two, as other theoretical positions also make clear.

Life and death come together in Laura Mulvey's recent view of cinema to generate an alternative description of Godard's definition of cinema as truth twenty-four frames per second (at its conventional celluloid projection speed). Mulvey speaks of death, rather than truth, at twenty-four frames per second (Mulvey 2006: 15). Following Bergson, who – as Deleuze reminds us – teaches us not to confuse movement with the space covered, if we select either life or death when designating film or photography, we reconstitute the mobility of the interval as two immobile sections labelled either "life" or "death".[5] The more enabling possibility here, then, would be to ask how we live a relation to the interval as we view film, while thinking its connection to the opening that death provides in Levinas's philosophy more generally. In keeping with this, work to date on Levinas and cinema has asked implicitly how the *entre temps* is brought back to the questions that Levinas asks with reference to being, or his challenge to ontology, as certain films have been explored in terms of the Levinasian themes that they feature. Celeste (2007) is closest to preserving film as an exemplification of the interval. Levinas's philosophy gives us pause if we are thinking film as a mobile life-force of duration, not only through his work on aesthetics, but also through his broader work on time.

As we have seen, in Levinas's work on death and time, death enters life through contact with others: in the face-to-face relation in *Time and the Other*, and through the death of others in "La Mort et le temps". This contact gives rise to a new subjectivity – a rebirth of the subject – in a time instituted and propelled by the relation to alterity: these are the terms of Levinas's ethics. As he writes in *Totality and Infinity*, there are ruptures in the continuity of time, but there is also continuation through these breaks (2007: 284). Death is rethought on the basis of time, not as an end, but as an encounter with uncertainty, with a future. To bring such Levinasian thinking

97

to film is to bring life to the interval, and to bring the interval to life. What is born through this encounter is another way of thinking about time. This is not to deny the properties of the *entre temps*, since these are precisely what have allowed me here to mark out a difference between life and death in their conventional association with the filmic and the photographic dimensions, respectively, along with the possibility of seeing more than relentless mobility and duration in film, even when it is at rest. For Levinas, in the artwork, death is never really ever dead enough and it is the inability to connect with the time of life that prevents film, among other arts, from entering the ethical dimension. But the interval, while located outside time in one respect, also contains the time of life in and through its images. L. B. Jefferies's relations to the others he watches and has more direct contact with in his flat may never change, however many times we view *Rear Window*, but these encounters in the aesthetic dimension are not entirely separated from similar ones that might take place beyond this realm.

To introduce Levinas's broader thinking on temporality to film, then, is to think time differently from within – rather than opposing it to – the interval that locates it between life and death. Levinas's philosophy opens discussions of the filmic and the photographic to a different future, in which temporality is born of an encounter with alterity, the model for which is the Levinasian conception of death. Death brings uncertainty, rather than immobility or temporal stasis, and makes duration thinkable. This duration does not head towards death or override it, but encounters it as uncertainty within life. Thought through in these Levinasian terms, death lies at the heart of cinematic duration, and time is not solely a function of movement or its absence. Time enters cinematic images from the outside: the life and death from which Levinas separates it. By introducing his broader thinking on time to cinema it is possible to reintroduce the temporality of life *and* death to film, and to stage an encounter between the Levinasian *entre temps* and ethics. This philosophical encounter with film realizes the paradox of locating the time of alterity within the instant that can stop. To think about cinema with Levinas is to be alive to temporal duration while marking time, and thus to participate in one of the many bloodstreams that circulate between art and life.

NOTES

1. See, for example, the range of articles published in S. Cooper (ed.), *Special Issue: The Occluded Relation: Levinas and Cinema*, Film-Philosophy **11**(2) (2007), www.film-philosophy.com/archive/vol11-2007/ (accessed July 2009). The introduction and the articles that constitute this special issue of *Film-Philosophy* give a broader sense of the scholars of Levinas and film who are working in this nascent field.
2. On this latter point of serialization, suspension between mortality and immortality, and the action film, see Reni Celeste's excellent article, "The Frozen Screen: Levinas and the Action Film", *Film-Philosophy* **11**(2) (2007), 15–36, www.film-philosophy.com/2007v11n2/celeste.pdf (accessed July 2009).
3. The two poles of such thinking within film theory derive broadly from the work of André Bazin and Gilles Deleuze. While Bazin binds cinema to the ontology of the photographic image, for Deleuze, and following the impetus of the Bergsonian *élan vital*, the immobility of the cinematic image is never fully equated with that of the photographic image, even though it may resemble it

at times. In this latter case, immobility is valorized for its potential becoming, rather than as a state in and of itself. Cf. A. Bazin, "Ontologie de l'image photographique", in his *Qu'est-ce que le cinéma?*, 9–17 (Paris: Éditions du Cerf, [1958] 2002); and G. Deleuze, *Cinema 1: The Movement-Image*, H. Tomlinson & B. Habberjam (trans.) (London: Athlone, 1986).

4. Cf. D. Green & J. Lowry (eds), *Stillness and Time: Photography and the Moving Image* (Brighton: Photoforum, 2006). For a fascinating theoretical attempt to think the stillness of the photographic image in ways that arrest neither time, nor the movement of thought, see Y. Lomax, "Thinking Stillness", in Green & Lowry (eds), *Stillness and Time*, 55–63. Lomax refers to Deleuze's own definition of an *entre temps*, translated as "the meanwhile", but notes, in contrast to my argument regarding the Levinasian *entre temps*: "this time – the meanwhile – does not belong to the eternal but, rather, becoming" (*ibid*: 59).

5. The view of film as a succession of immobile positions emerges in the fourth chapter of Bergson's *L'Évolution créatrice* (Creative evolution; Paris: Presses Universitaires de France, [1907] 1959) and is the source of Deleuze's critique of Bergson's explicit comments on cinema. In an interview with Michel Georges-Michel, published at the later date of 1914, and which Deleuze does not acknowledge, Bergson does, however, speak more positively about cinema. He notes that cinema could be of use to the intellectual, the historian or the artist in suggesting new ideas, most notably on the synthesis of memory and, even, of thought; cf. M. Georges-Michel, "Henri Bergson nous parle du cinéma", *Le Journal* (20 February 1914), 7.

9 ANDRÉ BAZIN

Hunter Vaughan

In the forty years of André Bazin's brief life (1918–58), he managed to re-map the relationship between the average moviegoing spectator, the film critic and the cinema industry, insisting that a thoughtful and demanding public could in fact shape the trajectory of cinema as an institution. Bazin developed a unique approach to the arts founded in a combination of Catholic mysticism, intellectual humanism and a combination of existentialism and phenomenology weaned from philosophers of the post-war period. Intellectuals of the French Resistance also instilled in Bazin a sense of activism that he directed towards his roles in the foundation of film clubs, the administration of France's first film school and the direct support of many founders of post-war European cinema, including Roberto Rossellini and Alain Resnais. As co-founder in 1951 and editor of the groundbreaking French journal *Cahiers du cinéma*, Bazin instilled film criticism with a profound humanism, and as the cultural godfather of his writing staff (including, among others, Truffaut, Godard, Rohmer, Chabrol and Rivette) Bazin exerted an incalculable influence on the cinematic explosion known as the French New Wave. At his death, Bazin left a range of uncollected and unpublished works, most of which are compiled into a multi-volume collection titled *What is Cinema?* (1958, 1959, 1961, 1962), as well as his lesser-read works: *Jean Renoir* (1971; English trans. 1973), *Orson Welles* (1972; English trans. 1978) and *The Cinema of Cruelty* (1975; English trans. 1982).

Bazin has received one of the most systematic drubbings in twentieth-century cultural studies. Noël Carroll, among others, challenges the extravagance of Bazin's metaphysical notion of cinematic essentialism, while purer structuralists have lambasted Bazin's idealism for what they claim to be a lack of historical or material criticism.[1] This is not an uncommon reaction to Bazin's work, a body of writing that is summarized by Bill Nichols as "a dual and perhaps contradictory approach of transcendent spiritualism and sociology" (1976: 151). But how could an approach so replete with sensitivity and humanism, and bearing such a positive influence on film history, be so vilified in retrospect? Indeed, Bazin's place in the evolution of film theory and the possible crossover between phenomenology and film aesthetics merits thorough reconsideration, which I hope to provide here in working toward an understanding of Bazin's multifold theory of cinematic immanence.

When attempting a survey of Bazin's film criticism, his own intellectual influences, his role in the genealogy of international and especially French film theory, as well as his historical context in general, we must begin with what brought him to film studies to begin with: philosophy. Dudley Andrew has single-handedly done the most to preserve both Bazin's legacy and the thread of phenomenology that can be found in Bazin's writing, and Andrew's *André Bazin* ([1978] 1990) charts the critical development of a young man coming of age at the edge of a historical precipice that would destroy many of humanity's assumptions about its relationship to the world. As such, it is understandable that Bazin's notion of the role of cinema and the role of art in general was heavily influenced by more sceptical thinkers of the century, such as Henri Bergson, Jean-Paul Sartre and Maurice Merleau-Ponty.

PHILOSOPHICAL ROOTS AND THE POLITICS OF CULTURE

According to Andrew, Bazin was greatly influenced early on by the philosopher Henri Bergson, who was lecturing in Paris when Bazin moved there in his teens (*ibid.*: 19). Such influence can be directly seen in Bazin's essay "A Bergsonian Film: *The Picasso Mystery*", in which Bazin uses Bergson to construct a theory of *durée* or duration (reprinted in *What is Cinema?* [Bazin 1967]). Bergson, whose influence on film theory has been fully realized through the impact of Gilles Deleuze's *Cinéma I* and *II* (1983, 1985), provided a radical departure from the twentieth century's dominant philosophical school of positivism.

Bergson's philosophy, less concerned with the facts surrounding existence than it is with the human *experience* of nature, would turn out to be a crucial stepping stone towards Bazin's appropriation of phenomenology. Andrew notes that, from Bergson to Merleau-Ponty, Bazin's affinities evolved from the complexity of the world to the ambiguity of our experience. In terms of these thinkers, "reality is not a situation available to experience but an 'emerging-something' which the mind essentially participates in and which can be said to exist only in experience" (Andrew 1978: 106). In Bazinian terms, phenomenology could therefore be defined as a study of the interactive and constantly developing relationship between human consciousness and objective reality.

In the influence of Bergson, Sartre and Merleau-Ponty, Bazin demonstrates an affinity for the central importance of the interactive relationship between elements, both of film and of life. However, Bazin could hardly be considered a straightforward phenomenologist – nor even a "philosopher" at that – and in order to systematize an understanding of his theory of immanence, one must also consider the other facets of his multifarious approach. From French writer Albert Béguin, Bazin inherited an existential filter for his Christianity, while Charles Péguy, intellectual avatar of the French Resistance, set Bazin on his path to use writing and thought as a weapon for sociopolitical change.

The social purpose of criticism was further instilled through Bazin's intense interest in the literary journal *Esprit*. Founded in 1932, *Esprit* brought Bazin under the wing of two great influences: editor Emmanuel Mounier, through whom Bazin would

101

cultivate a widely eclectic and interdisciplinary critical method, and Roger Leenhardt, *Esprit's* film writer. Leenhardt's writing, which proclaims that the proper role of *mise en scène* is not the production of complex meaning but the simple rendering of reality, can be detected at the heart of Bazin's opinionated view of the ontology of the image and his hierarchy of formal practices (cf. Leenhardt 1935).

The contributors of *Esprit* were greatly influential on Bazin not only because of their approach to cultural media, but because these approaches stemmed from a larger humanistic view of the world. This inseparability between art and life was central to Bazin's work, and explains his affinity for the theories of André Malraux and the writers of the journal *Les Temps Modernes*, including Sartre and Merleau-Ponty. As Andrew notes, Malraux "conceived of art as a transcendence of consciousness over circumstance through style" (1978: 68), a view that would be central to Bazin's theory of the immanence of artistic consciousness within the text. However, it is Sartre's work on the imaginary that would encourage Bazin's linkage of art and ontology, and Merleau-Ponty's phenomenology of perception that governed Bazin's insistence on the ambiguity of the human being's place in the world.

From these roots Bazin constructed an anomalous approach to film criticism that is as moving in its lyricism as it was relevant to the time and place of its production. Up until Bazin there had been no theoretical challenge to the nascent formalism developed by writers such as Sergei Eisenstein and Béla Balász.[2] The severe technocratic destruction produced by the Second World War caused many intellectuals and artists suddenly to challenge the philosophical and moral value of formalism and the manipulation of nature for the purposes of man, and Bazin tapped into this by developing a complex theory of cinematic realism. Bazin was not of course alone, as can be seen in the writings of German theorist Siegfried Kracauer, and both set their theories of realism atop principal assumptions that the specificity of cinema resides in the ontology of the photographic image (cf. Andrew 1978: 131–41).[3]

While Bazin's approach may differ from that of Kracauer, the two are similar in their insistence on an essentialism of cinematic form as well as a hierarchical assessment of film texts based on their utilization of certain tenets of realism, and it is for this somewhat biased passion that Bazin has been harshly criticized. English theorist V. F. Perkins points out that, while Bazin's stringent theory of realism helped to loosen the formalist stranglehold on film theory, he "mistook his own critical vocation to the defense of realism for the 'true vocation of cinema'" (1976: 421). While this may be true, Bazin's critical vocation does not exist in a void, and it is necessary to understand it in the context of a global political situation, a local intellectual history, and in relation to the state of international cinema during this very period.

Many writers – some in praise, some in scorn – claim that Bazin's work has neither a moral nor a political basis, but a phenomenological one (cf. Faulkner 2004: 179). However, Bazin can also quite rightly be accused of using the term "phenomenology" as a proxy to ameliorate the metaphysical and sometimes mystical or spiritual nature of his writiting. Critics such as James Roy MacBean accuse Bazin of exploiting this term in order "to cover up the absence of a materialist, process-oriented analysis of human society" (1976: 96) and Bazin's work is often chided for its de-historicization and de-politicization of films he discusses.

However, is such criticism of Bazin's work well founded? Does Bazin's praise of Jean Renoir, Orson Welles and Italian neo-realism not rest precisely in the texts' resistance to historical and political hegemony, in their insistence on bringing to light the very truth of the sociopolitical present? This contradiction of hegemonic practices is the very root of Bazin's praise for Rossellini's revolutionary humanism and the detailed realism he extracts from Welles and Renoir. Moreover, is Bazin's groundbreaking genre criticism (see e.g. "The Western, or the American Cinema *par excellence*", in *What is Cinema?*) not fundamentally a reading of how ideological forces in particular social institutions manifest themselves in genre cinema, and is his general approach not an attempt to analyse how underlying values and beliefs shape our personal, national and international symbolic?

THE POETICS OF IMMANENCE

As can be seen in the recent works of Stanley Cavell as well as in Deleuze's reading of Bazin in the opening of *Cinéma II*, Bazin's insights into film form in fact exist *only* within his historicization of the sociopolitical place of cinema in the world around it. In order to understand this, however, we must look at Bazin's underlying phenomenology not as a theory of transcendence, as MacBean claims, but instead as a multifold theory of *immanence*: the immanence of political history in the conventions of genre; the immanence of reality in the image; the immanence of a multitude of possible shots within the shot-sequence; and the immanence of artistic consciousness within the film text.

In this understanding, we could place Bazin's work, as Monica Dall'Asta points out, "in a specifically French genealogy of discourse" (2004: 86). Indeed, much of Bazin's concept of ontology evokes the memory of Louis Delluc and Jean Epstein's conceptualization of *photogénie*, which owes a common debt to Marcel l'Herbier's early theories about the photographic image. L'Herbier, like Delluc and Bazin to follow, framed the camera as a means for mechanical reproduction that, in avoiding the human intermediary necessary in other arts, holds a particularly objective connection with the reality it captures: according to l'Herbier, cinema produces an "imprint of life" whose purpose is "to transcribe as faithfully and truthfully as possible … a certain phenomenal truth" (quoted in *ibid.*).

That the vocabulary of this statement implies a latent phenomenological approach is no surprise, as the photographic image and the cinematic text have long been heralded for having the ability to uncover or to reveal some special, hidden truth in the world. This ability provides the foundation for Bazin's critical enthusiasm, and Bazin re-conceptualizes this unique characteristic on many levels, including the objectivity of the image and the humanitarian sensitivity of the camera, as well as the ability for the text to reveal the values of a society and to be a vessel for the consciousness of the artist, a critical technique developed in 1940s' Geneva and dubbed the "criticism of consciousness" because of its method of describing the world created by an author.

This method is evident in Bazin's numerous studies of directors such as Charlie Chaplin, Howard Hawks and Robert Bresson, his articles on the directors of Italian neo-realism, as well as in his collective *The Cinema of Cruelty* and more focused works, *Jean Renoir* and *Orson Welles*. Bazin's ability to transform auteur theory into a theory of immanence leads Andrew to conclude aptly that Bazin's work is the "closest thing we have to a phenomenological criticism in the manner of the Geneva School, for in all of these he strives to erase the distinction between such works and to join himself, as he was so able to do, to the creative energy of each auteur" (1985: 630). However, while it will be necessary to return to these studies in order to assess the realization of Bazin's theories, let us first begin with what are considered Bazin's seminal essays: "Ontology of the Photographic Image" and "The Evolution of Film Language".[4]

FROM ONTOLOGY OF THE IMAGE TO FILM LANGUAGE

In "Ontology of the Photographic Image", first outlined in an article in 1945, Bazin works to situate cinema according to its specific place in the historical evolution of the arts. He selects the photographic image, as a mechanical reproduction, as the definitive characteristic of cinema, thus putting him in line with l'Herbier and Kracauer, and laying the foundation for Stanley Cavell's writing on cinema. While critics such as Carroll and others are apt to challenge Bazin's monolithic deification of the photographic image (leading Brian Henderson to refer to Bazin's overall project as a "vague ontology" [1976: 392]), this plays an important role in Bazin's subsequent prioritization of certain stylistic elements over others, and in particular the decisive view that the deep-focus sequence shot is superior to the artificiality of montage.

Bazin asserts in this essay that from the early design of sarcophaguses to the contemporary use of photography, the purpose of the arts has essentially been "to preserve being through appearance", or to ward off death by guarding some sensory trace of our phenomenal existence ([1958] 2002a: 9). However, this attempt to make a reproduction of the world has, since the Renaissance, been challenged by the expressiveness of the arts, or the arrival of aesthetics (most notably manifested in the use of perspectival painting). Because of this, there has lingered a certain mistrust or doubt concerning the image, that is, at least, until the arrival of the photographic machine, a device that can exclude the human from the process of reproduction (*ibid.*: 12).

Unlike other art forms, photography and film actually guard a physically constructed imprint of the real object, or what Bazin refers to as a *fingerprint* (*ibid.*: 16). Through this, Bazin arrives at a conclusive maxim that serves as the bedrock for his theory and easy pickings for anyone hoping to challenge Bazin's ontology: "The originality of photography in relation to painting resides then in its *essential objectivity*" (*ibid.*: 13). This claim would form a crux of Bazin's theory of cinematic realism, so central to his approach that Eric Rohmer would without superlative refer to it as Bazin's *objectivity axiom*, an apt tribute to the characteristic of Bazin's criticism that would be most influential on such *Cahiers* avatars of the *nouvelle vague* as Godard.

The decades following Bazin would challenge the objectivity claim of any human creation, rightfully insisting that all texts are processes of signification that cannot shed the complex weight of ideological factors. When Bazin follows this to claim that cinema thus appears to be the achievement of this photographic objectivity with the added dimension of duration, he makes an essentialist claim all the more dubious by basing it on the presupposition of an essentialist claim about another medium! Needless to say, this seemingly shaky methodology has provided Bazin's posthumous reputation with an endless supply of opportunistic critics, all of whom seem stubbornly to ignore the final sentence of this essay: "On the other hand, cinema is a language" (*ibid.*: 17).

In other words, film is a process of signification. Many have accused Bazin of ignoring this, despite the fact that his entire body of work is based on attempting to understand the very junction of signification in film, the dialectic between the form and content of the text and between the spectator's imagination and the cinematic fable. While Bazin may have preceded semiotics as a widespread movement in cultural studies, he could hardly be interpreted as being negligent of cinema's process of creating meaning. However, he rests clearly and vociferously opposed to the production of meaning beyond the latent immanence of the filmed world, and for this he has been rightly accused of constructing an arbitrary hierarchy based on specific stylistic or formal characteristics, as is outlined in his "The Evolution of Film Language".

In this essay we find the reverberations of Bazin's most essential aesthetic arguments, primarily drawn according to the difference – clearly evoking the preferences of his mentor at *Esprit*, Leenhardt – between capturing and presenting reality as something meaningful, and using it as a factor in the production of a secondary signification. This is not the first time we encounter such a hierarchy in Bazin's work. Bazin announces this particular argument in "Montage Prohibited" (in Bazin 1967: 49–61), most notably in a comparison drawn concerning two films by documentarist Robert Flaherty: *Nanook of the North* (1922) and *Louisiana Story* (1948). Bazin cites the difference between the authenticity of the first, which uses a stationary long take in order to show an adventure in ice-fishing, and the artificiality of the second, which uses conventional editing techniques in order to produce a precise dramatic effect.

This differentiation becomes far more pronounced in "The Evolution of Film Language", which uses a summary of a number of directors (Erich von Stroheim, Renoir, Welles, Carl Theodor Dreyer, Bresson), directors who would provide the object for Bazin's larger *Cinema of Cruelty, Jean Renoir* and *Orson Welles*, in order to discuss the gradual movement of film language away from the editing mannerisms of D. W. Griffith and Eisenstein, and towards a cinema that returns the possibility of ambiguity to the image. Bazin opens this essay by claiming there to be a divide between directors: "directors who believe in the image, and directors who believe in reality" (1967: 24). More specifically, there are those for whom the raw truth of the real suffices, and those who must add meaning to it by means of plastic manipulation or editing: those for whom the final *signification* (Bazin does indeed use this word) resides in the organization of elements as opposed to the *objective content* of their images (*ibid.*: 65).

Reacting against the stylized interwar movements of Soviet montage, German expressionism, as well as the crystallization of narrative editing in American cinema, Bazin uses this text to herald in a different way of approaching cinema altogether. Here Bazin presents his two greatest directorial interests, Renoir and Welles, as manifestations of a new type of cinema, based not on the production of drama through editing but instead on the presentation of reality through the shot-sequence and use of deep focus, stylistic processes that respect the "continuity of dramatic space and naturally of its duration" (*ibid.*: 74). Depth of field, Bazin argues, affects the relationship between the spectator and the image by refusing to determine the attention of the viewer; it produces, instead, a more realistic relationship with the viewed space, and thus a more active mental role and even contribution on behalf of the spectator (*ibid.*: 75).

This is part and parcel, for Bazin, of yet another effect, this one being metaphysical: the presence of ambiguity, an immanent part of the real whose just replication is made possible through certain formal systems. Taking up the philosophical mantle of the sceptic, Bazin's rejection of certain forms of montage resides on two planes: defence of the fruitful polysemy of reality, and defence of the free and active spectator. As such, we arrive at a crux of the phenomenological in Bazin's work: the praise of ambiguity as a virtue of the real, and acknowledgement of our place not as distant observers of the world, but as being implicated in it. Bazin accentuates this point through an analysis of Renoir and then more so with Welles, who – alongside Renoir and the directors of Italian neo-realism – renders to film the sense of ambiguity inherent in our experience of the real (*ibid.*: 77).

This last point is crucial because it sets in motion the two major axes of Bazin's criticism: a clear stylistic hierarchy, and the oeuvres through which he will develop his critical approach. While all of Bazin's longer texts were unfinished and published posthumously, we can still discern a certain progression that carries from his study of the evolution of cinematographic language to a particular interest in the works of Italian neo-realism, followed by larger-scale works on particular film-makers. In "The Evolution of Cinematic Language", Bazin makes the claim that neo-realism is "a humanism before being a style of mise-en-scène" (*ibid.*: 70), a claim that belies the fundamental philosophical nature of Bazin's criticism and also reveals the affinity that this cinematic school will hold for the veteran from *Esprit*.

THE POLITICS OF FILM STYLE

In his essays on neo-realism, however, we also find that this philosophical nature is capable of producing a heavily biased politicization of the film sign, most clearly demonstrated in Bazin's insistence, clearly extending from his arguments concerning the historical role of art in "Ontology of the Photographic Image", that one can classify and even create a hierarchy of films based on a function of the degree of realism they represent (*ibid.*: 270). In "An Aesthetic of Reality: Cinematic Realism and the Italian School of the Liberation", Bazin introduces the object of his analysis that will take his writing most directly towards a phenomenological basis (1971: 16–40). Discussing the film-makers of the post-war generation in Italy, and especially Roberto Rossellini's war trilogy (1945; 1946; 1947), Bazin praises neo-realism because it does not merely utilize reality as a political sign, but preserves the real from such judgements in what he refers to as an act of "revolutionary humanism" (*ibid.*: 263). Bazin extends this theory of the fact in his analyses of Vittorio de Sica, acclaimed director of *Ladri di biciclette* (Bicycle thieves; 1948).

In his essay on de Sica, Bazin states his reasons for praising the works of Italian neo-realism. These films deserve such high praise, according to Bazin, because they do not subordinate reality to an *a-priori* point of view; instead, they take reality as it is, protecting its wealth of meaning within a framework of ambiguity that does not insist on determining the spectator's interpretation. In a most symptomatic and telling claim, Bazin states: "Neorealism knows only immanence ... It is a phenomenology" (1971: 64). Bazin's appraisal of neo-realism – that it knows only the immanence of pure appearances, that it refuses to interpret its content according to preconceived intentions, and that this refusal is expressed in terms not only of the content but also of how it is arranged through the form itself – presents us with the stipulations of Bazin's hierarchy, which he develops further in his larger studies of Welles and Renoir.

In *Orson Welles*, we find Bazin's clearest articulation of the immanence of artistic genius in his extended analysis of Welles's "logical progressions from intention to form" ([1972] 1991: 68). In such passages, Bazin constructs a multi-tier notion of immanence beginning with the immanence of the artist in the formal design of the text. From here he moves on to the immanence of implicit action and meaning within the action and meaning viewed by the spectator and, lastly, to the immanence of many possible shots within that great Wellesian device: the shot-sequence.

The shot-sequence (or *plan-séquence*) is Bazin's term for the use of deep focus and camera motion in order to avoid the necessity of editing. Originally developed in his writings on *Citizen Kane* such as we found in "The Evolution of Cinematic Language", Bazin extends his hierarchy of film style further still in what could be seen as his most touching and personal works: *Jean Renoir*. In this book, which François Truffaut touts as "the *best* book on the cinema, written by the *best* critic, about the *best* director" ([1971] 1992: 7), Bazin sets out to fully develop his notion of cinematic realism.

Bazin's conceptualization of realism, as Andrew clarifies, is a long way from the French tradition of *naturalisme* developed in the literature of Honoré de Balzac and Émile Zola. Instead, it is a realism based on the "phenomenology of everyday perception" (Andrew 1984: 50). Renoir, much like modern authors such as André Gide, Ernest Hemingway and Albert Camus, attests to the notion that artistic vision rests not in the *transformation of* reality, but in the artist's *selection from* reality (cf. D. Andrew 1976: 154).[5] "Empirical reality", Andrew writes of Bazin, "consists of correspondences and interrelationships which the camera can find", thus making cinema specifically capable of capturing the complex network of relations in spatiotemporal continuity (*ibid.*: 155). Nowhere is this approach more explicit than in Bazin's analysis of Renoir.

Evoking the writing of Merleau-Ponty and gestalt phenomenology in general, Bazin claims that Renoir's directorial power and aesthetic genius lie in "the attention he pays to the importance of individual things in relation to one another" (1992: 84). These relations make up what for Bazin is the *essential*, which is "everywhere in what is visible" and for which narrative action and drama are merely a pretext (*ibid.*: 32). However, this essence of the network of relations that make up our world is not available to all styles of filming: realism, Bazin argues, works "in relation to the freedom of the mise-en-scène" (*ibid.*: 29). In other words, as we have found constantly with Bazin, the phenomenological purity of the cinematic image rests entirely within the stylistic arrangement of elements. Nowhere is this connection between film form and the phenomenological importance of *correspondences* as evident, once again, as in the use of deep-focus cinematography, which "confirms the unity of actor and décor, the total interdependence of everything real, from the human to the mineral" (*ibid.*: 90).

As is clear in the pages of this work on Renoir, Bazin holds a strong affinity for the somewhat metaphysical notion of existential unity that can be found in both Emersonian transcendentalism and Merleau-Ponty's phenomenology: no doubt why some may accuse Bazin of a non-materialist metaphysics and, yet, also why I make here the argument for an understanding of Bazin's theory of immanence. For Bazin there is not only a *real* that is external to cinema, but also a reality in which cinema plays an important role, both as a recording device and also as a sociopolitical force. Bazin's notion of the real implicates the director, actor and spectator in the world around us, from which we are inseparable. In this way Bazin was well ahead of his time, constructing a philosophy of cinema based on the network of connections through which art, history and the praxis of production and viewing are immanent within every text.

NOTES

1. In *Theorizing the Moving Image* (Cambridge: Cambridge University Press, 1996) Carroll poses Bazin's cinematic realism as the type of "grand theory" (*ibid.*: xiv) that has retarded the clarity of film criticism over the years. Claiming that contemporary theorists "are correct to reject Bazin's metaphysics concerning the nature of the film image", Carroll rejects most specifically Bazin's specificity argument, which is based primarily on the ontology of the photographic image (*ibid.*: 78). Earlier structuralist arguments tend to take opportunistic approaches to Bazin's writings, ignoring his clear understanding of the sociohistoric praxis of film texts (hence his prophecies for Italian neo-realism) and also denying him his characteristic analysis of film texts as whole signifying networks.
2. The evolution from theories of formalism to those of realism is well documented in a multitude of texts, including V. F. Perkins's "A Critical History of Early Film Theory", in *Movies and Methods*, vol. 1, B. Nichols (ed.) (Berkeley, CA: University of California Press, 1976), 401–21), Dudley Andrew's *Concepts in Film Theory* (Oxford: Oxford University Press, 1984) and *The Major Film Theories* (Oxford: Oxford University Press, 1976), and Brian Henderson's "Two Types of Film Theory", Nichols (ed.), *Movies and Methods*, vol. 1, 388–400.
3. In general, it could be said that Kracauer's notion of cinematic realism is founded more in an exhaustingly rigorous reading of film history, while Bazin's provides a more lucid explanation of what the *real* is in terms of its relation to cinema.
4. "Ontologie de l'image photographique" and "L'évolution du langage cinématographique" both appear in Bazin's *Qu'est-ce que le cinéma?* (Paris: Éditions du Cerf, 2002), and translations here are mine in order to maintain the highest degree of accuracy.
5. We can see here a direct affinity between Bazin's literary influences and the literature that, only years after Bazin's death, Roland Barthes would theorize as *writing degree zero*.

10 ROLAND BARTHES

Colin Gardner

Roland Barthes (1915–80) studied Classsical Letters at the Sorbonne, Paris, from 1935 to 1939. Ill health kept him out of military service during the war. He taught at a number of institutes until 1977, when he began at the Collège de France in Paris (on the proposal of Michel Foucault) as the Chair of Literary Semiology from 1977. His works include *Writing Degree Zero* (1953; English trans. 1968), *Mythologies* (1957; English trans. 1972), *Criticism and Truth* (1966; English trans. 1987), his famous essay "The Death of the Author" (1967), *Empire of Signs* (1970; English trans. 1982), *S/Z* (1970; English trans. 1974), *A Lover's Discourse* (1977; English trans. 1979) and *Camera Lucida* (1980; English trans. 1981).

Given Roland Barthes' deep distrust of bourgeois myths and their attendant ortho-doxies, as well as his committed belief that the ostensible author of a given work is merely the contingent effect of a braid of separate texts, any attempt to systematically define his writings on film as a coherent body of work is inevitably doomed to failure. For better or worse, Barthes was an intellectual *flâneur* who persistently "wrote" (and "rewrote") his often "erotic" passion for literature, theatre, music, advertising, pop cul-ture and photography into a unique phenomenonology of both textual *and* somatic excess whereby he reversed the syntagmatic order of Maurice Merleau-Ponty's famous dictum in *Phenomenology of Perception*, "The theory of perception is already the theory of the body" (1989: 181).

Since his untimely death in 1980, most critical evaluations – notably Jonathan Rosenbaum (1982/3), Vlada Petric (1983) and Philip Watts (2005) – have stressed an almost schizophrenic disjuncture between, on the one hand, Barthes' undeniably seminal impact on the developing field of film studies and its related disciplines of ciné-semiology and structuralism in the 1960s and 1970s, and his own, academically non-specialist, "cinephobia" on the other. It is no secret that Barthes always preferred the incommensurability of the photographic fragment and the haiku – specifically the photographic object's ability to "unexpress the expressible" (where the latter stands for the entire realm of socially sanctioned and regulated meaning) – to the cinema's insistent, narratively homogenizing (and, by extension, scopically colonizing) continu-ity of metonymic images; "our French word for it, *pellicule*, is highly appropriate: a skin without puncture or perforation", he notes (Barthes 1977c: 54–5). In fact, he began his last book, *Camera Lucida: Reflections on Photography*, by admitting, "I decided I liked photography *in opposition* to the cinema, from which I none the less failed to separate it" (1981: 3). However, we should note that the latter half of this statement suggests less a binary opposition or simple dialectic between the two media than an *aporia* of *différance* (in Derrida's sense of a combination of difference *and* mutual deferral; cf. Derrida 1976).The reciprocrocity of Barthes' position may help us to creatively overcome their seeming contradictions in favour of positing a new type of cinematic paradigm: the *punctum* of photography (with its play of chance and subjective association) and the more conventionally coded *studium* that Barthes associated with narrative cinema become affective allies rather than ideological antagonists (Barthes 1981).

This ambivalent *aporia* is already apparent in "On CinemaScope", one of Barthes' earliest writings on cinema, first published in *Les Lettres nouvelles* in February 1954 (Barthes 1993a: 380). Although the essay on the new widescreen process was never included in Barthes' more famous collection of *Mythologies* in 1957, it nonetheless highlights his critical awareness of the insidious connections between the filmic apparatus and theatrical spectacle and, more importantly, the positioning of the spectator's body as both willing accomplice and naturalized (read, deluded) victim of a mythologizing postcolonial panopticon. As James Morrison points out, the essay

> is like a little anthology of the themes that would recur throughout his work. In condensed form, it's all there – the lure of asceticism against the sway of spectacle, the avid attunement to both the dangers and the pleasures of the text, the earnest crusade to expose the lies of Realism but have a little fun while you're at it. Perhaps the most interesting feature of the piece is the tantalizing balance it achieves, to be fulfilled in Barthes's late work, between critique and affirmation. Barthes has come to praise CinemaScope and to bury it at the same time. (1999)

Barthes thus affirms the screen process's ability – through binocular vision – to liberate the hitherto passive spectator from being "walled up in the darkness, receiving cinematic nourishment rather like the way a patient is fed intravenously" (Barthes 1999). Instead, echoing André Bazin's desire for a democratized, ontologically "Realist" image, the viewer's position is actively opened up: "I am on an enormous balcony, I move effortlessly within the field's range, I freely pick out what interests me" (*ibid.*). On the other hand, the circular sweep of the screen also envelops and entraps him: "I begin to be surrounded, and my larval state is replaced by the euphoria of an equal amount of circulation between the spectacle and my body". This sensation is both pleasurable – because it positions the viewer, "like a little god", as an active participant in the Epic theatre of History-as-spectacle (imagine yourself joining hands with the revolutionary insurgents in *Battleship Potemkin*, he enthuses) – and alarming, because ultimately scopic power depends on who controls the spectacle's means of production. Although the balcony of History is ready, "What remains to be seen is what we'll be shown there; if it will be *Potemkin* or *The Robe*, Odessa or Saint-Sulpice, History or Mythology" (*ibid.*).[1]

For Morrison, "On CinemaScope" is particularly important in the Barthes canon because it constitutes one of his earliest reflections on the phenomenology and erotics of his own body and its relation to the potentially mythic excess of the CinemaScope screen. It presages his later meditation on the body as itself a form of intentional excess in both *S/Z* – "There is one element *in excess*, and this untoward supplement is the body" (Barthes 1974: 28) – and "Upon Leaving the Movie Theater", where his resistance to the mythologizing diegesis becomes pleasurable simply by doubling the perversion of the scopic act. "It is by letting myself be *twice* fascinated by the image and by its surroundings, as if I had two bodies at once", explains Barthes:

> a narcissistic body which is looking, lost in gazing into the nearby mirror, and a perverse body, ready to fetishize not the image, but precisely that which exceeds it: the sound's grain, the theater, the obscure mass of other bodies, the rays of light, the entrance, the exit: in short, in order to distance myself, to "take off", I complicate a "relationship" with a "situation".
>
> (1980b: 4)

For Barthes, the body is always in excess because it intercedes between a pure one-to-one correspondence (and idealized transparency) between mind and text-as-sign. "Barthes's blissfully elegiac late work is a sustained effort to reconcile the material excess of the body with the pervasive but mercurial energies of the sign", argues Morrison:

> The critical mythologist comes face to face here with the passive subject of myth. Perhaps one reason this essay was not included in *Mythologies* was that it heralds a discovery the early Barthes had not yet made, one the late Barthes taught us again and again, and one post-colonial thought, in particular, dedicates itself to heeding: To expose a myth is not always to liberate one's own body from its power.   (1999)

The lifelong (and ultimately unsolved) question for Barthes then becomes: how can an aesthetics of the cinema utilize this *aporia* as a form of transformative, affective intensity instead of locking down the medium as a closed orthodoxy?

As one might expect, this artificial separation of "doxa"[2] (associated with the thinking body) from seduction and blissful excess (*jouissance*) is readily apparent in Barthes' more Marxist-inflected essays devoted to cinema in *Mythologies*, particularly "The Romans in Films" and "*Un Ouvrier sympathique*", Barthes' savage attack on Elia Kazan's *On the Waterfront* (1954) (Barthes 1993a. 603–4), in which Marlon Brando's Terry Malloy is seen less as a Christ-like martyr fighting the corruption of the union bosses than as a dupe of the management classes, who use him to orchestrate a return to "business as usual". Each of these essays utilizes demystification as a critique of artifice and false nature, thus setting up a standard of realism against the mythification of cinematic illusion and the star system (which Barthes invariably associates with the reification of capitalism and the culture industry in general). This is further manifested as a propagation of left-wing sobriety and restraint against the tautological overstatement of ideological excess (Barthes had yet to tie the latter to a politics of the body). Thus, as Watts points out, "[w]hile never espousing the cause of cinematic realism, the *Mythologies* depend upon an ideal of asceticism, of stylistic paring down, of an almost classical or rather Atticist aesthetic purity" (2005: 22).[3] This lip service to an ideal of Platonic essence is evident even in Barthes' otherwise carnal paean to the face of Greta Garbo. Describing her chalk-like visage in Rouben Mamoulian's *Queen Christina* (1933), he notes that her complexion has the snowy thickness of a mask. It is a face set in plaster, protected by the surface of the colour, not by its lineaments:

> Garbo offered to one's gaze a sort of Platonic Idea of the human creature, which explains why her face is almost sexually undefined, without how-ever leaving one in doubt ... Garbo still belongs to that moment in cinema when capturing the human face still plunged audiences into the deepest ecstasy, when one literally lost oneself in the human image as one would in a philter, when the face represented a kind of absolute state of the flesh, which could be neither reached nor renounced.   (Barthes 1972: 56)

To give him credit, throughout *Mythologies* Barthes eschews the strident polemics typical of much Marxist criticism in favour of a more light-hearted, decentred approach. Instead of focusing on the big picture – the analytical equivalent of CinemaScope – he teases out more marginal signifiers and drags them into the spotlight, all the better to show how they (co-)operate under the sway of a dominant code, which passes itself off as the natural order of things. Perhaps the most "infamous" example is Barthes' exploration of what constitutes "Romanness" in Joseph Mankiewicz's 1953 produc-tion of *Julius Caesar* through an examination of the actors' hair – or more specifically their fringes – the mainspring of the filmic spectacle and the guarantor of historical plausibility. This is a case of the sign, in effect, operating in the open, brazenly showing off its credentials as a scopic and ideological lure. Indeed, for Barthes, the film's true auteur is not Shakespeare or Mankiewicz but its hairdresser:

> The frontal lock overwhelms one with evidence, no one can doubt that he is in Ancient Rome. And this certainty is permanent: the actors speak, act, torment themselves, debate "questions of universal import", without losing, thanks to this little flag displayed on their foreheads, any of their historical plausibility. Their general representativeness can even expand in complete safety, cross the ocean and the centuries, and merge into the Yankee mugs of Hollywood extras: no matter, everyone is reassured, installed in the quiet certainty of a universe without duplicity, where Romans are Romans thanks to the most legible of signs: hair on the forehead.   (*Ibid.*: 26)

Barthes then proceeds to postulate an ethics of signs, all equally mythic:

> Signs ought to present themselves only in two extreme forms: either openly intellectual and so remote that they are reduced to an algebra, as in the Chinese theatre, where a flag on its own signifies a regiment; or deeply rooted, invented, so to speak, on each occasion, revealing an internal, a

hidden facet, and indicative of a moment in time, no longer of a concept (as in the art of Stanislavsky, for instance). (*Ibid.*: 28)

In contrast, the Hollywood sign, although equally mythic, represents a degraded spectacle,

> equally afraid of simple reality and of total artifice. For although it is a good thing if a spectacle is created to make the world more explicit, it is both reprehensible and deceitful to confuse the sign with what is signified. And it is a duplicity which is peculiar to bourgeois art: between the intellectual and the visceral sign is hypocritically inserted a hybrid, at once elliptical and pretentious, which is pompously christened "nature". (*Ibid.*)

This is the essence of bourgeois myth in the Hollywood film. It is what makes the spectacle seem real while at the same time indicating that it is fearful of the true reality – imperialism, capitalism, the division of labour – that underlies it.

By the early 1960s, Barthes had developed a much broader viewpoint on ideology in particular and "meaning" in general, less centred on the signified and more on the floating signifier, a concern that led him from a Saussure-based semiology into a Jakobson-grounded structuralism (and later poststructuralism; cf. Belsey [1980] 2002), spawning a critical dialogue with the contemporaneous work of Umberto Eco, Pier Paolo Pasolini (a Barthes admirer) and Christian Metz. In a 1963 interview with Michel Delahaye and Jacques Rivette for *Cahiers du cinéma*, Barthes outlined his initial attempts to frame cinema as a form of language. According to Barthes, the model for all languages is speech: articulated language. The latter is a code, using a system of signs that, because they are not analogical, means they are inherently discontinuous. Cinema is exactly the opposite: it presents itself as an analogical expression of reality that is also continuous and perpetually self-present, "and we don't know how to tackle a continuous and analogical expression in order to introduce, to initiate an analysis along linguistic lines; for example, how do you divide (semantically), how do you vary the meaning of a film, of a film fragment?" (Barthes 1985: 13). The critic would have to find in cinematic continuity elements that are not analogical, that is they must be deformed in such a way that they can be treated as fragments of language. This would require structuralist methods in order to discern the exact point where variations in the signifier also entail a variation in the signified. For Barthes it thus becomes an opposition between a micro- and a macro-semantics, solved by moving from the plane of denotation to that of connotation, where signifieds are global, diffuse and secondary. In this respect, Roman Jakobson's metaphoric and metonymic structural axes become an exemplary model: "We'd be tempted to say that in films, all montage, i.e., all signifying contiguity, is a metonymy, and since the cinema is montage, to say further that the cinema is a metonymic art (at least at present)" (*ibid.*: 15). In other words, film is governed by the syntagm, an extended, arranged fragment actualized by signs in and through montage. More importantly, as Barthes notes, "it is not things but the place of things which matters. The bond between the signifier and the signified is of much less importance than the organization of the signifiers among themselves" (*ibid.*: 16).

This is, of course, central to Barthes' subsequent move into poststructuralism with the publication of *S/Z* in 1970, and his shift in focus from treating film as a "work" (an ostensible imitation of reality producing a passive spectatorial response) to a "text" (a methodological "field of energy" constructed as a weave or tissue of significations that absorbs both writer and reader, film and spectator, into an active "writerly" engagement of meaning production). This is both anchored and relayed by five specific codes: (i) the hermeneutic or enigma code; (ii) the proairetic or action code; (iii) the semic code; (iv) the symbolic code; and (v) the referential or cultural code. Although Barthes himself effectively applied these codes to deconstruct Balzac's realist novella *Sarrasine* (1830), several film theorists have found his methodologies to be particularly useful in unpacking the latent contradictions of superficially seamless realist filmic texts such as Alfred Hitchcock's *North by Northwest* (1959) (Wollen 1982: 40–48) and Jean Renoir's *La Règle du jeu* (Rules of the game; 1939) (Lesage 1985: 476–500).

More importantly for validating Barthes' subsequent preference for photography over the cinema, however, was that this initial concern with the syntagm led him to renew his earlier interest in the epic theatre of Bertolt Brecht, culminating in his analysis (in his 1973 essay, "Diderot, Brecht, Eisenstein") of the "pregnant" moment in the theatrical tableau (Barthes 1977a: 69–78). Here, Barthes proposes a conception of representation less in terms of mimesis – the imitation of reality – than as a structured spectacle of unified *effects*. This positions the spectator at a distance, so that the representation may be securely appropriated as a series of instantaneities or snapshots, communicable at a glance (thus turning it into a fetish). The fetish – disavowing lack – places the subject in a position where identity is assured through the construction of a stable unity in relation to a fixed "reality" and gaze, such as in the paintings of Diderot's ideal artist, Jean-Baptiste Greuze (1725–1805). "The epic scene in Brecht, the shot in Eisenstein are so many tableaux", notes Barthes:

> they are scenes which are *laid out* (in the sense in which one says *the table is laid*), which answer perfectly to that dramatic unity theorized by Diderot: firmly cut out ... erecting a meaning but manifesting the production of that meaning, they accomplish the coincidence of the visual and the ideal *découpages*.
>
> (*Ibid.*: 70–71)

Barthes is thus able to draw a direct methodological relationship between the shot in Eisenstein, Greuze's pictorial composition and the scene in epic theatre. The main difference, however, is that Brechtian practice puts this unity in question, offering the tableau for ideological criticism instead of "blind" adherence. By distancing us still further from our pre-existing position of scopic distance, Brecht endlessly displaces identification and representation, thus forcing the spectator to understand the constructed nature of both. In an Althusserian sense, distanciation, through the tableau, "disinterpellates". This is again part of Barthes' objective to use art to "unexpress the expressible" (i.e. the "doxa" of officially sanctioned meaning). The result is a text of excessive bliss (*jouissance*) and overdetermination, which leaves culture and language in non-linear fragments. "There is no development, no maturation ..., no final meaning", states Barthes: "nothing but a series of segmentations each of which possesses a sufficient demonstrative power" (*ibid.*: 72). This disjuncture is experienced by the (politically aware) spectator not as loss but as the re-opening of blocked paths, a reformulated aestheticism.

Although it is commonly assumed that epic art harnesses the syntagm and tableau in order to generate a polemical didacticism, Barthes noted that it is also a meaning held in suspension or withheld:

> The work must ask the questions (in terms obviously chosen by the author: this is a responsible art), it is left to the public to find the answers (what Brecht called the *issue*); meaning (in the positive sense of the term) moved from the stage to the audience; to sum up, there is in fact, in Brecht's theater, a meaning and a very strong meaning, but it is always a question. This is perhaps what explains why this theater, although it is certainly a critical, polemic, committed theater, is not, however, a militant theater.
>
> (1985: 20)

The question remains: is this epic suspension – with its dependence on the frozen moment – translatable to the kinetic form of cinema itself? Although Barthes felt that, like literature, cinema was reactionary by its very nature, it did have this innate ability – in the right hands – to suspend meaning. This, however, "is an extremely difficult task requiring at the same time a very great technique and total intellectual loyalty. That means getting rid of all parasite meanings, which is extremely difficult" (*ibid.*: 21).

This preference for suspension is clearly the basis for Barthes' admiration for the work of Luis Buñuel (specifically *El Ángel exterminador* [The exterminating angel; 1962]) and Michelangelo Antonioni. In the former case, Barthes notes that the director's warning at the beginning of the 1962 film – "I Buñuel, say to you that this film has no meaning" – is no mere affectation, because at each moment meaning is suspended without ever being reduced to nonsense.

> It is not at all an absurd film; it's a film that is full of meaning; full of what Lacan calls "significance". It is full of significance, but it doesn't have *one* meaning, or a series of little meanings. And in that way it's a film which disturbs profoundly, and which forces you to go beyond dogmatism, beyond doctrines. (Barthes 1985: 21)

For Barthes, the innate "movement" of the film is this very notion of a perpetual dispatching at each and every instant, whereby the scenes (the syntagmatic fragments and tableaux), far from constituting immobile series (in the form of obsessional, metaphorical tropes), actually participate in the gradual transformation of a festive bourgeois society into one of pathological constraint: they form a duration that is inevitable and irreversible.

Similarly, in "Cher Antonioni", Barthes' open letter of appreciation to the Italian director, he discusses Antonioni and his modernism in terms that defy easy categorization: issues such as "fragility", "tenuousness", "wisdom" and "attentiveness".

Antonioni's phenomenology lies less in wilful intentionality than on the surface of things and in the interstices between them. Thus his *mise en scène* is only superficially "banal": material things cannot be easily explained away using conventional symbolic meaning or objective correlatives. Moreover, this methodology is innately political, for as Peter Brunette notes, quoting Barthes:

> the director's subtlety of meaning is politically decisive because "as soon as meaning is fixed and imposed, as soon as it loses its subtlety, it becomes an instrument of power. To make meaning more subtle, then, is a political activity, as is any effort that aims to harass, to trouble, to defeat the fanaticism of meaning".
>
> (Brunette 1998: 13–14)

However, Buñuel and Antonioni are rare beacons in Barthes' already threadbare cinematic pantheon. Indeed, it would be more accurate to say that his return to Brecht and his desire to capture a surplus of meaning, a semiological excess beyond signification (what Barthes calls a hallucination), brought him temperamentally closer to the anti-kinaesthetic characteristics of not only the tableau, but also, in the case of "The Third Meaning" (1970), the film still. Focusing specifically on Eisenstein's *Ivan Groznyy I* (Ivan the Terrible; 1944) and *Battleship Potemkin* (1925), Barthes analyses a selection of images featuring two courtiers as they rain gold down on to the young tsar's head, as well as grief-stricken mourners at the sailor Vakulinchuk's funeral. Barthes discerns three basic levels of meaning: (i) informational, on the level of communication, to be analysed by semiology; (ii) symbolic, on the level of signification, to be analysed by "the sciences of the symbol (psychoanalysis, economy, dramaturgy)" (1977a: 53); and (iii) the "obtuse meaning" or level of *significance*, which constitutes that surplus of meaning which cannot be exhausted or contained by the other two. Barthes discovers this "Third Meaning" in specific details (echoing his earlier analysis of Roman fringes and Garbo's face in *Mythologies*) such as the courtiers' pancake make-up and the mourners' hair and tightly woven buns as well as the ugliness of the character Euphrosyne, which "exceeds the anecdote, becomes a blunting of meaning, its drifting" (*ibid.*: 59). In short, "[t]he obtuse meaning is a signifier without a signified, hence the difficulty in naming it. My reading remains suspended between the image and its description, between definition and approximation" (*ibid.*: 61).

Although brilliantly argued, this essay makes clear that because he lacked a specific understanding of the kinetic properties of motion pictures (which includes sound as well as image), Barthes developed his concept of the nature of cinema negatively in relation to photography. He always considered the latter superior to film on a phenomenological level because it conserves the motionless *noema* of the referent captured by the camera – i.e. that which has been – instead of sweeping it away in a syntagmatic chain of images (a form of "present continuous"). Searching for a "totality of the image", Barthes inevitably found cinema incomplete and lacking simply because it *moves* and thus becomes something other:

> The photographic image is full, crammed: no room, nothing can be added to it. In the cinema, whose raw material is photographic, the image does

not, however, have this completeness (which is fortunate for the cinema). Why? Because the photograph, taken in flux, is impelled, ceaselessly drawn toward other views; in the cinema, no doubt, there is always a photographic referent, but this referent shifts, it does not make a claim in favor of its reality, it does not protest its former existence; it does not cling to me: it is not a *spectre*. Like the real world, the filmic world is sustained by the presumption that, as Husserl says, "the experience will constantly continue to flow by in the same constitutive style"; but the Photograph breaks the "constitutive style" (this is its astonishment); it is *without future* (this is its pathos, its melancholy); in it, no protensity, whereas the cinema is protensive, hence in no way melancholic (what is it, then? – It is, then, simply "normal", like life). Motionless, the Photograph flows back from presentation to retention.   (1981: 89–90)

For Barthes, pathos and melancholy (the corollary of the image's *punctum*) and the "spectralization" of people and objects can only result from the image's expulsion of temporality. Therefore, because it is simply an illusion, that is, phenomenologically too close to the perception of reality and thus the very opposite of an hallucination, film is incapable of producing a *punctum*.

This is obviously an extremely narrow, not to say misguided, reading of the very nature of film as a kinetic art. As Vlada Petric makes clear, "He theorises about those features of the motion picture image which are 'missing' and inessential to the medium, while at the same time he avoids addressing features intrinsic to cinema, properties which make it 'melancholic' in its own, dynamic way" (1983: 205). Barthes fails to make a valid distinction between the static and dynamic perception of an image and to explore them on their own terms. Instead, he dismisses film simply because it is too "normal" and "lifelike". Moreover, Petric rightly argues that Barthes puts himself in direct conflict with Eisenstein's intellectual montage and its aim of engaging the viewer so that he or she contemplates specific details of the depicted event during, but especially *after*, the screening as moments of deep melancholy. Eisenstein was fully aware of the hypnotic power of this auratic effect in conjunction with the intellectual elements of his montage of attractions. Thus Eisenstein's idea of excess – what he calls overtones and which are derived specifically from film form itself (associative montage, the artifical expansion of real time through editing, camera angle, lighting, depth of field, etc.) – is far removed from Barthes' desire to capture an already pre-fixed *punctum*.

Barthes' resistance to kinaesthetics is particularly galling because there are a number of contemporary film-makers – most notably Jean-Luc Godard (*Tout va bien* [Just great; 1972], *Passion* [1982a]), Terence Davies (*Distant Voices, Still Lives* [1988]), and Jesper Just (*No Man Is An Island II* [2004]) – who brilliantly conflate elements of both Brechtian and Greuzian tableaux, the photogramme and the affective properties of the soundtrack (to which Barthes seems to have turned a deaf ear) to create intensities that both touch the body and force it to think without resort to Barthes' spectatorial equivalent of a *doppelgänger*. In other words, photographs and a general slowing down of the pace of the filmic narrative can sufficiently immobilize time to

117

produce the very "completeness" of the image that Barthes so desired. This is particularly powerful in conveying a sense of affective violence in film, "not because it shows violent things, but because on each occasion *it fills the sight by force*, and because in it nothing can be refused or transformed" (Barthes 1981: 91). As Wendy Everett notes in respect to the use of the photograph and accompanying popular songs in Davies's *Distant Voices, Still Lives*:

> as point of violence and stasis, it has the ability to stop time, to rupture the flow of the film and thus to enact the moment of trauma. If the frozen attitude of the family reveals the extent of their continuing trauma, so powerful is this trauma that it has the power to halt the film, to take away the very movement that defines it, to disrupt its process of articulation. (2004: 76)

This is the essence of the affect- and time-images at work, but in order to theorize it, Barthes would have had to move closer to the Peircean semiotics of Deleuze and that, as they say, is another story.

NOTES

1. Given Barthes' deliberate contrast between socialist realism (Eisenstein's *Battleship Potemkin* [1925]) and Hollywood spectacle (Henry Koster's *The Robe* [1953]), Philip Watts is correct to position his film writings during this period – particularly in *Mythologies* – as an attempt to forge a non-aligned "Third Way" in response to cold war realpolitik (decolonization, the Korean War, capital–labour conflicts, the Americanization of European culture): what Barthes called "la grande contestation URSS–USA". See P. Watts, "Roland Barthes's Cold-War Cinema", *SubStance* **34**(3) (2005), 17–32.
2. "The *Doxa* ... is Public Opinion, the mind of the majority, petit bourgeois Consensus, the Voice of Nature, the Violence of Prejudice. We can call (using Leibniz's word) a *doxology* any way of speaking adapted to appearance, to opinion, or to practice" (*Roland Barthes*, R. Howard [trans.] [New York: Hill & Wang, 1977], 47).
3. Barthes' analysis of Robert Bresson's 1947 film, *Les Anges du péché* (Angels of the streets) is insightful in this regard; "On Robert Bresson's Film *Les Anges du péché*", in *Robert Bresson*, J. Quandt (ed.), R. Howard (trans.), 211–13 (Toronto: Toronto International Film Festival Group, 1998). He praises the film precisely because it avoids excess, taking pains to point out Bresson's directorial restraint and sobriety in performance, *mise en scène* and dialogue. In contrast, he criticizes Claude Chabrol's *Le Beau Serge* (Handsome Serge; 1958) because its "decriptive surface" eschews a "Flaubertian asceticism" (which is realistic only in so far as it signifies nothing) in favour of a false moralism. The result is an "art of the right" which always assigns meanings to human misfortunes without examining their reasons or consequences (Barthes 1993a: 787–9).

II POLITICS OF THE CINEMATIC CENTURY

Are you a theorist or a philosopher? Is it film-philosophy or film theory? Both areas have developed into heterogeneous disciplines. There are multiple ways in which these disciplines are conceived of and practised. Can you actually define and categorize the practice of engaging with screen forms and cinematic conditions? In Part II, a selection of philosophers and theorists who have been integral to providing accounts of twentieth-century cultures engage with the metaphysical account of what numerous theorists have referred to as the cinematic century (Daney 1991a; Godard & Ishaghpour 2005). As Garin Dowd reminds us in his chapter on legendary film critic Serge Daney, it was Daney who surmised that the history of the twentieth century "*was* the cinema" (Ch. 11). Dowd also marvellously points out some of the connections that can be drawn among the thinkers of the cinematic century: those who lived through the wars and understood the connections the cinema was making between the abstracted and new places where people found themselves to be located. New perspectives – from the air, from under the ground, from inside a concrete bunker, from the maritime space of the twentieth century, from the microcosmic, the invisible sites of new chemistry, new technologies – all of these places afforded a new metaphysics of the image. The post-war period also provided reflection on the nature of death, destruction and humankind's death drive. Further avenues for study in this regard would include Hannah Arendt's work.

New paradigms of theory and philosophy for critical analysis emerged in the late twentieth century. Rejecting diagnostic, rational, logocentric and gender-biased categorical analyses, these different forms of theory are commonly referred to as "contemporary" philosophy, or schools of critical thought. What contemporary philosophy produced was new ways of thinking: metacritical methods that provide critical analyses of traditional ways of doing philosophy and critiquing the criticism itself; classifications of knowledge; and, for the study of film forms and cinematic conditions, new distributions of the knowledge terms and new ways of understanding the semiologies of representation and how "normative" ideas are maintained. Twentieth-century philosophical and critical methods tested against cinematic conditions include: critical modes (inclusive of approaches to phenomenological, post-phenomenological, semiotic, structuralist, poststructuralist, cognitive, Marxist, feminist, queer, psychological, post-nationalist and decolonialist critiques, ethics and aesthetics issues); scientific philosophy (neurophilosophies that might engage cognitive-scientific theories such as mirror-neuron analysis, cognitive theorization of various forms of "embodied" vision, the affects of chemicals on corporeal receptors, etc.); and various vernacular philosophies (materialism, mathematics, feminism, existentialism). This list is indicative only (cf. Kearney & Rainwater 1996; Critchley 2001).

Variously, as described by the authors of each of the chapters in Part II, individual practices redefine metaphysics (the study of the nature of reality, the physics of forms and systems of movement) through the conditions of twentieth-century change, reflected in cinematic conditions. What is produced are new forms of film-philosophy and film theory: how these forms are articulated depends on how culturally sensitive criteria are engaged in order to position the operation of the intensive labour forms of film-making.

At the core of most film-philosophy lies an interest in approaching the philosophical possibilities offered by the screen form. Different practitioners engage in different ways, considering how, for example, the filmic mode produces, reduces, augments, limits, and/or disturbs, and so on, physical and mental assumptions and knowledge, mediating experience and perception. Further, film-philosophy generally articulates the terms of the shifts in that awareness when engaging such questions. The practice engenders new pathways of thinking as well as continuing core philosophical modes for study.

Dowd's chapter on Daney kicks off this section of practice with a development of André Bazin's realist aesthetics (Ch. 11). The notion of the cinema as a medium for "bearing witness" is extended in Daney's thinking, a common aspect for thinkers in this era, to realize that the "image" of the cinema can be located not only visually, but in sound, the voice or in disjunctions of various "non-human" kinds. The "reality" on screen, as each of the chapters in this part will describe, comes to determine history: a history that is the contingent and the causal politics of the twentieth century. Reality on screen is thus described in the purely aesthetic terms of non-representational forms or in the overt displays of political expression, or in the reflexive terms of both, such as we see in the work of director Jean-Luc Godard, as discussed by Zsuzsa Baross (Ch. 12). Bazin's question resonates in Godard's practice; like all New Wave thinkers (from all eras), he knows that he can create something different, redirecting "reality" out of the existing status quo, no matter what the circumstance or material details. This practice of redirection through writing practice is demonstrated in the chapter on Stanley Cavell by Rex Butler (Ch. 13). Cavell's work offers a bridging model for the analytic–continental methodological divide, as his work takes on the political and formal aesthetics of screen life, and cinematic conditions. Reality on screen also makes us consider the ways in which we view the world, and screen-worlds, as Cavell and Jean-Luc Nancy determine, articulating the phenomenological practice of cinema itself. Cinema forces us to account for the ways in which histories are determined, through the lens of experience of "reality", of "truth", of "ideas", provoked by sound and/or images. As Claire Colebrook discusses in her chapter on Nancy, for Nancy, the "world is *cinematic*" (Ch. 14). This entails a different form of conceptual image of and for the cinema from that of Jacques Derrida. Although he investigates concerns of "presence" that appear similar to Nancy's, Derrida is in fact in pursuit of an entirely different presence of celluloid: that of the "spectral", as Louise Burchill details (Ch. 15). For Derrida, the "eye" of the cinematic process of perception has shifted its technological purview, just as it does for Paul Virilio, where it becomes its own body of perception (Ch. 18). Like Henri Bergson's and Emmanuel Levinas's pursuit of the temporal in cinema, Derrida also considers the notion of duration as self-affective for consciousness and the apprehension of something via the cinematic: also one of the topics of Gilles Deleuze's theory of the cinema. John Mullarky, in his chapter on Deleuze, details Deleuze's "transcendental" theory of a cinema of the event (Ch. 16). Deleuze posits the cinema as a form "vital" for philosophical practice.

The creations Alfred Hitchcock bought to the screen figure, in particular *The Lady Vanishes* (1938), haunt the pages of Tom Conley's investigation into the original lady that vanished, Sarah Kofman (Ch. 17), and Laurence Simmons's discussion of Žižek's address of Hitchcock (Ch. 28). Conley's chapter take us to the heart of the practice of film-philosophy with the consideration of the self-situating concept of philosophical style and philosophical abstraction. The practice when writing philosophy becomes bound to the practice of creating a film, and what is at stake is the event of the "intolerable" (Ch. 17). That intolerable becomes, in Virilio's metaphysics, the end point to which all things are rushing, in a very fast movement towards death (Ch. 18). Bazinian "realism" becomes even more strange under the cinematic conditions described by Virilio. In the work of Jean Baudrillard, as Catherine Constable discusses, a new mode of "mythmaking" takes place, under the guise of simulacra theories that also push the Bazinian "real" (Ch. 19).

Part II concludes with chapters on some of the core theorists of the postmodern cinematic era of practice, Baudrillard, Jean-François Lyotard and Fredric Jameson, who develop feedback loops and aesthetic formal analysis, set up by earlier semiologists who offer film-philosophical commentary but are not included here: Jan Mukarovsky (1977), F. W. Galan (1985) and linguist Roman Jacobson (1971). As Lisa Trahair details, movement and the cinema remain central for the work of Lyotard (Ch. 19). Lyotard sought to chart movement in the cinema of various forms – libidinal, economic and so on – engaging the concept of the *dispositif* to describe filmic systems (e.g. as the marker of a temporal event such as a narrative structure, similar to Flusser's use of Jean-Louis Baudry's term; cf. Ch. 2).

Felix Guattari ends Part II; he is anti-"postmodern", instead offering a conception of the cinema that is "a-signifying" (Ch. 22). Guattari and Jameson are both advocates for cinema's attention to the politics of the marginal: the everyday, the intimate, the anti-authoritarian. This is staged as the "minor" in Guattarian terms, as Gary Genosko argues (Ch. 22), and for Jameson, as Scott Durham demonstrates, the "permanently provisional" site of non-centrist strategies of postmodernist production (Ch. 21). Like Siegfried Kracauer's and Theodor Adorno's, Guattari's film-philosophy describes how the technological organization of the cinema and its products can affectively alter sociopolitical structures and impact participants over the metaphysical relations of levels of experience (cf. Adorno 2000: 1–20). Cinematic conditions have redirected the experiences of the twentieth century.

11 SERGE DANEY

Garin Dowd

Serge Daney is widely recognized in his homeland as the most important French film critic after André Bazin. In a career devoted to criticism for *Cahiers du cinéma* and later *Libération* (where his remit widened to include other forms of journalism), including a key period as editor during the transition from the journal's French Communist Party and then Maoist phase beginning in 1973, Daney also held a lecturing position for a spell at the University of Paris III: Sorbonne Nouvelle. He was a significant public intellectual and featured in several documentaries, including Claire Denis' film *Jacques Rivette – Le veilleur* (Jacques Rivette – the night watchman; 1990). From 1985 to 1990 Daney presented a programme on cinema on the radio station France Culture. Following the publication of a book on Haitian politics in 1973 under the assumed name Raymond Sapène, Daney's journalism was collected in several volumes. He left *Libération* in 1981 to establish *Trafic*, a journal that, since his death from Aids in 1992, has continued his legacy. The only book-length English translation of Daney's writings to date – *Postcards from the Cinema* (2007) – is of the posthumously published *Persévérances*.

Ma page, c'était comme un film [My page was like a film].
(Daney 1999: 108)

The importance of Serge Daney's book lies in the fact that it is one of the few to take up the question of cinema–thought relations, which were so common at the beginning of reflection …, but later abandoned because of disenchantment.   (Deleuze 1989: 312 n.39)

Serge Daney was not a film theorist; nor was he a film critic in any ordinary sense of the term. Rather, he was engaged from the beginning to the end of his career, as Jacques Rancière asserts, in writing about "des actualités du cinéma" ("current cinema events") (Rancière 2001b: 142).[1] In the course of this project, which generated a substantial output, Daney would attract philosopher readers, invoke philosophical referents and make a significant contribution to the canon of philosophically minded writing on cinema. Daney's preferences in terms of philosophers are clearly signalled in his disdain for the *nouveaux philosophes* of his own generation, notably Bernard-Henri Lévy (often referred to as BHL). In his essay "Les Loges des intellectuels" (which plays on the title of a 1987 book by Lévy) Daney identifies BHL as a media phenomenon within a specific and mutating social, political and cultural context in France and beyond (summed up by Daney in the title *Les Fantasmes de l'info* [Information fantasies]), wherein the performance or *mediation* of intellectual, conceptual, political and military labour came to replace that labour itself (Daney 1991a: 141). During the 1980s his references to such contemporary thinkers as Gilles Deleuze, Jean Baudrillard, Jean-François Lyotard and Paul Virilio multiply. In particular, devoting a favourable book review to Deleuze's *Cinéma I: L'image-mouvement* (Cinema I: the movement image; 1983), Daney reciprocates the mutual admiration that would lead to an extended virtual dialogue (Daney and Deleuze met only twice) in the 1980s. He is, in this sense, partly located in that intellectual legacy known as *la pensée mai 68* against which the *nouveaux philosophes* such as BHL and Luc Ferry (also disparaged by Daney) would position themselves. The temptation to categorize Daney, however, should be tempered by the sort of caution commentators often exercise when approaching André Bazin, the thinker of cinema to whom he has often been compared. There is no overarching system and, although Daney was a meticulous tracker of his own career development, by his own account he reserved his capacity for systematic thought for reading others rather than for organizing himself.

As someone who spent most of his working life as a journalist, for Daney the speed of journalistic journey from conception to delivery meant, in Emilie Bickerton's words, an "absence of piety or permanence" (2006a: 11). This context continues to deliver its divided posterity in anglophone and francophone critical circles, respectively. In France he is lionized and his reputation as one of the central figures in what Philippe Roger calls *"la pensée-cinéma"* (cinema-thinking; 1991: 199) is cemented by his reception in philosophical and theoretical circles to the extent that, writing in a special issue on Daney of the journal *Trafic*, Sylvie Pierre can refer to "a certain hagiographic pedestalisation of Serge" in these milieus (2001: 22).[2]

THE CINEMATIC CENTURY

Daney belongs to the second generation of post-war *cinéphiles* brought up on the programming of Henri Langlois at the Cinémathèque Française. When, in response to a question by Roger, he states that little by little his generation realized that the history of the century *was* the cinema (1991a: 101), Daney makes one of the most condensed statements regarding his philosophical position on cinema. The latter is not to be thought of as detached from a supposed reality, from which it maintains a distance sustained *inter alia* by means of "escapism", idealism or abstraction. Rather, cinema offers an account of the century, and is, in some sense, to be thought of as an *embodiment* of it. In terms of political events, it is Roberto Rossellini's *Roma, città aperta* (Rome, open city; 1945) that performs the key role for Daney. Filmed in the year of his birth, 1944, that is, in the year the Nazi concentration camps came to the attention of the world, for Daney the film contributes to the dawning realization by his generation of the legacy to thought and artistic expression of the Holocaust. In this respect, if one is attempting to extract a narrative of Daney the film thinker, it will have to be in close proximity to the personal account that either Daney gave himself or was delivered by those drawn to him as a kind of guru of cinéphilia. In particular, when this "orphan" – Daney never knew his Jewish father, who was deported during the Occupation and presumably died in the camps – views Alain Resnais' *Nuit et brouillard* (Night and fog) in 1959, he realizes he could, conceivably, be viewing footage of the corpse of his own father. The event galvanized his Bazinian side: "I discovered cinema's capacity to say: this took place", he states in his interview with Regis Debray on the television programme *Océaniques* (Daney 1999: 38). The commemorative and archival function attributed to cinema also explains in part the virulence and relentlessness of Daney's later assaults on the aroma (memorably characterized as "*vichyssois*"; Daney 1991c), that he detects in Claude Berri's 1990 film *Uranus* and in Marc Caro and Jean-Pierre Jeunet's *Delicatessen* (1991). The famous polemic against the former was launched in *Libération*; at the time Daney would record the feeling of having been insufficiently supported by those he felt close to intellectually and politically (2007: 124). From the point of view of placing his position in the context of a broader intellectual framework in French philosophy, Daney himself notes that the foundations of his distaste for this aroma were laid by Michel Foucault's response to Louis Malle's *Lacombe Lucien* (1974) (in tandem with Cavani's *Il Portiere di notte* [The night porter; 1974]), which appeared in 1974 in *Cahiers du cinéma* during Daney's tenure as editor.[3] His disdain for the films of Marcel Carné and René Clair is in part founded on the analogy, in his extension of the Foucauldian commentary, whereby: "France is occupied and the studio represents the Occupation in the field of cinema" (1999: 40).

DANEY AND *LA PENSÉE MAI 68*

Cinéphilia for Daney is therefore always informed *and* qualified by significant political events. As he began to develop his voice as a film critic in the early 1960s, foremost among these was the banning of Jacques Rivette's *La Religieuse* (1966), which Daney cites as being responsible for his first politicization (Daney 1983: 150).[4] Also crucial is May 1968, including the "*affaire* Langlois".[5] The foundations thus laid, the single most defining characteristic of his generation, for Daney, seems to be less May 1968 itself than its aftermath. This aftermath is to be characterized by *expérience* (both experience and experimentation). Daney adds that rather an art that was *engagé* (politically engaged) in the Sartrian sense, what he had in mind was a combination of "drugs, travel, mysticism, political engagement, the couple, all self-dispossessions, the dandyism one sees in Eustache for example" (Daney, with Garrel 1991b: 59). Daney's own trajectory exemplified this aesthetics of existence: at this juncture, having abandoned his own and only attempted foray into film-making, he was active on the fringes of the Zanzibar group.[6] The group, centred on the editor Sylvina Boissonnas – later a key figure on the women's liberation movement – was dedicated to a profound disruption of the conventions governing cinema that would in its ambitions exceed the innovations and iconoclasm of the Nouvelle Vague (French New Wave) directors and some of their contemporaries. Experimentation on all levels was undertaken, including making films while using narcotics (as was the case with Philippe Garrel's

La Concentration [Concentration; 1968a] and *Le Révélateur* [1968b]), the eschewing of credits, improvisation based on minimal scripts and self-"distribution" – aside from some festival screenings, projection was limited to Langlois-programmed screenings at the Cinémathèque – and the rejection of linear narrative.[7]

TASK OF THE CRITIC

In a neat summation of his intellectual and ideological trajectory as a thinker of the image, Daney's response to the Gulf War as televised spectacle in 1991 was, by his own account, originally forged in embryo in reading Rivette's article "De l'abjection" on a film by Gillo Pontecorvo, *Kapò* (1960), for *Cahiers du cinéma* in 1961.

There Rivette had made a striking assertion of the intersection of technical, formal and political concerns that would remain a mantra for Daney until his death:

> Just look at the shot in *Kapò* where Riva commits suicide by throwing her-self on electric barbed wire: the man who decides at this moment to track forward and reframe the body in a low angle shot – carefully positioning the raised hand in the corner of the final frame – deserves only the most profound contempt.   (Daney 2007: 18)

Regardless of the political motivations of Pontecorvo (which Rivette notes are not themselves at stake and to which he may even be largely sympathetic) or his director of photography, in its abject surrender to the irresistible reframing, the film produces an interpretative quiescence and ethical short-circuit.

BAZIN AND HIS OTHERS

It is hardly surprising to note that Daney's writing is at its most polemical in the imme-diate aftermath of May 1968. Daney's points of contact with the thinking of Bazin, and with cinema itself (including his own abandoned film, rendered meaningless by *les événements* – the political events of May 1968 in France), are marked, as we have already observed, by the crucial events of May 1968 and it is in the immediate after-math of this that he formulates in print his response to Bazin, most prominently in the 1972 essay published in *Cahiers du cinéma*, "The Screen of Fantasy". There Daney challenges the Bazinian insistence on the integrity of the screen world, famously illus-trated in Bazin by the question of the presence of a dangerous wild animal and a human being in the same shot, versus the creation of the idea of their co-presence by way of editing. Bazin favours the former over the latter for its capacity to facilitate a better imprint of the material world within the cinematic frame. Daney takes Bazin to task for thereby (in a very Derridean formulation) "interning difference in self presence" (2003: 33). The integrity of frame and screen is not allowed to be compromised in Bazin's humbling of montage: "the screen, the skin, the celluloid, the surface of the pan, exposed to the fire of the real and on which is going to be inscribed – metaphorically and figuratively – everything that could burst them" (*ibid.*: 34–5). Daney, however, would later acknowledge and praise Bazin for his elevation of the non-human. This most supposedly anthropocentric of theorists had a hand in theorizing from an "other" point of view. Jacques Lacan, whose thought assisted Daney in his relentless taxonomies of three, would ultimately help Daney to square the two Bazins.

IMAGE, TECHNIQUE: *CINÉ-JOURNAL*

Daney contributed to *Cahiers du cinéma* during its French Communist Party and later Maoist phase but was also instrumental in the dismantling of this ideological apparatus in 1974 once he took on an editorial role whose guiding precept was the abandonment of the aspiration to create "un grand front culturel à la chinoise" ("a great cultural front Chinese-style") (1999: 91). In Daney's understanding of the "critical function", first outlined in the programmatic essay published in *Cahiers du cinéma* on his assumption of an editorial role in late 1973, criticism comes into its own when there is a *décalage* (discrepancy) between those who make images and those who observe them. The intervention of the critic should take place and occupy some of the space every time these two are not exactly facing each other (*ibid.*: 210). Among the essays from Daney's 1980s journalism that exemplify such a function, "Zoom interdit" (collected in the volume published as *Ciné-Journal*) arguably deserves to be as well known as Roland Barthes' rather more famous analysis (dating from 1957) of the front cover of *Paris Match* as put forward in "Myth Today" (Barthes 1972). The television representation of the public display of mourning and the posthumous decoration of fifty-eight French soldiers killed in 1983 in Beirut may be short because of the genre restrictions (journalistic reporting), but is nonetheless remarkably incisive. Daney's adherence to the insight, which he attributes to Godard, that *film is becoming television*, enables him to read in a television programme the moment when the programme-maker has no choice but to confront, in a self-critical, self-analytical manner, his own medium. The brief for the programme-maker would have been, he argues, to avoid anything that would detract or steal from the display of sobriety, grandeur and unity, and one of the techniques used is the specific trick of television: the zoom in. The absence of this modern device means that, in Daney's pithy formulation, "They filmed in 1983 a scene from 1883" (1986: 186).

Another review (from 1982) that retrospectively takes on a particular importance in following the development of Daney's thought in the *zappeur* (remote) era is of Francis Ford Coppola's *One from the Heart* (1982).[8] This text is important for its emphasis on a mannerist wave of US cinema, of which Coppola's film is regarded as the vanguard. Coppola, Daney argues, shows how "the never seen too quickly becomes the already seen" (1986: 123). In mannerist cinema, as defined by Daney, *nothing happens* to the characters; instead everything happens to the image. The decor and the characters do not belong to one another; they do not, unlike in Vincente Minnelli (a constant reference point for Daney in this decade), have the same weight as one another. The camera is in the sky, the characters in the rain, as the review puts it. Coppola, for Daney, films the Vietnam War "like a sequence of numbers at a musical revue" (*ibid*.: 125). He has the very Minnellian idea not to break the illusion but to multiply it. This leads logically to *One from the Heart*. The setting, Las Vegas, Daney argues, being the most false city in the US, becomes less false in being replicated by a zoetrope set: "Less multiplied by less equals more. False multiplied by false equals true" (*ibid*.).

As suggested by the fact that Deleuze provides a foreword to *Ciné-Journal*, the thinking of Daney at this time is very close to the author of *Cinéma I* and *Cinéma II*; close, then, to the Deleuze who would write a chapter on "The Powers of the False" for the second volume, in which we read: "contrary to the form of the true which is unifying ... the power of the false cannot be separated from an irreducible multiplicity" (1989: 133). Arguably, however, Daney's thought at this juncture chimes, more generally, with contemporary conceptions of postmodernism (as in the statement that video is a way of seeing the image as future anterior; 1986: 125) and theories of the hyper-real, associated with Lyotard and Baudrillard, respectively. The writings show traces of an emerging interest in the media complex beyond cinema, as in the statement "The image is (thanks to video) 'well treated' while the actors are (because of video) 'under surveillance'" (*ibid*.: 125), and it is not for nothing that Jonathan Rosenbaum recalled in a letter written in 2000 that Daney was one of the first and most rigorous thinkers to attempt to theorize the difference between film and video (Rosenbaum 2001).

DEVANT LA RECRUDESCENCE DES VOLS DE SACS À MAIN

Cinema, for Daney, should speak to our present condition (Rancière 2001b: 142). He was not of the view that the only readings of films were those locked in their historical period. The later reception of an old film was as worthy of discussion as contemporary responses. The film is not locked in to its original horizons. As he put it, writing on the re-release of the long version of Rivette's *L'Amour fou*, "Films, like paintings, move. And we, like films, also move" (Daney 2002b: 307, my trans.). One of the surprises for those who knew of Daney as the ultimate cinéphile was his year-long chronicle for *Libération* of his television viewing, later collected as *Les Fantômes du permanent*. Despite his trenchant criticisms of the society of the spectacle, and his insistence that television was part of the media complex (to adopt Virilio's term) that deprived us of images proper and replaced them with cliché, Daney approaches the task of reviewing films on television in a manner notable both for its eclecticism (Sylvester Stallone competes for attention with Luis Buñuel, for example) and its ability to reflect on effects produced by the specific form of viewing that is television broadcast.

In this connection, films are said by Daney to fall from the sky to television. This – highly Godardian – metaphor is designed to indicate a reduction in scale and in power (linked to his understanding of the art-historical period known as Mannerism), but also to gesture towards a theological dimension: films "sanctify" television, or at least this is the case when those films are by someone such as Luchino Visconti. Television, for Daney, has no between spaces; it deals only with a kind of toxic continuity. In this context *Diva* (dir. J.-J. Beineix, 1981) is an example, for Daney, of a mutation whereby aesthetic values of television infiltrate cinema and turn it into merely an enfeebled subsection of a voracious and pervasive media complex. The film flits about between objects and functions but forgets that there are *betweens* (Daney 1991a: 48). We did not need Jean-Jacques Beineix to give us this, however, as, after reviewing René Clair, Daney comes to characterize him as the grandfather of the "clip" (*ibid.*: 52).

Later, in his first text to be published in *Trafic*, Daney returns to the difference between Beineix and Carax. Today, he reflects:

> our rendezvous is not with the films, but with the sociological "happening" constituted by the encounter between product and consumer … A way of writing that takes these proceedings into account will have to be invented. A magazine is needed which would conduct traffic, as it were, among these singular figures and alien landscapes. (1991c: 44)

In his ongoing attempt to refine and define the critical function in a mutating media complex, Daney goes on to ask, "The question posed by these torpid times is, in fact, what can resist? What can withstand the market, the media, fear, cynicism, stupidity, indignity?", suggesting that there are two ways, one of them – echoing and transposing the ideas of Maurice Blanchot on literature – taking the shape of a resistance of the work in the film, a mode exemplified by Rivette (*ibid.*: 45). With Beineix and Annaud a pair of fish in hypermediated flux of the "ère du vide" ("the era of the void"), this leaves, for the Daney of 1991:

> Wenders and Carax. What resists in them? Not the work, not the cinema, not the artist, but an idea common to all of these, the idea of an image. A single image. An image that is just, finally becoming "just an image" … His lovers of the Pont-Neuf will be saved if the girl has time to offer the boy an image of himself which will reverse their common destiny … It is this sketch … which must become the "hero of our time" image: the one which must redeem its model. (*Ibid.*: 43)

The difference comes down to a particular ethics of cinema, which is inseparable from the technological prosthetic sensory apparatus on which it rests, and which his admiration for Rivette's response to *Kapò* would remain the touchstone.

Daney would agree with Vivian Sobchack that cinematic and electronic technologies of representation are "concrete and situated and institutionalized" (Sobchack [1994] 2004: 138). To take up the terms of reference of Sobchack's 1994 analysis, the differential is to be located in *transmission* in the electronic domain and *projection* in the cinematic. While for Raymond Bellour the television image can only ever be a ghost or a trace of what might have been cinematic, for Daney it offers a way to articulate a difference at quite a distinct level. Television is to be thought of not in terms of its deficiencies. Rather, it should be thought of in terms of its "perfections". The perfection derives from the absence of the *décalage* identified by Daney. This is what the artist François Bucher, taking Daney together with Deleuze and Giorgio Agamben, identifies as the "technical eye" of television. "The perfection of television has no supplement, no space for thought, no remainder" (Bucher 2005: 13): this, for Bucher, is one of Daney's most prescient formulations.

Daney had, in the course of his analysis of the 1985 television coverage of *Live Aid*, directed particular derision at "a dissolve [that] makes the dying and the famous dance together" (Daney 2007: 34). Fast-forwarding to another era in television coverage of war or disaster, Bucher asks how to resist the embedded reporter of our day. The pixellated image that the latter brings to us from the desert is absolutely available and resolutely meaningless (Bucher 2005: 11). It *tele-programmes* us, or formulates us as viewers from its "afar", which has collapsed into what Virilio calls telepresence. Writing from a Daneyian perspective, Bucher suggests the impossibility revealed, in reality television, of the *pre-televisual*: "At [*sic*] the end television always gets the distressing shriek of feedback, even when it places its subjects in the middle of the African wilderness" (*ibid.*).

DISJUNCTION OF SOUND AND IMAGE

The *Kapò* moment (technology and politics combine in what Rancière would call a *partage du sensible* [distribution of the sensible]) is also influential, this time in a more positive context, in Daney's reading of Robert Bresson's film *Le Diable probablement* (The devil probably; 1977). Here a technical decision – postsynchronization – becomes an ontological statement (2001c: 479). The influence of structuralist and poststructuralist philosophy on his mature thought may be seen in his attribution of a post-human quality to the "population" of Bresson's cinema. This is manifest only in part in the prominent role given to animals in his oeuvre – a point to which another of Daney's most famous essays, on Bazin and animals, returns – but is accounted for more generally by Bresson's orientation away from character as such; these are disposed of by "random, heterogeneous system of sounds", he writes, with reference to the cacophony of multi-layered sound in Bresson's sound mix, which places in dissonant arrangement the sounds of an organ and a vacuum cleaner (hence his essay title). Within such a set-up the "human encounter is hopelessly inadequate". Instead of being located in a character, in Bresson's cinema the voice is subject to what Daney calls "the Bressonian logic of sonic bodies" (*ibid.*: 477). Like many poststructuralist thinkers influenced by psychoanalysis, for Daney "the voice involves the entire body" (*ibid.*: 478).[9]

Bresson reverses the traditional metonymy of voice and body, unhinging the voice so that it becomes dislocated from the relation. In this respect Daney positions Bresson in a surprising lineage – surprising only for the reader unaware of the esteem in which the compared artist is held at *Cahiers du cinéma* (and by none more than Daney) – by stating that the director insists in realism in sound, and in this respect is like Jacques Tati (whose films and on-screen tennis, in the guise of M. Hulot, were both points of reference for Daney) (*ibid.*: 479). The realism in question has less to do with perhaps expected understanding of synchronized sound. This, in fact, would not amount to realism in Daney's sense. For, as he explains, the voice involves that which cannot necessarily be seen; in this context the reliance exclusively on post-synchronization, for

Bresson, facilitates the representation, or perhaps the presentation, of the aspect of the voice that makes it at once materially present but not visible or locatable, not anchored to a location in the frame (*ibid.*: 479). Bresson, in Daney's analysis, thereby contributes to what one of his models as a critic – Blanchot – described in the pithy formulation *"parler ce n'est pas voir"* (to speak is not to see). Bresson mounts his own challenge to the hegemony of the eye.[10] In a distinction that recalls aspects of Barthes' differentiation of a normative "pleasure of the text" and a transgressive *jouissance*, Daney identifies an out voice and a through voice (*ibid.*: 482). In the out voice, cinema fetishizes the emergence of the voice from the lips, from which, in his Lacanian formulation, the *objet a* separates. By contrast, the through voice renders the body in its opacity, where it functions as a stand-in, often filmed from behind. Such a voice tells the viewer: do not look for the originating locus of the voice.

This essay takes its place in a mini-pantheon of contributions by French theorists, among them Michel Chion and Pascal Bonitzer, to our understanding of sound, a pantheon that has the same Bresson film often in its sights. It would prove immensely influential on Deleuze, whose discussion of the "sound-image" in *Cinéma II* (especially in chapter nine) returns repeatedly to Daney, to whom he attributes in particular the theoretical innovation of returning sounds and images to their bodies. More generally, several chapters from the second half of his book take a significant part of their underpinning from Daney's thinking of cinema (in particular as this developed in his two allied "pedagogies", those of Godard and Jean-Marie Straub and Danièle Huillet, respectively), and might be regarded as the philosophical equivalent of Godard's on-screen tribute "from Diderot to Daney" (as the phrase appears in Godard and Anne-Marie Miéville's *Deux fois cinquante ans de cinéma français* (Twice fifty years of French cinema; 1995) and Godard's own *Histoire(s) du cinéma* (1988–98).[11]

ENDS OF CINEMA

For Deleuze, there is a combination of philosophical reflection and poetry in Daney's writing. This is abundantly evident throughout his oeuvre but might be exemplified in the extended metaphor (in response to a book by Gilles Lipovetsky) by means of which he produces an impressive montage of the 1980s at the end of that (and his own final) decade. This is a decade that is characterized by flux on every level: in finance, labour and the image, to name but three. It is a decade in which it was crucial to know how to swim (Daney 1991a: 162). The collapse of the Eastern bloc was under way; the maritime space that Virilio wrote of in relation to a "dromocractic" mutation in respect of ideas of location and circulation in the "fleet in being" (Virilio 1986: 40) of nuclear submarines produced a (perhaps surprising) context in which to contrast the contemporary cinema of Luc Besson and Nanni Moretti. Daney reveals himself as very close to Deleuze when he writes that a new hero emerges within this sea of images. In his *Grand Bleu* (The big blue; 1989) Besson in particular invents a "self-legitimating automaton" (*automate autolégitimé*) (Daney 1991a: 163), who dives into the big blue of the film with nothing to assist the viewer in the task of seeing. All that has happened is the elaboration of a "promoter's film" (*ibid.*). The film creates no *décalage*; by contrast, Moretti's *Palombella Rossa* (1989) is a cinema where the space of disjunction is manifest: "the natural habitat … of scintillating interfaces", in which the film creates a "dribble", testifies to the fact that, as Daney puts it, for Moretti it is important to note that "to float is still to work" (*ibid.*: 164–5).

In 1991, as the era of information made a rapid assault on the *zappeur*, the first Gulf War prompted the month-long series of essays by Daney and Paul Virilio writing in alternate entries for *Libération* (Virilio 2001a). It led Daney to formulate, in particular, a distinction between the image and the visual.[12] In the important essay "Montage obligé" (Montage obligatory; in 1991a; 2006), Daney argues that the war coverage was not coverage of a battle but of a victory. It gives us a world overdetermined by the logic of the one. It does not elicit montage from the viewer – it is a world without others. In this sense, in Daney's words, there is no Baghdad beneath the bombs.

Daney's importance for a thinking of the contemporary, abundantly demonstrated by more recent wars, continues to be signalled by appraisals such as those of Rosenbaum, whose review of the two-volume *La Maison cinéma et le monde* appeared in the *New Left Review* (Rosenbaum 2005), and Maurizio Lazzarato (a former activist in the Italian Autonomia movement), who cites Daney's theories of communication in support of his argument in "Strategies of the Political Entrepreneur" (Lazzarato 2007).

Daney was alert to the fact that his writing had philosophical underpinning. He stated that:

> between literature and philosophy (the essay) … Each article sketched something rough of a global nature, of which it contained the seed – and which would never come (because I have a systematic mind only to understand others). It is something eternally lacunary but which, in the end, wound up consisting. (Roger 1991: 221, my trans.)

There is a hint of Blanchot in this, an echo of the latter's notion of the work registering its lack of integrity on the author's self-evacuation from its orbit (Blanchot 1993: 54).[13] If one looks at the conceptual frameworks adopted in the late essays on Benetton advertising (Daney 1996) and the valedictory "Tracking Shot in *Kapò*", not only is the overlap of life and work – already endemic in a self-proclaimed *cinéfils*-critic – thoroughly in evidence, but it might be said that Daney came to bring his own writing on cinema to rest in an act of separation. It was of course in these late writings that he separated himself from the *maison cinéma* and positioned himself, with some bitterness but not resignation, in the *maison* of the mediated (and dislocated) world, the world picture in Heidegger's formulation.

NOTES

1. In 1974 the problem is formulated as follows: "How to contemplate a *critical and theoretical* journal, if not in terms of its capacity to respond, with its own weapons, to the issues raised by the ideological conjuncture and the struggles going on there?"; S. Daney & S. Toubiana, "Cahiers Today", in

Cahiers du Cinéma – Volume IV: 1973–1978: History, Ideology, Cultural Struggle, D. Wilson (ed.), 47–55 (London: Routledge, 2000), 53.

2. There are signs that the situation in anglophone circles is undergoing a shift. Romney, Darke, Rosenbaum and Martin, each in roles as film critics, have signalled their admiration for and advocacy of Daney in anglophone film journals and magazines. The translations of several of his articles in volumes III and IV of *Cahiers du cinéma* have been available since 2000. His belated but still frustratingly piecemeal recognition as a key thinker of the French post-war period (abetted by Deleuze's seal of approval) is signalled by the inclusion of an essay from his *La Rampe: Cahiers critique 1970–1982* (Paris: Gallimard/Cahiers du cinéma, 1983) in *Literary Debate: Texts and Contexts*, D. Hollier & J. Mehlman (eds) (New York: New Press, 1999). At the time of writing eleven arguably major essays have been translated, albeit not always in widely accessed publications. Since 2002, however, there has been a trickle of articles in English on Daney. His inclusion in *The French Cinema Book*, M. Temple & M. Witts (eds) (London: BFI, 2004) is significant, while the efforts of translators and in particular a blog devoted to keeping track of Daney in English run by Laurent Kretzschmar (http://sergedaney.blogspot.com) and the advocacy of the online journal *Rouge* (www. rouge.com.au) edited by Adrian Martin have continued to raise awareness. It is worth noting in passing that most of the contents of *La Rampe* have now been published in individual and scattered translations.

3. In his four-part velvet revolution essay on "La Fonction critique" published in *Cahiers du cinéma* from late 1973 and at intervals over the next twelve months, Daney would emphasize the importance of this response. The essay was an attempt to further the exploration outlined in an editorial of the need to differentiate, in a highly Foucauldian formulation, *statement* (what is said) from *enunciation* (when it is said and by whom); S. Daney, "The Critical Function", in *Cahiers du Cinéma – Volume IV: 1973–1978: History, Ideology, Cultural Struggle*, D. Wilson (ed.) (London: Routledge, 2000), 56–7).

4. As Emilie Bickerton, in one of the very few articles in English on Daney to date to be published in an academic journal, puts it, "The critical function, as Daney defined it, was thus the result of the disjunction between the first enchantment with cinema, the pure gaze, and the later sixties suspicion"; E. Bickerton, "A Message in a Bottle: Serge Daney's 'itinéraire d'un ciné-fils'", *Studies in French Cinema* **6**(1) (2006), 9.

5. For an account of both the banning of *La Religieuse* and the "*affaire* Langlois" see A. de Baecque, *Histoire d'une revue, tome II: Cinéma, tours, détours 1959–1981* (Paris: Éditions Cahiers du cinéma, 1991), 173–83.

6. Daney described his film as a "very masochistic short" rendered "ridiculous" by the events of May 1968; *Postcards from the Cinema*, P. Grant (trans.) (Oxford: Berg, 2007), 49.

7. See Garrel's contribution to "Quatre manifestes pour un cinéma violent"; N. Brenet & C. Lebrat (eds), *Jeune, dure et pure! Une histoire du cinéma d'avant-garde et experimentale en France* (Paris: Cinémathèque Française/Mazzotta, 2001), 298. A year before he died Daney conducted an important and revealing interview with Garrel, who is declared the most important film-maker of his generation (Daney, with Garrel 1991b: 58).

8. The "*zappeur*" is another of Daney's ways of characterizing himself in the 1980s, the beneficiary of a "*salaire du zappeur*" (a play on the title of Henri-Georges Clouzot's *Le Salaire de la peur* [The wages of fear; 1953]) paid by *Libération*.

9. Compare, for example, R. Barthes, *The Grain of the Voice: Interviews 1962–1980*, L. Coverdale (trans.) (New York: Hill & Wang, 1985), 182.

10. In his text "On Salador", Daney had quoted Derrida on photology and developed an argument about the hegemony of the eye; S. Daney, "On Salador", in S. Daney & J. P. Oudart, "Work, Reading, Pleasure", in *Cahiers du Cinéma – Volume III: 1969–1972: The Politics of Representation*, N. Browne (ed.), 306–24 (London: Routledge, 2000).

11. Two essays on Godard and Straub-Huillet (both in *La Rampe*) are important for their sketching out of the notion, which Daney himself later realized was quasi-Deleuzian, of images that achieved a density, opacity and potential for disjunction; *Devant la recrudescence des vols des sacs à main: Cinéma, télévision, information (1988–1991)* (Lyon: Aléas, 1991), 124.

12. Daney writes: "The visual is the verification that something functions. In that sense, clichés and stereotypes are part of the visual"; "Before and After the Image", in *Documenta X: The Book: Politics Poetics*, C. David & J. F. Chevrier (eds), 610–20 (Ostfildern: Cantz, 1997), 616.

13. The Blanchot reference is apposite. Daney reprinted Blanchot's 1950 essay "La Condition critique" in the second number of *Trafic* and refers to his writings, both fiction and critical, on several occasions. See, for example, the reference to the hero of *Thomas l'Obscur* (Daney, *Postcards from the Cinema*, 126).

12 JEAN-LUC GODARD

Zsuzsa Baross

Jean-Luc Godard (b. 1930) is a founding member, with François Truffaut, Jacques Rivette and Eric Rhomer, of the French New Wave movement in the 1950s, strongly influenced by the theoretical writing of André Bazin and the critical pedagogy of the founder of the Cinémathèque, Henri Langlois.

A continued experiment and innovation on film and video, the massive corpus of Godard is often discussed in four distinct periods. Works before 1968 (*Pierrot le fou*, *Week-End*, *Le Petit Soldat*, *Bande à part*, *Vivre sa vie*, etc.), despite their dark themes, are an exuberant celebration of the cinema. Under the radical influence of revolutionary movements, the spirit of 1968 and the Vietnam War, works after 1968 (*Le Vent d'est*, *One Plus One*, *Gay savoir*) set out to find, and reflexively critique, forms of direct political engagement. Godard forms the Dziga Vertov Group (*Struggles in Italy*, *Vladimir and Rosa*), collaborates with the Maoist film-maker Jean-Pierre Gorin (*Tout va bien, Letter to Jane*). In the third period, Godard retreats from the cinema: in collaboration with Anne-Marie Miéville, he turns to video and creates for television a series of complex visual essays on communication, the family, childhood (*Six fois deux/Sur et sous la communication, France/tour/détour/deux/enfants*). In the last melancholy phase in the 1980s, which also includes the massive *Histoire(s) du cinéma*, Godard returns to the cinema with profoundly philosophical and self-reflexive works (*Passion*, *Allemagne année 90 neuf zéro*, *In Praise of Love*, *Notre musique*), all marked by the sentiment that cinema failed to fulfil its role.

Godard's critical writings on the cinema from the period 1950–67 are collected in the book *Godard on Godard* (1968; published in English 1972). Godard's thoughts on the history of film are in the book *Cinema* (in conversation with Youssef Ishaghpour, 2000; published in English 2005).

PARADOXES

The most prodigious and prodigiously creative among the *auteurs* of the New Wave, if not in the whole short history of the cinema, Godard, or rather his cinema, is also the least known, seen, screened and, perhaps, understood. "I am an exile from the world of the cinema", he says of himself in one of the many films in which he appears in person (1982b). Yet his rich body of often difficult works constitutes a cinema – and I use this term as Godard himself prefers it, inclusive of writings, works on paper, the innumerable projects never to be realized, essays on film and video, works that pre-date the invention of found-footage – a corpus that is most self-conscious. Self-revealing – but this narcissism is intrinsic to the medium – it never ceases to turn back on to itself: show itself, give away its secrets. (Already in the much-celebrated sequence in *À bout de souffle* [Breathless; 1960], alone in the stolen car, Michel Piccard [Jean-Paul Belmondo] turns to speak directly to the camera.) If Serge Daney, the critic and theorist, speaks of a "Godardian pedagogy", it is because Godard's cinema makes itself visible, exhibits itself as cinema, as the *work* of the image – which may explain the unhappy experience of the common spectator, who, for the love of illusion, *unlearned to see* precisely the image. ("Ils ont désappris de voir", says one film [1988–98]; "when did the gaze collapse?" asks another [2001]).[1]

This self-consciousness is irreducible to a late or post- modernism, and is not confined to self-disruptive, deconstructive gestures, ubiquitous throughout his work, mocking the conventions that maintain the illusion of reality in narrative cinema. With Godard, rather, the question animating André Bazin's writing – "What is cinema?" – becomes a quest, a mission and a *permanent* problem (as the revolution was believed to be permanent) for the cinema itself. Despite Daney's reference to pedagogy, the uninterrupted turn to the medium is not didactic but purely cinematic. A *geste* in and by the cinema, it does not interrogate, reflect on or define what Erwin Panofsky called the "unique and specific possibilities of the new medium" (Cavell 1971: 30, paraphrasing Panofsky);[2] it rather creates them, creates them by actualizing them. Just like Cézanne, Godard no doubt knows very well that what is possible for the cinema "cannot be found except in the work at which he is at work" (Blanchot 1955: 246). The "true cinema", "our cinema", he whispers and covers his eyes in *Histoire(s) du cinéma* (hereafter *Histoire(s)*), has nothing to do with the "movies of Saturday": "already forgotten, still prohibited, always invisible – such is our cinema. One never saw it, one had to love it blindly, by heart" (3B).

In the work, and this is its postmodern dimension, the medium folds on to itself, becomes its own reflection or mirror image, perhaps a *crystal*, in Gilles Deleuze's definition of this term. But in between its (many) sides, and the adverbial phrase is a key operator in his work – in between sound and image, image and writing, voice and text, music and sound – something other than the disruption of the medium, the exposition of the machinery of the work in the work takes place: on a wholly other plane, there emerges a new creation and a pure film effect – Godard's cinema, which cannot be filmed. If it is also the most beautiful cinema in the world – it can bring "tears into the eyes," says Alain Bergala, one of the few connoisseurs of his work – it is because it actualizes a "faculty" that paradoxically is both intrinsic to the cinema and a pure creation (1999: 240). A form unique to the cinema, "seul le cinéma" ("only the cinema"), claims a chapter title in *Histoire(s)* (2A). At the same time, the beauty of this creation is impossible to dissociate from the condition – the malaise – of the cinema, in which the work is inscribed, which it diagnoses, laments and mourns: namely, the failure of the cinema to fulfil its role,[3] its refusal and/or forgetting that it is made for thinking, is an instrument of thought – in short, the disappearance (not the death) of the cinema.[4] If Godard's work situates itself at the limit of this failure ("I have shown and lived so many times this impossibility";

Godard 2006: 348), if it is cinema (always *cinema*) that retraces the retreat, mourns the forgetting of the cinema, it is also a cinema that does not (aspire to) negate or overcome, and even less so to replicate the latter. It converts it rather into the hollow ground of its possibility.

FORM

The question of the cinema for Godard is one neither of representation (of the world or the real or society or man) nor of narration ("Una storia! I need a story", cries out the unhappy producer in *Passion*). It is a question of thought "under a certain form of the visible". In a letter to Freddy Buache, he writes of one of his plans (one of many never to be realized) for a "film of pure thought, where pure thought is pure spectacle" (Godard 2006: 348). In his *JLG/JLG – Self-portrait in December* (hereafter *JLG/JLG*), in *Histoire(s) du cinéma*, among other places, he insists that the medium is a "form of thought, or rather, a form that thinks" (Godard 1995).

But the thought of what? To what concept of thought does the form cinema correspond? Printed in red on black screens of *Histoire(s)* is the prose poem, the threefold complication (folding) of Bazin's question: "What is cinema? / Nothing / What does it want? / Everything / What can it do? / Something" (3A). The three couplets delineate a field: in between "nothing" pre-established and "everything" desired, Godard's cinema gives birth to "something" new – a form that thinks, that is, itself is creative of something. For thought, and here Godard comes ever so close to Deleuze, does not represent or illuminate or reflect on the meaning of something that is. Just as philosophy's creation, the concept, the form-cinema is formative; it creates a possible world. (In the extraordinary film and crystalline structure *Scénario du film "Passion"* [1982b], Godard says that to create a scenario is to create not a world but the possibility of a world, which then the camera will actualize.)

MOVEMENT

In the limited space of this chapter I can approach this notion of a form that thinks, which I will do from the direction of movement, only with the aid of the following guiding hypothesis: it is movement that links the cinema to thought. Or to phrase this same proposition differently, in so far as the cinema is a form that thinks, it is also a quest, or as Godard himself would say, a "prayer" for movement ("make a camera movement, as if you were in prayer"; Godard 1982a). Thought and spectacle meet in the dimension or register of the movement each effectuates, and therein lies not their identity but profound affinity. In this register (which is temporal, not spatial), image and thought communicate or, rather, mutate, ex-change, metamorphose into one another, incessantly. Deleuze spoke of the "image of thought". On the reverse side of the thought that is image we will find, and this is my hypothesis, the form of the image that thinks.

But how are we to conceive this movement, as that which may or may not happen but on which everything depends? As something precarious – sought, awaited, hoped for, but never guaranteed? Analogous to the "radical incertitude" of which Blanchot (1955: 245) speaks as the work's work that escapes the one who creates it?

In the field of thought, there are familiar examples: Deleuze admires the speed with which Bergson's thought moves from one plane to another, from simpler to more complex formulations, crossing the interval that this very thought cuts into the fabric of thought. But we need not go further than Deleuze: he transports Bergson's three propositions on movement (indivisible, a mobile cut in duration, an expression of change in the whole) to the plane of the cinema, where he recapitulates them as the three aspects of the movement image (Deleuze 1986: cf. chs 1–4).

But how are we to conceive movement in the cinema as that which is wished for but may never take place, for it is not (a) given and may not be given by the cinema as apparatus? Is not the movement of the image (in the apparatus), or the movement (represented) in the image, or even the movement-image a temporal perspective, a mobile cut in duration?

With respect to thought, we may say that it moves or is not thought at all. The linguistic equivalent of non-thought is propositional discourse: dead blocks of mortifying phrases that firmly hold to their fixed stationary places, anchored as they are to their absent referents. Thought, on the other hand, is interior to discourse and passes (takes place) in between phrases. (Space does not permit me to cite here some of Derrida's most spectacular virtuoso passages, which rely on trajectories opened by language's metonymic chains, but the examples are well known [Derrida 1998].) Indivisible to stations, steps or elements, thought *is* the leap over the hiatus it opens, the indivisible movement (*élan*) of its passage. An analogy with the sense of the cinema – the "child born of montage" – already suggests itself, "the *coupling* of the first and the second element will be visible only in the third" (Godard 2006: 199). What we may take away from the movement of thought is that it must take place, or it is nothing. In so far as it is movement, it is not represented but present in the present tense. It is this quality of presentness, rather than presence, of taking place in the present, on the screen, that we must also look for in Godard's cinema.

EXCURSUS: GODARD, THE PAINTER

In the documentary film *La sociologie est un sport de combat* (dir. Pierre Carles 2001) we witness a curious scene and a precise symptom of Godard's condition in the world as exile: we are in the sociologist Pierre Bourdieu's office when a package arrives by messenger from Godard. Is it *Histoire(s) du cinéma?* Bourdieu does not tell. He opens the envelope and, while musing to his companion, perhaps a graduate student, "All this is mysterious. I do not understand a single sentence", he unceremoniously drops its contents in the waste-paper basket. In an interview, however, Godard recalls a more generous comment by Bourdieu, calling him a *painter*. This is a happy characterization, easy to embrace, even if Bourdieu may have meant to refer only to Godard's practice of digitally reworking images, borrowed and his own, often with bright colours (most spectacularly, perhaps, in the last part of *Éloge de l'amour* (2001), where images are being washed over with brilliant "chemical" colours whose fields shift and metamorphose, in the film's time, like the Northern Lights). But more significant than the digital brushstrokes, strikingly beautiful especially in the later work, is the *sense* of the image at work in the work of Godard. Whether a still life (a pair of domestic shoes set at the foot of his bed, a reading lamp in yellow competing with the twilight), or the famous cliché of the evening sky being traced by the white chalk of a jet liner (in *Passion* [1982a], for example, where it is filmed by Godard himself, with a camera especially designed for him), or that magnificent ruby-red robe in *The Bolero*, a film within a film (*For Ever Mozart*, 1996), spread out on a desolate beach in winter: an image by Godard bears the *promise* of happiness ("Oui, l'image est bonheur" [*Notre musique* (Our music), 2004]) – not ours, for it is indifferent, even oblivious of the subject. Hence its distance from that other cinema, which is about and for the desire of the subject and the subject of desire, whereas the force and (memory) work, but also the happiness of an image by Godard, are impersonal affects that bypass the subject.

The *geste* of this promise, we may say, is Godard's inimitable, ineffaceable signature: instantly recognizable without ever being the same, irreducible to something as predictable as "habitus", an image by Godard is testimony to a "vision". A glance has been cast on the world and extracted a singular image from it, which deserves the name – that is, is an image in so far as it owes nothing to its creator. Autonomous, it is something of the world, a phenomenon of nature – not the "snow flake" to which Bazin likens photography, but rather a force of nature, independent of the plans, projects, intentions of its creator (Bazin 1967: 9–16): in *Allemagne année 90 neuf zéro* (Germany year 90 nine zero; 1991), to give one example, an image as perfect as Vermeer's much-admired (by Proust, for example) *View of Delft*. The resemblance/remembrance is not by design, or imitation or allusion. It is anamnesis, the memory work of the image itself, which, according to the formula Godard borrows from Robert Bresson, recalls other images: inside the frame, Lemmy Caution (Eddie Constantine), the last secret agent, is seen moving away from us, crossing a frozen canal in Berlin. In the foreground, just as in Vermeer, a patch of yellowed winter grass covers an oval patch of dry land, in the distance, at the water's edge on the other side, tiny colourful figures are skating, and, even further, the contours of a red-brick building are outlined against the perfectly clear air rather than sky.

The same discerning eye is cast on the world of the image as well: photographs from the archives, innumerable clips and stills from the history of the cinema, Manet's paintings of modern life, Goya's prisoners, several works by Giotto, Rembrandt, Delacroix, and so on. In Godard's extraction and decoupage – the face of Kim Novak framed by the waves of San Francisco Bay (*Vertigo*, dir. A. Hitchcock, 1958), the skeletal hand of a Giacometti bronze, the angry face of an angel by Giotto, a horse's head by Ucello – the image is reborn. ("The order of the image is redemption" [*Histoire(s)* 3B].) Detached from its origin, it is no longer attributable; the question of origin simply falls away. (In the exhibition *Voyage(s) en Utopie* at the Centre Pompidou, Godard refused to identify the source for any of the numerous film and video clips that he simultaneously had playing on the tiny television screens placed all around on the walls of the exhibition space.) The three rough brushstrokes in blue, meeting in sharp angles, for example – which I think to attribute to Van Gogh's last work, with its inverted black Ws signalling rather than representing the black crows flying over the cornfield – the blue zigzag in Godard's extraction becomes an invocation. In chapter 3A of the *Histoire(s)*, it takes on the function of pure form, which metonymically links together as repetitions the tormented, martyred bodies in several distant images: a buckled corpse falling into a mass grave (documentary), another taken off the cross (gravure), a pair of emaciated legs of a half-naked prisoner in Dachau (filmed by George Stevens on 16mm film, in colour), an inverted W form, exposed from under a skirt, assaulted by a dog in the mud (Munk's *Pasażerka* [The passenger; 1963]), and so on.

The borrowed/extracted/reframed visions of another cinematographer or painter are often reworked, often simultaneously, often in the film's own time – their field washed over by colour and/or invaded by other distant images (the more distant an image, the more just is the idea). Pulsating, metamorphosing, invading, dissolving into one another, they yield a vision of an altogether different order, on another plane. The vision of no one, it is the pure work of the image.

But what is the significance of all this regarding the solidarity of image and thought?

First, movement (thought) passes by way of the image: it may be hoped for, even anticipated, but will not be preconceived first and actualized later. If and when it happens, if one image accords with another or others, when images contract to form something like a musical "accord" – it happens as if by miracle. *Histoire(s)* is entirely composed of such miracles (of montage). In one such magic (not an illusion of reality but the fraternity of fiction and the real), the window, whose dark secret a watchful L. B. Jeffries (James Stewart) tries to penetrate with the aid of the lens of his camera (*Rear Window*, dir. Hitchcock, 1954), holds not a domestic murderer but a youthful Hitler in its frame. "Signs among us", says one chapter title in *Histoire(s)*: the cinema does not read or interpret them, only registers and later projects them, as signs that have never been read or seen (which is proof of another "marvel": the cinema does not see what it looks at. "Ô quelle merveille que de pouvoir regarder ce qu'on ne voit pas" ["Oh the sweet miracle of our blind eyes"] [*Histoire(s)*, 1A]). It may be Godard who performs the coupling – Stewart/Hitler, the imaginary/the real, fiction/history – but it is an image (of Hitler) that spontaneously substitutes itself, slips into the place of another (a New York courtyard). Movement issues from within the space of the image; Godard is there only to witness it.[5] If it happens, it comes from the dimension of the unforeseeable (in another expression of Blanchot's "radical incertitude" of the future). If it does not, two images – mortifying "solitudes" – remain in indifferent contiguity, each fixed to its referent outside the frame.

Secondly, the thought of the cinema, of Godard's cinema, is not an abstraction. On the one hand, the "image is not born of a comparison" (*JLG/JLG*); on the other hand, the offspring of the montage that succeeds to bring together two distant realities ("the more distant, the more just" [*JLG/JLG*]) is not an analogy, allegory or metaphor giving expression to a concept or "idea" (Sergei Eisenstein's three rising lions standing in for the idea of revolution or uprising). When, again in *Histoire(s)*, Godard reworks three non-consecutive shots that he abducts from Hitchcock's *The Birds* (a cloud of black birds filling the frame and the sky; then, filmed from above [the sky], a column of terrified children fleeing from the birds – once towards, once away from the camera), the transport is non-linguistic, the movement(s) effectuated is (are) not in the direction of language or concept. Right on the screen, in the film's own time, the transfiguration(s) of the image take(s) place – in fact, of the whole film called *The Birds* – by way of the image. ("An image must be transformed by contact with other images as is a color by contact with other colors" [Bresson 1986: 9].) In one set of manipulations – multiple repetitions, redoubling, fragmentations, superimpositions, freeze-frame and so on – Hitchcock's originals are made to stagger and vibrate as if to the rhythm of the flapping of wings and the silent cries of the children below. In another, archival images of a single Second World War bomber both flash up between the fragments and are superimposed on, infiltrate, the now hysteric, trembling images of Hitchcock. In between the two sets of operations, in the flickering of their reciprocal after-image, the birds and the warplane trade places, without exchanging identities, without surrendering to a common meta-image (allegory or metaphor) their difference.

This is not a symbol or metaphor: of war in general, war as such. Nor is it a representation of one pointing to or finding the anchor of its support outside the image. An event of a different order, let us say provisionally (the reason for his caution will soon be apparent) an act of war, concrete and actual, takes place right on the screen, in the film's own time. This metamorphosis, moreover, is not the terminus of a thought (movement), as it would be in the case of metaphor or representation. It does not exhaust the capacity of the images to be affected by and to affect others. Godard often cites Bresson on this point: "if an image … will not transform upon contact with other images and other images will have no power over it … it is not utilizable in the system of cinematography" (*Histoire(s)* 1B; *Passion, JLG/JLG*; cf. Bresson 1986: 10). More receptive to contact, even more fertile after Godard's intervention (transfiguration does not give a new image; it maintains images in contact), the new sequence – for the sake of economy, let us call it Godard's *miniature* – gives birth to an open series of movements: expressions of the changes that transfigure relations in the whole.

In one direction, towards a cinematic past, the hystericized images of the children in flight activate the cinema's own memory, assemble in virtual montage with the countless images stored in the archive: columns of refugees fleeing a menace that arrives from the sky, in real and imaginary, historical and actual wars – filmed since the beginning of the history of the cinema, or perhaps of world history, as precisely this difference is blurred in our collective consciousness by the cinema.

In another direction, towards the future, projecting images yet to arrive when *The Birds* and Godard's little film are made, but since then played *ad nauseam* – exhausted, emptied of their force on our television screen – images of terrified New Yorkers fleeing from an enormous cloud of dust descending on the city, swallowing everything in its path, advancing like a tsunami with a terrifying speed.

PROJECTIONS

The cinema, as we know, not only screens but also projects. It screens images that themselves project, essentially two distinct realities: what cannot be filmed and what the cinema looks at but cannot see.

With respect to the first, what cannot be filmed is the purely cinematic, the pure film effect. This includes the *sense* of montage, the third element of Godard's celebrated formula: $1 + 1 = 3$, the *coupling* that appears in neither of its elements (Godard 2006: 199). "Montage, mon beau souci" ("montage my beautiful concern"), we read in texts, interviews and on the screen of *Histoire(s)*. But what could be the care of the one who is only a witness, a facilitator of the form? Not the fabrication of sense. As we said with regard to the *miniature* – and I will stay with this one example as space does not permit me to introduce others from the thousands of possibilities offered by the later work – the re-vision/perversion of Hitchcock is not in the direction of metaphor, allegory, nor in support of another interpretation of (the meaning of) the film. The *miniature* does not say: *The Birds* (dir. Hitchcock, 1963) projects not desire (the mother's for Mitch, his for Melanie, Melanie's for Mitch, etc.) but war. Instead, it *transports* Hitchcock's images to another plane, outside the field of interpretation and commentary; indeed, it itself constructs such a plane, is the creation of a possible *space* where the imaginary and the real show their "fraternity", without surrendering their distance (difference). Here the truth of one is neither subordinated to nor superordinates the truth of the other ("Equality and fraternity, between the real and fiction" [*Histoire(s)* 3B]).

So what sense is born of the fraternity of a hystericized imaginary (the birds' attack) and the archives (of a warplane)? Not yet another vision of war – so successfully fictioned, imagined and passively documented in and by the medium since the beginning. Whether fictional or real, war is always material, whereas the unfilmable of the *miniature* is immaterial sense (in another sense of this word), an affect that can only be projected: *menace* (just as Hitchcock's masterly *mise en scène* of the birds gathering in the schoolyard projects a temporality, *imminence*). Born of the coupling of the two *distant* realities, from the fraternity of killer birds and warplane, each operating on a different plane and maintaining their distance, is the *menace* of a catastrophe that arrives from the sky, from the dimension of the unforeseeable, and instantaneously changes: not the world but, as Karlheinz Stockhausen said so scandalously of 9/11, consciousness. In the film, it is the consciousness of birds. In the instant of recognition, which as always is delayed, an army of feathered weapons.

As it happens, the cinema and catastrophe share an anachronic dimension, a certain productive belatedness that is structural, which may explain their affinity. "One shoots today and projects tomorrow", says Godard of the cinema, whereas the disaster, and this is Blanchot's lesson, never takes place, "is always already past" (Blanchot 1986: 1). The traces of the one and of the other both become visible *a posteriori*, after the passage of another event: full-scale war in *The Birds*; the intervention in the dark room in the case of the cinema. The interval that separates the post-catastrophic present from the past will not be bridged or breached, just as the gap in time dividing the registration of the passing of the present and its projection as images will not be closed, as long as the image is by and of the cinema.

Visibility, appearance in the world in the phenomenological sense of the term, is an after-effect in both cases, a posthumous re-appropriation. This is precisely the manner in which Godard's little film transfigures, from a distance and long after *The Birds* is released in 1964, a crucial and very precise *mise en scène*, not included in the *miniature*: three quick shots in rapid succession – a gull in flight, the crash into Melanie's forehead, a gull flying away – which give the first air-borne attack by a solitary gull that draws Melanie's blood. To be sure, this short sequence, initially a freak incident, quickly forgotten, is already transfigured in the course of *The Birds*, whose narrative retrospectively recuperates it as the precise record of the invisible, the first sign (writing) of the disaster whose arrival remains *unseen*. But Godard's little film will transfigure this transfigured image: arriving from the future, it infects its pure timeless description of *menace*, which is at once imminent and already past, infects it with the *fraternity* of the birds and the plane, that is, the fraternity of the imaginary and history, of the cinema of Hollywood and the archives of history. This secondary transfiguration, which inscribes Hitchcock's imaginary in the time of history, turns the face of the latter towards the future, transforming it into a Cassandra face, a projective surface of the future.

The other reality concerns what the cinema does not see: "Signs among us". But Godard's *miniature* is also cinema. It projects but does not see that *The Birds* projects *images* of a future yet to come as memory. *Le Souvenir d'un avenir* (Remembrance of things to come), says the title of a film by Chris Marker and Yannick Bellon (2001). It traces *visions* (images) of a war yet to come inscribed in the photographs taken (registered as memory) by Denise Bellon years before the war. Now such a schism of time, as we learned from [Roland] Barthes, is structural to photography.[6] But the cinema is a projective apparatus. It registers first and projects later. One operation is separated from the other by an interval ("creative interval," says Deleuze) in a *relation* of repetition, *a posteriori* reappropriation. The projector does not hide what the "objectif", the lens of the camera, passively registers but does not see. *Cinematographic* projection is machinal: is a "machinism", as Deleuze says of the assemblage of movement-images that constitute the material universe (Deleuze 1986: 59). Constitutive of the apparatus cinema, it is the *dispositif par excellence* of the "signs among us", or what Benjamin calls the "secret historical index" inscribed on the interior of images. If they "accede to legibility only at a particular time" (Benjamin 1999a: 462), it is because they are missives from the past to a future or, better still, project the memories of a future yet to come.

Such is the nature of the cinematic apparatus that this projection itself can be archived (filmed). Godard's monumental *Histoire(s)* entails the production of precisely such an archive. In the case of *The Birds*, but also of Godard's own little film, the task falls on a third film-maker. With or without thinking with Godard, it is the found-footage film-maker Johan Grimonprez who, in *Double Take* (2009), develops this secret virtual correspondence, between *The Birds*, Godard's little film, and a future yet to come.[7] Grimonprez's own three-shot montage from *The Birds* shows with great precision that the images of 9/11 had been announced, were shown by Hollywood: from the close up of a dreamy Melanie crossing the bay (1), he cuts away to a slow panning shot of a jet liner in a distance, moving from left to right in the frame (2). Just before the plane would hit the tower, in view at the right-hand corner of the frame, Grimonprez cuts back to another close-up of Melanie (3), in the very instant that the seagull crashes into her forehead: entering the frame from left to right, the bird's flight seamlessly completes that of the jet liner in the previous image. The next frame (4) is not of the explosion, whose images will be recalled, projected by this montage – it is rather a visual echo of Blanchot's disaster: it shows from behind the behind of a very ordinary bird as it unceremoniously – perhaps indifferently would be a more precise word – flies away from the camera.

But to return to Godard, whose thesis is confirmed by both Marker and Grimonprez but finds a systematic demonstration only in *Histoire(s)*, if cinema is the prophet of the future, it is because "under a certain form of the visible" thought is (once again) a sort of anamnesis, an act of memory. This is not the form of memory (*Gedächtnis*) that is predicated on an archive, actual or virtual, Bergsonian or Platonic, which is then searched for a lost item, for a matching recollection, or a memory forgotten. It corresponds rather with movement, with the movements that characterize the form of memory for which English does not have a precise word: *ressouvenir* in French, *Erinnerung* in German, both of which preserve the memory of an act of repetition. A memory image surges up from the past and, just like the disaster, arrives from nowhere. This memory, however, does not imitate human recollection: the memory of the image is not of the world or the word but of other images. This is why under a certain form of the visible, thought will exceed both language and the "concept". It only moves towards language ("chemine *vers* la parole"; 1982a). However, in the case of Godard – but not for example of Harun Farocki's film essays or Péter Forgács' found-footage cinema – especially in the case of Godard, this thought is indissociable from an extraordinary aesthetic dimension, which is not the property or force of the image as such, the image *qua* image, but the singular force of Godard's cinema: "Yes, the image is happiness … and all its power can express itself only by appealing to it" ("Oui, l'image est bonheur … et toute la puissance de l'image ne peut s'exprimer qu'en lui faisant appel"; 1982a). The multiple affects it liberates or, to borrow another concept from Deleuze, the "percepts" it creates, are new every time, singular every time.

A field of such percepts, Godard's cinema will frustrate and escape writing every time – whether it hopes to speak for it, represent it or tries only to engage it.

NOTES

1. The eight-part video work *Histoire(s) du cinéma* was produced for ARTE, Canal+ and Gaumont between 1988 and 1998. It was followed by an edition of four volumes published by Gallimard, comprising a selection of video stills and excerpts from texts read on the soundtrack or printed on screen. The DVD edition by Gaumont, planned to coincide with the exhibition by Godard, *Voyage(s) en Utopie*, at the Centre Pompidou in 2006, appeared in the following year. References in the text are by chapter titles. Translations are mine.

2. See Stanley Cavell's discussion of this question (1971: 30). He paraphrases E. Panofsky, *Three Essays on Style*, I. Lavin (ed.) (Cambridge, MA: MIT Press, [1934–62] 1997).

3. "Le cinéma n'a pas su remplir son rôle", "le cinéma n'a pas joué son rôle d'instrument de pensée" ("The cinema did not know how to fulfil its role"; "the cinema has not played its role of an instrument of thought"); J.-L. Godard, *Godard par Godard*: volume 1, 1950–1984; volume 2, 1984–1998 (Paris: Éditions Cahiers du cinéma, 1998b), vol. 2, 335.

4. "Pas la mort, la disparition" (this untranslatable phrase plays with the two words French has to speak of death: "mort" and "disparition") (Godard, *Godard par Godard*, 409).

5. "C'est que c'est le film qui pense … il n'y a qu'un témoin de cette pensée. C'est ma satisfaction de faire du cinéma" ("It is the film that thinks … there is only a witness to this thought") ("Marguerite Duras et Jean-Luc Godard: entretien télévisé", *Godard par Godard*, vol. 2, 143).

6. For a discussion on the temporal dimension of photography in R. Barthes, *Camera Lucida: Reflections on Photography*, R. Howard (trans.) (New York: Farrar, Straus & Giroux, 1981), see my "Lessons to Live", *Deleuze Studies* (forthcoming).

7. The project in progress was presented by Johan Grimonprez at *Conférences – débats – rencontres*, Centre Pompidou, Paris, 4 June 2007), www.centrepompidou.fr/Pompidou/Manifs.nsf/0/8F8E01C1A1EF09CCC12572AA0032E572?OpenDocument&session M=2.10&L=1 (accessed July 2009).

13 STANLEY CAVELL

Rex Butler

Stanley Cavell (b. 1926) is an American post-analytic philosopher whose work crosses into aesthetics, literary criticism, psychoanalysis and film studies. After first teaching at the University of California, Berkeley, Cavell taught from 1963 to 1997 at Harvard University, where he became the Walter M. Cabot Professor of Aesthetics and the General Theory of Value. Chief among his philosophical works are *Must We Mean What We Say?* (1969), *The Claim of Reason* (1979) and *Philosophical Passages* (1995). Cavell has written a number of books on the New England Transcendentalists and the possibility of a distinctively "American" philosophy, including *The Senses of Walden* (1972), *In Quest of the Ordinary* (1988) and *Conditions Handsome and Unhandsome* (1990). He has also written three books on photography and film: *The World Viewed* (1971), *Pursuits of Happiness* (1981) and *Contesting Tears* (1996). More recently, Cavell has produced autobiographical reflection: *A Pitch of Philosophy* (1994). In retirement, he continues to write and publish prolifically, with *Cities of Words* (2004) and *Philosophy the Day After* (2005). Cavell has been extremely influential in American philosophical circles, with such thinkers as Hilary Putnam, Richard Rorty and Stephen Mulhall acknowledging his impact. He has also influenced a number of writers on the arts, most notably the art critic and historian Michael Fried and the film theorist William Rothman.

Cavell describes himself in interviews as an "ordinary-language" philosopher. He recalls that the decisive event in his intellectual life was his encounter with the English philosopher of speech acts J. L. Austin, when Austin came to Harvard in 1955 to deliver the William James Lectures. Cavell was at the time attempting unsuccessfully to complete his doctoral thesis, but it was only after hearing Austin that, as he says, "I found the beginning of my own intellectual voice" (Conant 1989: 36). The subject of Cavell's thesis, early versions of which formed his first book, *Must We Mean What We Say?*, is the question of how our words and actions mean. This was a common enough problem within post-Wittgensteinian philosophy, but Cavell brought a distinctively new approach to it. Breaking with the then-dominant idea that it would be necessary to reduce language to a set of unchanging rules in order to explain how it worked, Cavell proposed instead a series of what he called criteria or principles. As opposed to the philosophical ambition to answer the question in the abstract, Cavell insisted that the meaning of any particular word or action must be determined each time anew in different circumstances. Speech and actions follow, alter or even make up their rules depending on what they are wanting to say and to whom they are wanting to say it. The real breakthrough of "ordinary-language" philosophy as proposed by Austin lies in the attention it gives to specific cases of communication without seeking to generalize them. Each instance of communication is a matter not of obeying a pre-existing rule but of a negotiation with the prevailing conventions of language and the figuring out of a way to make oneself understood within them.

Understood in these terms, it is clear that from the beginning Cavell was already grappling with the problem of scepticism, which was to remain his principal philosophical concern for the rest of his career. Successful communication necessarily takes place against a background of potential misunderstanding or confusion: the inability to know or master the conventions that would allow us to say what we mean. The speaker cannot be certain that their words have conveyed the meaning they intended, that they have successfully communicated their message to others. But what they must do is to recognize or, to use Cavell's word, "acknowledge" those criteria or conventions that would help make them clearer and connect them to others. In the absence of normative rules that would tell them how to do this, they become responsible themselves for the way they mobilize the available resources in order to get their message across. And it is this their listeners respond to: not some unchanging meaning that remains the same in all circumstances, but the ongoing attempt to communicate in the always different circumstances they both inhabit. As Cavell writes of the experience of hearing another complain of pain: "Your suffering makes a claim upon me. It is not enough that I know (am certain) you suffer. I must do or reveal something. In a word, I must *acknowledge* it" (1969: 263). But, again, this doing away with certainty in communication also means that we can never be sure exactly what has been communicated. As Cavell brilliantly realizes, the desire that communication be certain is fundamentally no different from the sceptical complaint that communication can never be certain, that authentic communication never takes place. What both attitudes share, for all of their apparent opposition, is the assumption that communication is a matter of truth rather than, say, of meaningfulness. What both the sceptic and anti-sceptic do not see is that success and failure in communication cannot be separated: the failure to make oneself clear is not reason to give up but the very reason to keep on trying.

As Cavell's career continues, he progressively becomes more explicit about the social and political consequences of his argument. In his book *The Claim of Reason*, he disagrees with the common philosophical position that a proper morality must set out a code of conduct that is beyond dispute and that can be applied in all circumstances. On the contrary, for all of its seemingly apodictic quality, moral conduct is necessarily open to debate and disputation. We can still have an entirely acceptable morality, even though its rules and their application have not been absolutely determined. As Cavell writes: "Morality must leave itself open to repudiation" (1979a: 269). And in his later book *Conditions Handsome and Unhandsome*, Cavell finds the term "perfectionism" to speak of this project of the search for an always better morality, although he insists that the idea had been with him since at least *The Senses of Walden*. "Perfectionism" is, in fact, a doctrine associated with the nineteenth-century American poets and essayists Ralph Waldo Emerson and David Henry Thoreau, who founded the spiritual and philosophical movement transcendentalism in response to what they saw as Kant's dividing of the world up into the transcendental and empirical. In perfectionism – at least as seen through Cavell's eyes – there is a similar split in human beings, which might also be seen as that between acknowledgement and scepticism. And this notion of a constant search for shared criteria against the threat of dissension and disagreement has, as Cavell makes clear, political consequences. Emerson and Thoreau are the defining examples for Cavell of a distinctively American form of perfectionism: democracy. In democracy, we are always striving, against its inevitable failures and compromises, towards an increasing acknowledgement of the differences and idiosyncrasies of others. Indeed, democracy is the political system more than any other that operates as its own self-criticism, that is never achieved as such but exists only in process of its own endless testing and refinement.

For our purposes here, however, what is of most interest is the series of insightful and innovative readings of works of art that Cavell offers as a way of explaining his position. For Cavell, "modernism" in society and culture – a period marked in philosophy by Descartes' *Meditations* and in literature by the plays of Shakespeare – is a moment in which conventions in the form of tradition are no longer able to be taken for granted. In just the way that, Cavell argues, occurs in ordinary language, so in the arts after modernism individual artists in their works of art have to establish the criteria by which their work is to be judged in the absence of any universally agreed categories. In the essay "Music Decomposed" from *Must We Mean What We Say?*, Cavell addresses the problem of the potential "fraudulence" of so-called new music, in so far as without the recognized rules of tonality there is simply no way of knowing in advance what constitutes a successful piece of music. It is always possible that the composer has failed to communicate their intention, or indeed has nothing to say at all. This is also the problem raised with respect to the visual arts in the essay "A Matter of Meaning It". The artist must completely acknowledge, that is, is entirely responsible for, what they do in their work in the absence of pre-existing conventions that they can directly follow. But this does not mean – this is Cavell's objection to something like minimal art – that the artist can avoid or circumvent convention, which would be merely another form of scepticism. Rather, as Cavell puts it, "the task of the modernist artist, as of the contemporary critic, is to find what it is his art depends upon" (1979a: 219). Finally, in *Must We Mean What We Say?*, Cavell takes up these issues through a reading of two plays. In "The Avoidance of Love: A Reading of *King Lear*", he traces the tragic consequences of Lear being unable to acknowledge the love of his daughter Cordelia. And in "Ending the Waiting Game: A Reading of Beckett's *Endgame*", he examines the way in which Samuel Beckett's play dramatizes at once the irreducible ambiguity of everyday language and the equally irreducible desire to communicate despite this ambiguity.

Some two years after *Must We Mean What We Say?*, Cavell writes *The World Viewed*, which in some ways is an extension of the ideas addressed in relation to Beckett. Cavell makes the point with regard to *Endgame* that the characters in the play often point to the "theatrical" situation they find themselves in: they are on stage being beheld by an audience. Although this self-reflexivity, this drawing attention by the work to the medium in which it takes place, is what many critics mean by modernism, for Cavell something more is required. Indeed, this essentially sceptical understanding of the play is almost the opposite of what Cavell means by modernism. For while Beckett admits the theatrical set-up of his play, he ultimately seeks to overcome it by producing a situation in which there is no audience. Instead of directing attention to the barrier that separates actor and audience, the play attempts to do away with it or at least "extend" it, so that actors and audience, if only for a moment, share the same reality. Although Beckett has only the theatrical tools of scepticism at his disposal, his aim is for "theatre to defeat theatre" (1969: 160). And Cavell sees the same concerns played out in terms of photography and film in *The World Viewed*. To begin, unlike theatre, the viewer of a photograph or film is absent when the subject of the photograph or the actors in a film are present. They look on at a world from which they have been mechanically excluded. In this sense, as Cavell says, in a much-quoted phrase, film is a "moving image of scepticism" (1971: 188). The technical apparatus of both photography and film seems to correspond to the sceptical view that it is only through the denial of the human subject that the reality of the world can be achieved. And yet in the same way as Beckett, it is exactly through something like the admission of this scepticism, the essentially "selective" nature of reality, that they would also overcome it. Broadly sympathetic to the "realist" film aesthetic of such theorists as Rudolph Arnheim and André Bazin, Cavell argues that in the hands of the greatest film-makers events just appear to "happen", without having attention drawn to them by those cinematic devices that frame and make possible reality. In this way, the distance separating spectator and film disappears and both seem for a moment to be on the same side of the screen.

It is this same ambition of film to defeat scepticism that Cavell takes up in his later *Pursuits of Happiness*, one of the most inventive and enjoyable books on film ever written. In *Pursuits of Happiness*, Cavell identifies a series of seven Hollywood films made between 1934 and 1949 that feature in one way or another a couple in the process of separating and deciding whether to get back or a divorced couple having separated deciding whether to get remarried. In Frank Capra's *It Happened One Night* (1934), a journalist (Clark Gable) meets a society girl (Claudette Colbert) just after she has married, forcing her to choose whether she wants to go through with it. In Howard Hawks's *His Girl Friday* (1940), a newspaper editor (Cary Grant) attempts to get his ex-wife (Rosalind Russell) to remarry him while they work together on the story of an escaped murderer. In George Cukor's *Adam's Rib* (1949), two lawyers (Spencer Tracy and Katharine Hepburn) have to determine whether they want to remain together while they take opposite sides of a case involving a woman accused of shooting her husband. What is dramatized in each case is the ability of the couple in question to overcome the doubts they hold towards each other and form a lasting agreement, whose rules are not given in advance but have to be negotiated on a daily basis. This is why for Cavell is it always a question of *remarriage* or the decision to stay married. It is because with remarriage it is no longer a matter, as it is perhaps with marriage, of cultural habit or tradition but of what each party can make of marriage, what they can make marriage mean for both themselves and their partner. Remarriage, we might say, is the modernist state of marriage: it is an affirmation or acknowledgement that takes place only through and against a background of scepticism and prior disappointment.

In 1996, Cavell wrote the long-awaited follow-up to *Pursuits of Happiness*, *Contesting Tears*. In *Contesting Tears*, Cavell proposes an alternative dramatic possibility to that of the "comedies of remarriage", which he calls the "melodramas of the unknown women". Indeed, these melodramas operate, according to Cavell, as the "systematic negation" (1996: 115) of the comedies. In this cycle of films, it is a matter not of couples deciding to get back together, but of men and women remaining permanently estranged from each other. In the comedies, a series of unworldly or inexperienced women are educated by an older man, who in a sense takes the place of their father. In the melodramas, the woman is responsible for her own education or self-transformation, and the plot frequently revolves around the love between mother and daughter. No man is shown to be equal to the women in question, and they are destined to live alone and unacknowledged. In George Cukor's *Gaslight* (1944), Paula Anton (Ingrid Bergman) is driven mad by her husband's refusal to believe her and by his manipulation of the tokens of their shared reality. In Irving Rapper's *Now, Voyager* (1942), Charlotte Vale (Bette Davis) is shown spurning a number of apparently suitable suitors because at the deepest level none of them can recognize her for who she is. In King Vidor's *Stella Dallas* (1937), lower-class Stella Dallas (Barbara Stanwyck) is not only unappreciated by her upper-class husband, but she even deliberately seeks to alienate her own beloved daughter in order to produce a suitable match for her.

But, we might ask, what exactly is the relationship between the "comedies of remarriage" and the "melodramas of the unknown woman"? Some commentators have spoken of a "balance" (Eldridge 2003: 2) between the acknowledgement played out in the one and the scepticism played out in the other, but this is undoubtedly too simple. The first point to note is that the melodramas of the unknown woman *come after* the comedies of remarriage. Chronologically the two series of films virtually overlap, but within the logic of Cavell's analysis it is evident that the melodramas are a possibility inherent to the comedies that gradually comes to the fore as the genre develops. In the last entry in the series of remarriage comedies, *Adam's Rib*, Cavell will speak of Tracy's "villainy" and the film's quotation of melodrama; and the famous end to the film where Tracy says, in response to the question of whether the two sexes will ever understand each other, "Vive la différence!", might be seen to be a certain giving in to scepticism. And just as Cavell will at moments in *Pursuits of Happiness* speak of the way the remarriage comedies arise in response to female suffrage and the rising rate of divorce, so we might speculate that this shift from the comedies to the melodramas corresponds to the even greater independence of women and beyond that to the increasing cynicism and lack of belief that characterizes contemporary society.

However, for all of the obvious temptation to see the relationship between the two genres in this way, this cannot be the entire explanation. Even though we have the very strong sense – and he admits this – that Cavell could not have come to his insights regarding the melodramas except through the comedies, it is also true that these comedies themselves arise only in response to a prior threat of scepticism. The whole achievement of acknowledgement in the films, Cavell makes clear, would have no meaning outside the possibility that it might not occur. And, indeed, *Contesting Tears* is a continuation of Cavell's argument that it is not the final overcoming of scepticism that he wants, but a showing that scepticism must be taken into account within a wider economy of acknowledgement. That is, just as with Descartes, it is the admission of doubt itself that can become a principle of knowledge and conviction, if not truth and certainty. As Cavell will write of Greta Garbo, for him the greatest of the actresses of the genre of melodrama: "It is as if Garbo has generated this aptitude [for acting] beyond human doubting … so that the sense of failure to know her, of her being beyond us, is itself proof of her existence" (1996: 106). And, similarly, the point of Cavell's counter-intuitive reading of *Stella Dallas* as showing that Stella is well aware much earlier in the film than generally supposed of the effect her dressing is having on others is exactly a way of Cavell's recognizing a strategy on Stella's part that would otherwise have gone unnoticed, an acknowledgement that Cavell argues the film wants us to share.

In terms of criticism of Cavell, the most consistent line of argumentation against him has come not from analytic philosophy but from deconstruction. Drawing on Jacques Derrida's undoing of Austin's distinction between "serious" and "non-serious" speech acts, deconstructionists have argued that Cavell is ultimately unable to distinguish between acknowledgement and scepticism. Just as the non-serious, ironic or citational use of language is part of ordinary discourse, so the sceptical possibility always inhabits any acknowledgement. But this criticism would have to be understood very carefully, for Cavell does not obviously oppose acknowledgement and scepticism. Indeed, as we have seen, he sees the two as implying and unable to be separated from each other. Rather, the distinction between Cavell and Derrida might be put in the following terms: whereas in Cavell there exists, against the background of scepticism, the possibility of an act of authentic communication, in Derrida the authentic is inevitably accompanied by the inauthentic communication cannot in principle distinguish itself from what it tries to exclude. In Cavell, the conventions allowing a statement to be understood as intended can momentarily be settled, although they are constantly in the process of renegotiation. In Derrida, the conventions allowing a statement to be understood at the same time open it up to meanings never intended. As the philosopher Gordon C. F. Bearn writes: "The point of Cavell's work, its romantic goal, is to understand the conditions for the attainment of what Wittgenstein calls 'peace' … On the other hand, one face of Derrida's work, one of its antiromantic goals, is to understand the conditions of the impossibility of peace" (1998: 80).

Nevertheless, the more we look at the comparison between Cavell and Derrida, the closer they seem to each other. For it might be asked, against Bearn, is it simply the impossibility of "peace" that Derrida wants, and not also what makes it possible? And, likewise, is it not possible to read Cavell to be denying that we can at any moment separate acknowledgement and scepticism? In fact, pointing to the similarities between Cavell and Derrida, we might even reverse the usual deconstructive complaint against Cavell: it is not that Cavell does not sufficiently distinguish acknowledgement from scepticism but that *he does not even want to*. In a way, for all of Cavell's commendable stand against irony and lack of belief, he does not go far enough. There is still something in his work that is not acknowledged or taken account of. What could this be? It is not any new linguistic or artistic convention. As we know, Cavell proposes a "non-essentialist" notion of convention in which nothing is ruled out in advance. Nor is it simply some wider social or historical force outside language or artistic practice. Again, Cavell is right to argue that the shifting of conventions is not merely some intra-linguistic or intra-artistic game from which reality is excluded. The transformation of conventions *is* the way extra-linguistic forces register themselves on our lives. In a book like *Contesting Tears*, for example, Cavell is very particular to make the point that it is the felt "injustice" of the social situation of women that the films he is analysing are responding to, and that changes what can henceforth pass as a convincing depiction of the relations between men and women. (It is just this "injustice" that Cavell himself wants to rectify in his book by so dutifully acknowledging the work of female writers on film and by imitating what we must understand as a certain *écriture féminine* in his prose.)

It is neither any specific convention nor what produces changes in conventions that Cavell cannot account for in his work. It is exactly both of these that Cavell is wanting to capture by means of the ever-shifting relationship between acknowledgement and scepticism. It is rather what allows the space for this relationship between acknowledgement and scepticism, the social order in which it occurs and which for this reason cannot really be questioned. The comparison might be made here with the critique Slavoj Žižek makes of the work of such political theorists as Claude Lefort and Ernesto Laclau, who share broadly similar projects of hegemonic rearticulation, that is, the analysis of the essentially contingent master-signifier that binds together an otherwise heterogeneous series of ideological elements. Žižek's point against them is not merely to posit another master-signifier, but to ask what cannot be included within social space in order to allow this struggle for ideological supremacy. As he puts it: "How, through what violent operation of exclusion/repression, does this universal frame itself emerge?" (2008: 258). And the comparison with Cavell is even more pertinent, in so far as Lefort and Laclau too propose a kind of "radical" democracy, which cannot be realized and in which the position of the placeholder of power must remain empty. Democracy for Lefort and Laclau as well is utopian, transcendental, perfectionist. It lives on or is evidenced only in its failures or its own continual falling short of itself. But, if anything, we would say that Cavell, Lefort and Laclau are not sceptical enough here: for all of the doubts they harbour towards democracy, they do not seriously question its inherent perfectibility. To put it another way, although everything can be doubted in democracy, there is nevertheless one thing that cannot be: the very social space in which this doubt can be entertained and communicated to others. And this denial manifests itself in Cavell's work in the way that, as this activity of doubt is taking place, the social order is understood to remain unchanged. Cavell's work proceeds – this is its fundamental Cartesianism – under the guise of a provisional morality, in which public appearances are maintained while personal scruples are exercised. The "injustice" that Cavell identifies results only in the sort of private irony that he speaks of in *Contesting Tears* or the civil disobedience or withdrawal that he advocates in his work on Emerson and Thoreau. It is the traditional role of the philosopher as "gadfly": a permanent critic of the established order, but unwilling or unable to seize power themselves and ultimately acting only to rejuvenate the hold of those in authority.

It is something like this sense that the problematic of acknowledgement and scepticism does not go far enough that is to be seen in Lacanian critic Joan Copjec's extraordinary reading of *Stella Dallas* (Copjec 2002). In her reading, Copjec takes up the enigmatic and much-discussed last scene of the film, in which Stella looks on unnoticed through a window at the wedding of her daughter, a union that she has in effect allowed to come about by allowing her daughter to think that she has abandoned her. As Copjec explains, this extremely plausible conception of the film is to make Stella a *hysteric*. While endlessly complaining about the world, she remains secretly tied to it through her attempts to construct solutions to various problems, as though she had personally to make up for its failures. And this is in the end how Cavell sees Stella: like the hysteric, what Stella ultimately wants, for all of her apparent indifference, is to be recognized for the sacrifices she has made, if not by the world, then at least by the spectator. However, in her strong and uncommon reading of the film, Copjec argues that what the final shot of the film evidences is a *sacrifice* of this sacrifice, the giving up of the hysterical wish to have her self-sacrifice acknowledged by others (and this is part of Copjec's wider contention for the "absorptive" and not "theatrical" nature of the film, again implicitly against Cavell's reading of it as melodrama: that Stella wants to be part of the world and not to stand apart from it). Stella no longer believes that she is required to manipulate events from the outside or no longer acts with any sense that her actions will be registered by some Big Other. Instead, in Copjec's reading, she acts without any guarantee in the symbolic order, or she becomes this symbolic order itself.

It is perhaps in this light, finally, that we might look at a film like Lars von Trier's *Breaking the Waves* (1996), surely the great inheritor of the "melodramas of the unknown woman". In that film too, there is a kind of sacrifice of sacrifice, an acting beyond any recognition accorded to it by the one for whom it is intended. There is a certain "going beyond" of the whole problematic of acknowledgement, of the still necessary scepticism and distance towards the symbolic order that this entails. For the ringing of the bells at the end of the film is a kind of "answer of the real", in an overcoming of that mediation towards God that the official patriarchal religion in the film still requires. Instead, in that moment when the character Bess (Emily Watson) acts after she has been shunned by her community and when even her husband Jan (Stellan Skarsgård) has forsaken her, Bess in effect *becomes* God, directly embodies the symbolic order. She no longer is a hysteric or neurotically attempts to make up for the missing phallic power, but is a kind of psychotic, freely giving love without expectation of return. This perhaps what is also at stake in William Rothman's reading of *Psycho* (dir. A. Hitchcock, 1960) at the end of his *Hitchcock: The Murderous Gaze* (Rothman 1984). We might say that the passage from the "theatrical" to the "cinematic" traced in that book is a movement from the dialectic between acknowledgement and scepticism to a state beyond the symbolic. It is possible to argue, that is, that the well-known shot in the film when we see "mother" running out on to the landing from a bird's-eye point of view is meant to indicate Norman's (Anthony Perkins) identification with God – which is also his identification with his mother – as in that last shot from the sky in *Breaking the Waves*, in which we also impossibly hear God's voice. In both films, we no longer have a "sceptical" relationship to the symbolic order but a direct identification with the Other. And it is at this point that we see the limits to Cavell's problematic of acknowledgement and scepticism, his unspoken requirement that the place of the symbolic must remain empty in order for the social to remain possible, for that civilizing activity of doubt and the overcoming of doubt to still be possible.

14 JEAN-LUC NANCY

Claire Colebrook

Jean-Luc Nancy (b. 1940) is Professor of Political Philosophy and Media Aesthetics at the University of Strasbourg. He completed his doctoral dissertation in 1973 on Kant, under the supervision of Paul Ricoeur. In 1987 he received his Docteur D'Estat in Toulouse, published as *The Experience of Freedom* (1988; English trans. 1993). He has published more than twenty books on diverse topics of philosophy, including *The Speculative Remark* (1973; English trans. 2001), on G. W. F. Hegel, *Le Discours de la syncope* (1976) and *L'Impératif catégorique* (1983) on Immanuel Kant, *Ego sum* (1979) on René Descartes and *Le Partage des voix* (1982) on Martin Heidegger. Nancy has written a number of specific books on art and literature, such as *Les Muses* (1994), *The Ground of the Image* (2003; English trans. 2005) and a book on the Iranian film-maker Abbas Kiarostami, *The Evidence of Film* (2001). Other key works include *The Inoperative Community* (1982; English trans. 1991), *Being Singular Plural* (1996; English trans. 2000), *The Creation of the World or Globalization* (2002; English trans. 2007) and *Noli Me Tangere: On the Raising of the Body* (2008). Nancy has also collaborated with Philippe Lacoue-Labarthe on many works, including *The Title of the Letter* (1973; English trans. 1992).

The "and" of "philosophy and ..." is never a simple addition: never a question of having a fully formed philosophy and then proceeding to produce a philosophy "and politics", "and art", "and mathematics" or "and cinema". However one defines and practises philosophy will depend on how one creates links or relations to other modes of thinking. If one regards philosophy to be an enquiry into the universal, rigorous and formalized possibilities of thinking, then one will place formal knowledge and mathematics at the very heart of philosophy, and then establish relations with other manifestations of thinking and (possibly) doing (Badiou 1999). If, by contrast, one regards knowledge and action as possible only in certain historical and cultural contexts, and sees these in turn as effected through power relations, then philosophy is primarily politics. One would then read other forms of thought, such as art, through the lens of a philosophy that is attentive to power and the play of forces: "For politics precedes being" (Deleuze & Guattari 1987: 203). One of the ways in which continental philosophy, or poststructuralism, has been defined – especially on its own account and in relation to a history of metaphysics dominated by a striving for pure, present and unmediated truth – has been through the ideas of writing, language and structure. Such a genealogy is important for considering Jean-Luc Nancy's relation to philosophy, and the rela-tion he establishes to those other modes of thought concerned with images (such as cinema). If poststructuralism was dominated by an attention to mediating, differential and structured conditions through which presence was made possible, then Nancy could be seen to be post-poststructuralist, or post-deconstructive. The importance of cinema within his work would be more than that of an example or object considered *by* philosophy. Rather, the image, or the cinematic meditation on presentation, looking and manifestation is Nancy's response to the two philosophical problems that mark his corpus and that demand a radical reformulation of the very possibility of philosophy: the problem of phenomenology and the problem of deconstruction.

These two problems are at once the names of philosophical movements and the names of quite specific questions. The first is phenomenology (which includes both G. W. F. Hegel's phenomenology of spirit [Nancy 2002], and the twentieth-century movement running from Edmund Husserl and Martin Heidegger to the present). Phenomenology is not simply a movement or style of philosophy. It is an approach to philosophical possibility: philosophy is not some discipline or method added onto life. In so far as there is living, or the experience of being or existence, then there is something like manifestation or appearance. For Hegel it is naive or sensuous exist-ence that assumes that there is experience on the one hand, and then a world of external things or objects on the other. But, for Hegel, the next and inevitable stage of the world's appearance occurs when "we" realize that the external world is given only as it appears, in the form of images or as ideas. We then arrive at idealism: we only know the world as it is for us, never as it is in itself. Here, Hegel intervenes and argues that this sense that we are cut off from, or at one remove from, the world presupposes that there is a world that exists before all appearance and manifestation – before phenomena – and then there is the world after its appearing, as mere image or idea. Against this Hegel establishes philosophy as phenomenology or absolute idealism: there is not a world that then appears, for the world – what is – is *appear-ing*. The subject, or who "we" are, is not some being to whom or for whom the world appears; with philosophy as phenomenology we recognize that "we" are just this his-torical passage of the world's appearing, a passage that concludes with philosophical self-realization. It makes no sense to posit something that simply is – being – that would be absolutely in itself, and without relation; for the minute that we have any notion of being – that something *is* – then we are saying something about it, positing it, relating to it. There is not a being or existence that then relates to, or appears for, something like consciousness, mind or spirit. Rather, what is – being – is appearing, presencing, manifestation. This then means, in turn, that consciousness or spirit is not some contingent and particular substance that relates to the world in order to create an image of the world; as the medium that realizes the world as nothing more than images, consciousness *is* the world in its most proper appearing. Philosophy for Hegel is the science that comes to the realization that there is not the world on the one hand, and then knowledge on the other. The world is just that which comes to appearance and knowledge: knowledge of the world *as appearing* is consciousness, or what Hegel referred to as absolute idealism or absolute knowledge. This is not knowledge of some external and contingent outside, but knowledge that grasps that the world only is, and has being, in its coming forth in knowledge. Philosophy completes the world, brings spirit or consciousness and all that *is* to its highest and most self-conscious realization.

When phenomenology takes on its twentieth-century form, in Husserl and Heidegger, two key manoeuvres are undertaken that will be important for Nancy's understanding of philosophy and image. (Nancy will, though, remain Hegelian in his stress on a certain privilege of the image as idea – the image is that which gives forth the world and creates a relation between subject and object; the world is therefore *sense*, always given *as* this or that determined existence.) First, both Husserl and Heidegger rejected the primacy of consciousness or spirit in Hegel's phenomenology; both of their philosophical trajectories will result in a commitment to a being, existence or passivity that is beyond sense although known only through sense. Instead of arguing that the world is a process of appearing and becoming, with mind or consciousness being the point at which that process of appearing is reflected on and recognized, phenomenology "reduced" (Husserl) or "destroyed" (Heidegger) the notion of the subject. There is not a subject to whom the world appears, nor a consciousness or spirit that grasps being and becoming. Rather, there is appearing or revealing. Heidegger will therefore replace the word "man" or "subject" with *Da-sein*, "there-being" (Heidegger 1996) and define the world not as something that presents itself so much as a presencing that is given a "shining", "clearing" or word through the "dwelling" that "we" are (Heidegger 1971). That is, it is no longer possible to work with the normal subject–object structures of metaphysics or language; there is not a self to whom the world appears, not a "we" or humanity that must then come to understand itself and its world (Nancy 2000: 65, 71). Rather, there is a presencing, unfolding or appearing that we may passively witness or be affected by, even while all these terms of affect, active/passive, seeing/seen, suggest a self–world structure that is no longer appropriate if we aim to overcome the idea of a presence that is "in itself" and non-relational and that experience (also "in itself") must somehow bring forth as idea or image. Phenomenology is therefore an attention to appearing as such, without the commitment to a world, presence or real that would be before appearance.

Nancy's attention to images and his highly nuanced dedication to cinema are not, therefore, applications of philosophy *to* the image or the cinematic unfolding of a film's capacity to capture, display and mediate light. On the contrary, philosophy must always have been troubled by its propositional nature, its pronouncements *on* being, its statements about what is, and its assumption of a subject *who* philosophizes. And this problem for philosophy is also, in many ways for Nancy, the problem of the West, the problem of the world, and the problem of spirit: can it be said that there is a self or subject who then comes to experience a world? Certainly, in so far as there is a trajectory of monotheism – a trajectory that establishes a divine presence outside this world that would give the (absent, secret, hidden, unavailable) truth of the world (Nancy 2001: 32, 33) – then philosophy has been marked by "ontotheological" metaphysics. It has sought to give some truth or foundation to this world that appears, to establish a ground that can be grasped and held as true beyond, before or above images. Hegel wanted to establish one single history of philosophy as the realization of appearance; it would follow that art and religion would no longer be necessary in a world that had recognized itself as a process of appearing *as itself to itself.* For Hegel the images offered by art and religion are sensuous forms of what should properly be grasped, through philosophy, in concepts. Nancy, however, will carry the *phenomena* of phenomenology further: there is not spirit or consciousness to whom the world appears. There is appearing. Further, and far more importantly, there is no "we", "man" or clearing for whom, or through whom, the world appears. Rather, there are appearings, presencings, manifesations or disclosures, but these are never gathered, comprehended or exhausted by a single and fully aware consciousness. Nancy will therefore refer to dis(en)closure: no image is closed in on itself, and all disclosing is also a necessary limit or finitude that therefore also expresses other limited finite disclosures. On the one hand, it is not the case that there is a world above and beyond appearances: all there *is* is appearing. On the other hand, appearing is multiple, dispersed or dis-enclosed. That is, even if "we" can now abandon the idea of some absolute truth or presence beyond appearances, this does not mean that there is a "we" who can now recognize and master itself as the constructor or subject responsible for reality. Indeed, the "we" is itself for Nancy a dispersed, never centralized, never fully presented *inoperative* community, for the process of appearing to each other *that we are* is always open to what has not yet appeared, and there is no privileged or general community viewpoint that can grasp the whole (Nancy 1991). Cinema of a certain mode would therefore be one of the ways in which philosophy might overcome itself or realize itself *as phenomenology.* Nancy is not interested in those forms of cinema that are meta-cinematic, postmodern or critical. That is, he is not concerned with those moments in which there is, say, a film being shot within a film, or where characters are viewed in various ways as mediated images – in mirrors, through doorframes, reflected on surfaces or in photographs. Whereas Gilles Deleuze (1989) will privilege the cinema of Federico Fellini or Jean-Luc Godard, focusing on the scene of image production and the already-captured, screened and framed "shots" that any film-maker encounters before she begins to film the world, Nancy concentrates on a history of the world that is composed from a history of already frozen figures and types. This meta-cinematic style of cinema, in which the camera captures and re-presents the capacity for machines to produce images, is not the mode that Nancy presents as the cinema of a world that is in itself, and properly cinematic. Indeed, a certain notion of cinema that has been privileged in film theory – in which images are seen as simulacra (or copies/doubles of which there is no original) – consecrates a line of thinking that Nancy's work refuses to indulge:

> Cinema becomes the *motion* of what is real, much more than its representation. It will have taken long for the illusion of reality that held the ambiguous prestige and glamour if films – as if they had done nothing but carry to the extreme the old mimetic drive of the Western world – to disappear, at least in tendency, from an awareness of cinema (or from its self-awareness) and for a mobilized way of looking to take place. (Nancy 2001: 26)

Going to the very genesis of the phenomenological project, committed to the immanence of what appears without positing a foundation or being that would be the hidden truth of appearing, Nancy argues that a cinema of *evidence* is the best way in which thinking today can consider its own possibility. In his book on Abbas Kiarostami, Nancy (2001) acknowledges that while the films he is celebrating include images, such as torn photographs, portraits and television screens, this is not because all we have are mediated, doubled, created and secondary simulations of a reality that is never given in itself. On the contrary, reality is cinematic (*ibid.*: 14, 15). It is through the experience of cinema, and cinema *as experience* – the exposure of the viewer to the unfolding of images, and images as the very mobility of a world given in light and in the gaze – that "we" finally come to terms with Being: "The reality of images is the access to the real *itself*" (*ibid.*: 16, 17). Being is not a presence that is then given in re-presentation. And "we" are not some collection of subjects who must either find each other through experience, or experience through images. On the contrary, for Nancy, cinema helps us to work through and beyond a philosophical language and tradition that has posed false problems, such as the problem of how we come to know the world, or how we come to know each other, or even how we come to know ourselves, how the "I" comes to know itself. More importantly still, he rejects the twentieth- and twenty-first-century fetishization of the radical otherness of the other; this, he insists, follows only from a subject who constitutes himself from himself and in himself, and then is required to recognize the integrity of the other whose presentation will always belie and transgress their ipseity (Nancy 2000: 77). All these problems reach their limit in Hegel, for whom the self is at once established in relation to the other but who also arrives at a moment of the end of philosophy and community where relations of otherness are recognized as such in a final reflexive whole. For Nancy it is this striving for a system that recognizes and regards itself *as a system constituting itself* that, after Hegel, is opened through the necessarily fragmentary nature of the artistic image. As image the art object is essentially poetic, a created and detached existence that is no longer at one with its originating intention, the art object is also fragmentary, not in being a part of some completed whole, but only in its partiality. Considered in terms of contemporary aesthetics, then, Nancy insists that art is neither the figural revela-tion of a sense that could be given conceptually, nor a pure affect or sensibility that is radically other than sense. At the heart of Nancy's philosophy is a non-philosophical refusal of the distinction between form and matter, or meaning and singularity: it is not the case that there is a presence before all relations, and not the case that we live a world of singularities through processes of mediation and concepts that belie the world's intrinsic singularities; for Nancy the singular is given in relation, and rela-tions are always those of sense. The given is given in this particular relation, *as* this revelation, and is given elsewhere, otherwise in a different relation. This means that instead of cinema or art focusing on the system of mediation through which we know and image the world, cinema presents the world as in each case given in its own way, through this "here and now" relation of regard or evidence. Cinema that approaches reality as something essentially ungraspable and as existing beyond a world of signs and images within which we are imprisoned has not had the courage that Nancy celebrates in contemporary cinema. Rather than regarding the image as mediation, cinema begins with evidence: Nancy is indebted *that* the world presents itself, that being is there to be attended to, regarded, gazed on. Further, it is this experience of evidence that allows cinema to capture the truth of the world as image: that is, truth is not given *through* images. In the beginning is the image. This is to say, too, that there is not a self who experiences others, or even itself, through presenting an image of itself to itself, as there would be in those theories focusing on auto-affection (where identity is established by taking up a relation to oneself mediated by an image). For this would imply that there is initially a potentiality for relations – something like a consciousness, spirit, or being – and then the creation of a relation (an experience of otherness), and then a return where the self recognizes itself as constituted and lived through otherness. Nancy criticizes this primacy of the self, being or consciousness through two philosophical terms that trouble the very language of philosophy: "being singular plural" and "with".

Both of these terms not only provide a way for thinking philosophy differently in its response to cinema – by not imposing a philosophical method on the reading of cinema – but also demand a thought of the very possibility of cinema alongside the possibility of philosophy. For it is the very style and project of Nancy's philosophy that renders philosophy in its usual manner utterly impossible. If philosophy constitutes itself as the question of being as such, before any specific predication or particular being, then Nancy's response to that question is non-philosophical and, more importantly, cinematic. There can be no definition of being, not because there will always be a truth or ground of being that is hidden from the world of dispersed, multiple and singular images to which we are exposed. There is just this plurality of beings. This plurality is always given in singular, finite and dispersed images. This leads Nancy to attach a particular importance and sense to the notion of "with", which functions as a primordial term in his philosophy at the same time as it undoes the very possibility of philosophy: it is not the case that there are beings who then exist "with" each other, nor an overarching Being (such as community, humanity or even substance) that accounts for some whole within which singular beings are placed. In the beginning is the relation of "with", and there are neither beings *who* relate, nor a being that is related:

> Since it is neither "love," nor even "relation" in general, nor the juxtaposition of in-differences, the "with" is the proper realm of the plurality of origins insofar as they originate, not from one another or for one another, but in view of one another or with regard to one another. An origin is not an origin for itself; nor is it an origin in order to retain itself in itself (that would be the origin of nothing); nor is it an origin in order to hover over some derivative succession in which its being as origin would be lost. An origin is something other than a starting point; it is both a principle and an appearing; as such, it repeats itself at each moment of what it originates. It is "continual creation."
>
> If the world does not "have" an origin "outside of itself," if the world is its own origin or the origin "itself," then the origin of the world occurs at each moment of the world. It is the *each time* of Being, and its realm is the *being-with* of each time with every [other] time. The origin is for an by the way of the singular plural of every possible origin.   (Nancy 2000: 82–3)

These two notions – "being singular plural" and "with" – are at once the consequence of Nancy pushing his phenomenological philosophy to the point of deconstruction and a formation of a mode of deconstruction that is distinctly different from that of deconstruction's usually recognized inaugurator, Jacques Derrida.

Derrida also, like Nancy, begins from a commitment to philosophy as phenomenology: his first works on Husserl focused on philosophy's attention to grounding conditions, to pure truth, and to a refusal to accept any term as a foundation without giving a rigorous justification. Derrida, however, found this founding condition of philosophy to be both necessary and impossible. Necessary: all philosophy, and all experience in so far as it is experience *of* some world (and therefore "intentional") that aims at the revelation of presence. Philosophy's commitment to pure truth, presence and origins is therefore a hyperbolic extension of a possibility of all experience that, Derrida argues, opens to the infinite. However, such an opening to the infinite, or an experience aiming at a complete and full presence, is made possible only in finite conditions that render pure truth and presence impossible. Derrida will refer to this coupled possibility/impossibility as "writing" (as well as trace, *différance*, anarchic genesis, untamed genesis and a series of other terms): presence can only be experienced as determined, delimited and temporally located; but such a process of determination is possible only through traces that themselves cannot be presented or mastered. The condition for presence is itself unpresentable, and the task of philosophy (to ground itself and master itself) will always depend on finite, material and ungrounded/ungrounding events. For Derrida this results ultimately in a mode of deconstruction that is directly disruptive of phenomenology's commitment to presence. The lived, the present and the "now" are always haunted and disrupted by that which can never be lived; a certain death, non-presence or monstrosity occurs "beyond" or "before" all our meaningful notions of time and space. Derridean deconstruction, not surprisingly, has no direct relation to visual media or philosophies of the image. Indeed, in his writings on the work of Nancy, Derrida is insistently critical of Nancy's seeming return to a phenomenology of *touch itself*, and of Nancy's presentation of *the* sensible. This is because Derrida regards that which is touched, presented, seen or lived *as such and in its immediacy* as always already mediated.

Nancy, by contrast, makes several detours with regard to deconstruction by returning to phenomenology, going beyond deconstruction and, in ways that are problematic, exiting philosophical metaphysics in favour of "cinematic metaphysics". On the one hand, by *deconstructing* Christianity, Nancy argues that the idea of a divine, infinite, all-creating and absolute God who reveals himself in and through the world necessarily brings about its dissolution. Whereas pre-Christian pagan gods were within the world, and divinity was among and alongside the beings of this world, the Christian God is an infinite and absolute origin and source of revelation. This brings about a problematic trajectory: if God were truly infinite and absolute, then there could not be anything *other than* God; for that would set God apart from creation, thereby rendering him finite, and placing him in relation to what is not God. To carry the logic of monotheism to its conclusion, then, there cannot be an infinite that is *other than* the finite. Rather the infinite "is" only its revelation or dispersion in finite beings. Whereas Derrida insists on processes of trace, mediation and spacing that themselves are beyond all revelation, Nancy argues that there is only revelation, only presence, only this singular, finite and plural being: no infinite Other, or revealing origin beyond that which is always already originated, and which gives the birth of the world anew in each of its appearances. The deconstruction of Christianity is not, as it would be for Derrida, the marking out of a necessary impossibility, or a double bind: it is not the philosophical solicitation of a presence that can only show itself through that which remains absent. In this regard, Nancy marks a return to phenomenology, for he stresses the immanence of evidence and presentation, and insists that there is nothing other than the given (even though the given is never fully given, or intimates a further unfolding beyond this present). But this "return" to presence is also the sense in which Nancy is *post*-deconstructive, for he no longer accepts, as Derrida would do, that philosophy is a necessary impossibility at the very heart of experience. The very affect of experience – of feeling, touching, seeing or *being* oneself – requires, for Derrida, a relation to oneself, and therefore a medium, detour, gap or delay through which any being becomes present to itself. There is no touch *as such*, or touch in general, for every experience of touch has to be marked out, mediated and traced in the finite, even though this condition for thinking and living the finite is – according to Derrida (2005) – infinite. Mediation entails, always, a philosophical disturbance of any supposed pure immediacy, and precludes what Nancy would celebrate as an experience, evidence or disclosure that is no longer subjected to anything other than its own revealing and the relations it generates from itself. Christianity, for Nancy, not only *can* be deconstructed, but also must inevitably arrive at its deconstruction and does so – effortlessly – in cinema. Cinema does not come as some sort of technical intrusion into the world – mediating, representing or copying a world that otherwise remains present and within itself. On the contrary, the world *is cinematic*, and we come to realize that it is so, today, with cinema, and specifically with cinema of a certain type (non-narrative, non-postmodern or meta-cinematic cinema). When cinema becomes cinema in its proper mode, which for Nancy (2001: 38, 39) occurs when the camera dwells with a respectful gazing that allows the world to present itself in evidence, or in its singular presentation, then we arrive at Christianity's deconstruction. The divine is neither a part-intrusion into this world (as with pagan gods), nor a visitation by some force beyond this world: for the world is the totality of revelation, and is so only in so far as it reveals itself – because finite – as always more than its already pregnant presence (*ibid.*: 36, 37). Derrida, who insisted on radically non-living forces beyond all opposition between life and death, also understood images and the visual as essentially *blind,* as enabled only by a marking out, spacing or relation that could itself never be seen or touched (Derrida 1993). It is in response to Nancy's stress on touch itself, or the sensible itself – the singular that gives itself in finite relation – that Derrida (2005) responds by problematizing the notion of *touch in general*, or "the" singular. For Derrida, to speak or gesture to such a singular force as *the image* or *evidence* is to take up a relation towards that posited presence; it is, however falteringly, to determine, mark out and delimit that which cannot – for Derrida – present itself. There is no self-presentation without a detour through mediation, framing, tracing or marking. To *deconstruct* Christianity, or the commitments to an ultimate revelation and messianic presentation, would for Derrida amount to an abandonment of the ideal of the full gift of presence and a welcoming of that which arrives without sense. In terms of cinema or the visual arts, this has two broad consequences: first, the visual is rendered possible through the invisible, for that which is seen comes about through processes of tracing or marking ("writing") that never come to presence; secondly, the very notions of sense and world would be solicited by anarchic or untamed forces that are beyond sense.

For Nancy, by contrast, Christianity's positing of a God as an infinite being who is the creative source for finite being is deconstructed with the cinematic presence of sense, evidence, world and freedom. It is in the experience of the touch or sense of the world – in one's very finitude and relation to the world – that one may *live* the deconstruction of Christianity. In this presence of sense and evidence, in cinema's unfolding of the world as exposed to view, we live and feel this world as *all that is*: "Evidence refers to what is obvious, what makes sense, what is striking and, by the same token, opens and gives a chance and an opportunity to meaning. Its truth is something that grips and does not have to correspond to any given criteria" (Nancy 2001: 42–3). Cinema is, then, the completion of philosophy for Nancy. For if philosophy is a commitment to the truth of that which truly *is* (and not received opinion or dogma), then it is cinema that presents the world as it is given in mobile and located images, dependent also on light and film. It is cinema that is metaphysics: "Motion is the opening of the motionless, it is presence insofar as it is truly *present*, that is to say coming forward, introducing itself, offered, available, a site for waiting and thinking, presence itself becoming a passage toward or inside presence" (*ibid.*: 30, 31). This cannot be a narrative cinema, where the images serve to unfold a sense or *telos* beyond the image; it is a cinema of the image itself in its immanence. But whereas Nancy draws on a phenomenological tradition whereby philosophy completes *itself* – that is, where philosophy arrives at the pure truth it has always sought by recognizing that there is nothing other than experience in its revealing of the world – Nancy requires cinema to complete the trajectory of sense. For if it is the case that the world reveals itself through images – there is not some immobile and absolute being beyond the image – then, according to phenomenology from Hegel to Husserl, philosophy comes to maturity when it recognizes that the truth it sought beyond the world and appearance *is just that the world appears.* Nancy, however, precludes this truth of philosophy being given in a philosophical, propositional or prosaic form. This is because the truth of appearance – the truth of the given, of touch, of the sensible – is that there is non-appearing: not a non-appearing of some hidden ground or foundation, but a non-appearing *in* the appearing. An image appears at once as all that is, as the only world we have, *and* as an opening to further imaging.

Art, images, touch and the sensible were, for Derrida (and Hegel before him), essentially incomplete notions that would bring about their own surpassing: the idea that one touches or lives "this here" is already conceptual (for "this" is a marker of presence as such, and is repeatable beyond the "this"). In so far as "I touch" there is also a disruption of pure presence, established in the *relation* between the "I" who touches and that which is touched, and this relation of self to other, of finite subject to object, of the here to the "now", requires something like *meaning*, which for Derrida and Hegel entails some generalization, formalization or "death" of the purely singular.

Nancy, however, wants to avoid this passage to meaning and philosophy, this passage to contaminating every singularity with a concept. It is not the philosophical pronouncement that can arrive at this singularity; to write about the single image, about cinema itself, is already to generalize or depart from the presentation *itself*. On the contrary, it is not philosophy or theory that brings truth and meaning to cinema; cinema is the way in which the philosopher might be able to realize a sense or givenness that is not subsumed beneath the relations of meaning, that is not subjected to any criteria other than itself. Cinema, properly, is non-narrative and reflexive while not being self-reflexive. It presents images as nothing more than images.

15 JACQUES DERRIDA

Louise Burchill

Jacques Derrida (1930–2004) was born in Algiers and educated at the École Normale Supérieure and Harvard University. He held appointments teaching philosophy at the Sorbonne and École Normale Supérieure in Paris. In the United States he was a visiting Professor at Johns Hopkins University, Yale University, New York University, Stony Brook University, and The New School for Social Research. He was Professor of Humanities at the University of California at Irvine. Derrida was director of studies at the École des Hautes Études en Sciences Sociales in Paris. With François Châtelet and others he co-founded the Collège International de Philosophie (CIPH) in 1983 Derrida's extensive publications include *Writing and Difference* (1967; English trans. 1978), *Of Grammatology* (1967; English trans. 1976), *Speech and Phenomena* (1967; English trans. 1973), *Glas* (1974; English trans. 1986), *The Truth in Painting* (1978; English trans. 1987), *Right of Inspection* (1985; English trans. 1998), *Spectres of Marx* (1993; English trans. 1994) and *Archive Fever* (1995; English trans. 1996). He is co-author of *Echographies of Television* (1996; English trans. 2002).

DERRIDA AND THE (SPECTRAL) SCENE OF CINEMA

Derrida's scene of cinema is haunted, its every nook and cranny host to a pandemonium of phantoms, ghosts, shadows and spectres whose ethereal proliferation and enigmatic traces plot the space–time coordinates of not only the cinematic spectacle but its very "apparatus" as a repeated rerun of the (non-)living (non-)dead. Declaring the "cinematic experience" to partake, in its every aspect, of "spectrality", film in its very materiality, as projected on the screen, to be a "phantom", the screen itself to have a "structure of disappearing apparition" and the cinematic image a structure that is "through and through spectral", Derrida gestures towards a thought of cinema that is obviously irreducible to "crude phantasmagoria" or a thematic focus on the "representation of phantomality", as with horror films and their cortege of ghouls, vampires and the resurrected. In the conjunction of thought and cinema – where it is a matter of "the provocation to think" borne by cinema and of thought as exceeding philosophical discourse through its questioning the values of presence and being-present that define the latter – Derrida's contribution could, at first glance at least, be set down in a formula that immediately betrays the conjuration of phenomenology that forms its frame: "cinema *in its essence* is spectral". Having said this, however, when dealing

164

with the conjunction of Derrida's thought and cinema, we must be wary of entrusting ourselves to what is revealed "at first glance" – to what poses itself declaratively on the scene – and attend to more than the strict confines of what Derrida was to have said or written (if, indeed, he did ever write) on the cinema. The very fact that Derrida was to reflect so sparsely on film prompts us to further enquire as to what cinema might well provoke by way of a (re)thinking of certain key conceptual constellations within Derrida's work, with this, in turn, perhaps bringing into focus the logic of Derrida's cinematographic disinterest. In this way, too, what has been named the "structuring absence of Derrida within film theory" (Lapsley & Westlake 1988: 65), in the sense of this field's lack of reference to his work, might reveal itself to be much more of the order of a "palimpsestic" infiltration than non-referentiality or non-acknowledgement implies. Derrida's occulted and, indeed, nigh-disavowed "presence" (somewhat of the order of "a disappearing apparition"?) might itself be said to haunt the very same theoretical scene from which his work was supposedly excluded. That being the case, the confrontation of Derrida with his "ghostly double" has all the chances – as Sigmund Freud (1955) tells us in a text Derrida often cites with respect to cinema and spectrality – of proving to be distinctly ... *uncanny*.

"WERE I TO HAVE WRITTEN ON THE CINEMA ..."

As the author of some fifty books dealing with philosophy, of course, but also literature, history, psychoanalysis, politics, law, science, religion, anthropology, gender, aesthetics, painting, drawing, architecture, photography and so on, Derrida has been said to have written "on more or less everything under the sun" (Royle 2005). One would, then, have expected the "art of light and shadow" that is cinema to have been granted its subsolar place as well. Yet there is no text by Derrida on cinema, rendering him in this respect an exception among other French thinkers of his generation or, more precisely, his "philosophical sequence". Surprisingly, it would seem that Derrida alone wrote about more or less everything *except* cinema.[1] However, he did write about one particular film – Safaa Fathy's *D'ailleurs, Derrida* (Derrida's elsewhere; 1999).[2] Derrida also served as both actor and subject (or, as he puts it, "an Actor who plays the role of himself"; Derrida & Fathy 2000: 74) for three films – a documentary and two "docufictions", of which Fathy's film is one[3] – as well as appearing in a fiction film, once again in the guise of himself. The latter film, Ken McMullen's *Ghost Dance* (1983), forms, appropriately enough, the setting in which Derrida was to deliver his most incisive formulation of cinema's particular – or indeed *essential* – affinity with what he names "spectrality". In a scene that must surely qualify as a phantasmatic *mise en abyme*, Derrida first declares he himself to be a ghost, referring, as he glosses elsewhere, to the fact that, when filmed and aware of the images' vocation to be reproduced in one's absence, one is haunted in advance by one's future death such that, even before magically "re-appearing" on the screen, one is already "spectralized" by the camera (Derrida & Stiegler 1996: 131). Then, after adding that being haunted by ghosts consists in the memory of something never having had the form of being-present, he sets down as a literal formula: "*Cinema plus psychoanalysis equals a science of ghosts*". Some fourteen years after his apparition in McMullen's film, Derrida would reassert the basic coordinates of this formula in an interview he gave to the French film review *Cahiers du Cinéma* in 2001.

"Were [he] to have written on the cinema", as Derrida puts it in this interview, the subject explored would, indeed, have been cinema's relation to spectrality. Such a relation is not, though, specific to cinema alone. All the contemporary "teletechnologies" – consisting of the camera, cinema, television and photography, no less than the internet, digital imagery, and so on – partake of a "logic of spectrality" characterized principally by its blurring of distinctions as fundamental to traditional schemas of reasoning as sensible/insensible, real/virtual, living/dead and present/absent.[4] "A spectre is simultaneously visible and invisible, phenomenal and non-phenomenal: a trace marking in advance the present of its absence" (Derrida & Stiegler 1996: 131). That all the contemporary teletechnologies contribute to developing an experience of spectrality hitherto unprecedented in history is explained by Derrida in terms of these technologies' capacity to reproduce the "moment of inscription" – the event taking place – with an extraordinary "proximity", such that this appears "live", while transporting it an extraordinary distance, be this over space or time. Bringing together, then, the near and the far with an acceleration and amplification hitherto unknown, contemporary teletechnologies have the structural specificity of "restituting the living present" – albeit a "living present", as Derrida specifies, "of what is dead" in so far as death is structurally inscribed in any means of reproduction (*ibid*.: 48). As such, it is the (phenomenological) mode of presence of such a restitution that can be seen to obey the logic that Derrida names "spectral" to the degree that it is, at once, *both and neither*: visible and/nor invisible (nothing is presented in "flesh and blood"), sensible and/nor insensible, living and/nor dead, perceptual and/nor hallucinatory. Rendering, in short, the opposition between "effective presence" and its other – be this designated as absence, non-presence, ineffectivity, virtuality or simulacrum – non-operative, spectrality would ultimately scramble philosophy's determination of being as presence.

In this context it is important to grasp the intrinsic relationship the logic of spectrality bears to the major conceptual constellations of Derrida's thought overall and his "deconstruction" of phenomenology in particular. Indeed, while the theme of spectrality is a recurring one throughout Derrida's corpus, the book in which this theme is developed into a full-blown "logic" – *Spectres of Marx*, first published in French in 1993 – was described by Derrida as expressly continuing "the explication with phenomenology" he had initiated in texts such as *Speech and Phenomena* and *Of Grammatology* in the 1960s. Pursuing "the problematization of the values of presence, presentation and the living present" in the aim of distinguishing "the spectre" – and more broadly, the ludically baptized "hauntology" – from Western philosophy's traditional determination of being as being-present (*to ontōs*), the analyses of *Spectres of Marx* effectively echo the "final intention" of Derrida's 1967 *Of Grammatology*, the book undoubtedly most identified with his "philosophical project". This set out to "render enigmatic what one thinks one understands by the words 'proximity', 'immediacy', 'presence' (the proximate [*proche*], the own [*propre*], and the pre- of presence)" (1976: 70). Such a "rendering enigmatic" was to be wrought by a "deconstruction" – a dismantling and reconfiguration – by which any purported "presence" or "present entity" would be revealed as the product of a "non-presence", construed, though, not as a simple contrary or negative but as a point of leverage by which to overturn and reconfigure the entire system privileging the "presence" of the original "element". Drawing decisively, in this respect, on Ferdinand de Saussure's definition of language as a system in which there are only differences and no positive terms – a word only having meaning as a function of the differences it displays with respect to other terms of language and not from any positive content, such as a pre-existing concept – Derrida was to stress that the systematic play of differences conditioning the possibility of signification or conceptualization in general equally entails that meaning is endlessly "deferred" in an infinitely long chain of referrals; the "system" of meaning is neither closed nor synchronically present to itself. Giving to this systematic play of referrals or differences the name of "*différance*", Derrida insisted on the movement or force making of the latter that which "produces" the differences in play, while fuelling, by the same token, its dynamic aspect *qua* a "deferring", "delay", "detour" and "reserve": all operations encapsulated by that of "temporalization".

Deconstruction's constitutive relation to phenomenology is forged along this "temporalizing vector", brought to bear on Saussure's determination of signification under the influence of Edmund Husserl's analyses of temporality. Just as the latter dissected "inner-time consciousness" as a movement of temporalization in which the "present moment" or "living now" can appear as such only by its being continuously compounded with other "nows", past and future, so Derrida was to "inaugurally" define *différance* in phenomenological terms as the "'primordial' and irreducibly non-simple, and, therefore, in the strict sense non-primordial, synthesis of marks, and traces of retentions and protentions", which, constitutive of the present, is at once "spacing (and) temporalizing" (1973: 143, translation modified). Yet Derrida nonetheless considered Husserl's temporal syntheses, for all their complexity, to remain indebted to the traditional determination of the "now" as a "point of presence" in so far as they have their beginning in a "primordial impression" or "point-source". Although qualified by Husserl as a pure "creation" formed not by consciousness itself but by the passive reception of something foreign to the latter, the "primordial impression" is, in Derrida's view, central to Husserl's conception of consciousness as being "immediately" present to itself, without recourse to any form of sign or representation. Such a self-presence of experience would, Derrida argues, depend on the privileging of a punctiform "present of perception" since only on such a basis can Husserl affirm our mental acts to be lived by us in "the same instant" ("*im selben Augenblick*") as they are carried out. With Husserl rendering, in this way, the present of self-presence "as indivisible as a blink of an eye" (*ibid.*: 59) – as Derrida puts in a play on the German "Augenblick" the deconstruction of Husserl's transcendental phenomenology (positioned as the most rigorous modern version of philosophy's foundation of being as presence – in the form, namely, of self-consciousness) was to set itself the task of "troubling" just such an "eye blink".

Engaging as it does the question of perception – so central to considerations on the cinema – the way in which Derrida both introduces "duration to the blink" and deprives the eye of any form of opening on to perceptual presence is of pertinence here mainly in respect of his argument that the movement of temporalization (the continuity of the now and the not-now, perception and non-perception) must not only equally complicate the "punctuality" of primordial impression, such that consciousness's self-presence would no longer be im-mediate, but additionally makes primordial impression itself a creation of consciousness by which the latter *affects* itself. Primordial impression cannot, then, pretend to be a "source-point" engendered by the "presence" of something foreign to internal time consciousness: Derrida insisting, more radically than Husserl himself, on the consequences that ensue from the difference, or "phenomenological fold", between the "sensory appearing" (the world) and the "appearance" (the "phenomenological object" or "noema" constituted in the subjective process or lived experience), which comprises, as it were, phenomenology's "reduction" of the empirical world to the contents given to consciousness. A "Condition of all other differences" (1976: 65), this difference between sensory appearing and appearance determines the noema – in its singular status of an immanent moment of consciousness that no more belongs to the world than it "really" belongs to lived experience – as irreducible. It is a *trace* in relation to which there is no possibility of reanimating the manifest evidence of an "originary presence", which can as such only be "referred to" as an absolute past – a past that has never been present – within the very movement of *différance*. Yet, woven by intervals and reciprocal referrals, *différance* as temporalization is, no less irreducibly, a "spacing" that denies any closure within the im-mediacy of a pure proximity to consciousness through its enveloping within itself a "pure outside": time's "outside-itself as the self-relation of time" (Derrida 1973: 86). As such, Derrida can conclude his deconstruction of the self-presence of consciousness or the transcendental subject (understood – in distinction to any psychological attribution – as the subject that appears to itself and appears as what "constitutes", or gives sense to, the world) with a final twist of the trope of the eye, one that, with particular pertinence, beckons us back to the scene of cinema: consciousness's presence to itself "is not the inwardness of an inside that is closed upon itself; it is the irreducible openness in the inside; it is the eye and the world within speech. *Phenomenological reduction is a scene*" (*ibid.*).[5]

THE GHOST IN THE MACHINE

Absolutely everything Derrida was to advance concerning the essence of cinema as spectrality is informed by his deconstruction of Husserl's living present, as this appears in immediate proximity to a transcendental ego. Focusing particularly on the *credit* accorded to the cinematic image's "perceptual modality", he stipulates this, in the *Cahiers du Cinéma* interview, to require a radically new type of phenomenological analysis. Cinema, that is, would differ from all other teletechnologies of the image through its being spectral not simply by virtue of its technical apparatus – the operation of the camera, the projected image, the celluloid and the screen all marking in advance the presence of their absence – but by its equally engaging a modality of "belief", which, in an unprecedented way, suspends the distinction between imagination and the real, hallucination and perception, indeed, life and death, such that, by believing in the apparition on the screen, all while not believing, the spectator undergoes a vacillation of his or her own sense of identity.

This is where psychoanalysis – especially Freud's dissection of the experience of the "uncanny" – intersects with phenomenology as recast in Derrida's deconstruction. Couched in broad terms, cinematic perception mirrors, so to speak, the practice of psychoanalysis: both call on the processes of hypnosis, fascination and identification, while film's shifts in perceptual focus – notably the close-up – open on to the unconscious in a way similar to the psychoanalytic attention to slips of the tongue or other details previously unnoticed in the broad stream of perception. In stressing this shared attention to detail and to the "other scene" – another space and another time – thus opened up, Derrida's reference is to Walter Benjamin's very early, seminal analyses of the "phenomenological" revolution wrought by the two contemporaneous techniques of cinema and psychoanalysis. The reorganization of perception and the instituting of "new structural formations of the subject" that Benjamin limpidly related to the camera's introducing us to "unconscious optics as does psychoanalysis to unconscious impulses" ([1936] 1968: 237) equally call forth a new form of belief. Analysing the historical specificity of cinema to lie in its constructing a position for the spectator such that the latter completely identifies with the apparatus itself – by virtue of his or her eyes being situated on a line parallel with the camera lens and this eyeline then being reinforced in the editing process – Benjamin claims this yields an illusion of reality all the more potent for its seeming to be unmediated by artistic form. Interestingly, Benjamin casts this modality of illusion – which is no less one of belief – in terms that are almost identical to Derrida's analyses of cinema's specificity as residing in the restitution of the living present. Extracting, by its unprecedented technical prowess, "an apparatus-free aspect" from reality, cinema would proffer "the sight of immediate reality" in so "living" a restitution that this becomes, in Benjamin's vivid image, "an orchid in the land of technology" (ibid.: 233).

Like Benjamin, Derrida attributes the impression of reality (although the term is not one he uses) to an "effect of the subject" rather than engaging in any form of comparison between "representation" and "reality": both concepts subject to deconstruction in the analyses of mimesis Derrida undertakes elsewhere. Similar to the enchained spectators of Plato's cavern, mesmerized by the shadows of shadows flickering on the wall before them, the cinematic audience accords a credit to "something" that is there without being there, identifying thereby with simulacra of corporeal presence: sensible insensibilia. Of course, from Plato's "cavernous chamber" to the camera obscura, then to cinema itself, projected moving images have been likened over and over again to little ghosts (fantasma). Derrida would, however, have us understand the spectrality of the image and the credit accorded to it as partaking of the same logic: a logic in which the indistinction of hallucination and perception would, in fact, be prior to, and the condition of, any ascription of "reality", "verisimilitude", presence/ non-presence and so on.

Freud's notion of the uncanny proves, in this context, to be pertinent to Derrida's propositions not simply on the cinema but on spectrality in general. For Freud, the feeling of the uncanny, as a form of anguish or dread, involves a strange intermixture of the familiar and the unfamiliar – as, for example, the effect occasioned when, in strange surroundings, we unexpectedly encounter our own image in a reflecting surface but mistake it first for someone else. Of all the myriad circumstances that can give rise to the uncanny, it is the theme of the "return of the dead" that Freud deemed the most striking, indeed paradigmatic, instance. As such, he largely based his explanation of the uncanny on the mechanism he discerned to underlie the anguish aroused by the apparition of the dead, namely, the return of a belief that, once familiar to us, had been repressed in the unconscious or surmounted. Having once believed in spirits, during one's own infancy or the "infancy of humankind", so-called educated adults are – officially at any rate – no longer prone to crediting the dead with the ability to reanimate, resurrect or re-appear to the living. When, therefore, any such appearances do occur, the spectator is subject to intellectual uncertainty, the distinction between imagination and reality, perception and hallucination, being called into doubt.

> As soon as something actually happens in our lives which seems to sup-
> port the old, discarded beliefs, we get a feeling of the uncanny; and it is
> as though we were making a judgement something like this: ... "The dead
> do, then, continue to live and appear before our eyes on the scene of their
> former activities!" (Freud 1955: 249)

In short, for Freud no less than for Derrida, we are placed before a scene in which we believe without believing, and this is precisely the modality of our belief. Beyond this, however, in so far as the boundary between the imaginary and the real, fiction and non-fiction – in short, the "testing of reality" – no longer holds, not only are we, according to Derrida, ourselves projected within the scene of the unconscious, but the very structure of this scene is revealed to coincide with that of the spectral uncanny. Displaying a topology in which the "other" that suddenly surges before us is revealed to already reside inside us – more familiar to us than our very "selves", "an an-identity that ... invisibly occupies places belonging finally neither to us nor to it" (Derrida 1994: 172) – the uncanny accruing to the return of the dead shares with the unconscious a "spacing" that unsettles any and all notions of the subject as consisting of an identity persevering in the presence of self-relation.

This returns us to Derrida's deconstruction of phenomenology and the intrinsic relationship it bears to his logic of spectrality. Explicitly qualified as a "deconstructive logic" (Derrida & Stiegler 1996: 131), spectrality is positioned in *Spectres of Marx* as a radical potentiality contained within phenomenology itself. For "what is phenomenology", Derrida asks, "if not a logic of the *phainesthai* ['to shine, show oneself or appear'] and the *phantasma*, therefore of the phantom?" (1994: 122). Even before its determination as phenomenon or phantasm, and therefore as phantom, he continues, the *phainesthai* as such "is the very possibility of the spectre": a "phenomenology of the spectral", needing, in fact, only to realize the resources of Husserl's identification of the noema as an intentional but "non-real" component of lived experience or sub-jective processes. Neither "in" the world nor "in" consciousness, the noema "is the condition of any experience, any objectivity, any phenomenality"; it is "the very place of apparition, the essential, general, non-regional possibility of the specter" (*ibid.*: 135 n.6). With these analyses instating spectrality as partaking of the same structure as *différance*, what is particularly significant in the present context is the way the logic of spectrality thereby qualifies as the "new kind of phenomenology" that Derrida was to call for, in his *Cahiers du Cinéma* interview, in the context of cinema's modality of belief. Declaring the latter to require an absolutely original type of analysis, Derrida decisively specifies: "Such a phenomenology was not possible before cinematography because this experience of belief is linked to a particular technique, that of cinema, and it is historical through and through" (2001: 78, my trans.).

Such a statement on Derrida's part is truly momentous. He is not simply identifying cinema here with the logic of spectrality that only a new, deconstructive, kind of phenomenology is adequate to; he explicitly singles out the cinematic apparatus – the "particular technique of cinema" – to be what alone gives us the "experience" of *différance*, just as "cinematic perception is alone capable of making us understand through experience what a psychoanalytic practice is" (*ibid.*: 75, my trans.). The cinematic apparatus can alone, in other words, function as a "model" of *différance*, in the same way as Derrida's terms of spacing and "arche-writing" work (the "quasi-transcendental" "space of inscription" conditioning the operation of writing systems understood in the "narrow sense"). Despite, then, Derrida's avowed preference for the word over the image – "I won't hide from you that only words interest me, the advance and retreat of terms in the taciturn obsession of this powerful photographic machine" is a statement found, for example, in his text on Marie-Françoise Plissart's "photo-novel" in *Right of Inspection* (1985: III) – there would seem little doubt that, as regards the capacity of the two technologies of the image and the word to provide a "model" of the movement of *différance*, Derrida here is adjudicating in favour of the optical machine over the scriptural (*ibid.*, my trans.).

OCCULTED *MISE EN SCÈNE*

Attributing Derrida with having singled out as the "model" best equipped to represent the structure of *différance* an optical, rather than a scriptural, machine, poses, however, a seeming contradiction in respect of more than his "preference" for words and writing. In 1967 – alongside texts such as *Speech and Phenomena* and *Of Grammatology* destined to be revived in the logic of spectrality two and a half decades later – Derrida published an essay, "Freud and the Scene of Writing", the basic purport of which is that the best metaphorical model for what Freud named "the psychical apparatus" (and which Derrida relates to *différance*) is precisely not an optical mechanism but a graphic, writing, machine.

Freud's repeated recourse to optical models for the psyche the most famous of which, in *The Interpretation of Dreams*, consists of the proposition that "we should picture the instrument which carries out our mental functions as resembling a compound microscope or a photographic apparatus, or something of the kind" (1953: 574) – is, in fact, dismissed by Derrida in this text as blatantly inadequate. Optical mechanisms would not merely be incapable of fully accounting for the two distinct functions Freud assigned to the Perception-Consciousness and Memory systems but they would, thereby, fail to capture the "originary temporality" Derrida claims to be evinced by the psyche's structure. Only once Freud discovered a "writing machine of

171

marvellous complexity" (Derrida 1978: 200), the so-called "Mystic Writing Pad", would he cease to be "haunted" – as Derrida puts it – by his search for a model capable of representing the psyche's twofold capacity to, on the one hand, receive perceptions but retain no trace of them, remaining thereby perpetually open to the reception of fresh stimuli, and, on the other, transform the momentary excitations of the perceptual system into permanent memory-traces. While ultimately a simple device, composed of a wax slab of dark resin or wax and a surface "writing" sheet of celluloid lined by a layer of waxed paper, the Mystic Writing Pad is hailed by Derrida for its "*mise en scène*" of the psyche as a "spacing of writing", more fundamentally identified as "the movement of temporalization and self-affection". Whatever the grounds for such an interpretation, it leaves no doubt that, at the time he wrote "Freud and the Scene of Writing", Derrida himself considered the only possible metaphorical model of not only "psychical writing" but *différance* "itself" to be a scriptural one.

As such, it might seem well nigh uncanny that Derrida's own *mise en scène* of Freud's psychical apparatus as most definitely *not* lending itself to an optical model – such as the cinematographic one – should have inspired nothing less than the founding texts of the extremely influential current of writing on cinema known as "apparatus theory". In two seminal essays, "Ideological Effects of the Basic Cinematographic Apparatus" and "The Apparatus: Metapsychological Approaches to the Impression of Reality in the Cinema", written in the early 1970s, Jean-Louis Baudry (2004a, 2004b) was to set down a number of theses concerning the operations by which the cinematic apparatus mirrors the psychical structure of the spectator and, in this way, creates an impression of reality all the more "fascinating" for its satisfying formative desires. Despite the intense critical attention given to Baudry's theses, almost no mention has been made of their being cast within the conceptual framework of Derrida's text on Freud.[6] The opening sentences of Baudry's first text on the cinematographic apparatus, however, explicitly draw on Derrida's analyses to position Freud's recourse to optical models as betraying his failure to have as yet discovered an adequate representation of the psyche, which was not to eventuate, of course, until the discovery of a writing machine, "as Derrida has pointed out" (2004a: 355). Taking Derrida's interpretation as his point of departure, Baudry then nevertheless pursues the path of the optical model opened up by Freud in order to elucidate cinema's functioning as a "substitutive psychical apparatus". Proffering, in this sense, a form of counter-proof to Derrida's disqualification of the optical model, Baudry's analyses, at the same time, continually – if never again explicitly – re-stage Derrida's thought, such that not only does the cinematographic apparatus come to exemplify the workings of differance but the way in which it does so uncannily presages Derrida's own remarks in the *Cahiers du Cinéma* interview.

The confrontation of Derrida's thought to cinema staged in Baudry's texts first takes the form of what might best be described as a re-enactment of Derrida's deconstruction of Husserlian phenomenology. Cinema's specificity – for Baudry as for Benjamin – of attributing a position to the spectator whereby she or he is afforded a "limitless power of vision" by identifying with the camera's point of view, is understood by Baudry to technically transpose, as it were, the spectator within the phenomenological horizon of Husserl's transcendental subject. Objective reality is "phantasmatized", with the dreamlike images unfolding on the screen offering up objects that seem constituted for and by the "subject", endowed with a mastery unfettered by the laws of matter, time and corporeal existence. The effect of "plenitude" produced in this way, both on the level of vision and on the level of the (transcendental) subject/spectator, is, however, dependent on the material processes of editing and projection, which create an illusion of continuity out of the series of discontinuous images making up the film reel. Baudry's deconstructive gesture consists, in this respect, in breaking down the temporal and mobile coherence of what is perceived as a seamless continuity into its constitutive series of discrete units, which not only comport minute differences between themselves but are separated by intervening frames. While indispensable for the production of an illusion of continuity, this "spacing" of differences can only create such an impression on the condition that it is suppressed in favour of the relation between the images alone. "The individual images as such disappear so that movement and continuity can appear." "In this sense we could say that film – and perhaps this instance is exemplary – lives on the denial of difference: difference is necessary for it to live but it lives on its negation" (Baudry 2004a: 359). For this reason, Baudry claims the cinematographic apparatus – defined as encompassing all the various instruments and operations necessary to the production and projection of film, including the position given to the spectator – functions as a "substitutive psychical apparatus" that, denying the differential play of the unconscious, would serve to bolster the illusion of a transcendental subject, buoyed by the very values of presence and self-presence Baudry is obviously set on deconstructing.[7] Film's perceptual presence and the transcendental subject constituted in correlation to this are effectuated then only on the condition that the cinema denies its nature as *différance*.

Shifting away from the focus on cinema's idealist constitution of a subject situated as a transcendental gaze, Baudry's second article concentrates on the operations that precede and condition the instauration of such a subject. Crucially, this motivates Baudry to return to Freud's conception of the relation between perception/consciousness and the unconscious in order to advance the hypothesis that the cinematographic apparatus is alone capable of proposing an experience that would resemble that of the unconscious. In this context, Baudry now jettisons Derrida's interpretative schema, underlining, on the contrary, both the inability of writing machines such as the Mystic Writing Pad to reproduce memory's spontaneous restitution of its contents and Freud's return to optical models in his final texts. Given the cinematographic apparatus's capacity not only to continually receive fresh impressions and preserve memory-traces but, additionally, to reproduce these, Freud could even have turned to the cinema itself as a model for the psyche, Baudry suggests, were it not for its failure to fully represent the relations between perception and memory. Rather, though, than disqualifying the cinematographic "analogy", the fact of its falling short of Freud's conception of the psyche as differentiated into perception/consciousness and memory is taken by Baudry as revealing the cinematographic apparatus to correspond, in fact, to a stage of the psychical apparatus before any such differentiation comes into being. Drawing on Freud's metapsychological analyses of the dream, Baudry claims the cinematographic set-up would artificially transpose the subject back to a stage of his or her development when the boundaries between perception and hallucination, "external reality" and one's own body, were not as yet distinct, with desire therefore being able to find hallucinatory satisfaction, in so far as the spatial conditions governing the projection and reception of a film reproduce the structure of the psychical apparatus during sleep. The unique spatial arrangement of projection – the darkened cinema and the relative passivity of the immobilized spectators, isolated from all external sources of excitation other than the screen before them with its animated images – mirror, in other words, on Baudry's account, the conditions of the "dreamer". Yet where the dream proposes to its "subject" representations or images that present themselves as perceptions/reality in the absence of perception, the cinema offers images as perceptions/reality through the very means of perception. This is what explains the "subject-effect" of cinema's impression of reality: "the cinematographic apparatus is unique in that *it offers the subject perceptions 'of a reality' whose status seems similar to that of representations experienced as perceptions*" (2004b: 220). Beyond this, however, the cinematographic apparatus would also meet the desire of the unconscious for depictions of its "own scene": a scene, it should be specified, to be taken in its "literal sense" for Baudry in so far as the "unconscious disposes uniquely of visual representations" (*ibid.*: 215; translation modified). The superiority of the cinematographic apparatus over all precedent representations of the scene of the unconscious pertains not simply to its proposing the perception of images (as is also the case with Plato's allegory of the cave) but to these images having a phenomenal quality previously impossible to restitute. Derrida can, of course, be seen to say nothing other when asserting that "the cinema needed to be invented in order to satisfy a certain desire with respect of phantoms" (2001: 80, my trans.) or, again, when singling out the cinematographic apparatus as creating an experience of belief (Baudry's "impression of reality") analysable only by a logic, or phenomenology, of spectrality. "Because the spectral dimension is neither that of the living nor of the dead, neither that of hallucination nor that of perception, the modality of belief that is related to it must be analysed in an absolutely original way" (*ibid.*: 78, my trans.).

Given that Derrida was to analyse, like Baudry, the cinematographic apparatus in terms of a *mise en scène* of the unconscious, in which the latter, in its capacity of the condition of appearance and signification, displays an indifferentiation of hallucination and perception, objective reality and virtuality, such that we believe what we see, all while not believing, might he not – one is tempted to conclude – have written, had he written, something on cinema not all that disparate from Baudry's seminal texts? Indeed, given that the analyses of "Freud and the Scene of Writing" haunt Baudry's conceptualization of cinema from its very inception, could Derrida not pass, in a certain sense, as Baudry's ghostwriter: the unacknowledged author of a scenario that was to play itself out on the scene of English-language film theory during a decade? In such a case, Derrida's so-called "structuring absence" within that same scene would reveal itself to have a sense hitherto unsuspected.

Such conjecture seems far-fetched, however, for a number of reasons. Most fundamentally, there is a crucial difference between Derrida's defining *différance* (or spacing, arche-writing, the logic of spectrality …) pre-eminently in terms of temporalization and Baudry's conceptual framework, which suggests a notion of "spacing" that would not as yet display any form of temporalizing synthesis. In this respect, Baudry's analyses of the differential status of the frames constituting the film reel, before their "effacement" by projection's instauration of the dimension of time and continuity, take on a particular significance when read in conjunction with his "model" of the cinematographic apparatus as finally corresponding to a psychical state in which memory is not as yet distinguished from perception.

In fact, whereas Derrida ultimately dissolves the distinction of perception and memory in favour of a monism of the latter in its guise of an economy of the trace referring to an absolute past, Baudry advances a quite different temporal ordering when he too opts for the dissolution of any distinction between perception and memory. By conceiving of the cinema on the model of a psychic state neither differentiated into perception and memory nor permitting any distinction between the perceived and the represented, Baudry proposes what, strictly speaking, amounts less to a temporal ordering as such than an ordering outside time. On this conception – which accords with Freud's renowned description of the unconscious as a-temporal, taken precisely to task by Derrida – film is not, then, to be construed, contrary to the view adopted by many commentators, as rendering everything in the present tense or as making of everything a present of perception. Certainly, one can maintain that the operation of projection coincides with the "present tense of consciousness", but this is precisely the reason why Baudry claims that projection negates "difference" through its effacing of the multiplicity of images in favour of the relation between them. The "present" is dependent, we might therefore say, on the relation established between elements; outside this relation, the images as such, proposed to us by film, are no more intrinsically marked as "present" or "past" than they are as "representations" or "perceptions". Further, any claim of cinema's privileging the "present of perception" necessarily depends on a notion of the subject-as-"consciousness" that Baudry suspends, as it were, in his second article.

To rephrase this in terms drawing more concertedly on Baudry's conception of film's *material* status as the spacing of differential elements, the differences marked on the film reel are not constituted through the operation of reciprocal inter-reference – which is an operation dependent on a form of secondary circuit: projection and/or "proto-consciousness" – but through the fact of the camera lens's receiving light rays emanating from a source foreign to the camera itself. As such, the film reel's differences are material inscriptions of an irreducible relation to something (completely) other – comparable, in this sense, to Husserl's "point-source" – before they become differences in reciprocal relation to each other. Of course, the movement of the reel through the camera mechanism is necessary for the differentiation of photographic instants – which, failing this, would but yield a superimposition of indecipherable inscriptions – yet this differentiation by juxtaposition is not animated as much by continuity. Rather, the simple fact that the operation of "inscription" involves mobility does not, by itself, determine these inscriptions – or "instants extracted from 'reality'", as Baudry describes them (2004a: 358, trans. modified) – to be placed in relations of succession, or, for that matter, retention and protention. For relations such as the latter to be established, the camera's "perception" needs to be joined to projection, with this secondary circuit thus confirmed in its role of "temporal vector" assuring the opening of sense and appearance.

To the degree that this makes temporal synthesis dependent on a "doubling" or "repetition" whereby juxtaposition cedes to succession, Baudry's conception of the cinematic apparatus – in its correlation to the workings of the psyche/*différance* – can be interpreted in at least two quite different ways. On the one hand, Baudry can be seen as *complicating* Derrida's notion of *différance* – notably, by marking the irreducibility of a relation to an "other", which is, by the same token, the irreducibility of this relation to the inter-reference of differential elements between themselves – and, on the other, as "disavowing" *différance* by affirming not only the irreducibility of an opening on to the "presence" of something "other than *différance*" but, also, an ordering of "spacing" unable to be simply subsumed as "time's outside-itself as the self-relation of time" (Derrida 1967b: 86). Whether Derrida himself would have conceded Baudry's model of the cinematographic apparatus to confront him with something of the order of a "troubling" of *différance*, must, of course, remain a matter of speculation. That a confrontation to the cinema might, however, have led him beyond simply revising his conception of optical models' inability to transpose an "experience" of *differance*, to more profoundly rethink the very parameters of the space–time coordinates of the latter, seems a possibility both left "unthought" as such in the remarks he was to confide to the *Cahiers du Cinéma* and forcefully brought to light in Baudry's presaging of the latter.

A PARTING WINK

In this perspective one could ask, by way of conclusion, what Derrida's logic of spectrality – that version of *différance* pre-eminently called forth by cinema – might have made of a short cinematic sequence, the specific force of which comes from its presenting a "mode of perceptual presence" that is precisely set in contrast to the haunting, "spectral" quality of the rest of the film of which it constitutes the central turning point. Indeed, bar the three seconds of the sequence in question, the totality of the film – namely, Chris Marker's film *La Jetée* (1962) – is composed of still (optically printed) photographs that, although magisterially edited, via fades and dissolves as well as straight cuts, to yield an impression of flow, are nevertheless permeated with an overwhelming sense of stasis or capture in time, as is in keeping with the film's narrative purport.[8] Of the latter, all that is strictly pertinent to know here is that the film's protagonist, a "man marked by a childhood memory", is able to travel back in time in order to be reunited with the woman whose memory haunts him. Since his re-apparitions in the past are sudden and sporadic, the woman calls him her "spectre" or "ghost", while he himself continually queries her own mode of presence; might he not, after all, be simply hallucinating or dreaming of her? It is precisely while the voice-over relates the man's questioning the mode of belief he credits to her existence, that the woman – in the short three-second sequence referred to – is suddenly imbued with movement. As indicated, this is the only moment in the film composed not of a series of still photographs but of "normal cinematic movement", which, as such, entails that the images on the film reel not only succeed each other at the rate of twenty-four per second but that they differ between themselves. Orchestrated by a change of rhythm and use of dissolves, the transition from filmed stasis to filmed kinesis is almost imperceptible. A series of stills of the woman, asleep, in close-up, her face and shoulders as though enshrouded in the white of her bed cover and pillow, are projected in increasingly rapid succession all while dissolving so slowly one into another that they themselves seem to move as the woman's position in the bed changes. Finally, the succession of positions attains the rate of twenty-four per second, as the woman opens her eyes, to gaze at her ghost-lover, and to look out at us. "One snapshot literally coming alive" (Sellars 2000), "the girl awakes from slumber, and truly awakes, blinking and smiling" (Cruz 2008): "it is as though ... the film wakes up" (Kawin 1982: 18).

Cinema's capacity – as remarked by Derrida – to "restitute the living present" could scarcely find a better example than this sequence. Its interweaving of presence and non-presence, its synthesis of different rhythms and tempi, as, too, of "the living" and "the dead", seem to make it almost a crowning example of film's spectrality. Yet, as concerns the mode of presence conveyed by Marker's consummate mobilization of the *phenomenality* of the image, is there not something that the logic of spectrality would seem to occult? This is a sequence, after all, that knowingly plays with film's specificity of proposing to us perceptions of representations that present themselves as perception, exponentializing, as it were, the latter such that we are positioned as the percipients of representations no longer simply dissimulating as perceptions but claiming, on the contrary, to present something of the order of a perception of "perception itself". The fact that this presentation of "perception" occurs in the film's one sequence in which the series of photographically fixed instants on the reel results from the differential play of light flickering through the camera lens in conjunction with the flickering through the camera mechanism of the reel itself should surely give us cause for thought. There is, of course, no movement in the film, strictly speaking: cinematic technology does not present movement but, rather, *represents* it illusionistically through the projection of the reel's series of instants (Koch 1993: 213). The succession of photographic stills making up Marker's film, with the exception of the woman's eye-blink, equally, of course, obeys this logic of projection. For the three seconds of the fluttering of an eye, however, the film not only moved through the camera rather than remain static – as would a slice of celluloid serving as a palimpsest of superimpositions – but, equally, recorded a changing configuration of light received through the lens, giving rise thereby to the spacing of infinitesimally differentiated images. Before the play of temporalization insinuates itself within the spacing of these discontinuous images, each of these is a singular, instantaneous impression: what some may call an "immobilization of time", although, strictly defined, such instants forego any reference to the latter dimension. The repetition of the reel's unwinding via projection will establish relation and, with this, movement and the dimension of time, yet the workings of this secondary circuit find their condition first of all in the juxtaposition of synoptic impressions: like so many *Augenblicke*. When duration comes to close the eye in Marker's film, one is returned to the intrigues of memory and travelling in time. For one brief moment, though, a glimpse is offered, not of "reality" nor of "presence", but of the spacing of light.

NOTES

1. Note, however, that Peter Brunette and David Wills, the authors of the only book in English on Derrida and film theory, suggest, on the contrary, that all and everything Derrida wrote *potentially* touches on cinema; *Screen/Play: Derrida and Film Theory* (Princeton, NJ: Princeton University Press, 1989), 99.

2. Derrida's essay on Fathy's film is published in the book he co-authored with Fathy. *Tourner les mots: Au bord d'un film* (Paris: Galilée/Arte, 2000).

3. Respectively, J. C. Rosé's *Jacques Derrida* (1994) and K. Dick & A. Ziering-Kofman's *Derrida* (2005), in addition to Fathy's film.

4. Derrida's remarks on teletechnology are found in the series of (filmed) interviews he gave to Bernard Stiegler, subsequently published as *Echographies de la télévision: Entretiensfilmés* (Paris: Galilée/ INA, 1996), and later published in English as *Echographies of Television: Filmed Interviews*, J. Bajorek (trans.) (Cambridge: Polity, 2002). The references in the text are to the French edition, and quotations are my translation.

5. *"La réduction phénoménologique est une scène"* (*La Voix et le phénomène: introduction au probléme du signe dans la phénoménologie de Husserl* [Paris: Presses Universitaires de France, 1967], 96). In the English translation the word "scene" is followed by/glossed as "a theater stage".

6. One exception is Richard Allen's *Projecting Illusion* (Cambridge: Cambridge University Press, 1995), 49.

7. The English term "apparatus" covers, in fact, two disparate terms used by Baudry in French: *appareil*, which refers to all the technology and operations required to shoot, process, edit and project films, and *dispositif,* which relates more specifically to the set of perceptual, psychological, physiological and social mechanisms involved in projection as it encompasses the spectator. Baudry, nevertheless, defines the "basic cinematographic apparatus" (*l'appareil de base*) as englobing the two sets of meanings.

8. Thanks to Jennifer McCamley for suggesting consideration of this film and to Eon Yorck for his spectral input.

16 GILLES DELEUZE

John Mullarkey

Gilles Deleuze (1925–95) was Professor of Philosophy at the University of Vincennes in Saint-Denis from 1969 to 1987. He published extensively on the history of philosophy and on the concepts of the arts. His books include *Empiricism and Subjectivity* (1953; English trans. 1991), *Proust and Signs* (1964; English trans. 2000), *Bergsonism* (1966; English trans. 1988), *Difference and Repetition* (1968; English trans. 1994), *Spinoza and the Problem of Expression* (1968; English trans. 1988), *Francis Bacon* (1981; English trans. 2003), *Cinema 1* (1983; English trans. 1986), *Cinema 2* (1985; English trans. 1989); *Foucault* (1986; English trans. 1988) and *The Fold* (1988; English trans. 1993). In collaboration with the political psychoanalyst Félix Guattari he co-authored a number of works, including *Anti-Oedipus* (1972; English trans. 1977), *Kafka* (1975; English trans. 1986), *A Thousand Plateaus* (1980; English trans. 1987) and *What is Philosophy?* (1991; English trans. 1994).

Of all the film-philosophies of the twentieth century, it is perhaps Deleuze's that is most *of* the cinema. By that I mean that it attempts to *belong* to cinema rather than simply be *about* it. It shows us film thinking for itself. The magnanimity Deleuze shows to film's conceptual power is seen most clearly at the very end of his two-volume work on film (*Cinema 1: The Movement-Image* and *Cinema 2: The Time-Image*) when he writes that "cinema's concepts are not given in cinema. And yet they are cinema's concepts, not theories about cinema." Still, at every point and turn of his five hundred pages of text, films and their makers are continually compared with philosophical thinkers, only ones that "think with movement-images and time-images instead of concepts" (Deleuze 1989: 280). Nonetheless, it would be plain "stupid", as Deleuze remarked in one interview, "to want to create a philosophy of cinema": Deleuze is not trying to apply philosophy to cinema, but move directly from philosophy to cinema *and* from cinema to philosophy (Deleuze 2000: 366, 367). A philosophy *from* cinema, then, that belongs to it, is what we shall examine here.

The two essential things that come from cinema, in Deleuze's view, are movement and time, which is to say, the indirect and the direct presentation of time. This is what his books are about. Indeed, the story-arc of *Cinema 1* and *Cinema 2* is as dramatic as it is (narratively) classical. It begins with a state of nature, followed by its fall and subsequent redemption: there was once a cinematic image adequate to expression that then fell into crisis (the shattering of the movement-image) before its resurrection as a time-image, an image adequate to its time, even when it is a time of loss and decay. First act (*Cinema 1*), last act (*Cinema 2*), with the middle act coming in the transition between the two books. This short essay's purpose, then, is to explain the significance of movement and time both in cinema and for Deleuze. What we shall see in all of this is no mere philosophy of cinema, but how cinema gives us a new philosophy of subject and object and what moves between them: time.

BETWEEN SUBJECT AND OBJECT: IMAGE IS EVERY THING

The time-image in *Cinema 2* indicates the possibility of new images, new signs, a future art of cinema. But it is the task of *Cinema 1* to tell the story of the rise and fall of the movement-image – its various incarnations as perception-image, affection-image, impulse-image, action-image and mental-image – as well as the various signs related to them. We should first note that it is *images* that Deleuze writes about and not the *imaginary*; there is no gaze or look at work in Deleuze's approach, be it male or female, sadistic or masochistic. The image is for itself and not *for* a consciousness (as both phenomenology and Freud would have it). For, if Edmund Husserl claimed that consciousness is *of* the image (and the image is for consciousness), then Deleuze follows Henri Bergson's reply in *Matter and Memory* ([1896] 1994) that consciousness already *is* the image. There is an "eye" already "in things, in luminous images in themselves", for it is not consciousness that illumines (as phenomenology believes), but the images, or light, that already are a consciousness "immanent to matter" (Deleuze 1986: 60, 61).

Image as already consciousness, consciousness as already image. What is being iterated here is a materialist identity of brain and screen. It is a new form of material monism, going beyond phenomenology into an "extended mind", a mind as part of the world (cinema). The Deleuzian notion that "the brain is the screen" (Deleuze 2000) stems from Bergson's understanding of the material universe as an "*aggregate of images*" (Bergson [1896] 1994: 22) (which, in the modern parlance of philosophy of mind, makes him a "radical externalist"): "an image may *be* without *being perceived* – it may be present without being represented – and the distance between these two terms, presence and representation, seems just to measure the interval between matter itself and our conscious perception of matter" (*ibid*.: 35). Yet, despite the centrality of the Bergsonian image in his theory (one that would strike many as already veering back towards a phenomenology of appearances), Deleuze does not regard his approach as subjectivist. Image = consciousness = matter in an *objective* phenomenology (the flipside of Deleuze's thesis that the "brain is a subject") (Deleuze & Guattari 1994: 209–11). It is a phenomenology that transcends "normal", anthropomorphic, perception, showing us how things see themselves (and us), rather than how we (normally) see them. Whereas Lacanian theory proposes that we see the mirror *as if* it sees us, in Deleuze's world, the mirror, or the processes that comprise a mirror, *really do* see, and touch, us.

Nonetheless, Deleuzian images do have subjective and objective poles or profiles, which are themselves related to each other in different ways. These varied relations just are what Deleuze means by the perception-image, affection-image, action-image and so on. And how those different relations are generated is given to us in the story of images that Bergson provides in chapter one of *Matter and Memory*. This imagology provides the script for Deleuze's work too, from the movement-image, which gives us only an indirect representation of time (in so far as it depends on montage), to the time-image, which provides us a clear view of time in "false movements" that shatter our "sensory-motor schema" (Deleuze 1986: ix). Also in the script are all the permutations by which subject and object might connect with each other in between this alpha and omega. Although cinematic images do come with varying degrees of bias, sometimes leaning more to the object side (in the static frames of early cinema), sometimes more to the subject side (in the mental images of Alfred Hitchcock that bring movement-image cinema to its completion), they are never one or the other *entirely*.

Two things must be said here. First, if there is no independent reality to subject and object – they are merely the poles of the image – then there is nothing to stop us saying that cinema, with *its* images, gives us reality rather than some pale imitation of it. *Image is every thing.* The two ways it does this are through time and through movement, the latter being the indirect representation of the former. But irrespective of being direct or indirect, the movements shown in cinema are all real. And this is so not only on account of everything being an image. Hence the second point to be made, which compounds the first: *every thing is in motion*. In a universe where only "duration" (change) is real, the moving images of film have an equal claim on reality: films give us immediately self-moving images. That is why *Cinema 1* begins its study with real movement, understanding by this something totally unlike any subjective *impression* of movement. For this, says Deleuze, is exactly how Bergson understood images, as "mobile sections of duration"; duration itself being the Real (*ibid.*: 11). In fact, it is because of the ontological priority of change that the image is outlined by Deleuze as a set of relations between subjective and objective poles (in the perception-image, affection-image and so on), *as well as* being unopposed to reality (in virtue of the latter's own mobility). Mobility makes the image real (for the Real is change); and the mobility between subject and object makes the image real as well (for their variable relations are embodied in its various types).

These various types of image (perception-image, affection-image) do not, therefore, *represent* the relations between subject and object; rather, they *instantiate or exemplify* them. This is seen vividly (although also rather abstractly) at the beginning of *Cinema 1* in the relation between one or more images and the set of all images surrounding it (the Whole, which is itself incomplete or "Open"). Even in the relatively static framings of early cinema – which were often quite geometrical, with the use of golden sections (in Sergei Eisenstein), horizontals and verticals (in Carl Theodor Dreyer), and diagonals (in German Expressionism) – there is a relation with an out-of-field that is always *qualitative*. Alluding to Bergson's famous image in *Creative Evolution* of sugar dissolving in water, Deleuze talks of a variable thread linking the particular to the whole, a thread made manifest in the duration of this event (*ibid.*: 12–17). The local is never closed off: there is always a bi-directional movement that extends the *quantitative* change in the part to the *qualitative* state of the Whole. And this is plain to see in cinema, where the moving images on screen (a quantity) extend to an off-screen set of images (a quality). Indeed, in the simple shot we see "the essence" of the cinematic movement-image: it lies in the extraction from "moving bodies" the "movement which is their common substance, or extracting from [quantitative, partial] movements the [qualitative, holistic] mobility which is their essence" (*ibid.*: 23). This movement produces a qualitative feeling, a whole world, simply created from the way an actor might silently raise a hand during an otherwise static shot, or, in a modern movie, when a camera cranes high into the sky above its subject.

This thread or relation between part and whole is expressed even more clearly with the use of editing techniques, be it in the American, "organic", style of editing, Soviet "dialectical" montage, the "quantitative" style of pre-war French film-makers, or the "intensive" cutting of the German Expressionists (*ibid.*: 29–55). Montage – a new, aberrant, connection between images – releases even more the qualitative, holistic movement from the local (on-screen) movement-images in an indirect "image *of* time". This extension of the local to the whole is bi-directional, or reciprocally determining. The pure or qualitative movement also rebounds on the on-screen images before us. And it does so in different ways according to the different kinds of gap or "interval" expressed on screen between the actions and reactions displayed between images. This interval belongs to the interrelationship between the images as they frame each other: one shot calls for another kind of shot, one cut leads to another – actions and reactions – according to the interests of the film, in particular its directorial style. Crucially, these "interests" or selections are defined by Deleuze (after Bergson) *as forms of perception* (*ibid.*: 29–30, 62, 63). In other words, perception itself is an infra-imagistic delimitation, a further selection or filtering of images from the whole, although nonetheless still linked to the whole. Its link to the whole, therefore – that is, what it expresses of the whole by its infra-imagistic selection – itself constitutes a kind of (qualitative) image that Deleuze calls the "perception-image".

Like the movement-images, of which they are a subspecies, perception-images have their own variable characteristics, namely a bias towards passive *perception* at one limit, *action* at another, and the *affect* that occupies (without filling) the gap in between.[1] The perception-image, however, should not be regarded as subjective, but rather as an objective subjectivity (it is formed from the *real* auto-delimitation of images). With the perception-image, Deleuze tells us, "we are no longer faced with subjective *or* objective images; we are caught in a correlation between a perception-image and a camera-consciousness which transforms it" (*ibid.*: 72, 74).[2]

The action-image, on the other hand, expresses the well-organized, sensory-motor relationship between characters and the story-worlds that they inhabit. It is best typified by classical Hollywood narrative and the acting methods accompanying it (although, for Deleuze, narrative is derived from the images, not the other way round). Indeed, this organicism is said to culminate in the acting "Method" itself, whose rules apply not only to the actor but to "the conception and unfolding of the film, its framings, its cutting, its montage" (*ibid.*: 155). Here the sensory-motor schema takes "possession of the image" in two basic ways. Deleuze calls the first of these the "large form" (following Noël Burch's nomenclature), wherein situations lead to actions that then lead to altered situations, as seen in westerns and action films in particular. Things happen for a reason: framings and cuts expressing either the challenges an agent meets with, or how he or she responds to them. Deleuze gives this large form the formula SAS' (situation–action–new situation). Conversely, the other action-image follows the "small form" of ASA' (action–situation–new action) where small shifts in an agent's activity hugely alter the situation and so also the agent's next action. The small form is typically seen, according to Deleuze, in melodrama and burlesque (*ibid.*: 155, 141–3).

Finally, the affection-image – the in-between of perception and action – must not be understood as subjective any more than was the perception-image. Deleuze explains it as an inside made outside, expressed *par excellence* in the close-up of the face. Indeed, it is the face in close-up that is *the* model for all affection-images, even if these affection-images comprise close-ups of hands, knives, or guns. In each case, there is a facialization of the object, the face/close-up always being a disclosure of qualities or, rather, the passage from one quality to another in pathetic states such as wonder, anger or fear (*ibid.*: 87–90, 96–7).

CLICHÉ: THE CRISIS OF IMAGES

These different types of image, with their salient features (emphasizing agency or affect or milieu) also encompass and are intimately tied to their own respective forms of space and time, each of which possesses the same emphases.[3] Variously active, reactive or affective, antagonistic, melodramatic or comedic, such spaces nevertheless remain fairly complicit with the well-determined space–times of the movement-image, whose co-ordinates come from sensory-motor organization. The history of cinema in the first half of the twentieth century comprises all the various permutations that these images and their space–times can take on, the purpose of Deleuze's *Cinema 1* being to chart each and every one of them. Daunting though this objective is, it is not an infinite task, for after fifty years or so, Deleuze finds that cinema has exhausted all the variants of actual movement possible in the image. Indeed, the culmination of *Cinema 1* tells us that it was Alfred Hitchcock who brought these relations among images to their completion, directing the movement-image to its "logical perfection" (1986: 200, 205; 1989: 34). In Hitchcock's works, every variation of the movement-image, with biases towards one pole or the other, towards perception or action, is brought together and mentalized, filtered through the pole of intellect. Every permutation in plot and agency is explored and exhausted *in cerebro*. Hitchcock makes film think or, rather, he shows the calculative intellection involved in plotting a murder, an escape, a capture, a concealment, an evasion or a blackmail. He gives us the mental images (of movement) rather than the action-images themselves, virtual movement over actual movement. Characters and actions become specular, quasi-meditative – processed for their spectrality to create suspense or unease.

With this completion, though, also came the inevitable re-examination of the "nature and status" of the movement-images by theorists and film-makers alike (*ibid.*: 205). Just as the apparent completion of philosophy and history by G. W. F. Hegel brought about a crisis in Western thought, so also the completion of the first phase of cinema by Hitchcock occasioned new levels of critical re-examination. This second crisis, still current today according to Deleuze, concerns the uncreative, cliché-ridden nature of movement-image cinema (that is, Hollywood and its imitators). The question set at the end of *Cinema 1*, portentous though it may seem, is whether cinema

183

can "attack the dark organization of clichés" (*ibid.*: 210). Can cinema extract a new image from our clichéd world at the end of the movement-image? For the cliché is not just bare repetition; it also marks out our "mental deficiency", "organized mindless-ness" and "cretinization" (*ibid.*: 208–9, 210–211, 212; Deleuze 1995a: 60). It marks the stagnation of the brain, a generalized enslavement. The crisis for cinema, then, is also one for our culture and philosophy, for our ability, fundamentally, to think anew.

In *What is Philosophy?* Deleuze and Félix Guattari make it the artist's task to struggle against the clichés and repetitions of opinion (1994: 204, 214). And, after Hitchcock, after 1945, cinema certainly seemed in need of a new artistic image. Would one emerge to save it? Would film survive to fight the good fight against cliché? *Cinema 1* asks us to wait and see. We anticipate that it will survive, of course, as heroes always do. Yet the crisis of the image that Deleuze sets up between the last chapter of *Cinema 1* and the first chapter of its sequel, *Cinema 2*, does mark a crucial fissure, a genuine inter-mission, interval, or gap in Deleuze's own thought as well. Into the gap come many things: a real sense of anticipation (for the advent of the time-image), of suspense (over the life or death of cinema) and of animationness (how long before the sequel, *Cinema 2: The Time-Image*, would come out?). And alongside the cliffhanger ending and curtain-fall, there also comes a real crisis and gap in Deleuze's film-philosophy, although we shall have to wait until we have seen what the time-image does before we tackle that.[4] So what does it do? In a reflexive move typical of modernism, the time-image *thematizes* the lack of creativity in the movement-image, the historical exhaus-tion of the movement-image. The cliché is embraced in order to be resisted, by taking a failure of form as new content. The five characteristics of the new image, then, are "*the dispersive situation, the deliberatively weak links, the voyage form, the consciousness of clichés, the condemnation of the plot*" (1986: 210). Together, they transform a vice into a virtue, wresting a new image from the bare repetitions of Hollywood.

It can do this because, by thematizing a failure, the time-image gives us a *direct* representation of what reality is like itself: time as breakage, as wound, as fissure, as crack, as differential – all the features that Deleuze's process philosophy explores across its corpus. Time out of joint is true time, for time really is what puts things out of joint, what dismembers any organized situation. Deleuze is saying no more than what Friedrich Nietzsche, William James, Bergson and Martin Heidegger said before him: when something breaks, when a habitual act fails to find its target, it emerges (as it really is) into consciousness. When vision fails, we see (the truth of) vision, we see the searches in *L'Avventura* (The adventure; dir. M. Antonioni, 1960) or *Ladri di biciclette* (The bicycle thief; dir. V. De Sica, 1948). We see not the thing, but what it is to see (or not see) the thing. We see the *process* of seeing.

In one respect, *all* the movement-images, or set of action–reaction images, can be thought of as clichés because, following Bergson, Deleuze sees any perceived image as a selection and deletion of reality in accordance with *pre-set utilitarian formulae* (1989: 20). But these clichés become *too* formulaic if they cannot adapt to external changes impinging *on them*. They lose their utility when they cannot respond to the new challenges after 1945 (post-war European anomie and exhaustion, class upheaval, social reorganization, physical and spiritual dislocation, moral re-evaluation, vast eco-nomic migrations). This is the moment of transition when anything is possible, when all the normal motor-linkages, motivated actions, logical plots, rational cuts and well-organized spaces find no purchase. What Deleuze calls "any-space-whatevers" ("*espace quelconque*") arise (a concept he takes from the anthropologist Marc Augé; Deleuze 1986: 109).

Consequently, new images of a potentially more "readable" or "thinkable" nature can emerge because they are made thematic. Deleuze talks of a new breed of signs, "opsigns" and "sonsigns", where optical- and sound-images are directly apprehended: We *see* the actor seeing his seeing, hearing his hearing: it is an image *of* an image, a thematized image (1989: 69). In the comedies of Jacques Tati, for instance, we see (and read) what it is to be a sound, as when the sound of a swinging door becomes boredom itself in *Les Vacances de Monsieur Hulot* (Monsieur Hulot's holiday; 1953), or in the numerous false fidelities between sound and image (a car horn that is also a duck's quack, a door hinge that is a plucked cello) that make us hear and so think about sound as sound. Time, space and even thought itself are made perceptible in such time-images: they are made visible and audible by being thematized in the breakdown of "natural" sights, sounds, and actions (1989: 67, 18).[5] Direct time is the "out of joint" of perception, action and affect, and therefore, of all the dimensions of movement (*ibid.*: English preface, xi).

A NEW BELIEF

The new image, the time-image, was needed to meet the challenge of the cliché. It was born to restore our need to believe in the world, to awaken us from our cynical, hackneyed lives. Where the movement-image weakened itself in formulaic, "false" movements, it is superseded by and subordinated to the time-image. This is the power *of* the "false" as such: the power to create untruths, the power to *not* correspond (with the old "truth", the formulaic truth), but *to* respond to the world of change by instantiating it anew (cf. Bogue 2006: 212–13). Cinema tries to restore our belief in the world by creating reasons to believe in this world: "we need an ethic or a faith ... a need to believe in this world" (Deleuze 1989: 173). How is this done? By inventing new relationships between sound and vision, new types of space, and even new kinds of body (that correspond to a "genesis of bodies" rather than fixed organic coordinates). The power of the false is the power of creation, invention, novelty. New kinds of actor will also have to emerge, consequently: amateurs, "professional non-actors", or "actor-mediums", capable of "seeing and showing rather than acting" (*ibid.*: 20). The French New Wave gave us an instance of this with its "cinema of attitudes and postures" (*ibid.*: 193), going so far as to make even the scenery accord to the "attitudes of the body" (*ibid.*) (Deleuze is thinking of Jean-Pierre Léaud here, François Truffaut's cinematic alter-ego). A cinema of the body emerges in contrast to the old cinema of action, with a body that is caught up in "a quite different space"; "this is a space before action, always haunted by a child, or by a clown, or by both at once". This is the cinema of bodies, which is not sensory-motor, but "action being replaced by attitude" (*ibid.*: 276). It creates a "pre-hodological space", pointing to an "undecidability of the body", where any obstacle is dispersed "in a plurality of ways of being present in the world" (*ibid.*: 203).[6]

In all of this, time is weighty. Opsigns and sonsigns, being breaks with the sensory-motor, are glimpses of real time, the time that lies virtual behind all actual (move-ment) images. They find their "true genetic element when the actual optical image crystallizes with *its own* virtual image" (*ibid.*: 69). Indeed, Deleuze explains virtual ontology plainly: "for the time-image to be born ... the actual image must enter into relation with its *own* virtual image as such" (*ibid.*: 273). And this virtual, real time, which cannot occupy any actual present, must therefore occupy the past or "past in general" (a past that has no actual date) (*ibid.*: 79). In the cinematic time-image, past and present, virtual and actual, become indiscernible. The films of the Italian *neo*-realists, the French *New* Wave, *New* German Cinema, and the *New* Hollywood of the 1970s only give us glimpses of this virtuality, but they are direct glimpses all the same.[7] These "new", evidently, bring the virtual with them (*ibid.*). The cinematic glimpses of real time also come in various guises, some more and some less obviously temporal. With the work of Alain Resnais, for instance (*Je t'aime, je t'aime* [1968], *Hiroshima mon amour* [1959]), we "plunge into memory" (*ibid.*: 119): but it is not a present mem-ory or psychological recollection so much as a direct exploration of time: "memory is not in us; it is we who move in Being-memory, a world-memory" (*ibid.*: 98).

TIME AND ETERNITY: THE IRRATIONAL CUT AND THE EVENT

The locus of the indiscernibility of the virtual and actual is named (after Guattari) the "crystal-image" by Deleuze. But its ontology comes directly from Bergson's philosophy of time in *Matter and Memory* as well as his essay on *déjà vu*, "Memory of the Present and False Recognition" (Deleuze 1989: 81). Deleuze articulates it as follows:

> What constitutes the crystal-image is the most fundamental operation of time: since the past is constituted not after the present that it was but at the same time, time has to split itself in two at each moment as present and past, which differ from each other in nature, or, what amounts to the same thing, it has to split the present into two heterogeneous directions, one of which is launched towards the future while the other falls towards the past. ... Time consists of this split, and it is this, it is time, that we *see in the crystal.*
> (*Ibid.*: 81)

Because cinema is time itself in direct presentation, its time-images are glimmering instantiations of the "most fundamental operation of time". The past persists in the present, although we are never aware of this save for those rare moments of temporal paradoxs such as *déjà vu*.[8] But its persistence is what allows for change, its past is what makes each present *pass on*.[9] Once again, because the time-image (like every other image) is also a relation between subjective and objective tendencies or poles, it can present itself in two possible forms, one grounded in the past, the other in the present (*ibid.*: 98).

Film can explore Being-memory across a varied landscape formed with what Deleuze calls "peaks" and "plains" (or "sheets") of the past. Orson Welles's *Citizen*

Kane (1941) is a case in point of the co-presence of past and present, the famed depth of field photography expressing "regions of past as such … The hero acts, walks and moves: but it is the past that he plunges himself into and moves in: time is no longer subordinated to movement, but movement to time" (*ibid.*: 106). When Gregg Toland's camera bears down on Susan (Dorothy Comingore) at the club, for example, there is a "contraction" of "the actual present" in its "invitation to recollect" (*ibid.*: 109). Or, to take an example of our own, Jaco van Dormael's *Toto le héros* (Toto the hero; 1991) tells a story concerning the profound effects of an old man's past on his and others' present. This is a common storyline for many films, but *Toto le héros* achieves it as much with typical scenes of a man recollecting *his* past as by *showing* a continuity of past and present *in general* with resonating cuts, graphic matches and matches on action between different events. The "past in general" is here in the present *on screen*, or, rather, we are directly in the presence of the past on screen (*ibid.*: 101). From the Deleuzian position, therefore, it is a mistake to think that the film image is "by nature in the present" (*ibid.*: 105). Or, if it is, then at least it is not within a *simple* present, as *L'Année dernière à Marienbad* (Last year at Marienbad; 1961) demonstrates when its events derive from three types of present: that of the past, of the present and of the future.

Among the different kinds of time-image, the crystal-image itself maintains the closest link to the virtual. It is described as a kind of "expression" (Deleuze here shifting to his own Spinozist language; cf. Deleuze 1990b), be it the expression seen in the relation between past and present (or the virtual and the actual), or in other more oblique relations.[10] Various films provide examples of the different forms of the crystal's expression, some of them perfect (Max Ophüls' *La Ronde* [Roundabout; 1950]), some flawed (Jean Renoir's *La Règle du jeu* [The rules of the game; 1939]), some in the process of its composition (Federico Fellini's *Amarcord* [I remember; 1973]), some in the process of its decay (Luchino Visconti's *Il Gattopardo* [The leopard; 1963]). The curious fact about *Cinema 2*, however, is that the most powerful embodiment of the time-image throughout the book is not an image at all but the lack of one: the irrational cut. Indeed, the irrational cut is the paradigm case for Deleuze. It is more than just false continuity, though, for such cuts come in diverse forms, be it "the steady form of a sequence of unusual, 'anomolous' images, which come and interrupt the normal linkage of the two sequences; or in the enlarged form of the black screen, or the white screen, and their derivatives" (Deleuze 1989: 248–9).

What matters in each case is that the cut now exits for itself, no longer for what it conjoins, but for its own disjunctive value. The cut, being itself now cut through and broken (irrational), gives us a vision of real time. It captures the essence of how the movement-image differs from the time-image, the disjointedness of the latter being rendered fully in a mutilated joint.

This mutilation gives us real time, or the event – the time of eternity. Yet, what is an event for Deleuze? He writes: "I've tried in all my books to discover the nature of events; it's a philosophical concept, the only one capable of ousting the verb 'to be'" (Deleuze 1995a: 141): event as becoming *contra* being. Yet for Deleuze, the event is understood in terms of multiplicity rather than process. Time must be contained in eternity. Time cannot be time as *succession*: it is empty, the time of eternity. Ultimately, it is the Event. So, when does an event occur? The answer is that *it* (a static entity) could never *occur* (a process); to change is to stop being:

> The agonizing aspect of the pure event is that it is always and at the same something which has just happened and something about to happen; never something which is happening ... it is the present as being of reason which is subdivided *ad infinitum* into something that has just happened or is going to happen, always flying in both directions at once.
>
> (Deleuze 1990a: 63)

We keep missing the event. Or, rather, the event is in this constant *missing*, about to happen or having happened, but never happening. And cinema, modern cinema, *shows* this. Take Julio Medem's *Los Amantes del Círculo Polar* (Lovers of the Arctic Circle; 1998), a film all about missed identities and encounters. Not only do we have different actors playing the characters of Otto and Ana (a tactic of diffusion already used by Luis Buñuel in *Cet obscur objet du désir* (That obscure object of desire; 1977), but their names are palindromes: moving backwards and forwards, no less than time itself does in this film. The same occurrences are also populated by different characters/actors, a case in point being the line "it's the midnight sun" (above the Arctic Circle), which is spoken twice by different characters in different scenes communicating between two remote points in the film. There are also events – a chase through a forest/park, a fall through trees into snow, near-miss collisions – that repeat across the film, populating themselves with different individuals and settings each time they are "actualized". Finally, there are the numerous coincidences throughout that are not psychological premonitions (of the stag, for instance) but actual coexistences of different times gathered together by the same resonating names ("Otto the Piloto") and events (collisions, falls) where things and people do not *coincide*.

This is the Deleuzian event: above the Arctic Circle the sun never sets – a very Platonist idea evoking both the constancy of the atemporal event as well as the *circulation* of actions and individuals it keeps in play. But, and this is the crucial point, the series of repetitions is kept going by the *non-coincidence* of these two lovers who keep missing each other, even on their first night of love. Even at the end when Ana does meet her bus in a fatal collision, this one consummated act also stops her from meeting with Otto. Yet, it is such constant errancy and deflection in their lives that sustains their love (and the movie). Their evental difference resonates through all of the other moments, missed encounters, belated mourning and near-deaths.

Time in modern cinema, Deleuze tells us, "is no longer empirical, nor metaphysical; it is 'transcendental' in the sense that Kant gives this word: time is out of joint and presents itself in the pure state" (Deleuze 1986: 7, 46; 1989: xi, 271). In the history of cinema we see film repeat the history of philosophy. In a sense, though, it is only the same thing that is being said in different ways, and this is in line with Deleuze's theory of univocity (that Being is said in the same way of, and by, every different thing). There is but one Being, with many languages through which it may express itself. *Philosophia sive Cinema*. This is an inclusive disjunction: not a choice within a hierarchy of discourses, but different modes of expression. We can learn as much from what film shows as from what philosophy says: both are vital forms of expression for Deleuze.

NOTES

1. Each of these biases is itself expressed by a different type of film image: the perception-image as such (images that act on a central image), along with action-images (reaction of that centre to those images) and affection-images (the gap between that action and reaction, internal or undischarged reaction), as well as even further subdivisions (the impulse-image coming in between action and affect as a kind of virtual action, of potential acts more than actual ones).
2. Deleuze offers the example of "the obsessive framings" of Eric Rohmer's *Die Marquise von O...* (The marquis of O; 1976) as expressive of this objective phenomenology, or semi-subjectivity. Deleuze invokes Pier Paolo Pasolini's linguistic model of free indirect discourse to explain this transformation; *Cinema 1: The Movement-Image*, H. Tomlinson & B. Habberjam (trans.) (London: Athlone, 1986), 75, 78.
3. The affection-image, for instance, extracts the face, but also carries with that its own peculiar form of "space-time – a scrap of vision, sky, countryside or background" (Deleuze, *Cinema 1*, 108), as can be seen in Robert Bresson's *Procès de Jeanne d'Arc* ([*The Trial of Joan of Arc*] 1962) or in the tactile spaces of his *Pickpocket* (1959) (*ibid.*, 109).
4. Martin Schwab (2000: 134n.) argues that there is strong shift in theoretical orientation between the two *Cinema* books, *Cinema 2* largely ignoring the image-ontology set up in *Cinema 1*.
5. Other new signs enter into relation with a set of different types of time-image: readable and thinkable images or "chronosigns" (points of the present and sheets of the past), "crystal-images" (where actual and virtual are held together), "lectosigns" (readable images) and "noosigns" (signs that can only be thought); cf. Deleuze *Negotiations: 1972–1990*, M. Joughin (trans.) (New York: Columbia University Press, 1995), 53. With the lectosigns of modern cinema, for example, sounds now constitute an "autonomous sonic continuum", to use Ronald Bogue's phrase, while images constitute a separate visual continuum, the two being put into relation with one another through their *mutual differences* – their asynchrony rather than a synchrony; cf. R. Bogue, *Deleuze on Cinema* (New York: Routledge, 2003), 7–8.
6. With "in a plurality of ways of being present in the world", Deleuze is citing Gilbert Simondon, *L'individu et sa genèse physico-biologique* (Paris: Presses Universitaires de France, 1964), 233–4.
7. Although Deleuze says that there were earlier indications in Orson Welles, Yasujirō Ozu and Jacques Tati.
8. Indeed, Deleuze characteristically favours all the pathologies or failings of memory and recognition – *déjà vu*, dream-images, fantasies, visions of the dying – as the proper cinematic avatars of real time; cf. Deleuze, *Cinema 2: The Time-Image*, H. Tomlinson & R. Galeta (trans.) (London: Athlone, 1989), 39, 55. These pathologies are also Bergson's favourite *entrées* into time.
9. This argument comes directly from *Difference and Repetition*, P. Patton (trans.) (London: Continuum, 1994). Deleuze talks of the paradox of the present as the need for a time in which to constitute/synthesize time (past, present and future). So "*there must be another time in which the first synthesis of time can occur*" (*ibid.*, 79). That other time of passage is the past.
10. These others are that between the limpid and the opaque, and the seed and the environment (cf. *Cinema 2*, 74). Bogue reminds us that Deleuze alters Bergson to see "movement as the expression of *durée*" (rather than the same as it) (*Deleuze on Cinema*, 26).

17 SARAH KOFMAN

Tom Conley

Sarah Kofman (1934–94) was a French philosopher who held a Chair at the Sorbonne in Paris from 1991. She studied under Jean Hyppolite and Gilles Deleuze. She published more than twenty books of critical philosophy, including works on Freud, and Nietzsche, and a number of auto-biographical works concerning her life and the political culture of the twentieth century. These books include *The Childhood of Art* (1970; English trans. 1988), *Nietzsche and Metaphor* (1973; English trans. 1993), *Camera Obscura* (1973; English trans. 1998), *Aberrations* (1978), *The Enigma of Woman* (1980; English trans. 1985), *Le respect des femmes (Kant et Rousseau)* (1982), *Smothered Words* (1987; English trans. 1998), *Socrates* (1989; English trans. 1998), *Séductions* (1990) and *Rue Ordener, Rue Labat* (1994; English trans. 1996).

A LADY VANISHES

Towards the end of *Rue Ordener, Rue Labat* (1994), the terse and elegant autobio-graphical fiction she wrote just before terminating her life, Sarah Kofman inserts a brief episode relating her admiration for Alfred Hitchcock's *The Lady Vanishes* (1938). How or why Hitchcock's film appears in the fiction is uncanny. *Rue Ordener, Rue Labat* was the last book (of about twenty-five) the author had written prior to her suicide. The following year (1995) there appeared the posthumous *L'Imposture de la beauté*, a book of essays that the author had been crafting from six earlier articles or book chap-ters dating to 1990. On the verso of the title page, above the copyright line, is noted: "[t]his is Sarah Kofman's last book. She was at the point of completing it. Today we have done just that, in fidelity and in memory of an editorial friendship of more than twenty years."[1] The insertion implies that *L'Imposture de la beauté* marked the author's effort to put the remainders of her life together before taking leave of the world and to affirm that *Rue Ordener, Rue Labat* was in most likelihood her final work of integral and finished reflection. In all events, soon after the publication of the book of child-hood memories under the Occupation, *the lady vanishes*.

The film appears in the autobiography as a memory-flash having little to do with the narrative. It is not an episode the author locates in her childhood (although the film is roughly synchronous with her birth in the late pre-war years). Her recall of *The Lady Vanishes* becomes an anticipation or projection, even a telltale sign or hieroglyph alerting informed readers that she is turning a troubled – inspired and inspiring, but also traumatized and traumatizing – life into a work of art. With *The Lady Vanishes* she tells the world that she too will disappear. With her first overtly creative work and with Hitchcock she becomes an *auteur* in the strong cinematic sense of the word.[2]

The irruption of the film into an oeuvre in which film played little part affirms, paradoxically, how vital it is to life-writing in the mould of aesthetic philosophy. This becomes clear when the speculations of *L'Imposture de la beauté* (hereafter *L'Imposture*) are superimposed on *Rue Ordener, Rue Labat*: the former comprises six studies of works of art, philosophy and cinema. Its first and titular chapter, on Oscar Wilde's *Portrait of Dorian Gray*, makes no mention of the eponymous film of 1945 (dir. Albert Lewin), but in an unsolicited fashion this essay corresponds with the last essay, titled "Anguish and Catharsis", which takes up *The Lady Vanishes*. In the endnotes a list of sources for each of the essays reveals that the piece on Hitchcock "had been written for a special number of *Cahiers du cinéma* under the direction of Antoine de Baecque. This number was never published" (1995: 147). Thus the only really new or arresting piece in *L'Imposture* would have been this essay. Kofman might have left it to be published so as to allow readers – like those of this volume on philosophers and their movies – to contemplate where and how film works *with* (and not entirely *through*) philosophy and psychoanalysis. It allows the reader to see better how *Rue Ordener, Rue Labat* is crafted as a piece of cinematic writing, *ciné-écriture*, that its twenty-three paratactic "takes", each bearing a distinctly *visual texture* in its printed shape, can be appreciated as a future scenario for a film. Further still, given the compositional strategies of autobiography, they can be projected onto *L'Imposture* for the purpose of discerning how film riddles her other writings, whether on Freud's Michelangelo, Wilde, Kant or Nietzsche on Wagner and music in general.

It suffices to see how before why. *Rue Ordener, Rue Labat* departs from the style and tenor of much of Kofman's previous writing. It no longer follows, *à la* Gilles Deleuze and Jacques Derrida, a mode of free indirect philosophical discourse for which their schools were known. It is not that of a commentator who transposes the gist of the reasoning of authors under study into his or her own words for the purpose of modulating them or aiming them along new itineraries. It is not a montage that immediately yields, in the idiolect of her master-philosopher, the sights and sounds of *différance*. Unlike her other books, it never seeks to free the force of a concept or unveil an unconscious structure from other authors. In the earlier work Kofman often referred to the "hieroglyphics" of her philosophers – Friedrich Nietzsche and Sigmund Freud – who, like Pauline children, forever saw and wrote through "a glass darkly". She alternated between a free indirect style that Derrida had championed in his studies of Freud, in which, in order to depart from the founder of psychoanalysis he virtually "became" his master, and one that, in his work on cinema, Deleuze embodied through affiliation with Pier Paolo Pasolini's "free indirect" style of film and of writing (Deleuze 1983: 110–13), which went hand in hand with clarification and summary. A great comic philosopher, she was, like François Rabelais' alter ego, Alcofribas Nasier, an *abstractor of quintessence*: a scholar and a magus, a comedian and a commentator who abstracts truth from base material in the laboratory

191

of her wit; and who no sooner renders it abstract or enigmatic better to appreciate its unnameable quintessence.

In *Rue Ordener, Rue Labat* other issues are at stake. The prose is of arresting simplicity, of a simple confessional tenor. It refuses to analyse that of which it writes or even its own writing. In the fashion of Paul Valéry it can be taken as an *exercice de style*, an essay that undertakes risks by bringing forward to the reader, as if he or she were an analyst refusing to impose any moral judgement on the words, traumatic childhood memories. From the very first sentence the simplicity of the account beguiles:

> De lui, il ne me reste seulement le stylo. Je l'ai pris un jour dans le sac de ma mère où elle le gardait avec d'autres souvenirs de mon père. Un stylo comme l'on n'en fait plus, et qu'il fallait remplir avec de l'encre. Je m'en suis servie pendant toute ma scolarité. Il m'a "lâchée" avant que je puisse me décider à l'abandonner. Je le possède toujours, rafistolé avec du scotch, il est devant mes yeux sur ma table de travail et il me contraint à écrire, écrire. [Of him for me there remains only the pen. I took it one day from my mother's purse where she was keeping it with others of my father's souvenirs. A pen the way they are no longer made, that had to be filled with ink. I used it throughout my entire education. He "let me go" before I could decide to abandon him. I still own it, now pieced together with Scotch tape; it's before my eyes on my work desk, and it forces me to write, to write.]
>
> (1994: 9)

The first object in the fiction is the pen, and the first person who appears is the mother. She keeps memories of her husband (the child's father) in a handbag. The child pilfers a pen that later becomes a fetish. Kofman's habitual reader immediately remarks the presence of a *style* so limned and carefully wrought that the words and their spacings resemble hieroglyphs. The narratrix seems to commit – but the texture does not allow us to be sure – an original sin by stealing from her mother a vital and seminal object that had belonged to her father. As in a film, the deixis or delineation of subject-positions is indistinct in the midst of an almost blinding clarity. Her father let her go, but in the context he also "gave her over" before she could take it upon herself, in her coming of age, to detach herself from him, *to let him go*: but not entirely, because the pen as fetish-object, like the figurines on Freud's own writing desk in Vienna, remains eminently visible on hers. She does not write with it but, rather, uses its presence or visible evidence to inspire her writing. The syntax suggests that she possesses "him" (the father) through "it" (the pen). It is glued together with a product of the Minnesota Mining Company ("Scotch" being an *écho, escot* and an *escutcheon*, an emblem, but also a name that an inebriate reader would discern as a kind of whisky). Given the disposition of the whole chapter that stands as a picture on the page, both *he* and *it* lay before her eyes on her workbench that is the page itself, such that he and it oblige or dictate to her to write ... *to write*. The double iteration makes clear that the fetish imposes, like a memory of Moses, an injunction and a law that reassures ("I must write, it is my duty") but that disinters a deeply embedded fear ("Can I write, and if I can, how do I put pen to paper?"). The pen invokes a menacing presence eliciting a promise of pleasure. It is a complex scenario, not far from what Kofman elucidates in *L'Enfance de l'art* (her first book) and rehearses again in a chapter on Freud's reading of Michelangelo's statue of Moses (in *L'Imposture*, in which the analyst's first impression of the great statue inspires "crushing guilt"), when the figure seems ready to hurl the tables on the "atheist Jew" who beholds him (1995: 53). Which gives way to a second impression: as a statue Moses seems caught in his action, "forever seated and irritated" about his immobility.

Rather than elucidating what was the intolerable ambivalence felt in both the scene and its writing, Kofman prefers to hold (or, in the vocabulary of the psychoanalyst Nicholas Abraham [1987], "introject") the feeling of disquiet in the spaces marked between inverted commas. He "turned me over" or "gave me away". The flashback that follows in chapter two indicates that the past participle of *lâcher* redounds echoes of the father's canine obedience and unwarranted cowardice that went with his selfless and selfish act of turning himself over to the Nazis at the moment the police began to round up Jews in Paris (on 16 July 1942) under the directives of the Final Solution. The police arrive and the mother tries to convince the officer ("with a troubled smile") that her husband is at the synagogue before, suddenly, he emerges from an adjacent room and hands himself over. The child deduces that her mother committed a sin, a white lie that was to no avail, even when the agent did not want to shoulder the responsibility of reporting the man to the authorities. Today, writes Kofman, recalling the lamentations of Greek tragedy, she cannot fail to flash back to (*penser à*) "this scene of my childhood when six children, abandoned by their father (*abandonnés de leur père*) could only cry in suffocating, and with the certainty that she and the other siblings would never see him again: 'o papa, papa, papa'" (1994: 14). The father vanishes.

In the drift of the words cast between quotation marks on the first page the father "let [her] go" – to whom or to what? – before she could, it is implied, understand what it would mean to grieve. Without remaining in the grip of an incurable melancholy (which elsewhere Kofman sees afflicting Dorian Gray), the writer mystically "possesses" his ghost in the shape of the old pen, an element of style held together with Scotch tape. The scene sets the narration in motion at the same time as it embodies greater tensions in the shape of the writing. The scene is in the present. The pen incites memories that come "out of the past". The beginning anticipates the later flashback to *The Lady Vanishes*. The reader soon discovers that the latter arches back on the former so as to draw attention to the cinematic memory, much resembling what Freud in his work on dreams called *Bilderschriften*, moving hieroglyphs or pictured writings, which also run through *The Lady Vanishes*. As soon as Hitchcock's film figures in the text (in chapter nineteen), it goes without saying that each of the segments of the book resembles a *plan-séquence*.[3] Many of its unacknowledged effects inform the *ciné-écriture* with which Kofman constructs her memoir.

As in classical cinema, *The Lady Vanishes* owes much to Aristotelian poetics, which require a *trophy* or turning point to shift the tensions of the scenario at a median point of its development. It comes when Gilbert (Michael Redgrave), until then the nemesis of Iris (Margaret Lockwood), is won over to her cause in the pursuit of Miss Froy (Dame May Whitty), the good lady who has disappeared in a train, implied to be the Orient Express, on its return to London. Once their destiny of attraction is sealed, the two dashing characters solve the enigma and, wonder of wonders, share a love that dispels the "unhappy end" of the preordained marriage awaiting Iris on return to England. *Rue Ordener, Rue Labat* builds on the same structure through a graphic pattern indicating the presence of an "absent centre" or even a vanishing point in the textual design.[4] Composed of twenty-three chapters, it leaves at its axis, in the twelfth segment, set squarely between a "before" (chs 1–11) and an "after" (chs 13–23) a trophy-chapter titled "Métamorphose".[5] With oblique allusion to Kafka, it recounts how the author had to abandon her mother and take refuge with a Christian woman who eventually, as the final sentence of the book later underlines, "saved the life of a little Jewish girl during the war" (1994: 99). Spelled *mémé* in the text (unless at the head of a sentence), her name is in lower case, implying that she is a sort of *objet petit-m*, a lost m-object, a likely variant on Lacan's *objet petit-a*, the forlorn object that drives oral desire (or *appetite*, the *objet petit-a* in it is read backwards). In the guise of an ersatz mother, mémé wins the child's affection. She directs the little Jewish girl from what she calls (in Kofman's words) a "childhood pernicious to good health" (*ibid*.: 48) to a better state of being. Mémé gets her outdoors, introduces her to her saintly friend Paul (whose Christian name tells much about the ideology of faith, hope and charity), and habitually sets an elegant table at mealtimes. She embraces the child and ultimately awakens her to her senses.

Peu à peu mémé opéra en moi une véritable transformation (Little by little, mémé brought about in me a real transformation) (*ibid*.: 49, emphasis added). In its rapport with the chapter, the title indicates how a "bad" (Christian) surrogate mother is indeed a "good" counterpart to the "good" (Jewish) although "bad" biological mother who had been intolerably demanding of her daughter. Mémé brings the author to her life when, in the preterit, she *opéra* [operated] a (musical) transformation and also, in the distinctly Freudian gist of the text, becomes an unconscious substitute for the father, *père*, who had recently left her. One day in the hospital room, her tonsils removed, the author awakens to behold the two mothers at her bedside. One complains and makes a fracas in Yiddish to tyrannize a doctor. The other, calm and smiling, assures the child that ice cream is on the way. The last sentence of the axial chapter, the trophy itself, wins the day: "Je ressens vaguement ce jour-là que je me détache de ma mère et m'attache de plus en plus à l'autre femme" ("On that day I vaguely sense that I am detaching myself from my mother and attaching myself more and more to the other woman") (*ibid*.: 53).

At this juncture the title of the book is written into the text much as a "figure in a carpet" or a hieroglyph. Kofman had noted that the metro stop Rue Ordener was separated from the Rue Labat by one station. Adepts of the Parisian metro know well that the metro map is "a reminder, a pocket mirror on which are reflected – and lost in a flash – the skylarks of the past", and that certain stations and their names inform us of an "inner geology and subterranean geography of the city … where dazzling discoveries of correspondences promote recall of tiny and intimate tremors in the sedimentary layers of our memory" (Augé 2002: 4). For Kofman the names of the stations are points of a psychomachia in which a child is at odds between two mothers. The force of the autobiographical novel wells up in the toponyms and their proximity in the syntax. Kofman recalls with delight and disgust the shift from one regime to another. Under mémé's new management:

> Je dus m'accoutumer à un nouveau régime alimentaire. La viande saignante m'avait toujours été interdite. Rue Ordener, dans la cuisine, ma mère laissait dégouliner des heures entières des morceaux de boeuf salé qu'elle faisait ensuite bouillir. Rue Labat, je dus me "refaire la santé" en mangeant de la viande de cheval crue, dans du bouillon. Il me fallut manger du porc et me "faire" à la cuisine au saindoux.
> [I had to get accustomed to a new alimentary regime. Raw meat had always been forbidden. Rue Ordener: in the kitchen my mother let pieces of corned beef drip for hours on end that she then put to boil. Rue Labat: I had to "return to health" by eating raw horsemeat in bouillon. I was told to eat pork and "get used to" cooking with lard.]   (1994: 51)

The conversion to lard becomes an ultimate transgression, but it is also sign of the presence of the "good breast" (*sein doux*) of the new mother. Ordener, what in her life had been ordered and ordinary, seems *orde* or vile. Labat, what is "over there" (*là bas*), despite the sweet savour of the name for lard, also rings of the slaughterhouse, *l'abattoir*, a site of intolerable violence whence the horsemeat comes (as shown in Georges Franju's traumatizing *Sang des bêtes* [Blood of beasts; 1949] or in the writings of Georges Bataille, one of Kofman's formative authors). At no other point in the novel are the two names so visibly and immediately complementary in their opposition.

Much of what follows builds on the detachment and the residual guilt felt in the turn of events that concealed the girl from the fate of so many of her faith and kin. The narratrix works – or writes – with the founding ambivalence and separation through two memories. One (chapter eighteen) recalls the image on the cover of Kofman's first book, *L'Enfance de l'art* (1970) where she "chose to put a Leonardo, the famous 'London cartoon'" (*ibid.*: 73) of the Virgin and St Anne, shown almost arm-in-arm, who look over the infant Jesus who is playing with St John the Baptist. Implicitly alluding to Freud's 1907 "Leonardo da Vinci and a Memory of his Childhood" as if to suggest via the father of psychoanalysis that any writing of an early memory is a revision and reinvention bearing on tensions in the present. She quotes the essay in order, it seems, to put herself in the third person to show how this *je* of the autobiography is an *other* thanks to a distant memory that is both his (Freud's) and hers (Kofman's). She quotes Freud:

> Leonardo's childhood was as unique as this painting. He had two mothers, first his true mother, Caterina, from whom he was torn away between three and five years of age, and then a young and tender step-mother, the wife of his father, Donna Alibicia. ... When Leonardo, under the age of five, was received in the paternal grandparents' household, his young mother-in-law Albicia in most likelihood in his heart replaced mother.
> (*Ibid.*: 73–4, quoting Freud)

Kofman presents a *tableau vivant* of a relation with Leonardo and Freud that had been left latent in her critical studies. A veil is lifted, to be sure, but that veil gives way to another, the next chapter, that flashes back to a memory-image from *The Lady Vanishes*.

Freud, Leonardo's *Virgin and St Anne*, and *L'Enfance de l'art* are juxtaposed to the sudden and unforeseen remarks about *The Lady Vanishes*, "one of my favourite films" (*ibid.*: 75). Each time she sees the classic, "the same visceral anguish" overtakes her at the moment the "good little old lady, Miss Froy, seated in the compartment facing the heroine who has fallen asleep (a young English woman named Iris) disappears", especially when another woman made to resemble Miss Froy takes her place. The anguish reaches it apex when Iris, in pursuit of the motherly woman, returns to the compartment time and again, now half-convinced by a pseudo-doctor from Prague (whose accent in a requisitely grainy and baritone voice gives his assertions the ring of truth) telling her that the concussion she sustained when a pot of flowers fell on her head at the station prior to departure has caused hallucinations. Iris began to believe that Miss Froy never boarded the train and that the woman the conspirators put before her eyes had always been there. Kofman's words are of her own style and situation:

> L'intolérable, pour moi, c'est toujours d'apercevoir brutalement à la place du bon visage "maternel" de la vieille ..., l'intolérable, c'est d'apercevoir brusquement ce visage de sa remplaçante ..., visage effroyablement dur, faux, fuyant, menaçant, en lieu et place de celui si doux et si souriant de la bonne dame, au moment même où l'on s'attendait à la retrouver.
> [Intolerable for me is always to notice brutally in place of the good "natural" face of the old lady ..., [and] intolerable for me is brusquely to notice the face of the woman who replaces her ..., a frighteningly [*effroyablement*] hard, false, fleeting, menacing face in the space and place of that of the good lady, so sweet and smiling, at the very moment they expected to find her.]
> (*Ibid.*: 76–7)

Kofman concludes the chapter in a paragraph of a single sentence, a parting shot that arches uncharacteristically away from description and toward analysis (based on Melanie Klein): "the bad breast in place of the good breast, the one perfectly cleaved from the other, the one being transformed into the other" (*ibid.*: 77).

In their montage these two chapters appear as twin paratactic interruptions. They portray the rupture and contact of philosophy (in so far as Kofman had shown Freud's aesthetic philosophy to be more probing than Kant and the equal of Nietzsche) and cinema (Hitchcock but also Victor Sjöström, Louis Malle and Alain Resnais, directors of whom she writes or mentions elsewhere). The scene from *The Lady Vanishes* would be, like Leonardo's cartoon, the emblem of the lifesaving transformation she underwent between *Mère* and *mémé*. Nothing is said elsewhere to confirm the point. But the words that convey the impression bear, like the episode, and like the tenor of philosophy Kofman espouses, a double valence. First and foremost, the frighteningly obdurate face of the bad mother is contrived to bear the repressed presence of her counterpart in the volley of fricatives that draws the eye to the vanishing perspective of the good mother's name written into the face "*effroyablement* dur, faux, fuyant, menaçant ..." (emphasis added). The converse holds for Miss Froy, who carries the dubious traits of a liar, a double agent posing as a gentle governess.

In *Rue Ordener, Rue Labat*, no sign of the confluence of such opposites is made. They are shunted into the fiction at the end of chapter seventeen, in the episode recounting how the real mother fails to obtain Sarah's custody and what happens when two men brusquely tear the narratrix from mémé's arms. The bad mother yells in Yiddish, "I'm your mother, I don't give a damn about the court's decision, you belong to me" (*ibid.*: 71). There is another parting reflection: "Je me débattais, criais, sanglotais. Au fond, je me sentais soulagée" ("I was fighting with myself, I was crying, sobbing. In my heart of hearts I felt relieved") (*ibid.*: 71). The return to law and order at the Rue Ordener brings an inner calm. It is soon dissipated during the years of study under the real mother's aegis. It is the *cursus* that leads her to another life and to the end of the fiction in which – in the final parting shot – she recalls that the priest who spoke over mémé's burial reminded everyone present that she had saved a little Jewish girl.[6]

"Angoisse et catharsis", the final chapter of *L'Imposture de la beauté*, revises the scenario. The first two paragraphs (1995: 141–2) reproduce *verbatim* the decisive chapter of *Rue Ordener, Rue Labat*. A specialist in textual genesis would remark rightly how a snippet from a scholarly article destined for publication in a cinema journal utterly changes when placed in a montage of childhood memories. Much of the article is lopped away, ostensibly because the violence of the memory-image from Hitchcock is edulcorated when subjected to philosophical analysis.

Most of the article works with and through the same traumatic sequence. The montage is treated directly from the standpoint of ambivalence and, obliquely, from the position holding that Hitchcock's film inspires philosophical reflection. First, ambivalence: Miss Froy is not so innocent or "good" as she was in *Rue Ordener, Rue Labat*. She is a spy pitted against the enemy Kofman identifies as the Nazis. She has (unlike Kofman's father) "lied about her identity" (*ibid.*: 142). The image of the nasty woman obfuscates and soon contaminates the positive image she had drawn from the maternal figure. She no longer carries either "the purity of the ideal" or "its perfection". Having almost been murdered, the old lady loses her "productive powers". And, observes Kofman, Iris ultimately saves Miss Froy.[7] She further insists on the maternal agency of the film via François Truffaut, in his dialogues with the director, in *Hitchcock* (1985), that reveal how the seed of the narrative originated in Paris, in 1889, in a story telling of a mother and a daughter who come to the city where the elder falls ill in a hotel. The daughter seeks a doctor, who sends her off in search of medicine. Four hours later she returns and finds not only that the mother has vanished but also that she is accused of never having brought her there in the first place.

Secondly, reflection: hindsight of autobiography shows that the film "reads" or "analyses" the spectator's vital infantile anxieties. A "ritual of initiation" and "education in maternal ambivalence" (*ibid.*: 142), the film becomes a lesson in what might be called anxiety management. Iris, like Kofman, cannot recover the image of the "good" mother through that of her "bad" counterpart because the latter is too unstable – too fraught with contradictions – to allow her to "supporter l'intolérable de la transformation" ("support the intolerable nature of the transformation") (*ibid.*: 143).[8] The faces of the other travellers in the compartment convince the heroine that the maternal image was "indeed and only of a hallucinatory type" (*ibid.*). Her unconscious guilt over the transformation suffuses the film. The lawyer and his mistress are wrong to be in collusion; the two Englishmen's obsessions with the cricket match betrays a refusal to share concern about the political turmoil in their midst, much less to avow their own homoerotic fantasies. Even Iris had shown herself to be "intolerable" (*ibid.*) when she bribed the *maître d'hôtel* to be rid of Gilbert, the future hero, now a nonchalant musicologist who makes too much noise. In Kofman's terms, to have his room "emptied" would be tantamount to "emptying the maternal belly, to make it sterile" (*ibid.*). But her childish tantrum also signals that the episodes count among the heroine's various attempts to defer and to break up the marriage that awaits her at the end of the voyage. The instances of the death-drive (*pulsions de mort*) transform the other travellers into persecuting conspirators. What Kofman calls Iris's unconscious guilt in fact incites her to "repair the mother" with assistance of the clarinettist who had been her nemesis. Music, the bond that ties Miss Froy to Gilbert and to Iris and that brings the story to a happy end, draws Kofman into the story: for in the hieroglyphic register of the autobiography good food is indistinguishable from good music.[9]

In a first conclusion, Kofman remarks that *The Lady Vanishes* can be read as "the incarnation of the heroine's phantasms under the effect of her paranoid anguish and her unconscious guilt" (*ibid.*: 144). The film is a nightmare palliating the intolerable machinations it simultaneously brings forward. It seems that through the film Kofman "repairs" her relation with a maternal figure, but that she bumps against a white wall, a limit, where nothing more can be said: except to invent a contrary argument asserting that the *mise en abyme* of the title of the film within the film, seen in the name on a poster belonging to the paraphernalia of the Italian illusionist ("The Vanishing Lady"), would be an ultimate illusion of a cinematic illusionist.[10] Kofman deploys the second hypothetical conclusion to deconstruct her own "reductive, 'psychoanalytical'" (*ibid.*: 145) reading that would take itself too seriously. To this point the author notes how she *reads* the film and no sooner remarks that since she sees it over and again her identification with the heroine awakens in her "the most archaic anguish" and, she adds, borrowing a formula from Freud's "The Uncanny", "that has for a long time been surmounted" (*ibid.*). The illusionist's task, however, is to explode the anguish it engenders in a healthy burst of laughter or a resonant chord of music.[11]

Hitchcock taps into a deeply ambivalent maternal relation that seems to be part and parcel of Kofman's life (perhaps in ours as well), attesting to the intolerable difficulties that make life what it is. In the way it falls into the autobiography – next to Freud and Leonardo – and is treated in the posthumous essay at the end of *L'Imposture*, the film becomes more than a philosophical object. It obsesses. It reveals, dissimulates, clarifies and adjudicates. The webbing of relations it unveils, along with their traumatic underpinnings, is evident elsewhere in Kofman's writing. In the essay on Freud's *Moses and Monotheism* in *L'Imposture* Kofman writes of the intolerable incommensurability of a law with respect to a figure, like Michelangelo's statue, that would represent it. Kofman locates it in a maternal relation: "The figure of the law", she asserts, "can never be reduced to the figure of the mother, unless the latter figures what cannot be figured, in other words, sublimely" (1995: 68). *The Lady Vanishes* sustains that sublimity and indeed becomes the very enigma of art that, in Nietzsche's sense, is art because a maternal force engenders it. His artist, she adds, is he or she who is a "creator of affirmation of life, that is, the person who wants life with all its joy but also with everything that qualifies it to be terrible and intolerable" (*ibid.*: 112).

Why, now, after how: what enigma remains about *The Lady Vanishes* and Kofman's own vanishing? If Kofman took her life to be the matter of art and aesthetic philosophy, does the return of the film prompt a suicide enacted as a creative affirmation (much like that, a year later, of Deleuze), in which a life is taken to the letter of the film? Would Kofman's vanishing be catharsis after anguish? The proximity of the film to her last days and final ruminations would cast a response in the affirmative. It shows, beyond a shadow of a doubt, that Kofman affiliates cinema with the incommensurable measure of great art, art of a gauge that begs philosophical enquiry, and that no less engages the very lives of those who enquire of it.

NOTES

1. Here and elsewhere all translations from the French are mine.
2. The amateur of cinema recalls Jean-Luc Godard's *À bout de souffle* (1960), when director Jean-Pierre Melville, posing as the author of a controversial novel titled *Candida*, responds to a question posed by Jean Seberg (who plays at being a journalist): "Quel est votre plus grand désir dans la vie?" ("what is your greatest desire in life?"). The answer: "Devenir immortel et puis mourir" ("to become immortal and then die"). Kofman had not become immortal before she died. The suicide came, she had claimed to her close friends, at a moment when she avowed that she had nothing more to write. See "'My Life' and Psychoanalysis", in *Sarah Kofman: Selected Writings*, T. Albrecht (ed.) with G. Albert & E. Rottenberg (Stanford, CA: Stanford University Press, 2007), 250–51, in which, long before, she projects death at a point when she will no longer have "anything to say". Here and elsewhere all translations from the French are mine.
3. In *Casablanca*, a memoir that merits comparison with *Rue Ordener, Rue Labat*, Marc Augé becomes so Freudian that his own memories of the Occupation are shown inextricably woven into those of Michael Curtiz's film (1942), which appeared in France in 1946. It might be shown that the implicit cinema of Freud's writing *haunts* Kofman where Augé holds film as a memory-mirror to retrieve productive distortions of childhood memories. Augé writes, apropos his own relation with the Occupation, "film images swim through our heads like personal memories, as if they were part of our very lives, and moreover with this same degree of incertitude that often affects these memories and is sometimes revealed when we return to the places of our past or from a confrontation with the memories of another" (*Casablanca* [Paris: Éditions du Seuil, 2007], 25).
4. In my *Film Hieroglyphs: Ruptures in Classical Cinema* (Minneapolis, MN: University of Minnesota Press, 2006), the vanishing point is associated with analyst Guy Rosolato's notion of an *objet de perspective*: what clinical work draws from the experience of patients who "visualize or indicate through the bias of speech [certain] nodal points in their descriptive reltion to the world they see and live. ... it figures a concentrated point of attention that captures what a subject chooses to see, simply because in it resides what cannot, because of its paradoxical evidence and accessibility, be seen" (*ibid.*, xxvii–xxxviii). In *The Self-Made Map: Cartographic Writing in Early Modern France* (Minneapolis, MN: University of Minnesota Press 1996), 292–7, the concept is applied to the pictural and tabular design of Descartes' *Discours de la méthode*.
5. It is noteworthy that only roman numerals are set above the chapters. Named only in the list of contents, each chapter is set forward as an enigma.
6. Jean-Luc Nancy, "Foreword: Run, Sarah!", in *Enigmas: Essays on Sarah Kofman*, P. Deutscher & K. Oliver (eds), viii–xvi (Ithaca, NY: Cornell University Press, 1999) plays on Kofman who runs (*court*)

and who writes from the pleasure of her courses (*cours*). The hours she spends with books (a leit-motif in cinema of the New Wave) are the most engrossing and calming of her formative years.

7. "Iris" figures twice in *Rue Ordener, Rue Labat*, in the name of the flower (62, 65). The flower is associated with mémé and her world.

8. The French is cited because the adjectival substantive, *intolérable*, runs obsessively through Kofman's writing. *L'intolérable*, a word that the cinephile links with the hieroglyphics of Griffith's *Intolerance: Love's Struggle Through the Ages* (1916), translates the child's ever-renewed encounter with the menace of castration and death. It is also what cannot be thought, because the child is not at a stage where it can make use of its mediating virtues. Wherever Kofman writes of things intolerable, she signals a limit-situation, perhaps also Nietzsche's notion of a *Grenzsituation*, which she exhumes in her autobiography.

9. During the Occupation mémé taught the narratrix how to sift *la farine au son* (bran flour) through *un vieux bas de soie* (an old silk stocking) so that in the time of privation they could eat their daily "white brioche bread" (*Rue Ordener, Rue Labat*, 51). The act of sifting is the equal of creating and of measuring. *Farine au son* becomes a "good" bread because it is a flour endowed with sound, but then again the sound is sifted away. The motif of good and bad food, of digestion and indigestion, parallel in many respect to Kofman's relation with Hitchcock, is studied carefully in Kelly Oliver, "Sarah Kofman's Queasy Stomach and the Riddle of Paternal Law", in Deutscher & Oliver (eds), *Enigmas*, 184–7.

10. The reiteration of the title within a discourse can uncover the unconscious relation that the discourse holds to its title. It can range from guilt or indebtedness to disavowal. The reiteration is the topic of Jacques Derrida's "Le Titrier", in his *Parages*, rev. edn (Paris: Galilée, 2003). The concept returns in his untitled homage to Kofman in *Sarah Kofman: Selected Writings*, T. Albrecht (ed.) with G. Albert & E. Rottenberg, 1–34 (Stanford, CA: Stanford University Press, 2007), esp. 1–2, where he confesses that he cannot put a name or title to what would be a posthumous gift to the now-absent student, friend and colleague.

11. Yet in Kofman's other study of cinema, in an essay on Victor Sjöström's *He Who Gets Slapped* (1924), healthy laughter has its abject counterpart. The happy end of *L'Imposture de la beauté* is not so happy after all.

18 PAUL VIRILIO

Felicity Colman

Paul Virilio (b. 1932) was born in Paris and is a Professor of Architecture, a philosopher of technology and a humanitarian worker. Working across the field of urban studies and with the agency of the visual in society, his work has developed new paradigms of phenomenological perspectives of import for the analysis of screen-based works, including the notion of the *dromocratic condition*. Virilio co-founded the experimental *Architecture Principe Group* (1963–68) with architect Claude Parent. The group investigated new forms of architecture and urban orders that focused on the human body in its communal capacities. From 1973 Virilio was Professor of Architecture and Director of Studies of the École Speciale d'Architecture in Paris, where he was nominated Emeritus Professor on his retirement in 1998. He is a founding member of the Centre for Interdisciplinary Research in Peace Studies and Military Strategy (CIRPES).

The impact of Virilio's work was somewhat limited to a French-speaking audience until the early 1990s and 2000s, when English translations of major works and interviews broadened the knowledge of his work. A prolific author, Virilio develops his thesis on the relationships between activities of militarism, the visual (and in particular screen-based technologies) and human perception in a number of his books, including *War and Cinema* (1984; English trans. 1989), *Negative Horizon* (1984; English trans. 2005), *Strategy of Deception* (1999; English trans. 2000) and *Desert Screen* (1991; English trans. 2003). Virilio's thoughts and essays are also collected by James Der Derain in *The Virilio Reader* (1998), John Armitage in *Virilio Live* (2001) and in his discussions with Sylvère Lotringer in *Crepuscular Dawn* (2002).

> You go for a walk by the sea, and on the beach you watch the waves, as "The Day After," [dir. N. Meyer, 1983] not a bad film, either.
>
> (Virilio & Lotringer 2002: 64)

Virilio brings to the critique of screen-based and visual forms a polemic of how the developments in military and media technologies have radically determined forms of the body, and directed and contained the perceptual capacity of humanity. "It is thus our common destiny to *become film*", he argues (Virilio 2001b: 158). Through this process of "becoming film", Virilio describes a humanity that is driving itself to destruction. The spectacle of death is providing the ultimate trip. Throughout his work, Virilio describes a humankind that is the conduit of what he refers to as the *accident* (in its fullest etymological sense): the contingencies of change set off against humanity by humanity's pursuit of speed itself. Virilio's philosophy of film describes a *cinematic dromology*. Virilio brings to our attention the processes not just of movement in the world, and movement's determination of things in the world, but the consideration of *the speeds of movement* as governing forces, something to which few theorists of the moving image attend. Virilio developed a new form of phenomenology: a speed-phenomenology that he calls the study of speed, or *dromology*. Virilio subsumes the phenomenal body of the camera and of the human eye to its process of sight and the eye becomes an eye-body. The function of the eye is the historical site where the processes of war can be critiqued in Virilian terms. Collating and making visible those processes is to a large extent the project of his two key books for the study of the moving image: *War and Cinema: Logistics of Perception* ([1984] 1989) and *Negative Horizon: An Essay in Dromoscopy* ([1984] 2005). These books are usefully read together for a cartography of Virilio's thesis of technological processes of perception in the twentieth century.

Virilio's work has proved to be immensely influential to his and subsequent generations of thinkers. To canvass a few opinions: Sylvere Lotringer contends that "in his work, [Virilio] consistently adopted von Clausewitz's strategy of going to extremes" (Lotringer 2002: 11), and notes that his architectural interest has always been about the remains of the past and its impact on the political structures of the future, such as in his examination of the *"archaeology of violence"* (*ibid.*: 10). Philosopher Gilles Deleuze draws on Virilio's thesis in *War and Cinema* for his own conclusions concerning what Deleuze sees as cinema's death throes owing to two main factors: first, its "quantitative mediocrity", and secondly, the links Virilio provides between the film industry and the organization of militarisms; the "fascism of production" (Deleuze 1989: 164–5). Media theorist Eugene Thacker argues that "Virilio's rhetoric is constrained by his reference point, which is modern warfare between nation-states" (Thacker 2005: 241). Philosopher Ian James aligns Virilio's work with the personalist doctrines of Emmanuel Mounier. Developed in France from the 1930s onwards, personalism is a humanitarian, anti-liberalist movement that places the community above and against the values of capitalism (James 2007: 90). Steve Redhead argues that Virilio is to be understood as "an 'artist' rather than a social theorist in any conventional sense", as one who has made a significant contribution to "sociology of the accident" that is still in process of being analysed (Redhead 2006: 7). As theorists including John Armitage (2000), Redhead (2004) and James (2007) have discussed, Virilio's work extends much further than the classifications "poststructuralism" and "postmodernism" allow, and to gloss his work under these rubrics is to miss its theoretical function and implications. While these theorists have noted Virilio's key theoretical concepts, critical attention to Virilio's contribution to film-philosophy has thus far been scant.

Coming from a resolutely anarchic phenomenological position, he provides distinctive commentaries on the different screen media of film, television, new media art, computer games and screen technologies used for militaristic activities. Virilio's work has continually engaged questions of movement that have expanded the scope and practice of film-philosophy. The issues his work addresses include: the documentation of "reality" through the advent of photography, the history of the technologies of the moving image and in particular the study of the development of film for the purposes of militarism, the links between militarism and "entertainment", the hierarchy of mind–body, the psychology of the viewer and, finally, the influence of the cinema on the philosophy of phenomenology.

Virilio has referred to himself as "a critic of new technologies", of which we must include all senses of "cinema", in its ever-expanding technological pursuit of the image (David & Virilio 1996: 50). Of particular interest for film-philosophy is Virilio's *War and Cinema*. In this expansive work Virilio's dramatic style of writing links together phenomenological philosophy, informational media theory and material knowledge of the military and of film, tracing the systems of power and control in each. Through a largely phenomenal methodology he demonstrates that the citizen has been reduced to an image, a civil eye that is itself the governed and governing technology of our times. From there, the book examines how perceptual beings have been mobilized by commercial pursuits, which are in turn guided and formed by doctrines of militarism. Virilio elaborates how the perceptual war is being propelled through military gestalts that are enabled and fed by image technologies that are in total control – and continue to breed control – of the processes of the sentient eye.

A BODY OF PERCEPTION

Virilio's work asks: what did you do today, how did you do it and what drove you to do it? "Do we represent the construction, or construct the representation?" (1991b: 103). However, because humanity has been not just exposed to perceptual extremes, but *overexposed* and conditioned through visual and temporal disinformation, the conditions by which one might engage in life are confined by the processes of perception. As Virilio explains through his work, "our" subjectivity is mediated by technologies of architectures of perception. In an interview concerning the global economic collapse of 2008, Virilio noted that "the end is nearing capitalism", and that if we want to understand the current state of the world we would do best to focus on a study of the "ruptures in History" (Virilio 2008). Virilio's aesthetics are best understood through his own self-description as an "anarcho-Christian" (Armitage 2001: 20). Further, Virilio's art and architectural appreciation of sites, spaces and their critical territoriality lends a particular bent to his other influences: the scientific *epistēmē* of Albert Einstein (from whom he gleans the notion of the "information bomb" [Virilio in Armitage 2001: 98]), the phenomenological tradition of Maurice Merleau-Ponty, the dialogue with his colleague Jean Baudrillard. It is not out of place to situate Virilio within the anarchist field of thinkers such as Mikhail Bakunin. Across his work Bakunin described the synergistic relations levered by the technologies of culture and their effect on the individual in terms that underwrite all of Virilio's work: "Life dominates thought and determines the will. This is a truth that should never be lost sight of when we wish to understand anything about social and political phenomena" (Bakunin 1947: 2). Bakunin was here addressing a "class war" that involved differences of political opinion through social hierarchies. The classes that Virilio deals with are the consumers a century later, sated with industrialized "progress" and isolated in their consumption of "networked sys-tems". Virilio invokes a war of faith against the technologically produced world as the "pure war" that has altered the face of everyday life to an extreme state of civil warfare (Virilio & Lotringer 2008). Commenting in 2008, Virilio notes that the contempor-ary state of war has grown out of "Globalitarianism", which has produced "a change in scale", that is, a return to the "individual" who can effect a state of "total war", such as we see in history where individuals have held the power to affect the deaths of so many (*ibid.*: 11–13). This state of what Virilio terms a "fusion between hyper-terrorist civil war and international war" (*ibid.*) is the result of what he describes as the speed of sight, the temporality of the image and the cinematic control of the individual, which, over several of his volumes, are charted as the logistics of the control of the dimensions of visibility of war (1989). *"For men at war, the function of the weapon is the function of the eye"* (*ibid.*: 20).

Virilio often speaks of his own body and its youthful experiences as the phenom-enological catalyst for his research focus on the processual manipulations of sight itself by technologies of vision. The wars that took place in the twentieth century profoundly directed Virilio's thinking towards developing concepts that attest to mili-tarism's violent disturbance and reconfiguration of the social sites. As a youth in 1939, he was sent from Nazi-occupied Paris to Nantes in France, an event that proved to be a formative experience for his critical work as an architect and writer (Virilio 1994b; Virilio & Lotringer 2002: 23). Unlike the denial of Jean Cocteau, whose experience of the Second World War in Europe led to the extreme bliss-out of *La Belle et la Bête* (filmed in 1946; as Cocteau records in his diary of the time [Cocteau 1950], they had to cease shooting when the drone of overhead military aircraft disturbed the sound on set), Virilio decided to question what he termed the "metamorphism" of the "aes-thetics of war machines" (1991a: 103). Virilio saturates his writing with the "mobi-lization" of images of the sensorial intensities produced by the war event.[1] With his colleague and architectural partner Claude Parent, over the period 1963–9, Virilio developed the notion of oblique architecture, where the spatial masses around the bodies that inhabited that mass were considered as an "inclined" rather than "vertical sensibility" (Virilio & Parent 1996). This related to a sense of communal space, and to the organization of the total ecology surrounding the body (Virilio & Lotringer 2002: 52). Virilio's earlier training as a stained-glass painter, his work in the fields of archi-tecture and urbanism, and his anarchistic interest in Christianity led to the construc-tion of the "bunker church" of Sainte-Bernadette du Banlay at Nevers, France. Virilio comments: "Nevers was *Hiroshima Mon Amour*, the film by Marguerite Duras" (*ibid.*: 27). *Hiroshima Mon Amour* (dir. Alain Resnais, 1959) is a film that is a testimonial to one of the permanent psychological affects of war: a type of blindness of desire (as Virilio [1989: 14] cites Apollinaire's description of war). "For me, the architecture of war made palpable the power of technology – and now the infinite power of destruc-tion" (Virilio & Parent 1996: 11).

Throughout his writing on the subject, Virilio returns repeatedly to what we might refer to as Virilio's *perceptual faith*: a combination of critical-phenomenal and escha-tological Christianity. First, Virilio's Christian faith provides him with an apocalyptic proclivity ("God has come back into history through the door of terror" [Virilio &

Lotringer 2008: 143]; "One day the day will come when the day won't come" [Virilio 1997: vii]), but, Christianity's doctrinal history also provides him with a view to the sources of social organization: "God exists in the organization of time. They don't call it Eternity for nothing" (Virilio & Lotringer 2008: 140). Virilio's perceptual faith tends to see more darkness than light in the world (although he does advocate as "one of the best remedies" against "the dark" the tap-dancing American musical comedy of the Fred Astaire variety [1989: 10]). Secondly, Virilio continually stresses how all forms of "life" are enabled, changed, destroyed but, above all, *organized* by the visual activities of militarism:

> the soldier's obscene gaze, on his surroundings and on the world, his art of hiding from sight in order to see, is not just an ominous voyeurism but from the first imposes a long-term patterning on the chaos of vision, one which prefigures the synoptic machinations of architecture and the cinema screen.
> (*Ibid.*: 49)

Virilio argues that the "cottage industry" of sight was overtaken through the "industrialization of vision" (1997: 89). The body of the individual did not just disappear through the pathological conditions of war; it was mutated through its change of scale on the cinematic screen, an "instability of dimensions" (Virilio cites the case of the Hollywood star whose body is expanded on the big screen, folded into a magazine insert, painted on to bombs and warplanes [1989: 25–6]). In addition to physical exposure, the body is affected by war's "chemical, neurological processes" (*ibid.*: 6), "psychotropic derangement and chronological disturbance" (*ibid.*: 27–8), and the spatial situation of the body and its capacity to see and be seen are placed under scrutiny in militarized zones. Virilio says this "capacity to make the invisible visible" and "to find significance in what appears to be a chaos of meaningless forms … roots cinema in scientific discovery …" (*ibid.*: 26). The question arises: what is it that cine-science is trying to discover?

Virilio is attentive to the *tactics* of visually oriented technologies in order to discern how the often-contingent occurrences of the world (those produced by human-instigated interactions with the globe – the bombing of Hiroshima, the nuclear power station disaster at Chernobyl and the terrorist attacks on the World Trade Center) not only affect vision but propel a *mutant-spectator* to the service of the war. So Virilio follows the "spectacle" of a visioned body but, like his contemporary Deleuze, with whose cinema thesis Virilio's film model may be compared, Virilio looks to the use-value and not just the mechanics of this body-of-vision. Deleuze posits some form of "belief" in the "discourse to the body" against which Virilio's exposé of the cinema and militarism simply does not agree (Deleuze 1989: 171–3; Virilio 1989). Virilio applies a different type of method for thinking about the impact of visual stimulus to that of Sergei Eisenstein, for example, whose dialectical model of creating a montage of attractions has inspired formalist cinema and theories that focus on inventive functions. While Virilio deals with vision under a militarism body, his model of film-philosophy differs from the post-industrialized body of the consumer in Guy Debord's terms, where the society of the spectacle charted commodity consciousness (cf. Beller 2006: 106–7). Instead, Virilio's war of faith addresses the logistical Forms that perception produces and appends. In this thinking, we can discern the thoughts of Antonin Artaud, who was himself driven by the events of the war to come to a position that rejected cinema as a means to produce positive engagement in the world, but instead acts to co-opt individuals into militarist logic (cf. Artaud 1976j; Colman 2009; Virilio & Lotringer 2002: 132). Virilio discusses the ways in which we have lost our sight, owing to cinematic strategies of wars that have augmented physical sites and spaces, and in doing so have "deranged" appearances. Are there any positive outcomes to this governing of the masses through the cine-war machinery by those in control?

Virilio gives the example of how the loss of direct sight through the tactics of warfare in the Second World War was used by the British defence against the advancing German army as a means of protecting its territories. For example, as Virilio describes, the British military's deployment of the rule of "Fleet in Being" for this war included drawing from the Pimpernel tactics of visual subterfuge (1989: 62).[2] This is a technique not of camouflage but of "overexposure", where the enemy is offered a vast array of "visual disinformation" (*ibid.*). Virilio describes the East Anglian countryside of England, known for its air bases, being augmented with literal set-ups of the "scenery" of war – troops and equipment – so that it "came to resemble an enormous film lot complete with Hollywood-style props" (*ibid.*: 63). Virilio discusses a number of the war films of this period and their reception and relation to this strategy of overexposure: *The First of the Few* (dir. Howard, 1942), *To Be or Not To Be* (dir. Ernst Lubitsch, 1943), and *Alien* (dir. Ridley Scott, 1979). *Alien* was made in the same Shepperton Studios in Surrey, England, that had produced props for the 1940s army strategies, and which drew on the art direction of the militarism of the future perfected in *Dr Strangelove* (dir. Stanley Kubrick, 1964) (*ibid.*: 61–7).

The definition and filmic representation of a given reality, as Virilio details here, is thus expressive of the economic, political or organic situations of events that are bound by their modes of militarism. Whether they are deemed "positive" or "negative" depends on the political system in which you are placed. What gives us sight, and what directs our epistemological vision and ultimately interaction with the world, depends on how the body of that mode is itself figured in the world. How that perceptual faculty is given and determined in relation to historical events and possible futures is one of Virilio's central critiques. Under these conditions of overexposure and visual disinformation, an instability of sensorial dimensions is instigated, and new forms of war aesthetics are produced (*ibid.*: 19–25; 2005), directing the "relations of control" to new opportunities, such as those theorist Matthew Fuller has described in terms of the non-visibility of media ecologies (2005: 156). What type of opportunities exist under Virilio's terms are offered as a few glimmers of anarchic alternatives in *War and Cinema*, but they rest like gravestone epitaphs at the end of each uneasy chapter that provides case study after case study of the militarized capacity for perception. For Virilio *the brain is not the screen* (c.f. Deleuze 2000); rather, the brain is only an ocular support for directed perception. The speed at which the screen-images move causes unstable sensorial conditions for our perceptual activities and we are forced to engage through tactics of the screen-mediated body that organize our everyday experience into redundant forms of knowledge. Overexposure and the power of speed, as Virilio describes, have created the situation where "we are no longer truly seers (*voyants*) of our world, but already merely *reviewers* (*revoyants*)" (2005: 37). He continues:

> We pass our time and our lives in contemplating what we have already contemplated, and by this we are most insidiously imprisoned. This redundancy constructs our habitat, we construct an analogy and by resemblance, it is our architecture. Those who perceive, or build differently, or elsewhere, are our hereditary enemies.
>
> (*Ibid.*: 37)

Virilio makes some resolutely militant statements that critically damn the impact of technologies on the human body and its capacity to act, move and think. Because of this critique, his work is often sidelined or ignored by advocates of that system. Virilio refuses to compromise his value-ethics, which observe the detrimental effects of techno-culture on human life and the mutation of "democracy" by government organizations and the commercial media, which contribute in maintaining and managing the state of total war by making militarism a case of "perennial ordinariness" (1990: 35). Throughout his work, Virilio references the philosophical methodologies of the phenomenology of Edmund Husserl and Merleau-Ponty (with whom he studied phenomenology; Redhead 2004: 21). Of particular interest for the study of cinema are the ways in which Virilio develops the phenomenological position in relation to the study of movement. As we have seen with his discussion of the use of the tactic of overexposure by the British military in the Second World War, Virilio regards the phenomenal site as the experience of a (politically/aesthetically/theologically) determined space, which presents itself as a "self-enclosed system, a system of representation the exact configuration of which no one is ready to estimate" (1991b: 116).

Where Merleau-Ponty argues that "the screen has no horizons" (1962: 68) and sight of the horizon is what "guarantees the identity of the object" (*ibid.*), Virilio contends that our sight is organized by the non-form of the "negative horizon" that we rush towards under the directions of the perceptual management of globalized militarism. Objects are not static, and in the perceptual system of the military gestalt "speed appears as the primal magnitude of the image and thus the source of its depth" (1989: 16). The negative horizon evacuates the history of things and alters the configuration of space. Virilio proposes a new history here for reading the cinematic image. He cites the photographer Nadar from 1863 to describe how the view of a phenomenal definition of objects based on their relational resistance to each other – "one is only supported on what one resists" – has been *surpassed* by the acceleration of perspective: "space", he contends, "has become totally *dromogenous*" (2005: 146–7).

In *Negative Horizon: An Essay in Dromoscopy*, which acts as the companion volume to *War and Cinema* (both first published in 1984), Virilio explains his speed-phenomenology, and the dromogenous dimension. Virilio discusses his own phenomenal painting experiments: his attempts to understand the technology of his experience and perceptual expression of things. "The inanimate is merely a derogatory term used by those who read appearances", he cautions; "those who perceive trans-parence know well that nothing is immobile, that everything is always moving, that SENSE circulates among things like blood in the veins, in the forms of the frozen object" (2005: 26). Virilio argues that nothing is immobile, because our cultural destiny is always propelling us to our revisioning: in our redirection of things. Thus you may watch and revision a film over many years, and its forms will have changed their systematic sense as your perceptual situation of sense has been mobilized through time. Virilio gives the example of how a drawn line that might have gleaned itself from an experience of a material object may "reveal to us the nature of the void, the force of winds, the current of rivers" (*ibid.*: 27). The line, perhaps like a note of music that draws the length of a filmic scene and continues as a melody that lingers as a quality until long after the images have finished, is not an "abstract" thing at all; rather, it holds definite meaning, inflected by other experiences of things. "A forced cinematic reference, the line of the horizon", Virilio notes, "is the necessary condition of acceleration" (*ibid.*: 137).

To account for the concept of the range of speed and movements of things available in the twentieth century – of information (of events, of the appearance of things as they pass by) – Virilio invented the neologism "dromology", which refers to the logic of speed (Virilio 1986; 2005: 105–19). Virilio says that the "true 'seventh art'" was invented through the controlling device of this movement, which is "the dashboard" (2005: 105). He discusses "the philosophy of the windshield" as demanding "a precision far more than simple vision since the latter is distorted by the advancing movement, it is the future that decides the present of the course" (*ibid.*: 111). He takes us through the variations on the "screen of the *dashboard [tableau de bord]*" (*ibid.*: 110) where the "dromovisual apparatus" redirects vision, making it a control panel for all re/directors of movement: "the pilot"; "the *mise en scène* of the film of the windshield"; "the flight simulator" – all examples of where "the world becomes a video game" (*ibid.*: 106–7). In these terms, according to Virilio, the director becomes "the driver" of this movement, one who takes the "*seat of prevision*" (*ibid.*: 111). To describe the trajectory of the driver, Virilio indulges in a plethora of figures of speech that invoke the passenger: the racetrack; the hippodrome of old; the airport; the concentration camp; all along the watchtower; Martin Heidegger "in complicity with the philosophy of the Führer"; the "machines of war" (*ibid.*: 110–12).

The outcome of this acceleration of movement, argues Virilio, as all drivers of "the dashboard of everyday mobility" (*ibid.*: 109) know, is a perceptual take that is the *opposite* of an expansive cinematic cognition. Virilio writes, "the precipitation of images amounts to an evident telluric movement where the epicentre is situated at the blind spot of arrival" (*ibid.*). This is an "implosive" movement, where the redirector; the driver, becomes driven to enact a destructive passage. Virilio says this is caused through the law of dromology: "With the speed of the continuum it is the goal (*objectif*) of the voyage that destroys the road" (*ibid.*). Destination *is* everything, but that destiny is dependent on your body becoming dromogenous film: becoming a passage to destruction. Virilio quotes one of Nietzsche's optical homilies: "I see nothing but becoming" (*ibid.*: 139).

WAR IS THE THIRD DIMENSION OF CINEMA

We might now begin to answer Virilio's proposition and ask: how exactly does one "become film"? Like Merleau-Ponty, Virilio believes that perception is grounded in the body of the viewer. However, Virilio extends Merleau-Ponty's line to argue that sight is a wholly sensorial, affective experience that is largely denied by the speed of modes of the passage of images towards a destination. That destination is the system under which one lives, and *strives towards*. For instance, as Michael Degener has pointed out in relation to the politics of the "War on Terror" devised in the 2000s, America's *destiny* is to "export freedom to the rest of the world" (2005: 25). Virilio's thesis – "It is thus our common destiny to *become film*" – ties the process of movement with destination and/or destiny. It is from this critical position on film as the product of power that we can distinguish Virilio argument's concerning the outcomes of the concept of movement and the cinema from those thinkers of film-philosophy such as Merleau-Ponty or Deleuze.

In his subtitle for *War and Cinema – The Logistics of Perception* – Virilio reminds us of Merleau-Ponty's book *The Phenomenology of Perception* (1962). Virilio's argument lies in the differences of phenomenology and logistics. What is perception? In phenomenological terms, it is the apprehension of something – but that something is already given as a Form that may have achieved some state of autonomy – existing as it has been named and classified by a particular culture. For his architectural work, Virilio draws on Merleau-Ponty's notion of a body as a perceptual field in relation to architecture; this is the idea that it is not the eye that sees, but the body that can perceive as a receptive totality (cf. Merleau-Ponty 1968: 151; Virilio & Parent 1996). However, as we have seen, Virilio leaves behind Merleau-Ponty's stress of the perception of the whole in order to pursue a line of thinking that critiques the system that controls this receptive totality to show that perception is itself a technologically obsolete notion. Virilio questions how this condition has redetermined "reality". What does the cinematic situation imply for this reality where, through the means of commercial distribution, "a thousand film-goers [are turned] into a single spectator", and to what end does this commercially augmented perception serve in our society? (1989: 66–7). What is our ability to access a *vision* of life when our social capacity to *see* has been conscripted by the logistics of militarism and cultural contrivance?

Virilio's film-philosophy offers a contingency critique of perception itself (2005: 37–8). He treats film and new media as part of the social field that people use in order to modify and direct their own reality, a device that enables viewers to "sense the *differential time-span* borne by each technological object" (1989: 61). His work details the data that signal the impending apocalypse brought about through activities of militarism. However, in deciphering these activities not so much as proofs but as processes, Virilio's work offers a humanist conception of the technology of cinematic perception. Like Deleuze, Virilio separates the ways in which the world is perceived cinematically, according to the mediating factors of the types of recording technologies and cinema forms created at different junctures through different war events in the twentieth and twenty-first centuries. Virilio describes how the Second World War "was a world war in space" (Virilio & Wilson 1994: 4). However, since the advent of telecommunications technologies, such as the visible screen communication of the machinations and movements of military activities, which Virilio locates with the televised Vietnam War of the 1960s and 1970s, there has been what Virilio refers to as a spatial dislocation of the event. The medium of technology means that the event is located still in its place, but certainly not in its time; what has altered is the knowledge of movement, understanding of the values of perceptual psychology, the de-corporation of the human body and the resultant shifts in the conception of time. Virilio proposes that *"the history of battle is primarily the history of radically chang-ing fields of perception"* (1989: 7). We have only to look at war cinema to confirm this proposition. The shifts in the visual tactics of militarism are evident across the diversity of films, from *The General* (dirs Clyde Bruckman & Buster Keaton, 1927) to *Redacted* (dir. Brian De Palma, 2007). In all cases, what alters dramatically is not so much the forms of historically dated mediums of militarism, but the processes of the visual technologies of speed of perceptual attack. Virilio argues that this is because of "the eye's function being the function of the weapon" (1989: 3). The affect of this form of film, image and action of war causes a synthesis of perception: "Seeing and foreseeing therefore tend to merge so closely that the actual can no longer be distin-guished from the potential" (*ibid.*). Real-world applications of these tactics have long been taken up in the horror genre, particularly in sped-up zombie films such as *28 Days Later* (dir. Danny Boyle, 2002) or *Dawn of the Dead* (dir. Zack Snyder 2004), and in films that draw on "reality" styles for entertaining with the potential/actual scenario (the impending apocalypse coming to the mass cinemas of the early twenty-first century during the holiday season, when people have leisure time to "enjoy"). "Military actions take place 'out of view', with radio-electrical images substituting in real time for a now failing optical vision" (*ibid.*: 3) Thus, under Virilio's construction of the impact of war cinema on the perceptual body, the dimensions of time have also altered under dromology. Virilio argues that the part that the cinematic screen as a corpus of desocializing militaristic movement plays in the inevitable acceleration toward this "transpolitical eschatology" was enlarged through the twentieth century, to rapidly reach the time where the cinematically derived and deployed technology "exposes the whole world" (2005: 179; 1989: 88). In Virilio's terms, film-makers are co-opted by militarism's strategies of deception, and are thus bound with the continu-ing destruction of the world (cf. Virilio 2000b. Virilio's work serves as a primer for the political infantilization through *deceptive perceptual rhetoric* concerning the rea-sons surrounding the ongoing militarization of various zones, from border security at commercial airports to the Persian Gulf. The viewer becomes adept at recognizing the signs of any filmic encounter that produces events as identifiable genre texts. But it is not war that is generic but its iconography. That this iconography is one that is utilized in political campaigns to incite further conditions of war is a political hor-ror wrought on the bodies and lives of humanity. Under the dromocratic state, we are returned to the zombified state of living: a one-dimensional state of permanent militarized death-trajectory.

NOTES

1. Here I refer to another sociological field of work on the effects of militarism on the body of the participant: H. von Ernst Jünger, a German social theorist to whose work Virilio refers (*War and Cinema: The Logistics of Perception*, P. Camiller [trans.] [London: Verso 1989], 48, 93 n2). In *War and Cinema*, chapter four, "The Imposture of Immediacy", Virilio draws attention to the fact that many young recruits for the army respond to questions that "they cannot imagine what a war would be like" (*ibid.*, 47). Even with the large number of soldiers' blogs, posted online direct from the battlefields of the first decade of the twenty-first century, there is a sense that the experience of war is still eluding the visual. Virilio explains that despite the vast knowledge and documentation of war, and memorials that attest to its horrors, war is still able to be engaged: mobilized. I use the term "mobilization" here to refer readers to the term "Total Mobilization", from an essay by the same name in von Ernst Jünger's 1930 book on the ruinous results of the First World War for Germany, *Krieg und Krieger* (War and warrior) (Berlin: Junker & Dünnhaupt, 1930). Jünger's assertion is that war created an environment where, as John Armitage has described, "the visceral battle for existence over extinction literally blows every other historical and social concern apart" (*Virilio Live: Selected Interviews* [London: Sage, 2003], 194).
2. I use the term "Pimpernel tactics" in reference to Leslie Howard's development of his role in *The Scarlet Pimpernel* (dir. Harold Young, 1934) into his role in "*Pimpernel*" *Smith* (dir. Howard, 1941). Virilio discusses Howard's role in the latter in *War and Cinema*, 62.

19 JEAN BAUDRILLARD

Catherine Constable

Jean Baudrillard (1929–2007) studied with Henri Lefebvre and taught sociology at the Paris X University Nanterre from 1966 to 1987. From 1987 to 1997 he published critical articles in the Paris newspaper *Libération* (collected in *Screened Out* [2000; English trans. 2002]). From 1967 until the early 1970s Baudrillard was associated with the sociology of urbanism group, and the journal *Utopie*. Baudrillard published over thirty books on topics of philosophy and social theory, including *The System of Objects* (1968; English trans. 1996), *The Consumer Society* (1970; English trans. 1998), *For a Critique of the Political Economy of the Sign* (1972; English trans. 1981), *Symbolic Exchange and Death* (1976; English trans. 1993), *Seduction* (1979; English trans. 1990), *Simulacra and Simulations* (1981; English trans. 1994), *Fatal Strategies* (1983; English trans. 1990), *Cool Memories* (1990; English trans. 1996), *The Transparency of Evil* (1990; English trans. 1993), *The Gulf War Did Not Take Place* (1991; English trans. 1995), *Impossible Exchange* (1999; English trans. 2001) and *The Spirit of Terrorism* (2002). Baudrillard achieved global fame when Larry and Andy Wachowski accorded *Simulacra and Simulations* an on-screen role in *The Matrix* (1999).

This chapter will chart the diverse roles of cinema in the philosophical writings of Jean Baudrillard. This involves tracing Baudrillard's presentation of cinema as both a variant of pre-modern cultural forms and a gateway to the postmodern. American cinema plays a crucial role in Baudrillard's conception of the postmodern as nihilistic, underpinning key concepts such as simulation and the hyperreal, as well as major arguments such as the death of history. I will show that the comments on cinema also open up a positive way of reconceptualizing the hyperreal.

Unlike a number of his contemporaries, Jean Baudrillard does not provide a single, systematic theory of cinema. Instead, his comments are scattered across a range of works, taking the variant forms of brief asides, longer analyses and remarks made during interviews. Importantly, these fragments cannot be pieced together to form a consistent, coherent whole. Even Baudrillard's frequently professed "preference for American cinema" (Gane 1993: 67) is continually undercut by his negative assessment of "New Hollywood".[1] As William Merrin notes, "This preference is complicated … by Baudrillard's criticism of contemporary film-making and in particular of that style found precisely in the Hollywood films he … claims to prefer" (2005: 122). While this inconsistency might be dismissed as yet another instance of Baudrillard's deployment of wilful contradiction, I shall show that the diverse elements informing his analysis of Hollywood cinema actually offer very different ways of conceptualizing the advent of the postmodern.

Baudrillard's affection for New Hollywood is unusual in contemporary philosophy and cultural criticism. Interview material stresses the intuitive basis for his comments on Hollywood. "My relationship to the cinema is that of an untutored cinema-goer … and I have always wanted to keep it that way, never wanting to get into the analytic of it" (Baudrillard, in Gane 1993: 67). However, the division between the personal and the theoretical set up during this interview from the mid-1980s is not sustained. Indeed, Baudrillard's condemnation of *The Matrix Trilogy* for failing to present his ideas correctly clearly subjects the films to theoretical analysis (Baudrillard 2004).[2]

In contrast to Douglas Kellner's linear account of the development of Baudrillard's thought and ideas, I will show that Baudrillard's theorization of cinema keeps a number of conflicting modes of analysis in play simultaneously. This will be done by focusing on publications from the late 1970s and 1980s: specifically *Seduction*, which was first published in 1979 (English translation 1990), *Simulacra and Simulation* published in 1981 (English translation 1994), and *America* published in 1986 (English translation 1988), along with interviews from the mid-1980s (Gane 1993). Within film theory and cultural studies, Hollywood cinema has been conceptualized as the epitome of modernity (Hansen 2000). However, Baudrillard's analyses offer entirely different and contrary constructions of Hollywood as a variant of the pre-modern and the gateway to the postmodern.

In an article for the *International Journal of Baudrillard Studies*, Kellner argues that Baudrillard's work of the 1970s is marked by the development of two key distinctions: pre-modern versus modern, and modern versus postmodern (2006: 13). For Kellner, the first distinction is developed across a number of works, including *The Mirror of Production* (1975) and *Symbolic Exchange and Death* (1993). For Baudrillard, the modern is synonymous with the advent of capitalism and its associated values of "production, utility and instrumental rationality" (Kellner 2006: 11). By contrast, the pre-modern cultural forms of myth and ceremony are said to constitute modes of symbolic exchange that are outside capitalist production and the linear accumulation of meaning. "This is the metabolism of exchange, prodigality, festival – and also of destruction (which returns to non-value what production has erected, valorized)" (Baudrillard 1981, quoted in Kellner 2006: 10).

While the characterization of symbolic exchange as excessive and prodigal clearly draws heavily on Friedrich Nietzsche's conception of the Dionysian, Kellner notes that Baudrillard also takes up "Bataille's 'aristocratic critique' of capitalism" (2006: 10–11). As a result, capitalism is criticized for being "grounded in … crass notions of utility and savings rather than … 'aristocratic' notions of excess and expenditure" (*ibid*.: 10). Kellner thus positions Baudrillard's early work within a French tradition that valorizes features of "primitive" cultures. "Baudrillard's defense of symbolic exchange over production and instrumental rationality … stands in the tradition of Rousseau's defense of the 'natural savage' over modern man [and] Durkheim's posing organic solidarities of premodern societies against the abstract individualism and anomie of modern ones" (*ibid*.: 12).

Kellner argues that Baudrillard moves away from the discourse of symbolic exchange as an alternative to production, replacing it with the concept of seduction in his work of that name in 1979 (2006: 20). However, *Seduction* also takes up the previous distinction between the aristocratic and the bourgeois, reworking it as a division between two orders (Baudrillard 1990: 1). Seduction is the artificial "order ... of signs and rituals" epitomized by femininity, duelling, challenge and reversibility; whereas production is the natural order epitomized by the discourses of commerce and psychoanalysis (*ibid.*: 2, 39–43). The focus on artifice and ritual clearly links the concept of seduction with the pre-modern forms of myth, festival and ceremony. For Kellner, *Seduction* is a detour away from *Symbolic Exchange and Death* and *Simulacra and Simulation*, which set up the second key distinction between modern societies organized around capitalist production and postmodern societies structured around simulation (2006: 13–14).

In his account of Baudrillard, Kellner argues that the progression from the first distinction, pre-modern–modern, to the second, modern–postmodern, constitutes a crucial break. This is because the move into the postmodern is construed as the end of Baudrillard's presentation of viable alternatives to capitalism. In a media-saturated society, where the masses are fascinated by the endless play and proliferation of images, "the referent, the behind and the outside, along with depth, essence, and reality all disappear, and with their disappearance, the possibility of all potential opposition vanishes as well" (*ibid.*: 17–18). The artificial order of *Seduction* is dismissed by Kellner as "a soft alternative": a bad copy of the truly differential modalities of symbolic exchange (*ibid.*: 20). For Kellner, Baudrillard briefly hovers "between nostalgia and nihilism" between "a ... desire to return to pre-modern cultural forms" and the gleeful extermination of modern ideas: "the subject, meaning, truth, reality, society, socialism, emancipation", finally abandoning his "desperate search for a genuinely radical alternative ... by the early 1980s" (*ibid.*: 18).

While Kellner's article is one of the clearest accounts of the development of a challenging theorist, the division of Baudrillard's work into different epochs becomes much more difficult to sustain when focusing on the writing on cinema. Baudrillard relates cinema to the pre-modern forms of ceremony and myth as well as arguing that New Hollywood ushers in the postmodern era of simulation through its role in the creation of the hyperreal. Moreover, the conception of a clear break is problematic because key concepts associated with the pre-modern are used in Baudrillard's writing on cinema in the late 1970s and across the 1980s. In an interview from 1982, Baudrillard comments: "The Cinema is absolutely irreplaceable, it is our own special ceremonial ... The ceremonial of the cinema ... that quality of image, of light, that quality of myth, that hasn't gone" (Gane 1993: 31). Merrin argues that Baudrillard's conception of cinema's distinctive form of ceremonial draws on Émile Durkheim in that it constitutes a mode of "collective communion ... a ritual and mythic form actualizing ... the collective dreams ... of our society" (Merrin 2005: 122). Importantly, the sense of cinema as offering a pre-modern mode of collectivity is repeated in a later interview from 1984. Here Baudrillard recollects viewing *Star Wars* "in cinemas with 4,000 seats and everybody eating popcorn" as a moment in which he "caught a very strong whiff of *primitive cinema*, almost a communal affair but strong, intense" (Gane 1993: 67, emphasis added).

Baudrillard's characterization of cinema links its status as image to the realm of myth, repeating the following observation: "the cinema is … endowed with an intense imaginary – because it is an image. This is not simply to speak of film as a mere screen or visual form, but as a *myth*" (Baudrillard 1990: 162, repeated in Gane 1993: 69; Baudrillard 1994: 51). In *Seduction* the mythic aspect of cinema lies in its creation of stars, who constitute "our only myth in an age incapable of generating great myths or figures of seduction comparable to those of mythology or art" (1990: 95). Cinema is presented as a postmodern variant of pre-modern forms, combining and reworking myth and communion.[3] Baudrillard contrasts the "hot" seductions of ancient mythology with the "cold" seduction offered by contemporary stars who constitute "the intersection point of two cold mediums, … the image and … the masses" (*ibid.*). The cool allure of the female star is that of "a ritual fascination with the void … This is how she achieves mythic status and becomes subject to collective rites of sacrificial adulation" (*ibid.*).[4] Importantly, the fascination exerted by stars cannot be dismissed as mere delusion, "the dreams of the mystified masses" (*ibid.*), because Baudrillard presents seduction as the collective celebration of pure artifice from which there is no awakening to the truth.

Baudrillard's conception of both cinema and its stars as cool, shimmering, artificial surfaces (*ibid.*: 96) constructs them as key sites of the end of signification, in that they constitute the appearance of the signifier without the signified. Production rests on the concepts of exchange – goods for money, words for meanings – and accumulation – wealth, savings and full understanding. Seduction is the annulment of production, taking the linguistic form of "a radically different operation that absorbs rather than produces meaning" (*ibid.*: 57). The annulment of meaning is performed by key concepts, such as stars, which are repeatedly defined in terms of pure negation, as "void" or "absence" (*ibid.*: 95–6), thereby playing out the inversion of production: "[Great stars] … are dazzling in their nullity … They turn into a metaphor the immense glacial process which has seized hold of our universe of meaning … but … at a specific historical conjuncture that can no longer be reproduced, they transform it into an effect of seduction" (*ibid.*: 96). Baudrillard's words suggest that it is stars and the cinema that have transformed signs and images into the artificial order of the pure image: the depthless, fascinating, celluloid surface.

The analysis of the cinema as a realm of transformation is continued in *Simulacra and Simulation*. However, in the later work signs and metaphors become spectacle rather than artifice. Transformed into cinematic image, monstrosity is no longer threatening or mythic but spectacular: "a King Kong wrenched from his jungle and transformed into a music-hall star" (1994: 135). The loss of the construction of monstrosity as a "natural" threat is played out in Baudrillard's reading of *King Kong*.[5] Traditionally, the hero's annihilation or vanquishing of the monster constitutes the beginning of culture, suggesting that Kong's attack on the city marks the return of nature. However, the postmodern annihilation of the category of nature means that Baudrillard reads Kong's attack as an attempt to deliver us from a dead culture. Piling inversion upon inversion, Baudrillard reads the film as a key example of seductive reversibility. "The profound seduction of the film comes from this inversion of meaning: all inhumanity has gone over to the side of men, and all humanity has gone over to the side of captive bestiality … monstrous seduction of one order by the other" (*ibid.*).

Baudrillard's positive conception of cinema as a fascinating, seductive, artificial realm frequently occurs in tandem with negative analyses of the "new" medium of television. As pure image, the cinema "is blessed ... with an intense imaginary", its mythic qualities ensuring that it retains "something of the double, of the phantasm, of the mirror, of the dream" (*ibid.*: 51). By contrast, television "no longer conveys an imaginary, for the simple reason that *it is no longer an image*" (1990: 162). At stake here is the issue of distance, a gulf between the real and the image, or the division between the productive order of signs, signifiers and signifieds and the seductive order of pure images. As our phantasm/reflection/dream, the cinematic image offers us a separate double that is both ourselves and not ourselves, setting up a space for the play of the imaginary across the different orders. In an interview from 1984 Baudrillard adds: "in order to have an image you must have a scene, *a certain distance* without which there can be no looking, no play of glances ... I find television obscene, because there is no stage, no depth, no place for a possible glance and therefore no place ... for a possible seduction" (Gane 1993: 69, emphasis added).

Television is obscene because it elides distance and renders every intimate detail of life visible and immediate. The television screen is mesmeric because it is "immediately located in your head ... it transistorizes all the neurons and passes through like a magnetic tape – a tape not an image" (Baudrillard 1994: 51). Lacking the distance vital to the construction of the image and the imaginary, television reconfigures the subject as another screen and/or terminal. This analysis of the television screen underpins Baudrillard's later comments on computers in *Cool Memories II: 1987–1990*: "At the computer screen I look for the film and find only the subtitles. The text on the screen is neither a text nor an image – it is a transitional object ... which has meaning only in refraction from one screen to another, in inarticulate, purely luminous signalling terms" (1996: 2). The later argument utilizes the previous opposition between cinema and the screen, reworking it as the opposition between image and digital signal.

In the analyses of cinema versus the screen and/or terminal, Baudrillard presents the cinema as a different visual order. Cinema can offer a dialectical play between image and reality, or a seductive play of the surface that annuls the production of depth. The opposition cinema–television results in a particular invective against films that adopt "televisual" techniques of presentation (Gane 1993: 71). Thus, *Sex Lies and Videotape* (dir. Steven Soderbergh, 1989) is singled out for its reduction of the seductive cinematic image to a state of "video-indifference" through its thematic rendering of seduction via a video camera (Baudrillard 1996: 68). Importantly, the opposition cinema–television pivots on a key point: cinema is always associated with distance while television closes the gap, fusing the image and the real, and thus ushering in what Baudrillard terms the hyperreal (1994: 30; Gane 1993: 69). Key passages from *Seduction* and *Simulacra and Simulation*, coupled with interviews from the 1980s, clearly set up an opposition between cinema, which retains pre-modern elements of ceremony, ritual and myth, and the new medium of television, whose role in the creation of the hyperreal marks the break between the modern and the postmodern.[6]

The opposition cinema–television is (inevitably) checked and balanced by other analyses in *Simulacra and Simulation* in which cinema plays a crucial role ushering in the postmodern. In a chapter entitled "History: A Retro Scenario", Baudrillard argues that cinema and photography are responsible for the destruction of history and thus of myth. "History is ... perhaps, along with the unconscious, the last great myth. It is a myth that once subtended the possibility of an 'objective' enchainment of events and causes ... The age of history ... is also the age of the novel" (1994: 47). The passage marks a shift in the meaning of "myth" from the references to specific Greek myths in *Seduction* to a particular quality of narrative (1990: 67–9, 95). "It is this fabulous character, the *mythical energy* of an event, or of a narrative, that today seems to be increasingly lost" (1994: 47, emphasis added). Photography and cinema are responsible for the loss of the mythic form of history as narrative "by fixing it in its visible 'objective' form" (*ibid*.: 48). In this way, the flow and energy of narrative are frozen into stills and photomontages, which will act as true historical "data" from now on.

The initial shift from history as myth to history as data results in "the obsession with historical *fidelity*, with a perfect rendering" that is exemplified by the cinematic remake (*ibid*.: 47). The remake is a faithful rendition of a past that has already ossified into its objective form. For Baudrillard, such films act as evidence of a more widespread "negative and implacable fidelity to ... a particular scene of the past or of the present, to the restitution of an absolute simulacrum of the past or the present" (*ibid*.: 47). The perfect reconstructions offered by films such as *Chinatown* (dir. Roman Polanski, 1974), *Three Days of the Condor* (dir. Sydney Pollack, 1975), *Barry Lyndon* (dir. Stanley Kubrick, 1975), *All the President's Men* (dir. Alan J. Pakula, 1976) and *The Last Picture Show* (dir. Peter Bogdanovich, 1971) serve to play out the death of history twice over (Baudrillard 1994: 45). In offering reconstructions of a simulacral past, such films ensure that history can only make "its triumphal entry into cinema, posthumously" (*ibid*.: 44).

Baudrillard's presentation of cinema and photography as the media that killed history by turning myth into simulation intersects with another major line of argument about the advent of the postmodern. The move away from the modern is repeatedly presented as the result of the rise of new technologies and the concomitant fascination with technical and technological perfection. The film remake is thus the site of the resurrection of the ghost of history and a demonstration of new forms of technical perfection. Writing on *The Last Picture Show*, Baudrillard comments: "it was a little too good ... without the psychological, moral and sentimental blotches of films of that era. Stupefaction when one discovers it is a 1970s film, perfect retro, purged, pure, the hyperrealist restitution of 1950s cinema" (*ibid*.: 45). Importantly, the perfected form offered by the remake is repeatedly characterized in terms of absence and loss: no more errors, psychology or play of the imaginary and/or imagination. In an interview given the year after the publication of *Simulacra and Simulation*, Baudrillard adds: "Cinema has become hyper-realist, technically sophisticated, effective ... All the films are 'good' ... But they fail to incorporate any element of make-believe (*l'imaginaire*). As if the cinema were basically regressing towards infinity, towards ... a formal, empty perfection" (Gane 1993: 30).

The drive towards technical perfection obliterates both history and meaning. Directors who epitomize this tendency are characterized as overly logical, pursuing the "pleasure of machination" rather than aesthetics (Baudrillard 1994: 46). Thus Kubrick, "who manipulates his film like a chess player, who makes an operational scenario out of history" (*ibid.*), creates a product that is perfect yet empty. *Barry Lyndon* is said to mark the beginning of "an era of films that ... no longer have meaning strictly speaking, an era of great synthesizing machines of varying geometry" (*ibid.*). The quote characterizes contemporary films as both machinic and mathematical, their final form mirroring the qualities of their directors. Importantly, their synthesizing role is the antithesis of the differential nature of the structuralist model of opposition that is the basis of meaning creation in language. By bringing together opposing elements, contemporary films short-circuit the structures of meaning itself, thus becoming meaningless.

In a later discussion of Francis Ford Coppola in *Simulacra and Simulation*, Baudrillard draws together his key theses concerning the rise of new technologies and the consequent destruction of history and the structures of binary opposition. The brief analysis of *Apocalypse Now* (dir. Coppola, 1979) can also be seen as a prequel to Baudrillard's later work *The Gulf War Did Not Take Place* (1995). In summary, the argument is that both events, the Vietnam War and the later film, are rendered fundamentally equivalent in that they simply constitute test sites for new technologies.

> Coppola does nothing but ... test the impact of a cinema that has become an immeasurable machinery of special effects ... his film is really the extension of the war through other means ... The war became film, the film becomes war, the two are joined by their common hemorrhage into technology. (Baudrillard 1994: 59)

The commonality of the war and the film is not said to play out the destruction of meaning, but rather to mark the end of any moral distinction between good and evil. In this way, the loss of any ontological difference between the historical event of the war and the filmic images is also the loss of ethical difference in the form of an objective distinction between right and wrong. The similarity between the war and the film demonstrates "the reversibility of both destruction and production, of the immanence of a thing in its very revolution ... of the carpet of bombs in the strip of film" (*ibid.*: 60). Importantly, this instance of reversibility differs from seduction, whose process of annulment also marks the beginning of a different order. In this case, the reversibility is systemic, a turning inside out, which demonstrates the fundamental equivalence of both terms as products of the same system. It marks the loss of any possibility of revolution in that there is no way of accessing the outside or creating an alternative.

Baudrillard repeats the assertion that technological perfection marks the end of cinema as image in his later work from the 1990s. The key features of his line of argument reappear in an interview from 1991.

> As for the cinema, I am still very much in love with it, but it has reached a despairing state ... Here, too, huge machines are set up which possess great technical refinement. This is a racket on images, on the imaginary of people. Cinema has become a spectacular demonstration of what one

can do with the cinema .... Everything is possible, it's obvious ... there is no magic in it except, well, a mechanical magic ... there are only superb demonstrations; it's performance, that is all. (Gane 1993: 23)

The comment replays the move from the cinematic image to the machinic "racket on images" with its negative associations of noise and commercial racketeering. Cinema as spectacle can only demonstrate its own capabilities, marking the shift from the mythic to mathematical performance indicators. In this quotation, the annihilation of the pre-modern elements is presented as a loss of magic. Importantly, Merrin argues that such comments make it easy to predict Baudrillard's position on the current rise of computer-generated imagery (CGI) in Hollywood films. He suggests that the dominance of CGI would be regarded as a further example of the "hyperclean, hyperliteral perfection of the digital image", which destroys the image, the imaginary, the symbolic and illusion (Merrin 2005: 122–3).

Baudrillard suggests that it might be possible to conjoin his rather different theses about the nature of cinema by using them to form a single, linear model of development: "The cinema and its trajectory: from the most fantastic or mythical to the realistic and the hyperrealistic" (1994: 46). The shift to realism does not form a proper second stage because the attempt to capture "reality" through "banality, ... veracity, ... naked obviousness, ... boredom" and the endeavour to be "the real, the immediate, the unsignified" are dismissed by Baudrillard as "the craziest of undertakings" (*ibid.*: 46–7). Thus all efforts to capture and/or be the real simply result in its reconstruction as cinematic image. Moreover, in attempting to achieve "an absolute correspondence with the real, cinema also approaches an absolute correspondence with itself – and this is not contradictory: it is the very definition of the hyperreal ... Cinema plagiarizes and copies itself, ... remakes its classics, retroactives its original myths, ... etc." (*ibid.*: 47). In this comment the hyperreal is associated with the self-reflexive duplication of images. Thus the remake ushers in the hyperreal because it is a self-conscious, perfect copy of a previous film, rather than a perfect reconstruction of a simulacral historical era.

However, Baudrillard's brief assessment of the linear trajectory of cinema needs to be treated with caution. The singularity is misleading because there is more than one trajectory to the hyperreal. Within *Simulacra and Simulation*, films create the hyperreal through the destruction of history, the destruction of key oppositions underpinning our conceptions of meaning and morality, and the self-reflexive duplication of previous films. Moreover, in later books and interviews, Baudrillard argues that the cinema ushers in the hyperreal through an inversion of the standard mimetic relation between the image and reality (1988: 55–6; Gane 1993: 34). Instead of acting as a copy of the real, the cinematic image becomes the model through which we measure the real, a precession of simulacra that results in the cinematographization of reality. This view is most famously expressed in the travelogues in which Baudrillard cheerfully treats America as though it were a film.

It is not the least of America's charms that ... the whole country is cinematic. The desert you pass through is like the set of a Western, the city a screen of signs and formulas. The American city seems to have stepped straight out of the movies. To grasp its secret, you … should begin with the screen and move outwards to the city. (Baudrillard 1988: 56)

Importantly, this conception of the cinematographization of everyday life challenges the linear model of cinema's development because the move into the hyperreal does *not* constitute the end of the fantastic or the mythical. In *America*, Baudrillard argues: "the cinema does not assume an exceptional form, but simply invests the streets and the entire town with a mythical atmosphere" (*ibid.*). Interview material from 1984 also suggests that the cinematic hyperreal marks the conjunction of the postmodern with the pre-modern forms of communion and collectivity. "Cinema is the mode of expression one finds in the street, everywhere; life itself is cinematographic and, what's more, *that is what makes it possible to bear it*; otherwise the mass daily existence would be unthinkable. This dimension is part and parcel of collective survival" (Gane 1993: 71, emphasis added). This quotation differs from the ones discussed previously in that the ceremonial of cinema is not situated in the shared viewing experience of the audience. Interestingly, the analysis augments the Dionysian aspect of the pre-modern forms of symbolic exchange in that the account of the cinematic hyperreal closely resembles Nietzsche's analysis of the affirming power of the Apollonian as: "the countless illusions of the beauty of mere appearance that at every moment make life worth living at all and prompt the desire to live on" (1967: 143).

In linking the hyperreal with a positive mode of collectivity and an affirming model of illusion, Baudrillard breaks away from his typically nihilistic presentation of the postmodern. This particular model of life as cinema can therefore be seen to challenge Kellner's conception of Baudrillard as a theorist who hovers between a nostalgia for the pre-modern and a nihilistic extermination of the modern (2006: 18). At this point the conception of the postmodern as an ending is fundamentally reworked, reconstructing it as a new beginning. At the same time, the pre-modern forms to which we return, both Dionysian and Apollonian, have, in their turn, been reworked by their positioning within the advent of the postmodern and the formation of the hyperreal.

The diversity of Baudrillard's writing on cinema can therefore be seen to present key moments that do not conform to the lines of argument offered elsewhere in his writing. The presentation of the transformation of life into the cinematic image is utterly unlike the short-circuiting of the reality–image dichotomy offered by the tape and/or signal that constitutes television. In an interview from 1982, Baudrillard presents the cinematographization of everyday life as a productive interplay between the image and the real. Driving around Los Angeles or visiting the desert,

you … are in a film … sometimes you see scenes that begin strangely to resemble scenes in films. And this play … is one element of cinema … it is a role that has nothing to do with Art or Culture, but which is nevertheless deep: *cinema has a profound effect on our perception of people and things, and of time too.* (Gane 1993: 31, emphasis added)

In this quotation, the precession of the filmic image transforms our perception of the real, making reality strange, and thereby constructing another perspective on the world and others.

Importantly, the capacity of the filmic image to offer a different perception of reality constructs our entry into the hyperreal as a kind of perspectival shift. Kellner argues that Baudrillard's focus on the division between the modern and the postmodern marks the end of viable alternatives to the system in that we are all contained within "a carnival of mirrors, reflecting images projected from other mirrors onto the omnipresent television and computer screen and the screen of consciousness" (2006: 18). While it must be acknowledged that this analysis is broadly applicable to a number of Baudrillard's key arguments, including the end of history and the rise of technological perfection, it overlooks the ways in which the hyperreal itself is (occasionally) constructed as a differential mode of viewing. While there is no outside, there is depth, in that the shift of perspectives is presented as a profound change. For Kellner, change can lie only with the possibility of "disalienation, liberation and revolution" (2006: 18), an escape from the system itself. What Baudrillard's writing on life as cinema offers us is a rare sense of the hyperreal as a perspectival shift that affirms life – "makes it possible to bear it" (Gane 1993: 71) – and thus as a potential site of positive change.

NOTES

1. The term "New Hollywood" is used within film studies to refer to a time (beginning around the late 1960s and continuing to the present day) when economic and social factors led to the diminishment of the power of the studios. New Hollywood covers the development of aesthetic forms challenging the classical paradigm, and new economic forms such as the blockbuster and its related media tie-ins; G. King, *New Hollywood Cinema: An Introduction* (London: I. B. Tauris, 2007), 1–84.
2. For a different, positive analysis of the ways in which *The Matrix Trilogy* offers a complex take-up of Baudrillard's *Simulacra and Simulation* see C. Constable, *Adapting Philosophy: Jean Baudrillard and "The Matrix Trilogy"* (Manchester: Manchester University Press, 2009).
3. I have presented seduction as postmodern because production is clearly associated with the modern.
4. For a more detailed discussion of Baudrillard's figure of the seductress and female stars see my *Thinking in Images: Film Theory, Feminist Philosophy and Marlene Dietrich* (London: BFI, 2005), 138–62.
5. It is not clear whether this reference is to the RKO film of 1933 directed by Merian C. Cooper and Ernest Schoedsack or the 1976 film directed by John Guillermin. Given Baudrillard's preference for films of the 1970s, it is more likely to be the latter.
6. "The Orders of Simulacra" offers one of the few exceptions to the oppositional presentation of cinema and television. In this case, Baudrillard's analysis of film as a "test" that sets up a yes/no response is heavily reliant on Walter Benjamin (J. Baudrillard, *Simulations*, P. Foss, P. Patton & P. Beitchman [trans.] [New York: Semiotext(e), 1983], 117–19).

20 JEAN-FRANÇOIS LYOTARD

Lisa Trahair

Jean-François Lyotard (1924–98) was born in Versailles, France, and taught philosophy at boys' schools in Algeria and La Flèche before writing a masters thesis in literature and philosophy at the Sorbonne. In 1971, he received his *doctorat d'état* for *Discours, figure*. His first published writings were political in nature and concerned with the French colonization of Algeria. He was on the editorial committee of *Socialisme ou barbarie* and also contributed to *Pouvoir Ouvrir* until events of the late 1960s precipitated his disengagement from Marxism. From 1959 to 1966 he held the position of *maître-assistant* at the Sorbonne and then taught at the Paris X University Nanterre from 1966 to 1970. From 1970 he taught at the University of Vincennes in Saint-Denis. He was appointed Professor of Philosophy in 1972. From 1974 he simultaneously held numerous international posts in the US, Canada, Brazil, Denmark and Germany. Described as a polymath because of the broad disciplinary embrace of his endeavours (philosophy, literature, art, politics and ethics), he is most renowned for his work on postmodernism, particularly *The Post-Modern Condition* (1984), which was commissioned by the government of Quebec. Other works include *The Differend* (1988), *Phenomenology* (1954; English trans. 1991), *Dérive à partir Marx et Freud* (1973), *Des dispositifs pulsionnels* (1973), *Libidinal Economy* (1974; English trans. 1993), *Duchamp's TRANS/formers* (1977; English trans. 1990), *La Partie de peinture* (1980), *Les Immatérieux* (1985), *The Postmodern Explained to Children* (1986; English trans. 1992), *Heidegger and "the Jews"* (1988; English trans. 1990), *The Inhuman* (1988; English trans. 1991), *Lessons on the Analytic of the Sublime* (1991; English trans. 1994), *The Confession of Augustine* (1998; English trans. 2000) and *Misère de la philosophie* (2000).

Given the immensity of Jean-François Lyotard's contribution to understanding postmodernism and his many essays on art and aesthetics, it may be surprising to some that his comments on cinema are relatively scant. The two essays that explicitly address cinema derive from early experiments that attempt to reconfigure philosophical aesthetics by referring artistic practices to the psychoanalytic theory of the drives. "L'Acinéma" ("Acinema") was first published in *Revue d'Esthétique* in 1973 and in *Des dispositifs pulsionnels* the same year. It first appeared in English in 1978 in the American journal *Wide Angle*. "The Unconscious as Mise-en-scène" was published in 1977 in *Performance and Postmodern Culture*.

Read exactly thirty years after it first appeared in English, "Acinema" strikes one as a strange manner of beast. While the title and much of the essay suggest that Lyotard might be taking his first hesitant steps towards a theory of cinema, the extremely contracted nature of any examination of actual films – a brief discussion of a little-known film called *Joe* (dir. John G. Avildsen, 1970), a passing reference to E. H. Thompson's multi-lens camera and mere mention of early avant-garde film-makers Hans Richter and Viking Eggeling – occasion some doubt over the real target of his speculation. (Similarly, in "The Unconscious as Mise-en-scène", Lyotard's examination of film is limited to some closing remarks about Michael Snow's film *La Région Centrale* [1971].) The focus on movement as the self-defining or essential quality of cinema seems to be proffered less as a means of exploring the varieties of the cinematic image and more to contrast what cinema does with movement and how movement functions in other arts, or other kinds of art than narrative film.

As an art form whose primary expressive criterion is movement, cinema ought to provide the means of thinking through the parameters of movement. Cinema, Lyotard observes, is "an inscription of movement, a writing with movements" (1973a: 357, my translation). And it deals with movement at every level: things in the frame move (the actors, objects, lights, colours); at the level of the shot we detect the movement of the lens when it pulls focus and the frame when the camera moves; editing creates a movement between shots; and the film as a whole, "the spatio-temporal synthesis of the narration", inscribes self-movement (1989a: 169). It is thus not just the movement on the screen that concerns Lyotard but the kind of movement that circumscribes the location of the cinema in the world and that "positions" the spectator in relation to it. More broadly still, Lyotard's investigation of cinematic movement relates to the expenditure of psychical energy: different processes of movement give rise to different kinds of pleasure. While Lyotard's interest in the entire set-up of cinema seems to invoke the notion of the cinematic apparatus, the reader of the English translation of "Acinema" should be aware that the terms *arrangement* and *apparatus* exist in the French text as *dispositif* and that the latter has very specific conceptual parameters in Lyotard's early work.[1] The translator of *Libidinal Economy*, Iain Hamilton Grant, argues that to translate *dispositif* as set-up or apparatus gives an overly mechanistic gloss to what Lyotard is trying to conceive. The term also implies (de)positing and should invoke a "disposition to invest". In other words, its economic, dynamic and psychoanalytic connotations need to be kept in mind: "As such, the '*dispositif* is subject to economic movements and displacements, an aspect which the retention of the French term, by combining the dis-place with the dispose, movement with expenditure, helps to convey" (Lyotard 2004: xi). Most importantly the *dispositif* should not be understood simply as an apparatus circumscribing the subject–object relation. In the *dispositif*, the thetic subject is only a partial and momentary component of a more fundamental flow of cathectic energy.

"Acinema" is concerned with various *dispositifs* of movement. The organized movement of mainstream cinema is one *dispositif*, the non-utilitarian movement of firework displays suggests another. Significantly, the *dispositif* is not determined by the nature of the form or signification of the aesthetic object, and the same kind of *dispositif* can be found in works originating in quite different media. Lyotard, we shall see, finds the same *dispositif* to be operative in the Swedish practice of posering (cf. Lyotard 1989a: 177) as he does in the work of Pierre Klossowski and Marquis de

Sade. In a second instance, the same *dispositif* is envisaged in the paintings of Mark Rothko and Jackson Pollock, the films of Richter and Eggeling, and Noh Theatre.

The first *dispositif* that Lyotard elaborates is that of mainstream narrative cinema and is characterized by an *ordering* of movement. The interlocking schemas of representation, narration and form are combined to secure this ordering. For Lyotard, the ordering of movement achieved by these schemas binds cinema to the beautiful and to good form. They give rise to the unity of the whole.

Lyotard extends his thinking about cinema as an ordering of movement to the function of politics in capitalist liberal democracies, going so far as to suggest that film direction is not an artistic activity but "a general process touching on all fields of activity" (1989a: 175) and, moreover, political activity is "direction *par excellence*" (*ibid.*: 176). While politics and cinema are alike inasmuch as both are ordering activities that attempt to create unities out of partial components, Lyotard is less interested in the effects of the ordering (film as such or the body politic) and more concerned about the processes of elimination, effacement and exclusion on which it depends. "The central problem for both is not the representational arrangement and its accompanying question, that of knowing how and what to represent and the definition of good or true representation; the fundamental problem is the exclusion and foreclosure of all that is judged unrepresentable because non-recurrent" (*ibid.*).

What does Lyotard mean by elimination? With his sights set first of all on cinema, he gives what seems to be a common-sense answer: the kinds of movement that are eliminated are aberrant movements. Stated most simply, the repetition of takes in shooting and the scraps of footage left on the cutting-room floor testify to the necessary elimination of shots that are poorly framed, incorrectly exposed, depict unclear or indecipherable action, or include material that is confusing or fortuitous. Lyotard asks us to imagine, for example, a shot of a "gorgeous head of hair à la Renoir" suddenly interrupted by a montage sequence of various landscape shots (*ibid.*: 169). The latter shots are completely incongruous with the earlier one. Such aberration would undermine the integrity of the whole and its elimination is built into the process of ordering.

Yet Lyotard also suggests that a more profound kind of negation is at work in cinema, which is the negation of movement in-itself, the movement of sterile differences in the audio-visual field. The example here is movement wondered at when a child strikes a match, not for the sake of doing something with it, but purely for the pleasure of watching it burn, that is, to enjoy "the changing colours, the light flashing at the height of the blaze, the death of the tiny piece of wood, the hissing of the tiny flame" (*ibid.*: 171). Although consistent with the non-utility insisted on by Kant in judgements that can properly be understood as aesthetic, Lyotard associates the pleasure experienced in witnessing movement in-itself with libidinal gratification (*jouissance*) (*ibid.*).

Cinema effaces such useless movement. Movement in-itself – whether identified as gaps, jolts, postponements, losses or confusions – is rendered useful when it is utilized as a detour beneficial to the filmic totality (*ibid.*: 174). Lyotard notes, for example, how a symmetrical portrayal of two events, both murders, in a film of mostly conventional movement, is constructed by waiving the rule of representation that demands verisimilitudinal motion. The first murder is depicted by means of an *excess of mobility* "a hail of fists … [falls] upon the face of the defenceless hippie who quickly loses consciousness"; the second ends with a *freeze-frame* of the daughter "struck down in full movement" (*ibid.*: 174). The realist rhythm of action gives way to the organic rhythm of emotion. Although the good movement of representation is disfigured or deformed, it is to the benefit of the narrative order, which is thus rendered as "a beautiful melodic curve, the first accelerated murder finding its resolution in the second immobilized murder" (*ibid.*). This folding back of difference on to identity amounts to a securing of aberrant movement for a higher purpose. Aberrant movement, expressed as untimeliness at one level, produces rhythm at another level. Lyotard tells us repeatedly throughout the essay that the ordering of movement in cinema is nothing other than a return to the same. The syntheses of differences that occur in the various interlocking schemas follow the figure of return. From the organization of affective charges to the resolution of the intrigue, nothing is lost; everything is assembled in such a way that it transmits its value.

> Repetition, the principle of not only the metric but even of the rhythmic, if taken in the narrow sense as the repetition of the same (same colour, line, angle, chord) is the work of Eros and Apollo disciplining the movements, limiting them to the norms of tolerance characteristic of the system or whole in consideration.   (Lyotard 1989a: 172–3)

The third and final way that film direction involves movement is through the process of separation and the creation of exclusive zones. The cinematic frame institutes a split between the zone of reality on the one hand and the play space of the film on the other, circumscribing "the region of de-responsibility at the heart of a whole which *ideo facto* is posed as responsible (we call it *nature*, for example, or *society* or *final instance*)" (*ibid*: 175).

Significantly, the separation results in a devaluation of the "scene's realities", which are no longer considered for their aesthetic or artistic merits but come to be valued simply because of their capacity to represent "the realities of reality" (*ibid.*). At the same time, separation also forms a unity between the two zones because the conditions on both sides of the frame mirror each other. Here the exclusions performed in the zone of de-responsibility become invisibilities in the zone of reality:

> in order for the function of representation to be fulfilled, the activity of directing (a placing in and out of the scene, as we have just said) must also be an activity that unifies all movements, those on *both sides* of the frame's limit, imposing here *and* there, in "reality" just as in the reel, the same norms, the same ordering of all the drives, excluding, obliterating, effacing them no less in the scene than out. The references imposed on the filmic object are imposed just as necessarily on all the objects outside the film.   (Lyotard 1973a: 364, my translation)

Although Lyotard does not explicitly schematize it as this point, this separation entails another, which is that between the scene and/or screen and the spectator. He will, however, take up how such separation impacts on movement when he considers the acinematic *dispositifs*.

For Lyotard, commercial cinema partakes in the order of restricted economy in so far as it depends on the exclusion of movement in-itself: on noumenal movement if we want to consider it in relation to a Kantian schema, and abstract negativity if we want to push a Hegelian one. The effect is to ensure that all movements in the film have value. There is no waste in cinema, no useless expenditure, no movement for the sake of it. Contrasting with the restricted economy of commercial cinema, Lyotard explicates the general economy of two acinematic poles. Most simply, they are acin-ematic because they break with a representational depiction of movement: they no longer derive value from giving an "impression of reality" but explore the impact of the artifice of movement. One pole thus tends toward absolute immobility, the other toward excessive mobility.

In formulating these *dispositifs*, Lyotard extends his consideration of movement to include the mobility of the drives as they are understood in psychoanalysis. There are two points at which Lyotard invokes psychoanalysis here. The first is in order to understand the different kinds of pleasure at work in relation to movement: the useful and useless movements on the screen give rise, respectively, to normative and per-verse pleasure. In the second case, we move from a formulation of the movement of objects and images on the screen to the movement and cathexis of psychical energy. In this case, Lyotard speculates about how it is that the drives emanate from the body of spectator to "reunite" in the first place on the support (whether it is a mirror, screen, object or victim) and then in order to obliterate the support.

The first acinematic *dispositif* that Lyotard discusses is emblematized in the *tableau vivant*. The commercial practice popular in Sweden at the time known as "posering" allows him to schematize the distribution of immobility and its impact. The practice involves young girls participating in the sexual fantasies of their cli-ents by adopting poses stipulated by them. Most significantly, the erotic interaction between the girl and her client is limited by an explicit interdiction of any physical contact. As with cinema, a zone of de-responsibility is cordoned off from one of responsibility. Yet, in striking the pose the object/model tends towards the extrem-ity of immobility. Lyotard argues that by offering her self as a detached region, the prostitute/victim's "*whole person*" is humiliated and that humiliation is a necessary component in the *dispositif*: it adds to "the intensification since it indicates the ines-timable price of diverting the drives in order to achieve perverse pleasure" (Lyotard 1989a: 178). Extreme erotic intensification thus occurs in both zones. The immo-bilization of movement on the side of the girl is balanced, if not exceeded by, the "liveliest agitation" that overtakes the client and bursts forth in the sterile, useless movement of *jouissance* (*ibid*: 177).

Lyotard compares the *dispositif* of posering to the kind of immobilizing of the image that takes place in experimental cinema, arguing that the price the organic body pays is the same as cinema pays when the image is immobilized: the cost is the "the conventional syntheses that normally all cinematographic movements prolifer-ate" (*ibid*.: 178). Both examples (posering and experimental cinema) show that the cordoning off and immobilization of the detached region humiliate the whole.

While the regulated exchange of restricted economy is in this instance called into question, Lyotard nevertheless observes that representation still plays a vital role in this *dispositif*. The support is not itself subjected to perversion, only what is supported, that is, the simulacrum. "[T]he support is held in insensibility or unconsciousness" (*ibid.*).

The second acinematic *dispositif* is found in lyrical abstraction and excessive mobility. Lyotard is not here referring to anything like the rapid pans, undercranked images or violent cutting that we associate with contemporary cinematic techniques. Indeed, the quick camera movements and fast-paced editing of recent years demonstrate that the representational status of the image is only further consolidated by such speed; "the impression of reality" becomes the "information" of reality. In fact, the excessive mobility of acinematic movement is completely different from cinematographic movement. While the latter for Lyotard is always beautiful, in the former we approach the aesthetics of the sublime. Lyotard proposes that acinematic mobility arises "from any process which undoes the beautiful forms, ... from any process which to a greater or lesser degree works on and distorts these forms" (*ibid.*: 178–9). Mobility is excessive when it prevents identification, and hence representation. It may result in a disorder of iconic components, but the crucial point to understand is that the mobilization of the support means that artistic intervention cannot simply be sublated at the level of style.

The excess of mobility occurs not in relation to normal movement but at the level of the support. The body of the model associated with the first two *dispositifs* is no longer the site of the inscription of movement; the libidinal object is replaced by the plasticity of the celluloid. The support thus appears as if "touched by perverse hands" (*ibid.*: 178). Indeed, it is not agitation itself that Lyotard is attempting to understand, but the "price of agitation and libidinal expense" (*ibid.*). *Jouissance* is still caused by a disruption of a unified body, but this time it is the spectator's body. Lyotard explains how this happens by describing the kind of paralysis, somatic intensification and fragmentation that the viewer experiences as "the decomposition of his own organism" (*ibid.*: 179). "The channels of passage and libidinal discharge are restricted to very small partial regions (eye-cortex), and almost the whole body is neutralised in a tension blocking all escape of drives from passages other than those necessary to the detection of very fine differences" (*ibid.*).

It is arguable that Lyotard's essay is more concerned with understanding these "acinematic" possibilities than it is with cinema in general. And indeed it is because the span of his argument diverges so much from cinema in general while delving into other kinds of engagements (Sade and Klossowski, the nature of the simulacrum, the painting of Rothko and Pollock, the Swedish commerce in posering) that one begins to wonder whether the essay is about cinema at all. And yet the acinematic poles deserve to be understood with reference to cinema because they too are concerned with what is at stake in movement. We might surmise that the reason for Lyotard's apparent disinterest in the bulk of cinema is its unconcern with any aesthetic experimentation with the ontology of movement. Certainly his work has had more impact on the study of experimental cinema than it is has on mainstream cinema (cf. James 1989; Krauss 1994).

In 1973 Lyotard thus judged narrative cinema to be an exclusively representational medium, bound by the conditions of restricted economy, with the disciplining capacities of Eros and Apollo ensuring its compliance with good form. It was nothing other than "the orthopedic mirror" of the imaginary subject (*à la* Lacan) (Lyotard 1989a: 176). Experimentation with the acinematic poles of movement was the only means by which cinema could approach an aesthetics of the sublime. Yet within four years he extended his criteria of what could be reconciled with the libidinal economy of the *objet a* by reconceiving the nature of *mise en scène*. This, we shall see, also had implications for his understanding of film directing. In "The Unconscious as Mise-en-scène" Lyotard expands his earlier thesis concerning the intensification of detached regions by the investments of libidinal economy to come to the more radical view that the director creates what he calls a somatography: he takes the "message" of the poet and inscribes it on bodies in order to give it to other bodies.[2] He thus compares the staging of desire by the analysand and the staging undertaken by the director. In this analogy, "desire gives utterance" to the primary message while the unconscious stages it.

It is insignificant that Lyotard's opening reference to *mise en scène* is theatrical; the same things he says about theatre apply to cinema. His point is that *staging* in fact implies three different stages or phases. The initial stage entails everything that must come together for the performance, that is, "the heterogeneity of the arts": a "written drama, a musical score, the design of the stage and auditorium, the machinery at the disposal of the theatre" (1977: 87). Lyotard understands these as "groups of signifiers forming so many messages or constraints in any case, belonging to different systems" (*ibid*). The final stage is the performance itself.

Before providing details of the middle stage, Lyotard conjectures that the story itself (the written play or the film script) might provide a means of limiting the potential disorder that would result from the heterogeneity of the arts. The story would thus precede and contain (or frame) their differences. Although Lyotard seems to note this in passing and does not provide much comment on its position in the three-stage schema, the question of the story and its analogue in the possible existence of a primary text of desire, it is in fact a pivotal point in his argument.

In between the two stages is the coordination of the *mise en scène*: the stage in which the director makes a great number of decisions in order to execute the narrative, to give it life (*ibid*.: 88). To some extent, Lyotard revises his previously held view of the director: whereas in "Acinema" he refused to concede that directing was an aesthetic activity, he admits here that "[t]he intervention of the director is … no less creative than that of the poet or musician" (*ibid*.). And the significance of movement is not altogether absent from this essay. Indeed, Lyotard wrests from the static substantive concept of the *mise en scène* (that which has been put in the scene) not just a transitive, but a transformational dimension; it involves the entire process of taking something from a primary space and locating it in another space. What is put in the scene implies the verb, *mettre en scène*. Lyotard also insists that this somatography, this transcription of messages on to bodies that will in turn be relayed to still other bodies, be understood as a diagraphy, where the emphasis is on the "change in the space of inscription".[3]

Lyotard compares the coordination of the *mise en scène* with the role of the unconscious in psychoanalytic theory. The unconscious similarly stands between desire and

its staging, whether in hysterical symptoms, paranoid delusions, dreams or fantasies. And yet Lyotard is less concerned with how the hysteric makes use of her body
or the paranoiac the world to stage their desire than with the analysts' method of
interpretation. It is the nature of interpretation, its function in psychoanalysis and its
capacity for uncovering the truth, that Lyotard will ultimately bring to bear on the
meaning of aesthetic objects in order to question the claims of representation. Indeed,
he transposes his doubts over the interpretive method of psychoanalysis on to cinematic or theatrical direction. While "[t]he interpreter", he writes, "unravels what the
director has put together" (1977: 88–9), interpretation and *mise en scène*, he argues,
exist as recto and verso of the same principle of mistrust. The interpreter distrusts
the "inscription" because the unconscious works to disguise desire. The unconscious
is not just any director: it is a deceiving director, for it "disguises [messages] in order
to exhibit them on stage" (*ibid.*: 89). Lyotard reminds us that the colloquial French
expression for telling a hypocrite to "cut the act" is "arrête ton cinéma", implying that
performance only takes place in order to deceive (*ibid.*).

Lyotard equivocates about the pertinence of the view that intepretation should
serve to unmask deceitful appearances. He invokes Nietzsche here in a way that will
become important later, emphasizing his contention that mistrust lies at the origin
of the desire for knowledge, and questioning along with him "why it is better not to
be deceived than to be deceived … And above all: aren't we surely deceived by our
heeding only distrust?" (*ibid.*: 90).

Lyotard turns to Freud's account of the "Child is Being Beaten" fantasy in order to
contemplate further the implications of the notion that the *mise en scène* disguises
desire. The fantasy is a masturbation fantasy, apparently common with women, but
rarely acknowledged because associated with feelings of shame. It has three phases.
The first phase is recounted by the female analysand to her analyst and consists of
an authority figure beating some boys. Unlike the *tableau vivant dispositif* in the
"Acinema" essay, it is a girl who, at least initially, is "placed in the position of the
spectator" (*ibid.*: 91). In the process of analysis, the analyst and analysand working
together locate another scene behind the first one: "The father is beating the child
(that I hate)" (*ibid.*). Lyotard initially proposes that the primary message (the latent
content) is arrived at in the analysis, whereas the scene first described by the analysand is more like the final performance. But almost immediately he adds that the
process is complicated by a second phase emerging between the two. In this phase
"my father is beating me".[4] The supplementary phase is furnished by the analyst, and
the girl is absorbed into the picture. In his consideration of the fantasy, Lyotard insists
that one heed how the components of the fantasy – its objects, relations, content and
significance – undergo dramatic reconfigurations between the various stages. These
components are deemed equivalent to the heterogeneity of the arts that go into the
production of a film or a piece of theatre. Lyotard explains how they are subjected to
different operations in order to arrive at the final performance:

> For instance, from "the father is beating the child that I hate" to "my father
> is beating me," it is necessary that the patient, who was a spectator, become
> an actress, that the love of the father be turned into hatred, that the hatred

for the child be changed into the hatred the little girl feels for herself, that the initial jealously, which perhaps is not even sexualised, be replaced by a drive with a strongly anal component, that the sex of the victim be changed (from male to female), along with the position of the patient in relation to the stage. Likewise, to get from sentence no. 1 to sentence no. 3 requires linguistic transformations: the active voice in "The father is beating the child" becomes a passive voice in "A child is being beaten", the determinant *the* in *the child* is turned into *a*, and the part of the father is finally deleted.

(1977: 92)

Thus we see the importance of somatography: the *mise en scène*, "far from being a translation, would be a transcription of a pictorial text of virtual bodies, with effect on the real body of the spectator (masturbation)" (*ibid.*). Although Lyotard is not explicit about it, his later argumentation implies that *mise en scène* here can be understood in two ways. The fantasy functions to both exhibit and conceal an initial message (*ibid.*). The message concealed is the desire for the father, and the transformation of the components takes place in order to remove him from the picture. *Mise en scène* here would be understood negatively as a means of disguising a primary message. But how can we not also see that the *mise en scène* directed by Freud exhibits nothing other than the analyst putting himself into the picture through the proxy of the father?

The implication is that it is not simply a question of a static text (like a musical score or the written play) being interpreted differently at each stage of the fantasy. Lyotard suggests that Freud's ever more sophisticated theory of the drives and their vicissitudes gets in the way of understanding "the unconscious as mise-en-scène" as the concealment of a pre-existent discourse of desire. On the one hand, he observes that Freud seems to understand the phases of the fantasy chronologically, implying that one phase is but a representation of the prior one: "that the girl's masochism is a mise-en-scène of her initial sadism" (*ibid.*: 93). In which case, "the messages of desire" would have to be understood as themselves "already performances", and the structure being articulated would be a *mise en abyme*, a veritable vertigo of representation, a "causality which keeps endlessly multiplying mise-en-scène, changing representeds into representatives of other representeds" (*ibid.*). On the other hand, he suggests that Freud does not quite realize the implications of his own observations. Yet, by pointing to Freud's insistence on the fact that the primary processes responsible for the metamorphoses of the drives cannot be reduced to the categories of reason, Lyotard carves out another way of thinking about what is going on.

[A] drive-siege never lets up; the opposite or inverse investment which accompanies it does not suppress the first, does not even conceal it, but sets itself up next to it. All investments are, in this way, contemporaneous with each other: one loves and hates the same object at the same time and in the same respect, which is contrary to the rules of intelligibility and chronology.

(*Ibid.*: 94)

Drive-investments are "1) logically incompossible, 2) are simultaneous, and 3) concern the same regions of the body" (*ibid.*). There is no initially legible text that is subsequently disguised in order to elude censorship or the anti-cathexis of inhibition. Desire does not have to be disguised by the *mise en scène* to be represented, because it always was fractured, paralogical, distemporal, polytopical and serial.

Similarly, not all cinema is bound by the conditions of representation. At the very end of the essay Lyotard shows that Michael Snow's elimination of the frame in *La Région Centrale* deconstructs the separation of the unreal space of fantasy, the real space of the spectators and the hidden space of the machinery of construction. Lyotard argues that by creating space without framing, desire no longer has the means of disguising itself. It is thus not a question, he writes, of language being a technology for constructing truth and film one of disguising it. "Both are inexhaustible means for experimenting with new effects, never seen, never heard before. They create their own reference, therefore their object is not identifiable, they create their own addressee, a disconcerted body, invited to stretch its sensory capacities beyond measure" (*ibid.*: 96).

The operation of desire is no longer oriented toward the fulfilment of a wish (if it ever was) but is properly realized as a force. This is the point at which Lyotard finally reconfigures Freud's thinking along Nietzschean lines. And Snow's film stands as early evidence of what for Lyotard is at stake in postmodernism: "there is nothing but perspectives; one can invent new ones" (*ibid.*).

NOTES

1. Another important nuance that is lost in the English translation and that becomes problematic when one attempts to read this essay in relation to "The Unconscious as Mise-en-scène" is that in "Acinema", *mettre-en-scène* is translated as director and *mise-en-scène* as direction. References to the essay "Acinema" in this chapter are to the 1989 reprint in *The Lyotard Reader*, A. Benjamin (ed.), 169–80 (Oxford: Blackwell, 1989) unless otherwise stated.

2. The second stage is the final performance that "besieges our sensory body" by telling a story and thus "steers us along a course"; J.-F. Lyotard, "The Unconscious as Mise-en-scène", J. Maier (trans.), in *Performance in Postmodern Culture*, M. Benamou & C. Caramello (eds), 87–98 (Madison, WI: Coda Press, 1977), 87.

3. Those who have read *Discours, Figure* will not be surprised by this emphasis, although it is interesting that Lyotard has shifted his thinking about transcription significantly. In writing about the Freudian dream-work he goes to great lengths to point out that: " The dream-work does not relate to this primary discourse as another discourse, such as that of interpretation, might do; the gap between the latent content (*Traumgedanke*) and manifest content is not the empty distance, the transcendence separating a 'normal' discourse from its object (even if that object is itself a discourse), nor that which separates a text from its translation into another language. That difference is 'intrinsic' according to Freud. The problem of the dream-work is therefore to discover how, from the raw material of a statement, a qualitatively different though still meaningful object can be produced. The work is not an interpretation of the dream-thought, a discourse on a discourse. Neither is it a transcription, a discourse based on a discourse. It is its transformation" ("The Dream-Work Does Not Think", in Benjamin [ed.], *The Lyotard Reader*, 19–55, esp. 21). But there is also a sense in which the change of space signifies something quite different from the reduction of space that is entailed in condensation: "*Condensation* must be understood as a physical process by means of which one or more objects occupying a given space are reduced to a smaller volume, as is the case when gas becomes a liquid" (*ibid.*: 23).

4. It is surprising that neither Lyotard nor Jacqueline Rose in her subsequent commentary on the essay comment on this, especially considering that this is the masochistic phase of the fantasy. For her comments on the two essays discussed here see J. Rose, *Sexuality in the Field of Vision* (London: Verso, 1986).

21 FREDRIC JAMESON

Scott Durham

Fredric Jameson (b. 1934) is William A. Lane Professor of Comparative Literature at Duke University. After completing his doctorate at Yale, he taught at Harvard, Yale, the University of California, San Diego, and the University of California, Santa Cruz, before moving to Duke in 1985. His doctoral dissertation was published in 1961 as *Sartre: The Origins of a Style*. He has since published numerous books on literature, film, philosophy and cultural theory, including *Marxism and Form* (1971), *The Prison-House of Language* (1972), *The Political Unconscious* (1981), *Signatures of the Visible* (1990), *Postmodernism, or the Cultural Logic of Late Capitalism* (1991), *The Geopolitical Aesthetic* (1992), *The Seeds of Time* (1994), *Brecht and Method* (1998), *Archaeologies of the Future: The Desire Called Utopia and Other Science Fictions* (2005) and *The Modernist Papers* (2007).

Fredric Jameson is among the most prominent theorists of postmodernism and one of the foremost Marxist critics of his generation. In *Postmodernism, or the Cultural Logic of Late Capitalism* (1991), film occupies a central place in his account of the formal features of postmodernism and in his analysis of the relationship of postmodern culture to the social and economic forms of "late capitalism". In other works, such as *Signatures of the Visible* (1990) and *The Geopolitical Aesthetic* (1992), film is the focal point of his reflections on the fate of critical and utopian thought in postmodern culture, and of his evaluation of the possibilities and limits of various narrative and representational forms for imagining the place of individual experience in the new global system. Much of the power of Jameson's writings on postmodernism depends on his commitment to weaving these distinct levels of analysis into a coherent whole, thereby providing a global interpretation of postmodernism as the "cultural dominant" of "late capitalist" society. Thus the significance of this project – and the legitimacy of its philosophical, aesthetic and political claims – can only be fully understood within the broader framework of Jameson's rethinking of the problem of interpreting cultural history generally, which finds its most systematic elaboration in *The Political Unconscious* (1981).

"Always historicize!" (*ibid.*: 9). In the opening pages of *The Political Unconscious*, Jameson identifies this as the "one absolute" imperative of dialectical thought inherited from the Marxist tradition. But this task, Jameson argues, demands more of the interpreter of cultural artefacts than a reading of the work, as in traditional literary or film history, as a reflection of its political or cultural background. For Jameson, that background is never simply given to us immediately. While historical processes are, as Jameson acknowledges, far from being reducible to the stories we might tell about them, history is nonetheless accessible to us only in so far as it has passed through a "prior (re)textualization" (*ibid.*: 82). To be represented, in other words, history must first be rendered representable and the stories of its individual and collective characters imagined in terms of the repertoire of narrative schemas and generic formulas, conceptual oppositions, myths and stereotypes that, together, constitute the ideological horizon of a given historical moment.

It is, Jameson argues, only in and through such forms of narrative and thought that a society can attempt to represent its underlying contradictions and antagonisms, respond to the social anxieties and collective wishes to which those contradictions and antagonisms give rise, and imagine the possibility of their resolution. But since those forms, and their traditions of reception, have evolved in response to earlier historical moments of whose ideologies and collective fantasies they still bear the traces, they must themselves inevitably be rewritten or transformed in order to address the contradictions of the present. The text thus does not so much reflect history as work on and rewrite it, negotiating the relationship between the forms of social practice and experience, with their attendant fantasies and anxieties, that constitute its historical raw material, and the repertoire of narrative and representational strategies it has inherited, along with their ideological residues. From this perspective, the task of the critic is that of reconstructing the dynamic process by which the work writes a place for itself within those overlapping histories.

Jameson offers an exemplary reconstruction of this dynamic in a brief but richly layered account of the two first films of Francis Ford Coppola's *Godfather* trilogy (1972–90) in "Reification and Utopia in Mass Culture", which offers a condensed articulation of the interpretive method later elaborated in *The Political Unconscious*.[1] Of course, as Jameson acknowledges, *The Godfather* can, at the most immediate level, be considered a representation of actual historical events: the bloody struggles of the five great mob families, and the extension of their reach into the worlds of legitimate business, the entertainment industry and the political power structure. But the ideological work performed by the film will not turn so much on the truth or falsehood of its account of these events considered in and of themselves as on the transformations it brings about in the forms of narrative through which the historical events in question – as well as those of the broader history for which it serves as the allegorical figure – are imagined.

Thus our first clue as to what is at stake in *The Godfather*'s narration of the Corleone family's history is the way that its incorporation of this "Mafia material" becomes the occasion for reinventing the genre of the "gangster film", a genre whose transformations over the course of the century action "changing social and ideological functions" in response to "distinct historical situations" (1990: 30–31). For if, Jameson argues, the gangster film of the 1930s, responding to the moment of American New Deal populism, portrayed gangsters as "sick loners" lashing out at decent society and the "common man", and if "the post-war gangsters of the Bogart era" were loners of a different sort, imbued with a "tragic pathos" that resonated with the psychological wounds of veterans returning to confront a "petty and vindictive social order", the narrative of the Mafia family marks a shift away from the individualism that had marked the previous history of the genre. According to Jameson,

> this very distinctive narrative content – a kind of saga or family material analogous to that of the medieval *chansons de geste* with its recurrent episodes and legendary figures returning again and again in different perspectives and contexts – can at once be structurally differentiated from the older paradigms by its collective nature. *(Ibid.*: 31)

And this parallels "an evolution towards organizational themes and team narratives" (*ibid.*) in other subgenres (such as the western and the caper film) in the 1960s.

This shift in narrative form across generic boundaries would seem in itself to suggest, Jameson argues, a shift in the forms of social life that provide their raw material, one in which, in the age of the multinational corporation, the story of a mere individual can no longer credibly lay claim to the same significance. Coppola's reinvention of the myth of the Mafia – as "an organized conspiracy" (*ibid.*) extending its reach into all of our economic, cultural and political institutions – may be seen in this light as a mythic narrative through which this new form of social life can be represented in a form that is at once dramatic (in a way that the representation of the inner workings of a "legitimate" corporation is unlikely to be) and indirect, in so far as big business is represented here only through the displacement of its characteristics on to a Mafia family.

But if this substitution of organized crime for big business succeeds in endowing this material with the undeniable narrative fascination of the underworld and the evil that it presumably embodies, this same displacement also does the work of ideology, even, as Jameson remarks, if "organized crime has exactly the importance and influence in American life which such representations attribute to it" (*ibid.*: 32). For while it might be hoped that a direct representation of the dominant role of multinational corporations in our society could lead to a critique of the structures that perpetuate their dominance, the allegorical transposition of that dominance into a "'myth' of the Mafia" (*ibid.*: 30) encourages us to imagine the baleful effects of its invisible power as the product of a moral flaw in its perpetrators, rather than of undemocratic and exploitative social institutions themselves. The allegorical inscription of the contradictions of corporate America within the framework provided by the gangster genre (an inscription that, as we have seen, demands a reinvention of that genre) thus leads us to frame our objections to that system in the language of moral condemnation, rather than political critique. In this light, Jameson sees such films as carrying out a "strategic displacement" (*ibid.*: 32) of the anger that might otherwise be directed at the corporate masters of the universe – who, in fact, are pillars of the social order in its present form – on to criminal figures who appear as enemies of that order. Thus, Jameson concludes, in a historical moment where the Nixonian theme of law and order was a touchstone of the political right in America, Mafia films "project a 'solution' to social contradictions – incorruptibility, crime fighting, and finally law-and-order itself – which is evidently a very different proposition from that diagnosis of the American misery whose prescription would be social revolution" (*ibid.*).

These *Godfather* films, like other instances of mass culture analysed by Jameson, can thus be said to fulfil the ideological function that the structural anthropologist Claude Lévi-Strauss attributed to myth in the culture of tribal societies: that of offering an imaginary resolution of real social contradictions.[2] Such mass cultural myths, having tapped the affective reality of antagonism and fear generated by social relations of domination, contain them in a narrative form that, by representing the structural ills of that society as aberrations from the social order, leads us to imagine that the solution to those ills lies in the defence of that order.

But in addition to their performance of this ideological function, Jameson continues, such Mafia narratives also perform a "transcendent or Utopian function" (*ibid.*). For in shifting the genre away from its individualist narrative schemas to the representation of the collective as such, *The Godfather*'s rewriting of the gangster film incorporates the ethnic narrative of an immigrant and minority community, with its embedded memories and experiences. In the iconic wedding sequence of *The Godfather* (dir. Coppola, 1972), for example, Jameson observes that an "ethnic neighborhood solidarity" remains vivid and accessible to present memory in a way that the more distant memories of middle-American small-town life are not. Above all, the film brings before us the enduring image of "the Mafia family (in both senses)" (1990: 33) presided over by the patriarchal Godfather of the title. And this image, in a period in which social fragmentation is often blamed on the "deterioration of the family", unexpectedly provides the pretext for "a desperate Utopian fantasy", where the "ethnic group" seems "to project an image of social reintegration" no longer available in the present by resurrecting "the patriarchal and authoritarian family of the past" (*ibid.*: 33).

The power of such a "mass cultural artifact" (*ibid.*) as *The Godfather*, Jameson argues, thus depends first of all on its ability to serve as the means of expression for two opposing impulses at once. It must first respond to the ideological demand that the resolution of social contradictions be imagined without calling into question the underlying structures that give rise to them. But it must also, at the same time, express the ideologically inadmissible longing for another form of life, by entertaining the fantasy of a remembered or imagined collectivity beyond the contradictions of the present. Jameson's interpretation of the first *Godfather* film thus invites us to discern in it the overdetermined expression at once of "our deepest fantasies about the nature of social life, both as we live it now, and as we feel in our bones it ought rather to be lived", and of the ideological and generic constraints that allow this "ineradicable drive towards collectivity" to be expressed only in "distorted and repressed unconscious form" (*ibid.*: 34). The genius of the film would seem to lie, from this perspective, in its binding of these two seemingly incompatible impulses within a single generic structure, which allows each to serve as at once the pretext for and the mask of the other.

This argument is confirmed by the unravelling of this compromise in *The Godfather, Part II* (dir. Coppola, 1974). For as Jameson shows, the sequel's elaboration of both the utopian and ideological narrative strands of the film beyond the generic and historical limits of their framing in the reinvented gangster film unmasks each of these constituent dimensions of the earlier film. On the one hand, it retraces the historical origins of the future Godfather's familial bonds back to the repressive feudal social relations of pre-capitalist Sicily. On the other hand, it shows how the criminal conspiracy is gradually transformed into just the sort of capitalist enterprise of which it had been the displaced image in the first place. Having been forced to account for its history without the aid of the other, each is compelled, in the sequel, to confront as immediately historical content the contradictions that their displacement into allegorical narrative in the first film had served to transcend or contain. When, in the sequel, the family business grows into a corporate enterprise seeking foreign markets, it encounters in Cuba the same resistance confronted throughout the world by American political and economic power in the 1960s, thus allowing us to glimpse an "authentically Utopian vision of revolutionary liberation" (1990: 34). Similarly, as we move backwards to the Godfather's origins in feudal Sicily, "the degraded Utopian content of the family paradigm ultimately unmasks itself as the survival of more archaic forms of repression" (*ibid.*). In the sequel, both of these narratives, "freed to pursue their own inner logic to its limits, are thereby driven to the … historical boundaries of capitalism itself" (*ibid.*), the one resurrecting the memory of feudalism, the other conjuring up the spectre of socialist revolution.

Historical interpretation in Jameson might thus be said to pass through a series of expanding frames, each of which implies a different horizon of interpretation. On a first level, he examines the repressed collective wish or anxiety and its displaced expression through the individual work's rewriting of pre-existing narrative and representational forms. When Jameson focuses in this way on the individual work in and of itself, he interprets it as a discrete "symbolic act" (1981: 76), which not only serves to textualize underlying social contradictions, but also figures, often in allegorical form, the containment, resolution or transcendence of those contradictions by the fulfilment of a collective wish. From this perspective, the task of the critic, in Jameson's view, would be to identify the content of the underlying collective wishes expressed in the work and to show through what transformations of pre-existing cultural forms such wishes achieve indirect expression.

But since the pre-existing forms of representation mobilized by the work are rich in meanings accumulated over their previous history, Jameson also maintains that the critic cannot fully grasp the meaning of the work's symbolic act without reconstructing, in a broader frame, the implicit messages or presuppositions embedded in those forms themselves, which the individual work will either mobilize or suppress in making use of them in its new historical situation. This is particularly striking, as we have seen, in Coppola's rewriting of the gangster genre, which only becomes comprehensible in light of the critic's reconstruction of that genre's previous history. But it is also true of the pervasive motif of conspiracy cited by Jameson as providing the form of collective narrative that permits the Mafia to stand in for the corporation. This is just the sort of floating cultural trope – somewhere between an article of faith and a fantasy narrative – that Jameson calls an "ideologeme" (cf. *ibid.*: 87–8): part of a common stock of narrative situations, received ideas and stereotypes available for representing an invisible collective, of which the Mafia narrative is (along with the "paranoid" narratives discussed below) just one of many variants. In interpreting such pre-existing forms, the critic reconstructs the historical progression of a genre from one historical formation to the next, or maps out the alternative uses of the same ideologeme within a single moment. But here, as in the interpretation of the individual work as a symbolic act, the task of historical interpretation is to uncover the meanings alluded to in the text, in a succession of nested readings that add, with each new historical layer, another dimension of meaning.

It is on the basis of this greater "semantic richness" of his multi-levelled historical approach – and not on the basis of a claim to the superiority of Marxism as a political orientation or "master narrative" of history – that Jameson argues for "the priority of a Marxian interpretive framework" (*ibid.*: 10). But there is also a sense in which the very success of *The Godfather*, in carrying out its ideological and utopian vocations by weaving together elements drawn from multiple layers of history, requires the partial repression of that history. The success of the film as a projection of collective fantasy depends on a historical and geographical structure that allows for allusions to the Mafia's past in Sicilian feudalism and its future as big business without explicitly representing the dynamics of either of these moments. The full meaning of that fantasy must remain outside the frame – in the film's "political unconscious". That is why history re-enters the scene in Jameson's account of *The Godfather, Part II* as an unmasking: as a return of the repressed. In rendering explicit what was only evoked in the first, the second film unties the interwoven strands that gave the first its formal and ideological coherence. For that coherence turned on the exclusion of anything that might lead the viewer to question its illusory superimposition of the collective forms of the feudal family on the entirely different anti-individualism of corporations of the post-war period.

An essential strategy of Marxist critique – which Jameson refers to as an "imperative to totalize" (*ibid.*: 53) – is to move beyond the generic, historical or spatial limits of a given narrative or interpretive frame to make visible the text's repression of that inadmissible material which must be kept "beyond its boundaries" (*ibid.*) in order for the world it represents to maintain its narrative and ideological coherence. This ultimate form of reframing emphasizes not the richness of a text's multiple historical meanings, but the limits of what Jameson calls its "strategies of containment" (*ibid.*: 53): the ways in which a narrative or ideology gives the impression of being self-sufficient in its own terms, while repressing what cannot be thought without calling its underlying assumptions and narrative forms into question.

Nowhere is the tension between the semantic richness of a work's intertextual allusions, and the limits imposed on its frame by aesthetic form and ideology, more pronounced than in Jameson's analysis of postmodernism. No moment of cultural history would seem to be richer in its repetitions of multiple styles, languages, genres and cultural forms than is postmodernity. One of the key features of postmodernism is the "universal practice" of "pastiche" (1991: 16), in which the work, having abandoned any claim to the authority of a unique style or vision valorized by modernism, carries out a seemingly random cannibalization of the styles of a decontextualized past. Thus, in Jim Jarmusch's *Ghost Dog: The Way of the Samurai* (1999), to cite a more recent example, the contemporary language of hip hop coexists with the comically rendered *Godfather*-style gangster saga, alongside the otherwise now dead languages of the medieval samurai and the Betty Boop cartoon.

In postmodern pastiche, styles and images from every region and period coexist in the same space. But, as Jameson insists, this "omnivorous ... historicism" (1991: 18), far from representing a heightened consciousness of history, is the expression of "an age that has forgotten how to think historically ..." (*ibid.*: ix). For the historical past is not evoked in postmodern historicism as a different form of life or experience. It is accessible only at a second degree, through a recycling of its previous representations. Thus nostalgia films such as *American Graffiti* (dir. George Lucas, 1973) and *Chinatown* (dir. Roman Polanski, 1974), rather than representing the 1930s or the 1950s as historical contents, recycle through stylistic connotation the stereotypical concept of an eternal "'1930s-ness' or '1950s-ness'" (*ibid.*: 9).

For Jameson, the nostalgia film assimilates the styles of the past to its own "culture of the image" (*ibid.*: 6), foreclosing any relationship to the past in its difference from the present, and signalling a "crisis" of "historicity" (*ibid.*: 25) in postmodernism generally. This crisis is paralleled, at the level of individual narrative, by a fragmented and random ordering of events that permeates narrative in a culture of the image "dominated by space and spatial logic" (*ibid.*). Thus *Pulp Fiction* (dir. Quentin Tarantino, 1994), released a few years after the publication of Jameson's *Postmodernism*, can shuffle its images and their associated narrative events in any order, since that order is governed by no causal or experiential logic beyond the intensity of these images as such and the intertextual relations between them.

Postmodernism brings such formal features together in a single constellation as a "periodizing" concept (1991: 3), in which, Jameson argues, it replaces modernism as the "cultural dominant" (*ibid.*: 4) of the new phase of multinational or "late capitalism", which emerged after the Second World War. Jameson foregrounds two transformations that differentiate late capitalism from capitalism's previous forms. First, the distinction between the economic and the cultural considered as separate spheres – an opposition presupposed by the modernist notion of culture as a site of critique of, or compensation for, the dissatisfactions of modernity – is increasingly worn away. With the increasing centrality of images in consumer culture, both in the marketing of commodities and as commodities themselves, the economic becomes increasingly cultural. At the same time, the production of aesthetic objects themselves becomes increasingly integrated into commodity production. As a result, the content of social experience increasingly becomes indistinguishable from the cultural forms in which it is represented, and the forms of cultural representation themselves become the social reality they represent. In this situation, the only realism possible would seem to be that of citation: realism as pastiche.

Secondly, the global expansion of capital finally eradicates the last "precapitalist enclaves" (*ibid.*: 49) beyond the reach of capitalist modernity and, with them, the last forms of life and experience untouched by the market and instrumental reason. With this disappearance of the pre-modern (together with the "colonizing" of the unconscious by media images; *ibid.*), one could no longer credibly appeal to the Primitive, the Unconscious or Being as the ontological ground of a utopian or mythic alternative to the degraded experiences of modern life. All that will remain of the "authentic" experiences evoked by modernism will be the dead languages in which they were expressed. Meanwhile, this assimilation of its former peripheries into an expanded capitalist system exceeds the capacity of existing narrative and representational forms for situating the interactions of individual and collective actors within a now transnational social space. Postmodernism is thus born of the historical impossibility of reviving realism or modernism in late capitalism, even as the forms of postmodernism's predecessors persist, as so many dead languages within it.

Jameson's analysis of postmodernism as the cultural dominant of late capitalism encompasses the widest historical perspective discussed in *The Political Unconscious*: the ideology of cultural forms, in their dialectical relationship to the history of social formations. But in his most extended engagement with postmodern film, in *The Geopolitical Aesthetic*, Jameson offers analyses of how individual films textualize postmodernity's contradictions within the limits imposed by that historical conjuncture, while expressing its collective wishes and anxieties. The first section, "Totality as Conspiracy", examines North American conspiracy film (including such films as *Three Days of the Condor* [dir. Sydney Pollack, 1975], *The Parallax View* [dir. Alan J. Pakula, 1974], and *Videodrome* [dir. David Cronenberg, 1983]) as a form of "cognitive mapping": as "an unconscious, collective effort at trying to figure out where we are and what landscapes and forces confront us" in postmodernity (1992: 3). At one level, these films address a problem of textualization that Jameson explores elsewhere: how to concretely imagine "the essential impersonality and post-individualistic structure" through which political and economic power is exercised in an age of corporate dominance "while still operating among real people, in the tangible necessities of daily life" (1990: 48). In conspiracy film, this problem is managed by a continual shifting of gears between inherited narrative forms (such as those of the detective or espionage novel) where characters must be individuals, and the hidden conspiracy as an invisible collective character.

But such conspiracy narratives also elaborate an "unconscious meditation" (*ibid.*: 28), in the form of a myth or collective fantasy, on the fears and hopes aroused by a post-individual society. In Cronenberg's *Videodrome* (1983), sexually charged media images, through a hallucination-inducing technology, "colonize" the psychic interior of its anti-hero, Max, inducing him to play the roles, at various points, of investigator, victim and even perpetrator, of two conspiracies: a right-wing conspiracy of corporate elites and a millenarian utopian conspiracy. As Jameson points out, the dizzying rotation of Max's roles allows *Videodrome* to explore all the possibilities of paranoia as an ideologeme representing, through the "narrative category of the individual character" (1992: 34), collective processes incommensurate with individual experience. Meanwhile, the struggle between these two conspiracies, considered as collective characters, also provides a narrative apparatus in which opposing judgements concerning the ultimate nature of those social processes – as the utopian promise of a transfigured community or as an updated fascism – are juxtaposed. *Videodrome*, Jameson argues, does not ask us to decide between these visions of a post-individual world, but shows that they are "intimately intertwined" (*ibid.*: 28) in the same collective fantasy. The alternation between the two thus does not so much offer a mythic resolution of these contradictory aspects of postmodernity as lay bare before our eyes the narrative mechanisms of ideology itself.

But if such conspiracy narratives are to be understood as unconscious attempts to imagine the global totality from its North American "centre", in "Circumnavigations", the second half of *The Geopolitical Aesthetic*, Jameson explores how film-makers from Europe and the global South, who must think their distance from that centre, elaborate the most inventive strategies of resistance to postmodernity's social and cultural forms. In *Mababangong bangungot* (The perfumed nightmare; 1977), Kidlat Tahimik explores the relationship between his alter ego's life in a village in the Philippines and his implicit faith in the metropole's promise of technological and economic development. Kidlat's persona is a village jeepney driver. (Jeepneys are reconstructed and elaborately decorated surplus jeeps used for public transportation.) But he is also an avid listener to Voice of America, and founder of the Wernher von Braun Fan Club. Drawn to the European metropole by his dreams of the "developed" world, he is, ultimately, disillusioned with the ideology of development.

But Tahimik's critique of capitalist "overdevelopment" in this film – staged in a series of sketches and gags – cannot lay claim to some site of absolute otherness outside the global system. When, at the film's climax, Kidlat incongruously conjures up a great wind blowing against the empire, he cites, as Jameson acknowledges, a mythic language, expressing forces of revolt latent in the land. But, as Jameson insists, Tahimik foregrounds the incongruous and "unearned" (1992: 208) character of this mythic ending, which the film has not prepared by grounding it either in a natural or traditional world beyond the reach of Western technology, nor in any plausible alternative to global capitalism. Similarly, when Tahimik allegorizes Kidlat's situation on the periphery of the global system (as in Kidlat's series of attempts to pull a jeepney – first a tiny toy jeepney, then a larger one, ending, comically, with the massive thing itself – across the bridge leading from his village to the "developed" world beyond), he artfully deploys Brechtian effects of distanciation by adopting an aesthetic of formal "regression". This aesthetic, deftly staging the apparent unsophistication of a home movie or a child's game, is nonetheless valorized throughout the film as a "Utopian escape from commercial reification" (*ibid.*: 204).

Thus, when Tahimik takes up devices inherited from modernism, it is not in an attempt to invent an authentic alternative to postmodernism, but as part of a strategy of dislocation, where the oppositions of the modern to the natural or traditional, and of development to underdevelopment, are called into question. An analogous movement takes place thematically, as Kidlat leads us to rethink the opposition of periphery to centre in the world system. On his visit to metropolitan Paris, what most disillusions him is the destruction, in the name of development, of traditional neighbourhoods for the benefit of the corporate chains. Thus, through this witness from the periphery, we rediscover, in the metropole itself, the same sort of capitalist onslaught on pre-existing forms of life that might be denounced, in anti-imperialist terms, in the periphery.

Meanwhile, it is in the periphery that we discover a site that undoes, in a different way, the opposition of old to new, of invention to backwardness, of development to underdevelopment. This is the factory in which the jeepneys are reconstructed out of the scavenged parts of military machinery, to be refunctioned to a new purpose, but also individually and idiosyncratically painted, and thus transformed into aesthetic objects in their own right. Here, Jameson suggests, is a utopian image of "a space of human labor" which, without being traditional, is far from "the disembodied machinic forces of late capitalist high technology", a labour process that "does not know the structural oppression of the assembly line or Taylorization", but "is permanently provisional, thereby liberating its subjects from the tyrannies of form and of the pre-programmed": a form of work where, crucially, "aesthetics and production" are one (*ibid.*: 210). But Tahimik's film, Jameson argues, is itself a jeepney of this sort, a vehicle for the utopian reimagination of the postmodern practices of cannibalization and pastiche as seen from the periphery, but also for a reordering of the conceptual map of postmodernity, which "blasts apart the sterile opposition between the old and the new, the traditional and the Western, and allows its former components themselves to be cannibalized and conceptually resoldered" (*ibid.*: 209–10).

It is with this exemplary work of cognitive mapping – which, by widening the frame of postmodernism beyond the geographical limits of the metropole, shows us another way of imagining the interpenetration of the cultural and the economic – that Jameson concludes his most extended reflection on postmodern film. Tahimik's film does not move beyond the postmodern present to invoke another world beyond it. Nor does it, like a conspiracy film, dream of a commanding point of view from above, that would encompass the totality of the world system in a single gaze. But it produces, by the strategic displacement of postmodernity's geographical and conceptual space, a dialectical image of the limits we confront in this historical conjuncture, alongside its possibilities for resistance and invention. In this, it provides a fitting allegory for the work of Fredric Jameson himself.

NOTES

1. This 1979 essay appears in Jameson's first book on film, *Signatures of the Visible* (New York: Routledge, 1990), 9–34.
2. In his discussion of this aspect of myth in Lévi-Strauss, in which the mythic text is read as "a symbolic act, whereby real social contradictions, insurmountable in their own terms," are resolved "in the aesthetic realm" (F. Jameson, *The Political Unconscious: Narrative as a Socially Symbolic Act* [London: Methuen, 1981], 77–80, esp. 79), Jameson foregrounds the anthropologist's analysis of the facial decorations of Caduveo women in *Tristes Tropiques*, J. Russell (trans.) (New York: Atheneum, 1967), 173–80, as well as his classic essay, "The Structural Study of Myth," in *Structural Anthropology*, C. Jacobson & B. Grundfest Schoepf (trans.) (New York: Basic Books, 1963), 206–31.

22 FÉLIX GUATTARI

Gary Genosko

Félix Guattari (1930–92) worked as a psychoanalyst at the experimental psychiatric clinic La Borde in Cour-Cheverny, France. By 1953 he had entered the gravitational field of Jacques Lacan's seminar, and later became his analysand. Guattari participated in many far-left political organizations, engaged with the struggles of social movements such as anti-psychiatry, while not adopting the name, and turned to green politics in his later years. He supported the free radio movement in the mid 1970s, and assisted his Italian friends such as Antonio Negri and Franco Berardi in the autonomist movement during a period of state repression.

His books include *Psychanalyse et transversalité* (a collection of early articles published in 1972), *La Révolution moléculaire* (two different editions appeared in 1977; partial translation in 1984), *Les Années d'hiver* (occasional pieces from 1980–86), *Cartographies schizoanalytiques* (1989), *The Three Ecologies* (1989; English trans. 2000) and *Chaosmosis* (1992; English trans. 1995). Posthumously, his letters to Deleuze and preparatory notes were published in *The Anti-Oedipus Papers* (2004; English trans. 2006). Guattari collaborated with Gilles Deleuze on *Anti-Oedipus* (1972; English trans. 1977), *Kafka* (1975; English trans. 1986), *A Thousand Plateaus* (1980; English trans. 1987) and *What is Philosophy?* (1991; English trans. 1994). Guattari also collaborated with Antonio Negri on *Communists Like Us* (1990), and with Suely Rolnik on *Molecular Revolution in Brazil* (2008). Guattari's interview with Luiz Inácio Lula da Silva, current president of Brazil, is included *in The Party without Bosses* (Genosko 2003). Key edited collections include *The Guattari Reader* (1996a) and *Soft Subversions* (1996b).

Félix Guattari's most sustained comments on cinema consist of several interviews and occasional pieces dating from the 1970s gathered together in the Encres edition *of La Révolution moléculaire* (Molecular revolution) under the title "Cinema: A Minor Art" (Guattari 1977, reprinted in Guattari 1996b: 143–87). For Guattari, cinema is a privileged medium for minoritarian becomings that show a specific orientation towards the progressive goals of anti-psychiatric social and political practices. Guattari's approach to cinema through the minor is generally consistent with Deleuze's (1989: 221–4) deployment of the anti-colonialist, revolutionary Third Cinema; yet Guattari did not adopt this approach wholesale. He shared with Third Cinema progressive political goals and artistic experimentation; he did not accept the typology in Third Cinema between Hollywood's industrial model, auteur cinema (a miniature version of industry) and a valorized radical cinema that is grounded in anti-colonial struggles and the aspirations of emerging national cinemas (Solanas & Getino 1997).

Although the minor is not usually affixed to oppressed minorities (who might, on a restricted view of identity, author only marginal works), this does not change the fact that many people struggling with mental illness and poverty and racism – some treated in the films favoured by Guattari – are oppressed and socio-economically and psychically ghettoized. Guattari does not conflate minor and marginal. He is not making a socio-demographic claim, although the basis to do so surely exists in some cases. Marginal is distinguished from minor in Guattari's thought inasmuch as a minority (for example, first-wave gay rights activists in the US) refuse their marginality because it is tied to repressive recentrings on normative models of sexuality and lifestyle (Guattari 1977a: 185–6; 1978: 57). The transition from margin to minor may be used to describe numerous social movements that make significant gains for themselves and on this firmer ground are able to explore minoritarian and other becomings in the creation of new alliances, ultimately finding a receptive audience not yet formed, but which would hopefully participate in the labour of emancipation. Guattari cites the example of the occupation of Lincoln Hospital in the summer of 1970 by the Young Lords, a Puerto Rican group advocating self-determination and engaging in coordinated health activism with allies such as the Black Panthers. Although the occupation of the long-condemned facility lasted only a few weeks, the protest action had the goal of reorienting practice way from research and training to serving neighbourhood interests, agitating for a new building, linking housing and health, and reinventing the marginal as a vital force of social change and expression of collective values and tactical de-territorializations such as using former drug addicts to run the detox unit.

Guattari did not elaborate a comprehensive theory of the cinema and he discusses few films in depth. Minor cinema exudes the spirit of revolutionary politics in Guattari's working out of the minor's connectivity in a progressivist voice, indeed, in film's ability to give voice to workers themselves (for example Third Cinema theorists Fernando Solanas and Octavio Getino favourably cite Chris Marker's experiments in France to empower workers to film their own realities with 8mm equipment (Solanas & Getino 1997: 45). There is not, in Guattari, a straightforward valorization of documentary cinema, even though he cites a significant number of such films. Guattari's interest in a wide variety of documentary works within the stream of the anti-psychiatry movement is subject to the same criticisms he levels at the movement and its stars: creeping familial analysis (Oedipalism), reformist sentiments, a reactionary countercultural abdication of concrete struggle and taste for media spectacle. Even the intensity of these criticisms was tempered by exceptions, like the cinematic works dealing with the Italian situation of the movement and the institutional experiments of guerrilla psychiatrist Franco Basaglia (Guattari 1996a).

We need to take care when noting the affinities between minor cinema and Third Cinema. There is some continuity at the level of film praxis with a *cinema without bosses*, that is, of "total filmmakers", as Solanas (1970: 38) insisted, not directors, stars, studio mandarins and long lines of specialists, but revolutionaries prepared to tackle all of the dimensions of film production. To the extent that Guattari valorized a democratization of production and the responsible documentation, he is in line with Third Cinema objectives.

Deleuzian film critics point out that the major statements of Third Cinema by Solanas and Getino as well as Julio Garcia Espinoza's "For an Imperfect Cinema and Meditations on Imperfect Cinema ... Fifteen Years Later" are "movements" in which nomadic cinema participates, not in terms of representation, but along political lines of becoming (Andrew 2000b: 224–5). This takes place inside colonial situations, working against mastery, towards imperfection, carving out sites of struggle whose effects make beautiful, celebratory, commercial cinema with stars in its eyes and imported abstract standards take flight, forcing it out of its self-sufficiency and narcissism (Espinzoa 1997: 81).

Fifteen years after publishing "For an Imperfect Cinema", Espinoza clarified that one of the stakes of imperfection in a cinema of struggle was to find an audience not yet formed, and that perhaps never will be denumerable, but will hopefully "become conscious and participate with those who are making changes" (*ibid.*: 84).

Always changing shape, deviating, experimenting and giving the slip to dominant representations, a minoritarian cinema of producers, directors, actors, distributors and audiences, following Espinoza, "isn't the one that is participating in the changes, or isn't even potentially able to do so" (*ibid.*). It is an audience in formation, that still needs to be invented, that cannot be counted nor counted on in advance, but is becoming through contact with the vital part-signs of minor cinema's explorations of madness and commitment to struggle. On this point Guattari connects with Espinoza. Deleuze confronts the same problem as Espinoza: the people are missing in modern political cinema. This is political cinema's minor condition, and the condition of the minority's political predicament, and the task of the film-maker is to sow the "seeds of the people to come", to "prefigure a people" (Deleuze 1989: 220–21). In Deleuze the minor erases the distance between the private and political. This is especially the case in films concerning mental health in which the social character of illness, and the state of the family, is immediate. The political multiplies with the private, and peoples multiply to infinity; so the film-maker becomes a movement among other movements with no unifying consciousness. Yet the prefiguration of a people is carried by the film-maker's work, which, Deleuze explains, catalyses by expressing potential forces and collectively assembling movements (across the private and political), and in Third Cinema this is accomplished by exposing the dual impossibilities of living under the yoke of colonialism and raising the consciousness of a unified people because neither unity nor a people exist.

Guattari does not divide minor cinema into cinemas that display worker struggles and those that explore madness (and related conditions of epilepsy, autism and suicide) in documentary or fictional forms. Like Deleuze, Guattari sees political film's task in terms of the multiplication of connections between disparate fragments: between, for instance, anti-psychiatric struggles and the labour movement; between the family as a domain of containable private problems and dramas and as an already social and political entity. But at the core of Guattari's minor cinema is the idea that cinematic investigations of everyday struggles precipitate changes in those hitherto removed from them, removing the distance that separates private from political, issue from issue, and the many ways problems are swept from view in being compartmentalized. Guattari elegantly expresses this in terms of Jean Schmidt's film *Comme les anges déchus de la planète Saint-Michel* (Fallen angels from the planet St Michel; 1978). Guattari is struck by the immediately political effects of the homeless speaking freely about their lives; Schmidt "takes things as they come; he has not selected from their remarks in order to obtain the best effects of montage" (1977b: 348).[1] Instead, he includes tirades, racist outbursts and clichés alongside passionate and poetic statements. Guattari enumerates several kinds of dependencies that structure the lives of these marginal people subsisting in the centre of Paris: physiological (drugs, cold weather and alcohol); psychological or ethological (occupying precariously the territories populated by many different homeless and transients but also tourists – in the square before the Pompidou Centre, for example); institutional (the social services, jails, hospitals, shelters, benevolent organizations peddling false hope ...); and exhibitionist (the spectacles of street youth). No easy solutions are proffered; groups are shown to coalesce in collective projects and then decay into atoms of loneliness, delirium and violence. For Guattari, Schmidt "is not content with denouncing a scandal: he squarely puts the blame on sensibilities dulled, 'drugged', and infantilized by mass media, and by a public opinion that 'does not want to know about it'" (*ibid.*: 350).

Guattari champions minor cinema's ability to promote through a-signifying part-signs and ethically responsible film praxes the release of becomings-minor in the masses (or strains therein), or at least move towards this utopian goal that he shared with Espinoza. By promoting the release of creative potentialities, and examining how minor cinema extracts and communicates them, Guattari hoped they would mutate and emerge as components in new auto-modelizations of subjectivity. This way of establishing existential coordinates would include the ethico-political imperatives of an engagement with madness and poverty, as well as taking forward the references they trigger by all concerned, intimately and in terms of potential praxes.

Let us turn to the minor and consider how it conjoins with cinema. From *A Thousand Plateaus* (Deleuze & Guattari 1987) we learn that minorities are opposed to axioms. An axiomatic describes how a system such as capitalism works directly on decoded flows (the condition in which capital can become anything without regulatory reference points) regardless of their specific characteristics, domains in which they are realized and relations between such elements. The axiomatic is thus immanent (and not transcendent or perfect and thus closed) to the decoded flows and thus more flexible than coding operations, which are attached to specific domains and establish rules for relations among their elements. An axiomatic is aligned with the models of realization through which it is effectuated; the models differ widely but are all isomorphic (e.g. each different type of state and capitalism is different from the others but also corresponds to the others). Axiomatic capitalism may add new axioms in response to events or in order to master certain kinds of flows, and also subtract axioms. The nation-state in all its remarkable diversity is one model of realization for the capitalist axiomatic that Deleuze and Guattari note has the task of "crushing" its own minorities in an effort, for instance, to manage nationalist aspirations (*ibid.*: 456).

Minorities are not easily quashed, but they are captured in the name of an axiomatic of the majority that is countable and modelled by a standard form. A minority is not countable and thus has nothing to do with the smallness or largeness of its numbers but rests on the production of connections between its elements. To the extent that the axiom of the majority manipulates countable elements, non-countable minorities elude its grasp. New axioms are introduced in order to translate minorities into majoritarian clusters (e.g. granting some political autonomy and therein integrating them as an entity in a political union). The power of minorities rests with the multiplication of connections among their elements and the forging of lines of escape and errant trajectories, even though the assertion of such powers through demands (i.e. rights, territory, self-government) against the countable generates new axioms. In abstract terms, the opposition that Deleuze and Guattari (*ibid.*: 473) posit is between *revolutionary connections* of becoming minor available for all and the *conjugations of the axiomatic* that inflect and fix the flows.

For Guattari, cinema is a minor art that "perhaps serves the people who constitute a minority, and this is not at all pejorative. A major art is at the service of power ... A minor cinema for minorities ... and for the rest of us, too, since all of us participate in these minorities in one way or another" (Guattari 1996b: 180). A minor cinema precipitates becomings-minor in the mass. And to become minor is not to be in a minority or the representative of a minority or even to formally acquire the characteristics or status of a minority through some affiliation such as spouse, expert or even informant.

How is cinema minorized? How does it produce becomings with which everyone can connect? In order to answer this question we need to turn to some of the films that Guattari discusses within the terms of both the European anti-psychiatry movement and under the general heading of a cinema attuned to madness: a cinema that is not of a clinical, criteriological character, but that can open all of us to the exploration of our own anoedipal becomings, in the process of which normopathic subjecthood gives way to an inclusive and non-specific madness, not in accordance with a model, but by getting in touch with certain affective intensities made available through specific cinematic works. These affective intensities "start to exist in you, in spite of you" (Guattari 1995: 93).

How is cinema minorized by mental illness? How does it produce becomings that summon a people with whom it connects? The fundamental theoretical problem here is at the heart of what it means to summon a new people outside a political or messianic telos. After all, Guattari laments the popular "taste for morbidity" (1996b: 177) that brought psychiatric patients to the big screen in 1970s blockbusters (e.g. Milos Forman's *One Flew Over the Cuckoo's Nest* [1975]). This interest in madness was for him subsumable under the same impulse that made pornography and cop stories so successful. Less dejectedly, Guattari considers that during these decades non-spectacular (not on the order of May 1968) and softly subversive molecular disturbances across the sociopolitical spectrum were causing primary institutions of socialization to decay and reorganize themselves. These subversions were picked up on by film-makers, some of whom caught wind of developments in the anti-psychiatry and other social movements and took them beyond the discourses of professionals (analysts, doctors and nurses) as well as psychiatric survivors.

Guattari triumphed a cinema that provided the means for the multitude to connect with the struggles it communicated but not in the form of an ideological conversion or the dictates of a leadership caste. This simultaneously involved demystifying big studio representations of social issues and the pseudo-objectivity of *cinéma-vérité* that puts the struggles of minorities under its lens instead of putting the combatants and agitators themselves behind the camera lens. This is key to understanding Guattari's favourable mention of films such as Marin Karmitz's *Coup pour coup* (Blow by blow; 1972), in which non-professional actors who were engaged in a protracted labour struggle in a textile factory created a document of their own actions. Guattari is comfortable with a core idea of militant cinema: democratization of the means of production, specifically overcoming the barriers of specialization, technical and cost challenges by such actions as putting cameras in the hands of workers.

A further example of this democratization of the means of cinematic production in the service of summoning a people to come is found in Guattari's (2007) short reflection on hyperdense urban life in Tokyo and the district of Sanya in which foreign and day labourers live under the yoke of organized gangs. The cinematic significance of Sanya is that Sato Mitsuo, a Japanese documentary film director known for his social activism, was murdered during the making of his 1985 film *YAMA: An Eye for an Eye*; the colloquial name for Sanya is Yama. The film follows the struggles of the district's day labourers to organize themselves and the clashes they had with the local yakuza family, which led to the death by stabbing not only of Mitsuo: Yamaoka Kyoichi was a labour activist who took the reins of the project and saw it through to its completion after Mitsuo's murder, and he too was murdered. A becoming-minor may be effectuated in this instance through an ethics of film praxis that is built around respect for subjects and responsibility for the creation of documents.

Guattari (1996b: 164) theorizes how minor cinema "intervenes directly in our relations with the external world" and influences the semioticizations of viewers. Dominant and reactionary values are attacked in a variety of ways within film praxis. Guattari selected key early films by directors whose importance has grown over time as vital to minoritarian cinematic becomings. Guattari enthusiastically endorsed David Lynch, who, in *Eraserhead* (1977), has made "the greatest film on psychosis, alongside *Fists in the Pocket* (1965) by Marco Bellocchio. I find these two films overwhelming" (1990: 71).

Guattari's minor cinema is catalysed by the schizo process that escapes the semiotic subjugations of dominant cinematic representations and capitalist modes of production. Guattari's high praise for *Eraserhead* is evident enough in Henry Spencer's molecularizations: the "psychotic multiplicities of dispersion" (Deleuze & Guattari 1984: 375) in the eraser shavings that swirl around him. In Bellocchio's *Fists in the Pocket* there is a thorough critique of the claustrophobia of family values. Split by name – sometimes Ale, sometimes Sandro – Alessandro (Lou Castel) succumbs to his matricidal and fratricidal fantasies as he terrorizes the family's villa outside Piacenza, arranging the 'accidental' deaths first of his mother and then his mentally deficient brother, while attempting to smother his sister and kill his older brother, the family patriarch. Finally, Alessandro falls victim to a massive grand mal seizure, his psychosis orchestrated by a refrain of Verdi's *La Traviata*.

Generally Guattari (1996b: 162) considered most commercial cinema to be a drug whose trip is adaptation. However, for him one commercial film that displayed the textures of psychosis was Terence Malick's *Badlands* (1973), which displays the effects of *amour fou*: "the story is only there to serve as support for a schizophrenic journey" (Guattari 1996b: 167). In this respect Kit (Martin Sheen) was an abstraction from the intensities of *amour fou* released by Holly (Sissy Spacek) and the film is marked by vivid and intense blues, bizarre behaviours and circulation of objects (stones and toasters) in support of the schizo journey that follows intensities and desires that escape dominant values.

Guattari's focus on the minor within a diverse range of engaged cinemas runs all the way from the emotional textures of collective creation in *Germany in Autumn* (dir. Alf Brustellin *et al.*, 1978), which exposes the role of the mass mediatic machine in distributing subjugating affects through its reportage of acts of armed struggle in Germany in the late 1970s, staging the Manichean confrontation between a "monstrous state power and pathetic politico-military apparatuses" (Guattari 1996b: 187), to the documentary style of Raymond Depardon in *Urgences* (Emergencies; 1988). The twenty sequences shot at the emergency psychiatric service at Hôtel-Dieu in Paris not only interpellate viewers into the alienations and deceits of intake interview situations with psychotherapists and those suffering from everything from dereliction to psychosis, but also, Guattari believed, "the spectacle of these existential ruptures works directly upon our own lines of fragility" (1988: 22). Indeed, while struggling with his own depression, Guattari was deeply moved by the suicide of the soixante-huitard in Romain Goupil's *Mourir à trente ans* (Half a life; 1982).

Guattari's sense of minorization rests on the capacity of a-signifying part-signs. For Guattari, commercial cinema not only serves the interests of corporate power as a vehicle through which docile models of subjectivity are communicated by means of dominant signifying semiologies, but also reveals beyond its thematics (star system, studio moguls, static genres, hackneyed plots) militant becomings in the sociopolitical effects of its technological organization. Guattari sought a direct and efficacious contact between semiotic and material fluxes that he found in the free radio movement, for instance. The directness between semiotic and material fluxes (intense and multiple) is not diverted into a sphere of representation or signification (psychical quasi-objects such as the Saussurean sign consisting of sound-image and concept) that results in their mutual cancellation, which is how Guattari characterizes the condition of the subject in both structuralism and psychoanalysis; instead, the a-signifying particles, the most de-territorialized types of signs (not fully formed but part-signs), provide lines of escape from the snares of representation.

Guattari wants to outflank representation and its failures predicated on language altogether by focusing on a-signifying semiotics. And these signs play an important role in cinema. Guattari writes: "It is equally important to underline and insist on the independent status of what are called a-signifying semiotics. This will allow us to understand what permits cinema to escape from semiologies of signification and participate in collective assemblages of desire" (1996b: 149). First of all, signifying semiologies are based on dominant systems of encoding such as non-verbal codes, speech and writing, and thus constitute stable "centring" codes of fully formed substances indexed on individuated subjects (even if the non-verbal is, it is claimed, universally translatable into a linguistic-based semiology, and the letter insists in the unconscious). Guattari clarifies that a-signifying particle-signs "break the effects of significance and interpretance, thwart the system of dominant redundancies, accelerate the most 'innovative', 'constructive', and 'rhizomatic' components" (*ibid.*: 154 n.2). While signifying semiologies want to find meaning everywhere, and therefore refuse any independence to a-signifying semiotics that can function without them (but may make tactical use of them), Guattari resists embalming cinema in meaning, that is, in transcendent narratives and syntagmatic/paradigmatic chains of relations and clusters. Instead, he proposes that these incomplete part-signs, which are not interpretable and centred on the signifier but non-singularly expressive of the unformed signaletic matter of cinematic images, trigger a becoming-minor in those sensitive to their encounter with them. Dynamic cinematic particle-signs trigger becomings-minor in the same way that thought is forced or shocked in an immanent encounter.

A-signifying fragments populate the cinema as colours (or in black and white), non-phonic sounds, rhythms and facility traits: in short, in manifold modalities and expressive matters that are open, Guattari specifies, to "multiple systems of external intensities" (*ibid.*: 151). One does not connect with these ideologically, but rather is transported and reassembled by them, moved into configurations of components and new universes of reference because one's existential territory has been enriched by them. Such expressive matters, claims Guattari (*ibid.*: 150–51) quoting Christian Metz, have unbounded matters of content or "semantic tissue" that run beyond the reach of signifying semiologies and the dominant values that their encodings presume, like stereotypes (i.e. "normal", likeable, characters and model families) and behaviours (i.e. going to school, cooperating with authority). By the same token, Guattari adds that the textures and traits of expressive matter at the disposal of film-makers elude stabilizing codes or deep syntaxes that might still the restless deployment of heterogeneous semiotics and their creative constellations.

Cinema emits a-signifying particle-signs that trigger the desire to follow their leads. But what does this mean for film criticism? A good example is Spike Lee's *Do The Right Thing* (1989). Laleen Jayamanne (2001) displays acute attention to non-narrative rhythms and textures through the work of a-signifying signs in the film's visual and aural fluxes, focusing on the staking of territories by means of a sonic motif – blasts of Public Enemy's "Fight the Power" – and the dilly-dallying of Mookie in the sinuous everyday life on the block. These a-signifying particles have the power to throw one into becomings-minor that cannot be captured by the stock discourse of racial violence that took the film hostage shortly after its premiere.

Guattari's overt interest was in a cinema of madness. Peter Robinson's film about R. D. Laing, *Asylum* (1972), is included in a list of films that inaugurate something new: a minor cinema. *Asylum*, Guattari thought, found a significant audience and "indirectly revealed an anti-psychiatric current" (1996b: 177). Minor cinema probes a potential public, a public yet to come, with which it attempts to connect by bringing its a-signifying particle-signs flush with sensibilities not yet entangled in dominant modelizations of identity and social relations. The study of how subjectivity is modelled is, Guattari noted, really the sole question of schizoanalysis:

Schizoanalysis ... is not an alterative modelisation. It is meta-modelisation. It tries to understand how it is that you got where you are. What is your model to you? It doesn't work? then, I don't know, one tries to work together. One must see if one can make a graft with other models. It will be perhaps better, perhaps worse. We will see. There is no question of a standard model. And the criterion of truth in this comes precisely when the meta-modelisation transforms itself into auto-modelisation, or auto-gestation, if you prefer.   (1996a: 133)

Guattari enlisted the becomings-minor – which we can call "affective contaminations" after Guattari (1995: 92–3) – released by the cinema of anti-psychiatry for schizoanalysis's criticism of standard systems of modelization, but not towards a general model; rather, "as an instrument for deciphering systems of modelisation in diverse domains, in other words, a meta-model" (1989: 27) of subjectivity's autopoetic formation in context through the assemblage of heterogeneous coordinates on different levels and of various types and the discovery of consistency among its components by means of refrains: those felicitous "existential communicators" (a refrain is any iterative composition) catalysing passages into new universes of reference (*ibid.*: 27–8, 304). Minor cinema can and must contribute to a practical self-enrichment, either through making or viewing films.

The documentary *Asylum* undoubtedly impressed Guattari because of the intimacies of the household dramas it revealed in true *vérité* style, right down to the exposed microphones, in the context of Laing's post-Kingsley experiment in community care, Archway House. The commitment of the film-makers was evident inasmuch as they stayed in the therapeutic community for six weeks during the filming (echoing Mitsuo's commitment), and over this period they not only recorded but played active roles in the group problem-solving sessions. This community was itself questioning existing models of community and family and struggled with its own alternative auto-modelizations through the episodes of its key denizens. *Asylum* follows a schizoanalytic process of assisting in the discovery of passages between assemblages by releasing blockages.

Guattari focuses on the Italian strain of anti-psychiatric activity, particularly the work of Franco Basaglia and members of the *Psichiatria Democratica* movement. Anti-institutional struggle in Italy was necessary owing to the archaic nature of the asylum system and absence of patients' rights. An institution is negated, Basaglia explained, "when it is turned upside down, and when its specific field of activity is called into question and thereby thrown into crisis" (1987. 63). Guattari remained suspicious of this strategy, not because he believed that the hospitals in Gorizia and Parma were not totally repressive but because negation was not sufficiently anchored in extra-institutional social reality and tended to result in a denial or suppression of madness: in short, that negation overwhelmed madness, too (Guattari 1996a: 44). Yet to read Basaglia is immediately to acknowledge that the institutional experiments in 'negative thinking' undertaken by him parallel those of Guattari and Jean Oury at La Borde. Certainly the daily collective assembly at Gorizia in which patients and staff met voluntarily in a dehierarchized environment in which roles and uniforms were abandoned and topics for discussion came from the floor, were disorganized and at times confrontational; they were not as tightly semioticized as the table of work rotations on display at La Borde – the abstract machine that diagrammed that clinic. Notwithstanding this chaos, this was for many the first occasion they had to voice their concerns and needs and have them heard. It was the translation of these individual demands into a collective assumption of responsibility that could be addressed by changes in the institution itself.

Guattari praises the "exceptional" film *Matti da slegare* (Fit to be untied, 1976) made by the March 11 Collective (Silvano Agnosti, Marco Bellocchio, Sandro Petraglia, Stefano Rulli) about the hospital in Parma, where Basaglia had moved in 1969 (Guattari 1996b: 177–80). Guattari focuses largely on the youth and women in the film because their recounting of experiences of psychiatric repression in the hospital and triumphs in everyday life on the outside are the most moving, but he also notes how labour activists have come to integrate the psychiatricized and ex-patients into their political projects. This connection between mental health and industrial workers and patients was for Guattari one of the most remarkable features of the documentary because it provided evidence of new alliances across otherwise non-communicating sectors.

Guattari's praise for *Matti da slegare* is marked by provisos that should be read as general comments about how he tempers his enthusiasm for progressive documentary work in the anti-psychiatric milieu: that "truth" does not always come from the people, even if he is convinced that repression almost always comes from the caregivers; that good intentions and community actions are not enough to ameliorate the suffering of the mentally ill; that there are pressing issues within psychiatric hospital practice that need urgent revision.

European anti-psychiatry movements were dominated by leading radical psychiatrists and theorists whose ability to speak in the language of Michel Foucault's *History of Madness* (2006), appropriated for anti-psychiatry when it was originally published in 1961, often took precedence over making concrete interventions. A sophisticated social realist work on schizophrenia, such as Ken Loach's *Family Life* (1971), was brilliant but still short on concrete reforms, according to Guattari. Guattari makes no mention of classic anti-psychiatric documentaries such as Fredrick Wiseman's "reality fiction" about the conditions in Bridgewater State Hospital for the criminally insane, Massachusetts, *Titicut Follies* (1967). However, "popular" works such as these held promise because of the potential publics they catalysed that, Guattari hoped, would make new demands on the dominant commercial film industry to deliver radically different messages.

NOTE

1. All translations are my own unless otherwise indicated.

III CINEMATIC NATURE

The choices afforded by the praxes of thinking and creating have occupied philosophers for centuries, and cinema provides a new dimension to this practice: adding another perspective; articulating another configuration of "reality"; engaging a questioning of systems of science, judgement, knowledge and life. The instance, the vector or moment of conceptual choice (the technological and event epistemology) works on and off screen, creating new models that become the subject of study under film-philosophy.

Practices of film-philosophy have revived an interest in the technical epistemology of classical philosophers in a way that no other popular, commercially driven medium has been able to. For example, in the hands of film-philosophers, the ontological conditions of Plato's cave are redistributed into Hollywood, Aristotle's poetics take a spin around introductory classes on film form and style, and Descartes' "deception hypothesis" is supplanted with fictional filmic worlds.

In Part III, contemporary thinkers engage the technological and event epistemology of the theoretical and philosophical work done in the twentieth century in order to explore the cinematic (refer to the Introduction for further discussion of these terms). Film-philosophy is a hybrid discipline, and the many different methods of practising it covered in Part III can be characterized by their discrete use of technical and theoretical approaches to their subject, drawing as they do on various traditions and practices of thinking. As a practice, film-philosophy falls under a single disciplinary title, but as an approach and as a method (dependent on practitioner), theorists remain divided in their divergent interpretive modes over fundamental issues of analysis. Many quite dogmatic opinions are expressed under the rubric of the current discipline of film-philosophy, and despite its best intentions, internal limitations and empirically false positions can be noted as flaws that remain to be worked through as new research reformulates knowledge. Many of the film-philosophical and film-theoretical systems that developed in the twentieth century have produced themselves as *sui generis*. That is, they self-perpetuate under their own rules, despite external shifts. The content choices practitioners make when engaging this discipline serve many purposes. In itself, however, choice is a philosophical category that also requires analysis.

253

To begin this section are two examples of practices that investigate the essential nature of the cinematic, with philosophical ramifications for theories of "reality" and the very nature of the cinematic. Michael Goddard's chapter on Raymond Bellour in some ways returns us to thinking again of the issues of the era of Bazin and Daney. As Goddard explores, for Bellour the question of how to practise film-philosophy becomes central to the practice itself. Bellour's work becomes bound by the limitations of the screen form's physicality, as much as the potential of the activities of this limit devise new content for his analysis (Ch. 23). Bellour had worked with the semiotic theory of film devised by Christian Metz from Saussurian linguistics. But, as Richard Rushton explains in Chapter 24, it was Metz's psychoanalytic study of the cinematic signifier that had a significant impact on practices of film theory from the mid 1970s.

Patricia MacCormack's chapter on Julia Kristeva explores an example where the Barthesian strand of semiological analysis developed into a different mode of psychoanalytic critique (Ch. 25). Like Metz, Kristeva's practice investigates the construction of linguistic signifiers. However, Kristeva does not develop a theory of film *per se*, as MacCormack points out, although her work is regularly cited in cinema theory. What is useful to appreciate in film, theory and philosophy is how Kristeva's psychoanalytically informed critique of cinema as a category of "the imaginary" within a "symbolic order" is comparative to other critiques of the organizing frameworks of screen forms. Continuing to develop a practice of film-philosophy and theory engaging semiotic methods is Laura Mulvey. As David Sorfa describes in Chapter 26, her immensely popular and influential work stands as a testament to the hybrid nature of the discipline, and the eagerness to embrace new ideas in the hope of developing new systems of thinking about what cinema does.

In the middle section of Part III are variations of Lacanian and Lacanian-inspired psychoanalytic methodologies although, curiously, Jacques Lacan did not write directly about cinema. It is interesting to see how the convergences of theory develop, as with Lacan's own influential theoretical practice, which has now become philosophical practice. For example, Lacan provided a springboard for Félix Guattari's concepts to develop, in opposition. Patricia Pisters's chapter on Homi K. Bhabha demonstrates the value of Lacanian concepts for a postcolonial critical context for film theory (Ch. 27). As demonstrated in the work of the following chapters on Slavoj Žižek, Alain Badiou, Jacques Rancière and Giorgio Agamben, Bhabha's work has provided core event epistemology theories.

Laurence Simmons addresses the work of Žižek in terms of its psychoanalytical theoretical project, as one that enables a focus on the philosophical construction of subjectivity as made through the cinematic condition (Ch. 28). In another study of the convergence of psychoanalysis and the cinematic, Fred Botting's chapter on Stephen Heath offers a critique of Žižek's approach as well as offering a practice that was grounded in the Metzian era, but resonates with Maurice Merleau-Ponty's notion of the anchoring points required of perception (Ch. 29). Heath is also usefully read with Kristeva in terms of thinking further about the imaginary qualities of the cinematic.

Badiou offers a complete system for film-philosophy, where, as Stephen Zepke explores, cinema is the event, but one different to the Deleuzian event (Ch. 30).

Engaging forms of psychology and philosophy, practices of film theory and film-philosophy have been concerned to devise systematic and logical methodologies for screen analysis, but have also been very careful to qualify the dimensions of their categorization of screen qualities and tendencies. Badiou offers a formal method for analysis, through the device of mathematical set theory, which, like the work of Bellour and others in this volume, is attendant on the ontological dimensions of its own engagement.

In terms of the event epistemological approach, the final two chapters similarly offer events as "interventions" (as Zepke discusses). Sudeep Dasgupta (Ch. 31) positions the practice of Rancière to ask the question that by now we are all thinking: what does the film theorist want? Cinema wants to tell stories, explains Dasgupta, but, as Rancière's critique of film demonstrated, this is not necessarily by using the famed Aristotelian narrative method, which oversimplifies and overstates narrative into non-definitional cognition that tends to ignore the materiality of the image. In the hands of Rancière, film-philosophy can engage with the moving image as an aesthetic and politically situated thing.

Finally, it remains for Christian McCrea to provide us with a closing and eloquent chapter on the practice of Agamben (Ch. 32). Agamben's work provides some core terms for accessing the conditions of the practice of film-philosophy through his theorization of the events of the twentieth century, as well as a formal speculation on the technological epistemology of cinema (as one capable of producing new gestures, of summarizing meanings through the simplest of gestures), and speculating on the status of the object itself. This is film-philosophy at its pragmatic best.

23 RAYMOND BELLOUR

Michael Goddard

Raymond Bellour (b. 1939) is a film theorist and critic. From 1986, he taught in the department for cinema and audiovisual studies at the University of Paris III: Sorbonne Nouvelle, and he has also been a visiting professor at New York University and the University of California, Berkeley. He is the Director of Research Emeritus, Centre National de Recherches Scientifiques (CNRS), Paris. In 1991, with Serge Daney, he formed the journal *Trafic*. His published theory and critical work includes *Le Livre des autres, entretiens, 10/18* (1978), *The Analysis of Film* (1979; English trans. 1995), *Henri Michaux* (1986), *Mademoiselle Guillotine* (1989), *L'Entre-images: Photo. Cinéma. Vidéo* (1990), *Jean-Luc Godard: Son + Image 1974–1991* (1992), *Oubli , textes, La Différance* (1992), *L'entre-images 2* (1999), *Partages de l'ombre, textes, La Différance* (2002) and *Le Corps du cinéma* (2009).

INTRODUCTION

The image of the cinematic thought of Raymond Bellour in English-language contexts is an incomplete one, still framed to a large extent by the essays collected in the volume *The Analysis of Film* (Bellour 2000). There is a more limited awareness of Bellour's more recent work on cinema, owing to the translations in film journals of the research Bellour conducted into the relations between still and moving images as well as of his role as a key interlocutor of Michel Foucault and Gilles Deleuze.[1] This is not to mention Bellour's considerable reputation as a scholar of Henri Michaux, evidenced by his introduction to the latter's collected works, along with other engagements with literature. More importantly, many of the extraordinary essays in the two *Entre-images* collections (1999, 2002a) that assemble Bellour's work on the relations between cinema, photography, video art, painting, literature and philosophy since the 1980s remain unknown in an English-language context, despite the translations of a few of the key chapters. This leads to a distortion in the representation of Bellour's thought by means of which it remains associated with Metzian semiology of cinema and the practice of close filmic analysis, which did indeed characterize Bellour's thought and practice, but only up until the 1970s.

While Bellour has never renounced the importance of Christian Metz's semiological theories of cinema, even in the 1970s his practice as a film analyst tended to problematize them, if only by testing them via the crucible of practical film analysis.[2]

His more recent work, however, shows greater proximity to the cinematic thought of Deleuze on the one side and Serge Daney on the other, and is rather distant from the concerns of Metzian semiological analysis that were so foundational for 1970s film studies.[3] After all, as early as 1985 Bellour was already writing that the project, or rather the dream, of film analysis was already in flames and had become impossible for both theoretical and technical reasons: "Film analysis has become an art without a future. … There are no longer, or should no longer be, any analyses of films. There are just gestures" (2006: 121). In this chapter, therefore, the presentation of Bellour as a film-philosopher will begin with this impossible dream of film analysis but move through it fairly quickly, in order to bring out the less-known Bellour of the *Entre-images* project, who fully merits being included in a volume on film-philosophy.

THE ANALYSIS OF FILM

The Analysis of Film (2000) consists, for the most part, in a series of structural film analyses accompanied by frame enlargements and diagrams, usually of sequences from Classical Hollywood films, with a particular emphasis on Alfred Hitchcock, who accounts for four of the eight analyses. The analyses range from those of short sequences in a few pages to the magisterial analysis "Symbolic Blockage" (*ibid.*: 77–192), which exhaustively analyses Hitchcock's *North by Northwest* (1959) and takes the genre of film analysis to its limits by virtually reconstituting in the form of an analysis the entire system of the film. A short glance at these analyses is enough to reveal that they neither provide an imitable pedagogical example nor fulfil the usual functions of essayistic writing on films. Instead, they use a variety of analytic approaches that are rigorously oriented towards their objects and that produce interpretations of meaning only by means of a thorough presentation of the ways the films are structured through alternations, doublings and other patterns of development.

To get a broader perspective on this practice, it is necessary to turn to the dense essays that begin the book, "A Bit of History" (2000: 1–20) and "The Unattainable Text" (ibid.: 21–7). In the former, Bellour presents both the continuities and breaks between film criticism up until the 1960s and the new "science" of film semiology developed by Metz. Metz developed a general semiotic theory of film derived from linguistics and did not at first imagine "what was not yet called film analysis" (*ibid.*: 7). However, his theory called for a newly rigorous textual approach to cinema whose criticism was at that point dominated by auteurism. Bellour acknowledges rather than dismisses the pre-analytic history of film criticism as developed by the journal *Cahiers du cinéma*, Jean Mitry and other authors, while at the same time underlining the historical novelty and difficulty of textual analyses of film. The idea that films were signifying systems whose logics could be deciphered through a rigorous analytic practice may not have been an entirely new idea but actually carrying out such analyses, informed by the cultural and literary analyses of Claude Lévi-Strauss and Roland Barthes, certainly was. In an intriguing passage, Bellour recounts the failed attempt to do a film analysis together with Metz of a sequence from Hitchcock's *Suspicion* (1941). What emerges from this account is the specificity of Bellour's approach to film analysis, which, in a Barthesian fashion, privileges the fragment over the whole, whereas Metz was looking for a material basis for his general theories of the cinematic text: "Metz was looking for a concept (that of textual system), which had no need of any film … I, on the other hand, hoped that the 'desire of the film' would be concentrated in every fragment" (2000: 8). This difference, which we could characterize as that between a science of cinema semiology and a pragmatics of filmic, stylistic analysis, clearly informs Bellour's practice as a film analyst, at least in this period of his work.

The problematic nature of film analysis is especially highlighted in "The Unattainable Text". The *unattainability* of the filmic text had a first practical meaning of *unobtainability*; in the period in which Bellour was working, it was by no means easy to obtain a print of the film one wanted to work on, along with the conditions in which to analyse it, which depended on access to an editing table and the print for an extended period of time. All of this is quite hard to imagine in the era of the plenitude of video and DVD copies, not to mention the downloadability of cinematic materials, but in the late 1960s these were real material determinants of analytic practice. For example, Bellour had to abandon a planned analysis of Hitchcock's *Notorious* (1946) because the print was withdrawn from circulation by RKO.

But even given the contingent *obtainability* of the filmic text it remains *unattainable* for another reason: the impossibility of quoting fragments of the text as in the case of literary analyses. This may seem obvious but it is nevertheless crucial and definitive of the specificity of film analysis. Literature and literary analysis being conducted via the same medium of written language have been able to develop in tandem precisely because of this, which is what enabled the emergence of a literary meta-language. Filmic texts are not the only texts that lack this linguistic felicity of citation and Bellour points to the problems in the analysis of theatrical, musical and pictorial texts. However, these texts do not present the same problems as the filmic text, since they are all, however imperfectly, quotable. Film, on the other hand, is in the paradoxical situation of sharing the unquotability of performances while at the same time being an immutable finished work. The key problematic of film analysis is in the treatment of moving images. While cinematic images share with still pictures the presentation of a point of view, their existence in time associates them with literary narrative, while their segmentarity resembles the elements of a musical composition. This renders moving images particularly unquotable since, as Bellour puts it, "the reproduction of even many stills is only ever able to reveal a kind of radical inability to assume the textuality of the film. However, stills are essential" (2000: 25–6). In other words, film images can be rendered a quotable and analysable text only at the cost of stopping what gives them their specificity, namely movement. As Bellour puts it, "The frozen frame and the still that reproduces it are simulacra; … indispensable but already derisory" (*ibid.*: 6). It is this paradoxical dilemma of the unattainable filmic text that conditioned the desire for film analysis as Bellour practised it in *The Analysis of Film*, and accounts for why, according to Bellour, film analysis was always an art, rather than a scientifically delimited practice. What is also striking in this dense text is the rigorous attention to both the differences and continuities between cinematic images and other mediums of expression, an attention that would be developed throughout Bellour's later work. As Constance Penley points out in her preface to *The Analysis of Film* (2000), there are two modalities by means of which Bellour undertakes filmic analysis: a structural one evidenced by the studies in this book and an approach that focuses "more on figuration, the body and emotions, as well as the different logics of other photographic and digital media" (Penley 2000: xi). It is this second approach that Bellour would develop in his later work.

"ANALYSIS IN FLAMES" AND "THE PENSIVE SPECTATOR"

It is worth enquiring at this point what exactly led Bellour to the conclusion that film analysis was an art without a future. In the short essay "Analysis in Flames" (2006), the multiple reasons for this were spelt out very clearly. First of all there is the illusory nature of film analysis itself, which Bellour refers to as giving a sense of "false plenitude" (*ibid.*: 121). Essentially, film analysis was based on an interest in the cinematic signifier, bringing together a newly rigorous approach to film with a broader focus on textuality in many different fields. However, the polysemous and elusive body of the filmic text went beyond the linguistic capacities of film analyses, not because of any lack on the part of the analysts but simply because of the excess and resistance of filmic materials to linguistic procedures. This led film analysis to become a kind of hermetic field, comprehensible only to its adepts, rather than contributing to the broader spheres of film theory or textual analysis. However, for Bellour, the most important effect of the practice of film analysis was the emergence of what he calls a "free fascination" (*ibid.*: 122), achieved by the gesture of stopping films. In fact, rather than a methodology, Bellour sees in film analysis the condensation of a series of gestures that he elucidates as follows.

The first of these gestures is the above-mentioned stopping of motion: the freeze-frame immobilizing cinematic movement on an editing table, to be reproduced as the necessary visual accompaniment of written film analyses. For Bellour, this gesture is paradoxically destroyed by the invention of video, by means of which every moving image in every situation can be frozen, thereby generalizing and neutralizing the desire and singularity of film analysis. However, from this loss there are also gains, such as the use of video for film-analytic purposes in the seminar, a use of the medium certainly made by Bellour in his own teaching practice at University of Paris III: Sorbonne Nouvelle.[4] Another gain is the incorporation of this stopping of cinematic movement in the writing of some film critics such as Daney. Bellour describes Daney's writing on film in the following terms: "we see how certain stops in his sentences corresponds with freeze-frames that are projected into the reader's mind" (*ibid.*: 122). While this was perhaps always the case for good film criticism, the technical capacity of freezing cinematic images, both on the part of the writer and the viewer, has led to a new "determination, acuity … that assumes we have entered, vis-a-vis moving images, into another era" (*ibid.*).

The next gesture, which Bellour refers to as the third gesture, is the gesture of theorizing about cinema that, from now on, incorporates some of the procedures of film analysis without the "mad desire" (*ibid.*) to account for the whole system of the film.

In Bellour's words, "this excessive lack has disintegrated, like a love that dies from no longer repeating its gestures" (*ibid.*). This relaxation of the gesture of film analysis is especially associated by Bellour with the work of Jacques Aumont, who always retained a "sympathetic scepticism" (*ibid.*: 123) towards the textual analysis of films, while rigorously incorporating analytic strategies into his development of theories of imaging and montage. This relaxation is also something that clearly manifests itself in Bellour's own work, as we shall shortly see.

Finally there is what Bellour refers to as the dissolution of film analyses in film and video. Bellour had already anticipated this in "The Unattainable Text" when he referred to the possibility of the analysis of film through its own medium. Even at the time of this later essay these attempts still seemed inadequate, although Bellour would go on to analyse more successful examples such as the later film and video work of Chris Marker and Jean-Luc Godard. The latter's *Histoire(s) du cinéma* (1999) certainly seems like a direct fulfilment of this possibility. However, what is most interesting is Bellour's early realization that it is actually the invention of video, despite its destruction of the written genre of film analysis, that could allow for the continuation of film-analytic gestures. Referring to the video art of Thierry Kuntzel, Bellour sees the emergence of practices of video art in which the fusion of theory and the image that film analysis dreamed of could begin to be realized.

In the essay "The Pensive Spectator" (2007), Bellour made a first survey of what happens when the cinematic image stops moving: those moments in films when the spectator is presented with a photographic, still image rather than movement. It should be pointed out that this interest in the relations between photography and cinema, stasis and movement, was not in itself new but had been rigorously conducted only in a few instances. One of the most famous of these instances was the analysis of Sergei Eisenstein film stills by Roland Barthes, a significant influence on Bellour's earlier practice of film analysis.[5] But whereas Barthes was critically hostile towards cinematic movement, which he wanted to completely subtract from his engagement with Eisenstein's stills, Bellour aims to keep the dynamic interplay between stasis and movement alive by engaging with what happens in the spectator's sudden encounter with stasis in the middle of a flow of moving images. In other words, rather than the previous analytic gesture of stopping cinema there is an exploration of what happens when cinema stops itself, which leads directly to a previously lacking engagement with processes of cinematic spectatorship.

Bellour in fact begins the essay with a summary of "the line traced by Barthes" (2007: 119) between the apprehension of still and moving images. According to this optic, whereas moving images give a sense of the present, presence, illusion, flight and life, still images suggest the past, absence, ungraspability and death. The spectator of moving images adds nothing to them, has no time to close his or her eyes as the image perceived will already have been replaced by another. On the other hand, still images always invoke this closing of the eyes, a necessary supplement that the viewer must bring in order to enter the immobile image. But what interests Bellour is: what happens when the spectator of the moving image is suddenly confronted by a still image that suspends the unfolding of cinematic movement? For Bellour these moments not only attest to the fascination of the still image but also add something to cinema. In this situation, the viewer both recoils from the image and becomes more fascinated, a process Bellour traces through a number of cinematic examples. For Bellour, this fascination with the still image opens up another temporal dimension within the film, paradoxically by breaking spectatorial immersion in the unfolding of its narrative. While not giving rise to the same process as the contemplation of a still image, it paradoxically allows for a reflection that one is in the process of watching a film through the suspension of its normal temporal operations.

The irruption of a different, past temporality is more or less the model for Bellour's analysis of the examples cited in the essay. In these examples, the film is haunted by the photo as if by another dimension doubling the present temporality of the film itself. For Bellour, there is a more effective self-representation of cinema through the freeze-frame than via the representation of cinematic processes within a film since "when cinema looks at itself, it never sees itself as it does in the photograph" (*ibid*.: 122). There is, however, a quite different effect in films composed primarily of still images such as Marker's *La Jetée* (The jetty; 1962), in which there is a palpable shock from the one moving image that was included in the sequence of still images; the opening of an eye that is "the only vibration in a completely frozen world" (2007: 122). The basis of this film as a series of still images accompanied by voice-overs and music shows the nature of cinema as a medium based on time rather than movement. In short, the incorporation of still images in a film produces a kind of swerve that is enough to partially uncouple the viewer from the image, by the force of its added fascination. For this reason, Bellour refers to the photo as a stop within a stop, in which two types of time are blended without being confused; this renders the photo unique among the techniques that engender what Bellour is calling a pensive specta-tor. It also, without proposing the same historical sequence, resonates with Deleuze's conception of the Time-Image, a formulation that would have powerful effects on Bellour's *Entre-images* collections, both of which include essays either on Deleuze or using Deleuzian concepts.

L'ENTRE-IMAGES 1: PHOTO, CINEMA, VIDEO

In the last section we have already entered the *Entre-images* project in that the two essays referred to appear in the first volume. Whereas *The Analysis of Film* can be read as a response to the Bazinian question "What is cinema?", defining the nature of the cinematic medium in its difference from other textual practices, the *Entre-images* project looks at the relations between cinematic and other images, whether pre-existing ones such as in painting or photography or successors such as video. The shift is one both from identity to relations and from a focus on textual systems to particular images or sequences. This does not mean that there is no longer any film analysis but rather that this analysis is focused less on elucidating the system of a film than on the place cinematic images occupy within a broader field of image circulation; in the first volume this place is posited as the middle term in the series photo, cinema, video.

Bellour introduces the first collection with a poetic return to the magical act of stopping cinematic movement on an editing table, the analytic gesture *par excellence*.

However, now it is a case of seeing, through this gesture, two movements between cinema and photography, the first going from cinematic movement to the photogram and the second from the photograph to the imaginary film that would animate it. The first gesture is the familiar analytic one that Bellour illustrates with the example of Daney's citation of eight stills of the kiss from the end of Hitchcock's *North by Northwest* (Bellour 2002a: 12). The second gesture is illustrated by the photographer Robert Frank, who said that he would like to make a film combining his private life with his work, a "photo-film" to establish a dialogue between "the movement of the camera and the the freezing of the fixed image, between the present and the past, between the interior and the exterior and between the front and the back" (Frank, quoted in Bellour 2002a: 12).[6] What interests Bellour most about this citation is the emphasis on the "between". In the examples of Daney and Frank, Bellour discerns a "common gesture" (*ibid.*), taking place in the space between the photo and the photogram, which "has become one of the elective gestures of the consciousness of the image – of both its destiny and its survival" (*ibid.*: 13).

But the *Entre-images* project is by no means limited to consideration of the relations between cinema and photography. For Bellour, these relations, which only fully developed from the 1960s, during which there was an invasion of the cinematic image by still images, were not coincidentally accompanied by the developments summed up in the word "video", which encompasses the development of both television and video art. However, Bellour also states that *Entre-images* is not directly concerned with the transformation of images and reproducibility brought about by the invention and implantation of video technologies. Again, what Bellour is primarily interested in are relations: "what happened to cinema when it became impossible for it to separate itself from a double pressure: one that seemed to emerge from its own interior and the other one which modified it through its (direct or indirect) collusion with video" (*ibid.*: 14). In this regard, video art is of particular interest since, lacking any fixed identity, it is forced to fix on cinema along with other pre-existing artistic practices. According to Bellour, the force of video art "has been, is and will be to have operated as passages … between the mobile and the immobile, between the photographic analogy and that which transforms it" (*ibid.*). In other words, Bellour was already anticipating the convergent nature of digital technologies, their capacity to integrate all the others, even if this was only manifested at this point in the 1980s by the potential of all images to be shown on television or defined in resistance to this possibility. For Bellour, the space of what he calls "Entre-images" is precisely the space of all these passages. He describes it as being at once new enough to be approached as an enigma and well enough constituted that it can be circumscribed. Rather than giving either a history or a theory of this contemporary mixing of images, Bellour's declared aim is the more modest one of "seeking to formulate an experience [of Entre-images], in order to construct it little by little, beginning from the moment when it was admitted that we had entered, through video and everything that it brings, into another time of the image" (*ibid.*: 15).

The first *Entre-images* collection presents a rigorous examination of the relations between cinema and both photography and video, which is selected as the primary terrain, or the two faces, of Bellour's concept of Entre-images. However, the true force of the book lies in the radical effect on it of the phenomenon of video. Beginning with the second essay on Thierry Kuntzel (*ibid*.: 25–50) that was Bellour's first consideration of the medium to the final, long, poetic piece "Autoportraits", the first *Entre-images* collection is written under the exigency of responding to the new force of video. Nevertheless, this shock of video has effects not only on cinema but on all forms of representation, so that often both sides of the experience of Entre-images are at play within the same work, as Bellour says of Woody Vasulka's experimental video work *The Art of Memory* (1987) (Bellour 2002a: 201–17). Conceptually, one of the key aspects of the volume is its direct engagement with the thought of Deleuze, evident throughout the book, for example, in titles such as "Crystal-Duration" which is actually a consideration of the photo series (*ibid*.: 96–9). However, this confrontation is most directly addressed in the pivotal chapter, "Interruption, The Instant" (*ibid*.: 109–33). In an autobiographical preface, Bellour talks about how his interest in the photographic dimensions of cinema naturally led him towards Barthes, while at the same time he was fascinated by the displacements enacted on film theory by Deleuze's works on cinema. Despite the radical difference in the orientations of these two thinkers, Bellour discerns a common investment in the singularity of images at the precise point at which the cinematic is intimately linked by the photographic in the sense of being haunted by it. This position between Barthes and Deleuze, evident in this essay, is not a fixed one but rather gives a sense of Bellour's theoretical trajectory, which at this point is in passage not only between Barthes and Deleuze but also between the analysis of film as a separate entity and the new domain of Entre-images.

L'ENTRE-IMAGES 2: WORDS, IMAGES

In the "Note for a Century", written in 2002, which serves as the preface for the new edition of the first *Entre-images* collection (2002: 9–10), Bellour states that in both volumes it is a case of "discerning mixtures of images" (*ibid*.: 9). In the world of images, the only real change is one of acceleration, giving rise to "mixtures so diverse that words sometimes fail to name them" (*ibid*.). However, in relation to cinema there has been a change in that instead of confronting a single "intimate enemy" (*ibid*.), namely television, it now has two more, the computer and the museum. The first is in essence the new name for television, which it has, according to Bellour, devoured. The second, while appearing more friendly, is more sly; within the museum, cinema becomes on the one hand "really but only an art" (*ibid*.), while on the other it is framed within ever renewed foreign display apparatuses and, under the guise of being re-invented under other names, disappears. Bellour's project is inscribed within these passages but always with a privileged eye for what he describes as "that 'impure' art called cinema" (*ibid*.: 10).

The volume *L'Entre-images 2* (1999) covers a much wider field than the first, taking in relations not only with photography and video, but also with painting, literature, philosophy and the emergence of digital media. The engagement with the relations between words and images is something that can be traced back to the beginnings of Bellour's career when, as well as being a pioneer of film analysis, he was a scholar of literature, particularly of the the work of Henri Michaux. This interest in literature accompanied the whole of Bellour's work, not only through his numerous citations of literary theorists such as Barthes and Maurice Blanchot but also in his employment of a literary style even in his most structural analyses, and in fact his works include not only literary criticism but also novels. However, *L'Entre-images 2* is by no means a nostalgic return to language or literature but rather a response to new developments such as that of the computer and the convergence and coexistence of multiple representational techniques that have led to a situation in which "we know less and less what is *the* image, *an* image, what are *the* images" (1999: 9). As in the first volume, it is a case of discerning passages between images of which the diversity rather than the quantity or saturation is striking for Bellour. This circulation of images both in front of us and within us makes it ever harder to name them, hence implicating words and language in the problematic of *Entre-images.* Indeed, while many of the concerns of the first *Entre-images* project, such as the relations between cinematic images and other representational practices, now broadened to include painting and literature, are continued, as is the encounter with many of the same dramatis personae including Deleuze, Daney, Kuntzel, Godard, Bill Viola and even Metz, what is new is the pressure to rethink *Entre-images* against the horizon of the total synthesis of imaging and other representational practices that was at least foreshadowed by the emergence of the digital in the 1990s. The effect of this is a leap from Bellour's multiple engagement with the thought and practices of others to the development of a philosophy of the image that is articulated by Bellour through a reflection on the analogical functions of diverse imaging practices. This leads Bellour to the conception of images in terms of a "double helix" (*ibid.*: 9–41) that goes well beyond film theory into the constitution of a singular film-philosophy. The double helix accounts for the two operations of the technical image since the invention of cinema; namely, the photographic analogy that captures the world in the framework of "natural vision" and the cinematic analogy that captures movement by technically reconstituting it. Taken together, these two operations constitute what Bellour refers to as the "photographic", which is especially apparent during moments of stasis within the flow of moving images, giving rise to processes both of figuration and defiguration:

> The two modes of passage linked here in the image of the double helix constitute the actual–virtual boundaries or anchorage points, beginning from which one can conceive what passes and what is happening today between images. They have been strictly linked since the cinema of the 1920s which made them approach one another and vibrate in the production of images never before seen. But it is in modern cinema and the age of video that the link is tightened, explodes and accelerates around crossing points with an extreme violence – video which extends cinema, ends up dissolving it in a generality which has neither a number nor a name in the accounts of the arts.
>
> (*Ibid.*: 19)

This brief presentation does not do justice to the richness of the ideas developed in this essay, let alone the rest of the volume, which combines theoretical invention with the rigorous, detailed analysis of texts ranging from video installations to philosophy to Renaissance painting and of course the most interesting developments on the borders of what is still, despite everything, cinema, even if this is now qualified as "Cinema and …" (*ibid.*: 79–102) or "Cinema, Beyond" (*ibid.*: 103–12). This is not to mention Bellour's more recent work, which ranges from essays on cinematic emotion to detailed engagements with video artists to producing his own video installations. However, it is sufficient to show that through the *Entre-images* project, Bellour's thought is no longer that of a film analyst or theorist but a creative and innovative philosopher of film, images and representational practices, a transformation enacted through the creation and development of the concept of Entre-images.

NOTES

1. For the former see Raymond Bellour, *The Analysis of Film*, C. Penley (ed.) (Bloomington, IN: Indiana University Press 2007) and for the latter see G. Deleuze, *Negotiations: 1972–1990*, M. Joughin (trans.) (New York: Columbia University Press, 1995), 57–61, and Bellour, *Le Livre des autres: Entretiens avec M. Foucault, C. Lévi-Strauss, R. Barthes …* (Paris: UGE 10/18, 1978).
2. For Christian Metz's cinematic semiotics, see his *Psychoanalysis and Cinema: The Imaginary Signifier*, C. Britton & A. Williams (trans.) (London: Macmillan, 1982).
3. Bellour provided a homage to Metz in *Entre-images 2* that, while generously showing his appreciation of Metz, also indicated his distance from Metz's semiological project; Bellour *L'Entre-images 2: Mots, images* (Paris: POL, 1999: 79–102).
4. I attended seminars conducted by Bellour at University of Paris III: Sorbonne Nouvelle, in 2001 and 2002 focusing respectively on the freeze-frame and cinema and hypnosis.
5. See Barthes, "The Third Meaning: Research Notes on some Eisenstein Stills", in his *Image–Music–Text*, S. Heath (trans.), 52–68 (New York: Hill & Wang, 1977).
6. All citations from the *Entre-images* collections are the author's translations from the original French unless otherwise indicated.

24 CHRISTIAN METZ

Richard Rushton

Christian Metz (1931–93) was considered France's leading film theorist in the 1970s. His work on narrative structure, applied semiotics and psychoanalysis for film analysis had a major impact on film theory in France, Britain and the United States. Metz primarily engaged Ferdinand de Saussure's theories of semiotics to film, proposing a syntagmatic analysis as a system for categorizing scenes in films (which he called the Grande Syntagmatique). Metz also brought aspects of Sigmund Freud's and Jacques Lacan's psychoanalytic theories to film theory to explore the nature of the mass appeal of the cinema. His books include *Language and Cinema* (1971; English trans. 1974), *Film Language* (1971; English trans. 1974) and *The Imaginary Signifier* (1977; English trans. 1982).

Christian Metz was a pioneering film scholar. For many, his writings are the first rigorous examples of film studies in an academic sense, and the questions posed by his writings, especially those concerning the language of cinema and cinema spectatorship, are ones that are still central to film studies. Metz's writings on cinema can be separated into two strands, although these strands are closely related. On the one hand, most of his writings are directed towards issues of the semiotics of cinema derived predominantly from Saussurian linguistics (Metz 1968, 1971, 1972, 1974a, 1977a, 1991). On the other hand, Metz's most controversial work involved the use of psychoanalytic categories for the study of the cinematic *signifier* (Metz 1975, 1974a, 1979, 1982, 1985). My discussion here will focus on Metz's psychoanalytic study of the cinematic signifier, and most specifically on his essay "The Imaginary Signifier", first published in 1975 (translated in Metz 1982: 3–87). In order to further clarify what is at stake in the arguments contained in that article, I shall frame my discussion around one of the most astute critiques of Metz's essay. In one section of his groundbreaking *Mystifying Movies* (1988c), Noël Carroll offers some strong criticisms of Metz's arguments while at the same time offering some significant clarifications of Metz's position. I believe, however, that most of Carroll's criticisms of Metz are misguided, and I hope that by clarifying Carroll's misconceptions, the strength and coherence of Metz's position can be brought to light.

WHAT DOES CINEMA SIGNIFY?

Carroll rightly observes that Metz's engagement with psychoanalysis and cinema was not a radical departure from his previous researches on the semiology of cinema. Significantly, the kinds of questions Metz was trying to answer by enlisting the help of psychoanalytic theory were commensurate with the kinds of questions his work had always been asking: *why do we attend films* and *how are we able to understand films*? These are very specific questions, and Metz is keen to point out that such questions differ considerably from the kinds of enquiries many other authors have undertaken when approaching the relationship between psychoanalysis and cinema. Metz's study does not aim to allow us to understand "the unconscious" of the film text, nor is he interested in engaging in a psychoanalysis of the film director (cf. Metz 1982: 25–33). Rather, Metz is concerned with developing an understanding of the social activity called *cinema*. What do cinema-goers expect, what do they wish for, what do they hope to encounter when they go to the movies?

In posing such questions, is Metz trying to discover the essence of cinema? Are Metz's questions essentialist? Carroll certainly believes this to be the case: he refers to Metz's methodology as one that is "essentially essentialist" (1988c: 34). If one believes Metz's approach to be essentialist, however, then one misunderstands what it is that he is trying to do. He is trying to account not for cinema *per se*, but for the *cinematic signifier*. What this means is that Metz's argument, rather than being essentialist, is one that is quintessentially *historical*; he is trying to find out, at a particular historical moment in the young art of cinema, what the term "cinema" had come to signify (cf. Rodowick 2007: 22). In other words, his question is, for those who go to the cinema to see (and hear) films, what does "cinema" as a social, institutional, conventional experience mean, and how has it come to acquire that meaning? To underline the fundamental historicality of Metz's approach, we can point to his admission that at some time in the future the cinema might very well come to mean something entirely different (perhaps for us today it has already become something else) and furthermore that it has probably meant other things in the past (in an age, for example, that might be designated primitive or early cinema) (cf. Metz 1979: 22; 1982: 73).

One way in which Metz tries to account for the specificity of the cinematic signifier is by pointing out that, as cinema became a generalized cultural activity, audiences became accustomed to expecting a certain kind of experience from the cinema that was distinct from other experiences. One way in which he specifies what cinema had become is by conceiving of it as a conjoining of three interrelated machines. The first machine is that which produces films, that is, the studios, the equipment, the organizational institutions and technologies that create movies. The second machine emerges in tandem with the first and is probably the most important for Metz's argument in "The Imaginary Signifier": it is the *psychical* machine that is ticking inside us and that provokes in us a desire to go to the cinema. This desire is for *something*, for we are not forced to go to the cinema, and indeed, in most cases, we have to pay for it. Cinema's second machine is therefore a psychical one which creates in us the desire to go to the cinema on the basis of what we have imagined and continue to imagine cinema to be, and as a result of the pleasures it has delivered to us in the past. The third machine of cinema involves those who write about cinema: critics, historians, theoreticians. Metz thus considers the workings of cinematic institutions in a complex fashion and such claims place him a long way away from reducing cinema to any kind of essentialism.

PRESENCE AND ABSENCE, THEATRE AND CINEMA

Carroll is nonetheless correct to point out that one of the chief ways in which Metz tries to distinguish cinema from other forms of experience is by way of *the play of presence and absence*. Metz argues, in one of the standout features of his essay, that cinema offers a play of presence and absence that is quite specific. It is an experience that is distinct both from the other kinds of experiences available to human beings and from other art forms or cultural or social activities. Metz's main point of comparison is with the theatre: how is what audiences have come to expect from the theatre different from what audiences typically expect when they go to the cinema? What audiences are accustomed to expecting when they go to the theatre, he claims, is an array of props, sets and actors that perform a drama before the audience in a here and now. In other words, the action of a theatrical drama is one that is *present* before its audience. The actions of a film are, on the contrary, *not* present before the audience in a cinema: they are *absent*; they are mere projections of light on a screen. In support of this point, Metz calls on the example of a chair. If a chair appears in a stage drama, then that chair will take its place on stage and will be *present* to us in the same space we temporarily inhabit as a theatre audience. A similar presence does not, however, apply to cinema: the chair at which we look during a film will have been filmed at another time and place; it will be *absent* from the cinema auditorium (1982: 44).

Metz's point here does not appear to be a tremendously difficult one to grasp, yet Carroll is extremely critical of it; indeed, it is one of his major points of criticism. He frames his criticism of Metz in the following way:

> [I]f we are speaking of fiction – i.e., fiction film and fictional plays – then, ontologically, Shylock is no more present to the theatre spectator than Fred C. Dobbs is present to the film viewer. Neither Shylock nor Fred C. Dobbs can be hit by a disapproving spectator with a dissenting tomato ... Once we are considering the realm of fiction, it makes no sense to speak of the differences between cinema and theater in terms of what is absent to the spectator. In both fictional film and theatrical fiction, the characters are absent from the continuum of our world in the same way.
>
> (Carroll 1988c: 38)

Carroll is no doubt correct to point out that for fiction *per se* Metz's distinction does not hold. But for a range of other reasons, the distinction *does* hold, and Carroll substantially simplifies Metz's position in order to criticize it. Primarily, Metz's argument here holds on phenomenological grounds. The Shylock we see on stage during a theatrical production of *The Merchant of Venice* is phenomenologically different from the Fred C. Dobbs (Humphrey Bogart) we encounter during a projection of the film *The Treasure of the Sierra Madre* (dir. John Huston, 1948). If it is John Gielgud playing the part of Shylock in a stage production, then it is John Gielgud who is before us – *present* to us – while the character of Shylock is absent. By way of his presence as an actor, Gielgud will try to conjure up for us a presence of Shylock, but the character of Shylock will himself be absent. In the theatre, therefore, *the actor is present while the character is absent*. Bogart's portrayal of Dobbs is, on the other hand, of an entirely different order. Bogart is not present before us in the cinema auditorium: he exists merely as projected rays of light. Bogart is absent. But his character, Dobbs, is also absent. In the cinema, *both the actor and the character are absent*. What we see and hear on the screen is therefore doubly absent. While theatrical productions offer an experience of presence that refers to an absence, in the cinema we are presented with a projected absence that refers *also* to an absence.

It is on the basis of this doubled absence that Metz designates the cinematic signifier as *imaginary*. The Imaginary, as is well known, along with the Real and Symbolic, is one of the fundamental categories of unconscious structuration according to the psychoanalytic theories of Jacques Lacan. But it is not necessary to adhere to the precepts of Lacanian psychoanalysis in order to understand why Metz designates cinema's signifier as imaginary ("You know, I am not a Lacanian", he once quipped [1979: 8]). Much of Metz's argument relies on the assertion that what we experience at the cinema – the projection of images and sounds – can be regarded as primarily and fundamentally imaginary. Again, the contrast with theatre is pertinent: the common experience of the theatre is one in which there is a *combination of the real and the imaginary*: actors, sets and props that really are in front of us, which refer to imagined characters, actions and scenes. In the cinema, on the contrary, our experience is a *combination of the imaginary and the imaginary*: imaginary characters and scenes projected before us by virtue of a machine of the imaginary. Hence one of Metz's most controversial claims: "What is characteristic of the cinema is not the imaginary it may happen to represent, but the imaginary that it *is* from the start" (1982: 44). What is distinctive about cinema is not that it may give rise to fantastical, imaginary plots, but rather that the very means by which films are delivered to us is imaginary. Allied with Metz's claim, here is another notorious statement: "Every film is a fiction film" (*ibid.*). Again, this claim has nothing to do with the specific *content* of films, but rather is a claim regarding the way in which films are conceived and received by us; films do not unfold for us in a realm that is based on the presence of real objects, as in the theatre or in painting (paintings are made with "real" paint); instead, the modus operandi of films is itself fictional (for more on these points, see Rushton [2002]).

IDENTIFICATION

One of the ways in which Metz defines the imaginary signifier in cinema is by way of identification. In the wake of Metz's writings, many scholars have been critical of the use of the term *identification* in film theory. There is, however, still a great deal that is misunderstood about his conception, and clarifying these misunderstandings should demonstrate the strength of what it was that Metz was trying to say. He develops a very specific understanding of two cinematic modes of identification: *primary* and *secondary* cinematic identification. In order to point out what is at stake in these arguments, it is again opportune to examine Carroll's criticisms of those arguments. Carroll claims, against Metz, that we need not identify with anyone in order to comprehend a film:

> Metz holds that all communication requires a subtending process of identification … It is this commitment to the necessity of identification that drives Metz to explain film reception in terms of imaginary identification with the camera. But I think that it is outlandish to accept the general presupposition that every communication, in order to be intelligible, requires some subtending process of identification. I overhear a department store sales attendant tell a pregnant woman that maternity clothes are on the second floor. I understand these remarks, I find them intelligible, without in any meaningful sense of the word *identifying* with either the attendant or the woman. And even if identification were necessary it would be hard to come up with compelling reasons why I would have to identify with the attendant rather than the woman, or vice-versa.   (Carroll 1988c: 40–41)

Carroll's points here demonstrate substantial confusion, but he should not be seen as being alone in this respect, for interpretations of Metz's formulations of identification are clouded by confusion. First of all, Carroll points out that, for Metz, the cinema spectator identifies with the camera. Along with this, he adds that there is "a subtending process of identification" underlying the cinematic experience. However, Carroll then displaces these observations on to an apocryphal example and claims that in order to understand a conversation one does not need to identify with any of the people who are speaking in that conversation. Carroll's major point of confusion here is that he conflates primary identification – the subtending process of identification – with secondary identification – identification with characters, agents or persons.

Primary cinematic identification designates a spectator's identification with the camera. However, this process entails substantially more than *just* identifying with the camera. It is an identification with *the process by which the camera makes a cinematic universe available to the spectator*. To put it another way, it is an identification with the conditions of possibility that subtend (Carroll's word) any film. Indeed, this subtending condition of possibility can be fruitfully clarified with reference to Carroll's example. To understand the conversation he overhears, it is not necessary for him to identify with either of the conversants, but Carroll must identify with the presuppositions and codes that subtend that conversation and that are the conditions of possibility for understanding the communication that ensues. Carroll must identify with the characteristic formulations and enunciations of the English language; if our conversants were speaking in Finnish or Mandarin, for example, then Carroll would, I suspect, be entirely unable to understand their conversation. But he must also be able to understand the social codes that underpin the conversation: he must know what a department store is, and understand the kinds of activities associated with department stores; he must know what pregnancy is and how such things might be evident (for example, the specific abdominal bump indicative of pregnancy), and he must also understand that in certain societies there are specific types of clothing designated maternity clothes. He must also understand that there are such persons as sales attendants, what the function of such persons is, and the ways in which such persons are differentiated from other persons (customers, for example). Understanding the systemic underpinnings that subtend – which *make possible* – this communication is an *identification* with the framework or conditions of possibility that make the conversation intelligible to Carroll.

These are all examples of the complex ways in which identification functions in Carroll's example, but they also demonstrate that what Metz means by identification does not entail identifying with a person, agent or character. If Carroll's example shows us the kinds of processes of identification that function in overhearing a conversation, then Metz tries to convey in the notion of primary cinematic identification the processes by means of which cinema spectators make sense of and understand cinematic universes. In much the same way as one has to have lived during a particular historical period and in particular regions of the world (call them advanced Western societies) in which things called department stores, maternity clothes and sales assistants are meaningful, then so too have many people lived in societies in which "going to the cinema" can be understood to designate a specific kind of activity. Knowing what that activity is entails a subtending process of identification.

I cannot resist pushing a little further into Carroll's example. Why does he choose an example of commodity exchange? Would it be going too far to infer that Carroll identifies so closely and strongly with modes of commodity exchange that he feels there are no subtending processes: that the activities of commodity exchange are entirely natural, transparent, obvious and understandable without explanation? Carroll's apparent acceptance of the natural transparency of commodity exchange brings us face to face with one of Metz's overarching points: if the activity of going to the cinema had reached a point of obviousness for audiences, that is, if going to the cinema had reached a point in which there seemed to be *no* subtending processes of identification involved, then how could this seemingly natural act of going to the cinema be explained? Or, to put this another way, it is this very sense in which the activity of going to the cinema seemed to need no explanation that, for Metz, required explanation. "A film is difficult to explain because it is easy to understand" (1974a: 72), he writes at one point. In a very real sense, this is why he designates the cinematic signifier as *imaginary* rather than *symbolic*: we seem not to need a series of specially organized codes in order to understand a film in the way that we do in order to read novels (which requires specific textual codes – letters, grammar, sentences, and so on) or poetry (which typically requires sophisticated levels of symbolic decoding) or painting (much of the effect of which necessitates a knowledge of painting's history, historical developments and contextual underpinnings). Of course, we *do*, at some level, need to know what conventions and expectations subtend the activity of filmgoing, but such activities (at least at the time when Metz was writing) have less to do with learning an overtly signified system of symbolic codes and rather more to do with a fundamentally *unconscious* system of understandings rooted in the human subject's imaginary capacities at a specific historical juncture. This is certainly one reason Metz wants to call the cinematic signifier *imaginary*.

PRIMARY CINEMATIC IDENTIFICATION

Primary cinematic identification is the mode of identification by means of which the cinematic signifier is called imaginary. There are two key statements in Metz's "The Imaginary Signifier" that allow the imaginariness of this primary identification to be fleshed out. A first states that "the spectator *identifies with himself*, with himself as a pure act of perception (as wakefulness, alertness): as the condition of possibility of the perceived and hence as a kind of transcendental subject, which comes before every *there is*" (1982: 49). In what amounts to a complex formulation, Metz is here stating that the condition of possibility of cinema's ability to *be* cinema is that any audience member take him or herself precisely *as* the condition of possibility of any film's unfolding. Without a spectator to put the images of a film together, there is no film. And Metz's further point takes him close to territories defined by Kant and Lacan respectively: the ground of possibility of a film is any spectator's ability to assemble that film in his or her mind, just as, for Kant, the ground of possibility of experience *per se* is founded on certain transcendental principles by means of which human subjects have perceptual, cognitive and aesthetic access to the world. (For Kant, human beings might be said to identify with such transcendental principles as ones that subtend all human experiences; in Kant's words, "It must be possible for the 'I think' to accompany all my representations" [Kant 1929: 152–3]). Metz (although he does not explicitly refer to Kant) calls the spectatorial subject of cinema *transcendental*, not because such spectators possess any kinds of transcendent qualities, but rather because any spectator is himself or herself the underlying *condition of possibility* that enables any film to be experienced *as* a film. The Lacanian point is similar: by virtue of the "mirror stage", human subjects learn to make a distinction between an "I" that is the seat of experience and a world "out there" from which such subjects are separated (Lacan 2006). The result of this separation is that any experience of the world must be filtered through the perspective of this "I". For Metz, in making use of the Lacanian analogy, the spectator's relationship to the cinema screen sets into play something akin to a reinstatement of the subjective "I": as any film begins, each spectator enters a new kind of mirror stage in front of the screen, for on that screen any number of new worlds might come into being, new worlds that will require new "I"s through which the sense of those worlds can be made. ("It is I who make the film", Metz writes [1982: 48].)

Metz's second key statement on primary cinematic identification is no less easy to unpack:

> When I say that "I see" the film, I mean thereby a unique mixture of two contrary currents: the film is what I receive, and it is also what I release, since it does not pre-exist my entering the auditorium and I only need to close my eyes to suppress it. Releasing it, I am the projector, receiving it, I

am the screen; in both these figures together, I am the camera, which points
and yet which records.   (1982: 51)

Metz's central claim here is that the activity of the spectator is akin to that of the camera; hence primary cinematic identification entails an identification with the camera.
Carroll certainly takes issue with Metz's claims here. "If I truly identified with the
camera", Carroll writes,

> I suppose that I would experience the entire visual array of the projection
> as coextensive with my visual field. Yet, when I look at a film image, I only
> focus on part of it, usually upon what is represented in the foreground or
> upon that quadrant of the screen where the primary action of the narrative
> transpires.   (1988c: 40)

Carroll is certainly correct to observe that at the cinema we do not see exactly what
the camera sees, but in making such a point he sidesteps Metz's argument. Metz does
not argue that *we see what the camera sees*, but instead tries to infer that our activity of
perceiving, recording and processing filmic information is like that undertaken by the
cinema camera. To put it another way, while I watch a film I imagine I am a camera.
Or, as Edward Branigan has recently put it, "Metz believes that a camera does not stand
in by default for an absent observer but, rather, is embedded in the text as a 'purely
cinematographic' signifier linked through community rules to a narrative signified"
(2006: 88). One should not take Metz's analogy literally, for the camera acts for the
cinema spectator as a signifier, as an imagined way of organizing a spectator's modes
of viewing. In this way, identification with the camera provides an implicit interpretative schema for any cinema spectator. This implicit schema both enables and guides
any spectator's interpretative understanding of a film. The importance of Metz's point
here is that the spectator is engaged in a dual process of receiving, on the one hand,
and processing, on the other; both receiving *and* releasing; pointing *and* recording.
Hence Metz's point is not that we see only what the camera sees, but rather that at
the cinema we perceive and understand, as it were, in a manner that is like that of a
camera; we both introject and project, passively receive and actively impose forms on
what we see and hear.

THE METZIAN SPECTATOR: THE DUPE OF A PASSIVE ILLUSION

It strikes me as somewhat strange that Metz has often been accused of positing a
passive spectator, as though the kinds of spectators he proposed were incapable of
forming their own thoughts but instead passively had their thoughts formed for them
by the spectacle on which they gazed. However, the notion of the imaginary signifier presupposes a tremendous degree of psychological investment: in the social
formations or communities of meaning in which going to the cinema belongs. Such
investments amount to presuppositional schemas that underpin the kinds of cinematic engagements of which spectators are capable. As Metz pointed out, "I shall only

recall that the cinema was born in the midst of a capitalist epoch in a largely antago-nistic and fragmented society, based on individualism and the restricted family (= father–mother–children), in an especially super-egoistic bourgeois society" (1982: 64). Furthermore, Metz's insistence on the degrees to which both everyday spectators, on the one hand, and critics or scholars, on the other, go to great lengths to defend what they believe to be "good" films over those that they consider "bad" cannot fail to elicit far-reaching degrees of individual, personal – that is, *active* – responses to the films they see. Indeed, one ought to consider, quite contrary to prevailing misunderstand-ings of Metz, that he in fact posits a model of a very *active* spectator.

Carroll nonetheless sees Metz's spectator as a passive entity. He writes that "there is a general tendency in contemporary film theory to maintain that film spectators are rapt in the illusion that what is represented – the cinematic referents – are really present" (1988c: 43), a point he infers from Metz's formulations.[1] But there is no such explicit claim in Metz's writings. Indeed, there are more explicit suggestions that, because of its psychical proximity to such prohibited or repressed acts such as sco-pophilia, voyeurism, fetishism and observation of the primal scene, cinema presents far more scope for undermining the strength of the symbolic order. To be "rapt in the illusion that the cinematic referents are really present", as Carroll suggests, might come to mean for Metz that the cinema allows us to perceive, and to be in the pres-ence of, visions and exhibitions that are normally prohibited in general daily life. "For the vast majority of the audience", writes Metz,

> the cinema (rather like the dream in this) represents a kind of enclosure or "reserve" which escapes the fully social aspect of life although it is accepted and fully prescribed by it: going to the cinema is one lawful activity among others with its place in the admissable pasttimes of the day or the week, and yet that place is a "hole" in the social cloth, a *loophole* opening onto something slightly more crazy, slightly less approved than what one does the rest of the time. (1982: 66)

It is in this way, then, that the cinema presents a very particular kind of imaginary illusion for Metz (where "illusion" need not be understood as a negative trait). Indeed, from Metz's perspective, the cinema might provide something akin to an illusion or impression of *reality*, but such illusory impressions are in no way grounded in *real-ism*, especially if one means by realism an "indexical" realism where the signifier is a transparent effect of reality. For Metz, something other than realism is at work with the cinematic signifier, a point that separates his position from so-called apparatus theorists. Indeed, this is a point emphasized by Ben Singer when writing about Metz some years ago, noting that at the cinema,

> [the] illusion that the viewer is the perceptual source of the image is much stronger than in photography, to the extent of eclipsing any significant awareness of the original instance of recording ... The truth-value of the indexical force of the cinematic medium does not impress itself on us [as] an indexical recording process, and instead affirms it as a sight we generate

ourselves, a sight gathered by natural perception … The film is not coated
with a sheen of indexical believability.   (Singer 1988: 19–20)

Perhaps this, then, is the final point we can take from Metz: films do not emerge from a
fundamental indexicality – they are not the causal effect of a prior reality – but instead
emerge as a consequence of the spectator's own imaginary engagement, an identification with the "I" that is also at one and the same time an identification with the camera.
Belief in the cinema is of the order of that which is imagined: the fetish, the primal
scene, often of things that are prohibited by everyday social reality. That, if nothing else,
is the lesson we should begin with when considering the work of Christian Metz.

NOTE

1. The notion that Metz was an "apparatus theorist" seems to be taken as something of a given for
    most film scholars today. For example, Tom Gunning has no hesitation in declaring that Metz, like
    other "apparatus theorists … would see realism as a dangerous ideological illusion"; "Moving Away
    from the Index: Cinema and the Impression of Reality", *Differences: A Journal of Feminist Cultural
    Studies* **18**(1) (2007), 41. This is emphatically wrong; see Metz, "The Cinematic Apparatus as a Social
    Institution: An Interview with Christian Metz", *Discourse: Journal for Theoretical Studies in Media
    and Culture* **3** (1979), 30.

25 JULIA KRISTEVA

Patricia MacCormack

Julia Kristeva (b. 1941) was born in Bulgaria, and moved to Paris for her doctoral studies in phil-osophy. In 1965 she became a member of the Tel Quel Group in Paris, important for their work on the production of writing as a political activity. In 1974 she was appointed Chair of Linguistics at the University of Paris. In 1979 she completed her training in psychoanalysis. Her published the-ory works include, *Desire in Language* (1969; English trans. 1980), *Powers of Horror* (1980; English trans. 1982), *Black Sun* (1989; English trans. 1992), *Nations without Nationalism* (1993), *Time and Sense* (1996), *Crisis of the European Subject* (2000), *Female Genius: Life, Madness, Words* (1999; vol. 1, English trans. 2001). Her works of fiction include *The Old Man and the Wolves* (1991), *Possessions* (1996) and *Murder in Byzantium* (2004). Kristeva's exploration of language as a fluid semiology accesses the chora or "woman's" space of the in-between to challenge and interrogate the arbi-trary nature of language and the symbolic. By experiencing film through a semiotic navigation of corporeality, materiality and affect, the spectator opens up to the possibility of experiencing and encountering film differently, and thus the way film both informs and creates meaning can be used experimentally rather than reifying established power structures. Salient to the feminist semiotics, Kristeva's work on the abject similarly investigates the risks and revolutions of those elements of language, including the language of images, when they exceed boundaries, col-lapse borders and involute language with flesh, logic with bodies. Her work on semiotics and the abject thus can be used towards a feminist ethics of spectatorship.

It is tempting to transplant Julia Kristeva's work on language to the language of film. Kristeva's work emphasizes that the semiotic and the space of corporeal *jouissance* (joy/ecstasy) are not bound within the text as the work but come from between the text and reader relation, as process. The content of art as transcendentally meaning-ful or signifying dissipates into its affective potential. Art is not an object of analysis or transmission but an ignition of *jouissance* in the subject. Kristeva sees cinema as the central place of the imaginary in modern culture (2002a: 68). The question is not to what extent cinema allows mastery over the imaginary towards a totalizing sym-bolic view of society simultaneous with that of self in the mirror stage, but to what extent cinema invokes the liminal encounter between the imaginary as the time of undifferentiated drive converted in adulthood to the unconscious mediated through symbolization. The imaginary, the point where the ego begins to form as mastery over forms, for Kristeva, is converted from apprehension to creativity through art, so nei-ther the self nor images are symbols but both form a unique desiring space-between. As I shall explore here, Kristeva argues that a-signified drive and thus a-signifying image is not infantile but a schizoid, "de-structuring and a-signifying machine of the unconscious ... schizophrenic flow ... [not] schizophrenic blockage, is a structuring and destructuring *practice*, a passage to the outer *boundaries* of the subject and society. Then – and only then – can it be *jouissance* and revolution" (1984: 17).

Desire for images and films is an ethical tactic of apprehension. Ethics demands an address to relations of difference that will necessarily dismantle and reform the subject and thus desire for images is ethical to the extent that the spectator mobilizes sub-jective transformation. Femininity as arguably the first point of difference asks, "are women not already participating in the rapid dismantling that our age is experiencing ... and which poses the *demand* for a new ethics?" (Kristeva 1986: 211). Following Kristeva's critical position on the ethics of constructed discourses that engage notions of representation, the medium of film is likewise engaged in an ethics of desire. Desire constitutes the experience of films and the extent to which spectators view poeti-cally comes from flesh and selves in relation to images as potentials for *jouissance*. Celebrating spectatorship as *jouissance* offers a revolution in images not for what they show but for the pleasures they elicit and spectatorship as an act of poetic revolt. *Jouissance* found in not what images show but the pleasures they mobilize offers the spectator dialectic as a form of revolt. "I see revolt as a dialectical process ... Revolt ... refers to a state of permanent questioning, of transformation, change, an endless probing of appearances" (2002b: 120). By dialectic Kristeva means ethics as relation, her Spinozan interpretation (1986: 211), not Hegelian dialectics, which involves mas-tery/transmission of meaning and submission/reception of meaning. From Kristeva, film theorists would argue that reading forms, justifying or repudiating metonymic relations, focusing on noun–verb narratives is not an objective practice but makes the spectator as accountable as the image. Spectator *jouissance* orients and is oriented by the signification of enfleshed subject and the corporeal materiality of images: not reflections or representations of reality but creators of materially affective realities. The way spectators navigate images constitutes the way they navigate all significa-tion, which is all they are but which is always in excess of itself. Revolution comes from the ethics of perceiving ourselves *as already in* poetic language: an ethics of desire. Perceiving the possibility of transcendental signifiers identifies transcendental subjectivity through observation of transcendental elements: words, images, bod-ies. Reading is prevented if a language is not known to the reader, whereas a visual language, while always different in disparate cultures and countries, is ubiquitously resonant with the way speaking subjectivity is apprehended through the flesh. The subject emerges and is then recognized via corporeal signifiers of gender, race, age and various other elements.

Kristeva's work resonates around the rupture of subjectivity in relation to lan-guage and desire as the crucial nexus of the encounter between language and aes-thetic encounter and the notion of *jouissance*. Kristeva's work has been historicized as structuralist (or deconstructivist in relation to her work on Jacques Derrida) and psychoanalytic epistemologies. She turns frequently to Jean-Paul Sartre and Roland

Barthes, Jacques Lacan and Sigmund Freud. Kristeva studied under Barthes and was a member of *Tel Quel*, the avant-garde assemblage of writers who renegotiated science, literature and art. Kristeva's association with the group is remarkable to the extent that she was one of the (very) few women in the group and certainly the only woman who appears regularly in collective writings.

However, particularly in her studies of literature, Kristeva emerges as one of the continental philosophers who move beyond the deconstruction of language and the psyche. Her discussions on corporeality and *jouissance* in relation to the market value of women's sexuality (particularly in "Stabat Mater"; 1986; 1996: 273) align her with Luce Irigaray. She is interested in the gestural, disjunctive rhythmic and other asemiotic elements in language (1980: 29–33) that Félix Guattari (1995, 1996b) similarly explores in reference to cinematic images. Her concept of harmony without melody (1980: 88–9) encounters Gilles Deleuze's (2001) work on Leibniz; she claims "drive denotes waves of attack against stases" (1984: 28) connecting her with Michel Serres' studies of physics, the clinamen and equilibrium as death (cf. Serres 2000). She references Maurice Blanchot's (2003) concept of fascination (Kristeva 1980: 104) and the becoming of literature and, extending these becomings, her literary analyses (more correctly a-analyses or mediative extensions; *ibid.*: 71–2) resonate with the work on literature of Deleuze and Guattari – the shift from the symbolic psyche-subject of sciences, including psychoanalysis, to the schizoid-subject of art. This is Kristeva's first privileged site of semiotics – madness (1980: 29; 1986: 91).

Psychoanalysis attempts to repair the body and psyche of the fractured subject. Kristeva's preferred privileged site of social revolution catalysed through aesthetics is poetic writing (Joyce, Celine, Mallarmé) just as the relation between poetics and desire is one of inscribed flesh rather than enunciating and enunciated subject. This is Kristeva's second site: poetics. Where the subject can only emerge as language, a result of the conversion (and thus extravasation [1984: 22]) of drives to empty endlessly deferred symbols – making a "sentence" (in both senses) of desire – poetry stretches the limit by celebrating the failure of signification. Kelly Oliver, a key theorist of Kristeva's work, states "poetry is a type of borderline case that calls into question all that is central to representation" (Oliver 1993: 2). Signifying practices are the limit and limiting of subjectivity, thought and ideology. They claim to observe, describe and reflect on "things" without acknowledging the processes that constitute objects of analysis. Literature is the missing link of the human sciences because it focuses on *process*, which, from the French, means subject in process and to succeed and/or to become successive; so "questionable and unsettling" (Kristeva 1980: 17). Thus an ethics of reception of literature takes as its first requirement the unsettled subject. For these reasons Kristeva's work can be considered alongside those theories that go beyond interrogating the structures of language and subjectivity towards a vitalistic philosophy, which, through poetry, pleasure and the body, show language and other art as extensive, neither transgressive nor conservative but revolutionary, through the ways they explore and eventually explode the excesses of subjectivity.

Where signification converts drive to symbol, poetics emphasizes the risks of pleasure found in letting go of signification and its constitution of the subject, so pleasure itself must be deconstitutive of subjectivity. The poetic relies on a-signifying corporeal elements, verbs without nouns. Signification and the normalizing systems it serves ablate the flesh: science extends subjectivity through manipulating mortal bodies, religion repudiates the body for transcendental eternal spirit and capitalism makes the body a reproductive machine through family and a valuable object through fetishes of consumption that adorn and thus define the myth of self-styled social identity. "Poetic discourse measures rhythm against the meaning of language structure and is thus always eluded by meaning in the present while continually postponing it to an impossible time to come" (1980: 33), so is historical while guaranteeing the future. If poetic texts mourn the impossibility of discourse as pure signifier, *what* is that mourning for? The speaking subject is not present in poetry because poetry and thus the subject become fragmented, fleeting and affective. Does poetry actually point to the inevitable presence of a failed speaking subject, like the signifier itself, dead before it arrives and impossible to come?

Extending Kristeva's work on poetry and literature to her concept of abjection, this mourning is for a "death", but to "the place where [language] kills, thinks and experiences *jouissance* all at the same time" (1982: 206). Death is therefore simultaneous with love as "the subversion of language [is] the amorous state" (2002a: 120). The subject is not autonomous but amorous. In her work she explores literature as constituted by homology between body–dream–language–desire, destruction of the person, social activity. After Mikhail Bakhtin (1968) she contrasts dialogism with dialectics:

> Dialogism replaces [dialectic] concepts by absorbing them within the concept of relation [the becomings of text and reader]. It does not strive towards transcendence but rather toward harmony [but *not* melody], all the while implying an idea of rupture (of opposition and analogy) as a modality of transformation. (1980: 88–9)

Then, through the concept of holiness, Kristeva shifts the notion of pleasure from a higher-order coming, not through God or the Father but through undifferentiated desire that recalls the pre-symbolic maternal relation, an overwhelming joy within the inflection and not extrication between subject and art. The excesses of poetics make the subject exceed itself and become lost to itself in an ecstatic *jouissance*. The subject moves outside syntax to the spatial moment of ecstasy. This is Kristeva's third privileged site of semiotics: pleasure as holiness.

Film as a legible reflective language defers endlessly the (impossibility of) the apprehension of images as always symbolic, psychically striated, indexed to the conversion from *jouissance* to symbol. Kristeva associates dreams and poetry with transgression and revolution, not dreams as convertible to the symbolic to access the unconscious drives but dreams as these boundaries, neither above or below, "out" or "in", a terrain of *chora* where no distinction is acknowledged. The chora is the space where the subject is constituted through discursive processes *as* mobile and provisional. Chora, like poetry, is the "spatial intuition … as rupture and articulations (rhythm), precedes evidence, verisimilitude, spatiality and temporality" (1984: 26). It is maternal because it is the terrain that nurtures the possibility of signification but is not signification. In cinema studies this would be called virtuality. Unlike

Metz's spectator bent on reading images, spectatorship describes an intuitive space of schizoid desire (MacCormack 2008). Rhythmic articulation is harmony over melody: images are evidence of nothing but the affects they produce with the spectator. Images are not verisimilitude of ideas or social objects. They may be perceived as unfurling in movement and duration; however, space is neither paradigmatic nor time syntagmatic. Spectatorship *jouissance* occurs when images are perceived free from necessary bonds between asemiotic adjectival elements – sound, colour, gesture, inflection, angle and so forth – and form. Thus, under Kristeva's analysis, no connections are unreal or impossible. Interpretation nomenclatures *jouissance*: "Interpretation as pardon is manifested first as the establishment of a form" (2002a: 20). Any apprehension of a form resolves that form for the perceiver in order to pardon it. The incommensurable cannot be pardoned because it cannot be interpreted as a commensurable form. Symbols are "*units of restriction* ... the good and the bad are incompatible ... The contradiction, once it appears, immediately demands resolution. It is thus concealed, 'resolved', put aside" (1980: 38–9). Symbolically, opposition is resolvable because the meaning of each is clear and one must be better, truer and so on. Symbolic opposition is made resolvable because the meaning of each unit is able to be interpreted through established forms that can be deemed better or truer. Resistance to form, perhaps what could be called a *poethics*, is the pardoning of the unformed or un-form-able. Drawing on Augustine, Kristeva describes the image without, formed by a sensible body and succeeded by a similar vision within. "This internal vision (an essential element of our 'intimate') is warehoused in the memory and becomes 'vision in thought' only when recollection seizes it" (2002a: 46). But recollection always seizes it as "something else"; thus the mode by which subjects recollect is the ethical turn or the point of the shift from knowing to thinking. This recollection is also evidence of the impossibility of time Augustine laments because one is always recollecting as soon as one is vision-ing.

Any event of apprehension is oriented around previous modes of perception. The act of seeing is the act of negotiating how to see. Does the spectator judge an image based on their memory of similar images and their significations – the belief that images are transcendental and ahistorical signifiers? Or is an image exploited for the elements that exceed memories of comparative images, where every image is always new and signifying that image creates a new signification but, because it cannot be deferred, it is image without signification, present and affective nonetheless – semiotic. The spectator asks not "What does this image mean?" but "What does this image do?" Claims to "know" what an image means extract the spectator from the responsibility of perception emergent through the subjective history that is always present in seeing images. A memory of affect creates possible open futures. Forgiveness comes from the accountable acceptance and celebration of residues of desire that flaw history as memory: poetic immanence inherent in chrono-linearity. Spectators forgive the image's incapacity to ever communicate and their own incapacity to receive transcendental meaning. The spectator can mediate meaning with subjective memory rather than observe as truth. Thus images are events and born of memories of events. To remember forgives the self that can never re-know. Timelessness is not an image that transcends change; timelessness *is* modification. It makes time and images existent only as immediacy, elucidating all history, memory and image as events of now.

From Proust's rereading of Kant's taste as style, style is a mode of intimacy for Kristeva (from judgement to inclination/quality of apprehension). Kristeva addresses the ethical impossible imperative of style as almost a responsibility, linking style with "the unnameable and to the pain of the intimate" (2002a: 53). Using Kristeva, spectator-ship shifts from a dialectic to a dialogism. An ethics of literature, cinematic encounter or other encounter with art spans the becomings of text and reader. The relationship between spectator and image is similarly not monological, which is based on the logic of demarcation of things and their opposition. The way an image is apprehended as open-affective-potential emerging through the spectator as a semiotic intensity – not a sign with one meaning and in opposition to the spectator – facilitates the becom-ing of the image. Images rupture signification, through disjunctive poetic narrative, forms, colours, sonorities, angles and elements that do not inform the spectator of meaning and function but are disanchored as semiotic particles of intensity from the nouns and acts to which we are compelled to annex them. Rupturing affective quali-ties facilitate the becoming of the spectator, no longer able to orient the image and thus the "I", which knows how to perceive that image based on a sense of reified sub-jectivity, the logic of being – frequently, and particularly in feminist psychoanalytic film theory, structured on the sexuality and gender of subjects understood as rela-tively stable. Within and between these two unique becomings is the point of dialo-gism: perception as a dialogue between the two becomings in process. The between functions as a semiotic revolt-trajectory because, as the third element in excess of each becoming, it dissipates the two elements differently into the world.

Philosophical explorations of cinema as a developmental intensification of desire shift the focus from image content to the subjectivity of spectatorship as semiotic space. "The issue of ethics crops up wherever a code (mores, social contract) must be shattered in order to give way to the free play of negativity, need, desire, pleasure, and jouissance" (1980: 23). If film language is codified representation, then the relation-ship of pleasure between the spectator and internal cinematic codes shifts from one of objective content apprehension to subjective negotiation of pleasure. In Kristevean terms this is an ethical encounter. In Lacanian terms, pleasure requires an object of desire be chosen, which necessitates the possibility of a demarcated ego who chooses. The drive for an object towards satisfaction maintains the observing subject in rela-tion to a not necessarily consensual object: non-consensual not in relation to the desiring subject but to the codes within which the desiring structure exists. Spectator *jouissance* renegotiates the solitary desiring subject through the affects they emit and the way they open up to the affects of images. Speech is poetic when desiring struc-tures contort and distort, just as poetry contorts and distorts language. Distortion creates new possibilities for the future of language and images and is considered malevolent only by those subjects who benefit most from the maintenance of belief in transcendentally signifying language. As for Georges Bataille, ecstasy for Kristeva occurs where self is lost but also lost to self, the contract one of continuum rather than oscillating mastery between ego and object. What Kristeva calls *rhythmic rapture* opposes the ego. It is the place where language fits the individual only after a hundred thousand experiments. She uses the sun as the great symbol of the father for poets, which means illuminating the un-illuminable. "Solar mastery cuts off rhythm" (1980: 29). Images understood as invocations towards different modes of desire rather than forms illuminated herald the shift from paternal author-izers to experimental poets: the space of semiotics as maternal and fluid, recalling the fluidity between mother and child before the symbolic break. Fluidity emphasizes the need to break down and see desiring structures occurring within the space between rather than between two objects in space. Kristeva's maternal neither fetishizes nor remembers mother-hood (and thus is not a lamentation of lost-mother love, which imprints the symbolic dialectic on the pre-Oedipal relation). As feminist theorist Sylvie Gambaudo states, "Kristeva is now clearly pointing the finger at a breakdown of the paternal function, not at the actual mother, and explaining how this paternal function affects and is effected by actual men and women but also symbolic entities (state, school etc.)" (2007: 97). However, the maternal function is not, as Gambaudo claims, metaphoric (*ibid.*), but is material and actual, just as the paternal function actualizes reality. The maternal function is more than, in excess of and demythologizes the imperative of the paternal function. The functive-realization of the actual mirrors the text and image as material just as the subject is symbolic. Cinema realizes, not reflects, the world, within the spectator. There is no demarcation between the actual and metaphoric because pleasure experiences signification materially.

The extent to which an ego opens up to negotiating fluidity with intensities of desire – found in all art poetics – constitutes revolt and revolution. Revolution is the relation of desire to content, not content within and for itself. It is tempting to offer abjection as a possible entry point into revolt through extreme or unpalatable images. Images of gore and those that emphasize the (always corporeally) oriented abject force the spectator to make a choice: face the abject and lose the ego or turn away and lose the abject, which is the mortal and visceral inevitability of the flesh that the ego repudiates, the flesh that sickens and kills the ego but where *jouissance* resides. Before extreme images of abjection, however, comes the female and particu-larly maternal flesh, which is forbidden desired flesh that threatens the rigid male ego found in rigid male flesh and described by rigid signifiers including visual forms. The phallus depends on form being rigid, illuminated and demarcated. Image-relation as dialogism not dialectic threatens the ego as its own transcendental signifier, thus is abject, maternal and poetic. Revolution in poetic language comes from desire found by the reader, or spectator, in that language and revolution are always about the rela-tion to language as much as the revolutions language elicits in itself. Is all language potentially poetic? Film language multiplies the sentence. Within any frame are forms that exist in relation to each other paradigmatically as a single plane, and cinema as art in motion metonymically relates the functive-acts of each element-form as the narrative or frames unfurl. The sentence of the painting and the semiotic imagistic nature of poetry coalesce. The phallus in literature is the word and the work. The crucial visual nature of the phallus demands that planes of cinema be understood as a series of demarcated forms with limited capacities to act in particular ways. As the symbol of logos, patriarchy and masculinity, the actual corporeal organ, the penis, need not be seen if significations of phallologicentrism are present – to act and look as a man – not performative, but in the spectator's belief in the logic of certain characters and images emergent only through the commensurability between form and act. The very style of image apprehension is phallologic: to look for forms the spectator believes must be there. Frames teem with forms and forms have commensurable functions and capacities. Planes of colour, abstract images, elements that directly affect the flesh of the spectator revolt against film language. The spectator chooses to privilege elements of any image. Poetic revolt occurs in perception so an image need not be abstract to be abstracted from its signifying chain. If the spectator seeks form and function in abstract images, it is the practice of looking that selects signification over *jouissance*-semiosis in the excessive and escapist qualities of all images.

The idea of a *work* always includes its own death through the impossibility of transparent signification/meaning. Like the demarcated and transcendentally independent signifier, the notion of "the" work by "the" author is constituted traditionally as a kind of parthenogenic event. Like Barthes, Kristeva urges a shift from the production of the author to focus on textual productivity, no longer narrative/phenomenon or literature/discourse (1980: 57), which is the bounded text. The transgressive text is a refusal of isomorphism or oppositional logic not because it operates by selecting the "other" term but because it functions within another law(s) – what Kristeva calls polyphonics. The spectator and reader must be included as part of this productivity and, in being so, through desire and pleasure, find ecstasy in the leaking, ambiguous rupturing elements of signification, just as feminism finds these elements in female bodies and pleasure. This mode neither replaces nor repudiates monological experiences of works but includes the compulsion towards monological relation as always a decision born of desire. Ethics comes from an accountability for this compulsion as it is most often desire that emerges through pleasure in control, repression of the feminine, maternal, semiotic and *jouissance*. As Kristeva sees the experience of art as one of desire, monology can be described as monogamy. The heroines of the works she explores see heroines oppressed by (always a one-way-enforced) monogamy. Political theorist of Kristeva's work Carol Mastrangelo Bové claims the heroine in poetic literature attempts to free herself "from monogamy's constraints in an effort to give expression to the physical and emotional life threatened by her relationship to a man … a struggle to transform a dangerous monogamous relationship" (Bové 2006: 63). Compulsory dialectic relations within phallologic structures are dangerous to the feminine, damming up *jouissance* and limiting desiring women to desired objects to be "had". Relations that emphasize flesh and emotion are associated with poetry as neither can access description of objective and visually apprehensible reality, so both are abstract, abstract reality and show reality as always abstract – dangerous to transcendental subjectivity. Kristeva states that abjection is the state of "perpetual danger" (1982: 9). The question is, dangerous to whom?

Polyamoury, like polyvocality, is not many love objects but multiple connections between possible intensities, ruptures and fissures in meaning, language and images. What constraints does interpretive spectatorship force on desiring subjects and what modes of revolutionary perception of images exploit emotion and corporeality? Experiencing images monogamously as objects of desire makes demands on us to interpret in a limited restrictive way that objectifies subject *jouissance*. There are no good or bad, right or wrong films: examples of horror films appear abject because literally revolt-ing; romance films demand courtly self-objectification that cut off *jouissance*. However, there are revolutions in all images; indeed, it could be argued, it is more important to view trite and repetitive representations of dialectic desire through poetic structures to show the revolution potential within all representation.

Asking a question of the other populates that other (Kristeva 1980: 152–3). The compelling psychoanalytic question "What do women want?", which amounts to a demand to convert *jouissance* to subject/object desire-satisfaction, can also be asked of the work. "What does this work want?" simultaneously ponders "What do I want from this work?" Signification is always within the reader and spectator, not the work. This is not the same as the reader-as-author claims of structuralism, as interpreting subjectivity is not a failure or necessary evil. In spectator *jouissance* the meditative and destabilizing elements of the experience of a work are celebrated, accessing pleasure rather than lamenting the object as ultimately never true, thus never satisfying. The "I" loses itself in (political, logical and art) events (*ibid.*: 171). The I that emerges through revolt reception comes from speech, which is "painful and deadly negative drive, capable of provoking schism … the 'I' emerges again, speaking and musicating [*sic*], so as to reveal the material truth of the process that brought it to the brink of its shattering into a whirlwind of mute particles. The schizoid regains consciousness" (*ibid.*: 185). Where is the musicality in a form, the gestural in an enunciation, the adjective intensity of an image, the muteness in sound that always exceeds limits and borders of a bound object?

Recognition is "intellectual speculation" (2002a: 73). For Kristeva, "of my dreamed body [cinema] offers only what the doctor's speculum maintains: a de-eroticized surface that 'I' concede to him in the wink of an eye by which 'I' make him believe that he is not another, that he has only to look as 'I' would if 'I' were him" (*ibid.*). Of film's capacity to invoke fear, using horror and pornography, she says "the stupider it is the better, for the filmic image does not need to be intelligent" (*ibid.*: 77). This addresses the bourgeois compulsion to "get" ambiguous and confounding films, more as a technique of self-realization within a particular intelligent community than as *jouissance*. The struggle to "get" (and be got by and know there is no final getting) is the event of semiotic pleasure, not the result that binds the image as intelligible. This suggests that abjection seems most appropriate to the very films that are considered the lowest of the low: gore, pornography and so on. Kristeva also describes as stupid (not evaluative but rupturing) asemiotic elements that are often the most frightening in dreams – shapes, saturation of colour, tones – poetic ruptures, the pleasures of which are as ambiguous as their de-formalized nature. In dream or the imaginary, adjectives are intensities (not informants) and movement is gestural (not inter-action between forms). Kristeva suggests that cinema is evil when it represents evil, not because it shows evil but because it expresses it as banal. Within this system evil is found not in representation but in the extent to which visuals explore and explode traditional signification: debanalizing the world and thus invoking thought rather than recognition. Poetic language reception causes "a perturbation, this plunge, this 'I am another' … rhythms, melodies, scansions – so many presyntactic, semiotic approaches" (*ibid.*: 120).

Kristeva explores the breakdown of contracts, where one party creates the mores and law to which the other party must agree and speak within in order to enter into relations. All contracts are enforcements of a desiring monology. A contract is an agreement between two parties on a truth. In cinema it is the agreement between the image showing a "true" thing and the spectator not only recognizing it *as* true. Recognition needs to believe something is true to occur. "Truth" overrides (the ethics of acknowledging) speaking positions. Pleasure and *jouissance* are found in the incommensurabilities between parties and truth as a process of tactical relation. The space between where incommensurabilities occur ruptures the contract that social structures demand and by which subjects serve those structures. The subject needs the object to maintain its power of objectification, and its truth to maintain the subject as true. Unbound desire has no need for a true thing. Love for poetry, for film, is simply undifferentiated need: the need for the relation, not the work. Pleasure is inherent in ethics and *jouissance* negotiates pleasure, not closing systems. Pleasure revolts. Social constraint constrains not subject but language and thus speaking positions are limited (1980: 25).

The tension towards unity "is accompanied by centrifugal forces of dissolution and dispersion" (2002a: 7). Unity is found in all (always failed) signifiers – from ego to image and word form. Unity is not limited to the psyche, the work or the word; it is a structuring element and thus is neither organic nor inorganic. The image is flesh and pleasure semiotic. "Flesh is the ultimate feeling of incompletion that sensation gives me … is it my flesh or the flesh of the world? In the end they are one and the same" (1996: 273).

26 LAURA MULVEY

David Sorfa

Laura Mulvey (b. 1941) is Professor of Film and Media Studies at Birkbeck College, University of London. She is the author of *Visual and Other Pleasures* (1989), *Fetishism and Curiosity* (1996), *Citizen Kane* (1992) and *Death 24x a Second* (2006). She is the director of a number of avant-garde films made in the 1970s and 1980s, made with Peter Wollen and Mark Lewis. Mulvey's essay "Visual Pleasure and Narrative Cinema" (1975) has had a major impact on the course of film scholarship. Mulvey's interests are broad, ranging from contemporary art to the introduction of sound in cinema, from Douglas Sirk to Abbas Kiarostami.

It would be difficult to argue that Laura Mulvey's work over the past four decades presents a coherent philosophy in the sense of a developed and argued *Weltanschauung*. Mulvey's published work consists almost entirely of reviews and articles, many of which have been collected in the three books for which she is well known: *Visual and Other Pleasures* (1989), *Fetishism and Curiosity* (1996) and *Death 24x a Second* (2006). The only single-topic book Mulvey has written is her short *Citizen Kane* for the BFI Film Classics series in 1992. Mulvey herself writes that she has "remained an 'essayist' and, … with no intended self-denigration, a dilettante" (1996: xii). In this chapter I shall highlight a number of themes and obsessions that run throughout Mulvey's writing and I shall contend that the lack of a central, overriding theory may in fact be the very philosophical point for which she is striving. However, I shall also discuss the possible problems with such an eclectic approach with specific reference to her writing on Iranian cinema. In addition to her written work, Mulvey has produced a number of films, although these are not easily or commercially available and are perhaps mostly known through Mulvey's own published commentaries on them.[1]

It is clear that the most iconic of Mulvey's articles is "Visual Pleasure and Narrative Cinema", first published in *Screen* in 1975 (reprinted in *Visual and Other Pleasures* along with "Afterthoughts on 'Visual Pleasure and Narrative Cinema' inspired by King Vidor's *Duel in the Sun* (1946)"). Mulvey herself has often referred back to this article and I shall discuss this self-criticism in the next section on the so-called "gaze". Mulvey's work has been overshadowed by this single piece of youthful polemic (the author was in her early thirties on publication) but "Visual Pleasure" does highlight issues of concern that continue to run through her subsequent work. Most obviously these include feminism and psychoanalysis, and it is these two branches of twenti-eth-century thinking, alongside Marxism, that most consistently inform her philo-sophical approach to film and art. A number of other broad areas are of obvious and continuing interest to Mulvey. These include photography (particularly ideas of stillness and delay) and contemporary art (with an emphasis on women artists and artists who could broadly be described as "postmodern"). Increasingly her work has reflected her interest in death and the Freudian compulsion to repeat. Her interest in cinema covers a surprisingly narrow range, with an overwhelming emphasis on popular Hollywood cinema from around 1930 to 1960, melodrama (particularly the films of Douglas Sirk and Rainer Werner Fassbinder) and, more recently, Iranian cin-ema. There are a small number of films to which she dedicates extended discussions – *Morocco* (dir. Josef von Sternberg, 1930), *Citizen Kane* (dir. Orson Welles, 1941), *Viaggio in Italia* (Journey to Italy; dir. Roberto Rossellini, 1954), *Imitation of Life* (dir. Sirk, 1959), *Psycho* (dir. Alfred Hitchcock, 1960), *Angst essen Seele auf* (Fear eats the soul; dir. Fassbinder, 1974), *Xala* (dir. Ousmane Sembene, 1975) and *Blue Velvet* (dir. David Lynch, 1986) – to some of which she returns repeatedly throughout her writing.

Mulvey's interest in Hollywood cinema can be understood as part of a certain antagonistic approach that characterizes her relationship with popular culture. In an internal pamphlet on the history of the British Film Institute (BFI) Education Department, Mulvey writes that film criticism as practised in the BFI from the 1960s onwards moved away from "concepts of value" (Mulvey is possibly thinking of the sort of criticism associated with V. F. Perkins and the *Movie* critics, a position per-haps most cogently argued in Perkins's *Film as Film* [1972]) and "turned to theories of semiotics and structuralism" that validated the discussion of the low culture of Hollywood cinema through "French ideas" (Mulvey 1994: 2). Here we can also see the beginnings of so-called Screen Theory associated with the journal *Screen* and with Mulvey herself during the 1970s. This validation initially provided film criticism with a way of taking Hollywood seriously by reacting against the snobbery of English critics. Mulvey writes:

> The combination of popular cinema from across the Atlantic and theory from across the channel amount to [a] slap in the face to the traditional Englishness, that was, in many ways, characteristic of this generation [i.e. 1950s and 1960s UK critics], and constituted a rejection of English isola-tionism and chauvinism. (*Ibid.*: 2–3)

Thus it is in reaction to English small-mindedness that Hollywood and semiotics were combined in the late 1960s to allow a way of thinking that moved beyond the mere exaltation or denigration of individual films. It is within this context that we can place Mulvey's collection of essays on Sirk published as part of a retrospective of his films at the 1972 Edinburgh Film Festival. In their introduction to the book, which includes the famous essay by Fassbinder on Sirk, Mulvey and John Halliday claim Sirk as an "undoubted *auteur*" but also as a film-maker whose films "raise a number of complex critical and aesthetic problems in a particularly clear and conscious manner"

(1972: vi). Sirk's cinema, then, is seen as providing an auto-critique of the conventions of Hollywood cinema and it is here that we can see one of the problems in Mulvey's thinking: to what extent can a film simultaneously be a product and a critique of the same system? Sirk could be seen as exceptional because he is "so familiar with the avant-garde theatre of Europe in the early decades of this century [the twentieth] and also familiar with painting, poetry and music" and, in addition, "his work shows an aware and clear conception of cinematic values" (*ibid.*). Sirk therefore comes from a tradition outside Hollywood and thus his films bring an extrinsic criticism to the facile form of melodrama.[2]

It is in the early 1970s that Mulvey began to re-evaluate her relationship to Hollywood cinema, because of her greater involvement with feminism and, increasingly, psychoanalysis. In her introduction to *Visual and Other Pleasures* she writes:

> Before I became absorbed in the Women's Movement, I had spent almost a decade [during her twenties in the 1960s] absorbed in Hollywood cinema. Although this great, previously unquestioned and unanalysed love was put in crisis by the impact of feminism on my thought in the early 1970s, it also had an enormous influence on the development of my critical work and ideas and the debate within film culture with which I became preoccupied over the next fifteen years or so. (1989: xiii)

Her work begins to concentrate on analysing the ways in which women are represented in popular and art culture. She takes part in the demonstration against the Miss World competition held in London's Royal Albert Hall in 1970, and this action also points to a concern that runs throughout her work: the relationship between theory and practice (Mulvey 1989: 3–5). Mulvey sees that it is necessary to understand and analyse the ideological precepts of contemporary culture, while also realizing that one should contribute to or intervene in that culture itself in order to bring about change. From the direct action of a stage invasion, Mulvey's analysis of films informs her own film-making practice (see note 1) in the 1970s and 1980s. More recently her basic experiments with digital editing inform her analytic writing. In "The Possessive Spectator", for instance, she "digitally re-edited a 30-second sequence [from *Gentlemen Prefer Blondes* (dir. Howard Hawks 1953)] in order to analyse the precision of Marilyn Monroe's dance movements and as a tribute to the perfection of her performance" (Mulvey 2006: 172). Thus there remains a tension between "doing" and "analysing" that is never resolved in Mulvey's work.

In the sentence quoted above, however, we can also see another duality within Mulvey's thinking and that is in the desire to both exalt Hollywood ("perfection") and to keep a critical distance from it ("analyse the precision"). Since Mulvey comes from a self-confessed uncritically cinephiliac position to one in which her former "good object" becomes a "bad object", it is not surprising that the tension between love and hate is one that characterizes her most famous essay, "Visual Pleasure and Narrative Cinema" (1975). While I will go on to discuss the ubiquitous "gaze", I wish here to foreground what Mulvey herself calls, in the final sentence of the essay, "sentimental regret" (1989: 26). In "Visual Pleasure and Narrative Cinema", Mulvey characterizes the viewer of cinema as being caught within the "patriarchal order" and, in accordance with a certain feminist identity politics, postulates an "alienated subject" (*ibid.*: 16) that exists prior to the establishment of such an order. It is to the possibility of this romantic individual and his or her liberation from that order that the essay is addressed. Mulvey explains that Hollywood, and crucially its visual style (which we can broadly understand as the style expounded by David Bordwell *et al.* [1985]), is to a large extent dedicated to the "skilled and satisfying manipulation of visual pleasure" (Mulvey 1989: 16). There is almost a sense of paranoid joy in the existence of such a paranoid and powerful opponent (and I wonder whether Mulvey's own fascination with the drama of the Oedipal complex is not echoed in her own struggle with Hollywood) and she gleefully writes, adopting the impersonal tone of myth, that: "It is said that analysing pleasure, or beauty, destroys it. That is the intention of this article" (*ibid.*).

Her stated aim in "Visual Pleasure and Narrative Cinema" is not only to analyse the way in which pleasure has been organized and used by Hollywood in the service of patriarchy, but to destroy that pleasure (despite any lingering "sentimental regret" for the enjoyment that cinema had previously afforded), and not only to destroy past pleasure but to "make way for a total negation of the ease and plenitude of the narrative fiction film". This rebellion will transcend "outworn or oppressive forms" and will "conceive a new language of desire" (*ibid.*). This language is to be understood in formal, structural terms, which will then inform the new cinema that is to come. This burnt-earth policy is complicated by Mulvey's own contention that Hollywood is not as straightforwardly monolithic as she makes it appear here, but "Visual Pleasure and Narrative Cinema" should be understood as a polemic rather than as a nuanced argument. For instance, she writes in 1989: "As time passes and the historical gap between the films produced by the studio system and now, I feel that I overemphasized Hollywood's transparency and verisimilitude, and underestimated its *trompe l'oeil* quality and its propensity to flatten the signified into the signifier" (*ibid.*: 250). Mulvey's later position is to try to rescue Hollywood from her own critique.

In *Spectatorship: The Power of Looking On*, Michele Aaron provides a succinct overview of the issues raised in Mulvey's article (2007: 24–35) and summarizes her conclusions usefully as follows:

> One, women cannot be subjects; they cannot own the gaze (read: there is no such thing as a female spectator). Two, men cannot be objects; they cannot be gazed at, they can only look, and only at women (read: there is no such thing as a male spectacle). Three, the only way to evade conclusions one and two, for spectatorship to be liberated from patriarchal ideology, was via a film practice that operated in opposition to narrative cinema.
>
> (*Ibid.*: 34)

Clearly Mulvey hoped that her own films would be a part of this new cinema but it is evident from the continued dominance of "traditional" fiction film that the pleasures that she hoped to destroy keep coming back. Whether this is because the patriarchal system is indeed unbreachable or whether it indicates a flaw in her own argument is something that must be explored further elsewhere. However, I would argue that the fault lies in Mulvey's necessary simplification, which subordinates critical insight to political expediency. Nevertheless, it is clear that "Visual Pleasure and Narrative Cinema" will inevitably be remembered for its formulation of the "male gaze".

THE GAZE AND CURIOSITY

The phrase "male gaze" occurs only twice in "Visual Pleasure and Narrative Cinema" (1989: 19, 22) but has become the shorthand for describing the main point of the essay (undergraduates particularly seem to like referring to "the male gaze theory"). While Mulvey uses a seemingly complex psychoanalytic structure to explain the objectification of women, not only within the narrative but also within the stylistic codes of Hollywood film-making, it strikes me that her use of the term "scopophilia" is given too much weight, since Freud himself never really discusses the idea in much detail (it is not even listed in J. Laplanche and J.-B. Pontalis's definitive *Language of Psychoanalysis* [1973]). While the term "love of looking" makes an expedient link for a discussion centring around cinema, it seems clear that Mulvey is in fact discussing sadism and masochism: the desire to inflict harm or to have harm inflicted on the self. However, using the bridge of "scopophilia", Mulvey quicky arrives at Freud's structure of fetishism, since the "gaze" finds within its object a disquieting lack (the infamous "castration anxiety") and moves beyond this anxiety by, paradoxically, overvaluing (fetishizing) the object, which then, of course, means that the object is once again examined and found wanting, and the circle of anxiety and pleasure continues. Taking issue with her understanding of fetishism, Lorraine Gamman and Merja Makinen argue that Mulvey

> tends to conflate the terms voyeurism and scopophilia with fetishism, and that these terms, at times, appear to be used interchangeably. Mulvey suggests that "scopophilic" pleasure arises principally from using another person as an object of sexual stimulation through sight. Voyeurism and scopophilia for most cinematic viewers rarely replace other forms of sexual stimulation, nor are they preferred to sex itself. Thus these forms of pleasure cannot be encompassed within our definition of fetishism.
>
> (1994: 179)

However, it is not necessary to go down this rather absolutist route around the definition of the fetish in order to say that Mulvey's insight that women tend to be treated as sexualized objects in Hollywood films does not really require the clumsy psychoanalytic mechanism of scopophilia/voyeurism (and Gamman and Makinen go on to say that they feel that Mulvey actually means "objectification" rather than "fetishism"; *ibid.*: 180). Mulvey, however, goes on in her later work to develop her discussion of fetishism in terms of what she calls "curiosity", and I wish to briefly discuss this now.

Curiosity is Mulvey's non-gendered version of fetishism's fraught relationship to knowledge best summed up in Octave Mannoni's formulation: "Je sais bien, mais quand même ..." (I know very well, but all the same ...) (1985: 9–33). Mulvey attempts to move beyond this Freudian paradox by concentrating on the drive to knowledge, which she understands as the desire to solve puzzles and understand enigmas (problematically, perhaps, festishistic disavowal – the act of believing two contradictory elements simultaneously – is itself unsolvable in the traditional sense of arriving at a single conclusion). In *Death 24x a Second*, Mulvey writes that after "Visual Pleasure and Narrative Cinema" she tried

> to evolve an alternative spectator, who was driven, not by voyeurism, but by curiosity and the desire to decipher the screen, informed by feminism and responding to the new cinema of the avant-garde. Curiosity, a drive to see, but also to know, still marked a utopian space for a political, demanding visual culture, but also one in which the process of deciphering might respond to the human mind's long standing interest and pleasure in solving puzzles and riddles. (2006: 191)

Mulvey had expanded on the theme of curiosity, which is also an explanation of her own academic "drive to see", in *Fetishism and Curiosity* (1996) and in what follows I will explicate some of her arguments of this book.[3]

Mulvey argues that "if a society's collective consciousness includes its sexuality, it must also contain an element of collective unconsciousness" (1996: xiii). This leads her to the conclusion that, since she is interested in the cinema's "ability to materialise both fantasy and the fantastic", the cinema is "phantasmagoria, illusion and a symptom of the social unconscious" (*ibid.*: xiv). For Mulvey, then, cinema functions much like the speech of the analysand on the psychoanalyst's couch: what we see on the screen can be interpreted as containing a latent meaning that reflects the desires and problems of that cinema's contemporary society. Mulvey writes:

> Psychoanalytic film theory suggests that mass culture can be interpreted similarly symptomatically. As a massive screen on which collective fantasy, anxiety, fear and their effects can be projected, it speaks the blind-spots of a culture and finds forms that make manifest socially traumatic material, through distortion, defence and disguise. (*Ibid.*: 12)

This understanding of meaning as being on two levels (the conscious and the unconscious) is one that permeates Mulvey's thinking and is fundamental to her understanding of "curiosity".

It is the curious interpreter who is able to read the hidden messages within culture and its products, and so she sees that culture as a "fetish" that hides within itself the truth of its production. She writes, "The 'presence' can only be understood through a process of decoding because the 'covered' material has necessarily been distorted into the symptom" (*ibid.*: xiv). This argument allows Mulvey to conclude: "The fetish is a metaphor for the displacement of meaning behind the representation in history, but fetishisms are also integral to the very process of the displacement of meaning behind representation. My interest here is to argue that the real world exists within its representations" (*ibid.*). There is a problem with the use of the phrase "real world" here.

If there is such a thing as the "real world", the existence of which is manifest only in readings of the representations of that "real world", how would one be sure that one has managed to find the "real" and correct interpretation of those representations and thus be able to claim knowledge of the "real world"? She speaks of the "incontrovertible reality of intense human suffering" and proclaims that "the Gulf War did happen, in spite of what Baudrillard may claim" (*ibid.*: xiv–xv). This anxious call to the real is a reflection of Mulvey's roots in second-wave feminism and the direct action of the women's movement in the 1970s and her own desire to bridge the gap between cinema theory and practice.

It is in this argument that Mulvey refers to a third term that I think is intrinsic to her understanding of interpretation: difficulty. "And over the human tragedy, like a nuclear cloud, hang the difficult to decipher complexities of international politics and economics" (*ibid.*: xv). It is in this difficulty, in the representation's unwillingness to easily provide meaning, in the dream's recalcitrance in the face of the analyst, in cinema's refusal to be unproblematically understood, that Mulvey finds the exhilaration that gives her work its force.

Throughout *Fetishism and Curiosity*, Mulvey uses a number of similes and metaphors – fetishism "like a grain of sand in the oyster that produces the pearl" (*ibid.*: 3) or "The Hollywood cinema of the studio system had as many separate but intermeshed layers as an onion" (*ibid.*: 25) – but the two images to which she constantly returns are those of the carapace and the hieroglyph. The *Oxford English Dictionary* (OED) prosaically defines a carapace as "the upper body-shell of tortoises and of crustaceans", and Mulvey uses this image of a hard outer layer covering an inner "soft" truth as the primary metaphor for femininity and its fetishization. Using Julia Kristeva's definition of abjection and Barbara Creed's later application of this to horror film, Mulvey characterizes the cinema star's "glossy surface" as a "fragile carapace" that

> shares the phantasmatic space of the fetish itself, masking the site of the wound, covering lack with beauty. In the horror genre, it can crack open to reveal its binary opposition when, for instance, a beautiful vampire disintegrates into ancient slime; or in film noir, when the seductive powers of the heroine's beauty mask her destructive and castrating powers.
>
> (*Ibid.*: 13)

Mulvey is especially interested in those moments when the carapace cracks: "When the exterior carapace of feminine beauty collapses to reveal the uncanny, abject maternal body it is as though the fetish itself has failed" (*ibid.*: 14). It is this moment of failure that is fascinating, and it is difficult to tell whether Mulvey feels that that failure is inherent within the structure of the fetish as carapace or whether it is the task of the interpreter, of Mulvey herself, to take up the lobster hammer of critical interpretation and smash open the beautiful object to reveal the putrid interior (as always, extended metaphors seem to lead to rather odd illogical moments, for it is the meat within the crustacean that is white and highly sought after).

The carapace is often aligned with "masquerade", a term that Mulvey uses in her description of Marilyn Monroe in her third chapter, "Close-Ups and Commodities":

Marilyn's image is an ethnic image; her extreme whiteness, her make-up, her peroxide blonde hair bear witness to a fetishisation of race. But its cosmetic, artificial character also bears witness to an element of masquerade. Her image triumphantly creates a spectacle that holds the eye and distracts it from what should not be seen. (*Ibid.*: 48)

Beneath the beauty of the sex goddess lies the dual horror of sexism and racism. This fascination with the hidden abject is continued in "Pandora's Box: Topographies of Curiosity": "The surface is like a beautiful carapace, an exquisite mask. But it is vulnerable. It threatens to crack, hinting that through the cracks might seep whatever the 'stuff' might be that it is supposed to conceal and hold in check" (*ibid.*: 63). Here, Mulvey seems to be implying that the carapace is always on the edge of self-destruction and the cinematic image that comes to my mind is that of the huge insect-like alien covering itself uncomfortably with human skin in *Men in Black* (dir. Barry Sonnenfeld, 1997).

The interior/exterior model explored in *Fetishism and Curiosity* could be explained by a term such as "false consciousness", or even "ideology", and in this sense it can be linked back to Mulvey's preoccupation with the "real". In order to be able to sustain an intellectual project based on the moral worth of interpretive activity, the critic cannot interpret blindly but must have as a goal the elucidation of the "real" and of "truth". This truth lies beneath the carapace created by another (presumably evil) power. Critical activity becomes a crusade against hypocrisy and oppression where the avant-garde (whether it be artistic or interpretive) is the only position from which an attack on the carapace is possible.

It is the importance of interpretation that lies behind Mulvey's other, less frequent, metaphor in *Fetishism and Curiosity*: that of the hieroglyph, one of the meanings of which is "a secret or enigmatical figure" (OED). She writes of three processes that the hieroglyph evokes:

a code of composition, the encapsulation, that is, of an idea in an image at a stage just prior to writing; a mode of address that asks an audience to apply their ability to decipher the poetics of the "screen script"; and, finally, the work of criticism as a means of articulating the poetics that an audience recognises but leaves implicit. (1996: 118)

For Mulvey, the process of the formation of meaning is quite straightforward. There is an idea that exists, which is then translated into a form that demands to be deciphered but which can be properly understood only by a small group of critics who will come and explain to the general public the true message of any "mode of address". This final reading of the hieroglyph would constitute the failure of the fetish and the final cracking of the carapace. Presumably, this explanation of the processes that underpin popular culture and consumer culture in general will have some sort of liberating effect on general society. The problem that faces the critic is difficulty itself.

Mulvey returns to the problematic of difficulty again and again throughout these essays. She writes that:

> it may always be difficult to decipher the place of labour power as the
> source of value. (*Ibid.*: 5)

> A shared sense of addressing a world written in cipher may have drawn
> feminist film critics, like me, to psychoanalytic theory, which has then pro-
> vided a, if not the, means to cracking the codes encapsulated in the "rebus"
> of images of women. (*Ibid.*: 27)

> The enigmatic text [*Citizen Kane*] that then gradually materialises appeals
> to an active, curious, spectator who takes pleasure in identifying, decipher-
> ing and interpreting signs. (*Ibid.*: 99)

In the introduction she writes:

> History is, undoubtedly, constructed out of representations. But these rep-
> resentations are themselves symptoms. They provide clues, not to ultimate
> or fixed meanings, but to sites of social difficulty that need to be deci-
> phered, politically and psychoanalytically ... even though it may be too
> hard, ultimately, to make complete sense of the code. (*Ibid.*: 11)

The difficulty of interpretation would appear to be the ultimate impossibility of combining theory and practice. Mulvey seems to come to the conclusion that reality, while
always the necessary yardstick of interpretation, cannot in the end be understood
through curiosity. It is in her book on *Citizen Kane* that Mulvey explores the pleasures of interpretation for its own sake and ends with the observation that there "are
two retreats possible: *death* and *the womb*" (1992: 83). If we can understand her work
to have been concerned with "the womb" (the origins and interpretation of reality),
perhaps her most recent book deals with the other retreat: death.

In *Death 24x a Second*, Mulvey shifts her attention to the freeze-frame, or the
slowed image, and to the image of death. She explores what she terms the "death drive
movie" (2006: 86) epitomized by *Psycho* and *Viaggio in Italia*. Her ruminations on
C. S. Peirce's semiotic triangle of icon, index and symbol try once again to come to
terms with the relationship between representation and reality and her focus on the
index, which is "a sign produced by the 'thing' it represents" (*ibid.*: 9) like a footprint
or shadow. Here she concentrates on photography more than cinema and is indebted
to Roland Barthes' linking of the photograph with death in *Camera Lucida* (1981).
She also discusses the uncanny at some length. She sums up her project in *Death
24x a Second* thus: "The cinema combines ... two human fascinations: one with the
boundary between life and death and the other with mechanical animation of the
inanimate, particularly the human figure" (2006: 11).

Mulvey is also fascinated by the impact of digital technologies on the moving
image but does not really explore this beyond the analogue possibility of freezing the
image on screen. She formulates two new models of spectatorship – the pensive and
the possessive spectator – but neither of these are fully articulated in any convincing manner. Rather than examining the details of her argument in this book, which

are perhaps even less clearly formulated than in her other episodic works, it may be worth noting Mulvey's rather world-weary tone and her emphasis on death.

The book does, however, contain an essay on the Iranian film-maker Abbas Kiarostami, whose work she terms as a cinema of "uncertainty" and of "delay". For Mulvey, Kiarostami's films appear to be an elegy for cinema itself, which is now in its final death throes. This approach seems uncannily to echo Mulvey's 1970s "negative aesthetics" approach that film as it exists should be destroyed, with only a vague sense of "sentimental regret". It is this emotion that seems to pervade *Death 24x a Second*. Finally, Mulvey cannot reconcile pleasure, or even life, and reality. At this stage of her work reality equals death.

In her afterword to a collection of essays on the new Iranian cinema Mulvey explicitly addresses the issue that her feminist stance in the 1970s is echoed in Islamic censorship of cinema:

> Islamic censorship reflects a social subordination of women and, particularly, an anxiety about female sexuality. But it then produces, as a result, a "difficulty" with the representation of women on the screen which has some – unexpected – coincidence with the problems feminists have raised about the representations of women in the cinema.   (2002: 258)

Mulvey is puzzled by the fact that both oppression and liberation may result in exactly the same aesthetic object and her proposed solution is that it is this puzzlement, this curiosity, this call to "the process of deciphering", that will move us away from being transfixed by "the fascination of the spectacle" (*ibid.*: 261). However, it is difficult not to be left with a certain sense of pessimism.

NOTES

1. Mulvey co-directed the following films with Peter Wollen: *Penthesilea: Queen of the Amazons* (1974), *Riddles of the Sphinx* (1977), *The ELEVENTH HOUR: AMY!* (1980), *Crystal Gazing* (1982), *Frida Kahlo and Tina Modotti* (1982) and *The Bad Sister* (1982). A film on Soviet sculpture, *Disgraced Monuments* (1993), was directed with Mark Lewis. Eleanor Burke provides a brief overview of the films in her biography of Mulvey, "Mulvey, Laura (1941–)", *Screenonline*, www.screenonline.org.uk/people/id/566978/ (accessed August 2009). See also Erika Wolf's review of *Disgraced Monuments* in which Wolf criticizes the film for "the failure to discuss representations of women and works by prominent women sculptors"; "Review: *Disgraced Monuments*", *American Historical Review* **103**(1) (1998), 310.
2. Hollywood's many émigré film-makers, including Sternberg, Billy Wilder, Fritz Lang and Hitchcock (not to mention various non-American stars and other crew), could therefore explain why Hollywood appears to be able to carry out a complex self-criticism during the studio era and beyond. In her book on *Citizen Kane* (directed by the theatrical Welles) Mulvey claims that the film "cuts across conventional Hollywood investment in the visualisation of the feminine" and that it "seems strikingly anti-Hollywood"; *Citizen Kane* (London: BFI, 1992), 16–17.
3. The following section is based on my much longer review essay on the book, "Hieroglyphs and Carapaces: Laura Mulvey's *Fetishism and Curiosity*", *Film-Philosophy* **5**(5) (2001), www.film-philosophy.com/vol5-2001/n5sorfa.html (accessed August 2009).

27 HOMI K. BHABHA

Patricia Pisters

Homi K. Bhabha (b. 1949) was educated at the University of Bombay and the University of Oxford, and is the Director of the Humanities Center at Harvard University and Distinguished Visiting Professor in the Humanities at University College, London. His works include *Nation and Narration* (1990), *The Location of Culture* (1993), *Cosmopolitanism* (co-edited with C. Breckenridge *et al.,* 2002) and *Edward Said* (co-edited with W. J. T. Mitchell, 2005).

When historical visibility has faded, when the present tense of testimony loses its power to arrest, then the displacements of memory and the indirections of art offer us the image of our psychic survival. To live in an unhomely world, to find its ambivalences and ambiguities enacted in the house of fiction, or its sundering and splitting performed in the work of art, is also to affirm a profound desire of social solidarity: I am looking for the join … I want to join … I want to join.   (Bhabha 1994: 27)

In his epistemological work on colonial and postcolonial discourse, cultural translation, hybridity and ambiguity, Homi Bhabha gives a central place to culture. Bhabha refers regularly to literature and (albeit to a lesser extent) to cinema. Speaking from a profoundly humanities perspective, and influenced by Sigmund Freud, Jacques Lacan, Frantz Fanon and Jacques Derrida, Bhabha argues that in a postmodern, postcolonial world, art, including cinema, has a very specific political function to show the underlying structures of thoughts of the relationship between words, stories, images and the world, and to call for social solidarity (Bhabha 2006). Theoretically Bhabha's work has made two important contributions in film studies debates. In the midst of academic discussions on sexual representations in *Screen* theory at the beginnings of the 1980s, Bhabha asked "The Other Question" (1983), looking at ambiguous racist stereotypes. And a few years later, in the context of the revival of questions of Third Cinema, Bhabha introduced the notion of Third Space and emphasized a "Commitment to Theory" (1989). In this essay I shall look at these two key interventions of Bhabha in film-theoretical debates by referring regularly to filmic examples and by thus reconstructing a narrative of Bhabha's key concepts. I shall argue that these concepts are particularly relevant for contemporary globalized image culture.

ECHOES IN THE KERNEL OF COLONIAL DISCOURSE

In October 2001 Homi Bhabha gave a video conference at the Documenta 11 in the House of Cultures in Berlin (Bhabha 2001). Because of security measures after the 9/11 attacks Bhabha was unable to travel outside the United States. Obviously affected by the terrible events, he starts his lecture by drawing attention to the underlying political narrative of the clash of civilizations, also expressed in many Hollywood terrorist action films that framed the event, and by calling for other political narratives that can provide us with lessons of empathies. These other narratives, according to Bhabha, are best learned from the colonized and enslaved worlds. He makes a strong case for seeing contemporary globalization in conflictual contiguity with colonization, slavery and diaspora, which are all earlier forms of globalization. Bhabha refers to Allan Sekula's *Fish Story* series of photographs, showing harbours with container ships full of global goods in transnational movements that relate obliquely to the deadly directions of the global economy of illegal immigrants and asylum seekers.[1] These unequal and unjust relations, Bhabha argues, are the antagonisms of the global world that have to be thought as agonizing continuations of old regimes of power rather than in terms of great dialectics of social and political contradictions.[2] This conflictual contiguity is the reason why, throughout his work, Bhabha frequently refers to colonial history and colonial discourse. Therefore, before introducing Bhabha's intervention into film-theoretical debates, I shall start retracing Bhabha's main concepts and thoughts by looking at another important text on colonial discourse from *The Location of Culture*.

In the chapter "Articulating the Archaic: Cultural Difference and Colonial Nonsense", Bhabha is concerned with cultural difference and how colonialism dealt with cultural difference at those moments when meaning got lost in translation or even never reached translation (1994: 175–98). Bhabha's starting-points are events described in colonial literature where meaning starts to collapse and that witness "an uncertain colonial silence that mocks the social performance of language with their non-sense; that baffles the communicable verities of culture with their refusal to translate" (*ibid.*). In E. M. Forster's novel *A Passage to India* (1924), Bhabha's main reference in this article, the echo in the Marabar Caves is the "primal scene" for such a non-sensical moment. The story of *A Passage to India* starts when two English ladies, Mrs Moore and her daughter-in-law-to-be Adela Quested, arrive in India in the mid 1920s and are shocked by the racism of the English elite. They try to connect to the Indian people and are invited by Dr Aziz, an Indian doctor, to a picnic at the mysterious Marabar Caves. Here the central non-sensical scene takes place, when Adele gets confusingly overwhelmed by a cave's echo right after she walks into the caves with Aziz. I shall return to this scene, but for now it is important to see that the echo of the cave turns every sound into a non-sensical sound: "Boum, ouboum is the sound as far as the human alphabet can express it" (Forster, quoted in Bhabha 1994: 176). "Boum, ouboum" expresses the loss of meaningfulness in cross-cultural interpretations.

Bhabha relates this scene to Lacanian alienation of the Subject in the Other, who can never be known entirely and is always based on a kernel of non-sense, mystery and ambiguity (which makes the Other at the same time strangely unfamiliar and desirable). This position of undecidability and confusion of the "ouboum echo" in the caves in *A Passage to India* is foreshadowed in an earlier scene, where Adela, freshly arrived in Chandrapore, discovers by accident the hidden ruins of ancient temples in the tropical forest. In the very faithful and much-acclaimed filmic adaptation of *A Passage to India* (1984), director David Lean breathtakingly shows how Adela is fascinated by the erotic postures of the God-statues that we see as her points of view. Her face tells us she is deeply affected and confused by these statues as she begins to discover the sexuality within herself. Then all of a sudden a group of monkeys discovers her and aggressively chases her away. Shocked and scared, Adela gets away and returns home. In an earlier scene she had announced to her English fiancé that she would *not* marry him; now she suddenly changes her mind and asks for his protection in marriage. In an allegorical way the scene shows how confusingly desire and fear operate in colonial discourse in order to sustain the colonial order.

The cave scene shows a similar ambiguity between desire and normative cultural codes. During their climb to the caves Adela starts asking questions about Aziz's wife and love life; she clearly finds Aziz attractive (and conveys her desire to him). Aziz is clearly shocked by her questioning and needs some time to get himself together. Adela thinks of her own loveless engagement with her English fiancé that she has just agreed on (binding her to normative cultural codes). When Adela enters one of the caves she gets frightened, as in the earlier temple/monkey scene. In the next scene we see her in panic running downhill. Back with the English, she seems to hallucinate (she complains of an echo in her head) and accuses Aziz of sexual assault. It is only in court that she acknowledges that she actually does not know what happened in the cave, thus clearing Aziz of the charges against him, a deed that is considered by the English as a betrayal of her race. This rare and courageous acknowledgement of undecidability and not knowing the truth (or the sense) of an event is an example of a general (but mostly disavowed) epistemological structure in colonial discourse that Bhabha describes as "the enunciatory disorder of the colonial present … [that] lies in the staging of the colonial signifier in the narrative uncertainty of culture's in-between: between sign and signifier, neither one nor the other, neither sexuality nor race, neither simply, memory nor desire" (1994: 180).

The "in-between" in this quote should not be regarded as a dialectic synthesis or higher merging between two oppositions, but should be understood as a Derridean *entre* that "sows confusion between opposites and stands between oppositions at once. The colonial signifier … is an act of ambivalent significations, literally splitting the difference between the binary oppositions or polarities through which we think cultural difference" (*ibid.*: 182). In this sense Bhabha is not saying that in the echo of the cave the oppositions between the English and Indians become confused and are therefore sublated. According to the Derridean implications of the "in-between", the "ouboum" that confuses the opposition between the English and the Indians at the same time sustains them. It is this uncertainty at the heart of the colonial project, the uncanny and traumatic problem of the untranslatable that haunts cultural authority time and again, that Bhabha distinguishes as one of the legacies of colonial discourse that in contemporary global culture is still operative. I shall return to this point at the end of the chapter.

AMBIVALENCE OF COLONIAL STEREOTYPES

Bhabha's seminal article "The Other Question", which appeared in *Screen* in 1983, introduces his ideas on colonial discourse and knowledge construction into film-theoretical debates. Following Laura Mulvey's "Visual Pleasure and Narrative Cinema" (1975), film-theoretical debates focused for a large part on questions of gender and sexuality. In "The Other Question", Bhabha introduces his particular angle on the emerging debates on race, colonialism and cinema in screen theory.[3] Bhabha again emphasizes the importance of recognizing ambiguity and confusion at the heart of colonial discourse but here he focuses on racist stereotypes: "the stereotype [is] an ambivalent mode of knowledge and power". One should not understand the stereotype normatively as negative or positive, nor as a fixed and secure point of reference, Bhabha argues, but as "the process of subjectification made possible (and plausible) through stereotypical discourse" (1994: 95).

Methodologically, Bhabha performs a deconstructive reading against the grain of several (film-)theoretical texts in order to articulate more sharply notions of differences of race. Stephen Heath's (1975) analysis of Orson Welles's *Touch of Evil* (1958) is Bhabha's first reference. He draws attention to the elements in Heath's analysis of the structuration of the Mexican/US border that generated the least attention, namely its racial implications and the issue of cultural differences.[4] Bhabha highlights an underdeveloped passage in Edward Said's *Orientalism* (1978) that indicates the relationship between racism and sexuality. Inspired then by Fanon and Freud, Bhabha proposes to see the stereotype in terms of fetishism. Acknowledging the obvious differences between the sexual fetish (disavowing something "invisible") and the racial or epidermic fetish (always visible), Bhabha emphasizes the relationship between fantasy/desire and subjectification/power in colonial discourse. Just as the sexual fetish facilitates sexual relations by disavowing sexual difference, the racist stereotype also "facilitates colonial relations, and sets up a discursive form of racial and cultural oppositions in terms of which colonial power is exercised" (1994: 112). The racist stereotype, however, is not based on disavowal value; it has knowledge value. Colonial discourse needs discrimination and the constant recognition of difference in order to create a certain type of knowledge that justifies the colonial system. Freud's assertion that fetishism provides a form of knowledge that "allows for the possibility of simultaneously embracing two contradictory beliefs, one official and one secret" is important to Bhabha (*ibid.*: 115). It explains how knowledge and fantasy, power and pleasure, are so profoundly connected to the visual regime of colonial discourse.

One can look again at *A Passage to India* and see how stereotypes function here. Considering the portrayal of Aziz, it is very clear that he embodies mixed stereotypical beliefs. On the one hand he is seen as a most dignified and docile colonized subject who adapts to the customs and rules of the English. On the other hand Aziz *has* to be accused of sexual harassment because that provides affirmation of the stereotype of the dangerous and sexually uncontrollable black man, which is needed to sustain the colonial authority. In fact, the outcome of the trial was already decided by the English regime before it even started. Hence the subversive and "betraying" act of Adela to withdraw her accusations. Many other examples could be given. And since stereotypes operate so much within the visual regime, Bhabha's intervention has been important for the critical development of postcolonial film studies.

POLITICS AND THEORY: THIRD CINEMA AND THIRD SPACE

Another contribution that Bhabha has made in film-theoretical debates is his contribution to the Edinburgh "Third Cinema Conference" (1986). In "The Commitment to Theory" (1989), Bhabha warns against a certain rejection of theory among the participants of the conference on political militant cinema: "[It is said that] theory is necessarily the elite language of the socially and culturally privileged. It is said that the place of the academic critic is inevitably within the Eurocentric archives of an imperialistic or neo-colonial West" (1989: 111).[5] Bhabha strongly argues against this binarism of (European) theory versus (developing world) politics and activism. According to Bhabha it is precisely a politics of *cultural* production (such as cinema) that gives depth to and extends the domain of "politics" in other directions than only social and economic forces. Beyond the simplistic opposition of the West and the developing world, Bhabha draws attention to the complex and uneven interplays between developed and developing worlds. The West has great symbolic capital, as is clear from the example of an Indian film that wins a Western film festival, which then opens up distribution facilities in India (*ibid.*: 113). But this does not mean the West and India have a pure oppositional relationship. Rather, this relationship should be seen as a process of (often agonizing and traumatic) negotiations.

In a similar vein, theory and political action are not opposed, but are mutually implicated. In the first place this is because the textuality of theory is not "simply a second-order ideological expression or a verbal symptom of a pre-given political subject" (*ibid.*: 115). Rather, the political subject should be seen as a discursive event that emerges in writing and political enunciation. As with the "non-sense" in colonial discourse and the ambivalence of stereotypes, Bhabha emphasizes the fantasmatic ambivalence of the text that infuses the political fact. So for Bhabha the oppositions between appearance and reality, fantasmatic and factual, theory and practice, are false oppositions. They are always already mutually implicated in a process of negotiation. Bhabha calls this the temporality of negotiation and translation. This temporality, to which I shall return in the next paragraphs more elaborately, has two important implications signalled by Bhabha:

> First, it acknowledges the historical connectedness between the subject and object of critique so that there can be no simplistic, essentialist opposition between ideological miscognition and revolutionary truth. ... [Secondly,] the function of theory within the political process becomes double-edged. It makes us aware that our political referents and priorities – the people, the community, class struggle, anti-racism, gender difference, the assertion of an anti-imperialist, black or third perspective – are not "there" in some primordial, naturalistic sense. Nor do they reflect a unitary or homogeneous political object. They "make sense" as they come to be constructed

in the discourses of feminism or Marxism or the Third cinema or whatever, whose objects of priority – class or sexuality or "the new ethnicity"
(Stuart Hall) – are always in historical and philosophical tension, or cross-
reference with other objectives.   (*Ibid.*: 118)

All these different political groups come into being, or make sense in the discourses they construct in relation to specific historical and philosophical references.
Each political position, Bhabha argues, is always a process of translation and transference of meaning. No position can claim a natural and timeless truth. And it is this
emphasis on the construction of discourses that is the main contribution of theory's
vigilance that "never allows a simple identity between the political objective (not
object) and its means of representation" (*ibid.*: 119). Bhabha is thus concerned with
the knowledge that emerges in the encounter between theory and politics. Theory
cannot claim a meta-position that presents a more general or total view, nor is it an
elitist perspective outside the political. Rather, it is an actor in the process of negotiation and translation that is never closed, finished or total.

The most important theoretical concept that Bhabha proposes in "The Commitment
to Theory" is the concept of the Third Space of enunciation, "which represents both
the general conditions of language and the specific implication of the utterance in
a performative and institutional strategy of which it cannot 'in itself' be conscious"
(*ibid.*: 129). This Third Space makes meaning an ambivalent process, not a fixed reference. Third Space in itself is not representable; it is not an actual space, but it is caused
by the openness of signs, symbols and culture that can be "appropriated, translated,
rehistoricised, and read anew" (*ibid.*: 130). It is a space of hybridity in and between
cultural differences. Going back to *A Passage to India* once more, we can now see how
it is precisely the confusing and traumatic moment of the echo in the cave that allows
for appropriation, first by the hegemonic discourse of the English, who want to make
sense of this scene by fixing Aziz in the stereotypical place of the sexually uncontrollable Other. But as Adela re-opens the meaning of the mystery of the cave by acknowledging that she does not know what happened, new meaning can be assigned to it
and the Indian population turns it into a discourse of victory and possible change. In
respect to questions of Third Cinema, Bhabha has clearly given theory a new place,
beyond the oppositions between theory and political practice, showing that meaning
is always a site of struggle, traumatic negotiation and open transference of meaning,
precisely in the act of filming and the (theoretical) production of discourses.

"GHOST STORIES" ON THE NATIONAL SCREEN

As one reads Bhabha's work in total, one is struck by the meticulous coherence of
his system of thought. It is as if every article or chapter develops another piece of his
reasoning, but always connected to his main principle of cultural difference and the
ambiguity of signification and cultural authority. In "The Commitment to Theory"
Bhabha indicated that in the process of enunciation there is a split between two different types of time: on the one hand, the traditional cultural demand for a fixed

model, tradition and stable references (mythical time); on the other hand, the space for negotiating new cultural demands, changes, resistances (time of undecidability, time of liberation). Bhabha develops this idea of "double time" with respect to the idea of the modern nation in his article "DissemiNation" (1994: 199–244). Here Bhabha moves from colonial discourse and the imperial situation to the condition of migration and diaspora in postcolonial nation states. Obviously Bhabha plays here in Derridean fashion with the word DissemiNation, completely in line with his argument that the homogeneous narrative of the modern Western nation is displaced and "disseminated" by other narratives, narratives from the marginalized, migrants and minorities.

The nation is constructed in a double time, a double act of writing that splits the national subject. There is a homogeneous time of a pedagogy of the nation that narrates and signifies the people as a historical sedimentation. But at the same time the nation has to construct it itself time and again from the patches of daily life in the performance of the narrative in the present. This performative "introduces a temporality of the 'in-between'" (*ibid*.: 212). This double temporality of pedagogy and performance of the nation creates a space where minority discourses emerge (*ibid*.: 222). Bhabha refers to the Black Audio and Film Collective's *Handsworth Songs* (dir. John Akomfrah, 1986) to indicate how a film can function as a performative act that questions the pedagogy of the nation. Dealing with the riots of 1985 in the Handsworth district of Birmingham in England, the film is, according to Bhabha's analysis, haunted by two moments: "the arrival of the migrant population in the 1950s, and the emergence of a black British people in diaspora" (*ibid*.: 223). The film can be considered as a Third Cinema film that aims at raising cultural and political awareness of British minorities. The archival footage of the arrival of migrants, full of hope and singing the English national anthem, introduces itself between the pedagogical narrative of the sedimented nation and the contemporary reality of the migrant's minority position. Images of the riots of 1985 demonstrate how times change and how the riots contain "the ghosts of other stories" that are hidden within the national narrative (*ibid*.: 224).

The homogeneous time of the pedagogy of the nation entails a huge "effort" of forgetting, the forgetting of the real origins of the narrative of the Western nation, which excludes the violence of imperialism and the role of "Others" in the creation of the nation. It excludes the fact that large parts of the history of the nation happened overseas, outside the territory of the nation itself. It is impossible here not to refer to another film that precisely raises the ghosts of other stories in the homogenized image of the nation, Michael Haneke's *Caché* (Hidden; 2005). The film has been widely discussed and commented on, but in connection to Bhabha's concept of the double time of the nation it is striking to see how this film is almost a literal act of ghostly repetition and doubling of time, expressed at the level of the image. The coherent life of the French bourgeois television presenter and actress is profoundly disturbed by the anonymous video recordings of their house they receive in their mailbox, which literally doubles the filmed image of their house with the more ghostly video recordings of it. In the search for the sender of these images, the largely forgotten or disavowed history of the Algerian War of Independence emerges.

Bhabha ends his essay on the double time of the nation by referring to Salman Rushdie's evocation of the English weather in the *Satanic Verses*: "The trouble with the English was ... in a word ... their weather" (quoted in Bhabha 1994: 242). Bhabha explains that the English weather with its notorious rain is the most changeable and immanent sign of national difference. It evokes England, but also "revives memories of its demonic double: the heat and dust of India" (*ibid.*). In that sense *Handsworth Songs* tropicalizes London. And is it also obvious that the English rain at both the beginning and end of *A Passage to India* is closely connected to the heath in India as an allegory of the double temporal inscriptions of the nation.

AGENCY IN THE PERFORMATIVE SPACE OF CINEMA

The double time of the nation raises the question of agency from a minority perspective. This question is addressed in "The Postcolonial and the Postmodern" (1994: 245–82), where Bhabha reformulates and extends the times of pedagogy and performance of the nation into a temporality of Casablanca and a temporality of Tangiers. Bhabha now looks at the transformation of the notion of time itself, rather than at the narrative of the nation as in "DissemiNation":

> To reconstitute the discourse of cultural difference demands not simply a change of cultural contents and symbols; a replacement within the same time-frame of representation is never adequate. It requires a radical revision of the social temporality in which emergent histories may be written, the rearticulation of the "sign" in which cultural identities may be inscribed. (*Ibid.*: 246)

Bhabha emphasizes the importance of culture as a strategy of survival and argues that this strategy is both transnational and translational. It is transnational because contemporary discourses are rooted in specific histories of cultural displacements of various sorts (imperial, slavery, migratory, exilic). It is translational because such dynamic histories make the question of how culture signifies, certainly in times of global media communication, a complex matter.

In order the address these questions of transnationality and translationality, Bhabha refers to Roland Barthes' visits to Tangiers. Tangiers was very instructive for the white French semiotician because it enabled him to open up hegemonic language (French) for transnational and translational revisions. Bhabha recalls how Barthes describes his Tangiers experience: "Half-asleep on a banquette in a bar, of which Tangiers is the exemplary site, Barthes attempts to 'enumerate the stereophony of languages within earshot': music, conversations, chairs, glasses, Arabic, French", when suddenly he feels how the sentence is opened up with the carnality of the voice and the incomprehensibility of language (*ibid.*: 258). "I was myself a public place, a souk; words, small syntagmas, bits of formulations, and no sentence could be formed" (Barthes 1979: 79, my trans.). This is what Barthes calls "the outside of the sentence" and what Bhabha renames the "temporality of Tangiers", a temporality that is changing and open, full of ambiguities.

Bhabha contrasts this temporality of Tangiers with the temporality of Casablanca, for which he refers not so much to the city itself as, significantly, to the film *Casablanca* (dir. Michael Curtiz, 1942): "In Casablanca the passage of time preserves the identity of language; the possibility of naming over time is fixed in the repetition. ... 'Play it again, Sam' which is perhaps the Western world's most celebrated demand for repetition, is still an invocation to similitude, a return to eternal verities" (Bhabha 1994: 261). Casablanca could be seen as a sign for a nostalgic time of the pedagogy of the nation; Tangiers is the sign of the "non-sense", the sign that marks the "time-lag" between the event of the sign itself and its discursive eventuality (*ibid.*: 263). In the space of this time-lag, negotiations of meaning and agency are possible. By referring to Hannah Arendt's concept of the intersubjective space of "human inter-est" that are opened by this temporality of Tangiers, Bhabha sees the possibility for agency: "When the sign ceases the synchronous flow of the symbol, it also seizes the power to elaborate – through the time-lag – new and hybrid agencies and articulations. This is the moment for revisions" (*ibid.*: 275).

Elsewhere I have elaborated on these moments of revision by analysing filmic representations of Tangiers in a double time structure, demonstrating that the time of Casablanca structures nostalgic filmic discourses about the city as international zone. And a temporality of Tangiers can be discovered in both Third Cinema films about boat refugees that hide in Tangiers harbour and the films of French film-maker André Téchiné.[6] Here I would like to look once more at *A Passage to India* and see whether this film allows agency in a temporality of Tangiers. Clearly, the time of Casablanca is present in the rules and traditions of the English, which are set up to remain eternally the same, keeping the same structures of power and pleasure in place. It is with the arrival of Mrs Moore and Adela Quested that (both symbolically and effectively) a different temporal order is introduced into the imperial nation. Tangiers-like, Mrs Moore and Adela question the lack of intersubjective encounters and inter-est in the Indian people. Mrs Moore opens up this intersubjective space by talking as a friend to Aziz and inviting him to the English club, and Adela by grasping Aziz's hand (in close-up in the film) to climb the rocks. These are moments of transformation of temporalities where India is no longer a fixed signified but becomes openly (and no longer deeply disavowed and hidden) a much more ambiguous space. I have already indicated how on the part of Adela this leads to a moment of "non-sense" and an echo in her head. This confusing moment where signification is suspended is immediately appropriated by the English to re-install the time of Casablanca. But it also opens up the possibilities of agency on the part of the Indians, since it is from now on that the Independence Movement becomes more prominent in the film, which eventually leads to Aziz's empowerment as an Indian, instead of as a colonized subject.

FROM POSTCOLONIAL HYBRIDITY TO GLOBAL AMBIVALENCE

In November 2007, Bhabha gave a lecture "On Global Ambivalence" in the Van Abbe Museum in Eindhoven, the Netherlands. Here Bhabha directly addressed global image culture. Concerned about the omnipresence of the image, he asked how it is possible to make distinctions in the vast wall of information that keeps on disappearing and yet makes an intervention (Bhabha 2007). In line with his assertion in Berlin that contemporary culture has to be seen in conflictual contiguity with earlier structures of colonial and postcolonial discourse, Bhabha emphasizes once more the ambivalent moments in culture that ask for critical reflection and commitment in both theoretical and political senses. But yet again, his focus has slightly shifted. Bhabha's concern is now more clearly related to image culture and its relation to memory and memory sites. A personal experience that Bhabha shared with the audience in Eindhoven is very telling of his position. During a visit to the Nuremberg fields in Germany, now completely empty and overgrown with weeds, Bhabha noticed that in this empty space the memories of several films started to replay in his mind; *Judgment at Nuremberg* (dir. Stanley Kramer, 1961) and *Brutalität in Stein* (Brutality in stone; dirs Alexander Kluge & Peter Schamoni, 1961), which he saw many years before in Bombay, brought back the question of the "banality of evil" and resuscitated the voices of Hitler and Himmler. Cultural memory, particularly cinema in this case, exceeds the historical event.

Bhabha has always emphasized the role (location) of culture, but now that everything is immediately translated into images or other digital codes, this fact becomes even more pertinent, complex and full of ambivalences that have to be acknowledged. On the one hand contemporary image culture provides us with an endless digital hall of mirrors and pictures that never go away (Bhabha refered in his lecture to the images of Abu Ghraib in particular), and on the other hand these images call for an ethics of memory, as the cultural sites of memory in image culture are increasingly ambiguous. As there were in colonial and postcolonial times, Bhabha argues for alternative spaces of narration and revisions and for the "right to narrate".

But Bhabha's earlier concepts on colonial and postcolonial discourse are also relevant for globalized media culture. The insistence on a kernel of "non-sense" and "untranslatability" in intercultural relationships should warn us of too simple translations of one discourse into the other. For instance, Western media emphasize the Western values of democracy and freedom of speech and treat them as transparent fixed values. On the one hand, this leads to unbridgeable gaps in creating sensitivities to other political and cultural situations, and on the other hand, this same ambiguity of the terms leads to perverse appropriations of the freedom of speech translated into a political right to insult.[7]

Bhabha's analysis of the ambivalent and double function of stereotypes is just as important today as in colonial discourse. Minorities and (illegal) immigrants are still discriminated and stereotyped in order to sustain certain empowering "knowledges" and justify government policies. And these stereotypes are increasingly created and sustained in images that travel in ever growing quantities and speed across the globe. The temporality of Tangiers that allowed for the revision of history and the re-inscription of subaltern agency in postcolonialism is a process that is continuing in contemporary globalized media culture, where the fight between "Casablanca" (the myth of eternal origins) and "Tangiers" (transformations) is continuous in all societies.

One could argue that in contemporary image culture the internet, and especially YouTube, has become a sort of symbolic Third Space, where meanings are constantly negotiated and translated into all kinds of other meanings. If Third Space is fundamentally open, it implies that meaning can be transferred in all kinds of directions, not only between the colonial and the colonized, but between many different enunciatory positions and meanings. But this does not mean that everything becomes meshed in a hybrid, happy common space, as the concepts of hybridity have often been considered in critiques on Bhabha's postmodernism.[8] Things are more complicated and agonizing. Bhabha has always emphasized that the synthetic "merging" view of developed and developing world encounters does not correspond to his ideas. Bhabha is concerned to show how culture is a contested location: an ambivalent place that is open for complex and often agonizing negotiations in which balances are not even and pleasure and power always play confusing roles.

Although Bhabha's conception of cinema is part of a much larger field of artistic cultural interventions, he has made several important theoretical contributions to film-theoretical debates, drawing attention to the ambiguous process of signification in colonial and postcolonial discourses. In today's audio-visual culture his ideas seem all the more important; his continuing call for theoretical reflections from a humanities perspective, especially, seems of a much larger significance. As he argues, scholarly knowledge is not in opposition to the world, but

> through a process of conceptualization the empirical world comes to be represented in linguistic signs, scientific formulae, resonant symbols, or digital images. Humanists reflect as much on these processes of mediation as on the outcome of knowledge. They draw attention to the frames, maps, or tables with which we construct our access to reality at one remove.
>
> (Bhabha 2006)

The location of cinema as one of the most influential art forms in contemporary globalized media culture, but also as the basis for political activism of all sorts, asks for reflection on its ambivalent implications for cultural knowledge and strategies of survival.

NOTES

1. In the introduction to *The Location of Culture* (London: Routledge, 1994), 11, Bhabha also refers to *Fish Story*.
2. Bhabha's concept of dialectic seems to be always very Hegelian in that he conceives it as great contradictions that lead to a teleological synthesis. At several instances, such as in this lecture, Bhabha rejects this kind of dialectic. However, as Fredric Jameson has argued, there are several ways of defining dialectics and Bhabha does seem to be dialectic in a Marxist sense, in that he favours a logic of (changeable) situation or historicity, that he looks for alternative historical narratives and emphasizes antagonist views instead of a unified story, looks for material grounding of analysis and finally aims to "transform the present into future"; X. Zhang, "Marxism and the Historicity of Dialectics: An Interview with Fredric Jameson", *New Literary History* **29**(3) (1998), 353–83.
3. Bhabha's "The Other Question: Stereotype, Discrimination and the Discourse of Colonialism" is reprinted in his *The Location of Culture*, 94–120. Page references are to this edition.
4. The main reading of the border is directed by feminist discourse, to see it as a struggle between the Ideal Father and the Phallic Mother, with Susan as a "good object" that delivers Vargas from his racial mixedness.
5. Bhabha's "The Commitment to Theory" is reprinted in *The Location of Culture* , 28–56. References are to the version in *Questions of Third Cinema*, J. Pines & P. Willemen (eds), 111–32 (London: BFI, 1989), which addresses explicitly the conference context.

6. See my "Filming the Times of Tangier: Nostalgia, Postcolonial Agency and Preposterous History", in *Cinema at the Periphery: Industries, Narratives, Iconography*, D. Iordonova, D. Martin-Jones & B. Vidal (eds) (Detroit, MI: Wayne State University Press, forthcoming) for an elaborate analysis of cinematographic temporalities of Tangiers.

7. I am referring here to the Dutch situation, where an extreme right-wing politician claims the right to make a *film* about the fascistic nature of the Koran.

8. Marjory Perloff, for instance, gives a typical example of this type of critique: "In its general outlines, Bhabha's hybridity paradigm has enormous appeal: we want to believe, after all, that the postcolonial location is one where the binary opposition of oppressor and oppressed, male and female, master and victim, has become irrelevant, that the new playing field is one of performative contestation rather than ethnic or national separation and rivalry"; "Cultural Liminality/Aesthetic Closure? The 'Interstitial Perspective' of Homi Bhabha", *Literary Imagination: The Review of the Association of Literary Scholars and Critics* **1**(1) (Spring 1999), 109–25, www.epc.buffalo.edu/authors/perloff/bhabha.html (accessed August 2009).

28 SLAVOJ ŽIŽEK

Laurence Simmons

Slavoj Žižek was born in 1949 in Ljubljana, Slovenia. He was a candidate for the presidency of the Republic of Slovenia in 1990. He is the founder and president of the Society for Theoretical Psychoanalysis, Ljubljana. Žižek was a visiting professor at the Department of Psychoanalysis, the University of Paris VIII in 1982–3 and 1985–6; the Centre for the Study of Psychoanalysis and Art, SUNY Buffalo, in 1991–2; the Department of Comparative Literature, University of Minnesota, Minneapolis, in 1992; Tulane University, New Orleans, in 1993; Cardozo Law School, New York, in 1994; Columbia University, New York, in 1995; Princeton University in 1996; the New School for Social Research, New York, in 1997; the University of Michigan, Ann Arbor, in 1998; and Georgetown University, Washington, in 1999. He is a returning faculty member of the European Graduate School. He is a prolific author. His works include *For they Know Not What they Do* (1991), *Enjoy Your Symptom!* (1992), *Everything you Always Wanted to Know About Lacan (But were Afraid to Ask Hitchcock)* (1992), *Tarrying with the Negative* (1993), *The Metastases of Enjoyment* (1994), *The Ticklish Subject* (1999), *The Fragile Absolute* (2000), *The Art of the Ridiculous Sublime* (2000), *The Fright of Real Tears* (2001), *The Neighbor* (2006), *The Parallax View* (2006) and *In Defense of Lost Causes* (2007).

We need the excuse of a fiction to stage what we really are.
(Slavoj Žižek, in The Pervert's Guide to Cinema
[dir. Sophie Fiennes, 2005])

Would you allow this guy to take your daughter to a movie? Of course not. [*Laughs*]
(Ibid.)

LOST HIGHWAY

One of the early sequences of Sophie Fiennes's film *The Pervert's Guide to Cinema* (2006) opens with Slovenian cultural analyst and philosopher Slavoj Žižek dressed in a yellow shirt, sitting a little uncomfortably at the helm of a motorized dingy, which, he declares, is floating in the middle of Bodega Bay, the location for Alfred Hitchcock's film *The Birds* (1963). The sequence then cuts back and forth between scenes from

The Birds and Žižek's animated explanations of how the Oedipal tensions between the central character Mitch (Rod Taylor) and his mother underpin an explanation of why the birds inexplicably attack; they are, he suggests, "raw incestuous energy". A little later, with the outboard engine now running, relaxing into his role, Žižek turns to the camera and declares: "You know what I am thinking now? I am thinking like Melanie, I am thinking I want to fuck Mitch". This sequence of Fiennes's film illustrates the almost perfect conflation of "Žižek the person" with "Žižek the scholar" and now "Žižek the film star". The characteristic frenzy of his tics and spasms, the wild gesticulations of his hands and tugging at his beard, the ever-increasing circles of sweat widening under his arms, his strong Central European accent in English, and above all his outrageous and unselfconscious bad taste in jokes and examples, scatological as well as sexual, all translate directly into print and now on to screen. On screen we have a sense of the unrestrained energy of Žižek's published ideas, which rush ahead of themselves and frenetically dissipate into a web of disseminated connections, of what Robert Boynton calls a "trademark synthesis of philosophical verve and rhetorical playfulness" (1998: 42–3). Žižek the film star also plays to the marketing on the back covers of his books – "The Elvis of Cultural Theory" and "An academic rock star"[1] – and to Žižek the global academic, who is feted on the international academic conference circuit, has run for the office of President of Slovenia, written copy for the catalogue of American outfitters Abercrombie and Fitch, collaborated with experimental punk rock band Laibach and has featured in no fewer than five films.

However, among many film theorists Žižek's status as film critic (and film star) is that of a clown: the Charlie Chaplin of film theory! This is not only the result of his distinctive personality but also the product of his prolific writing, which employs the thrust of "cut and paste"; articles, essays, chapters, bad jokes and film examples get re-used time and time again, forcing his reader to tease out a philosophical argument from among the asides and at times dubious vignettes.[2] Indeed, towards the end of another documentary, *Žižek!* (dir. Astra Taylor, 2005), in which he also stars, Žižek himself wonders in a psychoanalytic vein whether the attempts to turn him into a figure of fun may represent in fact a deep resistance to taking him seriously.

Most film critics have been scathing of what they see as Žižek's utilitarian plundering in a "machinic" fashion of, in the main, Hollywood feature films to advance and illustrate aspects of his Marxist and psychoanalytical theoretical project. His references to film, it is consistently argued, are merely incidental illustrations, which show little concern for or interest in the fundamental basics of film study.[3] We might cite the only one of Žižek's monographs dedicated to an individual film as such, *The Art of the Ridiculous Sublime* (2000b), on David Lynch's *Lost Highway* (1997), as a case in point since it fails to address significant aspects of the film text in favour of an extended exploration of the Lacanian position on fantasy. About one-third into *Lost Highway* the protagonist, Fred (Bill Pullman), who has been sentenced to death for the murder of his unfaithful wife, Renée (Patricia Arquette), inexplicably transforms into another person, Pete (Balthazar Getty), in his prison cell. It is a transformation from the dull, drab existence of the impotent husband with a mousy non-communicative wife to the exciting and dangerous life of the young virile Pete, who is seduced by the sexually aggressive femme fatale blond reincarnation of Renée named Alice and uncannily played by the same actress. The problem of the film is: how are we to understand this inexplicable ("unreal") transformation? We can understand it, suggests Žižek, not through any exploration of a formal distinctiveness but by understanding the film as an illustration of the Lacanian notion of "traversing the fantasy", the re-avowal of subjective responsibility that comes at the end of the psychoanalytic cure. *Traversing the fantasy* means the recognition that in the long term, Žižek argues, in order to avoid a clash of fantasies we have to acknowledge that fantasy functions merely to screen the abyss or inconsistency in the Other, and we must cease positing that the Other has stolen the "lost" object of our desire. In "traversing" or "going through" the fantasy all we have to do is experience how there is nothing "behind" it, and how fantasy masks precisely this "nothing". In *Lost Highway*, Lynch achieves resolution of the contradiction by staging two solutions one after the other on the same level: Renée is destroyed, killed, punished; Alice eludes the control of the male protagonist and disappears triumphantly along the lost highway.

THE PARALLAX VIEW

One of the most sustained criticisms of Žižek's (lack of) film criticism has come from veteran cognitivist and post-theorist David Bordwell (2005), who attacks Žižek with the charge of fundamentally lacking responsibility to scholarly process and serious engagement with the nuts and bolts of film studies. This attack is prompted in no small part by Žižek's scathing, and far wittier, dismantling of post-theory in the opening pages of his only complete "film book", *The Fright of Real Tears* (2001), before he offers, through analysis of the films of Krzysztof Kieślowski, the alternative of a later Lacanian reading of the film text's organization of enjoyment. Of course, such oppositions, deconstructionists versus cognitivists or Lacanians versus post-theorists, are dialectical, and Žižek's understanding and exploitation of dialectics underpins his entire project. However, Žižek rereads the traditional dialectical process of Hegel in a more radical fashion. In Žižek's version, the dialectic does not produce a resolution or a synthesized viewpoint; rather, it points out that contradiction is an internal condition of every identity. An idea about something is always disrupted by a discrepancy, but that discrepancy is necessary for the idea to exist in the first place. For Žižek, the truth is always found not in the compromise or middle way but in the contradiction rather than the smoothing out of differences.

The importance of the revised dialectic is paralleled by the Žižekian notion of "the parallax view", which he defines as follows:

> The standard definition of parallax is: the apparent displacement of an object (the shift of its position against a background), caused by a change in observational position that provides a new line of sight. The philosophical twist to be added, of course, is that the observed difference is not simply "subjective", due to the fact that the same object which exists "out there" is seen from two different stances, or points of view. It is rather that, as Hegel would have put it, subject and object are inherently "mediated", so

that an "epistemological" shift in the subjects point of view always reflects an "ontological" shift in the object itself. Or – to put it in Lacanese – the subject's gaze is always-already inscribed into the perceived object itself, in the guise of its "blind spot", that which is "in the object more than the object itself", the point from which the object returns the gaze.

(2006a: 17)

Žižek is interested in the "parallax gap" separating two points between which no synthesis or mediation is possible, a gap linked by an "impossible short circuit" of levels that can never meet. At the root of this category is the gap or split (*béance*) within human subjectivity identified by Jacques Lacan, where the split or barred subject (symbolized by the matheme $) denotes the impossibility of a fully present self-consciousness. How can one read a book like *The Parallax View* (2006a) except with a parallax view – by reading, that is, what seems to be there but is never there? The early responses to Žižek's book, and several bloggers' websites, have lamented the fact there is not one mention of Alan J. Pakula's film *The Parallax View* (1974), which is obviously the source of Žižek's title. How might we explain the perversity of Žižek naming a monumental book that he describes as his "magnum opus" after a film and then not discussing it? And there is also the odd fact that, given that it is an optical phenomenon under discussion, the film references in *The Parallax View* are minimal. But it would seem that the parallax in Žižek's sense is present in the film, and the book, in the gap between explanations that account for the immediacy of an event and explanations that account for the totality of forces behind them; or, perhaps, better, in the way that investigating a crime or matter shifts imperceptibly into becoming part of the very crime or matter. Warren Beatty's character in Pakula's film moves from being a reporter to being part of the situation, to being involved, hence suggesting the presence of the observer within the frame. Similarly, for Žižek the shift is from cognitive responses to the moving image (what the screen places in our heads) to an interest in cinema as the screen onto which we project our desires.

A similar "parallax view" marks Žižek's ambivalent relationship to cultural studies. It might seem that Žižek's interest in mass-cultural objects such as *Titanic* (dir. James Cameron, 1997), or the novels of Stephen King, are merely part of a recent "turn" to the study of popular culture. By locating his theorizing within popular culture Žižek would seem to share this approach and the assertion that, in Raymond Williams's (1958) words, culture is "ordinary". Indeed, the charge of Bordwell and others is that with Žižek we have an emphasis of context above text, and that the film text for Žižek is significant not for its own sake, its aesthetic greatness, but for what it might reveal to us about the cultural context from whence it came. However, cultural studies is the object of some of Žižek's most scathing criticism. Žižek approaches the popular from the opposite (parallax) angle: rather than treating high works of art as if they were popular, Žižek treats the popular work of art as if it were "high"; the popular texts in some way transcend their context and testify to some truth that the context obscures. Take his response to the liberal claim that the film *Fight Club* (dir. David Fincher, 1999) is pro-violence and proto-fascist. Žižek counters that the message of the film is not about "liberating violence" and that it is the reality of the appearance that "violence hurts" that is its true message after all. The fights are "part of a potentially redemptive disciplinary drive ... an indication that fighting brings the participants close to the excess-of-life over and above the simple run of life" (2004: 174).

THE LADY VANISHES

For Lacan there are two steps in the psychoanalytic process: interpreting symptoms and traversing fantasy. When we are confronted with the patient's symptoms, we must first interpret them, and penetrate through them to the fundamental fantasy, as the kernel of enjoyment, which is blocking the further movement of interpretation. Then we must accomplish the crucial step of going through the fantasy, of obtaining distance from it, of experiencing how the fantasy-formation is just masking, filling out a certain void, lack, an empty place in the Other. But even so there were patients who had traversed the fantasy and obtained distance from the fantasy-framework of their reality but whose key symptom still persisted. Lacan tried to answer this challenge with the concept of the *sinthome*. The word *sinthome* in French is a fifteenth- and sixteenth-century way of writing the modern word *symptôme* (symptom). By suggesting a word that is derived from an archaic form of writing Lacan also shifts the inflection of the term to the letter rather than the signifier (as message to be deciphered). The letter as the site where meaning becomes undone is, for Lacan, a primary inscription of subjectivity. The pronunciation *sinthome* in French also produces the associations of *saint homme* (holy man) and *synth-homme* (synthetic [artificial] man). When it occurs, a symptom causes discomfort and displeasure; nevertheless, we embrace its interpretation with pleasure. But why, in spite of its interpretation, does the symptom not dissolve itself? Why does it persist? The answer, of course, is enjoyment. The symptom is not only a ciphered message; it is a way for the subject to organize his or her enjoyment. Treatment is not strictly speaking directed towards the symptom. The symptom is what the subject must cling to since it is what uniquely characterizes him or her. Žižek's film example is from Ridley Scott's *Alien* (1979): the figure of the alien, while it is external to the crew on board the spaceship, is also what, by virtue of its threat to them, confers unity on the spaceship crew. Indeed, the ambiguous relationship we have to our *sinthomes* – one in which we enjoy our suffering and suffer our enjoyments – is like the relationship of the character Ripley (Sigourney Weaver) to the alien, which she fears but progressively identifies with (we need only think of the famous scene at the end of the film where she "undresses" for the alien).

Let us take Hitchcock's *The Lady Vanishes* (1938), and Žižek's influential interpretations of Hitchcock's films in general, as further illustrations of this ambiguity. The existence of an old lady is understood, or made to pass, as a hallucination of the central character Iris. The old woman, Miss Froy (May Whitty), is a mother-figure to – but also a counterpart/mirror of – the young woman, Iris (Margaret Lockwood), who is the "ideal woman", the ideal partner in the sexual relation. Iris is returning to London to be married to a boring father figure whom she does not love. His name, Lord Charles Fotheringale, tells us everything. Iris in fact is the woman who, according to Lacanian theory, does not exist. The attraction of the theme is that through the disappearance of her double (mOther), Miss Froy, she is "made to exist". Žižek suggests that the woman who disappears is always "the woman with whom the sexual relationship would be possible, the elusive shadow of a Woman who would not just be another woman" (1991: 92). At the end Iris falls for Gilbert (Michael Redgrave), who throughout the film has played the role of naughty child (without a father). Hitchcock's films are full of "the woman who knows too much" (intellectually superior but sexually unattractive, bespectacled but able see into what remains hidden from others: Ingrid Bergman as Alicia in *Spellbound* [1945]; Ruth Roman as Anne in *Strangers on a Train* [1951]; Barbara Bel Geddes as Midge in *Vertigo* [1958]). How can we interpret this motif? These figures are not symbols but, on the other hand, they are not insignificant details of individual films; they persist across a number of Hitchcock films. Žižek's answer is that they are *sinthomes*. They designate the limit of interpretation, they resist interpretation; they fix or tie together a certain core of enjoyment.

SOLARIS

Žižek pursues the difference between the early structuralist Lacan of the 1950s and the late Lacan of the fundamental recalcitrance of the Real of the 1960s on. The Lacanian concept of the Real – the most under-represented component of the triad of the Real, the Symbolic and the Imaginary[4] – provides another way to approach that which cannot be spoken (drawn into the Symbolic), because it eludes the ability of the ontological subject to signify it. The Real is the hidden/traumatic underside of our existence or sense of reality, whose disturbing effects are felt in strange and unexpected places. For Žižek, material contained within the pre-ontological, like abject material, can and does emerge into the ontological sphere and once there, however troubling or traumatic, it is made meaning of. Žižek's examples are the Mother Superior who emerges at the close of *Vertigo*, who "functions as a kind of negative *deus ex machina*, a sudden intrusion in no way properly grounded in the narrative logic, the prevents the happy ending" (2002: 208); and the swamp that Norman (Anthony Perkins) sinks Marion's (Janet Leigh) car into in *Psycho* "is another in the series of entrance points to the preontological netherworld" (*ibid.*). Nevertheless, despite its irruption into the film text, the Real resists every attempt to render it meaningful and those elements that inhabit it continually elude signification. As such, it is a version of the mythic creature called by Lacan the lamella. On the one hand, the lamella is a thin plate-like strata, like those of a shell or the layers found in geological formations; on the other, it can refer to flat amoeba-like organisms that reproduce asexually. Žižek notes, "As Lacan puts it, the lamella does not exist, it insists: it is unreal, an entity of pure semblance, a multiplicity of appearances that seem to enfold a central void – its status is purely phantasmatic" (2006b: 62). In its materializations the lamella marks an Otherness beyond intersubjectivity. Lacan's description, Žižek declares, reminds us of the creatures in horror movies: vampires, zombies, the undead, the monsters of science fiction. Indeed, it is the alien from Scott's film that may conjure up the lamella in its purest form. Uncannily, Lacan writes in Seminar 11, a decade before the film appeared, "But suppose it comes and envelopes your face while you are quietly asleep" (Lacan 1979: 197); "it is as if Lacan somehow saw the film before it was even made", suggests Žižek (2006b: 63). We think immediately of the scene in the womb-like cave of the unknown planet when the alien leaps from its throbbing egg-like globe and sticks to Executive Officer Kane's (John Hurt) face. This amoeba-like flattened creature that envelops the face stands for irrepressible life beyond all the finite forms that are merely its representatives. In later scenes of the film the alien is able to assume a multitude of different shapes; it is immortal and indestructible. The Real of the lamella is an entity of pure surface without density, an infinitely plastic object that can change its form. It is indivisible, indestructible and immortal, like the living dead, which, after every attempt at annihilation, simply reconstitute themselves and continue on.

With regard to science fiction film, Žižek talks about the Lacanian notion of the Thing (*das Ding*), used by Freud to designate the ultimate object of our desires in its unbearable intensity, a mechanism that directly materializes the impenetrability of our unacknowledged fantasies. In the film *Solaris* (dir. Andrei Tarkovsky, 1972), for example, it relates to "the deadlocks of sexual relationship" (Žižek 1999: 222). A space agency psychologist is sent to an abandoned spaceship above a newly discovered planet. Solaris is a planet with a fluid surface that imitates recognizable forms. Scientists in the film hypothesize that Solaris is a gigantic brain that somehow reads our minds. Soon after his arrival Kelvin (Donatas Banionis), the psychologist, finds his dead wife at his side in bed. In fact his wife had committed suicide years ago on Earth after Kelvin deserted her. The dead wife pops up everywhere, sticks around and finally Kevin grasps that she is a materialization of his own innermost traumatic fantasies. He discovers that she does not have human chemical composition. The dead wife, because she has no material identity of her own, thus acquires the status of the Real. However, the wife then becomes aware of the tragedy of her status, that she only exists in the Other's dream and has no innermost substance, and her only option is to commit suicide a second time by swallowing a chemical that will prevent her recomposition. The planet Solaris here, Žižek argues, is the Lacanian Thing (*das Ding*), a sort of obscene jelly, the traumatic Real where Symbolic distance collapses: "it provides – or rather imposes on us – the answer before we even raise the question, directly materialising our innermost fantasies which support our desire" (1999: 223).

WILD AT HEART

Žižek can be credited with a revival of interest in specifically Lacanian psychoanalytical film criticism, but, as we have seen, his approach also represents a decisive shift from Laura Mulvey's analysis of the gaze of mastery (1975) and Jean-Pierre Oudart's notion of suture and cinematic identification (1977–8), to focus on questions of fantasy and spectator enjoyment. Thus concepts of the gaze and identification in Žižek's film commentary are linked to issues of desire and the fantasmatic support of reality as a defence against the Real.[5] A case in point is Žižek's repeated analysis of the sexual assault scene from Lynch's *Wild at Heart* (1990).[6] In this scene Bobby Peru (Willem Dafoe) invades the motel room of Lula Fortune (Laura Dern) and after repeated verbal and physical harassment coerces her into saying to him, "Fuck me!" As soon as the exhausted Dern utters the barely audible words that would signal her consent to the sexual act, Dafoe withdraws, puts on a pleasant face and politely retorts: "No thanks, I don't have time today, I've got to go; but on another occasion I would do it gladly." Our uneasiness with this scene, suggests Žižek, lies in the fact that Dafoe's "unexpected rejection is his ultimate triumph and, in a way, humiliates her more than direct rape" but also that "just prior to her 'Fuck me!', the camera focuses on [Dern's] right hand, which she slowly spreads out – the sign of her acquiescence, the proof that he has stirred her fantasy" (2006a: 69).

A keystone to Žižek's edifice is the Lacanian notion of *jouissance*, which, character-istically, he simply translates as "enjoyment".[7] For Žižek, *jouissance* is both a feature of individual subjectivity, an explanation of our individual obsessions and investments, and a phenomenon that best describes the political dynamics of collective violence; for example, it is the envy of the *jouissance* of the Other (as neighbour) that accounts for racism and extreme forms of nationalism. What gets on our nerves about the Other is his or her enjoyment (smelly food, noisy conversation in another language), strange customs (chador) or attitudes to work (he or she is either a workaholic steal-ing our jobs or a bludger living off our benefits) (see Žižek 1993: 200–205). One of Žižek's central concerns is the status of enjoyment within ideological discourse, where, in our so-called permissive society, there is an obscene command to enjoy that marks the return of the Freudian superego. For example, there is a paradox between the greater possibilities of sexual pleasure in more open societies such as ours and the pursuit of such pleasure, which turns into a duty. The superego stands between these two: the command to enjoy and the duty to enjoy. The law is a renunciation of enjoy-ment that manifests itself by telling you what you cannot do; in contrast the superego orders you to enjoy what you can do – permitted enjoyment becomes an obligation to enjoy. But of course, Žižek notes, when enjoyment becomes compulsory it is no longer enjoyment.

It is the relational and paradoxical understanding of enjoyment that renders it important for an understanding of film spectatorship. Again, one detects Žižek's interpretive revision of the stereotypical Hegelian dialectical progression from thesis, through antithesis to synthesis at work here. In Hitchcock's *Marnie* (1964), Marnie (Tippi Hedren) does not want to be touched and it is this desire to touch the human being who does not want to be touched that paradoxically animates a system of look-ing. At one point in the film Mark Rutland (Sean Connery) describes an object that seems to be a flower until one reaches out and touches it and perceives that it is in fact a conglomeration of insects. During the first kiss between Mark and Marnie in the midst of a thunderstorm, Hitchcock's camera comes in to a close two-shot and then a very tight zoom that ends up obliterating all but facial fragments. It is as if the flesh of the characters is made to cover the film frame. Throughout the film there is a need for Hitchcock's camera to possess Marnie, to offer her up as "something" that can not only be viewed but also physically touched. Marnie's stealing is a symptom of some-thing she does not know or understand and her *jouissance* is almost excessive. What is the nature of her enjoyment and why do we retain our sympathy with the character of Mark Rutland when he appears to rape her? His relationship duplicates Marnie's relationship with her mother (Mark=Marnie, Marnie=Mother). He is not simply her antagonist but a double in terms of the film's motif of touch and desire. Mark wants to touch Marnie who wants to touch her mother, a prostitute, who makes her living from the touch of men. Žižek explores how the Lacanian concept of *jouissance* provides for a re-reading of the femme fatale (Marnie) of film noir. In the traditional reading the femme fatale is the embodiment of the fear of emancipated femininity perceived as a threat to male identity. But this, Žižek proposes, misses the point. All the features denounced as the result of male paranoia (woman as inherently evil, as the seductress whose hate and destruction of men express, in a perverted way, her awareness of how her identity depends on the male gaze, and who therefore longs for her own annihilation) account for the figure's charm, as if the theorizing provides an alibi for our enjoyment of the femme fatale. And this in turn, for Žižek, makes sense of Lacan's pun *jouis-sens* (enjoy-meant).[8]

A PERVERT'S GUIDE TO CINEMA

We might question whether what is at stake in Žižekian film criticism is a pervert's guide to cinema or a cinema guide for perverts. There is the fact or possibility of Žižek's cinematic perversion, which, as we have seen, is a mainstay of many responses from within film studies to his texts, but what if it were possible for this perversion to be more complex than might initially appear, and, secondly, for it to serve a critical and heretical function? Here Žižek's own thoughts on the relationship between cinema and perversion prove illuminating. Žižek's use of Lacan's definition of perversion hinges on the structural aspect of perversion: what is perverse in film viewing is the subject's identification with the gaze of an other, a moment that represents a shift in subjective position within the interplay of gazes articulated by the cinematic text. Utilizing an example from Michael Mann's *Manhunter* (1986), Žižek comments that the moment Will Graham (William Petersen), the FBI profiler, recognizes that the victims' home movies, which he is watching, are the same films that provided the sadistic killer with vital information, his "obsessive gaze, surveying every detail of the scenery, coincides with the gaze of the murderer" (1991: 108). This identification, Žižek continues, "is extremely unpleasant and obscene … [because] such a coincidence of gazes defines the position of the pervert" (*ibid.*). As Will examines home movies, seeking as a profiler whatever they have in common, his gaze shifts from their content to their status as home movies, thereby coinciding with the gaze of the murderer; in so doing he identifies the form of the movies he is watching and with them. It is their very status as home movies that is the key to unravelling the mystery of *Manhunter*.

But is such perverse spectatorship more than simply a rupture in the old psychoanalytical suture of conventional film narrative? Since the pervert for Lacan and Žižek "does not pursue pleasure for his own pleasure, but for the enjoyment of the Other" (*ibid.*: 109), the perversely situated spectator is forced suddenly to recognize that the drive to satisfaction, ordinarily rendered possible through the standard conduit of narrative and spectatorship, is actually oriented towards the service and satisfaction of an "Other" that remains forever beyond the ability of the spectator (or the film, for that matter) to conceptualize and, hence, contain. To conclude we might turn to Žižek's own commentary on the importance and general objective of his work. In *The Fright of Real Tears* (2001) he suggests his aim is not so much to argue for the reality of fictions as to "make us experience reality as a fiction". To adapt another of his book titles, it is because film keeps us "looking awry" on reality, that

> if our social reality itself is sustained by a symbolic fiction or fantasy, then the ultimate achievement of film art is not to recreate reality within a narrative fiction, to seduce us into (mis)taking a fiction for reality, but, on the contrary, to make us discern the fictional aspect of reality itself, to experience reality itself as a fiction.   (*Ibid.*: 77)

NOTES

1. See, for example, the back cover of his recent *Violence: Six Sideways Reflections* (London: Profile, 2008).
2. For example, it is with characteristic perversity that Žižek cites *The Fountainhead* (dir. King Vidor 1949) as the best American movie of all time.
3. Stephen Heath expresses concern that Žižek "has, in fact, little to say about 'institution', 'apparatus', and so on, all the concerns of the immediately preceding attempts to think cinema and psychoanalysis" ("Cinema and Psychoanalysis: Parallel Histories", in *Endless Night: Cinema and Psychoanalysis, Parallel Histories*, J. Bergstrom [ed.], 25–56 [Berkeley, CA: University of California Press, 1999], 44). Vicky Lebeau argues that "it is the specificity of cinema that seems to go missing in Žižek's account" (*Psychoanalysis and Cinema: The Play of Shadows* [London: Wallflower, 2001], 59). These points have been made and summarized by Todd McGowan, "Introduction: Enjoying the Cinema", *International Journal of Žižek Studies* **1**(3) (2007) www.zizekstudies.org/index.php/ijzs/article/view/57/119 (accessed June 2009).
4. Žižek explains these three levels as follows:
   This triad can be nicely illustrated by the game of chess. The rules one has to follow in order to play it are its symbolic dimension: from the purely formal symbolic standpoint, "knight" is defined only by the moves this figure can make. This level is clearly different from the imaginary one, namely the way in which different pieces are shaped and characterized by their names (king, queen, knight), and it is easy to envision a game with the same rules, but with a different imaginary, in which this figure would be called "messenger" or "runner" or whatever. Finally, real is the entire complex set of contingent circumstances that affect the course of the game.
   (*How to Read Lacan* [London: Granta, 2006], 8–9)
5. Todd McGowan maintains that Žižek "elaborates an entirely new concept of suture" ("Introduction: Enjoying the Cinema", 4).
6. Analysis of this scene occurs in Žižek's *The Plague of Fantasies* (London: Verso, 1997), 186–7, *The Art of the Ridiculous Sublime: On David Lynch's Lost Highway* (Seattle, WA: Walter Chapin Simpson Center for the Humanities, 2000), 11, *The Fright of Real Tears: Krzystof Kieslowski between Theory and Post-theory* (London: BFI, 2001), 131, and *The Parallax View* (Cambridge, MA: MIT Press, 2006), 69–70, as well as *The Pervert's Guide to Cinema* (dir. S. Fiennes, 2006).
7. Dylan Evans notes: "The French word *jouissance* means basically 'enjoyment', but it has a sexual connotation (i.e. 'orgasm') lacking in the English word 'enjoyment', and is therefore left untranslated in most English editions of Lacan" (*An Introductory Dictionary of Lacanian Psychoanalysis* [London & New York: Routledge, 1996], 91).
8. *Jouis-sens* relates to the demand of the superego to enjoy, a demand that the subject will never be able to satisfy. According to Lacan, *jouis-sens*, the *jouissance* of meaning, is located at the intersection of the Imaginary and the Symbolic.

29 STEPHEN HEATH

Fred Botting

Stephen Heath was one of the founders of *Screen*, the British journal of film criticism and theory. He is Professor of English and French Literature and Culture at University of Cambridge. He is the author of *The Nouveau Roman* (1972), *Questions of Cinema* (1981), *The Sexual Fix* (1982) and *Gustave Flaubert* (1992). Heath edited and translated Roland Barthes' *Image–Music–Text* (1977). An influential early essay for cinema is Heath's "Notes On Suture" published in *Screen* 18 (1977–8). He has co-edited *The Cinematic Apparatus* (with Teresa De Lauretis, 1980) and *Cinema and Language* (with Patricia Mellencamp, 1983).

"Stephen Heath" signifies, not an author, but something like a "text" (Barthes 1977a: 157). A text takes the form of a weave, a multiplicity, entwining aesthetic, social, political and historical systems of signification. Noting that "fiction film" works to produce a "homogeneity", "Heath" (still in quotation marks) writes that "in no way can it exhaust the textual system – the filmic process, the relational movement – which is precisely the term of its production" (1981: 133). In a review of *Questions of Cinema*, Heath's major collection of writings on film, Dana Polan sympathizes with the book's refusal of humanist concerns and notes both its focus on a new problematic (the articulation of Althusserian ideology, psychoanalysis and semiotics) and the writer's curious institutional position: "a writer on cinema and French theory in a department dedicated to Eng. Lit., Heath would appear to have the worst of the humanist tradition" (1985: 160). There is also movement, a "crossing" ("between Eng. Lit. and film, between the US and France and Great Britain") and a "crossing over" from dominant representational models to new systems of discourse, which present theory as "an affiliative process" most effective when "in-between, in transit, moving" (1986: 163–4). Situated in a crossing of languages and cultures, Heath also performs a traversal of disciplinary boundaries (English and French literature; film and cultural studies) and critical discourses (Marxism, feminism, semiotics, psychoanalysis). His writings pursue questions of subjectivity, ideology and sexuality across various histories and cultural forms, interrogating relations and differences, maintaining irreducibility, while exploring the ramifications of particular conjunctions.

CINEMA *AND* PSYCHOANALYSIS

In an essay charting their "parallel histories" across a century, Heath (1999) reviews the asymmetrical conjunction of cinema and psychoanalysis. Hungarian psychoanalyst Sándor Ferenczi (1873–1933) apparently became boyishly excited at the prospect of going to the movies, while Russian-born psychoanalyst and author Lou Andreas-Salomé (1861–1937) offered a number of more considered reflections on the usefulness of cinema in promoting the understanding of psychoanalysis. In contrast, neither Sigmund Freud nor Melanie Klein showed any inclination to take film seriously, remaining suspicious of cinema as a mechanism to explain or illustrate psychoanalytic concepts (the former even refused to take part in a film, fearing that pictorialization would betray the unrepresentable concepts of his discourse). Almost at the start of psychoanalysis, the question of the visibility of its key terms splits its advocates: the tendency to look to film as an illustration of psychoanalytic insights and manifest psychoanalytic principles is resisted as a trajectory of misrepresentation. If anything conjoins the projects of cinema and psychoanalysis, it is something unseen: the analyst's "compulsion to visibility" paralleled by cinema and "haunted by the possibility of something more than vision" (*ibid.*: 34).

Reviewing the ways cinema and psychoanalysis have been conjoined in making the unseen visible – the notion of the "dream screen" in particular – Heath goes on to trace the fortunes of different psychoanalytic concepts in film studies in the wake of the journal *Screen*, which transformed the anglophone field in the 1970s: "suture is no longer doing well, nor, on the whole, is fetishism; the phallus is mostly holding up, while fantasy is fine but prone to disparate appreciations; as for real and symptom, they have come up strong indeed" (*ibid.*: 33). Thirty years later in the 2000s the shares, suture in particular, of which Heath was a major stockholder are down in current prices; those associated most closely with the Žižek brand – Real and Symptom – are doing well. Heath describes a trend in film criticism that reduces the spectatorial relation to one of "pure specularity, effectively suturing cinema into an ideology of the subject that takes little account of the complexity of the latter's constitution" (*ibid.*). Identifying with figures on screen, readily eliding them with culturally typed positions, and easily recognizing particular concepts, tends to homogenize and flatten relations. In line with this tendency, psychoanalysis serves "as interpretive source" and "enclosing imaginary", working "illustratively, resolving things into the confirmation of a set of themes, a repeatable story duly repeated" (*ibid.*: 35). Yet psychoanalysis argues that the mirror enables subjective identity to be formed on the basis of *misrecognition*: the subject sees itself, whole for the first time, in an inverted place where he/she is not, and on this basis organizes a fragmented sense of body and psyche into a singular entity, an individual able to say "I" and assume social/symbolic roles. An arrested development allows the film critic to find "him or herself everywhere on screen", with "no trouble between film and interpreter that is not already contained within the interpretative circle" (*ibid.*). Psychoanalysis does not, in theory at least, allow such ready assimilations: it founders "ceaselessly on the bedrock impasse" of sexual difference and feminine resistance, on the divisions and gaps entailed in the constitution of subjectivity (*ibid.*: 35–6).

Another tendency in film studies is the phenomenon of "Žižek-film", in which, beyond mirroring, cinema provides the illustration of psychoanalytic concepts: "it itself *shows* and can be *shown to show*" the truth of psychoanalysis. Heath describes Slavoj Žižek, in full conference mode, making his point: "'If a student asks "What is the psychoanalytic Thing?" show him *Alien*', Žižek will exclaim in a lecture, arm flung screenward as the parasite viscously bursts through human flesh" (*ibid*.: 36). Excess is everywhere visible: on screen, in its affect and in the demonstration of that non-object of excess, the Thing, crucial to Lacanian formulations. Through excess, cinema moves beyond exposition and into experience "on the edge of the real, at an extreme of psychoanalytical shock"; it "exceeds" psychoanalysis to the extent that "Žižek-film" "realizes the unrepresentable" (*ibid*.: 36–7). Where interpretation, tying and untying the threads of the text, attends to interplays of signification and relations between images and spectator, the demonstrations of "Žižek-film" involve fantasy in a specifically Lacanian sense: fantasy fills the (shock of) the real with an object, a Thing, to which it repeatedly turns, screening off the absence. Žižek-film's recourse to the Thing is interpreted as an excessive visualization of what is, psychoanalytically speaking, unrepresentable. In repeatedly returning to the Thing as a general manifestation, Žižek-film's fantasy appears: for all the social antagonism supposed to cohere and unravel around the place of the Thing (a site of fantasms, projections and cultural elaborations in Lacan [1992]), there is a sense of non-specificity and ahistoricity – "a prehistoric Other, the primordial mother-Thing, alien and threatening, the traumatic embodiment of an impossible jouissance" (Heath 1999: 41). Overemphasizing the Thing as "an unhistorical kernel that stays the same" precludes all contestation of phallic order and pre-empts any challenges to its authorizing function. It is significant, Heath continues, that terms such as "institution" and "apparatus" are absent from the Žižek-film (*ibid*.: 44): these terms point to the social, psychic and ideological fields beyond cinema where gaps between spectator and subject, screen and reality, cinema and theory are maintained and challenged in various material and historical contexts.

The problem of psychoanalysis and representation for Lacan, Heath argues, concerns what is not represented. The subject designates "the impossibility of its own signifying representation". Nor is there any "signifying representation of jouissance", nor any representation of the gap that symptoms and fantasies serve to hide. The real, moreover, is beyond symbolization; the Thing manifested only as a void (*ibid*.: 42). Žižek-film, however, does not bother with questions of representation and employs Lacanian psychoanalysis "as basis for truth-claiming propositions". Its illustrations leave no room for surprises in and of cinema, to the extent that cinema falls out of the picture: the "reduction of psychoanalysis to a platitude of representation" entails a "similar reduction of cinema by psychoanalysis" (*ibid*.: 49). One collapses on the other in a flattening that occludes differences – of interpretation, politics, history, subject-formation. Perhaps the flattening has its own conditions of emergence: the move to postmodernist practices, as Jameson suggests, diminishes the capacity for critical distance and depth in that its playful aesthetic surfaces recycle histories, and multiply and disorient subject positions. In terms of film, the emergence of post-Classical Hollywood cinema eschews narrative coherence, unified character and single perspective frameworks and evokes a sense of excess and "engulfment" (Elsaesser 1998). In a culture dominated by the excessive global flows of commodities, capital and desire, the structures of modernity, like repression or the Oedipal model of the family, no longer hold; nor do their media apparatuses require or produce a centred and rational subject linked to a social or national whole (Polan 1986: 178–83).

SUTURE

Implicitly, Heath's critique of Žižek involves a return to those terms that have fallen out of favour in film studies. The notion of suture examines the articulations of cinema and subjectivity, articulations (through montage and editing) that occur within films and (through identification, signification and ideology) between film, spectatorial positions and social subjects. It is drawn from Lacanian psychoanalysis to denote the point at which subject and sense appear in relation to the system of signifiers, linked to the "anchoring point" by which different levels of signification are tied together: the signifier, a "sound-image", is connected to other signifiers in chains whose relations are differential and associative and from which subject and sense are excluded, to appear on another level – that of the signified (meaning or concept). At a certain point, the chain of signifying association is arrested, and meaning is recognized retroactively by the subject, linking the level of signifier with that of signified. In Jacques-Alain Miller's account, suture involves the "lack" associated with subjectivity: individuals are not whole entities but split between being and structures of language (the Other; system of signifiers; chain of discourse spoken by and speaking the subject). That split, between self and self-image, I and unconscious, is, for psychoanalysis, constitutive of subjectivity and its relation to language and meaning, a relation underpinned by lack or absence.

In terms of the subject's relation to film, absence forms the space for the operations of suture. Every filmic field is echoed by an absent field: every shot signifies absence (the image is the absence of a real object; a look of a character indicates something viewers cannot see) as much as the presence of an image, pointing to the cuts between shots, to what is out of frame and to the space Jean-Pierre Oudart designates as that of the "Absent One". The latter is the lack-in-vision within film made evident as the place from which identification can proceed. This absence, separating film from reality, requires the intervention of a structure that anchors signifiers in the visual field, articulating images in narrative and offering the spectator a position to make sense of what is passing before his or her eyes. The absent space is crucial as the basis for cinema:

> prior to any semantic "exchange" between two images … and within the framework of a cinematic *énoncé* constructed on a shot/reverse-shot principle, the appearance of a lack perceived as a Some One (the Absent One) is followed by its abolition by some-one (or something) placed within the same field. (Oudart 1977–8: 37)

321

Shot/reverse-shot is held up as a prime example of suture, the latter, according to editing conventions, serving to close the gap opened by the former (a character's look, down and off screen is completed by a shot of the object viewed). The filmic field, its systemic articulation of images and cuts, is also a space of enunciation, working – imaginarily – at the level of meaning and enabling the spectator to make sense of the sequence of images. For Oudart, the articulation of what is shown (statement) and the context in which it is shown (enunciation) means suture has a "dual effect", anticipatory in terms of the signifier (the images on screen) and retroactive at the level of the signified (when the spectator recognizes the meaning linking images). Through absence, films leave a place for the subject, its images, cuts and narrative composition organizing a viewing position from which sense can be established. At the same time, this space remains to announce the difference between the subject position offered by the film to the spectator and the ideological subject position (in culture, society and history) that the spectator also, by virtue of being a subject, occupies outside the cinema. In Daniel Dayan's reading of suture, the two positions are moved closer together: suture is regarded as the "tutor-code" through which ideological effects can be exerted in cinematic form.

Heath, having translated Miller's and Oudart's essays for *Screen*, negotiates the three positions in his "Notes on Suture". Distinguishing Miller's psychoanalytic emphasis on the constitution of subjectivity in respect of discourse from Oudart's stress on the imaginary with its dual inflections (a psychoanalytic sense of the mirror phase and a cinematic relation of the spectator to image and absence), Heath notes how the overlap of subject formation and spectatorial relation induces misrecognition on two levels: one shaping individuals in relation to the rules of social discourse (symbolic/Other), the other articulating spectator with the images on screen. At stake, Heath continues, is "the understanding of cinema as discourse" (1977–8: 63). His discussion opens on to the issue of ideology, as developed by Dayan, and the problems arising from different conceptions of suture as a specific relation to a particular film or a feature of the general operations of cinematic production. Heath cites objections to the shot/reverse-shot model of suture as too limiting and simple (see Rothman), objections claiming that suture can be generalized to refer to any form of montage, any joining of images that establishes continuity and positional unity for the spectator. This unity remains imaginary, constantly traversed and destabilized by the movement of images and the gap between the look of the spectator, the looks on screen and the look of the camera itself. All these looks open, beyond the imaginary, to the symbolic dimension of structure, cinematic and social conventions and differences.

For Heath, a spectator's position is never simply imaginary, never utterly absorbed in the totality of the images on screen: as a speaking subject of culture and ideology s/he is already situated in a symbolic order and already furnished with assumptions, expectations and modes of understanding. At the other end of the spectrum, the issue of suture engages questions of the way this already-formed being is enlisted or ideologically addressed by cinema. In between lies the structure of the filmic text itself, a text that both invites subjective identification and announces the gaps and divisions of a signifying heterogeneity irreducible finally to a simple unification of subject and spectator. Irreducibility remains key for relations that are sustained in their difference:

ideology cannot be reduced to the imaginary register since it manifests itself in relation to, and in the separation from, images, reality and language (Heath 1981: 5). The imaginary fills a gap, projecting unity in a space of division. The symbolic, although necessary to ideology, also remains distinct: while no ideology can operate without the symbolic framework of language and meanings, it is "never simply not ideological", that is, there is no pure outside – a direct expression of nature, say – that remains unaffected by (ideologically informed) understanding (1977–8: 73). Suture remains a "dual process of multiplication and projection" in operation at various levels. As such, it remains a "crucial difficulty" in the analysis of film, indicating that subjectivity is never unified but itself a process, a heterogeneous site of the crossing of images, signifiers, meanings, identifications and structures; it is moreover a joining that is never only in the film itself – suture operates within a particular film, but also between it, spectator and social formation.

Heath distinguishes three main areas for consideration: "preconstruction" (designating the film's adoption of specific positions and meanings), "construction" (the ending and direction of the overall film) and the "passage" (the film's performance) (*ibid.*: 74). As a process in which ideology is reproduced, the focus on suture demands that any film analysis attend to interrelationships involved in cinematic production (the ordering of images on screen and positioning of spectators) and cultural reproduction (the values, meanings and expectations circulated beyond and with which film necessarily interacts). "In a sense", Heath comments, "the cinematographic apparatus itself is nothing but an operation of suture" (1981: 14). A term for the joining of elements in a film together and with extra-cinematic positions, suture serves as a point where specific relationships can be located and unravelled: the "apparatus" of cinema signifies the systems of signification and subjection as well as the technical operations of shooting, recording and screening, and thus a general, and open, arrangement linking cinema, subjectivity and culture.

The notion of suture remains an important term for understanding film in that it articulates differences without collapsing them: theory, analysis, the filmic text, the conditions of production and circulation, the spectatorial position and ideological address are acknowledged as not just overlapping but, in their relations, as productive of the apparatus's overall effect. With suture, meaning, affect or significance are never simply a property of textual structure, material historical conditions or spectatorial position: although analysis might project (in both senses) what appears as unity, might have a distinct aesthetic project, the heterogeneity of the elements it combines and the relations it involves render any single meaning assigned to it provisional, always subject to the imaginary process of identifying – and misrecognizing – unity. While the psychoanalytic notion of the imaginary remains crucial, it does not tell the whole story: as "the stand-in, the sutured coherence, the fiction of anticipated totality", it "functions over and against the symbolic, the order of language, the production of meanings, with which the subject is set as the place of an endless movement (identifying a function of repeated difference) and from which, precisely, there is image and desire and suture" (*ibid.*: 15). Relations, differences, desires and excesses are sustained by suture. As a process, as Heath goes on to develop the term, it involves narrative as both structure and spacing, allowing imaginary unities to be perceived as an effect of gaps and differences underlying narrative and image flow, and the framings, cuts, intermittences and absences (*ibid.*: 13).

What Heath calls "narrative space" is a process of linking the entirety of shots composing a film within a frame that, despite the flickering of absence and discontinuity, provides coherence and contains the mobility of images and associations, thereby enabling the film to be understood or read (*ibid.*: 33). Conventions of genre are part of this process of framing, as are the compositional rules of cinematography – the variations of scale of shot, the matching of action and eye line, the 180 and 30 degree rules and the use of field/reverse field (*ibid.*: 41). In framing and centring an image (which is never "immediate or neutral"), narrative space depends on a perspective system that ties the spectator to a specific place, setting the scene for him or her in a way that sustains coherence despite the potential of film to move in diverse "ways and directions", with a variety of "flows and energies" and as a "veritable festival of affects" (*ibid.*: 53). In this model, film narrative – and its pleasures – operates as containment: the discontinuities (of time and space), movements (of images), excesses (of affect and looks) and negativities (of absence) underlying the process are ordered and imaginarily resolved in a rhythm of loss and recovery – "films are full of fragments, bits of bodies, gestures, desirable traces", a ceaseless sliding of image and desire that narrative only imaginarily and temporarily makes appear whole (*ibid.*: 183). Classic cinema employs narrative to provide an "order of bearable repetition", coherence established through a "sustained equilibrium", a rhythmic oscillation in which excess appears and is resolved: "narrativization is scene and movement, movement and scene, the reconstruction of the subject in the pleasure for that balance (with genres as specific instances of equilibrium) – *for* homogeneity, containment" (*ibid.*: 154).

Excess, lack, desire, as inescapable as they are ungraspable, underpin the cinematic relation and announce, crucially for any approach engaging with psychoanalysis, the question of sexuality and femininity. Female sexuality is more than an object to be mastered in psychoanalysis, more than a figure of castration and male pre-eminence: it marks a site of resistance and relation, a locus of excess and deficiency that opens up the whole process of analysis. So, too, does cinema, employing the image of woman as object of a gaze it repeatedly escapes, of a desire it cannot master, of exchanges that open up structures of representation and looking to a lack that is endlessly made visible and screened out. In terms of narrative, sexuality is often presented as the locus where narrative order is disrupted: in the transformation through which a story moves from one state to another, the process marks an interruption of homogeneity and a subsequent return to it, a process in which objects and meanings are seen to be out of place. In the long tracking shot that opens *A Touch of Evil* (dir. Orson Welles, 1958), a shot that is about to end with a kiss, the moment of harmony is broken by an explosion that sets off, out of kilter, the train of events composing the narrative. The kiss, interrupted by the violence of the explosion, signals that law – and its object, woman – is pushed from its place. In the figure of Susan (Janet Leigh), woman is marked as the object of law: she is the wife of the detective, Vargas (Charlton Heston). Female sexuality, when freed from its social and moral constraints, is associated in the semiotics of the film with conflagration, fire, excess and evil. Narrative closure, in bringing female sexuality back into its conventional subordinate relationship to masculinity, re-establishes law. As object of exchange between men, and as site of law, female sexuality is never simply secondary, since it continues to threaten law and narrative order with an excess that cannot be mastered, and only imaginarily, narratively – and temporarily – contained. A similar duality is evident in images of women on screen: noting how Lisa (Joan Fontaine) is presented in Max Ophüls's *Letter from an Unknown Woman* (1948) as the very image of femininity, the "image of female beauty", Heath detects an ambivalence in her figuring of "the desired and untouchable image, an endless *vision*". She is there only as image, as an object on which to gaze, arresting the gaze and around which the moving series of images seems to rest. As vision, "desired and untouchable", the image also foregrounds the process of vision in stimulating and deferring desire. Cinema is an apparatus for screening desire, and sexuality describes "the 'more' the look elides" (Heath 1981: 146): it exceeds the gaze it attracts, arrests and captivates, drawing out the differences of looks entailed in looking at an image on screen that solicits and diverts looks. The "more" declares there is something else, something lacking in and excessive about the look of the image on screen when it comes to addressing sexuality. "More" announces an incompletion, a lack, and the continuance of desiring; it locates desire, not at the centre of any subject, but beyond it, in relations outside its mastery.

Significantly, "more" defines the absence of any sexual relationship in Lacan's (1998) discussion of female sexuality: "woman" is not a man's complement, but a supplement; "she" exists (constructed as other, object and figure of excess/*jouissance*) in a fantasy of completion sustained in the face of differences and divisions by which masculine subjects misrecognize their place in symbolic structures of desire, both sexes separated and defined by the function of the phallic signifier (Heath 1978). The fantasy of femininity insubstantially incarnated in the image of woman thus occludes the lack integral to all subjects, the internal divisions and gaps between being and language that mean all individuals are alienated in signification: if "woman", as cultural and cinematic construction, is repeatedly deployed as object and image for a male subject's gaze, any sense of fullness, of unity, remains imaginary. At the outer edges of symbolization, feminine *jouissance* is located beyond comprehension, refusing containment and closure in an idealized or romanticized coupling, and pointing to the gaps in subjectivity, the failure of any male assumption of mastery or phallic power, and leaves something more to be desired.

In the scene from *Letter from an Unknown Woman* in which Joan Fontaine is modelling dresses, woman is not just an image of beauty, but seems to know herself as such, fully aware of the looks she draws: a scene of modelling is all about looks, attracting looks, looking good, drawing attention to the artifice, the performance entailed in looking. Cinema does not just present a picture of sexualized looking, it seems, but verges on over-presenting it, almost to the point that one begins to see sexuality as nothing but an orchestrated set of looks in which performance – a "masquerade" – comes to the fore. Joan Riviere suggested that womanliness, in patriarchal culture, is very much a masquerade, a performance of conventional signifiers of femininity aimed at resolving tensions caused by women who occupy roles traditionally associated with masculinity. Riviere discusses the case of one woman, "a university lecturer in an abstruse subject which seldom attracts women", who, when working, wears "particularly feminine clothes" and behaves with inappropriate flippancy and jocularity, treating "the situation of displaying her masculinity to men as a 'game', as something *not real*, as a 'joke'" (Riviere 1986: 39). This conventional sexual perform-ance does more than defuse tense situations: in turning normal sexual roles into the unreality of a game, it discloses the artifice that supports them. In disclosing there is no difference between womanliness and the masquerade, Heath argues, Riviere "undermines the integrity of the former with the artifices of the latter": "in the mas-querade the woman mimics an authentic – genuine – womanliness but then authen-tic womanliness is such a mimicry, *is* the masquerade ('they are the same thing'); to be a woman is to dissimulate a fundamental masculinity, femininity is that dissimula-tion" (Heath 1986: 49–50). In psychoanalytic terms, the masquerade sees "woman" becoming the phallus: "she", Heath glosses, "becomes the woman men want, the term of phallic identity, phallic exchange" (*ibid.*: 52). Hence, translating Lacan's "Encore", "the woman" is a "male fiction, construction, condition"; it is another fantasy occlud-ing the absence of sexual relationship, the gap in subjective and sexual formation. The game played in the masquerade of femininity extends to masculinity, of course, reflecting its own artifices and unreality. Marlene Dietrich (Heath cites her perform-ance in *Morocco* [dir. Josef von Sternberg, 1930]) exemplifies its excessive possibil-ity: in her poses and her actions she "wears all the accoutrements of femininity *as* accoutrements", a wearing that seems to wear thin the fantasy construction in that she "gives the masquerade as excess", performs too much, wearing out the surfaces of the image on which the gaze is supposed to rest, "holding and flaunting" it so that its superficiality becomes evident (Heath 1986: 57).

"The masquerade is obviously at once a whole cinema". Heath's discussion of femi-ninity and the masquerade pertains not only to images of women, but cinema gener-ally in all its specular attractions:

> cinema has played to the maximum the masquerade, the signs of the exchange of femininity, has ceaselessly reproduced its – their – social cur-rency, from genre to genre, film to film, the same spectacle of the woman, her body highlighted into the unity of its image, this cinema image, set out with all the signs of femininity.   (*Ibid.*: 57)

The relation to cinema, the looks, desires, misrecognitions it invites, depends, it seems, on a spectacle of sexuality, of a sexual non-relation played out to the full in which the persistence and historical weight of cultural conventions, stereotyp-ing and divisions form the basis of its entire operation: a slide from images to the imaginary in a recalcitrant reinforcement and occlusion of the real; the seductions of femininity, the lure of the screen, the avoidance of artifice in its very performance. This cine-masquerade cuts two ways, falling back on familiar types and images to shore up representational norms, and pushing at the limits of the artifices and fan-tasmatic scenarios it feeds and feeds on, a doubling in which one remains irreducible to other.

30 ALAIN BADIOU

Stephen Zepke

For the French philosopher Alain Badiou (b. 1937), cinema constitutes itself in an act of purification, it emerges by throwing off its non-artistic elements and develops by using the other arts in
an impure way. This, according to Badiou, produces a cinematic "visitation" of a universal Idea. This
"event" marks a new mixture of the other arts, and reveals what had previously been impossible
for cinema to express, being an irruption of something unprecedented and new. For Badiou, then,
cinema is a poetics of movement that exposes the passage of an Idea, an Idea that is an immobile
singularity and universality, but which cinema's "false movement" has nevertheless brought into
the world. This process of creation reveals what will-have-been, a retrospective void that defines
a new present and gives cinema a political dimension as important as its aesthetic and ontological aspects. Here, cinema assaults the status quo by producing "illegal" images that escape
their non-artistic conditions within the popular imaginary and the market for clichés. As a result,
cinema operates within the artistic and political registers, both of which are also ontological in
their processes. In this, Badiou's cinematic philosophy delivers what seems a dominating desire
of contemporary thought: the immanence of aesthetic and political practice within an ontological process. From 1968 to 1999 Badiou served on the faculty in the Department of Philosophy
at the University of Paris, VIII. He has taught philosophy at the École Normale Supérieure (ENS)
since 1999, and also teaches at the Collège International de Philosophie in Paris. He has published
many papers and books concerning the ontology of mathematics and the "truths" of philosophical discourses. Some of his works include *The Concept of Model* (1969; English trans. 2007), *Being
and Event* (1988; English trans. 2005), *Metapolitics* (2006) and *The Century* (2007).

"We must begin," Badiou tells us in a lecture on art, "from the beginning" (2005a).
The beginning, for cinema as much as for philosophers, is marked by the oldest question: "What is being?" Being, Badiou argues, is pure multiplicity untroubled by any
distinction between whole and part, a multiple of multiples "without any foundational
stopping point" (2005b: 33). Thus, this beginning of philosophy already catches it in
an impasse according to Badiou, inasmuch as the ontology of multiplicity implies that
what we take to be "*a* thing", a "one", *is not*, and only exists as an *operation*: what Badiou
calls the "count-as-one" (*ibid.:* 24). This operation is what presents the multiplicity of
being in a situation, and what causes the multiple to "split apart" (*ibid.:* 25) into the
inconsistent multiplicity, or non-one, of being, and its presentation or count-as-one

as a consistent multiplicity. The ontology of multiplicity is therefore the re-beginning of philosophy based on the assumption that the one is not, and that being *qua* being is neither present in a thing, nor in this thing's presentation (the operation of the count). As a result, if what exist in the world are consistent multiplicities, then being as inconsistent multiplicity does not exist in the world, and is, strictly speaking, *nothing*; it *is* "void". As Badiou puts it: "it is only in completely thinking through the non-being of the one that the name of the void emerges as the unique conceivable presentation of what supports, as unpresentable and as pure multiplicity, any plural presentation, that is, any one-effect" (*ibid.*: 36). As void, then, being is always already "subtracted" from any "count-as-one", a subtraction that is achieved in the very operation of presentation as such, inasmuch as being *qua* inconsistent multiple cannot be counted-as-one. Badiou claims that it was the mathematician Georg Cantor who both recognized this paradox and offered a way out of it by "creating the mathematical theory of the pure multiple" known as "set-theory" (*ibid.*: 38).

Cantor's set theory allows us to count-as-one everything that exhibits a certain property. But what is counted here is not a thing (a "one") but a set (a multiple), making set theory the condition of Badiou's rather startling claim that "the thinking of a pure multiplicity is finally mathematics" (2005c).[1] Set theory, then, is the means to formalize presentation and its operative counts-as-one, but in doing so it also performs a crucial ontological operation: it "fixes the point of non-being from whence it can be established that there is a presentation of being" (2005b: 42). Ontology, *as* mathematics, is therefore the presentation of presentation, which set theory will go on to axiomatize in the work of Ernst Zermelo and Adolf Fraenkel. These axioms will determine the possible relations of belonging and inclusion defining a set (a consistent multiplicity), and hence the possible conditions of the presentation of being. Being does not precede its presentation, however, but instead emerges in a situation as the result of the count-as-one operations, as what is always already foreclosed by these operations, but as what they must nevertheless assume; what "must-be-counted". "It is this latter", Badiou argues, "which causes the structured presentation to waver towards the phantom of inconsistency" (*ibid.*: 52). This means, within the situation, relations of belonging and inclusion (given in the axioms of set theory) define when a multiplicity can be "counted as one" as a consistent multiple, while what evades the count – the void of the not-one, or inconsistent multiple – is subtracted from it. Subtraction makes the void a conditional subset of any set, a "universal inclusion" (*ibid.*: 87), but it includes the void only as lack, as what avoids any count of positive terms and so cannot belong to a set.[2] To be counted as one is therefore the *law* of presentation (*ibid.*: 25), but like all laws this one can be broken. Indeed, there is always the "danger" of an inconsistent multiplicity "*haunting*" the situation as such, as the presentation of subtraction itself (*ibid.*: 94). This is the possibility inherent in the fact that subtraction is the "suture" of being (*qua* inconsistent multiple) and its presentation (*qua* consistent multiple) an ambiguous double movement of rejection and embrace. The danger is that it is in the uncounted nature of the count itself that the void inheres. To innoculate the structure against such a possibility there must be a "count of the count", as Badiou calls it, a "metastructure" within which all the axioms of presentation can be counted as one in order to "secure" the structure against the void. This metastructure establishes a *"state of the situation"* (*ibid.*: 95) and inaugurates "the reign, since completeness is numbered, of the universal security of the one" (*ibid.*: 98). To be counted as one means a multiple is presented as belonging within a situation, but when this count is itself counted, and so included within the situation, the multiple is *represented*. Representation is therefore the "fiction" by which the one attains being, by which what is included in the situation are only the one-multiples that belong to it, meaning the void is "banished" (*ibid.*). To both belong (presentation) and be included (representation) in a situation is to be "normal", to be represented but not be presented is to be an "excrescence", and to be present in a situation, but not be represented by the state marks a "singularity". These last two excessive terms name the suture of the void and its presentation, and appear, as we shall see, as what cannot be counted as one by the state. Excrescence and singularity will be the names of both ontological emergence and aesthetic creation (which, as we shall see, are essentially the same thing), as well as being the conditions of any genuine political resistance.

The appearance of a singularity is fleeting and rare, and is what Badiou calls an "event". Within the world of structured presentation and representation, an event – by definition cataclysmic – presents an "inconsistent multiplicity" as an "ultra-one", and includes the "void" of the situation – what had, in psychoanalytical and political terms, been *repressed* – as "retroactively discernible" (*ibid.*: 56). This militant event is the genetic moment of Badiou's ontology, erupting within science, politics, art and love (*ibid.*: 341). These are the four faculties of the noumenal void that create themselves in creating new truths, new retroactive namings of what was not. The event therefore illuminates and incinerates in its explosion the axioms acting as the contemporary conditions of appearance, the current "logical grammar" (*ibid.*: 287) of belonging. These conditions are "natural" inasmuch as everything they include can be counted as one.[3] The state polices or, the same thing, *produces* "nature" by numbering and ordering all situations into subsets representable in language. There is no room here for a "singularity" that cannot be represented (included) within an existing social subset. The state, Badiou provocatively argues, is not founded on a social bond, but on the prohibition and prevention of "un-binding" maintained through its "administrative and management functions" (*ibid.*: 108). These representative functions do not deal with individuals but with "sub-multiples" or "classes", and in maintaining the "natural" order "the State is the State of the ruling class" (*ibid.*: 105). This means that today the state reproduces the situation as it has been structured by capitalism, and protects the interests of the capitalist class. Under these conditions "politics can be defined as an assault against the State, whatever the mode of that assault might be, peaceful or violent" (*ibid.*: 110).[4] This assault on the state in the name of the event – the irruption of the void – will be a necessary criterion for Badiou's cinema, as it will for science, the other arts and lovers everywhere. This "assault" is the only option for politics given that it is impossible for the state to produce an event, making not only the politically committed, but artists, scientists and lovers too all "activists", "patient watchmen of the void" who are able to illuminate "if only for an instant, the site of the unpresentable, and the means to be thenceforth faithful to the proper name that, afterwards, he or she will have been able to give to – or hear, *one cannot decide* – this non-place of place, the void" (*ibid.*: 111, emphasis added). This makes creation, the invention of a new truth, a fundamentally criminal act. The naming of the event "is essentially illegal in that it cannot conform to any *law* of representation" (*ibid.*: 205).

This name – the appearance of politics as such – is a singular inconsistent multiple whose elements do not belong to the situation, appearing instead at an "*eventual site ... on the edge of the void*" (*ibid.*: 175). The site belongs to the situation, but what belongs to it does not. This event can only be counted "as the arrival in being of non-being, the arrival amidst the visible of the invisible" (*ibid.*: 189). This is a glorious arrival, a naming of the event that forces the situation to "confess its own void, and to thereby let forth, from inconsistent being and the interrupted count, the incandescent non-being of an existence" (*ibid.*: 183). This existence is first of all a "generic truth", a part of the situation that marks its "fundamental inconsistency". "A truth is this minimal consistency (a part, a conceptless immanence), which certifies in the situation the inconsistency from which its being is made" (1999: 107). This "truth" is generic because once it appears it exists in every situation, it is universal, eternal and belongs to everyone. "The generic is *egalitarian*" (2005b: 409). Politics for Badiou is in this sense "a communism of singularities" (1999: 108) inasmuch as truth is "*indifferent to differences [... and] the same for all*" (2001: 27). Indeed, difference – multiculturalism and postmodernism are Badiou's examples (*ibid.*: 22) – is "precisely what truths depose, or render insignificant" (*ibid.*: 27). The power of political truth, or as we shall see of political cinema, is not in representing differences, which "hold no interest for thought" (*ibid.*: 26), but in recognizing what is the same, what is eternally true for all, in its assault on the state. It is this event the state attempts to repress – "the void avoided" (*ibid.*: 74) – because it signals a new egalitarianism, a new "justice" founded in truth. There is something both liberating and disturbing in this political imperative to create truth. Championed by the likes of Slavoj Žižek, Badiou's concept of truth "aims at the very heart of politically correct radical intellectuals, undermining their mode of life".[5] This is a major break with a postmodern politics privileging difference, and, of course, a major break with much recent film criticism that is based on it.

The event is first of all an "intervention" that "consists in identifying that there has been some undecidability, and in deciding it belongs in the situation" (2005b: 202). This decision takes the form of a nomination, a name, but how can such a naming be possible when it is precisely as void that the event appears?[6] Badiou argues that this requires a subject prepared to contest the law, and to agitate on behalf of an "illegal" name that is not allowed within representation. Rather than counting as one within the situation, the intervention names the event according to a different logic, that of the two, by which the event is both absent and present in a "supernumerary name" (*ibid.*: 205), a name that is both an "anomaly" within the state, and an enigma. The militant announces this enigmatic name of the event through a set of procedures Badiou calls "fidelity". Fidelity is a militant naming by which the event appears within the situation, thus creating a revolutionary "counter-state" (*ibid.*: 233). "A fidelity is definitively distinct from the state if, in some manner, it is *unassignable* to a defined function of the state, its result a particularly nonsensical part" (*ibid.*: 237). The fidelity of a subject to an event traces its trajectory from unassignable enigma to a new truth defining existent multiples.[7] This "procedure" transforms the situation by "forcing" it to encompass a new truth. At this point the two outsides of the situation, the event as "singularity" and the "excrescent" generic procedures that force a new truth into the situation, come together, and the new emerges in all its revolutionary brilliance.[8] "As such, art, science and politics do change the world, not by what they discern, but by what they indiscern therein. And the all-powerfulness of a truth is merely that of changing what is, such that this unnameable being may be, which is the very being of what-is" (*ibid.*: 343).

Let us narrow our focus from the infinite expanse of the event horizon and take a look at the appearance of "art". "Art", Badiou tells us, "presents the sensible in the finitude of a work, and destines the infinite to the finite" (2006b: 143). The artist's decision to remain faithful to an event results in an infinite "Idea", or "truth", appearing within the situation in a finite and sensible being. Art understood in this sense is an "aristocratic truth procedure" inasmuch as "the artist ultimately needs no one" (*ibid.*: 142). Indeed, art takes nothing but truth into account, and this produces its "proletarian aristocratism" (2006a: 147); it exists for all without consideration for any special interests. The art work, then, is not an event; it is a "local instance" of truth – a "subject of art" (cf. 2005c) – an ongoing "artistic procedure" acting in fidelity to the event, and forcing a new "artistic configuration" or "art-truth" into the situation (2005a: 12). This configuration is not an art form, a genre, a period in art history, or – significantly for cinema – a technical *dispositif* (*ibid.*: 13). It is an "identifiable sequence" extending from the event in "faithful procedures" dedicated to introducing "great aesthetic transformations" (2005c: 340). Some of Badiou's examples are Greek tragedy, the "Classical style" of music (2005a: 13), cubism and Cezanne (2005c: 329) or Malevich (Badiou 2007: 56).[9]

A configuration thinks in the works that compose it and art "is in each and every one of its points the thinking of the thought that it itself is" (2005a: 14). Art, for Badiou, exists as thought's immanence with being *qua* being, inasmuch as it marks the appearance of a new art-Idea *qua* void. In this way, art thinks itself by creating itself anew, by forever discovering its truth as what (it) *is not*. This distinguishes Badiou's account of art from both its Classical and Romantic relations to truth. It is no longer ostracized from truth for being an imitation of the (Platonic) idea, nor worshipped as the body of truth in its post-Kantian incarnation.[10] Nor is its exteriority to truth "cathartic", making art an Aristotelean therapeutic. Instead, Heidegger's "anti-aesthetic" subtraction of the work of art from the realm of knowledge and its emergence – in-itself – as a procedure producing truth marks, for Badiou, the onset of modernity.[11] Modernity, in Badiou's sense, is defined by art's anti-mimetic foundation in the event-void and the fact that these ideas, proper to art alone, emerge from art's self-critique as something absolutely new.[12] Nevertheless, Badiou categorically condemns modernism's most critical mechanism, the avant-garde. The avant-garde, he argues, attempts to mediate Platonic and Romantic conceptions of art, overcoming the former's ostracism of art from truth by destroying its autonomy, and then confirming the latter in demanding art be reborn as the living expression of the absolute. This is "desperate and unstable" (*ibid.*: 8). Badiou claims that avant-garde artists remain "partisans of the absoluteness of creative destruction" (*ibid.*).[13] The artist, for Badiou, is instead the adherent of the creative event.

As much as Badiou rejects the avant-garde attack on art (interpreting, as we have seen, its ambitions towards the everyday as an anti-Romantic *disincarnation*), he also rejects any defence of art's purity, or of its essential being. Art's truth is in this respect entirely immanent: a work materializes an infinite truth when it is able to stage the "minimal difference" between itself and the event of its founding subtraction. As a result, Badiou's "modernist" sensibilities tend towards the aesthetics of emptiness (Malevich, Webern) where minimal difference is materialized as the real of lack. Similarly cinema, he argues, is essentially impure, being both saturated by the market forces determining its production (Hollywood), and in a constant relation with the other arts. Indeed, a "'pure cinema' does not exist, except in the dead-end of avant-garde formalism" (2004: 111). Badiou's strange modernism therefore rejects formalism, while still searching for cinema's own defining ideas: "Artistic activity can only be discerned in a film as a process of *purification of its own immanent non-artistic character*" (*ibid.*). Unlike the formalism of "high" modernism, however, and echoing his comments on the readymade's effect in art, this process begins within the common imagery constituting cinema as a mass-art, and guaranteeing its universal address. Cinema's modernist "immanent-critique" therefore begins with the purification of the visible and audible of representation, identification and realism, and continues with the purification of the clichés that make it an object of capitalist Spectacle. In cinema there are five "privileged operators" of the Spectacle: "pornographic nudity, the cataclysmic special effect, the intimacy of the couple, social melodrama, pathological cruelty". By purifying the film of these operators cinema will produce a new "cinema-idea" (*ibid.*: 114).[14] In fact, cinema is an art of "visitations" that "organize within the visible the caress proffered by the passage of the idea" (2005a: 78). Modern cinema in its sensible materiality, that is, in its *thought*, is a fidelity to such visitations that reject the aesthetic and political state of the "contemporary" situation, forcing its change. "A film operates", Badiou tells us, "through what it withdraws from the visible" (*ibid.*). This "cut" is carried out as much by framing as it is by editing and, as Badiou puts it, cinema's "flowers" (ideas), in their "captivity to the cut", are both singular and ideal (*ibid.*). This "idealism" of cinema nevertheless remains entirely immanent to cinema, while rejecting any account that would see cinema's operations as essentially material or affectual. Such "cinematic idealism" clearly runs counter to much contemporary cinema theory.

Badiou claims that cinema's modernity is in fact a "*post-classicism*" (*ibid.*: 123). Cinema has come to the end of its modernist subtractions, but as yet no new configuration (event) is perceptible, leaving us drowning in a proliferation of "pre-existent schemas". Post-classicism responds to this situation with the moving camera, which seeks to join together "visible configurations which are disparate, or classically non-unifiable". This "contemporary formalism" cannot encounter the real and has already given rise to a kind of academicism. Cinema is *neo*-classical inasmuch as it seeks to purify this dead end of academic reaction, but it does so on the basis of a saturated modernism, from within the realm of the popular itself. Badiou's examples are "the best sequences of *The Titanic*, or even *Brassed Off*" (*ibid.*: 124).

Art, for Badiou, involves "the destitution of the category of objectivity" (2004: 97), meaning there is neither a film "object", nor a subject as its (productive or receptive) condition of possibility (see also Badiou 2005c). As a result, Badiou rejects the possibility of a contemporary *auteur*, leaving us with "an inquiry into the details" (2004:

115). "The basic unit of investigation is not so much the film in its totality as some moments of film, moments within which an operation is legible" (*ibid.*: 114). The operations of an event appear in cinema through their negation of the non-art of the market; they "discredit ordinary industrial materials" (*ibid.*: 115) and avoid the "dominant motifs, more or less coded within genres" (*ibid.*: 116). This puts cinema into a permanent rebellion against its contemporary commercial conditions as well as against its current theoreticizations, and defines cinema's creative operations as those producing an eternal truth. Nevertheless, despite modern cinema being the permanent negation of its contemporary situation, it must not be forgotten, Badiou tells us, "that it is the films of Oliveira, of Kiarostami, of Straub, of the early Wenders, of a certain Pollet, of some Godards, etc." – a short and tantalizing list – that allow us to identify "everything" new in the situation (*ibid.*: 110). These directors are the measure of the new because they were the new, providing a brief genealogy of its emergence. Despite the elitist feel of this list, an aspect it shares with most of Badiou's pronounced preferences in art, what its members share is the way they disrupt the smooth consumption of cinema's "genres". These genres involve some narrative elements, but are mainly defined as political conflicts over the state's power of representation.

To begin, Badiou asks about the possibility of purified sexual images "proving an exception to the contemporary subsumption of love by the functional organization of enjoyment" (*ibid.*: 116). With the unfortunate ubiquity of pornography, Badiou concludes that "as yet no conclusive work has been done on this point" (*ibid.*: 117). In the genre of "extreme violence, cruelty, … [and] variations of putting to death" (*ibid.*) there has, however, been considerable research. The point, Badiou argues, is whether "embryonic operations exist which announce that all this material – which acts like an urban mythology for today – will be integrated into attempts at a baroque tragedy" (*ibid.*: 118). Despite this evocative description, no examples are given. The next genre is the figure of the worker, and the problem for cinema is to create a "subjective generalization" of the worker's "autonomy". "What is at stake is the very possibility of a real encounter of cinema and politics" (*ibid.*). A long history of such encounters already exists, and today cinema must strip itself of any nostalgia in order for the worker to appear as the film's "unfigurable real point" (*ibid.*). The example is Denis Levy's *L'École de Mai: 1968–1978* (1979). Next comes the millenarian motif. Here the problem is to purify the special effect of the "planetary catastrophe" signifying our helplessness in the face of globalization, by transmitting "the idea that the world is prey to Capital in an unbridled form, and by this very fact rendered, globally, foreign to the very truths that it detains in its midst" (*ibid.*: 119). This would require a "hero" whose "truth procedures confidence in themselves" were able to force this rather remarkable new truth on us. Once more, there are no examples.[15] The final genre Badiou mentions is the "petite-bourgeois comedy" representing love through the various states of marriage. Here it is a question of a "subjective ex-centring" of the "dominant conceptions" (*ibid.*: 120), with Éric Rohmer being "superior to his descendants" (*ibid.*: 120). As well as working within/against these "genres", cinema also mounts other assaults, such as Jean-Luc Godard's transformation of the "permanent rhythmic background" of youth into an "adulterated murmer", or Abbas Kiarostami or Manoel de Oliveira's use of the car chase to change "a sign of speed into a sign of slowness, constraining what is an exteriority of movement to become a form of reflexive or dialogic interiority" (*ibid.*: 112). In all these cases cinema defines itself anew through its subtractive appearance, avoiding the cliché and commercialism of the mass-art, while nevertheless achieving a universal address proper to truth.

Cinema is also impure in relation to the other arts, being the seventh art only in the sense of being every art's "plus-one". Cinema is "parasitic and inconsistent" (2005a: 83) and "operates on the other arts, using them as its starting point, in a movement that subtracts them from themselves" (*ibid.*: 79). The relation to music, for example, circles the use of rhythm that gives cinema "the tonality of the movement" within the "general pulsation of filmic transitions" (2004: 121). Cinematic rhythm may therefore begin from its music, but also includes editing, colours and acting. In the twenti-eth century ("the century of cinema") music has three lines of development, two of which cinema has appropriated. First, a post-Romantic music still operating under "the artifices of the finishing tonality" (*ibid.*) has had an important place in cinema music. Badiou's example is Luchino Visconti's *Morte a Venezia* (Death in Venice; 1971). Here the idea linking "amorous melancholy, the genius of the place, and death" (2005a: 80) becomes visible in a space opened by Mahler's melodies, a space where music and cinema's "pictorial stability" annul and dissolve each other. "These trans-ferences and dissolutions are the very thing that will have ultimately constituted the Real of the idea's passage" (*ibid.*). Secondly, Badiou traces a line from jazz to "youth music", "from rock to techno", a line also often utilized in cinema and identified with the "post-classical" frenetic camera. And finally, the site of "veritable musical creation", Arnold Schoenberg's rupture with the tonal system introducing a "universe of musical singularities" (2004: 121). It remains, however, for a cinematic rhythm comparable to serial and post-serial music to emerge, and cinema must, Badiou claims, take some blame for this failure. Oliveira and Jean-Marie Straub are exceptions proving the rule. Another example of cinema's status as the "plus-one" of the other arts is its relation to theatre, a relation embodied by the actor, whose Hollywood form must be purified. The actor must refuse being animated by capitalist neuroses, must escape normal-ized subjectivity, in order to "*divert* the evidence of the image" by poeticizing it (*ibid*: 123). Finally, and in relation to literature, cinema separates "the novelistic from itself by something that we could call a theatrical sampling, and opens up a space between theatre and the novel as a passage between them" (2005a: 79). Here, as with all the other examples, the "impurity" of cinema appears in the way it "extracts" something from the other arts, diverting both itself and them in a mutual "subtraction", which is also a "passage". Cinema therefore appears only in its relation to the other arts, as their plus-one, but this addition is a subtraction, the paradoxical movement of cin-ema's impurity *and* self-purification establishing its "truth". "These transferences and dissolutions are the very thing that will have ultimately constituted the Real of the idea's passage" (*ibid.*: 80).

This movement marking the passage of an idea has three aspects. First, cinema is the global movement of the visitation, the event-site of an idea. Secondly, cinema's "generic" self-purification becomes visible in "acts of local movement" (*ibid.*: 79). Thirdly, there is within cinema an "impure circulation" of the other arts, giving rise to "transferences and dissolutions". These three "movements" constitute the "poetics of cinema", a poetics of the visitation of the idea in the sensible. This is not, Badiou the resolute atheist insists, an incarnation. Cinema is not a sensible form of the idea, and does not endow the latter with a body. "The idea is not separable – it exists only for cinema in its passage" (*ibid.*: 80). In fact, cinema's ideas become visible in these three "movements": in the event, in its "truth procedure" within language, and in its relations to the other arts. In this sense, Badiou gives us, quite precisely, an *idea* of cinema that finds its principle in (a distinctly Lacanian) topology rather than movement. Indeed, cinema is a "knot" tying together its three *false* movements (*ibid.*: 82). Global movement is false because no measure is adequate to the event. Local movement is false because it is the effect following the subtraction of an image from itself. And impure movement is "falsest of all" because there is no way of completing the move from one art to another. "The arts are closed" (*ibid.*). As a result, "formal considerations – cutting, shot, global or local movement, color, corporeal agents, sound and so on – must be referred to only inasmuch as they contribute to the 'touch' of the Idea and to the capture of its native impurity" (*ibid.*: 85).

Despite the eternal essence of any "idea", we must always remember that in cinema it refers only to its contemporary conditions, only to everything in the current situation that *is not*. Although this adds a powerful contemporaneity to cinema's ontology, Badiou's "axiomatic discussion of film" does raise the problem, as he readily admits, "of speaking about it qua *film*" (*ibid.*: 86). The cinematic idea – the *truth* of cinema – appears through a process of subtraction (from commercialized genre effects, from the other arts, and from what already makes up cinema "itself") that is finally both a new and exciting philosophy of cinema and a rather restricting approach. It is restricting because, despite the often acute readings he gives of films, Badiou is only interested in cinema *qua idea*, rather than *qua film*. This means that when they appear, discussions of formal, material or historical aspects of cinema are entirely subordinated, and usually replaced, by a description of an idea. These descriptions vary in nature, sometimes proceeding according to the strictly subtractive methodology of the axiom, as in Badiou's account of cinematic genre, but often adopting a poetic methodology of the "impure", which tends towards the metaphoric. In Visconti's *Morte a Venezia*, for example, the film's grand accumulation of cultural references leads to a "decomposition by excess" (2005a: 86) as a metaphor for the main character's melancholy "adventure", presenting a "visitation of a subjective immobility" (*ibid.*: 87). It is no longer clear how cinema here aspires to, or indeed creates, the new. On the other hand, when Badiou places cinema as a mechanism of subtraction from its contemporary capitalist capture, and sees these operations as intervening at the level of popular culture, he offers an exciting role to cinema as mass-art. Here cinema is less art than politics, inasmuch as "an event is political if its material is collective" (2006b: 141). In this sense cinema's "impurity" seems to disengage it from the other arts, for it is its impurity that places its production within the economic realm of capital rather than the creative (not to mention Romantic) subjectivity of the artist.[16] These are the moments when Badiou's analysis of cinema tends more towards the question of what is to come – towards the cinematic *act* – than to the analysis of what has already been achieved, and when he considers the contemporary conditions of cinema in political terms (the representation of sex and violence, for example) rather than in terms of its historical achievements. At these moments Badiou's examples tend towards the popular (John Woo, *Titanic* [dir. James Cameron, 1997], *Brassed Off* [dir. Mark Herman, 1996]) rather than the canon (Visconti, Orson Welles, F. W. Murnau), and so move away from modernism's formal and elitist constraints to explore the political potential of cinema's refusal of capitalism's miserable conflation of *what is* with *what can be*.[17]

This is finally the gift Badiou offers, a gift both exciting and generous: cinema as a truth procedure, cinema as a *poetic* politics acting against Capital's saturation of everything, against its capture of the future. "When the situation is saturated by its own norms, when the calculation of itself is inscribed there without respite, when there is no longer a void between knowledge and prediction, then one must be *poetically* ready for the outside-of-self" (2004: 100). This is the role of cinema: to subtract itself from the representational logic of the Capitalist ruling class in order to offer a new truth, a new *image* of the collective.

NOTES

1. "Ontology," Badiou writes, "axiom system of the particular inconsistency of multiplicities, seizes the in-itself of the multiple by forming into consistency all inconsistency and forming into inconsistency all consistency. It thereby deconstructs any one-effect; it is faithful to the non-being of the one, so as to unfold, without explicit nomination, the regulated game of the multiple such that it is none other than the absolute form of presentation, thus the mode in which being proposes itself to any access" (*Being and Event*, O. Feltham [trans.] [London: Continuum. 2005b], 30).

2. This will imply, as Badiou writes, "the unpresentable is presented, as a subtractive term of the presentation of presentation" (*Being and Event*, 67). This is the axiom of the void set, and is written as: "$(\exists\beta)[\sim(\exists\alpha)(\alpha\in\beta)]$" (*ibid.*, 68).

3. For Badiou, "'nature' and 'number' are substitutable" (*Being and Event*, 140, 189).

4. Badiou is unapologetic about the violence of radical politics. In defence of Maoism he writes: "But the acts of violence, often so extreme? The hundreds of thousands dead? The persecutions, especially against intellectuals? One will say the same thing about them as about all the acts of violence that have marked the history, to this very day, of any expansive attempts to practice a free politics. The radical subversion of the eternal order that subjects society to wealth and to the wealthy, to power and to the powerful, to science and to scientists, to capital and to its servants, cannot be sweet, progressive and peaceful. There is already a great and rigorous violence of thought when you cease to tolerate that one counts what the people think for nothing, for nothing the collective intelligence of workers, for nothing, to say the truth, any thought that is not homogenous to the order in which the hideous reign of profit is perpetuated. The theme of total emancipation, practiced in the present, in the enthusiasm of the absolute present, is always situated beyond Good and Evil, because, in the circumstances of action, the only known Good is what the status quo establishes as the precious name of its own subsistence. Extreme violence is therefore reciprocal to extreme enthusiasm, because it is in effect, to speak like Nietzsche, a matter of the transvaluation of all values" (*The Century*, A. Toscano [trans.] [Cambridge: Polity, 2007], 62–3).

5. From the back covers of *Infinite Thought, Truth and the Return to Philosophy*, O. Feltham & J. Clemens (trans.) (London: Continuum, 2004) and *Metapolitics*, J. Barker (trans.) (London: Verso, 2006).

6. "The striking paradox of our undertaking is that we are going to try to *name* the very thing which is impossible to discern. We are searching for a language for the unnameable" (*Being and Event*, 376).

7. "[A] *truth groups together all the terms of the situation which are positively connected to the event*" (*ibid.*: 335). This procedure is that of "subjectivization" as "the rule of the infra-situational effects of the supernumerary name's entrance into circulation". The subject, in this sense, is "an occurrence of the void" (*ibid.*: 393) and "measures the *newness* of the situation-to-come" (*ibid*: 406).

8. The generic procedure is included in the situation (as a representational operation) but does not belong to it (it has no object, or its object is the *void*), making it an "excrescence", while the event itself belongs to the situation but is not included (represented) in it, making it a "singularity". Through the action of the Subject the truth announced in the event (the void of the situation) enters the situation: "A faithful generic procedure renders the indiscernible immanent" (*ibid.*: 342).

9. For a long list of proper names designating artistic "events" see "Third Sketch of a Manifesto of Affirmationist Art", in *Polemics*, S. Corcoran (trans.) (London: Verso, 2006), 141–2.

10. In Romanticism: "Art is the absolute as subject – it is *incarnation*" ("Art and Philosophy", in his *Handbook of Inaesthetics*, A. Toscano [trans.], 1–15 [Stanford, CA: Stanford University Press, 2005], 3). In as much as Romanticism affirms the descent of the idea into the finite artwork, Badiou must detach it from his account of contemporary artistic practice. Doing so involves "deconstructing" the artwork, removing it from its Romantic tendencies (especially those vitalist experiments generated from the Deleuzian refrain of "We don't know what a body can do" (*Polemics*, 137) and replacing these with works exploring the Duchampian readymade, and other "temporary installations" (*The Century*, 154). By bringing the art object into the everyday, the Ideal and infinite realm of its truth achieves a "*disincarnation*" in which "The infinite is not captured in form, it *transits through form*. If it is an event – if it is *what happens* – finite form can be equivalent to an infinite opening" (*ibid.*, 155). The modern art work rejects Romantic incarnation by opening on to the infinite and Ideal through the "active finitude" (*ibid.*, 159) of the art work itself, which becomes oriented in the twentieth century towards "a sort of generalized theatricality" (*ibid.*, 156).

11. Although Badiou acknowledges that Heidegger's radical critique of aesthetics begins modernity, he nevertheless rejects Heidegger's own "poetico-natural orientation, which lets-be presentation as non-veiling, as the authentic origin" (*Being and Event*, 125). Here, Heidegger remains a Romantic ("Art and Philosophy", 6) and by giving the rights to truth to art he "*hands philosophy over to poetry*" (*Manifesto for Philosophy*, N. Madarasz [trans.] [Albany, NY: SUNY Press, 1999], 74). Art is not and cannot be the usurpation (or worse, the "truth") of philosophy, but equally the opposite holds too, maintaining each in their area of expertise. Badiou offers not an "aesthetics", then, but an "inaesthetics": "a relation of philosophy to art that, maintaining that art is itself a producer of truths, makes no claim to turn art into an object of philosophy. Against aesthetic speculation, inaesthetics describes the strictly intraphilosophical effects produced by the independent existence of some art works" (as Badiou's self-penned epitaph to *Handbook of Inaesthetics* puts it ["Art and Philosophy", 1]). In fact, philosophy does not produce any truth. "It seizes truths, shows them, exposes them, announces that they exist. In so doing, it turns time towards eternity – since every truth, as a generic infinity, is eternal" (*ibid.*: 14). As a result, "Philosophy is the go-between in our encounters with truths, the procuress of truth" (*ibid.*: 10).

12. In a fascinating critique of Badiou's inaesthetics Jacques Rancière calls it a "twisted modernism" ("Aesthetics, Inaesthetics, Anti-Aesthetics", in *Think Again, Alain Badiou and the Future of Philosophy*, P. Hallward [ed.], 218–31 [London: Continuum, 2004], 221) because its attempt to combine modernism with Platonic ideas requires a condemnation of Romanticism that is both "summary" and somewhat hypocritical. Rancière argues that Badiou constantly "circles" the empty sepulchre, Hegel's "core-image of Romantic art" (*ibid.*: 223), marking the re-ascension of the idea and the disappearance of the body. In Badiou art is "forever caught between the muteness of material and the return to itself of thought" (*ibid.*). This, for Rancière, is finally the paradoxical result of an art that produces ideas as subtractions that are simultaneously inscribed in a name. For Badiou's comments on Rancière's work see *Metapolitic*, chs 7 and 8.

13. Badiou's position on the avant-garde seems to vary with the context. In *Being and Event*, "intervention is always the affair of the avant-garde" (*Being and Event*, 219). But this "avant-garde" is not artistic *per se*, and at other points, such as in "Art and Philosophy", Badiou strongly attacks avant-garde artistic movements as failed attempts to merge didactic and Romantic positions on art. More recently, in *The Century*, however, Badiou claims the avant-gardes as an important symptom of the century's desire for the real. As a result: "We've re-thought the fate of the avant-gardes, and hailed, for all time, their splendid and violent ambition" (*The Century*, 152). Here the avant-garde is celebrated as the modern response to Romanticism, while in "Third Sketch of a Manifesto of Affirmationist Art", Badiou returns to the criticisms he made in his essay "Art and Philosophy" both quoting and confirming them (*Polemics*, 135).

14. Elsewhere Badiou calls this a new Academicism or "Pompierism" (*Polemics*, 136) constituted by violent technological affects and a grandiose decorative style.
15. Badiou does mention John Woo as attempting to purify the special effect through "a type of slowed calligraphy of general explosions" (*Infinite Thought*, 113).
16. For the distinction between "individual" (love), "mixed" (science and art) and "collective" (politics) situations, see Badiou, *Being and Event*, 340.
17. This formulation comes from "Philosophy and Politics", in *Infinite Thought, Truth and the Return to Philosophy*, O. Feltham & J. Clemens (trans.) (London: Continuum, 2004), 74.

31 JACQUES RANCIÈRE

Sudeep Dasgupta

Jacques Rancière (b. 1940) is Emeritus Professor of Philosophy at the University of Paris (St Denis). Rancière co-authored *Reading Capital* (with his teacher Louis Althusser, and Etienne Balibar *et al.*, 1968). Rancière is known for his work on labour historiography, political pedagogy, literature, film and the politics of aesthetics. Rancière has published many books in French, most of which have been translated into English, including *The Nights of Labour* (1981; English trans. 1989), *The Philosopher and his Poor* (1983; English trans. 2004), *The Ignorant Schoolmaster* (1987; English trans. 1991), *On the Shores of Politics* (1992; English trans. 1995), *The Names of History* (1992; English trans. 1994), *Disagreement* (1995; English trans. 1999), *Mallarmé* (1996), *The Flesh of Words* (1998; English trans. 2004), *Film Fables* (2001; English trans. 2006), *The Politics of Aesthetics* (2000; English trans. 2004), *The Future of the Image* (2003; English trans. 2007) and *Hatred of Democracy* (2005; English trans. 2007).

Jacques Rancière's engagement with philosophy has been marked by scrupulous and sustained critique. This critique is one node of a much larger network of work that spans and questions the fields of literature, history, pedagogy, art and cinema. Rancière's engagement with film cannot thus be cast as that of a philosopher applying a "framework" to the study of film, for he reworks philosophy as much as film, within an a-disciplinary project that has linked the question of aesthetics to politics (cf. Dasgupta 2007; Rancière 2006a). Rancière's engagement with cinema is less that of a "film theorist" than a cinephile's poetic engagement with the history of cinema. Through his close readings of films and film theorists, Rancière produces both a mode of reading cinema that is crucial in developing a certain notion of aesthetics, and a reading of aesthetics that expands the perspectives on film. The notion of aesthetic play, the material specificity of cinema, and the relation between image and world are all central to this engagement with film. Explicitly eschewing the temptation to begin by asking "What *is* film?", Rancière's reading of film history begins with the question "What does the film theorist *want*? What can film make possible?"

No questions are innocent, of course, and by posing the question of the film theorist's desire, Rancière lands on a particular moment, and figure, in film history where the expectations *of* film will come to structure his own reading of film's productivity. The title of his book on cinema, *Film Fables* (2006a) leads to an answer to the question "What does the film-maker/theorist want *of* film?" It is with Jean Epstein, and his understanding of the fable in *Bonjour Cinéma* (1921), that Rancière's formulation of an answer to this film-theoretical/historical question begins. For Epstein, film promises the registration of pure materiality *sans* subjective intervention. The mechanical eye of the camera, Epstein believes, promises liberation from the story (fable), the subjective imprinting of form on matter. Epstein argues that the dispassionate eye of the camera will record the muteness of naked materiality. "Cinema is true. A story is a lie" (2006a: 1), as Rancière's epigraph to *Film Fables* ends, quoting Epstein. By starting with Epstein, Rancière provides an answer to the question "What does the film-maker want?": "cinema is to the art of telling stories (*l'art des histoires*) what truth is to lying" (*ibid.*). Rancière *begins* his own engagement with film with Epstein's expectation that film will discard the Aristotelian fable, "the arrangement of necessary and verisimilar actions that lead the characters from fortune to misfortune, or vice versa, through the careful construction of the intrigue (*nœud*) and denouement" (*ibid.*). Paraphrasing Epstein, Rancière argues: "life is not about stories, about actions oriented towards an end, but about situations open in every direction. Life has nothing to do with dramatic progression, but is instead a long and continuous movement made up of an infinity of micro-movements" (*ibid.*: 2). Further, film becomes the art in "which the intelligence that creates the reversals of fortune and the dramatic conflicts is subject to another intelligence, the intelligence of the machine that wants nothing, that does not construct any stories" (*ibid.*).

Rancière is constructing his own story of cinema by beginning with Epstein's expectation that cinema will annul the Aristotelean fable. If Epstein's (hi)story of cinema begins with a fulfilment of a desire (the annulment of the story), Rancière will thwart this narrative of cinema to construct another story of cinema, one that paradoxically does annul any Aristotelian fable *of* cinema, and instead puts the powers of cinema into play. Rancière first overturns, then puts into play the opposition between matter and meaning, object and subject, mute materiality and subjective intention that undergirds Epstein's argument. Epstein's expectation that cinema will overturn authorial subjectivity in favour of pure materiality ("the writing of movement with light … the suspension of specks of dust, the smoke of a cigar"; *ibid.*: 3) is overturned in Rancière's reading. If the machine-eye does not "want anything", it is precisely for the reason that it is *made to* want something by the film-maker. Subjective intention triumphs precisely because "the camera cannot be made passive, it is passive already, because it is of necessity at the service of the intelligence that manipulates it" (*ibid.*: 9). The thwarting of the fable in cinema becomes the thwarting of the fable *of* cinema. The (hi)story/fable (*histoire*) of cinema is not one of gradual progression or of a fall; rather, it is one of the continual play between the oppositions of form and matter, subject and object, the conscious and the unconscious. For the history of cinema, when read with Epstein's expectations of it as the starting-point, is also the betrayal of his desire. Cinema soon subsumed the materiality of the image to the logic of the plot. The "coherence of the plot (*muthos*)" ends up predominating the "spectacle's sensible effect (*opsis*)" (*ibid.*: 2).

However, Rancière argues, cinema can never completely annul the power of the image to testify to the muteness of materiality. The image becomes the site and surface on which the play between muteness and loquaciousness, matter and form, coexist in multiple ways. The overturning of Epstein's desire does not mean that the final word on cinema is the death of a dream/desire born at cinema's inception. Rather, Rancière holds in tension and puts into play the annulment of the pure passivity of the camera eye *and* its ability to register "the infinity of movements that gives rise to a drama a hundred times more intense than all dramatic reversals of fortune" (*ibid.*). It is through a reading of the cinematic *image*, and images in general, that the notion of play between opposites is developed. The notion of play is central to Rancière's understanding of cinema, and a longer philosophical tradition from which he borrows, and develops, his understanding of aesthetics.

AESTHETICS, FILM AND THE ROMANTICS

... everything speaks ...   (Novalis)

In the Introduction to *Film Fables*, Rancière argues that "cinema, in the double power of the conscious eye of the director and the unconscious eye of the camera is the perfect embodiment of Schelling's and Hegel's argument that the identity of conscious and unconscious is the very principle of art" (2006a: 9). Cinema is not just an art, but an idea of art, and its successful embodiment. As Rancière puts it, "Cinema seems to accomplish naturally the writing of *opsis* that reverses Aristotle's privileging of *muthos*. The conclusion, however, is false, for the very simple reason that cinema, being by nature *what the arts of the aesthetic age* strive to be, invariably reverts the movement" (*ibid.*, emphasis added). Rancière calls up a particular idea of art, which frames his reading of cinema, to then undermine any temptation to subsume cinema as an exemplification and accomplishment of that idea's desire to see art as the perfect "identity of conscious and unconscious". Film remains caught within this desire and its failed fulfilment – and this failure is precisely what is *productive* in film. By framing his reading of film within "the arts of the aesthetic age", Rancière explores the interpretive, aesthetic and political possibilities that open up by playing with this irresolvable tension between *muthos* and *opsis*, form and matter, the subject and the object. What, then, is the aesthetic age, and what ideas of art played a part in philosophy?

The "aesthetic age" is a term that Rancière coins, and refers to the period around the beginning of the nineteenth century and the philosophical circle that developed around Schelling, the Schlegel brothers, Hegel, Schiller, Novalis and Goethe among others (cf. Früchtl 2007: 213–15). In the introduction to his *System of Transcendental Idealism* (hereafter *System*; [1800] 1978), Schelling addresses the antinomy of subject and object that has marked philosophical thought. Schelling's *System* aims at transcending the dualisms of man and nature, form and matter, the subject and object, by "identifying an identity of the non-conscious activity that has brought forth nature, and the conscious activity expressed in willing" (*ibid.*: 12). Rancière's discussion of Epstein can be understood as a film-specific argument that is linked to this longer and broader philosophical interest in the dualism of subjective intention and "non-conscious" nature. Schelling argues that "this coming-to-be reflected of the absolutely non-conscious and non-objective is possible only through an *aesthetic act* of the imagination" (*ibid.*). Schelling elaborates:

> [A]ll philosophy is *productive*. Thus philosophy depends as much as art does on the productive capacity, and the difference between them rests merely on the different direction taken by the productive force. For whereas in art the production is directed outwards, so as to reflect the unknown by means of products, philosophical production is directed immediately inwards, so as to reflect it in intellectual intuition. The proper sense by which this type of philosophy must be apprehended is thus the *aesthetic* sense, and that is why the philosophy of art is the true organon of philosophy.
>
> (*Ibid.*)

The products of art (such as film) concretize this identity of conscious and non-conscious of which philosophical concepts are the internalization. As Rancière demonstrates through all of his writing on aesthetics and politics, philosophy needs art precisely because the apprehension of this unity of conscious and non-conscious needs the externalization of these opposites and their embodiment in the "products" of art. Romantic poetry (Hölderlin, in particular) is central to the formulation of aesthetics as an idea of art. Hegel's *Aesthetics: Lectures on Fine Arts* (1975) are an elaboration of this changing relation. Further, Rancière's emphasis on play between form and matter, subject and object, which he develops through a reading of the Romantics, also extends *across* the arts, including literature, cinema and painting.

Rancière's aesthetic framing of film through its connection to Schelling links Epstein's expectations of the cinematic cancellation of subjective intervention, and the emergence of the pure presence of objective materiality, to a more extended philosophical discussion going back to the Romantics, of the *union* of the opposites of form and matter, subject and object. If Rancière thwarts Epstein's overcoming of this dualism through the *submission* of conscious to unconscious, he will also thwart Schelling's desire for the successful union of form and matter in art. Through a reading of Schiller's *On the Aesthetic Education of Man* ([1793] 1967), Rancière will maintain a productive tension that ensures that the attempted overcoming of the dualism is a continuous process; in fact, film becomes one of the most recent artistic practices in the process of overcoming the dualism of form and matter that marks the aesthetic age inaugurated at the dawn of the nineteenth century. Central to Rancière's deployment of Schiller in developing his notion of the aesthetic regime is the concept of "play". Echoing and extending Schelling's concerns, Schiller famously states:

> let there be a bond of union (*Gemeinschaft*) between the form-drive (*Formtrieb*) and the material-drive (*Stofftrieb*); that is to say, let there be a play-drive (*Spieltrieb*), since only the union of reality with form, contingency with necessity, passivity with freedom, makes the concept of human nature (*Menschheit*) complete.
>
> (*Ibid.*: 103)

The play-drive mediates between matter (*Stoff*) and form, preventing both the subservience of reality to the law of form, and the chaos of pure formless matter. The aesthetic distinction between form and matter must be understood as also a reference to *social* life and human community (*Menschheit*). The play-drive has an explicitly political, as well as aesthetic, role in relation to the oppositions it seeks to unite, a point that will influence Rancière's political reading of film, and the arts in general, as we shall discuss below.

Aesthetic play is the continual process that attempts to unite the oppositions of form and matter. In Letter Fifteen, Schiller provides the example of the sculpture of Juno Ludovisi, although the ongoing play between form and matter is concretized across the art forms. Film, when framed within the notion of play, exemplifies the process of overcoming the dualisms that were exercised by Schelling, Schiller and Hegel (particularly in Hegel's *Lectures on Aesthetics*). The dialectical overcoming of the dualism of form and matter, intrinsic to the Romantic conception of art, also derails artistic specificity. The play of opposites is transcended only at the expense of art losing its specificity in relation to other art forms. As Rancière, referring to Epstein and Bresson, argues,

> all these great figures of a pure cinema whose fables and forms would be easily deducible from its essence do no more than offer up the best examples of the film fable, split and thwarted: *mise-en-scène* of a *mise-en-scène*, counter-movement that affects the arrangements of the incidents and shots, automatism separating image from movement ... cinema can only make the games it plays with its own means intelligible to itself *through the games of exchange and inversion* it plays *with* the literary fable, the plastic form, and the theatrical voice.   (2006a: 15, emphasis added)

Rancière's readings of films are examples of these games film must play with itself. This is an auto-ludic process of negotiating between the plot and mute matter, the image and its movement, that is at the same time related to the games film must play with the other arts, including literature, painting, theatre and dance. The dialectics of this auto-ludic "essence" of cinema is understood by Rancière as an ongoing process that maintains the tension between the opposites of the form-drive and the material-drive through the mediation of the *Spieltrieb* that seeks to unite them in art. The dialectic between opposites will never result in Hegelian terms to sublation (*Aufhebung*), that is, the transference to a *higher* level of both the contradiction and its annulment. Hence Rancière's focus on play (*Spiel*), rather than on the overvaluation of matter (*Stoff*), on which Epstein and later Gilles Deleuze rely. The tension between the opposites is never overcome or transcended (hence Rancière's aversion to aesthetic theories that assert either the fulfilment of transcendence, or the impossibility of play).[1] As Rancière argues,

> Cinema literalizes a secular idea of art in the same stroke that it actualizes the refutation of that idea: it is both the art of the afterwards that emerges from the Romantic de-figuration of stories, and the art that returns the

work of de-figuration to classical imitation. Hence the paradoxical nature of the continuity between cinema and the aesthetic revolution that made it possible. Even though the basic technical equipment of the cinema secures the identity of active and passive that is the principle of that revolution, the fact remains that cinema can only be faithful to it if it gives another turn of the screw to its secular dialectics. (2006a: 11)

We can name three aspects of aesthetic play that Rancière addresses. The *first* dimension of aesthetic play is one that finds its scene of gaming within the specificity of the medium of film itself: despite itself, film must thwart what its own technical specificity promises to make possible – the overcoming of opposites of active and passive. Further, aesthetic play underlines the borrowings *between* the arts. Rancière's framing of film thus suggests not just a reworking of a philosophical lineage going back to the nineteenth-century Romantics' concern with the unity of opposites, but also a cross-disciplinary understanding of aesthetic play that is relevant to the materiality of all art forms. This interplay was central to the Romantics (the Schlegel brothers in particular), where the essence of a medium is only "intelligible to itself *through* the games of exchange and inversion" (*ibid.*: 15). This seemingly paradoxical, cross-disciplinary articulation of play evokes a *non-sublatable* dialectic formulation: an essence, understood as necessarily internal to an object, comprehensible only through its connections to what is beyond the object. This *second* aspect of play in Rancière's reading of film, cross-disciplinarity, precludes the temptation of ontological arguments around the filmic image, for example, without sacrificing the requisite specificity (e.g. "technical equipment") crucial to an informed analysis. It forces film theory to be wary of technological determinism, and encourages an analysis of the arts in comparative perspective without collapsing them all together.

A *third*, related, element of play, which radicalizes artistic hybridity, is the internal dissolution of each of the art forms: what Rancière calls "la reconstitution d'un système des genres tombé en désuétude" (the reconstitution of a now obsolete system of genres) (1998: 28),[2] with reference to the Schlegel brothers. "Le roman", Rancière argues, describing this Romantic conception, "est le genre de ce qui est sans genre" (The novel … is the genre without genre) (*ibid.*: 29). The novel is deprived of "une nature fictionnelle déterminée" (a specific fictional nature) (*ibid.*). Rather, the ruination of genre produces an "anarchy", such as aspired to by Gustave Flaubert (*ibid.*). An idea of pure art is an idea of art purified from determinations of appropriate subjects and their proper representation. An Absolute style, exemplified in a book *about nothing*, Flaubert's dream, is an example of this idea of art given birth within Romanticism.

The aesthetic relationship that Rancière forms between Flaubert's dream of "an Absolute perspective on things" *sans* determinations of events and their mode of representation, and Epstein's privileging of film *sans* story (fable) and subjective intervention through narrative, should now be apparent. Both Flaubert and Epstein's conceptions share an overcoming of any normative relationship between object/ event in reality, and its representation. Epstein's desire for cinema's possibilities to erase subjectivity in favour of pure objectivity, and Flaubert's desire to overcome the representational logic that limits language to representation, are part of the break inaugurated by the Romantics' heralding of the "aesthetic age". Epstein's borrowing of film fragments to produce his own fable of film continues an idea of art's non-generic indifference as it plays form against matter. As Rancière argues, this tendency is also identifiable in Hegel's method, where he attempted to establish "le bon rapport entre le savoir et le non-savoir, entre la manifestation langagière du sens et le mutisme de la pierre" (the solid relation between knowing and not-knowing, between senses and language-related manifestation to see, and the silence of stone [Victor Hugo's *Notre dame de Paris*]) (*ibid.*: 57). Hegel articulates the possibility of overcoming such dualities in a "poésie generalisée" (a generalized poetry) of the aesthetic age, in "une figure nouvelle de l'art d'écrire" (a new form of the art of writing). Rancière argues that it is this form of language/writing that is indeed "*capable de poétiser toute chose*, de faire de toute réalité finie le hiéroglyphe de l'infini" (able to render everything poetic, to turn all of finite reality into the hieroglyph of infinity) (*ibid.*: 57–8, emphasis added), and which develops into the category "literature" two centuries later. Cinema is a continuation of this understanding of a language that attempts to unite the conscious and unconscious, the muteness of stone and the chatter of words. To "poetize everything" necessarily implies no estimation of either genre-specificity or of a division between the arts. This is also why Rancière argues: "*Cinema*, like *painting* and *literature*, is not just the name of an art whose processes can be deduced from the specificity of its material and technical apparatuses. Like painting and literature, cinema is the name of an art whose meaning cuts across the borders between the arts" (2006a: 4). Just as Flaubert's *Madame Bovary* attends to the details of the interior of a room or the plants outside her window with the equal attention granted to human passions and the unfolding of the narrative, cinema is capable of capturing the drop of the ink at the tip of a pen, the cigar burning at the edge of the ashtray: what Rancière refers to as "the splendor of the insignificant" (*ibid.*: 8).

Non-generic thinking marks Romantic thought, violates the borders that separate the arts, and makes anything and everything possible for appropriation.[3] This aspect of the "aesthetic regime", while not central to Schiller's notion of aesthetic play, is integral to how Rancière understands the productive aesthetic and political possibilities of cinema. While attending to the medium-specificity of film, Rancière deepens the possibilities of the medium to be "productive", in the sense that Schelling articulates. Thus it is striking that across the different readings of film, Rancière pays absolutely no heed to the traditional generic divisions in film studies, unlike the method of a film philosopher such as Stanley Cavell (1996).

It is in the work of Gilles Deleuze (1986, 1989), a reading of whose *Cinema* books occupies the mid-section of *Film Fables*, and the cinephile and film-maker, Jean-Luc Godard, with whom the book closes, that Rancière's engagement with the Romantics is most closely connected to a sustained analysis of film's aesthetic turn, and it is developed most recently in *The Future of the Image* (2007a). Epstein's importance for Rancière, in beginning his discussion of film as a thwarted fable (*fable contredite*), enables a broaching of the "identity of opposites" question that exercised the Romantics around 1800. If Epstein's answer to that conundrum at the dawn of cinema was to suggest the overcoming of the opposition in favour of the object (over the subject), Deleuze's engagement with film *as thought* some eighty years later is a return to that very question, and a similar (although not the same) answer. Deleuze's two books, *Cinema 1: The Movement-Image* and *Cinema 2: The Time-Image*, can be seen as marking not just two "ages of cinema" (part of the title of Rancière's essay on Deleuze), but also a *reversal* of the history of images according to the opposition Epstein sets up. If the "movement" of the plot subsumes the image to the logic of the narrative (*pathos* succumbing to *muthos*, in Aristotelian terms), the upsurge of the image as op-sign and son-sign in Deleuze's concept of the "time-image" marks the overturning of the priority of the plot over the pure materiality of image.

After first reminding us that Deleuze's history of images should not be mistaken for a history of the relations between representation and the real world, but a history of images *as part of the real world*, Rancière conducts an astute reading of the impulse and desire that marks such a history of images in Deleuze. If the development of cinema was to betray Epstein's desire to see it as the overcoming of the tyranny of the plot and the intervention of the film-maker, Deleuze's own history of cinema counters this historical betrayal by saving Epstein's dream. Yet Rancière shows how Deleuze's supposed overturning of the matter–form dichtomy is itself predicated on reinstalling the subjective intervention of the director, through Deleuze's continual reference to plot and narrative in his examples, and the growing incoherence of the relation between image category and historical period. Deleuze's redemption of cinema from subjective intervention is predicated on the director's subjectivity he claims to have annuled in his history of images in the world.

AESTHETICS, POLITICS AND FILM

> An artistic intervention can be political by modifying the visible, the ways of perceiving and expressing it, of experiencing it as tolerable or intolerable.
> (Rancière 2007b: 259)

Rancière's contemporary stature as a philosopher is integrally linked to his *critique* of philosophy. In particular, Rancière (1995, 1996, 2001a) attacks philosophy for playing the role of partitioning social space and human capacities according to the order of its own discourse. The contemporary consensual form of politics, shorn of all conflict, is what Rancière calls the "police order" (1996: 30). By articulating the norms for the establishment of proper relationships between aptitudes and social positions, it provides a false legitimacy to a social order always threatened by disagreement (*mésentente*), the practice of equality that threatens conventional separations and exposes the groundless ground of political philosophy. This process of disagreement that counters the police regime Rancière calls "politics" (*ibid.*): "Politics is the art of warped deductions and mixed identities" (*ibid.*: 139). It is paratactical in the sense of combining and mixing identities that do not obey the logic of political representation.[4] "Politics", Rancière argues, "has an aesthetic dimension: It is a common landscape of the given and the possible, a changing landscape and not a series of acts that are the consequence of 'forms of consciousness' acquired elsewhere" (2007b: 259).

The fields of intervention and the details of the arguments Rancière develops within philosophy and art criticism are distinct, and cannot be collapsed on to each other. Yet, for him, they are integrally *linked*. His politico-philosophical argument around the "police regime" can be said to be homologous to his articulation of the representative regime of art, which establishes the conventions that govern the subjects of art and their "proper" mode of representation. The dis-articulation of this regime by the "aesthetic revolution" (Rancière 2002), which disobeys generic classifications and thwarts artistic purity through "mixed identities", can also be seen to be homologous with Rancière's understanding of "politics", which disobeys the rules and conventions that demarcate social space. Flaubert deranges the ordering discourse of conventional propriety by an indifferent equalization, by treating the rationality and flights of fancy of the village doctor's wife in the same way as the writer of the age of belles-lettres represented the lives of the aristocracy.[5] Further, the art of the aesthetic age explores the "splendor of the insignificant" (2006a: 8): "a little dust shining in the sun, a drop of melted snow falling on the moiré silk of a parasol, a blade of foliage on the muzzle of a donkey" (2007a: 44). There is a politics to Flaubert precisely because he equalizes the dignity of human subjects with the materiality of their surroundings: both are equally worthy of the writer's pen and eye, *contra* the conventions of the norms of the representative regime. The splendour of the "insignificant" is a polemical articulation, for by according the insignificant significance (meaning, but also importance), it disrupts the boundary between what is worth representing and what is not.

The politics of aesthetics lies in this disrespect toward conventional boundaries and the making available of anything and everything, anyone and everyone to the dignity of a work of art: "each element in this [aesthetic] regime is at once an image-material susceptible to infinite transformations and combinations, and an image-sign capable of designating and interpreting every other" (2006a: 178). The universe of artistic practice is potentially infinite; in Godard's omnivorous appropriation of text and image *Histoire(s) du cinéma* (History(s) of the cinema; 1988–98) and of the history of all the arts we see a similar disregard for artistic purity or medium-specificity. Godard turns images "into units caught up in a double relationship – with all the things that have left their impressions on them, and with all other things with which they compose a specific sensorium, a world of inter-expressivity" (Rancière 2006a: 174). The film image is an interface, which by borrowing indiscriminately and reworking "all other things" composes a "world", stages a mode of being-in-common based on the absolute equality of all things.[6] That is what Rancière means by the "radical innocence of the art of the moving image" (2006a: 171): lacking any ontology based on properties, essences or norms, it becomes the site and surface of possibility by borrowing from anything and everyone to produce a specific "sensorium". Rancière, of course, does not legislate what kind of sensorium. The politics of polemical equalization is an open politics, just as the politics of the aesthetic age is one of possibility.

Through the concept of "equality", Rancière's critique of political philosophy provides the condition of possibility for the potential of all art, including the art of the moving image, to produce a possible world through its capacity to indifferently borrow materials, techniques and logics of all the arts without respect for generic differences or technological specificity. By creating and thwarting expectations, by polemically

347

configuring spaces and forms, images are aesthetic and political. If politics is the para-tactical staging of a common world, cinema as an art of the aesthetic age provides one of the multiple surfaces of play for countering consensus through the staging of disagreement.

NOTES

1. By holding on to the promise of reconciliation between the general and the particular, Theodor Adorno, *Aesthetic Theory*, R. Hullot-Kentor (trans.) (London: Continuum, 2002) comes closest to Rancière's own argument. Jean-François Lyotard's deployment of Adorno to ultimately articulate a catastrophic reading of art through what Rancière insists is a mistaken reading of the Kantian sublime is precisely what Rancière rejects; see *L'Inhumain* (Paris: Galilée, 1988). See Rancière, "Les Antinomies du modernisme", in *Malaise dans l'esthétique*, 85–141 (Paris: Éditions du Seuil, 2004), and in particular the section "Lyotard et l'esthétique: un contre-lecture de Kant", 119–41.
2. Thanks to Charles J. Stivale and Jacques Rancière for assistance with translations of this passage.
3. The discussion of lyric poetry, for example, in Rancière's *The Flesh of Words: The Politics of Writing*, C. Mandell (trans.) (Stanford, CA: Stanford University Press, 2004), 10–15.
4. Cf. Rancière for an analysis of the "perpetual flight of identities" that disrupts a formalization of class identity (*The Philosopher and His Poor*, A. Parker [trans.] [Durham, NC: Duke University Press, 2004], 90–104, esp. 99).
5. See Rancière, "Le Cinéaste, le peuple et les gouvernants", in his *Chronique des temps consensuels*, 109–14 (Paris: Éditions du Seuil, 2005) for a critique of the contemporary deployment of film and new technology through a reading of Eric Rohmer's film *L'Anglaise et le duc* (The lady and the duke; 2001). The latter stabilizes the disruptive force of the aesthetic regime of art, identifiable in Flaubert. Rancière is himself explicit about the *possibilities* opened up by new technology including video and digital techniques, although of course, unlike Walter Benjamin, he does not believe a technology is intrinsically linked to a particular kind of politics. See for example Solange Guénoun, "An Interview with Jacques Rancière: Cinematographic Image, Democracy and the 'Splendor of the Insignificant'", *Sites: The Journal of Twentieth-Century Contemporary French Studies/Revue d'études françaises* **4** (2000), 249–58.
6. Cf. Philip Watts's suggestive reading of Rancière on images: "Images d'Égalité", in *La Philosophie déplacée: Autour de Jacques Rancière*, L. Cornu & P. Vermeren (eds), 361–70 (Paris: Horlieu, 2004).

32 GIORGIO AGAMBEN

Christian McCrea

Giorgio Agamben (b. 1942) is an Italian philosopher best known for his political treatises in which the decay of the citizen and the abolition of civil rights are held to account, in such works as *The State of Exception* (2003; English trans. 2005), *Homo Sacer* (1995; English trans. 1998), *Stanzas* (1977; English trans. 1993), *Means Without End* (1996; English trans. 2000) and *Remnants of Auschwitz* (1998; English trans. 1999) . Agamben is Professor of Aesthetics at the University of Verona, Italy. He holds the Baruch Spinoza Chair at the European Graduate School in Saas-Fee, Switzerland and also teaches philosophy at the Collège International de Philosophie in Paris and at the University of Macerata in Italy. His fascination with the power of images, and their relationships to gestures and language, is marked throughout his writings, and he has published some brief essays concerning cinema, "Notes on Gesture" (1992), "Difference and Repetition: On Guy Debord's Films" (1995) and "The Six Most Beautiful Minutes in the History of Cinema" (2007).

The Italian philosopher Giorgio Agamben has been rapidly taken up by scholars working in a variety of fields in the past decade as his work concerns some of the most pressing and complex elements of contemporary life. While the rethinking of sovereignty and the rights of the individual are his most famous philosophical enquiries, his work traverses many fields, including biblical research, aesthetics and art history. Agamben has received a great deal of critical attention for his work on "bare life" and the reframing of our collective subjectivity given the contemporary status of the refugee.

Agamben's *Homo Sacer* (1998) is a concise and deeply political examination of the ways in which life is bound by law, and how exceptionality – especially the figure of the refugee – became weaponized underneath contemporary capitalism. Disputed borders and no-man's-lands between them, for example, open up the broader question about what it means to be a citizen. Agamben's contribution to these themes continues in *The Man Without Content* (1999b), *Means Without End* (2000), *Remnants of Auschwitz* (1999d), *The Open* (2004), *State of Exception* (2005a) and *The Time That Remains* (2005b).

Throughout these political works, Agamben's preference for the dialectic, the double and the opposing pair becomes more than clear. In many of his situations, he uses negative and positive poles as a way to explore the machinations of the globalizing systems that sit at the centre of his study. *The Coming Community* (1993a) was rooted in a series of these relationships; blessed and damned, potentiality and actuality, common and proper. While Roland Barthes, Jacques Derrida and Gilles Deleuze (among many others) gained considerable traction in their discovery of deeper meaning-systems that disavow the need of anything as absolute as a pair of opposing ideas, this resurgent polar rhetorical technique, in many ways, identifies Agamben's idiosyncratic mode of writing.

There is another Agamben, however: the Agamben of poetics, culture and signification. In the books *Stanzas: Word and Phantasm in Western Culture* (1993c), *Idea of Prose* (1995b), *The End of the Poem: Studies in Poetics* (1999a), *Potentialities: Collected Essays in Philosophy* (1999c) and *Profanations* (2007a), another history emerges. Naturally, it is here that Agamben's interests in cinema are more visible, and from these texts that a cultural Agambenism – a "thinking texts through" his work – might become possible. Of special interest to the aesthetic Agamben are ongoing questions of status in the literal sense: how do objects become sacred, and what is their power when they are? How might another object profane against the first and disrupt the contingent authority? Answers inevitably arise from disaffection, and energized dissimulation through art for Agamben. Although his appreciation of film does not span the breadth and depth of the form, his formulation of the status of the image (and the avant-garde image in particular) proves itself invaluable in furnishing discourse.

There is also an opportunity to use his commentary on cinema to take on the other, political, Agamben in the simple dialectic, and pose the question: why retain the simple dualisms when they are lost to so many others? Throughout *Stanzas*, "poetry" and "philosophy" emerge as devices to unravel the status of the written and spoken word, reassembling semiotics around the two supposed opposites and in a spectrum between them (1993c: 45). It is imagining them as *limit cases* rather than opposites, or as being diametrically related, that creates Agamben's potential movements in discourse: in seeing the poetic as a marked point towards which acts and gestures only point, and philosophy a marked point to which words and formulations only hint. These are the terms that Agamben's readers are involved with; certainly throughout the political writing and explicitly in *State of Exception* (2005a), the non-state and the limit case are made to be politically potent and potentialized. When poetry and philosophy are limit cases, event horizons to which only signals can be ascribed, they retain some of the digestive, open qualities of the philosophies more readily ascribed to Agamben's contemporaries.

Where Micheal Hardt and Antonio Negri's searing critique of contemporary capitalism fuels their collaborations *Empire* (2000) and *Multitude* (2004), and Slavoj Žižek (2002) stridently asserts a new psychological status for images, moving and otherwise, Agamben – or at least the aesthetic and cultural Agamben – can be best conceptualized in the tradition of Walter Benjamin. As in that earlier critic, the state of meaning-making itself is constantly under enquiry, from which each medium can be made to speak either directly or indirectly to the conditions under which signs and power find themselves. Agamben seeks, in a sense like Barthes' preference for the "puncture or perforation" in the photographic image, to slip underneath the surface of the image and come to terms with the frame.

Agamben is not in the practical sense a philosopher of the cinematic, but his work refers to a cinema that is completely unlike those of other contemporary thinkers. This ongoing look at the status of the image – this intense glare – is deployed with reference to film images in order to unravel the status of images more generally. It is under this type of philosophy, then, at several points in both writerly histories, the philosophical and the aesthetic, that Agamben cuts across them to furnish a new history of the image. Cinema's power for Agamben – and especially in the cases that this chapter will focus on – is the continual reformulation of representation, of ruptures slowly recaptured and symbols made speechless. The cinematic Agamben, assembled out of frames and gestures at several key moments in his writing, presents to us a unique and powerful language for decoding what may be otherwise indecipherable: the sensation of cinema speaking to itself.

THE GESTURAL HOMELAND

Working on the historical evolution of the status of the image, Agamben's essay "Notes on Gesture" in *Infancy and History: the Destruction of Experience* constructs a history of the depletion of the gestural world in everyday life. In this history, neurologist Gilles de la Tourette and the photographer Eadweard J. Muybridge are sympathetically linked as gesture's pallbearers (1993b: 134). For Agamben, Tourette's breaking up of physiological movements into segments and sections, with some becoming unruly, mechanized previously smooth and continuous human movements. Muybridge's serial photography of faces going through complex speech and breakdowns of the human stride offered a companion project: a capturing of the elemental atoms of movement. Imagined together by Agamben through admitted coincidence, we develop a new and material prehistory of the cinematic image. More than as just a historical task, Agamben sees questions of materiality as how cinema itself speaks: the most striking cinematic images are those in which the circumstances of its construction are completely laid bare.

In crediting the work of Tourette as possessing a gaze "already prophetic of the cinema" and a more precise social examination than even Balzac (*ibid.*: 135), Agamben refers to a series of experiments that involved measuring the markings of patients' feet once they were covered with powdered iron sesquioxide. Describing the growth of the experiments as they begin to organize and comprehend many types of movements, Agamben looks to Tourette's mapping of the "involuntary spasms and mannerisms that can be defined only as a generalized catastrophe of the gestural sphere" (*ibid.*). This "generalized catastrophe" is explained as the collapse of the assemblages of movement and the casting out of gesture from social behaviour. For Agamben, the birth of modernity and mechanized work practices also mechanized gestures into their components: the business handshake, the salute, the hand on the hip. The growth of signs and photographic images makes it impossible to feature subtlety in these gestures, as their permanency eliminates the natural gait, the lilt, the error. The core of the gestural life, the ritualized personal expression of movement, is increasingly parsed, corrected and tested under Agamben's modernity.

What occurs alongside this shift from a personal and specific gestural sphere to a collapsing, flattening one is "that the bourgeoisie – which, only a few decades earlier, had still been firmly in possession of its symbols – falls a victim to interiority and entrusts itself to psychology" (*ibid.*: 134). There is little doubt from the text of "Notes on Gesture" that Agamben speaks to this particular appreciation of history with a degree of sadness.

As the apparatus of continuance, cinema occupies the central problematic of this disappearing act. If we accept that "a society that has lost its gestures seeks to reappropriate what it has lost while simultaneously recording that loss" (*ibid.*: 137), then the history of cinema begins with two gestural images of its own: the return to the family home and the funeral. The motions of Muybridge's experiments – the "man running with a rifle", the "woman walking and picking up a jug" – are empowered precisely because they memorialize what is fading away into the world of ultimately meaningless "use". Where is the soldier going? What is inside the jug?

Because Agamben is speaking so generally here about the status of cinema at its birth as a way to reconceive of the evolution of the image, it is a way to speak about cinema outside the image: that is, "gesture rather than image is the cinematic element" (*ibid.*: 136). Theorist Benjamin Noys wrote around Agamben's cinematic thinking in an article for *Film Philosophy* that: "The power of cinema, and the power of cinematic montage, is to free the image from its frozen state and transform it back into gesture. It can reveal the potential of the image, and release what has been frozen in the image" (Noys 2004).

The gestural cinema is not a historical rewriting, but an unravelling and unspooling of film that recapitulates the materiality of movement in frame over the materiality of the eye. The potential of the image, the return of meaning, which Agamben calls "Messianic" in his "Difference and Repetition" (1995a), is that we may see powerful, affective, distancing elements – human or abstract gestures – that work to undermine the category of the image itself: that is, to remind us of the funereal quality of the cinematic apparatus, the burial of gesture.

Agamben's 1995 essay generates a more detailed conception of the gestural cinema, again deftly read by Noys (2004) as showing that "philosophy and cinema converge on the gesture, on the loss of the gesture, and on recovering the gesture as the realm of both the ethical and the political". While Agamben concentrates here on Guy Debord's formal and material interventions into film practice, and continues a line of questions that posits montage as a polar limit case of one type of cinematic image rather than a practice, he retains throughout a fascination with the status of the image.

> There's no need to shoot film anymore, just to repeat and stop … The compositional technique has not changed, it is still montage, but now montage comes to the forefront and is shown as such. That's why one can consider that cinema enters a zone of indifference where all genres tend to coincide, documentary and narrative, reality and fiction. Cinema will now be made on the basis of images from cinema. (Agamben 1995a: 315)

This is not a call merely for anti-formalist avant-garde experimentalism, although the strategies of Debord and Godard are specifically mentioned. Agamben calls for a political cinema that can disarm the indifference and coincidence of the form itself; new images, new scenes may not be enough. What is required is a deep reworking of the relationship of the image and the gestures within it, of the relationship between digital, discrete instances and analogue, flowing consistencies. He seeks a battle, in short, with careless coincidence. Agamben refers to the end of Debord's short film *In Girum Imus Nocte Et Consumimur Igni* (We spin around the night consumed by the fire; 1978), which ends not on "end", but on "to be taken up again at the beginning" as a palindromic act. It is also a chant or mantra, as repetition possesses qualities of its own. To repeat the film at its end is not a smooth, continuous act, but a layering one. Agamben situates repetition and stoppage as the key tools of his desired cinema, or the "coming cinema". "By placing repetition at the centre of his compositional technique, Debord makes what he shows us possible again, or rather he opens up a zone of undecidability between the real and the possible" (1995a: 316). When we see an image once, we presume it has passed, but should it repeat, a fracturing of the relationship between present and past opens up – and we anticipate a repeat. Debord's films are not political because they attempt to convince; they are rather as formal and tactical as his famous and devout love of chess. (His first film, *Hurlements en faveur de Sade* [Howlings in favour of de Sade; 1952], consists of alternating black and white frames while found text fragments are read.) His films are all possessed with a critique of mediation; *La Société du spectacle* (Society of the spectacle; 1973) famously equips itself with Marx's assault on commodity fetishism while stroking women and cars alike in their idealized forms. In Debord's method, images haunt; they never merely appear. *In Girum Imus Nocte Et Consumimur Igni* opens with a still image of a happy middle-class family from a high, isometric view, while Debord speaks: "Separated from each other by the general loss of any language capable of describing reality". There is no contradiction between Debord's use of stillness and when Agamben says that "the specific character of cinema stems from montage" (1995a: 315), as we recall that the two conditions are repetition and its equally powerful apostate, stoppage.

Consider also the films of Viennese experimental film-maker Martin Arnold, such as *Passage à l'acte* (1993), which explodes a few seconds of *To Kill A Mockingbird* (dir. Robert Mulligan, 1962) into a glossolalic tempest. Gestures repeat ad infinitum, until the children at the table crescendo in a unconscious, Tourette-like cycle: "Hurry up / I'm trying to / Hurry up / I'm trying to / I'm try / I'm try / I'm try / Hur / Hur / Hur". But it is film that suffers the neurological condition, not the characters. Film cannot help but try to express the inexpressible, it feels the heat and, eventually, the outburst will come. Arnold's history, avowedly drawing on Maya Deren, whose own films take place deep in the gestural homeland, is one of seeking out something that is opposed – radically opposed – to the image itself.

The aesthetics and politics of these questions are yet too indeterminate to form a sense of cinema more broadly, without first creating a meaningful body. Noys describes the processes at work in Agamben's formula, which contains two types of cinema (recalling the fascination for dualisms and dialectics):

One is pornography or advertising, in which the image is revealed as deficient, exposed as such, but only to lead us on to more images. There are
always more images promised that will fulfill our desire but this image as
such is not it. The other way, Debord's way, is to exhibit the image and so
to allow the appearance of "imagelessness". In this case there is no longer
some other image but the end of the image. (Noys 2004)

As crippling as any duality is, there emerges in this particular point in Agamben's
argument a potent clarification on the avant-garde gesture (and image) more generally: "The expressive act is fulfilled when the means, the medium, is no longer perceived as such", he writes, but "on the contrary, the image worked by repetition and
stoppage is a means, a medium, that does not disappear in what it makes visible"
(1995a: 318). There is doubtless a predilection for avant-gardism in Agamben; the
privilege of distancing techniques seems to disallow narrative cinema any of the credit
given to Debord's revolutionary project. Thankfully, Agamben is careful to open the
discourses of gesture and image across cinematic experiences, and situates the return
to the gestural outside texts. His love for analysis-as-spectrum here opens up, rather
than closes down, possibilities for reading. Here the Agambenian method of simple
dualistic dialectics is a way to pose an impossible problem in the present, and display
a means by which to recapture, recapitulate and disrupt the collective history, and
then onwards to disturb the present in turn. Agamben's reading of Debord poses
cinema against media as spectral limit cases of gestural subjectivity (1995a: 316). The
media subject is ever-present, ever-indignant, but ever-powerless, while the cinematic subject has to the power to repeat and stop the past, and in so doing realize the
repetition and stoppages in the present.

What Agamben seeks, then, is a cinema of pure means. It does not appear, nor
can it be said to really exist, in one director's history, but it is somewhere in the
melee of gestures. Agamben makes specific reference to Ingmar Bergman's *Sommaren
Med Monika* (Monika, the story of a bad girl; 1953a), and the experience of watching
actress Harriet Andersson staring back at the camera as a way to read across both
Bergman's films and into a gestural undertow of images more generally. Agamben
refers to Bergman's own belief of the importance of this moment, but the splitting of
reality from its mirrors need not be so direct. Only five years later, Bergman directed
Ansiktet (The magician; 1958), in which Max Von Sydow played Albert Vogler, a
depressive travelling trickster figure attempting to bamboozle a new town before the
plot unravels in farce and ferocity. Albert spends much of the film stony-faced and
silent, and comes to the act of expression after a long, harrowing shot where he stares
at his own clawing hand, in dismay. Albert's "Magical Health Theatre" comprises a
small troupe whose own means are shown for what they are: purposeful and to an end,
any end. The trick of the magic acts performed interpolates the trick of the attempt to
swindle the townspeople of their money. The rumours that begin the townspeople's
vulnerability is not that Albert's tricks are real, but more that serious unexplained
phenomena occur around his performances. A procession of sleights of hand quickly
overlap until we begin to watch the gestures to catch the tricks (of Albert, of his
enemies, of Sydow, of Bergman), enmeshing ourselves with the despicable and dozy

critics and science-avowed members of the town's aristocracy. In this film, images are disavowed and gestures reclaimed, although perhaps not fully in the "messianic" mode that Agamben anticipates; we do not necessarily expect anything but a final return to fiction, to normalcy. As the character Johan Spegel (Bengt Ekerot) dies, he professes: "I've prayed one prayer in my life: Use me, O God! But He never understood what a devoted slave I'd have been. So I was never used … But that too is a lie. Step by step you go into the dark. The movement itself is the only truth." The trick has always already been played; we imagine ourselves in images rather than as gestural beings, insulating ourselves against ruptures. So when one of the troupe, Manda Vogler (Ingrid Thulin) asks the Minister of Health, Dr Vergerus (Gunnar Björnstrand), to leave them alone and cease his inquisition of their group, he simply says "I can't. You represent what I detest most of all … the unexplainable." The real and the possible are best turned in on each other, for the minister and for the pornographic/advertising image of Agamben's formula. "Doesn't cinema always just do that, transform the real into the possible and the possible into the real?" (1995a: 316) This is the zone of indifference from which escape is impossible but necessary.

Bergman's intense interest throughout many of his films of this period, through *Gycklarnas Afton* (Sawdust and tinsel; (1953), *Smultronstället* (Wild strawberries; 1957) and *Jungfrukällan* (The virgin spring; 1960) is not in what is hidden, but "hiddenness" itself. What re-emerges later in his film-making as more overt breaks with continuity and contingency bubbles through films such as *Ansiktet*, just beneath the surface. These films, to a lesser or greater extent, are not merely cinema but occur in *a medium that does not disappear in what it makes visible*. We are always perceiving too much to be contained in a fiction, but never enough for the well to overflow completely into chaos. Returning to Agamben's fixation on the political task of history, we can see past acts and events unfurl and open up even as we experience the present, giving us a growing sense of opportunity, of a break in the melancholy into something more irruptive. We fixate, like Albert on his hand, rise, and speak for the first time.

CONFRONTING THE IMAGE, OR "WHEN ARE YOU GOING TO FINISH *DON QUIXOTE?*"

In the opening lines of "Difference and Repetition", Agamben asks us to do away with the idea of the work entirely and instead come down to the question of action: "Rather than inquiring into the work as such, I think we should ask about the relation between what could be done and what actually was done" (1995a: 313). Potentiality, then, makes another leap from the political to the aesthetic Agamben. If there can be a theorizing of unfinished cinema, then it could be of gestures – gaits, lilts, errors – that are not accompanied by images at all. Like Johan, step by step we go into the dark, where movement itself is the only truth. Yet, in an essay called "In Praise of Profanation" (in Agamben 2007a), Agamben returns to the pornographic video as a site of unmasking imagery, asking how the images within might be unmade, or regain their power to properly profane against the sacred itself (2007a: 65). How do they become images that do not lead on to other images, in infinite regress, disappointment and delay?

Cervantes' story *Don Quixote* is the gesture from which images are wrung only after a fight. Orson Welles and Terry Gilliam are the most famous of film-makers to fail to complete a film of the novel, but the story of Quixote's world overlapping with Sancho Panza's forms an immediate problem for the process of representation. The more vivid scenario cannot be; the real and the possible cannot attach properly and feed into each other – and by Agamben's conception, the very idea of cinema would be impossible in the first place. So it is that readers of the novel never equate delusion with falsity. Welles worked on his film at various points in his life, from principal shooting in 1955 until his death in 1985, and the film was subsequently re-cut by cult horror director Jesus Franco in 1992, who worked on the set with Welles and at some points in the intervening years.

Of all Giorgio Agamben's cinema writing, none is more passionate, gnomic or arresting than the simple 273-word essay simply called "The Six Most Beautiful Minutes in the History of Cinema" (2007b: 196), which focuses on a sequence from Welles's *Don Quixote*. Nowhere else is Agamben's interest in the cinematic clearer: a seeking out of a final confrontation with the status of the image that is literal, but never absolute.

In the scene in question, Don Quixote sits in a provincial cinema, agape at the screen. The light flickers excessively as we watch Panza stumble in, grotty, chubby and confused. Up above, the balcony is stacked with young boys looking down. Our Dulcinea is a young girl of seven or eight, blonde and pigtailed, armed with lollipop and piercing eyes. She watches the scene unfold before it truly unfolds, as Sancho sits next to her and they share a moment enjoying the spectacle of the film. Don Quixote, of course, sees only what he sees, and rises up to stand before the images. Frustrated at their lifelike nature, he slashes at the canvas, cutting into horses and pirates as the balcony erupts in outrage and laughter, egging him on. Dulcinea looks up at Quixote, reproachful. Agamben's reading of this scene is a gesture in itself, a sprinkle of iron sesquioxide on the feet to watch where the heel steps deepest, and we come to a very different approach from the one chasing Debord's politics:

> What shall we do with our fantasies? Love them, believe them – to the point where we have to deface, to destroy them. But when they prove in the end to be empty and unfulfilled, when they show the void from which they were made, then it is time to pay the price for their truth, to understand that Dulcinea – whom we saved – cannot love us. (*Ibid.*)

The image thus confronted, a turnabout is possible, even if it means standing up to its projection physically. The real and the possible here, and in Quixote, are shown to be not at odds, but merely limit cases, walking in the desert heat, keeping each other company. "For in every image there is always a kind of *ligatio* at work, a power that paralyses, whose spell needs to be broken; it is as if, from the whole history of art, a mute invocation were raised towards the freeing of the image in the gesture" (1993c: 136). So despite the case for gestural cinema and avant-gardism, another political task is possible: the freeing of image from gesture in turn – but one that has ultimately caressed modernity and its haidmaiden, capital. Quixote tilts at this windmill himself, looking not just to slash away at the fleeting impressions on the canvas, but to make his beloved Dulcinea possible, and the girl Dulcinea impossible again. The difficulty Welles experienced in completing the film is all too real, but there is also a gesture of stoppage involved from our vantage point in the present. We see collected images, snippets, reels, and assemble for ourselves the author as we expect and demand him to be reformed and reborn. In sympathy with Deleuze, Agamben notes that: "[T]he image in cinema – and not only in cinema but in modern times more generally – is no longer something immobile, it is not an archetype, but nor is it something outside of history; rather, it is a cut which itself is mobile, an image-movement, charged as such with a dynamic tension" (1995a: 314). Yet, in privileging gesture, such as the soldier with his gun, or the carried jug, it seems impossible to avoid the creation of archetypes – of using the quest for gestures as shorthand for another quest – beauty. That, too, can be subject to the material questions of the apparatus, to stoppage and repetition, which split up our sense of viewership from our sense of place. We sympathize with Sancho Panza, who knows reality well enough to enjoy the image for what it is, and to form a friendship with Dulcinea. However, Don Quixote is under our care, our fate bound with his; his madness quickly becomes our duty of care. In either limit case, there is a confrontation with the image – one with the sword taken up to make real out of the possible, and the other a smiling Panza, enjoying the possible formed from the real.

Agamben's gestural politics of the cinema is not especially bound up in ideas of the body, or even its movements. Gesture, generally framed as it is with Agamben, is everything that the conception of the "image" is not, or what the image has profaned and taken away from the past. The philosophy espoused throughout his work is that the construction of the image is the portal through which meaning makes itself, or "Because it is centrally located in the gesture, not the image, cinema essentially ranks with ethics and politics (and not merely with aesthetics)" (1993b: 136). The political task of cinema for Agamben is to begin to come to terms with all the potentials of the apparatus, and undo its own damage: slash at itself while at the same time attempting a rescue. The energy of that division forms not one avant-garde reading and tradition, but really two: one making sense of form and another interpreting only information coming in through the non-senses.

Speaking to Aristotle's poiesis and praxis division, Agamben seeks a form of cinema that follows an end other than itself. So that "what characterizes gesture is that in it there is neither production nor enactment, but undertaking and supporting. In other words, gesture opens the sphere of ethos as the most fitting sphere of the human" (*ibid.*: 135). The key expressive power of the moment – never the moment as a spectacular, memory-forming palace, but as humble, simple, repetitive, stilted and sometimes stopped – is to generate both doubt and action: to draw us in, and to demand of us something radical.

This type of philosophy presents formal plays with the cinematic apparatus as a history and tradition on its own. Agamben's cinema is both a homeland for the gestural, and its funeral. The impossibility of being able to represent abstracts forces the hand of the artist to present pure possibilities in their stead. A cinema is always coming, but never on time for a philosopher such as Agamben, for whom an "idea" is "a constellation in which phenomena are composed in a gesture" (*ibid.*).

FILMOGRAPHY

28 Days Later, D. Boyle (dir.) (British Film Council/DNA Films, 2002).
À bout de souffle [Breathless], J.-L. Godard (dir.) (Les Productions Georges de Beauregard/Société Nouvelle de Cinématographie [SNC], 1960).
The Act of Seeing with One's Own Eyes, S. Brakhage (dir.) (Canyon Cinema and The Criterion Collection, 1971).
Adam's Rib, G. Cukor (dir.) (Loew's, 1949).
Alien, R. Scott (dir.) (Brandywine Productions/Twentieth Century-Fox Productions, 1979).
All the President's Men, A. J. Pakula (dir.) (Warner Bros. Pictures/Wildwood, 1976).
Allemagne année 90 neuf zéro [Germany year 90 nine zero], J.-L. Godard (dir.) (Antenne-2/Production Brainstorm/Gaumont/Périphéria, 1991).
Altered States, K. Russell (dir.) (Warner Bros. Pictures, 1980).
Amarcord [I remember], F. Fellini (dir.) (F. C. Produzioni/PECF, 1973).
Los Amantes del Círculo Polar [Lovers of the Arctic Circle], J. Medem (dir.) (Canal+/Sociedad/Sociedad General de Televisión SA (Sogetel), 1998).
American Graffiti, G. Lucas (dir.) (Lucasfilm/The Coppola Company/Universal Pictures, 1973).
L'Amour fou, J. Rivette (dir.) (Cocinor/Les Films Marceau/Sogexportfilm, 1969).
El Ángel exterminador [The exterminating angel], L. Buñuel (dir.) (Producciones Gustavo Alatriste, 1962).
Les Anges du péché [Angels of the streets], R. Bresson (dir.) (Synops, 1947).
L'Anglaise et le duc [The lady and the duke], E. Rohmer (dir.) (Compagnie Eric Rohmer [CER]/Pathé Image Production, 2001).
Angst essen Seele auf [Fear eats the soul], R. W. Fassbinder (dir.) (Filmverlag der Autoren/Tango Film, 1974).
L'Année dernière à Marienbad [Last year at Marienbad], A. Resnais (dir.) (Cocinor/Terra Film/Cormoran Films/Precitel/Como Film Production/Argos Films/Les Films Tamara/Cinétel/Silver Films/Cineriz, 1961).
Ansiktet [The magician], I. Bergman (dir.) (Svensk Filmindustri [SF], 1958).
Apocalypse Now, F. F. Coppola (dir.) (Zoetrope Studios, 1979).
The Art of Memory, W. Vasulka (dir.), www.vdb.org/smackn.acgi$artistdetail?VASULKAW (accessed July 2009) (1987).
Asylum, P. Robinson (dir.) (Peter Robinson Associates, 1972).
L'Avventura [The adventure], M. Antonioni (dir.) (Cino del Duca [co-production]/Produzioni Cinematografiche Europee [PCE]/Société Cinématographique Lyre, 1960).
Babettes gæstebud [Babette's feast], G. Axel (dir.) (Panorama Film A/S/Det Danske Filminstitut/Nordisk Film/Rungstedlundfonden, 1987).
The Bad Sister, L. Mulvey & P. Wollen (dirs) (Moving Picture/Modelmark, 1982).
Badlands, T. Malick (dir.) (Badlands Co./Warner, 1973).
Barry Lyndon, S. Kubrick (dir.) (Peregrine/Hawk Films, 1975).
Battleship Potemkin, S. Eisenstein (dir.) (Goskino, 1925).
La Belle et la Bête [Beauty and the beast], J. Cocteau (dir.) (DisCina, 1946).
Le Beau Serge [Handsome Serge], C. Chabrol (dir.) (Ajym Films/Coopérative Générale du Cinéma Français, 1958).
Ben Hur: A Tale of the Christ, B. Niblo (dir.) (Metro-Goldwyn-Mayer [MGM], 1925).
Berlin: Die Sinfonie der Großstadt [Berlin: symphony of a great city], W. Ruttmann (Deutsche Vereins-Film/Les Productions Fox Europa, 1927).

The Birds, A. Hitchcock (dir.) (Universal Pictures (presents)/Alfred J. Hitchcock Productions, 1963).

Birth of a Nation, D. W. Griffith (dir.) (David W. Griffith Corp./Epoch Producing Corporation, 1915).

Der Blaue Engel [The blue angel], J. von Sternberg (dir.) (Universum Film [UFA], 1930).

Blue Velvet, D. Lynch (dir.) (De Laurentiis Entertainment Group, 1986).

Brassed Off, M. Herman (dir.) (Channel Four Films/Miramax Films/Prominent Features, 1996).

Breaking the Waves, L. von Trier (dir.) (Argus Film Produktie/Arte/Canal+/CoBo Fonds/Det Danske Filminstitut/ Eurimages/European Script Fund/Finnish Film Foundation/Icelandic Film [as Icelandic Film Corporation]/La Sept Cinéma/Liberator Productions/Lucky Red/Media Investment Club/Memfis Film/Nederlands Fonds voor de Film/Nordisk Film- & TV-Fond/Northern Lights/Norwegian Film Institute/October Films/Philippe Bober/SVT Drama [Stockholm]/Svenska Filminstitutet [SFI]/TV1000 AB/Trust Film Svenska/VPRO Television/Villealfa Filmproduction Oy/Yleisradio [YLE]/Zentropa Entertainments/Zweites Deutsches Fernsehen [ZDF], 1996).

Brutalität in Stein [Brutality in stone], A. Kluge & P. Schamoni (dirs) (Alexander Kluge Filmproduktion/Dieter Lemmel Kurzfilmproduktion/Peter Schamoni Film, 1961).

Das Cabinet des Dr Caligari [The cabinet of Dr Caligari], R. Wiene (dir.) (Decla-Bioscop AG, 1920).

Caché [Hidden], M. Haneke (dir.) (Les Films du Losange/Wega Film/Bavaria Film/BIM Distribuzione/Uphill Pictures, 2005)

Casablanca, M. Curtiz (dir.) (Warner Brothers Pictures, 1942).

Cet obscur objet du désir [That obscure object of desire], L. Buñuel (dir.) (Greenwich Film Productions/In-Cine Compañía Industrial Cinematográfica/Les Films Galaxie, 1977).

La chienne [Isn't life a bitch?], J. Renoir (dir.) (Les Établissements Braunberger-Richebé, 1931).

Chinatown, R. Polanski (dir.) (Long Road/Paramount Pictures/Penthouse, 1974).

Citizen Kane, O. Welles (dir.) (Mercury Productions/RKO Radio Pictures, 1941).

City Lights, C. Chaplin (dir.) (Charles Chaplin Productions, 1931).

A Clockwork Orange, S. Kubrick (dir.) (Warner Bros./Hawk Films, 1971).

Coffee and Cigarettes, J. Jarmusch (dir.) (Asmik Ace Entertainment/BIM/Smokescreen Inc., 2003).

Comme les anges déchus de la planète Saint-Michel [Fallen angels from the planet St Michel], J. Schmidt (dir.) (Atelier 8, 1978).

La concentration [Concentration], P. Garrel (dir.) (Zanzibar Films, 1968).

La Coquille et le clergyman [The seashell and the clergyman], G. Dulac (dir.) (Délia Film, 1928).

Coup pour coup [Blow by blow], M. Karmitz (dir.) (Cinema Services, 1972).

Crystal Gazing, L. Mulvey & P. Wollen (dirs) (BFI Production, 1982).

D'ailleurs, Derrida [Derrida's elsewhere], S. Fathy (dir.) (La Sept/ARTE/GLORIA Films, 1999).

Dawn of the Dead, Z. Snyder (dir.) (Strike Entertainment/New Amsterdam Entertainment/Metropolitan Filmexport/Toho-Towa, 2004).

The Day After, N. Meyer (dir.) (ABC Circle Films, 1983).

Days of Heaven, T. Malick (dir.) (Paramount Pictures, 1978).

Delicatessen, M. Caro & J.-P. Jenuet (dirs) (Constellation/Union Générale Cinématographique/Hachette Première/Sofinergie Films/Sofinerge 2/Investimage 2/Investimage 3/ Fondation GAN pour le Cinéma/ Victoires Productions, 1991).

Derrida, K. Dick & A. Ziering-Kofman (dirs) (Jane Doe Films, 2005).

Deux fois cinquante ans de cinema Français [Twice fifty years of French cinema], J.-L. Godard & A.-M. Miéville (dirs) (BFI/La Sept-Arte/Peripheria/Vega Film, 1995).

Le Diable probablement [The devil probably], R. Bresson (dir.) (GMF/Gaumont Films/Sunchild Productions, 1977).

Disgraced Monuments, M. Lewis & L. Mulvey (dirs) (Mark Lewis & Laura Mulvey/Broadcast Channel 4 TV, 6 June, 1994).

Distant Voices, Still Lives, T. Davies (dir.) (British Film Institute (BFI)/Channel Four Films, 1988).

Diva, J.-J. Beineix (dir.) (Les Films Galaxie/Greenwich Film Productions (as Greenwich Film Production)/ Antenne-2, 1991).

Do the Right Thing, S. Lee (dir.) (40 Acres and a Mule Filmworks, 1989).

Double Take, J. Grimonprez (dir.) (Zap-O-Matik/Nikovantastic Film/Volya Films, 2009).

Dr Strangelove or: How I Learned to Stop Worrying and Love the Bomb, S. Kubrick (dir.) (Hawk Films, 1964).

Duel in the Sun, K. Vidor (dir.) (Vanguard Films/The Selznick Studio, 1946).

L'École de Mai: 1968–1978 [*May school: 1968–78*], D. Levy (dir.) (Collectif Réalisation Audiovisuel Cinéma, 1979).

The ELEVENTH HOUR: AMY!, L. Mulvey & P. Wollen (dirs) (Modelmark, 1980).

Éloge de l'amour [In praise of love], J.-L. Godard (dir.) (Avventura Films/Peripheria/Canal+/arte France Cinéma/ Vega Film/Télévision Suisse-Romande/ECM Records/Studio Canal/Deutsches Film Insititut/Studio Images 6, 2001).

Eraserhead, D. Lynch (dir.) (American Film Institute, 1977).

Eyes Wide Shut, S. Kubrick (dir.) (Hobby Films/Pole Star/Stanley Kubrick Productions/Warner Bros. Pictures, 1999).

Family Life, K. Loach (dir.) (EMI Films, 1971).

Fight Club, D. Fincher (dir.) (Art Linson Productions/Fox 2000 Pictures/Regency Enterprises/Taurus Film, 1999).

The First of the Few, L. Howard (dir.) (British Aviation Pictures, 1942).

Fists in the Pocket, M. Bellocchio (dir.) (Doria, 1965).

For Ever Mozart, J.-L. Godard (dir.) (Avventura Films/Peripheria/Centre Européen Cinématographique Rhône-Alpes/France 2 Cinéma/Canal+/Centre National de la Cinématographie/Vega Film/Télévision Suisse-Romande/Eurimages/Deutsches Film Insititut [DFI], 1996).

The Fountainhead, K. Vidor (Warner Bros. Pictures, 1949).

Frida Kahlo and Tina Modotti, L. Mulvey & P. Wollen (dirs) (Modelmark, 1982).

Gaslight, G. Cukor (dir.) (Metro-Goldwyn-Meyer [MGM], 1944).

Il Gattopardo [The leopard], L. Visconti, (dir.) (Titanus [Rome]/Société Nouvelle Pathé Cinéma [as S. N. Pathé Cinéma]/SGC [Paris], 1963).

The General, C. Bruckman & B. Keaton (dirs) (Buster Keaton Productions/Joseph M. Schenck Productions, 1927).

Gentlemen Prefer Blondes, H. Hawks (dir.) (Twentieth Century-Fox Film Corporation, 1953).

Germania anno zero [Germany, year zero], R. Rossellini (dir.) (Produzione Salvo D'Angelo/Tevere Film, 1947).

Germany in Autumn, A. Brustellin, H. P. Cloos *et al.* (dirs) (Filmverlag der Autoren, 1978).

Ghost Dance, K. McMullen (dir.) (Looseyard for Channel 4/ZD, 1983).

Ghost Dog: The Way of the Samurai, J. Jarmusch (dir.) (Pandora Filmproduktion/Arbeitsgemeinschaft der öffentlich-rechtlichen Rundfunkanstalten der Bundesrepublik Deutschland [ARD]/Degeto Film/Plywood Productions/Bac Films/Canal+/JVC Entertainment, 1999).

Les Glaneurs et la glaneuse [The gleaners and I], A. Varda (dir.) (Ciné Tamaris, 2000).

The Godfather, F. F. Coppola (dir.) (Paramount Pictures, 1972).

The Godfather: Part II, F. F. Coppola (dir.) (Paramount Pictures/The Coppola Company, 1974).

The Godfather: Part III, F. F. Coppola (dir.) (Paramount Pictures/Zoetrope Studios, 1990).

The Gold Rush, C. Chaplin (dir.) (Charles Chaplin Productions, 1925).

Le Grand bleu [The big blue], L. Besson (dir.) (Gaumont/Les Films du Loup, 1989).

Gycklarnas Afton [Sawdust and tinsel], I. Bergman (dir.) (Svensk Filmindustri [SF], 1953).

Handsworth Songs, J. Akomfrah (dir.) (Black Audio Film Collective, 1986).

He Who gets Slapped, V. Sjostrom (dir.) (Metro-Goldwyn-Mayer [MGM], 1924).

Her Sweetness Lingers, S. Mootoo (dir.) (Vancouver/Video in Studios/Video Out Distribution, 1994).

Hiroshima mon amour, A. Resnais (dir.) (Argos Films/Como Films/Daiei Studios/Pathé Entertainment, 1959).

His Girl Friday, H. Hawks (dir.) (Columbia Pictures, 1940).

Histoire(s) du cinéma, J.-L. Godard (dir.) (Canal+/Arte/Gaumont, 1988–98).

Histoire(s) du cinema, J.-L. Godard (dir.) (Canal/Centre National de la Cinématographie [CNC]/France 3 Cinéma/JLG Films/La Sept Cinéma/Société des Etablissements L. Gaumont/Vega Film Productions, 1999).

Histoire(s) du cinema, DVD, J.-L. Godard (dir.) (Gaumont, 2007).

Hurlements en faveur de Sade [Howlings in favour of de Sade], G. Debord (dir. & prod.) (1952).

Imitation of Life, D. Sirk (dir.) (Universal International Pictures, 1959).

In Girum Imus Nocte Et Consumimur Igni [We spin around the night consumed by the fire], G. Debord (dir.) (Simar Films, 1978).

Intolerance: Love's Struggle Throughout the Areas [also known as *Intolerance*], D. W. Griffith (dir.) (Triangle Film Corporation/Wark Producing, 1916).

Irréversible, G. Noé (dir.) (120 Films/Eskwad/Grandpierre/Les Cinemas de la Zone/Nord-Ouest Productions/Rossignon/Studio Canal, 2002).

It Happened One Night, F. Capra (dir.) (Columbia Pictures, 1934).

Ivan Groznyy I [Ivan the Terrible], S. Eisenstein (dir.) (Alma Ata Studio, 1944).

Ivan Groznyy II: Boyarsky zagovor [Ivan the Terrible: Part II: The Boyars' plot], S. Eisenstein & M. Filimonova (dir.) (Alma Ata Studio, 1958).

Jacques Derrida, J. C. Rosé (dir.) (INA, 1994).

Jacques Rivette – Le veilleur [Jacques Rivette – the night watchman], C. Denis & S. Daney (dirs). Produced for the television series "Cinéma, de notre temps". (Le Sept/Arte/Centre Nationale de la Cinématographie/Ministère des Affaires Étrangères/Intermédia, 1990).

La Jetée [The jetty], C. Marker (dir.) (Argos Films, 1962).

Je t'aime, je t'aime, A. Resnais (dir.) (Les Productions Fox Europa/Parc Film, 1968).

JLG/JLG – autoportrait de décembre [JLG/JLG – self-portrait in December], J.-L. Godard (dir.) (Gaumont International, 1995).
Joë, c'est aussi l'Amérique [Released in the US as *Joe*], J. G. Avildsen (dir.) (Metro-Goldwyn-Mayer [MGM], 1970).
Judgment at Nuremberg, S. Kramer (dir.) (Roxlom Films Inc., 1961).
Julius Caesar, J. Mankiewicz (dir.) (Metro-Goldwyn-Mayer [MGM], 1953).
Jungfrukällan [The virgin spring], I. Bergman (dir.) (Svensk Filmindustri [SF], 1960).
Kapò, G. Pontecorvo (dir.) (Vides Cinematografica/Zebra Films/Francinex/Lovcen Film/Cineriz, 1960).
King Kong, M. C. Cooper & E. B. Schoedsack (dirs) (RKO Radio Pictures, 1933).
King Kong, J. Guillermin (dir.) (Dino De Laurentiis Company/Paramount Pictures, 1976).
Lacombe Lucien, L. Malle (dir.) (Hallelujah Films/Nouvelles Éditions de Films/Universal Pictures France [UPF]/Vides Cinematografica, 1974).
Ladri di biciclette [The bicycle thief], V. De Sica (dir.) (Produzioni De Sica, 1948).
The Lady Vanishes, A. Hitchcock (dir.) (Gainsborough Pictures, 1938).
The Last Picture Show, P. Bogdanovich (dir.) (BBS Productions/Columbia Pictures Corporation, 1971).
Letter from an Unknown Woman, M. Ophüls (dir.) (Rampart Productions, 1948).
Lost Highway, D. Lynch (dir.) (October Films/CiBy 2000/Asymmetrical Productions/Lost Highway Productions LLC, 1977).
Louisiana Story, R. Flaherty (dir.) (Robert Flaherty Productions Inc., 1948).
M, F. Lang (dir.) (Nero-Film AG, 1931).
Mababangong bangungot [The perfumed nightmare], K. Tahimik (dir.) (Tahimik, 1977).
Mädchen in Uniform [Girls in uniform], L. Sagan (dir.) (Deutsche Film-Gemeinschaft, 1931).
Manhunter, M. Mann (dir.) (De Laurentiis Entertainment Group (DEG)/Red Dragon Productions S.A., 1986).
Marnie, A. Hitchcock (dir.) (Universal Pictures, 1964).
Die Marquise von O ... [The Marquis of O ...], E. Rohmer (dir.) (Les Films du Losange/Filmproduktion Janus/Artemis/Hessischer Rundfunk [HR]/Gaumont, 1976).
The Matrix, A. Wachowski & L. Wachowski (dirs) (Warner/Village Roadshow/Groucho II, 1999).
The Matrix Reloaded, A. Wachowski & L. Wachowski (dirs) (Warner/Village Roadshow/NPV, 2003).
The Matrix Revolutions, A. Wachowski & L. Wachowski (dirs) (Warner/Village Roadshow/NPV, 2003).
Matti da slegare [Fit to be untied], S. Agnosti, S. & M. Bellocchio (dirs) (11 Marzo Cinematografica, 1975).
Men in Black, B. Sonnenfeld (dir.) (Amblin Entertainment/Columbia Pictures, 1997).
Morocco, J. von Sternberg (dir.) (Paramount Pictures, 1930).
Morte a Venezia [Death in Venice], L. Visconti (dir.) (Alfa Cinematografica, 1971).
Mourir à trente ans [Half a life], R. Goupil (dir.) (MK2 Productions, 1982).
Nanook of the North, R. Flaherty (dir.) (Les Frères Revillon/Pathé Exchange, 1922).
Neptune's Daughter, H. Brenon (dir.) (Universal Film Manufacturing Company, 1914).
No Man Is An Island II, J. Just (dir.), www.jesperjust.com/nomanisanisland2.html (accessed June 2009) (Copenhagen: Galleri Christna Wilson/New York: Perry Rubenstein Gallery, 2004).
North by Northwest, A. Hitchcock (dir.) (Metro-Goldwyn-Mayer [MGM] [as Loew's Incorporated], 1959).
Nosferatu, eine Symphonie des Grauens, F. W. Murnau (dir.) (Jofa-Atelier Berlin-Johannisthal/Prana-Film GmbH, 1922).
Notorious, A. Hitchcock (dir.) (Vanguard Films (uncredited) (for) RKO Radio Pictures, 1946).
Notre musique [Our music], J.-L. Godard (dir.) (Avventura Films/Les Films Alain Sarde/Périphéria/France 3 Cinéma/Canal+/Télévision Suisse-Romande [TSR]/Vega Film, 2004).
Now, Voyager, I. Rapper (dir.) (Warner Bros. Pictures, 1942).
Nuit et brouillard [Night and fog], A. Resnais (dir.) (Argos Films, 1959).
On the Waterfront, E. Kazan (dir.) (Horizon Pictures/Columbia Pictures Corporation, 1954).
One Flew Over the Cuckoo's Nest, M. Forman (dir.) (Fantasy Films, 1975).
One from the Heart, F. F. Coppola (dir.) (Zoetrope Studios, 1982).
Paisà [Paisan], R. Rossellini (dir.) (Organizzazione Film Internazionali [OFI]/Foreign Film Productions, 1946).
Palombella Rossa [Reb lob], N. Moretti (dir.) (Banfilm/La Sept Cinéma/Palm Rye Productions/ Radiotelevisione Italiana/Sacher Film/So. Fin. A., 1989).
The Parallax View, A. Pakula (dir.) (Doubleday Productions/Gus/Harbor Productions/Paramount Pictures, 1974).
Pasażerka [The passenger], A. Munk (dir.) (Zespol Filmowy "Kamera", 1963).
Passage à l'acte, M. Arnold (dir.) (Sixpack Film, 1993).
A Passage to India, D. Lean (dir.) (EMI Films/Home Box Office (HBO)/Thorn EMI Screen Entertainment, 1984).
Passion, J.-L. Godard (dir.) (Film et Vidéo Companie/Films A2/JLG Films/Sara Films/Sonimage/Télévision Suisse-Romande [TSR], 1982).

La Passion de Jeanne d'Arc [The passion of Joan of Arc], C. T. Dreyer (dir.) (Société générale des films, 1928).

Penthesilea: Queen of the Amazons, L. Mulvey & P. Wollen (dirs) (Laura Mulvey–Peter Wollen, 1974).

Persepolis, M. Satrapi & V. Paronnaud (dirs) (2.4.7 Films/Kennedy/Marshall Company/France 3 Cinéma/French Connection Animations/Diaphana Films/Celluloid Dreams/Sony Pictures Classics/Sofica Europacorp/ Soficinéma/Centre National de la Cinématographie [CNC]/Région Ile-de-France/Fondation GAN pour le Cinéma/Procirep/Angoa-Agicoa, 2007).

The Pervert's Guide to Cinema, S. Fiennes (dir.) (Lone Star, Mischief Films, 2005).

Pickpocket, R. Bresson (dir.) (Agnès Delahaie/Compagnie Cinématographique de France, 1959).

"Pimpernel" Smith, L. Howard (dir.) (British National Films, 1941).

Il Portiere di notte [The night porter], L. Cavani (dir.) (Italonegglio Cinematografico/Lotar Film Productions, 1974).

Portrait of Dorian Gray, A. Lewin (dir.) (Metro-Goldwyn-Mayer (MGM)/Loew's, 1945).

Procès de Jeanne d'Arc [The trial of Joan of Arc], R. Bresson (dir.) (Agnès Delahaie, 1962).

Psycho, A. Hitchcock (dir.) (Universal Pictures (presents)/Alfred J. Hitchcock Productions, 1960).

Pulp Fiction, Q. Tarantino (dir.) (A Band Apart/Jersey Films/Miramax Films, 1994).

Les Quatre cents coups [The 400 blows], F. Truffaut (dir.) (Les Films du Carrosse/Sédif Productions, 1959).

Queen Christina, R. Mamoulian (dir.) (Metro-Goldwyn-Mayer [MGM], 1933).

Rear Window, A. Hitchcock (dir.) (Paramount Pictures/Patron Inc., 1954).

Redacted, B. DePalma (dir.) (Film Farm/The HDNet Films, 2007).

La Région Centrale, M. Snow (dir.) (Canadian Filmmakers' Distribution Centre, 1971).

La Règle du jeu [The rules of the game], J. Renoir (dir.) (Nouvelle édition française, 1939).

La religieuse, J. Rivette (dir.) (Rome Paris Films/Société Nouvelle de Cinématographie, 1966).

Le Révélateur, P. Garrel (dir.) (Zanzibar Films, 1968).

Riddles of the Sphinx, L. Mulvey & P. Wollen (dirs) (British Film Institute Production Board, 1977).

The Robe, H. Koster (dir.) (Twentieth Century-Fox Film Corporation, 1953).

Roma, città aperta [Rome, open city], R. Rossellini (dir.) (Excelsa Film, 1945).

La Ronde [Roundabout], M. Ophüls (dir.) (Films Sacha Gordine, 1950).

Russkiy kovcheg [Russian ark], A. Sokurov (dir.) (State Hermitage Museum, The Hermitage Bridge Studio/Ministry of Culture of the Russian Federation [in association with, as Ministry of Culture of the Russian Federation, Department of the Stage Support of Cinematography]/Mitteldeutsche Medienfürderung Filmboard Berlin Brandenburg [in association with]/Kulturelle Filmförderung des bundes Filmlörderung Hamburg [in association with]/Filmbüro Nordrhein-Westfalen Kulturelle Filmborderung Sachsen-Anhalt [in association with]/ WDR/Arte [in association with]/Fora Film [in association with]/Koppmedia [in association with]/NHK [in association with]/Seville Pictures [in association with]/YLE TV1 [in association with, as YLE/TV1]/Danmarks Radio [DR] [in association with, as DR 1]/AST Studio [in association with]/Mariinsky Theatre [in association with]/Egoli Tossell Film, 2002).

La Salaire de la peur [The wages of fear], H. Georges-Clouzot (dir.) (Compagnie Industrielle et Commerciale Cinématographique/Filmsonor/Vera Films/Fono Roma, 1953).

Le Sang des bêtes [The blood of beasts], G. Franju (dir.) (Forces et voix de la France, 1949).

The Scarlet Pimpernel, H. Young (dir.) (London Film Productions, 1934).

Sex, Lies and Videotape, S. Soderbergh (Outlaw Productions/Virgin, 1989).

Si j'avais quatre dromadaires [If I had four dromedaries], C. Marker (dir.) (APEC/NWDR, 1966).

The Silence of the Lambs, J. Demme (dir.) (Orion Pictures Corporation/Strong Heart/Demme Production, 1991).

Silly Symphonies, www.disneyshorts.org/miscellaneous/silly.html (accessed June 2009) (Walt Disney Productions, 1929–39).

Singin' in the Rain, S. Donen & G. Kelly (dirs) (Metro-Goldwyn-Mayer [MGM], 1952).

Smultronstället [Wild strawberries], I. Bergman (dir.) (Svensk Filmindustri [SF], 1957).

La Société du spectacle [Society of the spectacle], G. Debord (dir.) (Simar Films, 1973).

La sociologie est un sport de combat [Sociology is a martial art], P. Carles (dir.) (C. P. Productions/V. F. Films Productions/Icarus Films, 2001).

Solyaris [Solaris], A. Tarkovsky (dir.) (Creative Unit of Writers & Cinema Workers/Moxfilm/Unit Four, 1972).

Sommaren Med Monika [Monika, the story of a bad girl], I. Bergman (dir.) (Svensk Filmindustri [SF], 1953).

Le souvenir d'un avenir [Remembrance of things to come], C. Marker & Y. Bellon (dirs) (Les Films de l'Equinoxe, 2001).

Spellbound, A. Hitchcock (dir.) (Vanguard Films for Selznick International Pictures, 1945).

Star Wars, G. Lucas (dir.) (Lucasfilm/Twentieth Century-Fox Film Corporation, 1977).

Steamboat Bill, Jr, C. Reisner (dir.) (Buster Keaton Productions/Joseph M. Schenck Productions, 1928).

Stella Dallas, K. Vidor (dir.) (Samuel Goldwyn Company, 1937).

Strangers on a Train, A. Hitchcock (dir.) (Warner Bros. Pictures, 1951).

Suspicion, A. Hitchcock (dir.) (RKO Radio Pictures, 1941).

Symphonie Diagonale, V. Eggeling (dir.) (Art Production Fund, 1992).

Ten Canoes, R. de Heer & P. Djigirr (dirs) (Adelaide Film Festival/Fandago Australia/Fandango/Vertigo Productions/Special Broadcasting Service (SBS), 2006).

The Terminator, J. Cameron (dir.) (Hemdale Film/Cinema 84/Amblin Entertainment/Euro Film Funding/Pacific Western, 1984).

Terminator 2: Judgment Day, J. Cameron (dir.) (Amblin Entertainment/Canal+ (as "Le Studio Canal+")/Carolco Pictures/Lightstorm Entertainment/Pacific Western/T2 Productions (uncredited), 1991).

Terminator 3: Rise of the Machines, J. Mostow (dir.) (C-2 Pictures/Intermedia Films/IMF Internationale Medien und Film GmbH & Co. 3. Produktions KG/Mostow/Lieberman Productions, 2003).

Terminator Salvation, McG (dir.) (The Halcyon Company/Wonderland Sound and Vision, 2009).

Three Days of the Condor, S. Pollack (dir.) (Dino De Laurentiis Company/Paramount Pictures/Wildwood Enterprises, 1975).

Titanic, J. Cameron (dir.) (Twentieth Century-Fox Film Corporation/Paramount Pictures/Lightstorm Entertainment, 1997).

Titicut Follies, F. Wiseman (dir.) (Zipporah Films, 1967).

To Be or Not To Be, E. Lubitsch (dir.) (Romaine Film Corporation, 1943).

To Kill A Mockingbird, R. Mulligan (dir.) (Brentwood Productions, 1962).

Toto le héro [Toto the hero], J. Van Dormael (dir.) (Cama;+/France 3 Cinéma/Het Ministerie van Cultuur van de Vlaamse Gemeenschap/Iblis Films/La Direction de L'Audiovisuel de Communauté Française de Belgique/Les Entrepeneurs de l'Audiovisuel Européen/Metropolis Filmproduction/Philippe Dussart/Programme MEDIA de la Communauté Européene/Radio Télévision Belge Francophone (RTBF)/Zweites Deutsches Fernsehen (ZDF), 1991).

Touch of Evil, O. Welles (dir.) (Universal International Pictures [UI], 1958).

Touch the Sound, T. Riedelsheimer (dir.) (Filmquadrat/Skyline Productions, 2006).

Tout va bien [Just great], J.-L. Godard (dir.) (Anouchka Films/Empire Films/Vieco Films, 1972).

Traité de bave et d'éternité [Tract of drool and eternity], I. Isou (dir.) (Films M.-G. Guillemin, 1951).

The Treasure of the Sierra Madre, J. Huston (dir.) (Warner Bros. Pictures, 1948).

Trois couleurs: Blanc [Three colours: white], K. Kieslowski (dir.) (MK2 Productions/Paris: France 3 Cinéma/CAB Productions/Zespol Filmowy "Tor" [as "TOR" Production – Varsovie]/Canal+ [participation]/Eurimages [as Fonds EURIMAGES]/Conseil de l'Europe, 1994).

Trois couleurs: Bleu [Three colours: blue], K. Kieslowski (dir.) (Canal+/Conseil de l'Europe [financial support]/CAB Productions/CED Productions/Eurimages/France 3 Cinéma/MK2 Productions/Zespol Filmowy "Tor", 1993).

Trois couleurs: Rouge [Three colours: red], K. Kieslowski (dir.) (CAB Productions/Canal+/France 3 Cinéma/MK2 Productions/Télévision Suisse-Romande (TSR)/Zespol Filmowy "Tor", 1994).

Uranus, C. Berri (dir.) (DD Productions/Films A2/Investimage 2/Investimage 3/Renn Productions/Soficas Sofi Ano, 1990).

Urgences [Emergencies], R. Depardon (dir.) (CNC, 1988).

Les Vacances de Monsieur Hulot [Monsieur Hulot's holiday], J. Tati (dir.) (Cady Films/Specta Films, 1953).

Vertigo, A. Hitchcock (dir.) (Alfred J. Hitchcock Productions/Paramount Pictures, 1958).

Viaggio in Italia [Journey to Italy], R. Rossellini (dir.) (Italia Film/Junior Film/Sveva Film/Les Films Ariane/Francinex/SGC, 1954).

Videodrome, D. Cronenberg (dir.) (Canadian Film Development Corporation (CFDC)/Famous Players/Filmplan/Guardian Trust Company/Victor Solnicki Productions, 1983).

Wild at Heart, D. Lynch (dir.) (PolyGram Filmed Entertainment/Progaganda Films, 1990).

Xala, O. Sembene (dir.) (Films Domireew/Ste. Me. Production du Senegal, 1975).

YAMA: An Eye for an Eye, S. Mitsuo (dir.) (YAMA Production and Exhibition Committee, 1985),

Žižek!, A. Taylor (dir.) (Zeitgeist Films, 2005).

BIBLIOGRAPHY

[Anon.] 1989. "Laura Mulvey". *Camera Obscura* **20–21**: 248–52.

Aaron, M. 2007. *Spectatorship: The Power of Looking On*. London: Wallflower.

Abraham, N. 1987. *L'Ecorce et le noyau*. Paris: Flammarion.

Adorno, T. W. 1976. *Introduction to the Sociology of Music*. New York: Seabury Press.

Adorno, T. W. [1967] 1983. *Prisms*, S. Weber & S. Weber (trans.). Boston, MA: MIT Press. Originally published in German as *Prismen: Kulturkritik und Gesellschaft* (Frankfurt: Suhrkamp, 1955).

Adorno, T. W. 1991a. *The Culture Industry: Selected Essays on Mass Culture*, J. M. Bernstein (ed.). London & New York: Routledge.

Adorno, T. W. 1991b. "Trying to Understand *Endgame*". In his *Notes to Literature*, vol. 1, 241–75. Cambridge: Cambridge University Press.

Adorno, T. W. 1991c. "The Curious Realist: On Siegfried Kracauer", S. Weber Nicholsen (trans.). *New German Critique* **54**: 159–77.

Adorno, T. W. 2000. *Metaphysics: Concepts and Problems*, E. Jephcott (trans.). Stanford, CA: Stanford University Press. Originally published in German as *Metaphysik: Begriff und Probleme* (Frankfurt: Suhrkamp, 1965).

Adorno, T. W. 2002. *Aesthetic Theory*, R. Hullot-Kentor (trans.). London: Continuum. Originally published in German as *Ästhetische Theorie*, G. Adorno & R. Tiedemann (eds) (Frankfurt: Suhrkamp, 1970).

Adorno, T. W. & H. Eisler [1947] 2005. *Composing for the Films*. London: Continuum.

Adorno, T. W. & M. Horkheimer 1997. *Dialectic of Enlightenment*, J. Cumming (trans.). London: Verso. Originally published in German as *Philosophische Fragmente* (New York: Social Studies Association, 1944), and revised as *Dialektik der Aufklärung* (Amsterdam: Querido, 1947).

Agamben, G. 1991. *Language and Death: The Place of Negativity*, K. E. Pinkus & M. Hardt (trans.), Theory and History of Literature, 78. Minneapolis, MN: University of Minnesota Press.

Agamben, G. 1993a. *The Coming Community*, M. Hardt (trans.). Theory Out of Bounds, 1. Minneapolis, MN: University of Minnesota Press. Originally published in Italian as *La Comunità che viene* (Turin: Giulio Einaudi, 1990).

Agamben, G. 1993b. *Infancy and History: Essays on the Destruction of Experience*, L. Heron (trans.). London: Verso.

Agamben, G. 1993c. *Stanzas: Word and Phantasm in Western Culture*, R. L. Martinez (trans.). Theory and History of Literature, 69. Minneapolis, MN: University of Minnesota Press. Originally published in Italian as *Stanze: la parola e il fantasma nella cultura occidentale* (Turin: Guilio Einaudi, 1979).

Agamben, G. 1995a. "Difference and Repetition: On Guy Debord's Films". In *Guy Debord and the Situationist International: Texts and Documents*, T. McDonough (ed.), 313–20. Cambridge, MA: MIT Press.

Agamben, G. 1995b. *Idea of Prose*, M. Sullivan & S. Whitsitt (trans.). Albany, NY: SUNY Press. Originally published in Italian as *Idea della prosa* (Milan: Feltrinelli, 1985).

Agamben, G. 1998. *Homo Sacer: Sovereign Power and Bare Life*, D. Heller-Roazen (trans.). Stanford, CA: Stanford University Press. Originally published in Italian as *Homo sacer* (Turin: Giulio Einaudi, 1995).

Agamben, G. 1999a. *The End of the Poem: Studies in Poetics*, D. Heller-Roazen (trans.). Stanford, CA: Stanford University Press. Originally published in Italian as *Categorie Italiane: studi di poetica* (Venice: Marsilio, 1996).

Agamben, G. 1999b. *The Man Without Content*, G. Albert (trans.). Stanford, CA: Stanford University Press. Originally published in Italian as *L'uomo senza contenuto* (Milan: Rizzoli, 1970).

Agamben, G. 1999c. *Potentialities: Collected Essays in Philosophy*, D. Heller-Roazen (trans.). Stanford, CA: Stanford University Press.

Agamben, G. 1999d. *Remnants of Auschwitz: The Witness and the Archive*, D. Heller-Roazen (trans.). New York: Zone Books. Originally published in Italian as *Quel che resta di Auschwitz: L'archivio e il testimone* (Turin: Bollati Boringhieri, 1998).

Agamben, G. 2000. *Means Without End: Notes on Politics*, C. Casarino & V. Binetti (trans.), Theory Out of Bounds, 20. Minneapolis, MN: University of Minnesota Press. Originally published in French as *Moyens sans fins: Notes sur la politique* (Paris: Payot et Rivages, 1995).

Agamben, G. 2004. *The Open: Man and Animal*, K. Attell (trans.). Stanford, CA: Stanford University Press. Originally published in Italian as *L'aperto: L'uomo e l'animale* (Turin: Bollati Boringhieri, 2002).

Agamben, G. 2005a. *State of Exception*, K. Attell (trans.). Chicago, IL: University of Chicago Press. Originally published in Italian as *Stato di Eccezione* (Turin: Bollati Boringhieri, 2003).

Agamben, G. 2005b. *The Time that Remains: A Commentary on the Letter to the Romans*, P. Daly (trans.). Stanford, CA: Stanford University Press. Originally published in Italian as *Il Tempo che resta: Un commento alla Lettera ai romani* (Turin: Bollati Boringhieri, 2000).

Agamben, G. 2007a. *Profanations*, J. Fort (trans.). New York: Zone Books.

Agamben, G. 2007b. "The Six Most Beautiful Minutes in the History of Cinema". In his *Profanations*, J. Fort (trans.), 196. New York: Zone Books.

Agnosti, S., M. Bellocchio, S. Petraglia & S. Rulli (dirs) 1975. *Matti da slegare* [Fit to be untied]. 11 Marzo Cinematografica.

Akomfrah, J. (dir.) 1986. *Handsworth Songs*. Black Audio Film Collective.

Allaire, E. B. [1963] 1998. "Bare Particulars". In *Contemporary Readings in the Foundations of Metaphysics*, S. Laurence & C. Macdonald (eds), 248–54. Oxford: Blackwell.

Allen, R. 1995. *Projecting Illusion*. Cambridge: Cambridge University Press.

Alliez, E. 2004. "Existe-t-il une esthétique rancièrenne?". In *La Philosophie déplacée: autour de Jacques Rancière*, L. Cornu & P. Vermeren (eds), 271–87. Paris: Horlieu.

Andrew, J. D. 1976. *The Major Film Theories: An Introduction*. Oxford: Oxford University Press.

Andrew, D. 1978. *André Bazin*. New York: Columbia University Press.

Andrew, J. D. 1984. *Concepts in Film Theory*. Oxford: Oxford University Press.

Andrew, D. 1985. "The Neglected Tradition of Phenomenology in Film Theory". See Nichols (1985), 625–31.

Andrew, D. 2000a. "The 'Three Ages' of Cinema Studies and the Age to Come". *PMLA* **115**(3): 341–51.

Andrew, D. 2000b. "The Roots of the Nomadic: Gilles Deleuze and the Cinema of West Africa". See Flaxman (2000), 215–49.

Andrew, J. D. 1976. "Hugo Münsterberg". In his *The Major Film Theories: An Introduction*, 14–26. Oxford: Oxford University Press.

Antonioni, M. (dir.) 1960. *L'Avventura* [The adventure]. Cino del Duca (co-production)/Produzioni Cinematografiche Europee (PCE)/Societé Cinématographique Lyre.

Armitage, J. 2000. *Paul Virilio: From Modernism to Hypermodernism and Beyond*. London: Sage.

Armitage, J. 2001. *Virilio Live: Selected Interviews*. London: Sage.

Arnheim, R. 1957. *Film as Art*. London: Faber. Rewritten from the original publication in German as *Film als Kunst* (Berlin: Ernst Rowohlt, 1932), and translation into English as *Film*, L. M. Sieveking & I. F. D. Morrow (trans.) (London: Faber, 1933).

Arnheim, R. 1963. "Melancholy Unshaped". *Journal of Aesthetics and Art Criticism* **21**(3): 291–7.

Arnold, M. (dir.) 1993. *Passage à l'acte*. Sixpack Film.

Artaud, A 1958. *The Theatre and its Double*, M. Richards (trans.). New York: Grove. Originally published in French as *Le Théâtre et son double* (Paris: Gallimard, 1938).

Artaud, A. 1976a. *Antonin Artaud: Selected Writings*, S. Sontag (ed.), H. Weaver (trans.). Berkeley, CA: University of California Press.

Artaud, A. 1976b. "Introduction to *The Seashell and the Clergyman*". See Artaud (1976a), 49–50.

Artaud, A. 1976c. "Eighteen Seconds". See Artaud (1976a), 115–18.

Artaud, A. 1976d. "Art and Death". See Artaud (1976a), 121–38.

Artaud, A. 1976e. "Cinema and Reality". See Artaud (1976a), 150–52.

Artaud, A. 1976f. "Reply to a Questionnaire". See Artaud (1976a), 181–2.

Artaud, A. 1976g. "Interview with *Cinémonde*". See Artaud (1976a), 182–5.

Artaud, A. 1976h. "The Theatre and its Double" See Artaud (1976a), 215–76.

Artaud, A. 1976i. "The Premature Old Age of the Cinema". See Artaud (1976a), 311–14.

Artaud, A. 1976j. "To be Done with the Judgment of God". See Artaud (1976a), 555–71.

Artaud, A. [1971] 1976k. *The Peyote Dance*, H. Weaver (trans.). New York: Farrar, Straus & Giroux. First published in French as *Les Tarahumaras* (Geneva: L'Arbalète, 1955)

Artaud, A. [1999] 2004. "Sorcery and Cinema". In *The Screaming Body: Antonin Artaud – Film Projects, Drawings and Sound Recordings*, S. Barber, 37–9. San Francisco, CA: Creation Books.

Atkins, P. W. 1984. *The Second Law*. New York: Scientific American Library.

Augé, M. 2002. *In the Metro*, T. Conley (trans.). Minneapolis, MN: University of Minnesota Press.

Augé, M. 2007. *Casablanca*. Paris: Éditions du Seuil.

Avildsen, J. G. (dir.) 1970. *Joë, c'est aussi l'Amérique* [Released in the US as *Joe*]. Metro-Goldwyn-Meyer (MGM).

Axel, G. (dir.) 1987. *Babettes gæstebud* [Babette's feast]. Panorama Film A/S/Det Danske Filminstitut/Nordisk Film/Rungstedlundfonden.

Badiou, A. 1999. *Manifesto for Philosophy*, N. Madarasz (trans.). Albany, NY: SUNY Press.

Badiou, A. 2001. *Ethics: An Essay on the Understanding of Evil*, P. Hallward (trans.). London: Verso.

Badiou, A. 2004. *Infinite Thought, Truth and the Return to Philosophy*, O. Feltham & J. Clemens (trans.). London: Continuum.

Badiou, A. 2005a. "Art and Philosophy". In his *Handbook of Inaesthetics*, A. Toscano (trans.), 1–15. Stanford, CA: Stanford University Press.

Badiou, A. 2005b. *Being and Event*, O. Feltham (trans.). London: Continuum. Originally published in French as *L'Être et l'Événement* (Paris: Éditions du Seuil, 1988).

Badiou, A. 2005c. "The Subject of Art". *The Symptom* **6** (Spring), www.lacan.com//symptom6_articles/badiou.html (accessed June 2009).

Badiou, A. 2006a. *Polemics*, S. Corcoran (trans.). London: Verso.

Badiou, A. 2006b. *Metapolitics*, J. Barker (trans.). London: Verso.

Badiou, A. 2007. *The Century*, A. Toscano (trans.). Cambridge: Polity.

Badiou, A. "Fifteen Theses on Contemporary Art". *Lacanian Ink* **23**, www.lacan.com/frameXXIII7.htm (accessed June 2009).

Baecque, A. de 1991. *Histoire d'une revue, tome II: Cinéma, tours, détours 1959–1981*. Paris: Éditions Cahiers du cinéma.

Baecque, A. de 1996. "Le Temps perdu du cinéma". In *Le Retour du cinéma*, A. de Baecque & T. Jousse (eds), 11–47. Paris: Hachette.

Bakhtin, M. 1968. *Rabelais and His World*, H. Iswolsky (trans.). Cambridge, MA: MIT Press.

Bakunin, M. [1870] 1947. "The Class War". In his *Mikhail Bakunin Reference Archive: 1817–1876*, 1–3. New York: Modern Publishers. Available online at www.marxists.org/reference/archive/bakunin/works/writings/ch06.htm (accessed June 2009).

Barber, S. 1999. *The Screaming Body: Antonin Artaud – Film Projects, Drawings and Sound Recordings*. London: Creation Books.

Barthes, R. 1972. *Mythologies*, A. Lavers (trans.). New York: Hill & Wang. Originally published (Paris: Éditions du Seuil, 1970).

Barthes, R. 1974. *S/Z*, R. Miller (trans.). New York: Hill & Wang. Originally published (Paris: Éditions du Seuil, 1970).

Barthes, R. 1977a. *Image–Music–Text*, S. Heath (trans.). New York: Hill & Wang.

Barthes, R. 1977b. "The Grain of the Voice". In his *Image–Music–Text*, S. Heath (trans.), 179–89. London: Fontana.

Barthes, R. 1977c. *Roland Barthes*, R. Howard (trans.). New York: Hill & Wang.

Barthes, R. 1979. *Le Plaisir du texte*. Paris: Éditions du Seuil.

Barthes, R. 1980a. *La Chambre Claire: Note sur la photographie*. Paris: Éditions du Seuil.

Barthes, R. 1980b. "Upon Leaving the Movie Theater". In *Apparatus*, T. H. K. Cha (ed.), B. Augst & S. White (trans.), 1–4. New York: Tanam Press.

Barthes, R. 1981. *Camera Lucida: Reflections on Photography*, R. Howard (trans.). New York: Farrar, Straus & Giroux.

Barthes, R. 1985. *The Grain of the Voice: Interviews 1962–1980*, L. Coverdale (trans.). New York: Hill & Wang.

Barthes, R. 1993a. *Œuvres complètes, tome I, 1942–1965*, É. Marty (ed.). Paris: Éditions du Seuil.

Barthes, R. [1957] 1993b. "Myth Today". In his *Mythologies*, A. Lavers (trans.), 109–59. London: Vintage.

Barthes, R. 1995. *Œuvres complètes, tome III, 1974–1980*, É. Marty (ed.). Paris: Éditions du Seuil.

Barthes, R. 1998. "On Robert Bresson's Film *Les Anges du péché*". In *Robert Bresson*, J. Quandt (ed.), R. Howard (trans.), 211–13. Toronto: Toronto International Film Festival Group.

Barthes, R. 1999. "On Cinemascope", J. Rosenbaum (trans.). *Jouvert: A Journal of Postcolonial Studies* **3**(3), http://english.chass.ncsu.edu/jouvert/v3i3/barth.htm (accessed July 2009).

Basaglia, F. 1987. *Psychiatry Inside Out: Selected Writings of Franco Basaglia*, N. Scheper-Hughes & A. M. Lovell (eds), A. M. Lovell & T. Shtob (trans.). New York: Columbia University Press.

Baudrillard, J. 1975. *The Mirror of Production*, M. Poster (trans.). St Louis, MO: Telos Press.

Baudrillard, J. [1973] 1981. *For a Critique of the Political Economy of Signs*, C. Levin (trans.). St Louis, MO: Telos Press.

Baudrillard, J. 1983. *Simulations*, P. Foss, P. Patton & P. Beitchman (trans.). New York: Semiotext(e).

Baudrillard, J. 1988. *America*, C. Turner (trans.). London: Verso. First published in French as *Amérique* (Paris: Grasset, 1986).

Baudrillard, J. 1990. *Seduction*, B. Singer (trans.). London: Macmillan. First published in French as *De la séduction* (Paris: Galilée, 1979).

Baudrillard, J. [1976] 1993. *Symbolic Exchange and Death*, I. Hamilton Grant (trans.). London: Sage.

Baudrillard, J. 1994. *Simulacra and Simulation*, S. F. Glaser (trans.). Ann Arbor, MI: University of Michigan Press. First published in French as *Simulacres et simulation* (Paris: Galilée, 1981).

Baudrillard, J. [1991] 1995. *The Gulf War did not Take Place*, P. Patton (trans.). Bloomington, IN: Indiana University Press.

Baudrillard, J. 1996. *Cool Memories II: 1987–1990*, C. Turner (trans.). Cambridge: Polity.

Baudrillard, J. 2000. *The Vital Illusion*, J. Witner (ed. & trans.). New York: Columbia University Press.

Baudrillard, J. 2004. "*The Matrix* Decoded: Interview with *Le Nouvel Observateur*", G. Genosko & A. Bryx (trans.). *International Journal of Baudrillard Studies* **1**(2) (July), www.ubishops.ca/baudrillardstudies/vol1_2/genosko. htm (accessed June 2009).

Baudry, J.-L. 1978. *L'Effet cinéma*. Paris: Albatros.

Baudry, J.-L. 2004a. "Ideological Effects of the Basic Cinematographic Apparatus". In *Film Theory and Criticism: Introductory Readings*, 6th edn, L. Braudy & M. Cohen (eds), 355–65. New York: Oxford University Press. Originally published in French as "Effets idéologiques produits par l'appareil de base", *Cinéthique* **7/8** (1970), 1–8.

Baudry, J.-L. 2004b. "The Apparatus: Metapsychological Approaches to the Impression of Reality in the Cinema". In *Film Theory and Criticism: Introductory Readings*, 6th edn, L. Braudy & M. Cohen (eds), 206–23. New York: Oxford University Press. Originally published in French as "Le dispositif: approches metapsychologiques de l'impression de réalité'", *Communications* **23** (1975), 56–72.

Bazin, A. 1967. *What is Cinema? Vol. 1*, essays selected by H. Gray (trans.). Berkeley, CA: University of California Press. Essays selected from his *Qu'est-ce que le cinéma? tome 1: Ontologie et langage* (Paris: Éditions du Cerf, 1958) and *Qu'est-ce que le cinéma? tome 2: Le Cinéma et les autres arts* (Paris: Éditions du Cerf, 1959).

Bazin, A. 1971. *What is Cinema? Vol. 2*, essays selected by H. Gray (trans.). Berkeley, CA: University of California Press. Essays selected from his *Qu'est-ce que le cinéma? tome 3: Cinéma et sociologie* (Paris: Éditions du Cerf, 1961) and *Qu'est-ce que le cinéma? tome 4: Une esthétique de la Réalité: le néo-réalisme* (Paris: Éditions du Cerf, 1962).

Bazin, A. [1975] 1982. *The Cinema of Cruelty*, S. d'Estrée (trans.). New York: Seaver Books.

Bazin, A. [1972] 1991. *Orson Welles: A Critical View*, J. Rosenbaum (trans.). Venice, CA: Acrobat Books.

Bazin, A. [1971] 1992. *Jean Renoir*, W. W. Halsey & W. H. Simon (trans.). New York: De Capo Press.

Bazin, A. [1952] 2002a. *Qu'est-ce que le cinéma?* Paris: Éditions du Cerf.

Bazin, A. [1945] 2002b. "Ontologie de l'image photographique". In his *Qu'est-ce que le cinéma?*, 9–17. Paris: Éditions du Cerf.

Bazin, A. [1957] 2008. "*De la politique des auteurs*". In *Auteurs and Authorship: A Film Reader*, B. K. Grant (ed.), 19–28. Oxford: Wiley–Blackwell.

Bearn, G. C. F. 1998. "Sounding Serious: Cavell and Derrida". *Representations* **63** (Summer): 80.

Beineix, J.-J. (dir.) 1991. *Diva*. Les Films Galaxie/Greenwich Film Productions (as Greenwich Film Production)/ Antenne-2, 1991.

Beller, J. 2006. *The Cinematic Mode of Production: Attention Economy and the Society of the Spectacle*. Hanover, NH: Dartmouth College Press.

Bellocchio, M. (dir.) 1965. *Fists in the Pocket*. Doria.

Bellour, R. 1978. *Le Livre des autres: Entretiens avec M. Foucault, C. Lévi-Strauss, R. Barthes …*. Paris: UGE 10/18.

Bellour, R. 1986. "Serge Daney". *Magazine littéraire* **232** (July): 15.

Bellour, R. 1999. *L'Entre-images 2: Mots, images*. Paris: POL.

Bellour, R. 2000. *The Analysis of Film*, C. Penley (ed.). Bloomington, IN: Indiana University Press.

Bellour, R. 2001. "L'effet Daney ou l'arrêt de vie et de mort". *Trafic* **37**: 75–86.

Bellour, R. 2002a. *L'Entre-images: Photo, cinéma, vidéo*. Paris: Éditions de la Différence.

Bellour, R. 2002b. "Le Dépli des émotions". *Trafic* **43** (Autumn): 93–128.

Bellour, R. 2006. "Analysis in Flames". In *Kino wie noch nie: Cinema Like Never Before*, A. Ehmann & H. Farocki (eds), 121–4. Vienna: Generali Foundation.

Bellour, R. 2007. "The Pensive Spectator". In *The Cinematic*, D. Campany (ed.), 119–23. London: Whitechapel.

Belsey, C. [1980] 2002. *Critical Practice*, 2nd edn. London & New York: Routledge.

Benjamin, W. [1936] 1968. "The Work of Art in the Age of Mechanical Reproduction". In *Illuminations*, H. Arendt (ed.), H. Zohn (trans.), 217–52. New York: Harcourt, Brace & World.

Benjamin, W. 1999a. *Arcades Project*, H. Eiland & K. McLaughlin (trans.). Cambridge, MA: Harvard University Press.

Benjamin, W. 1999b. *Illuminations*, H. Arendt (ed.), H. Zohn (trans.). London: Pimlico.

Bennington, G. 1988. *Lyotard: Writing the Event*. Manchester: Manchester University Press.

Bergala, A. 1999. *Nul mieux que Godard*. Paris: Éditions Cahiers du cinéma.

Bergman, I. (dir.) 1953a. *Sommaren Med Monika* [Monika, the story of a bad girl]. Svensk Filmindustri (SF).

Bergman, I. (dir.) 1953b. *Gycklarnas Afton* [Sawdust and tinsel]. Svensk Filmindustri (SF).

Bergman, I. (dir.) 1957. *Smultronstället* [Wild strawberries]. Svensk Filmindustri (SF).

Bergman, I. (dir.) 1958. *Ansiktet* [The magician]. Svensk Filmindustri (SF).

Bergman, I. (dir.) 1960. *Jungfrukällan* [The virgin spring]. Svensk Filmindustri (SF).

Bergson, H. [1932] 1948. *Les deux sources de la morale et de la religion*. Paris: Presses Universitaires de France.

Bergson, H. [1907] 1959. *L'Évolution créatrice* [Creative evolution]. Paris: Presses Universitaires de France.

Bergson, H. [1911] 1983. *Creative Evolution*, A. Mitchell (trans.). Boston, MA: University Press of America.

Bergson, H. [1888] 1991. *Essai sur les données immédiates de la conscience*. Paris: Presses Universitaires de France.

Bergson, H. 1994. *Matter and Memory*, N. M. Paul & W. S. Palmer (trans.). New York: Zone Books. Originally published in French as *Matière et mémoire: Essai sur la relation du corps à l'esprit* (Paris: F. Alcan, 1896).

Bergson, H. [1896] 1995. *Matière et mémoire: Essai sur la relation du corps à l'esprit*. Paris: Presses Universitaires de France.

Bergson, H. 1999. *Duration and Simultaneity*, M. Lewis & R. Durie (trans.). Manchester: Clinamen Press.

Bergson, H. 2007. *Mind-Energy*, K. Ansell Pearson & M. Kolkman (eds), H. W. Carr (trans.). Basingstoke: Palgrave Macmillan.

Berri, C. (dir.) 1990. *Uranus*. DD Productions/Films A2/Investimage 2/Investimage 3/Renn Productions/Soficas Sofi Ano.

Bersani, L. & U. Dutoit 2004. *Forms of Being: Cinema, Aesthetics, Subjectivity*. London: BFI.

Besson, L. (dir.) 1989. *Le Grand bleu* [The big blue]. Gaumont/Les Films du Loup.

Best, S. & D. Kellner 1991. *Postmodern Theory*. Basingstoke: Macmillan.

Bhabha, H. 1983. "The Other Question: Stereotype, Discrimination and the Discourse of Colonialism". *Screen* **24**(6), special issue, "Racism, Colomialism and Cinema": 18–36.

Bhabha, H. 1989. "The Commitment to Theory". In *Questions of Third Cinema*, J. Pines & P. Willemen (eds), 111–32. London: BFI.

Bhabha, H. 1994. *The Location of Culture*. London & New York: Routledge.

Bhabha, H. 2001. "Democracy De-realized". In *Platform 1, Documenta 11*, www.documenta12.de/archiv/d11/data/english/platform1/index.html (accessed June 2009).

Bhabha, H. 2006. "Humanities at Harvard", www.hno.harvard.edu/multimedia/2006/humanities/intro.html (accessed June 2009).

Bhabha, H. 2007. "On Global Ambivalence". Lecture in Caucasus series "Becoming-Dutch", 17 November, Van Abbe Museum, Eindhoven.

Bickerton, E. 2006a. "A Message in a Bottle: Serge Daney's 'itinéraire d'un ciné-fils'". *Studies in French Cinema* **6**(1): 5–15.

Bickerton, E. 2006b. "Adieu *Cahiers*: Life-cycle of a Film Journal". *New Left Review* **42** (November–December): 69–97.

Blanchot, M. 1955. *L'Espace littéraire*. Paris: Gallimard.

Blanchot, M. 1986. *The Writing of the Disaster*, A. Smock (trans.). Lincoln, NE: University of Nebraska Press.

Blanchot, M. 1993. *The Infinite Conversation*, S. Hanson (trans.). Minneapolis, MN: Minnesota University Press.

Blanchot, M. 2003. *The Book to Come*, Charlotte Mandell (trans.). Stanford, CA: Stanford University Press.

Bogdanovich, P. (dir.) 1971. *The Last Picture Show*. BBS Productions/Columbia Pictures Corporation.

Bogue, R. 2003. *Deleuze on Cinema*. London & New York: Routledge.

Bogue, R. 2006. "Fabulation, Narration, and the People to Come". In *Deleuze and Philosophy*, C. Boundas (ed.), 202–23. Edinburgh: Edinburgh University Press.

Bordwell, D., J. Staiger & K. Thompson 1985. *The Classical Hollywood Cinema: Film Style and Mode of Production to 1960*. London: Routledge & Kegan Paul.

Bordwell, D. 2005. "Slavoj Žižek: Say Anything", www.davidbordwell.net/essays/zizek.php (accessed June 2009).

Bové, C. 2006. *Language and Politics in Julia Kristeva: Literature, Art, Therapy*. Albany, NY: SUNY Press.

Boyle, D. (dir.) 2002. *28 Days Later*. British Film Council/DNA Films.

369

Boynton, R. S. 1998. "Enjoy your Žižek: A Profile of Slavoj Žižek". *Lingua Franca*, www.robertboynton.com/articleDisplay.php?article_id=43 (accessed June 2009).

Braidotti, R. 2006. *Transpositions: On Nomadic Ethics*. Cambridge: Polity.

Brakhage, S. 1967. "The Camera-Eye". In *New American Cinema: A Critical Anthology*, G. Battcock (ed.), 211–25. New York: Dutton.

Brakhage, S. (dir.) 1971. *The Act of Seeing with One's Own Eyes*. Canyon Cinema/The Criterion Collection.

Brakhage, S. 1982. "Interview with Richard Grossinger". In his *Brakhage Scrapbook: Collected Writings 1964–1980*, 190–200. New York: Documentexte.

Branigan, E. 2006. *Projecting a Camera: Language-Games in Film Theory*. London & New York: Routledge.

Brenet, N. & C. Lebrat (eds) 2001. *Jeune, dure et pure! Une histoire du cinéma d'avant-garde et experimentale en France*. Paris: Cinémathèque Française/Mazzotta.

Brenon, H. (dir.) 1914. *Neptune's Daughter*. Universal Film Manufacturing Company.

Bresson, R. (dir.) 1947. *Les Anges du péché* [Angels of the streets]. Synops.

Bresson, R. (dir.) 1959. *Pickpocket*. Agnès Delahaie/Compagnie Cinématographique de France.

Bresson, R. (dir.) 1962. *Procès de Jeanne d'Arc* [The trial of Joan of Arc]. Agnès Delahaie.

Bresson, R. (dir.) 1977. *Le Diable probablement* [The devil probably]. GMF/Gaumont Films/Sunchild Productions.

Bresson, R. 1986. *Notes on the Cinematographer*, J. M. G. Le Clézio (trans.). London: Quartet Encounters.

Bruckman, C. & B. Keaton (dirs) 1927. *The General*. Buster Keaton Productions/Joseph M. Schenck Productions.

Brunette, P. 1998. *The Films of Michelangelo Antonioni*. Cambridge: Cambridge University Press.

Brunette, P. & D. Wills 1989. *Screen/Play: Derrida and Film Theory*. Princeton, NJ: Princeton University Press.

Brustellin, A., H. P. Cloos *et al.* (dirs) 1978. *Germany in Autumn*. Filmverlag der Autoren.

Bucher, F. 2005. "Television (An Address)". *Journal of Visual Culture* **4**(1): 5–15.

Buñuel, L. (dir.) 1962. *El Ángel exterminador* [The exterminating angel]. Producciones Gustavo Alatriste.

Buñuel, L. (dir.) 1977. *Cet obscur objet du désir* [That obscure object of desire]. Greenwich Film Productions/In-Cine Compañía Industrial Cinematográfica/Les Films Galaxie.

Burch, N. 1973. *Theory of Film Practice*, H. R. Lane (trans.). New York: Praeger.

Burke, E. n.d. "Mulvey, Laura (1941–)". *Screenonline*, www.screenonline.org.uk/people/id/566978/ (accessed August 2009).

Butler, A. 2002. *Women's Cinema: The Contested Screen*. London: Wallflower.

Cameron, J. (dir.) 1984. *The Terminator*. Hemdale Film/Cinema 84/Amblin Entertainment/Euro Film Funding/Pacific Western.

Cameron, J. (dir.) 1991. *Terminator 2: Judgment Day*. Amblin Entertainment/Canal+ (as "Le Studio Canal+")/Carolco Pictures/Lightstorm Entertainment/Pacific Western/T2 Productions (uncredited).

Cameron, J. (dir.) 1997. *Titanic*. Twentieth Century-Fox Film Corporation/Paramount Pictures/Lightstorm Entertainment.

Capra, F. (dir.) 1934. *It Happened One Night*. Columbia Pictures.

Carles, P. (dir.) 2001. *La sociologie est un sport de combat* [Sociology is a martial art] C. P. Productions/V. F. Films Productions/Icarus Films.

Caro, M. & J.-P. Jenuet (dirs) 1991. *Delicatessen*. Constellation/Union Générale Cinématographique/Hachette Première/Sofinergie Films/Sofinerge 2/Investimage 2/Investimage 3/ Fondation GAN pour le Cinéma/Victoires Productions.

Carroll, N. 1988a. *Philosophical Problems of Classical Film Theory*. Princeton, NJ: Princeton University Press.

Carroll, N. 1988b. "Film/Mind Analogies: The Case of Hugo Münsterberg". *Journal of Aesthetics and Art Criticism* **46**(4) (Summer): 489–99.

Carroll, N. 1988c. *Mystifying Movies: Fads and Fallacies in Contemporary Film Theory*. New York: Columbia University Press.

Carroll, N. 1996. *Theorizing the Moving Image*. Cambridge: Cambridge University Press.

Carroll, N. 2008. *The Philosophy of Motion Pictures*. Oxford: Blackwell.

Carroll, N. & J. Choi (eds) 2006. *Philosophy of Film and Motion Pictures: An Anthology*. Oxford: Blackwell.

Casebier, A. 1991. *Film and Phenomenology: Toward a Realist Theory of Cinematic Representation*. Cambridge: Cambridge University Press.

Casetti, F. 1999. *Theories of Cinema, 1945–90*, F. Chiostri (trans.). Austin, TX: University of Texas Press.

Cavani, L. (dir.) 1974. *Il Portiere di notte* [The night porter]. Italonegglio Cinematografico/Lotar Film Productions.

Cavell, S. 1969. *Must We Mean What We Say?* New York: Scribner's.

Cavell, S. 1971. *The World Viewed*. New York: Penguin.

Cavell, S. 1979a. *The Claim of Reason*. Oxford: Clarendon Press.

Cavell, S. 1979b. *The World Viewed: Reflections on the Ontology of Film*, enlarged edn. Cambridge, MA: Harvard University Press.

Cavell, S. 1996. *Contesting Tears*. Chicago, IL: University of Chicago Press.

Celeste, R. 2007. "The Frozen Screen: Levinas and the Action Film". *Film-Philosophy* **11**(2): 15–36, www.film-philosophy.com/2007v11n2/celeste.pdf (accessed July 2009).

Cha, T. H. K. (ed.) 1981. *Apparatus, Cinematographic Apparatus: Selected Writings*. New York: Tanam Press.

Chabrol, C. (dir.) 1958. *Le Beau Serge* [Handsome Serge]. Ajym Films/Coopérative Générale du Cinéma Français.

Chaplin, C. (dir.) 1925. *The Gold Rush*. Charles Chaplin Productions.

Chaplin, C. (dir.) 1931. *City Lights*. Charles Chaplin Productions.

Charney, L. & V. Schwarz 1996. *Cinema and the Invention of Modern Life*. Berkeley, CA: University of California Press.

Chion, M. 1982. *La Voix au cinéma*. Paris: Éditions Cahiers du cinéma.

Clément, C. & J. Kristeva 2001. *The Feminine and the Sacred*, J. M. Todd (trans.). Basingstoke: Palgrave.

Coates, P. 2002. "Kieslowski and the Anti-Politics of Color: A Reading of the 'Three Colors' Trilogy". *Cinema Journal* **41**(2): 41–66.

Cobb, A. 2007. "Cinema of Pre-predication: On Stan Brakhage and the Phenomenology of Maurice Merleau-Ponty". *Senses of Cinema* 44 (July), www.sensesofcinema.com/contents/07/44/brakhage-merleau-ponty.html (accessed July 2009).

Cocteau, J. (dir.) 1946. *La Belle et la Bête* [Beauty and the beast]. DisCina.

Cocteau, J. 1950. *Beauty and the Beast: Diary of a Film*. London: Dennis Dobson.

Cohen-Séat, G. 1946. *Essai sur les principes d'une philosophie du cinéma*. Paris: Presses Universitaires de France.

Colapietro, V. 2000. "Let's All Go to the Movies: Two Thumbs Up for Hugo Münsterberg's *The Photoplay* (1916)". *Transactions of the Charles S. Peirce Society* **36**(4) (Fall): 477–501.

Colman, F. 2009. "Affective Imagery: Screen Militarism". In *Gilles Deleuze: Image and Text*, E. W. Holland, D. W. Smith & C. J. Stivale (eds), 143–59. London: Continuum.

Conant, J. 1989. "An Interview with Stanley Cavell". In *The Senses of Stanley Cavell*, R. Fleming & M. Payne (eds), 21–72. Lewisburg, PA: Bucknell University Press.

Conley, T. 1996. *The Self-Made Map: Cartographic Writing in Early Modern France*. Minneapolis, MN: University of Minnesota Press.

Conley, T. [1991] 2006. *Film Hieroglyphs: Ruptures in Classical Cinema*. Minneapolis, MN: University of Minnesota Press.

Constable, C. 2005. *Thinking in Images: Film Theory, Feminist Philosophy and Marlene Dietrich*. London: BFI.

Constable, C. 2009. *Adapting Philosophy: Jean Baudrillard and "The Matrix Trilogy"*. Manchester: Manchester University Press.

Cooper, M. C. & E. B. Schoedsack (dirs) 1933. *King Kong*. RKO Radio Pictures.

Cooper, S. (ed.) 2007. *Special Issue: The Occluded Relation: Levinas and Cinema*. *Film-Philosophy* **11**(2), www.film-philosophy.com/archive/vol11-2007/ (accessed July 2009).

Copjec, J. 2002. "The Invention of Crying and the Antitheatrics of the Act". In her *Imagine There's No Woman: Ethics and Sublimation*, 108–31. Cambridge, MA: MIT Press.

Coppola, F. F. (dir.) 1972. *The Godfather*. Paramount Pictures.

Coppola, F. F. (dir.) 1974. *The Godfather: Part II*. Paramount Pictures/The Coppola Company.

Coppola, F. F. (dir.) 1979. *Apocalypse Now*. Zoetrope Studios.

Coppola, F. F. (dir.) 1982. *One from the Heart*. Zoetrope Studios.

Coppola, F. F. (dir.) 1990. *The Godfather: Part III*. Paramount Pictures/Zoetrope Studios.

Critchley, S. 1992. *The Ethics of Deconstruction: Derrida and Levinas*. Oxford: Blackwell.

Critchley, S. 2001. *Continental Philosophy: A Very Short Introduction*. Oxford: Oxford University Press.

Crome, K. & J. Williams (eds) 2006. *The Lyotard Reader and Guide*. Edinburgh: Edinburgh University Press.

Cronenberg, D. (dir.) 1983. *Videodrome*. Canadian Film Development Corporation (CFDC)/Famous Players/Filmplan/Guardian Trust Company/Victor Solnicki Productions.

Cruz, O. 2008. "Lessons from the School of Inattention". Available online at www.oggsmoggs.blogspot.com/2008/04/la-jete-1962.html (accessed June 2009).

Cubitt, S. 2001. *Simulation and Social Theory*. London: Sage.

Cubitt, S. 2004. *The Cinema Effect*. Cambridge, MA: MIT Press.

Cukor, G. (dir.) 1944. *Gaslight*. Metro-Goldwyn-Meyer (MGM).

Cukor, G. (dir.) 1949. *Adam's Rib*. Loew's.

Currie, G. 1995. *Image and Mind: Film, Philosophy and Cognitive Science*. Cambridge: Cambridge University Press.

Curtiz, M. (dir.) 1942. *Casablanca*. Warner Brothers Pictures.

Dall'Asta, M. 2004. "Debates: Thinking about Cinema: First Waves". See Temple & Witt (eds) (2004), 82–9.

Daly, F. & G. Dowd 2003. *Leos Carax*. Manchester: Manchester University Press.

Daney, S. 1983. *La Rampe: Cahiers critique 1970–1982*. Paris: Gallimard/Cahiers du cinéma.

Daney, S. 1986. *Ciné-Journal 1981–1986*. Paris: Éditions Cahiers du cinéma.

Daney, S. 1991a. *Devant la recrudescence des vols des sacs à main: Cinéma, télévision, information (1988–1991)*. Lyon: Aléas.

Daney, S., with P. Garrel 1991b. "Dialogue, propos recueillis par Thierry Jousse". *Cahiers du cinéma* **443/4**: 58–63.

Daney, S. 1991c. "Journal de l'an passée". *Trafic* **1**.

Daney, S. 1996. "Baby Seeking Bathwater", B. Holmes (trans.). In *Documenta Documents 2*, 22–31. Ostfildern: Cantz. Originally published in French in two parts as "Bébé cherche eau du bain", *Libération* (30 September/1 October 1991).

Daney, S. 1997. "Before and After the Image". In *Documenta X: The Book: Politics Poetics*, C. David & J. F. Chevrier (eds), 610–20. Ostfildern: Cantz.

Daney, S. 1999. *Itinéraire d'un ciné-fils*, transcript of an interview by R. Debray & C. Delage (eds). Paris: Jean Michel Place.

Daney, S. 2000a. "The Critical Function". In *Cahiers du Cinéma – Volume IV: 1973–1978: History, Ideology, Cultural Struggle*, D. Wilson (ed.), London: Routledge: 56–71. Originally published in French as "La Fonction critique", *Cahiers du cinéma* **248/249/250/253** (1973–4).

Daney, S. 2000b. "Theorize/Terrorize (Godardian Pedagogy)". In *Cahiers du Cinéma – Volume IV: 1973–1978: History, Ideology, Cultural Struggle*, D. Wilson (ed.), 116–23. London: Routledge. Originally published in French as "Le Thérrorisé (pédagogie godardienne)", *Cahiers du cinéma* **262** (1976); reprinted in *La Rampe* (Paris: Gallimard, 1983).

Daney, S. 2000c. "On Salador". In S. Daney & J.-P. Oudart, "Work, Reading, Pleasure", 115–23. In *Cahiers du Cinéma – Volume III: 1969–1972: The Politics of Representation*, N. Browne (ed.), 115–36. London: Routledge. Originally published in French in *Cahiers du cinéma* **222** (1970); reprinted in *La Rampe* (Paris: Gallimard, 1983).

Daney, S. 2001a. "Biofilmographie [imaginaire] de Patrick Deval". In *Jeune, dure et pure! Une histoire du cinéma d'avant-garde et experimentale en France*, N. Brenez & C. Lebrat (eds), 317. Paris: Cinémathèque Française/Mazzotta.

Daney, S. 2001b. *La Maison cinéma et le monde, tome 1: Le Temps de Cahiers 1962–1981*. P. Rollet, J.-C. Biette & C. Manon (eds). Paris: POL.

Daney, S. 2001c. "The Organ and the Vacuum Cleaner". In *Literary Debate: Texts and Contexts, Postwar French Thought*, vol. II, D. Hollier & J. Mehlman (eds), 474–86. New York: New Press. Originally published in French as "L'Orge et l'aspirateur", *Cahiers du cinéma* **279/80** (1977), 19–27; reprinted in *La Rampe*, 138–48 (Paris: Gallimard, 1983).

Daney, S. 2002. *La Maison cinéma et le monde, tome 2: Les Années Libé 1981–1985*. P. Rollet, J.-C. Biette & C. Manon (eds). Paris: POL.

Daney, S. 2003. "The Screen of Fantasy", M. A. Cohen (trans.). In *Rites of Realism: Essays on Corporeal Cinema*, I. Margulies (ed.), 32–41. Durham, NC: Duke University Press. Originally published in French as "L'Écran du fantasme", in *Cahiers du cinéma* **236/7** (March–April 1972), 30; reprinted in *La Rampe*, 34–42 (Paris: Gallimard, 1983).

Daney, S. 2004. "La guère, le visuel, l'image". *Trafic* **50**: 439–44.

Daney, S. 2006. "Montage Obligatory: The War, the Gulf and the Small Screen", L. Kretzschmar (trans.). *Rouge* **8**. [First published in *Libération* (April 1991) and reprinted in his *Devant la recrudescence des vols de sacs à mains: cinéma, télévision, information*, 187–96 (Lyon: Aléas, 1991).]

Daney, S. 2007. *Postcards from the Cinema*, P. Grant (trans.). Oxford: Berg. [Contains "The Tracking Shot in *Kapò*", originally published in *Trafic* **4** (1992), and a translation of *Persévérances* (Paris: POL, 1994).]

Daney, S. & J. P. Oudart [1972] 2000. "The Name of the Author (on the 'place' in *Death in Venice*)". *Cahiers du Cinéma – Volume III: 1969–1972: The Politics of Representation*, N. Browne (ed.), 306–24. London: Routledge. [First published as "Le nom-de-l'auteur", *Cahiers du cinéma* **234** (February) (1972).]

Daney, S. & S. Toubiana 2000. "Cahiers Today". In *Cahiers du Cinéma – Volume IV: 1973–1978: History, Ideology, Cultural Struggle*, D. Wilson (ed.), 47–55. London: Routledge. Originally published in French in *Cahiers du cinéma* **250** (May) (1974), 5–10.

Dardenne, L. 2005. *Au dos de nos images*. Paris: Éditions du Seuil.

Darke, C. 2001. "Cinema *sans papiers*: Writing on French Cinema". In his *Light Readings: Film Criticism and Screen Arts*, 69–75. London: Wallflower Press.

Dasgupta, S. 2007. "Jacques Rancière en de spiraal van het denken over politiek en esthetiek". In Jacques Rancière, *Het Esthetische Denken*, W. van der Star (trans.), 147–77. Amsterdam: Valiz.

David, C. & P. Virilio 1996. "The Dark Spot of Art". In *Documenta documents 1*, C. David (ed.) J. C. Bailly (contrib.), 47–67. Ostfildern: Cantz.

Davies, T. (dir.) 1988. *Distant Voices, Still Lives*. British Film Institute (BFI)/Channel Four Films.

Davis, C. 2007. "Levinas, *Nosferatu*, and the Love as Strong as Death". *Film-Philosophy* 11(2): 37–48, www.film-philosophy.com/2007v11n2/davis.pdf (accessed July 2009).

Dayan, D. 1985. "The Tutor-Code of Classical Cinema". See Nichols (1985), 438–51.

Debord, G. (dir. & prod.) 1952. *Hurlements en faveur de Sade* [Howlings in favour of de Sade]. Films Lettristes.

Debord, G. (dir.) 1973. *La Société du spectacle* [Society of the spectacle]. Simar Films.

Debord, G. (dir.) 1978. *In Girum Imus Nocte Et Consumimur Igni* [We spin around the night consumed by the fire]. Simar Films.

Degener, M. 2005. "Translator's introduction: Seven Minutes". In *Negative Horizon: An Essay in Dromoscopy*, P. Virilio (ed.), M. Degener (trans.), 1–25. London: Continuum.

Deleuze, G. 1983. *Cinéma I: L'Image-mouvement*. Paris: Les Éditions de Minuit.

Deleuze, G. 1985. *Cinéma II: L'Image-temps*. Paris: Les Éditions de Minuit.

Deleuze, G. 1986. *Cinema 1: The Movement-Image*, H. Tomlinson & B. Habberjam (trans.). London: Athlone.

Deleuze, G. [1986] 1988. *Foucault*, S. Hand (trans.). Minneapolis, MN: University of Minnesota Press.

Deleuze, G. 1989. *Cinema 2: The Time-Image*, H. Tomlinson & R. Galeta (trans.). London: Athlone.

Deleuze, G. 1990a. *The Logic of Sense*, C. Boundas (ed.), M. Lester with C. Stivale (trans.). New York: Columbia University Press. Originally published in French as *Logique du sens* (Paris: Éditions de Minuit, 1969).

Deleuze, G. 1990b. *Expressionism in Philosophy: Spinoza*, M. Joughin (trans.). New York: Zone Books. Originally published in French as *Spinoza et le problème de l'expression* (Paris: Éditions de Minuit, 1968).

Deleuze, G. 1994. *Difference and Repetition*, P. Patton (trans.). London: Continuum. Originally published in French as *Différence et Répétition* (Paris: Presses Universitaires de France, 1968).

Deleuze, G. 1995a. *Negotiations: 1972–1990*, M. Joughin (trans.). New York: Columbia University Press. Originally published in French as *Pourparlers, 1972–1990* (Paris: Éditions de Minuit, 1990).

Deleuze, G. [1990] 1995b. "Letter to Serge Daney: Optimism, Pessimism and Travel". In his *Negotiations 1972–1990*, M. Joughin (trans.), 68–79. New York: Columbia University Press.

Deleuze, G. 2000. "The Brain is the Screen: An Interview with Gilles Deleuze", M. T. Guirgis (trans.). See Flaxman (2000), 365–73.

Deleuze, G. 2001. *The Fold: Leibniz and the Baroque*, T. Conley (trans.). London: Athlone. Originally published in French as *Le Pli: Leibniz et le baroque* (Paris: Minuit, 1988).

Deleuze, G. 2003. *Francis Bacon: The Logic of Sensation*, D. W. Smith (trans.). London: Continuum.

Deleuze, G. & F. Guattari [1977] 1984. *Anti-Oedipus*, R. Hurley, M. Seem & H. R. Lane (trans.). London: Athlone. Orginally published in French as *L'Anti-Œdipe: Capitalisme et schizophrénie* (Paris: Minuit, 1972).

Deleuze, G. & F. Guattari [1975] 1986. *Kafka: For a Minor Literature*, D. Polan (trans.). Minneapolis, MN: University of Minnesota Press.

Deleuze, G. & F. Guattari 1987. *A Thousand Plateaus*, B. Massumi (trans.). Minneapolis, MN: University of Minnesota Press. Originally published in French as *Mille Plateaux* (Paris: Minuit, 1980).

Deleuze, G. & F. Guattari 1994. *What is Philosophy?* H. Tomlinson & G. Burchell (trans.). New York: Columbia University Press. Originally published in French as *Qu'est-ce que la philosophie?* (Paris: Minuit, 1991).

Demme, J. (dir.) 1991. *The Silence of the Lambs*. Orion Pictures Corporation/Strong Heart/Demme Production.

Denis, C. & S. Daney (dirs) 1990. *Jacques Rivette – Le veilleur* [Jacques Rivette – the night watchman]. Produced for the television series "Cinéma, de notre temps", Le Sept/Arte/Centre Nationale de la Cinématographie/Ministère des Affaires Étrangères/Intermédia.

Dennison, S. & S. H. Lim 2006. *Remapping World Cinema: Identity, Culture and Politics in Film*. London: Wallflower.

De Palma, B. (dir.) 2007. *Redacted*. Film Farm/The HDNet Films.

Depardon, R. (dir.) 1988. *Urgences* [Emergencies]. CNC.

Der Derian, J. 1998. *The Virilio Reader*. Oxford: Blackwell.

Derrida, J. 1967. *La Voix et le phénomène: introduction au problème du signe dans la phénoménologie de Husserl*. Paris: Presses Universitaires de France.

Derrida, J. 1973. *Speech and Phenomena and Other Essays on Husserl's Theory of Signs*, D. B. Allison (trans.). Evanston, IL: Northwestern University Press..

Derrida, J. 1976. *Of Grammatology*, G. C. Spivak (trans.). Baltimore, MD: Johns Hopkins University Press. Originally published in French as *De la grammatologie* (Paris: Les Éditions de Minuit, 1967).

Derrida, J. 1978. "Freud and the Scene of Writing". In *Writing and Difference*, A. Bass (trans.), 197–8. Chicago, IL: University of Chicago Press. *Writing and Difference* was originally published in French as *L'écriture et la différence* (Paris, Éditions du Seuil, 1967).

Derrida, J. 1985. "Lecture de Droit de Regards". In *Droit de Regards*, M.-F. Plissart (photography), I–XXXVI. Paris: Éditions de Minuit. Published in English as *Right of Inspection* (New York: Monacelli Press, 1998).

Derrida, J. 1993. *Memoirs of the Blind*, P.-A. Brault & M. Naas (trans.). Chicago, IL: University of Chicago Press.

Derrida, J. 1994. *Spectres of Marx: The State of the Debt, the Work of Mourning and the New International*, P. Kamuf (trans.). London: Routledge. Originally published in French as *Spectres de Marx: l'état de la dette, le travail du deuil et la nouvelle Internationale* (Paris: Galilée, 1993).

Derrida, J. 1998. *Archive Fever*. E. Prenowitz (trans.). Chicago, IL: University of Chicago Press.

Derrida, J. 2001. "Le Cinéma et ses fantômes", Interview with A. de Baecque & T. Jousse. *Cahiers du cinéma* **556** (April): 75–85.

Derrida, J. 2003. "Le Tritier". In his *Parages*, rev. edn. Paris: Galilée.

Derrida, J. 2005. *On Touching*, C. Irizarry (trans.). Stanford, CA: Stanford University Press.

Derrida, J. 2007. Introduction [untitled] in *Sarah Kofman: Selected Writings*, T. Albrecht (ed.) with G. Albert & E. Rottenberg, 1–34. Stanford, CA: Stanford University Press.

Derrida, J. & S. Fathy 2000. *Tourner les mots: Au bord d'un film*. Paris: Galilée/Arte.

Derrida, J. & B. Stiegler 1996. *Echographies de la télévision: Entretiensfilmés*. Paris: Galilée/INA. [Published in English as *Echographies of Television: Filmed Interviews*, J. Bajorek (trans.) (Cambridge: Polity, 2002).]

De Sica, V. (dir.) 1948. *Ladri di biciclette* [The bicycle thief]. Produzioni De Sica.

DeWitt, R. 2004. *Worldviews: An Introduction to the History and Philosophy of Science*. Oxford: Blackwell.

Dick, K. & A. Ziering-Kofman (dirs) 2005. *Derrida*. Jane Doe Films.

Dissanayake, W. (ed.) 1994. *Colonialism and Nationalism in Asian Cinema*. Bloomington, IN: Indiana University Press.

Doane, M. A. 2002. *The Emergence of Cinematic Time: Modernity, Contingency, the Archive*. Cambridge, MA: Harvard University Press.

Donen, S. & G. Kelly (dirs) 1952. *Singin' in the Rain*. Metro-Goldwyn-Mayer (MGM).

Dreyer, C. T. (dir.) 1928. *La Passion de Jeanne d'Arc* [The passion of Joan of Arc]. Société générale des films.

Dulac, G. (dir.) 1928. *La Coquille et le clergyman* [The seashell and the clergyman]. Délia Film.

Durie, R. 1999. "Introduction". In Henri Bergson, *Duration and Simultaneity*, M. Lewis & R. Durie (trans.), v–xxiii. Manchester: Clinamen Press.

Eggeling, V. (dir.) 1992. *Symphonie Diagonale* [Diagonal symphony]. Art Production Fund.

Eisenstein, S. (dir.) 1925. *Battleship Potemkin*. Goskino.

Eisenstein, S. (dir.) 1944. *Ivan Groznyy I* [Ivan the Terrible]. Alma Ata Studio.

Eisenstein, S. 1949. *Film Form: Essays in Film Theory*, J. Leyda (trans.). New York: Harcourt Brace Jovanovich.

Eisenstein, S. & M. Filimonova (dir.) 1958. *Ivan Groznyy II: Boyarsky zagovor* [Ivan the Terrible: Part II: The Boyars' plot]. Alma Ata Studio.

Eldridge, R. 2003. "Introduction". In his *Stanley Cavell*, Cambridge: Cambridge University Press.

Elsaesser, T. 1987. "Cinema – The Irresponsible Signifier or 'The Gamble with History': Film Theory or Cinema Theory". *New German Critique* **40**: 65–89.

Elsaesser, T. (ed.) 1990. *Early Cinema: Space, Frame, Narrative*. London: BFI.

Elsaesser, T. 1997. "Zwischen Filmtheorie und Cultural Studies: Mit Kracauer (noch einmal) im Kino". In *Idole des deutschen Films: Eine Galerie von Schlüsselfiguren*, T. Koebner (ed.), 22–40. Munich: text + kritik.

Elsaesser, T. 1998. "Specularity and Engulfment: Francis Ford Coppola and *Bram Stoker's Dracula*". In *Contemporary Hollywood Cinema*, S. Neale & M. White (eds), 191–208. London & New York: Routledge.

Elsaesser, T. 2005. *European Cinema: Face to Face with Hollywood*. Amsterdam: Amsterdam University Press.

Epstein, J. 1921. *Bonjour Cinéma*. Paris: Sirène.

Espinoza, J. G. 1997. "For an Imperfect Cinema and Meditations on Imperfect Cinema … Fifteen Years Later". In *New Latin American Cinema*, vol. 1, M. I. Martin (ed.), 71–85. Detroit, MI: Wayne State University Press.

Evans, D. 1996. *An Introductory Dictionary of Lacanian Psychoanalysis*. London: Routledge.

Everett, W. 2004. *Terence Davies*. Manchester: Manchester University Press.

Fassbinder, R. W. (dir.) 1974. *Angst essen Seele auf* [Fear eats the soul]. Filmverlag der Autoren/Tango Film.

Fathy, S. (dir.) 1999. *D'ailleurs, Derrida* [Derrida's elsewhere]. La Sept/ARTE/GLORIA Films.

Faulkner, C. 2004. "Critical Debate and the Construction of Society". See Temple & Witt (eds) (2004), 172–80.

Fellini, F. (dir.) 1973. *Amarcord* [I remember]. F. C. Produzioni/PECF.

Fielding, H. 2006. "White Logic and the Constancy of Colour". In *Feminist Interpretations of Merleau-Ponty*, D. Olkowski & G. Weiss (eds), 71–89. University Park, PA: Pennsylvania State University Press.

Fiennes, S. (dir.) 2005. *The Pervert's Guide to Cinema*. Lone Star, Mischief Films.

Fincher, D. (dir.) 1999. *Fight Club*. Art Linson Productions/Fox 2000 Pictures/Regency Enterprises/Taurus Film.

Flaherty, R. (dir.) 1922. *Nanook of the North*. Les Frères Revillon/Pathé Exchange.

Flaherty, R. (dir.) 1948. *Louisiana Story*. Robert Flaherty Productions Inc.

Flaxman, G. (ed.) 2000. *The Brain is the Screen: Deleuze and the Philosophy of Cinema*. Minneapolis, MN: University of Minnesota Press

374

Flittermann-Lewis, S. 1996. "The Image and the Spark: Dulac and Artaud Revisited". In *Dada and Surrealist Film*, R. Kuenzli (ed.), 110–27. Cambridge MA: MIT Press.

Flusser, V. 1973. *Le Monde condifié*. Paris: Institut de l'Environnement.

Flusser, V. 1975. "Fred Forest, or the Destruction of Established Points of View", www.webnetmuseum.org/html/en/expo-retr-fredforest/textes_critiques/auteurs/flusser_en.htm#text (accessed July 2009).

Flusser, V. 1977. *L'Art sociologique et vidéo à travers la démarche de Fred Forest* [Sociological art and video through the work of Fred Forest]. Paris: UGE.

Flusser, V. 1988. "Vilém Flusser interviewed by Miklós Peternák". At "Intersubjectivity: Media Metaphors, Play & Provocation", 6th International Vilém Flusser Symposium and Event Series, 15–19 March 1997, Budapest, Hungary. www.c3.hu/events/97/flusser/participantstext/miklos-interview.html (accessed July 2009).

Flusser, V. 1991. *Gesten, Versuch einer Phänomenologie*. Düsseldorf & Bensheim: Bollmann.

Flusser, V. 1999. *The Shape of Things: A Philosophy of Design*, A. Mathews (trans.). London: Reaktion. Originally published in German as *Vom Stand der Dinge: Eine kleine Philosophie des Design* (Göttingen: European Photography, 1993).

Flusser, V. 2000. *Towards a Philosophy of Photography*, A. Mathews (trans.). London: Reaktion. Originally published in German as *Für eine Philosophie der Fotografie* (Göttingen: European Photography, 1983).

Flusser, V. 2006. "De la Production et de la consommation des films" [On the production and consumption of films]. In *La Civilisation des médias*, C. Maillard (trans.), 75–88. Belval: Circé.

Flusser, V. forthcoming. "On the Production and Consumption of Films", A. Martin (trans.). *Rouge*, www. rouge. com.au/.

Forbes, J. 1992. "The Heritage of the Nouvelle Vague". In her *The Cinema in France After the New Wave*, 125–37. Basingstoke: Macmillan.

Forman, M. (dir.) 1975. *One Flew Over the Cuckoo's Nest*. Fantasy Films.

Forster, E. M. 1924. *A Passage to India*. London: E. Arnold.

Foucault, M. [1969] 1972. *The Archaeology of Knowledge*, A. M. Sheridan Smith (trans.). London: Tavistock.

Foucault, M. [1984] 1986. *The History of Sexuality, Vol. 3: The Care of Self*, R. Hurley (trans.). London: Routledge.

Foucault, M. [1974] 1989. "Film and Popular Memory". In *Foucault Live – Interviews 1966–84*, S. Lotringer (ed.), M. Jordin (trans.), 89–106. New York: Semiotexte. [First published as "Entretien avec Michel Foucault", *Cahiers du cinéma* **251/2** (1974), 5–15.]

Foucault, M. 2006. *History of Madness*, J. Murphy & J. Khalfa (trans.) London: Routledge.

Frampton, D. 2006. *Filmosophy*. London: Wallflower.

Frampton, H. 1983. *Circles of Confusion: Film, Photography, Video: Texts, 1968–1980*. Rochester, NY: Visual Studies Workshop Press.

Franju, G. (dir.) 1949. *Le Sang des bêtes* [The blood of beasts]. Forces et voix de la France.

Freud, S. 1953. *The Interpretation of Dreams*. In *The Standard Edition of the Complete Psychological Works of Sigmund Freud*, vols IX & V, J. Strachey (ed. & trans.). London: The Hogarth Press and the Institute of Psychoanalysis. Originally published in German as *Die Traumdeutung* (Leipzig & Vienna: Franz Deuticke, 1900).

Freud, S. 1955. "The Uncanny". In *The Standard Edition of the Complete Psychological Works of Sigmund Freud*, vol. XVII, A. Strachey & J. Strachey (trans.), 217–56. London: The Hogarth Press and the Institute of Psychoanalysis. Originally published in German as "Das Unheimliche", *Imago* **5** (1919).

Freud, S. [1925] 1971. "Note on the Mystical Writing Pad". In *Collected Papers*, vol. 5, J. Strachey (ed. & trans.), 175–80. London: The Hogarth Press and the Institute of Psychoanalysis.

Früchtl, J. 2007. "'Auf ein Neues': Ästhetik und Politik. Und dazwischen das Spiel. Angestoßen durch Jacques Rancière". *Deutsche Zeitschrift für Philosophie* **55**(2): 209–19.

Fuller, M. 2005. *Media Ecologies: Materialist Energies in Art and Technoculture*. Cambridge, MA: MIT Press.

Gaines, J. M. 2002. "Everyday Strangeness: Robert Ripley's International Oddities as Documentary Attractions". *New Literary History* **33**(4): 781–801.

Galan, F. W. 1985. *Historical Structures: The Prague School Project, 1928–1946*. Austin, TX: University of Texas Press.

Gambaudo, S. 2007. *Kristeva, Psychoanalysis and Culture: Subjectivity in Crisis*. Aldershot: Ashgate.

Gamman, L. & M. Makinen 1994. *Female Fetishism: A New Look*. London: Lawrence & Wishart.

Gane, M. (ed.) 1993. *Baudrillard Live: Selected Interviews*. London: Routledge.

Gane, M. 2003. *French Social Theory*. London: Sage.

Gardner, C. 2004. *Joseph Losey*. Manchester: Manchester University Press.

Gargett, A. 2001. "Doppelganger: Exploded States of Consciousness in *Fight Club*". *Disinformation*, www.disinfo.com/archive/pages/article/id1497/pg1/index.html (accessed July 2009).

Garrel, P. (dir.) 1968a. *La concentration* [Concentration]. Zanzibar Films.

Garrel, P. (dir.) 1968b. *Le Révélateur*. Zanzibar Films.

Genosko, G. 2001. *The Uncollected Baudrillard*. London: Sage.

Genosko, G. 2002. *Félix Guattari: An Aberrant Introduction*. London: Athlone.

Genosko, G. 2003. *The Party Without Bosses*. Winnipeg, MB: Arbeiter Ring.

Georges-Clouzot, H. (dir.) 1953. *La Salaire de la peur* [The wages of fear]. Compagnie Industrielle et Commerciale Cinématographique/Filmsonor/Vera Films/Fono Roma.

Georges-Michel, M. 1914. "Henri Bergson nous parle du cinéma". *Le Journal* (20 February).

Godard, J.-L. (dir.) 1960. *À bout de souffle* [Breathless]. Les Productions Georges de Beauregard/Société Nouvelle de Cinématographie (SNC).

Godard, J.-L. (dir.) 1972. *Tout va bien* [Just great]. Anouchka Films/Empire Films/Vieco Films.

Godard, J.-L. (dir.) 1982a. *Passion*. Film et Vidéo Companie/Films A2/JLG Films/Sara Films/Sonimage/Télévision Suisse-Romande (TSR).

Godard, J.-L. 1982b. *Scénario du film "Passion"*. Unpublished script.

Godard, J.-L. (dir.) 1988–98. *Histoire(s) du cinéma*. Canal+/Arte/Gaumont.

Godard, J.-L. (dir.) 1991. *Allemagne année 90 neuf zéro* [Germany year 90 nine zero]. Antenne-2/Production Brainstorm/Gaumont/Périphéria.

Godard, J.-L. (dir.) 1995. *JLG/JLG – autoportrait de décembre* [JLG/JLG – self-portrait in December]. Gaumont International.

Godard, J.-L. (dir.) 1996. *For Ever Mozart*. Avventura Films/Peripheria/Centre Européen Cinématographique Rhône-Alpes/France 2 Cinéma/Canal+/Centre National de la Cinématographie/Vega Film/Télévision Suisse-Romande/Eurimages/Deutsches Film Insititut (DFI).

Godard, J.-L. 1998a. *Histoire(s) du cinéma*. Paris: Gallimard.

Godard, J.-L. 1998b. *Godard par Godard*: volume 1, 1950–1984; volume 2, 1984–1998. Paris: Éditions Cahiers du cinéma.

Godard, J.-L. (dir.) 1999. *Histoire(s) du cinéma*. Canal/Centre National de la Cinématographie (CNC)/France 3 Cinéma/JLG Films/La Sept Cinéma/Société des Etablissements L. Gaumont/Vega Film Productions.

Godard, J.-L. (dir.) 2001. *Éloge de l'amour* [In praise of love]. Avventura Films/Peripheria/Canal+/arte France Cinéma/Vega Film/Télévision Suisse-Romande/ECM Records/Studio Canal/Deutsches Film Insititut/Studio Images 6.

Godard, J.-L. (dir.) 2004. *Notre musique* [Our music]. Avventura Films/Les Films Alain Sarde/Périphéria/France 3 Cinéma/Canal+/Télévision Suisse-Romande (TSR)/Vega Film.

Godard, J.-L. 2006. *Documents*. Paris: Éditions Centre Pompidou.

Godard, J.-L. (dir.) 2007. *Histoire(s) du cinema*. DVD version, Gaumont.

Godard, J.-L. & Y. Ishaghpour 2005. *Cinema: The Archaeology of Film and the Memory of a Century*, J. Howe (trans.). Oxford: Berg. Originally published in French as *Archéologie du cinéma et mémoire du siècle: dialogue* (Paris: Farrago, 2000).

Godard, J.-L. & A.-M. Miéville (dirs) 1995. *Deux fois cinquante ans de cinéma Français* [Twice fifty years of French cinema]. BFI/La Sept-Arte/Peripheria/Vega Film.

Goupil, R. (dir.) 1982. *Mourir à trente ans* [Half a life]. MK2 Productions.

Grant, P. D. 2007. "Introduction: The History of an Absence". In *Postcards from the Cinema*, S. Daney, 1–10. Oxford: Berg.

Greco, J. & E. Sosa (eds) 1999. *The Blackwell Guide to Epistemology*. Oxford: Blackwell.

Green, D. & J. Lowry (eds) 2006. *Stillness and Time: Photography and the Moving Image*. Brighton: Photoforum.

Griffith, D. W. (dir.) 1915. *Birth of a Nation*. David W. Griffith Corp./Epoch Producing Corporation.

Griffith, D. W. (dir.) 1916. *Intolerance: Love's Struggle Throughout the Areas* [also known as *Intolerance*]. Triangle Film Corporation/Wark Producing.

Grimonprez, J. 2007. *Conférences – débats – rencontres*. Centre Pompidou, Paris. (June 4), www.centrepompidou.fr/Pompidou/Manifs.nsf/0/8F8E01C1A1EF09CCC12572AA0032E572?OpenDocument&sessionM=2.10&L=1 (accessed July 2009).

Grimonprez, J. (dir.) 2009. *Double Take*. Zap-O-Matik/Nikovantastic Film/Volya Films.

Guattari, F. 1972. *Psychanalyse et transversalité*. Paris: Maspero.

Guattari, F. 1977. "Le Cinéma: un art mineur". In his *La Révolution moléculaire*, 203–38. Fontenay-sous-Bois: Recherches.

Guattari, F. 1978. "Revolution and Desire: An Interview with Félix Guattari", with H. Levin & M. Seem (interviewers). *State and Mind* **6**(4) & **7**(1) (Summer/Fall): 53–7.

Guattari, F. 1980. *La Révolution moléculaire*, 2nd condensed and augmented edn. Paris: Union Générale d'Éditions.

Guattari, F. 1984. *Molecular Revolution*, R. Sheed (trans.). Harmondsworth: Penguin.

Guattari, F. 1986. *Les Années d'hiver 1980–86*. Paris: Barrault.

Guattari, F. 1988. "Urgences: la folie est dans le champ". *Le Monde* (9 mars): 22.

Guattari, F. 1989. *Cartographies schizoanalytiques*. Paris: Galilée.

Guattari, F. 1990. "La machine à images". *Cahiers du cinéma* **437** (November): 70–72.

Guattari, F. 1995. *Chaosmosis*, P. Bains & J. Pefanis (trans.). Bloomington, IN: Indiana University Press.

Guattari, F. 1996a. *The Guattari Reader*, G. Genosko (ed.). Oxford: Blackwell.

Guattari, F. 1996b. *Soft Subversions*, S. Lotringer (ed.). New York: Semiotext(e).

Guattari, F. 2000. *The Three Ecologies*, I. Pindar & P. Sutton (trans.). London: Athlone.

Guattari, F. 2006. *The Anti-Oedipus Papers*, K. Gotman (trans.). New York: Semiotext(e).

Guattari, F. 2007. "Tokyo, the Proud", G. Genosko (trans.). *Deleuze Studies* **1**(2): 96–9.

Guattari, F. & A. Negri 1990. *Communists Like Us*, M. Ryan (trans.). New York: Semiotext(e).

Guattari, F. & S. Rolnik 2008. *Molecular Revolution in Brazil*, K. Clapshow & B. Holmes (trans.). New York: Semiotext(e).

Guénoun, S. 2000. "An Interview with Jacques Rancière: Cinematographic Image, Democracy and the 'Splendor of the Insignificant'". *Sites: The Journal of Twentieth-Century Contemporary French Studies/Revue d'études françaises* **4**: 249–58.

Guerin, M. A. 2004. "Le première personne". *Trafic* **37**: 117–25.

Guillermin, J. (dir.) 1976. *King Kong*. Dino De Laurentiis Company/ Paramount Pictures.

Gunning, T. 2007. "Moving Away from the Index: Cinema and the Impression of Reality". *Differences: A Journal of Feminist Cultural Studies* **18**(1): 29–52.

Hallward, P. (ed.) 2004. *Think Again, Alain Badiou and the Future of Philosophy*. London: Continuum.

Haneke, M. (dir.) 2005. *Caché* [Hidden]. Les Films du Losange/ Wega Film/Bavaria Film/BIM Distribuzione/ Uphill Pictures.

Hansen, M. B. 1997. "Introduction". In *Theory of Film: The Redemption of Physical Reality*, vii–xlv. Princeton, NJ: Princeton University Press.

Hansen, M. B. 2000. "The Mass Production of the Senses: Classical Cinema as Vernacular Modernism". In *Reinventing Film Studies*, C. Gledhill & L. Williams (eds), 332–50. London: Arnold.

Hansen, M. 2004. "The Time of Affect, or Bearing Witness to Life". *Critical Inquiry* **30**(3): 584–626.

Haraway, D. 1997. *Modest_Witness@Second_Millennium.FemaleMan©_Meets_OncoMouse™*. London: Routledge.

Harding, S. 1991. *Whose Science? Whose Knowledge?: Thinking from Women's Lives*. Ithaca, NY: Cornell University Press.

Hardt, M. & A. Negri 2000. *Empire*. Cambridge, MA: Harvard University Press.

Hardt, M. & A. Negri 2004. *Multitude: War and Democracy in the Age of Empire*. New York: Penguin.

Harvey, R. & L. R. Schehr 2001. "Editors' Preface". *Yale French Studies* **99**, "Jean-François Lyotard: Time and Judgment": 1–5.

Hawks, H. (dir.) 1940. *His Girl Friday*. Columbia Pictures.

Hawks, H. (dir.) 1953. *Gentlemen Prefer Blondes*. Twentieth Century-Fox Film Corporation.

Heath, S. 1975. "Film and System, Terms of Analysis". *Screen* **16**(2): 91–113.

Heath, S. 1977–8. "Notes on Suture". *Screen* **18**(4): 48–76.

Heath, S. 1978. "Difference". *Screen* **19**(3): 51–112.

Heath, S. 1981. *Questions of Cinema*. Basingstoke: Macmillan.

Heath, S. 1982. *The Sexual Fix*. Basingstoke: Macmillan.

Heath, S. 1985. "*Jaws*, Ideology, and Film Theory". See Nichols (1985), 509–14.

Heath, S. 1986. "Joan Riviere and the Masquerade". In *Formations of Fantasy*, V. Burgin, J. Donald & C. Kaplan (eds), 45–61. London: Methuen.

Heath, S. 1987. "Male Feminism". In *Men in Feminism*, A. Jardine & P. Smith (eds), 1–32. London: Methuen.

Heath, S. 1999. "Cinema and Psychoanalysis: Parallel Histories". In *Endless Night: Cinema and Psychoanalysis, Parallel Histories*, J. Bergstrom (ed.), 25–56. Berkeley, CA: University of California Press.

Heer, R. de & P. Djigirr (dirs) 2006. *Ten Canoes*. Adelaide Film Festival/Fandago Australia/Fandango/Vertigo Productions/Special Broadcasting Service (SBS).

Hegel, G. W. F. 1975. *Hegel's Aesthetics: Lectures on Fine Art*. Oxford: Oxford University Press.

Heidegger, M. 1971. *Poetry, Language, Thought*, A. Hofstadter (trans.). New York: Harper & Row.

Heidegger, M. 1996. *Being and Time*, J. Stambaugh (trans.). Albany, NY: SUNY Press.

Heinrich, B. & T. Bugnyar 2007. "Just How Smart are Ravens?". *Scientific American* (April): 64–71.

Henderson, B. 1976. "Two Types of Film Theory". See Nichols (1976), 388–400.

Herman, M. (dir.) 1996. *Brassed Off*. Channel Four Films/Miramax Films/Prominent Features.

Herzog, A. 2000. "Images of Thought and Acts of Creation: Deleuze, Bergson, and the Question of Cinema". *Invisible Culture: An Electronic Journal for Visual Studies*, **3**, "Time and the Work", R. Celeste (ed.), www.rochester.edu/in_visible_culture/issue3/herzog.htm (accessed July 2009).

Hitchcock, A. (dir.) 1938. *The Lady Vanishes*. Gainsborough Pictures.

Hitchcock, A. (dir.) 1941. *Suspicion*. RKO Radio Pictures.

Hitchcock, A. (dir.) 1945. *Spellbound*. Vanguard Films for Selznick International Pictures.

Hitchcock, A. (dir.) 1946. *Notorious*. Vanguard Films (uncredited) (for) RKO Radio Pictures.

Hitchcock, A. (dir.) 1951. *Strangers on a Train*. Warner Bros. Pictures.

Hitchcock, A. (dir.) 1954. *Rear Window*. Paramount Pictures/Patron Inc.

Hitchcock, A. (dir.) 1958. *Vertigo*. Alfred J. Hitchcock Productions/Paramount Pictures.

Hitchcock, A. (dir.) 1959. *North by Northwest*. Metro-Goldwyn-Mayer (MGM) (as Loew's Incorporated).

Hitchcock, A. (dir.) 1960. *Psycho*. Universal Pictures (presents)/Alfred J. Hitchcock Productions.

Hitchcock, A. (dir.) 1963. *The Birds*. Universal Pictures (presents)/Alfred J. Hitchcock Productions.

Hitchcock, A. (dir.) 1964. *Marnie*. Universal Pictures.

Hollier, D. & J. Mehlman (eds) 1999. *Literary Debate: Texts and Contexts*. Postwar French Thought, II. New York: New Press.

Howard, L. (dir.) 1941. *"Pimpernel" Smith*. British National Films.

Howard, L. (dir.) 1942. *The First of the Few*. British Aviation Pictures.

Husserl, E. 1970. *The Crisis of European Sciences and Transcendental Phenomenology*, D. Carr (trans.). Evanston, IL: Northwestern University Press.

Husserl, E. [1893–1917] 1991. *On the Phenomenology of the Consciousness of Internal Time*, J. B. Brough (trans.). Dordrecht: Kluwer.

Husserl, E. 1997. *Thing and Space: Lectures of 1907. Collected Works VII*, R. Rojcewicz (trans.). Dordrecht: Kluwer.

Huston, J. (dir.) 1948. *The Treasure of the Sierra Madre*. Warner Bros. Pictures.

Huyssen, A. 1986. *After the Great Divide: Modernism, Mass Culture, Postmodernism*. Bloomington, IN: Indiana University Press.

Isou, I. (dir.) 1951. *Traité de bave et d'éternité* [Tract of drool and eternity]. Films M.-G. Guillemin.

Jacobson, R. 1971. *Studies in Verbal Art: Texts in Czech and Slovak Languages*. Ann Arbor, MI: University of Michigan Press.

James, D. E. 1989. *Allegories of Cinema: American Film in the Sixties*. Princeton, NJ: Princeton University Press.

James, I. 2007. *Paul Virilio*. London: Routledge.

Jameson, F. 1981. *The Political Unconscious: Narrative as a Socially Symbolic Act*. London: Methuen.

Jameson, F. 1984. "Postmodernism, or the Cultural Logic of Late Capitalism". *New Left Review* **146**: 53–92.

Jameson, F. 1990. *Signatures of the Visible*. London & New York: Routledge.

Jameson, F. 1991. *Postmodernism, or the Cultural Logic of Late Capitalism*. Durham, NC: Duke University Press.

Jameson, F. 1992. *The Geopolitical Aesthetic: Cinema and Space in the World System*. London: BFI.

Jarmusch, J. (dir.) 1999. *Ghost Dog: The Way of the Samurai*. Pandora Filmproduktion/Arbeitsgemeinschaft der öffentlich-rechtlichen Rundfunkanstalten der Bundesrepublik Deutschland (ARD)/Degeto Film/Plywood Productions/Bac Films/Canal+/JVC Entertainment.

Jarmusch, J. (dir.) 2003. *Coffee and Cigarettes*. Asmik Ace Entertainment/BIM/Smokescreen Inc.

Jayamanne, L. 2001. "Forty Acres and A Mule Filmworks: Do the Right Thing – A Spike Lee Joint: Blocking and Unblocking the Block". In *Micropolitics of Media Culture: Reading the Rhizomes of Deleuze and Guattari*, P. Pisters (ed.), 235–49. Amsterdam: Amsterdam University Press.

Just, J. (dir.) 2004. *No Man Is An Island II*, www.jesperjust.com/nomanisanisland2.html (accessed June 2009) (Copenhagen: Galleri Christna Wilson/New York: Perry Rubenstein Gallery, 2004).

Kant, I. 1929. *Critique of Pure Reason*, N. Kemp Smith (trans.). London: Macmillan.

Karmitz, M. (dir.) 1972. *Coup pour coup* [Blow by blow]. Cinema Services.

Kawin, B. 1982. "Time and Stasis in 'La Jetée'". *Film Quarterly* **36**(1) (Autumn): 15–20.

Kazan, E. (dir.) 1954. *On the Waterfront*. Horizon Pictures/Columbia Pictures Corporation.

Kearney, R. & M. Rainwater (eds) 1996. *The Continental Philosophy Reader*. London: Routledge.

Kellner, D. 1998. "Virilio on Vision Machines". *Film-Philosophy: Electronic Salon*, www.film-philosophy.com/vol2-1998/n30kellner.html (accessed September 2009).

Kellner, D. 2006. "Jean Baudrillard After Modernity: Provocations on a Provocateur and Challenger". *The International Journal of Baudrillard Studies* **3**(1), 1–41, www.ubishops.ca/baudrillardstudies/vol3_1/kellner.htm (accessed Jul 2009).

Kennedy, B. 2000. *Deleuze and Cinema: The Aesthetics of Sensation*. Edinburgh: Edinburgh University Press.

Kessler, F. 2007. "The Cinema of Attractions as *Dispositif*". In *The Cinema of Attractions Reloaded*, W. Strauven (ed.), 57–69. Amsterdam: Amsterdam University Press.

Kieslowski, K. (dir.) 1993. *Trois couleurs: Bleu* [Three colours: blue]. Canal+/Conseil de l'Europe (financial support)/CAB Productions/CED Productions/Eurimages/France 3 Cinéma/MK2 Productions/Zespol Filmowy "Tor".

Kieslowski, K. (dir.) 1994a. *Trois couleurs: Blanc* [Three colours: white]. MK2 Productions/France 3 Cinéma (Paris)/CAB Productions/Zespol Filmowy "Tor" (as "TOR" Production – Varsovie)/Canal+ (participation)/ Eurimages (as Fonds EURIMAGES)/Conseil de l'Europe.

Kieslowski, K. (dir.) 1994b. *Trois couleurs: Rouge* [Three colours: red]. CAB Productions/Canal+/France 3 Cinéma/ MK2 Productions/Télévision Suisse-Romande (TSR)/Zespol Filmowy "Tor".

King, G. 2007. *New Hollywood Cinema: An Introduction*. London: I. B. Tauris.

Kluge, A. & P. Schamoni (dirs) 1961. *Brutalität in Stein* [Brutality in stone]. Alexander Kluge Filmproduktion/ Dieter Lemmel Kurzfilmproduktion/Peter Schamoni Film.

Koch, G. 1993. "Cosmos in Film: On the Concept of Space in Walter Benjamin's 'Work of Art' Essay". In *Walter Benjamin's Philosophy: Destruction and Experience*, A. Benjamin & P. Osborne (eds), 206–15. London & New York: Routledge.

Koch, G. 2000. *Siegfried Kracauer: An Introduction*, J. Gaines (trans.). Princeton, NJ: Princeton University Press.

Kofman, S. 1994. *Rue Ordener, Rue Labat*. Paris: Galilée.

Kofman, S. 1995. *L'Imposture de la beauté*. Paris: Galilée.

Kofman, S. 2007. "'My Life' and Psychoanalysis". In *Sarah Kofman: Selected Writings*, T. Albrecht (ed.) with G. Albert & E. Rottenberg, 250. Stanford, CA: Stanford University Press.

Koster, H. (dir.) 1953. *The Robe*. Twentieth Century-Fox Film Corporation.

Kracauer, S. 1947. *From Caligari to Hitler: A Psychological History of German Film*. Princeton, NJ: Princeton University Press.

Kracauer, S. 1960. *Theory of Film: The Redemption of Physical Reality*. Princeton, NJ: Princeton University Press.

Kracauer, S. 1969. *History: The Last Things Before the Last*. New York: Oxford University Press.

Kracauer, S. 1995. *The Mass Ornament: Weimar Essays*, T. Y. Levin (trans.). Cambridge, MA: Harvard University Press.

Kracauer, S. 1998. *The Salaried Masses: Duty and Distraction in Weimar Germany*, Q. Hoare (trans.). London: Verso. Originally published in German as *Die Angestellten. Aus dem neuesten Deutschland* (Frankfurt: Societäts, 1930).

Kracauer, S. 2004. *Kleine Schriften zum Film*, 3 vols, I. Mülder-Bach (ed). Frankfurt: Suhrkamp.

Kramer, S. (dir.) 1961. *Judgment at Nuremberg*. Roxlom Films Inc.

Krauss, R. E. 1994. *The Optical Unconscious*. Cambridge MA: MIT Press.

Kristeva, J. 1980. *Desire in Language: A Semiotic Approach to Literature and Art*, T. Gora, A. Jardine & L. S. Roudiez (trans.). Oxford: Blackwell. Originally published in French as *Séméiôtiké: recherches pour une sémanalyse* (Paris: Éditions du Seuil, 1969).

Kristeva, J. 1982. *Powers of Horror*, L. Roudiez (trans.). New York: Columbia University Press. Originally published in French as *Pouvoirs de l'horreur: essai sur l'abjection* (Paris: Éditions du Seuil, 1980).

Kristeva, J. 1984. *Revolution in Poetic Language*, M. Waller (trans.). New York: Columbia University Press. Originally published in French as *La Révolution du langage poétique: l'avant-garde à la fin du xixe siècle*, Lautréamont et Mallarmé (Paris: Éditions du Seuil, 1974).

Kristeva, J. 1986. *The Kristeva Reader*, R. Moi (ed.), S. Hand (trans.). New York: Columbia University Press.

Kristeva, J. 1987. *In the Beginning was Love*, A. Goldhammer (trans.). New York: Columbia University Press. Originally published in French as *Au commencement était l'amour: psychanalyse et foi* (Paris: Hachette, 1985).

Kristeva, J. 1996. *Time and Sense: Proust and the Experience of Literature*, R. Guberman (trans.). New York: Columbia University Press.

Kristeva, J. 2000. *The Sense and Nonsense of Revolt*, J. Herman (trans.). New York: Columbia University Press. Originally published in French as *Sens et non-sens de la révolte* (Paris: Fayard, 1996).

Kristeva, J. 2002a. *Intimate Revolt*, J. Herman (trans.). New York: Columbia University Press. Originally published in French as *La Révolte intime: discours direct* (Paris: Fayard, 1997).

Kristeva, J. 2002b. *Revolt, She Said*, Brian O'Keeffe (trans.). New York: Semiotext(e).

Kubrick, S. (dir.) 1964. *Dr Strangelove or: How I Learned to Stop Worrying and Love the Bomb*. Hawk Films.

Kubrick, S. (dir.) 1971. *A Clockwork Orange*. Warner Bros./Hawk Films.

Kubrick, S. (dir.) 1975. *Barry Lyndon*. Peregrine/Hawk Films.

Kubrick, S. (dir.) 1999. *Eyes Wide Shut*. Hobby Films/Pole Star/Stanley Kubrick Productions/Warner Bros. Pictures.

Lacan, J. 1979. *The Four Fundamental Concepts of Psycho-Analysis*. Harmondsworth: Penguin.

Lacan, J. 1992. *The Ethics of Psychoanalysis*, D. Porter (trans.). London & New York: Routledge.

Lacan, J. 1998. *Encore*, B. Fink (trans.). New York: Norton.

Lacan, J. 2006. "The Mirror Stage as Formative of the *I* Function as Revealed in Psychoanalytic Experience". In *Écrits: The First Complete Edition in English*, B. Fink (trans.), 75–81. New York: Norton.

Lang, F. (dir.) 1931. *M*. Nero-Film AG.

Langdale, A. 2002. "S(t)imulation of Mind: The Film Theory of Hugo Münsterberg". In *Hugo Münsterberg On Film: The Photoplay – A Psychological Study and Other Writings*, A. Langdale (ed.), 1–41. London & New York: Routledge.

Laplanche, J. & J.-B. Pontalis [1967] 1973. *The Language of Psychoanalysis*, D. Nicholson-Smith (trans.). London: Karnac.

Lapsley, R. & M. Westlake 1988. *Film Theory: An Introduction*. Manchester: Manchester University Press.

Laurence, S. & C. Macdonald (eds) 1998. *Contemporary Readings in the Foundations of Metaphysics*. Oxford: Blackwell.

Lazzarato, M. 2007. "Strategies of the Political Entrepreneur". *SubStance* **112**(36.1): 87–97.

Lean, D. (dir.) 1984. *A Passage to India*. EMI Films/Home Box Office (HBO)/Thorn EMI Screen Entertainment.

Lebeau, V. 2001. *Psychoanalysis and Cinema: The Play of Shadows*. London: Wallflower.

Lee, S. (dir.) 1989. *Do the Right Thing*. 40 Acres and a Mule Filmworks.

Leenhardt, R. 1935. "Le Rhythme cinématographique". *Esprit* **3** (September): 631–2.

Leighton, T. & P. Büchler (eds) 2003. *Saving the Image: Art After Film*. Glasgow: Centre for Contemporary Arts/ Manchester: Manchester Metropolitan University.

Lesage, J. 1985. "*S/Z* and *The Rules of the Game*". See Nichols (1985), 476–500.

Levin, T. Y. 1995. "Introduction". In *The Mass Ornament: Weimar Essays*, S. Kracauer, 1–30. Cambridge, MA: Harvard University Press.

Levinas, E. 1981. *Otherwise than Being or Beyond Essence*, A. Lingis (trans.). Dordrecht: Kluwer. Originally published in French as *Autrement quêtre, ou au-delà de l'essence* (The Hague: Martinus Nijhoff, 1974).

Levinas, E. 1987. *Time and the Other*, R. Cohen (trans.). Pittsburgh, PA: Duquesne University Press. Originally published in French as *Le Temps et l'autre* (Paris: Arthaud, 1948).

Levinas, E. 1989. "Reality and its Shadow". In *The Levinas Reader*, S. Hand (ed.), 129–43. Oxford: Blackwell. Originally published in French as "La Réalité et son ombre", in *Les Temps Modernes* **38** (1948), 771–89.

Levinas, E. 1998. *Entre Nous: Thinking-of the-other*, M. B. Smith & B. Harshaw (trans.). London: Continuum. Orginally published in French as *Entre Nous: Essais sur le penser-à-l'autre* (Paris: Grasset, 1991).

Levinas, E. 2000. *God, Death, and Time*, B. Bergo (trans.). Stanford, CA: Stanford University Press. Originally published in French as *Dieu, la mort et le temps* (Paris: Grasset, 1993).

Levinas, E. 2003. On Escape, B. Bergo (trans.). Stanford, CA: Stanford University Press. Originally published as "De l'évasion", *Recherches Philosophiques* **5** (1935/6): 373–92.

Levinas, E. 2007. *Totality and Infinity: An Essay on Exteriority*, A. Lingis (trans.). Pittsburgh, PA: Duquesne University Press. Originally published in French as *Totalité et Infini: essai sur l'extériorité* (The Hague: Martinus Nijhoff, 1961).

Lévi-Strauss, C. 1963. *Structural Anthropology*, C. Jacobson & B. Grundfest Schoepf (trans.). New York: Basic Books.

Lévi-Strauss, C. 1967. *Tristes Tropiques*, J. Russell (trans.). New York: Atheneum.

Lévy, B.-H. 1987. *Éloge des intellectuels*. Paris: Grasset.

Levy, D. (dir.) 1979. *L'École de Mai: 1968–1978* [*May school: 1968–78*]. Collectif Réalisation Audiovisuel Cinéma.

Lewin, A. (dir.) 1945. *Portrait of Dorian Gray*. Metro-Goldwyn-Mayer (MGM)/Loew's.

Lewis, B. 1980. *Jean Mitry and the Aesthetics of Cinema*. Ann Arbor, MI: UMI Research Press.

Lewis, M. & L. Mulvey (dirs) 1994. *Disgraced Monuments*. Mark Lewis & Laura Mulvey/Broadcast Channel 4 TV, 6 June.

Lindsay, V. 1915. *The Art of the Moving Picture*. New York: Macmillan.

Lipovetsky, G. 1983. *L'Ére du vide: Essais sur l'individualisme contemporain*. Paris: Gallimard.

Loach, K. (dir.) 1971. *Family Life*. EMI Films.

Lomax, Y. 2006. "Thinking Stillness". In *Stillness and Time: Photography and the Moving Image*, D. Green & J. Lowry (eds), 55–63. Brighton: Photoforum.

Lotringer, S. 2002. "Introduction: Time Bomb". In *Crepuscular Dawn*, P. Virilio & S. Lotringer (eds), M. Taormina (trans.), 7–17. New York: Semiotext(e).

Lotringer, S. & P. Virilio 2005. *The Accident of Art*. New York: Semiotext(e).

Lowry, E. 1985. *The Filmology Movement and Film Study in France*. Ann Arbor, MI: UMI Research Press.

Lubitsch, E. (dir.) 1943. *To Be or Not To Be*. Romaine Film Corporation.

Lucas, G. (dir.) 1973. *American Graffiti*. Lucasfilm/The Coppola Company/Universal Pictures.

Lucas, G. (dir.) 1977. *Star Wars*. Lucasfilm/Twentieth Century-Fox Film Corporation.

Lynch, D. (dir.) 1977. *Eraserhead*. American Film Institute.

Lynch, D. (dir.) 1977. *Lost Highway*. October Films/CiBy 2000/Asymmetrical Productions/Lost Highway Productions LLC.

Lynch, D. (dir.) 1986. *Blue Velvet*. De Laurentiis Entertainment Group.

Lynch, D. (dir.) 1990. *Wild at Heart*. PolyGram Filmed Entertainment/Progaganda Films.

Lyotard, J.-F. 1973a. "L'Acinéma". *Revue d'Esthétique* **26**(2–4): 357–369.

Lyotard, J.-F. 1973b. *Des dispositifs pulsionels*. Paris: Union générale d'éditions.

Lyotard, J.-F. 1977. "The Unconscious as Mise-en-scène", J. Maier (trans.). In *Performance in Postmodern Culture*, M. Benamou & C. Caramello (eds), 87–98. Madison, WI: Coda Press.

Lyotard, J.-F. 1988. *L'Inhumain*. Paris: Galilée.

Lyotard, J.-F. 1989a. "Acinema". In *The Lyotard Reader*, A. Benjamin (ed.), 169–80. Oxford: Blackwell. Also published in *Wide Angle* **2**(3) (1989): 52–9.

Lyotard, J.-F. 1989b. "The Dream-Work Does Not Think". In *The Lyotard Reader*, A. Benjamin (ed.), 19–55. Oxford: Blackwell.

Lyotard, J.-F. 2004. *Libidinal Economy*, I. H. Grant (trans.). London: Continuum.

MacBean, J. R. 1976. "*Vent d'Est* – Godard and Rocha". See Nichols (1976), 91–106.

MacCormack, P. 2008. *Cinesexuality*. Aldershot: Ashgate.

Malick, T. (dir.) 1973. *Badlands*. Badlands Co./Warner.

Malick, T. (dir.) 1978. *Days of Heaven*. Paramount Pictures.

Malle, L. (dir.) 1974. *Lacombe Lucien*. Hallelujah Films/Nouvelles Éditions de Films/Universal Pictures France (UPF)/Vides Cinematografica.

Mamoulian, R. (dir.) 1933. *Queen Christina*. Metro-Goldwyn-Mayer (MGM).

Mankiewicz, J. (dir.) 1953. *Julius Caesar*. Metro-Goldwyn-Mayer (MGM).

Mann, M. (dir.) 1986. *Manhunter*. De Laurentiis Entertainment Group (DEG)/Red Dragon Productions S.A.

Mannoni, O. 1985. *Clefs pour l'imaginaire ou L'Autre Scène*. Paris: Éditions du Seuil.

Marciniak, K., A. Imre & Á. O'Healy 2007. *Transnational Feminism in Film and Media*. Basingstoke: Palgrave Macmillian.

Marcuse, H. 1964. *One-dimensional Man*. London: Routledge & Kegan Paul.

Margulis, L. & D. Sagan 1997. "The Universe in Heat". In their *What is Sex?* New York: Simon & Schuster.

Marker, C. (dir.) 1962. *La Jetée* [The jetty]. Argos Films.

Marker, C. (dir.) 1966. *Si j'avais quatre dromadaires* [If I had four dromedaries]. APEC/NWDR.

Marker, C. & Y. Bellon (dirs) 2001. *Le souvenir d'un avenir* [Remembrance of things to come]. Les Films de l'Equinoxe.

Marks, L. U. 2000. *The Skin of the Film: Intercultural Cinema, Embodiment, and the Senses*. Durham, NC: Duke University Press.

Martin-Jones, D. 2006. *Deleuze, Cinema and National Identity: Narrative Time in National Contexts*. Edinburgh: Edinburgh University Press.

McG (dir.) 2009. *Terminator Salvation*. The Halcyon Company/Wonderland Sound and Vision.

McGowan, T. 2007. "Introduction: Enjoying the Cinema". *International Journal of Žižek Studies* **1**(3), www.zizek-studies.org/index.php/ijzs/article/view/57/119 (accessed June 2009).

McMullen, K. (dir.) 1983. *Ghost Dance*. Looseyard for Channel 4/ZDF.

Medem, J. (dir.) 1998. *Los Amantes del Círculo Polar* [Lovers of the Arctic Circle]. Canal+/Sociedad/Sociedad General de Televisión S.A. (Sogetel).

Merleau-Ponty, M. 1962. *Phenomenology of Perception*, C. Smith (trans.). London: Routledge & Kegan Paul. Originally published in French as *Phénoménologie de la perception* (Paris: Gallimard, 1945).

Merleau-Ponty, M. [1948] 1963. "Le Cinéma et la nouvelle psychologie", *Sens et non-sens*, 61–75. Paris: Nagel.

Merleau-Ponty, M. 1964. "The Film and the New Psychology". In *Sense and Non-Sense*, H. Dreyfus & P. A. Dreyfus (trans.), 48–59. Evanston, IL: Northwestern University Press.

Merleau-Ponty, M. 1966. *Sens et Non-Sens*. Paris: Nagel.

Merleau-Ponty, M. 1968. *The Visible and the Invisible*, A. Lingis (trans.). Evanston, IL: Northwestern University Press. Originally published in French as *Le Visible et l'invisible, suivi de notes de travail*, C. Lefort (ed.) (Paris: Gallimard, 1964).

Merleau-Ponty, M. 1989. *Phenomenology of Perception*. London & New York: Routledge. Originally published in French as *Phénoménologie de la perception* (Paris: Gallimard, 1945).

Merleau-Ponty, M. 2003. *Nature: Course Notes from the Collège de France*, R. Vallier (trans.). Evanston, IL: Northwestern University Press.

Merrin, W. 2005. *Baudrillard and the Media*. Cambridge: Polity.

Metz, C. 1968. *Essais sur le signification au cinéma, tome 1*. Paris: Klincksieck.

Metz, C. 1971. *Language et cinéma*. Paris: Librairie Larousse.

Metz, C. 1972. *Essais sur le signification au cinéma, tome 2*. Paris: Klincksieck.

Metz, C. 1974a. *Film Language: A Semiotics of the Cinema*, M. Taylor (trans.). New York: Oxford University Press.

Metz, C. 1974b. *Language and Cinema*. The Hague: Mouton.

Metz, C. 1975. "Le significant imaginaire". *Communications* **23**: 3–55.

Metz, C. 1977a. *Essais Sémiotiques*. Paris: Klincksieck.

Metz, C. 1977b. *Le Signifiant imaginaire: Psychanalyse et cinéma*. Paris: Union générale d'éditions.

Metz, C. 1979. "The Cinematic Apparatus as a Social Institution: An Interview with Christian Metz". *Discourse: Journal for Theoretical Studies in Media and Culture* **3**: 7–38.

Metz, C. 1982. *Psychoanalysis and Cinema: The Imaginary Signifier*, C. Britton & A. Williams (trans.). London: Macmillan.

Metz, C. 1985. "Photography and Fetish". *October* **34**: 81–90.

Metz, C. 1991. *L'Énonciation impersonnelle, ou le site du film*. Paris: Klincksieck.

Meyer, N. (dir.) 1983. *The Day After*. ABC Circle Films.

Michel, G.-M. 1914. "Henri Bergson nous parle du cinéma". *Le Journal* (20 February).

Miller, J.-A. 1977–78. "Suture (Elements of the Logic of the Signifier)". *Screen* **18**(4): 24–34.

Mitry, J. [1963] 2000. *The Aesthetics and Psychology of the Cinema*, C. King (trans.). Bloomington, IN: Indiana University Press.

Mitsuo, S. (dir.) 1985. *YAMA: An Eye for an Eye*. YAMA Production and Exhibition Committee.

Mootoo, S. (dir.) 1994. *Her Sweetness Lingers*. Vancouver/Video in Studios/Video Out Distribution.

Moretti, N. (dir.) 1989. *Palombella Rossa* [Reb lob]. Banfilm/La Sept Cinéma/Palm Rye Productions/Radiotelevisione Italiana/Sacher Film/So. Fin. A.

Morin, E. [1956/1978] 2005. *The Cinema, or, the Imaginary Man*, L. Mortimer (trans.). Minneapolis, MN: University of Minnesota Press.

Morrison, J. 1999. "On Barthes On CinemaScope". *Jouvert: A Journal of Postcolonial Studies* **3**(3), http://english.chass.ncsu.edu/jouvert/v3i3/barth.htm (accessed July 2009).

Mostow, J. (dir.) 2003. *Terminator 3: Rise of the Machines*. C-2 Pictures/Intermedia Films/IMF Internationale Medien und Film GmbH & Co. 3. Produktions KG/Mostow/Lieberman Productions.

Mukarovsky, J. 1977. *Structure, Sign, and Function: Selected Essays*. J. Burbank & P. Steiner (eds & trans.). New Haven, CT: Yale University Press.

Mulhall, S. 2005. "In Space, No-one Can Hear You Scream: Acknowledging the Human Voice in the Alien Universe". In *Film as Philosophy: Essays on Cinema After Wittgenstein and Cavell*, R. Read & J. Goodenough (eds), 57–71. Basingstoke: Palgrave Macmillan.

Mulligan, R. (dir.) 1962. *To Kill A Mockingbird*. Brentwood Productions.

Mulvey, L. 1975. "Visual Pleasure and Narrative Cinema". *Screen* **16**(3): 6–18.

Mulvey, L. 1989. *Visual and Other Pleasures*. Basingstoke: Macmillan.

Mulvey, L. 1992. *Citizen Kane*. London: BFI.

Mulvey, L. 1994. "A Short History of the BFI Education Department". Unpublished pamphlet. London: British Film Institute.

Mulvey, L. 1996. *Fetishism and Curiosity*. London: BFI.

Mulvey, L. 2002. "Afterword". In *The New Iranian Cinema: Politics, Representation and Identity*, R. Tapper (ed.), 254–61. London: I. B. Tauris.

Mulvey, L. 2006. *Death 24x a Second: Stillness and the Moving Image*. London: Reaktion.

Mulvey, L. & J. Halliday (eds) 1972. *Douglas Sirk*. Prescot: Edinburgh Film Festival 72 in association with the National Film Theatre and John Player & Sons.

Mulvey, L. & P. Wollen (dirs) 1974. *Penthesilea: Queen of the Amazons*. Laura Mulvey–Peter Wollen.

Mulvey, L. & P. Wollen (dirs) 1977. *Riddles of the Sphinx*. British Film Institute Production Board.

Mulvey, L. & P. Wollen (dirs) 1980. *The ELEVENTH HOUR: AMY!* Modelmark.

Mulvey, L. & P. Wollen (dirs) 1982. *Crystal Gazing*. BFI Production.

Mulvey, L. & P. Wollen (dirs) 1982. *Frida Kahlo and Tina Modotti*. Modelmark.

Mulvey, L. & P. Wollen (dirs) 1982. *The Bad Sister*. Moving Picture/Modelmark.

Munk, A. (dir.) 1963. *Pasażerka* [The passenger]. Zespol Filmowy "Kamera".

Münsterberg, H. 1916. *The Photoplay: A Psychological Study*. New York: D. Appleton. Republished as *The Film: A Psychological Study* (New York: Dover, 1970).

Münsterberg, H. [1917] 2002. *Hugo Münsterberg On Film: The Photoplay – A Psychological Study and Other Writings*, A. Langdale (ed.). London & New York: Routledge.

Murnau, F. W. (dir.) 1922. *Nosferatu, eine Symphonie des Grauens*. Jofa-Atelier Berlin-Johannisthal/Prana-Film GmbH.

382

Naficy, H. 2001. *An Accented Cinema: Exilic and Diasporic Filmmaking*. Princeton, NJ: Princeton University Press.

Nancy, J.-L. 1991. *The Inoperative Community*, P. Connor, L. Garbus, M. Holland & S. Sawhney (trans.). Minneapolis, MN: University of Minnesota Press.

Nancy, J.-L. 1999. "Foreword: Run, Sarah!". In *Enigmas: Essays on Sarah Kofman*, P. Deutscher & K. Oliver (eds), viii–xvi. Ithaca, NY: Cornell University Press.

Nancy, J.-L. 2000. *Being Singular Plural*, R. D. Richardson & A. E. O'Byrne (trans.). Stanford, CA: Stanford University Press.

Nancy, J.-L. 2001. *L'Évidence du film, The Evidence of Film: Abbas Kiarostami*, C. Irizarry & V. A. Conley (trans.). Brussels: Yves Gevaert.

Nancy, J.-L. 2002. *Hegel: The Restlessness of the Negative*, J. Smith & S. Miller (trans.). Minneapolis, MN: University of Minnesota Press.

Nancy, J.-L. 2003. *A Finite Thinking*, S. Sparks (ed.). Stanford, CA: Stanford University Press.

Nancy, J.-L. 2005. *The Ground of the Image*, J. Fort (trans.). New York: Fordham University Press.

Nancy, J.-L. 2008. *Dis-enclosure: The Deconstruction of Christianity*, B. Bergo, G. Malenfant & M. B. Smith (trans.). New York : Fordham University Press.

Niblo, B. (dir.) 1925. *Ben Hur: A Tale of the Christ*. Metro-Goldwyn-Mayer (MGM).

Nichols, B. (ed.) 1976. *Movies and Methods*, vol. 1. Berkeley, CA: University of California Press.

Nichols, B. (ed.) 1985. *Movies and Methods*, vol. II. Berkeley, CA: University of California Press.

Nietzsche, F. 1967. *The Birth of Tragedy*, W. Kaufmann (trans.). New York: Vintage.

Noé, G. (dir.) 2002. *Irréversible*. 120 Films/Eskwad/Grandpierre/Les Cinémas de la Zone/Nord-Ouest Productions/Rossignon/Studio Canal.

Noys, B. 2004. "Gestural Cinema? Notes On Two Texts by Giorgio Agamben". *Film Philosophy* 8(22) (July), www.film-philosophy.com/vol8-2004/n22noys.html (accessed August 2009).

Oliver, K. 1993. "Introduction: Julia Kristeva's Outlaw Ethics". In her *Ethics, Politics and Difference in Julia Kristeva's Writing*, 1–22. London & New York: Routledge.

Oliver, K. 1999. "Sarah Kofman's Queasy Stomach and the Riddle of Paternal Law". In *Enigmas: Essays on Sarah Kofman*, P. Deutscher & K. Oliver (eds), 174–88. Ithaca, NY: Cornell University Press.

Olkowski, D. 2006. "Maurice Merleau-Ponty: Intertwining and Objectifcation". *Phanex, the Journal for Existential and Phenomenological Theory and Culture* 1(1) (November): 113–39.

Olkowski, D. 2007. *The Universal (in the Realm of the Sensible): Beyond Continental Philosophy*. Edinburgh: Edinburgh University Press.

Ophüls, M. (dir.) 1948. *Letter from an Unknown Woman*. Rampart Productions.

Ophüls, M. (dir.) 1950. *La Ronde* [Roundabout]. Films Sacha Gordine.

Oudart, J.-P. 1977–8. "Cinema and Suture". *Screen* **18**(4): 35–47. [First published in French in *Cahiers du cinéma* **211/212** (April and May) (1969).]

Pakula, A. (dir.) 1974. *The Parallax View*. Doubleday Productions/Gus/Harbor Productions/Paramount Pictures.

Pakula, A. J. (dir.) 1976. *All the President's Men*. Warner Bros. Pictures/Wildwood.

Panofsky, E. [1934–62] 1997. *Three Essays on Style*, I. Lavin (ed.). Cambridge, MA: MIT Press.

Pasolini, P. P. 1988. *Heretical Empiricism*, L. K. Barnett (ed.), B. Lawton & L. K. Barnett (trans.). Bloomington, IN: Indiana University Press.

Pawley, M. 1999. "Introduction". In V. Flusser, *The Shape of Things: A Philosophy of Design*, A. Mathews (trans.), 7–16. London: Reaktion.

Penley, C. 2000. "Preface". In R. Bellour, *The Analysis of Film*, C. Penley (ed.), ix–xviii. Bloomington, IN: Indiana University Press.

Perez, G. 1998. *The Material Ghost: Films and their Medium*. Baltimore, MD: Johns Hopkins University Press.

Perkins, V. F. 1972. *Film as Film: Understanding and Judging Movies*. Harmondsworth: Penguin.

Perkins, V. F. 1976. "A Critical History of Early Film Theory". See Nichols (1976), 401–21.

Perloff, M. 1999. "Cultural Liminality/Aesthetic Closure? The 'Interstitial Perspective' of Homi Bhabha". *Literary Imagination: The Review of the Association of Literary Scholars and Critics* 1(1) (Spring): 109–25, www.epc.buffalo.edu/authors/perloff/bhabha.html (accessed April 2008).

Petric, V. 1983. "Barthes Versus Cinema". *Sight and Sound* **52**(3) (Summer): 205–7.

Phillips, J. (ed.) 2008. *Cinematic Thinking: Philosophical Approaches to the New Cinema*. Stanford, CA: Stanford University Press.

Pierre, S. 2001. "Rio Daney Bravo". *Trafic* **37**: 13–26.

Pisters, P. (ed.) 2002. *Micropolitics of Media Culture: Reading the Rhizomes of Deleuze and Guattari*. Amsterdam: Amsterdam University Press.

Pisters, P. 2003. *The Matrix of Visual Culture: Working with Deleuze in Film Theory*. Stanford, CA: Stanford University Press.

Pisters, P. forthcoming. "Filming the Times of Tangier: Nostalgia, Postcolonial Agency and Preposterous History".

In *Cinema at the Periphery: Industries, Narratives, Iconography*, D. Iordonova, D. Martin-Jones & B. Vidal (eds). Detroit, MI: Wayne State University Press.

Plate, S. B. (ed.) 2003. *Representing Religion in World Cinema: Filmmaking, Mythmaking, Culturemaking*. Basingstoke: Palgrave Macmillan.

Plato 1945. *The Republic of Plato*, Gilbert Highet (trans.). Oxford: Oxford University Press.

Polan, D. 1985. "The Critique of Cinematic Reason: Stephen Heath and the Theoretical Study of Film". *Boundary 2* **13**(2/3): 157–71.

Polan, D. 1986. "Brief Encounters: Mass Culture and the Evacuation of Sense". In *Studies in Entertainment: Critical Approaches to Mass Culture*, T. Modleski (ed.), 157–71. Bloomington, IN: Indiana University Press.

Polanski, R. (dir.) 1974. *Chinatown*. Long Road/Paramount Pictures/Penthouse.

Polkinghome, J. 2002. *Quantum Theory: A Very Short Introduction*. Oxford: Oxford University Press.

Pollack, S. (dir.) 1975. *Three Days of the Condor*. Dino De Laurentiis Company/Paramount Pictures/Wildwood Enterprises.

Pontecorvo, G. (dir.) 1960. *Kapò*. Vides Cinematografica/Zebra Films/Francinex/Lovcen Film/Cineriz.

Porton, R. 1999. *Film and the Anarchist Imagination*. New York: Verso.

Powell, A. 2005. *Deleuze and Horror Film*. Edinburgh: Edinburgh University Press.

Powell, A. 2007. *Deleuze, Altered States and Film*. Edinburgh: Edinburgh University Press.

Prigogine, I. & I. Stengers 1984. *Order Out of Chaos: Man's New Dialogue with Nature*. New York: Bantam. Originally published in French as *La Nouvelle alliance: Métamorphose de la science* (Paris: Gallimard, 1979).

Pursley, D. 2005. "Moving in Time: Chantal Akerman's 'Toute une Nuit'". *MLN* **120**(5): 1192–205.

Quine, W. V. O. [1951] 1998. "On What There Is". In *Contemporary Readings in the Foundations of Metaphysics*, S. Laurence & C. Macdonald (eds), 32–45. Oxford: Blackwell.

Rancière, J. 1995. *On the Shores of Politics*, T. Heron (trans.). London: Verso.

Rancière, J. 1996. *Disagreement: Politics and Philosophy*, J. Rose (trans.). Minneapolis, MN: University of Minnesota Press.

Rancière, J. 1998. *La Parole muette: Essai sur les contradictions de la littérature*. Paris: Hachette.

Rancière, J. 1999. *Disagreement: Politics and Philosophy*, J. Rose (trans.). Minneapolis, MN: University of Minnesota Press.

Rancière, J. 2001a. "Ten Theses on Politics", R. Bowlby & D. Panagia (trans.). *Theory and Event* **5**: 3.

Rancière, J. 2001b. "Celui qui vient après: Les antinomies de la pensée critique". *Trafic* **37**: 142–50.

Rancière, J. 2002. "The Aesthetic Revolution and its Outcomes: Emplotments of Autonomy and Heteronomy". *New Left Review* **14** (March/April): 133–51.

Rancière, J. 2004a. "Aesthetics, Inaesthetics, Anti-Aesthetics". In *Think Again: Alain Badiou and the Future of Philosophy*, P. Hallward (ed.), 218–31. London: Continuum.

Rancière, J. 2004b. *The Flesh of Words: The Politics of Writing*, C. Mandell (trans.). Stanford, CA: Stanford University Press.

Rancière, J. 2004c. *Malaise dans l'esthétique*. Paris: Éditions du Seuil.

Rancière, J. 2004d. *The Philosopher and His Poor*, A. Parker (trans.). Durham, NC: Duke University Press.

Rancière, J. 2005. "Le Cinéaste, le peuple et les gouvernants". In his *Chronique des temps consensuels*, 109–14. Paris: Éditions du Seuil.

Rancière, J. 2006a. *Film Fables*, E. Battista (trans.). Oxford: Berg.

Rancière, J. 2006b. "Thinking between Disciplines: An Aesthetics of Knowledge", J. Roffe (trans.). *Parrhesia* **1**: 1–12.

Rancière, J. 2007a. *The Future of the Image*, G. Elliot (trans.). London: Verso.

Rancière, J. 2007b. "The Art of the Possible: Fulvia Carnevale and John Kelsey in Conversation with Jacques Rancière". *Artforum* (March): 254–69.

Rapper, I. (dir.) 1942. *Now, Voyager*. Warner Bros. Pictures.

Read, R. & J. Goodenough (eds) 2005. *Film as Philosophy: Essays on Cinema After Wittgenstein and Cavell*. Basingstoke: Palgrave Macmillan.

Redhead, S. 2004. *Paul Virilio: Theorist for an Accelerated Culture*. Toronto: University of Toronto Press.

Redhead, S. 2006. "The Art of the Accident: Paul Virilio and Accelerated Modernity". *Fast Capitalism* **2**(1): 1–12, www.fastcapitalism.com/ (accessed June 2009).

Reisner, C. (dir.) 1928. *Steamboat Bill, Jr.* Buster Keaton Productions/Joseph M. Schenck Productions.

Renoir, J. (dir.) 1931. *La chienne* [Isn't life a bitch?]. Les Établissements Braunberger-Richebé.

Renoir, J. (dir.) 1939. *La Règle du jeu* [The rules of the game]. Nouvelle édition française.

Resina, J. R. 1998. "Historical Discourse and the Propaganda Film: Reporting the Revolution in Barcelona". *New Literary History* **29**(1): 67–84.

Resnais, A. (dir.) 1959. *Nuit et brouillard* [Night and fog]. Argos Films.

Resnais, A. (dir.) 1959. *Hiroshima mon amour*. Argos Films/Como Films/Daiei Studios/Pathé Entertainment.

Resnais, A. (dir.) 1961. *L'Année dernière à Marienbad* [Last year at Marienbad]. Cocinor/Terra Film/Cormoran Films/Precitel/Como Film Production/Argos Films/Les Films Tamara/Cinétel/Silver Films/ Cineriz.

Resnais, A. (dir.) 1968. *Je t'aime, je t'aime*. Les Productions Fox Europa/Parc Film.

Riedelsheimer, T. (dir.) 2006. *Touch the Sound*. Filmquadrat/Skyline Productions.

Rio, E. del 2000. "The Body of Voyeurism: Mapping a Discourse of the Senses in Michael Powell's 'Peeping Tom'". *Camera Obscura* **15**(3): 115–49.

Rio, E. del 2005. "Alchemies of Thought in Godard's Cinema: Deleuze and Merleau-Ponty". *SubStance* **34**(3): 62–78.

Rivette, J. 1961. "De l'abjection". *Cahiers du cinéma* **126** (December): 54–5.

Rivette, J. (dir.) 1966. *La Religieuse*. Rome Paris Films/Société Nouvelle de Cinématographie.

Rivette, J. (dir.) 1969. *L'Amour fou*. Cocinor/Les Films Marceau/Sogexportfilm.

Riviere, J. 1986. "Womanliness as a Masquerade". In *Formations of Fantasy*, V. Burgin, J. Donald & C. Kaplan (eds), 35–44. London: Methuen.

Robinson, P. (dir.). 1972. *Asylum*. Peter Robinson Associates.

Rodowick, D. N. 1997. *Gilles Deleuze's Time Machine*. Durham, NC: Duke University Press.

Rodowick, D. N. 2001. *Reading the Figural, or, Philosophy after the New Media*. Durham, NC: Duke University Press.

Rodowick, D. N. 2007. *The Virtual Life of Film*. Cambridge, MA: Harvard University Press.

Roger, P. 1991. "Du casse à la passé". In *Devant la recrudescence des vols de sacs à main: Cinéma, télévision, information (1988–1991)*, S. Daney, 199–223. Lyon: Aléas.

Rohdie, S. 1990. *Antonioni*. London: BFI.

Rohmer, É. (dir.) 1976. *Die Marquise von O ...* [The Marquis of O]. Les Films du Losange/Filmproduktion Janus/Artemis/Hessischer Rundfunk (HR)/Gaumont.

Rohmer, É. (dir.) 2001. *L'Anglaise et le duc* [The lady and the duke]. Compagnie Eric Rohmer [CER]/Pathé Image Production.

Rollet, P. 2002. "Preface". In *La Maison cinéma et le monde 1*, P. Rollet, J. C. Biette & C. Manon (eds), 7–15. Paris: POL.

Rose, J. 1986. *Sexuality in the Field of Vision*. London: Verso.

Rosé, J. C. (dir.) 1994. *Jacques Derrida*. INA.

Rosenbaum, J. 1982/3. "Barthes and Film: 12 Suggestions". *Sight and Sound* **52**(1) (Winter): 50–53.

Rosenbaum, J. 2001. "Daney in English: A Letter to *Trafic*". *Trafic* **37**. Reprinted in *Senses of Cinema*, www.sensesofcinema.com/contents/01/13/daney.html (accessed June 2009).

Rosenbaum, J. 2005. "The Missing Image". *New Left Review* **34**: 145–51.

Rosenbaum, J. & A. Martin 2003. *Movie Mutations: The Changing Face of World Cinephilia*. London: BFI.

Rossellini, R. (dir.) 1945. *Roma, città aperta* [Rome, open city]. Excelsa Film.

Rossellini, R. (dir.) 1946. *Paisà* [Paisan]. Organizzazione Film Internazionali (OFI)/Foreign Film Productions.

Rossellini, R. (dir.) 1947. *Germania anno zero* [Germany, year zero]. Produzione Salvo D'Angelo/Tevere Film.

Rossellini, R. (dir.) 1954. *Viaggio in Italia* [Journey to Italy]. Italia Film/Junior Film/Sveva Film/Les Films Ariane/Francinex/S.G.C.

Rothman, W. 1984. *Hitchcock: The Murderous Gaze*. Cambridge, MA: Harvard University Press.

Rothman, W. 1985. "Against 'The System of Suture'". See Nichols (1985), 451–9.

Royle, N. 2005. "Blind Cinema". In *Derrida: Screenplay and Essays on the Film*, K. Dick & A. Ziering Kofman (eds), 10–21. Manchester: Manchester University Press.

Rushdie, S. 1992. *The Wizard of Oz*. London: BFI.

Russell, K. (dir.) 1980. *Altered States*. Warner Bros. Pictures.

Rushton, R. 2002. "Cinema's Double: Some Reflections on Metz". *Screen* **43**(2): 107–18.

Ruttmann, W. (dir.) 1927. *Berlin: Die Sinfonie der Großstadt* [Berlin: symphony of a great city]. Deutsche Vereins-Film/Les Productions Fox Europa.

Sagan, L. (dir.) 1931. *Mädchen in Uniform* [Girls in uniform]. Deutsche Film-Gemeinschaft

Said, E. 1978. *Orientalism*. New York: Pantheon.

Satrapi, M. & V. Paronnaud (dirs) 2007. *Persepolis*. 2. 4. 7. Films/Kennedy/Marshall Company/France 3 Cinéma/French Connection Animations/Diaphana Films/Celluloid Dreams/Sony Pictures Classics/Sofica Europacorp/Soficinéma/Centre National de la Cinématographie (CNC)/Région Ile-de-France/Fondation GAN pour le Cinéma/Procirep/Angoa-Agicoa.

Schelling, F. W. J. [1800] 1978. *The System of Transcendental Idealism*, P. Heath (trans.). Charlottesville, VA: University Press of Virginia.

Schiller, F. [1793] 1967. *On the Aesthetic Education of Man*, E. M. Wilkinson & L. A. Willoughby (trans.). Oxford: Clarendon Press.

Schlüpmann, H. 1987. "Phenomenology of Film: On Siegfried Kracauer's Writings of the 1920s", T. Y. Levin (trans.). *New German Critique* **40**: 97–114.

Schlüpmann, H. 1991. "The Subject of Survival: On Kracauer's *Theory of Film*", J. Gaines (trans.). *New German Critique* **54**: 111–26.

Schlüpmann, H. 1994. "Re-reading Nietzsche Through Kracauer: Towards a Feminist Perspective on Film History", I. Flett (trans.). *Film History* **6**: 80–93.

Schlüpmann, H. 2007. *Ungeheure Einbildungskraft: Die dunkle Moralität des Kinos*. Frankfurt: Stroemfeld.

Schmidt, J. (dir.) 1978. *Comme les anges déchus de la planète Saint-Michel* [Fallen angels from the planet St Michel]. Atelier 8.

Schroeder, F. 2005. "The Old and the New and the New Old: A Conceptual Approach Towards Performing the Changing Body". *HZ* **7** (December), www.hz-journal.org/n7/schroeder.html (accessed June 2009).

Schwab, M. 2000. "Escape from the Image: Deleuze's Image-Ontology". See Flaxman (2000), 109–40.

Scott, R. (dir.) 1979. *Alien*. Brandywine Productions/Twentieth Century-Fox Productions.

Sellars, S. 2000. "Retrospecto: La Jetée". Available online at www.simonsellars.com/retrospecto-la-jetee/ (accessed June 2009).

Sembene, O. (dir.) 1975. *Xala*. Films Domireew/Ste. Me. Production du Senegal.

Serres, M. 2000. *The Birth of Physics*, J. Hawkes (trans.). Manchester: Clinamen Press.

Shaviro, S. 1993. *The Cinematic Body*. Minneapolis, MN: University of Minnesota Press.

Silly Symphonies 1929–39. Walt Disney Productions. www.disneyshorts.org/miscellaneous/silly.html (accessed June 2009).

Simondon, G. 1964. *L'individu et sa genèse physico-biologique*. Paris: Presses Universitaires de France.

Singer, B. 1988. "Film, Photography, and Fetish: The Analyses of Christian Metz". *Cinema Journal* **27**(4): 4–22.

Sirk, D. (dir.) 1959. *Imitation of Life*. Universal International Pictures.

Sjostrom, V. (dir.) 1924. *He Who gets Slapped*. Metro-Goldwyn-Mayer (MGM).

Snow, M. (dir.) 1971. *La Région Centrale*. Canadian Filmmakers' Distribution Centre.

Snyder, Z. (dir.) 2004. *Dawn of the Dead*. Strike Entertainment/New Amsterdam Entertainment/Metropolitan Filmexport/Toho-Towa.

Sobchack, V. 1991. *The Address of the Eye: A Phenomenology of Film Experience*. Princeton, NJ: Princeton University Press.

Sobchack, V. [1994] 2004. "The Scene of the Screen: Envisaging Photographic, Cinematic and Electronic Presence", revised from his 1994 essay. In his *Carnal Thoughts: Embodiment and Moving Image Culture*, 135–62. Berkeley, CA: University of California Press.

Soderbergh, S. (dir.) 1989. *Sex, Lies and Videotape*. Outlaw Productions/Virgin.

Sokurov, A. (dir.) 2002. *Russkiy kovcheg* [Russian ark]. State Hermitage Museum, The Hermitage Bridge Studio/ Ministry of Culture of the Russian Federation (in association with) (as Ministry of Culture of the Russian Federation, Department of the Stage Support of Cinematography)/Mitteldeutsche Medienfürderung Filmboard Berlin Brandenburg (in association with)/Kulturelle Filmförderung des bundes Filmlörderung Hamburg (in association with)/Filmbüro Nordrhein-Westfalen Kulturelle Filmborderung Sachsen-Anhalt (in association with)/WDR/Arte (in association with)/Fora Film (in association with)/Koppmedia (in association with)/NHK (in association with)/Seville Pictures (in association with)/YLE TV1 (in association with) (as YLE/TV1)/Danmarks Radio (DR) (in association with) (as DR 1)/AST Studio (in association with)/Mariinsky Theatre (in association with)/Egoli Tossell Film.

Solanas, F. 1970. "Fernando Solanas: An Interview". *Film Quarterly* **24**(1), 37–43.

Solanas, F. & O. Getino 1997. "Towards a Third Cinema: Notes and Experiences for the Development of a Cinema of Liberation in the Third World". In *New Latin American Cinema*, vol. 1. M. I. Martin (ed.), 33–58. Detroit, MI: Wayne State University Press.

Sonnenfeld, B. (dir.) 1997. *Men in Black*. Amblin Entertainment/Columbia Pictures.

Sontag, S. 1979. *On Photography*. Harmondsworth: Penguin.

Sorfa, D. 2001. "Hieroglyphs and Carapaces: Laura Mulvey's *Fetishism and Curiosity*". *Film-Philosophy* **5**(5), www.film-philosophy.com/vol5-2001/n5sorfa.html (accessed August 2009).

Stengers, I. 2000. *The Invention of Modern Science*, D. W. Smith (trans.). Minneapolis, MN: University of Minnesota Press.

Sternberg, J. von (dir.) 1930. *Der Blaue Engel* [The blue angel]. Universum Film (UFA).

Sternberg, J. von (dir.) 1930. *Morocco*. Paramount Pictures.

Stiegler, B. 1998. *Techniques and Time, 1: The Fault of Epimetheus*, R. Beardsworth & G. Collins (trans.). Stanford, CA: Stanford University Press. Originally published in French as *La technique et le temps, 1: La faute d'Épiméthée* (Paris: Galilée, 1994).

Sullivan, D. 1997. "Noemata or No Matter?: Forcing Phenomenology into Film Theory". *Film-Philosophy* **1**(3) (July), www.film-philosophy.com/vol1-1997/n3sullivan.htm (accessed July 2009).

Szaloky, M. 2002. "Sounding Images in Silent Film: Visual Acoustics in Murnau's 'Sunrise'". *Cinema Journal* **41**(2): 109–31.

Tahimik, K. (dir.) 1977. *Mababangong bangungot* [The perfumed nightmare]. Tahimik.

Tarantino, Q. (dir.) 1994. *Pulp Fiction*. A Band Apart/Jersey Films/Miramax Films.

Tarkovsky, A. (dir.) 1972. *Solyaris* [*Solaris*]. Creative Unit of Writers & Cinema Workers/Moxfilm/Unit Four.

Tati, J. (dir.) 1953. *Les Vacances de Monsieur Hulot* [Monsieur Hulot's holiday]. Cady Films/Specta Films.

Taylor, A. (dir.) 2005. *Žižek!* Zeitgeist Films.

Taylor, R. (ed.) 1998. *The Eisenstein Reader*, R. Taylor & W. Powell (trans.). London: BFI.

Taylor, V. E. & G. Lambert (eds) 2006. *Jean-François Lyotard: Critical Evaluations in Cultural Theory*. Abingdon: Routledge.

Temple, M. & M. Witts (eds) 2004. *The French Cinema Book*. London: BFI.

Thacker, E. 2005. *The Global Genome: Biotechnology, Politics, and Culture*. Cambridge, MA: MIT Press.

Toubiana, S. 2007. "Preface to the French edition". In *Postcards from the Cinema*, S. Daney, P. Grant (trans.), 11–14. Oxford: Berg.

Trahair, L. 2007. *The Comedy of Philosophy: Sense and Nonsense in Early Cinematic Slapstick*. Albany, NY: SUNY Press.

Truffaut, F. (dir.) 1959. *Les Quatre cents coups* [The 400 blows]. Les Films du Carrosse/Sédif Productions.

Truffaut, F. 1985. *Hitchcock*, rev. edn, F. Truffaut & H. Scott (trans.). New York: Simon & Schuster.

Van Dormael, J. (dir.) 1991. *Toto le héro* [Toto the hero]. Cama;+/France 3 Cinéma/Het Ministerie van Cultuur van de Vlaamse Gemeenschap/Iblis Films/La Direction de L'Audiovisuel de Communauté Française de Belgique/Les Entrepeneurs de l'Audiovisuel Européen/Metropolis Filmproduction/Philippe Dussart/Programme MEDIA de la Communauté Européene/Radio Télévision Belge Francophone (RTBF)/Zweites Deutsches Fernsehen (ZDF).

Varda, A. (dir.) 2000. *Les Glaneurs et la glaneuse* [The gleaners and I]. Ciné Tamaris.

Vasulka, W. (dir.) 1987. *The Art of Memory*. Available from Video Data Bank, Chicago, www.vdb.org/smackn. acgi$artistdetail?VASULKAW (accessed August 2009).

Vidor, K. (dir.) 1937. *Stella Dallas*. Samuel Goldwyn Company.

Vidor, K. (dir.) 1946. *Duel in the Sun*. Vanguard Films/The Selznick Studio.

Vidor, K. (dir.) 1949. *The Fountainhead*. Warner Bros. Pictures.

Virilio, P. 1986. *Speed and Politics: An Essay on Dromology*, M. Polizzotti (trans.). New York: Semiotext(e). Originally published in French as *Vitesse et politique: essai de dromologie* (Paris: Galilée, 1977).

Virilio, P. 1989. *War and Cinema: The Logistics of Perception*, P. Camiller (trans.). London: Verso. Originally published in French as *Guerre et cinéma 1: Logistique de la perception* (Paris: L'Etoile, 1984).

Virilio, P. 1990. *Popular Defence and Ecological Struggles*. New York: Semiotext(e).

Virilio, P. 1991a. *The Aesthetics of Disappearance*, P. Beitchman (trans.). New York: Semiotext(e). Originally published in French as *Esthetique de la disparition* (Paris: Balland, 1980).

Virilio, P. 1991b. *The Lost Dimension*, D. Moshenberg (trans.). New York: Semiotext(e). Originally published in French as *L'Espace critique* (Paris: Christian Bourgois, 1984).

Virilio, P. 1994a. *The Vision Machine*. Bloomington, IN: Indiana University Press.

Virilio, P. 1994b. *Bunker Archaeology*, G. Collins (trans.). New York: Princeton Architectural Press.

Virilio, P. 1997. *Open Sky*, J. Rose (trans.). New York: Verso.

Virilio, P. 2000a. *A Landscape of Events*, J. Rose (trans.). Cambridge, MA: MIT Press.

Virilio, P. 2000b. *Strategies of Deception*, C. Turner (trans.). London: Verso.

Virilio, P. 2001a. "Le Mur de la lumière". *Trafic* **37**: 225–9.

Virilio, P. 2001b. "The Last Vehicle". In *Hatred of Capitalism: A Semiotext(e) Reader*, C. Kraus & S. Lotringer (eds), 151–60. New York: Semiotext(e).

Virilio, P. 2002. *Desert Screen: War at the Speed of Light*, M. Degener (trans.). London: Continuum.

Virilio, P. 2003. *Art and Fear*, J. Rose (trans.). London: Continuum.

Virilio, P. 2005. *Negative Horizon: An Essay in Dromoscopy*, M. Degener (trans.). London: Continuum. Originally published in French as *L'horizon négatif* (Paris: Galilée, 1984).

Virilio, P. 2008. "Le krach actuel représente l'accident intégral par excellence", www.lemonde.fr/opinions/article/2008/10/18/le-krach-actuel-represente-l-accident-integral-par-excellence_1108473_3232.html (accessed July 2009).

Virilio, P. & S. Lotringer 2002. *Crepuscular Dawn*, M. Taormina (trans.). New York: Semiotext(e).

Virilio, P. & S. Lotringer 2008. *Pure War: Twenty-five Years Later*, M. Polizzotti, B. O'Keeffe & P. Beitchman (trans.). New York: Semiotext(e).

Virilio, P. & C. Oliveira 1996. "The Silence of the Lambs: Paul Virilio in Conversation". *Cultural Theory* **19**(1–2).

Virilio, P. & C. Parent 1996. *The Function of the Oblique: The Architecture of Claude Parent and Paul Virilio 1963–1969*. London: Architectural Association.

Virilio, P. & P. Petit 1999. *Politics of the Very Worst*. New York: Semiotext(e).

Virilio, P. & L. Wilson 1994. "Cyberwar, God and Television: Interview with Paul Virilio". *ctheory* **62**: 1–7, www.ctheory.net/articles.aspx?id=62 (accessed June 2009).

Visconti, L. (dir.) 1963. *Il Gattopardo* [The leopard]. Titanus (Rome)/Société Nouvelle Pathé Cinéma (as S. N. Pathé Cinéma)/S.G.C. (Paris).

Visconti, L. (dir.) 1971. *Morte a Venezia* [Death in Venice]. Alfa Cinematografica.

von Ernst Jünger, H. 1930. *Krieg und Krieger* [War and warrior]. Berlin: Junker & Dünnhaupt.

von Trier, L. (dir.) 1996. *Breaking the Waves*. Argus Film Produktie/Arte/Canal+/CoBo Fonds/Det Danske Filminstitut/Eurimages/European Script Fund/Finnish Film Foundation/Icelandic Film (as Icelandic Film Corporation)/La Sept Cinéma/Liberator Productions/Lucky Red/Media Investment Club/ Memfis Film/ Nederlands Fonds voor de Film/Nordisk Film- & TV-Fond/Northern Lights/Norwegian Film Institute/ October Films/Philippe Bober/SVT Drama (Stockholm)/Svenska Filminstitutet (SFI)/TV1000 AB/Trust Film Svenska/VPRO Television/Villealfa Filmproduction Oy/Yleisradio (YLE)/Zentropa Entertainments/Zweites Deutsches Fernsehen (ZDF).

Wachowski, A. & L. Wachowski (dirs) 1999. *The Matrix*. Warner/Village Roadshow/Groucho II.

Wachowski, A. & L. Wachowski (dirs) 2003. *The Matrix Reloaded*. Warner/Village Roadshow/NPV.

Wachowski, A. & L. Wachowski (dirs) 2003. *The Matrix Revolutions*. Warner/Village Roadshow/ NPV.

Wartenberg, T. 2007. *Thinking on Screen: Film as Philosophy*. London & New York: Routledge.

Watts, P. 2004. "Images d'Égalité". In *La Philosophie déplacée: Autour de Jacques Rancière*, L. Cornu & P. Vermeren (eds), 361–70. Paris: Horlieu.

Watts, P. 2005. "Roland Barthes's Cold-War Cinema". *SubStance* **34**(3): 17–32.

Welles, O. (dir.) 1941. *Citizen Kane*. Mercury Productions/ RKO Radio Pictures.

Welles, O. (dir.) 1958. *Touch of Evil*. Universal International Pictures (UI).

Wheeler, J. A. 1990. *A Journey into Gravity and Spacetime*. New York: Scientific American Library.

Wicclair, M. R. 1978. "Film Theory and Hugo Münsterberg's *The Film: A Psychological Study*". *Journal of Aesthetic Education* **12**(3) (July): 33–50.

Wiene, R. (dir.) 1920. *Das Cabinet des Dr. Caligari* [The cabinet of Dr. Caligari]. Decla-Bioscop AG.

Williams, J. S. 2004. "The Exercise was Profitable, Monsieur Daney". See Temple & Witt (eds) (2004), 265–72.

Williams, L. 2008. *Screening Sex*. Durham, NC: Duke University Press.

Williams, R. 1958. "Culture is Ordinary". In his *Resources of Hope: Culture, Democracy, Socialism*, 3–14. London: Verso.

Wilson, D. (ed.) 2000. *Cahiers du Cinéma – Volume IV: 1973–1978: History, Ideology, Cultural Struggle*. London & New York: Routledge.

Wiseman, F. (dir.) 1967. *Titicut Follies*. Zipporah Films.

Wolf, E. 1998. "Review: *Disgraced Monuments*". *American Historical Review* **103**(1): 310–11.

Wollen, P. 1982. *Readings and Writings: Semiotic Counter-Strategies*. London: Verso.

Wollen, P. 2001. "Conférence de Rotterdam". *Trafic* **37**: 59–74.

Woodward, A. 2006. "Jean-François Lyotard (1924–1998)". In *The Internet Encyclopedia of Philosophy*, www.iep.utm.edu/l/Lyotard.html (accessed June 2009).

Yeghiayan, E. "Jean-François Lyotard: A Bibliography". *The Critical Theory Institute*. Irvine, CA: University of California. Available online at www.lib.uci.edu/libraries/pubs/scctr/Wellek/lyotard/index.html (accessed September 2009).

Young, H. (dir.) 1934. *The Scarlet Pimpernel*. London Film Productions.

Zepke, S. 2005. *Art as Abstract Machine: Ontology and Aesthetics in Deleuze and Guattari*. London & New York: Routledge.

Zhang, X. 1998. "Marxism and the Historicity of Dialectics: An Interview with Fredric Jameson". *New Literary History* **29**(3): 353–83.

Žižek, S. 1991. *Looking Awry: An Introduction to Jacques Lacan through Popular Culture*. Cambridge, MA: MIT Press.

Žižek, S. 1993. *Tarrying with the Negative: Kant, Hegel and the Critique of Ideology*. Durham, NC: Duke University Press.

Žižek, S. 1997. *The Plague of Fantasies*. London: Verso.

Žižek, S. 1999. "The Thing from Inner Space: On Tarkovsky". *Angelaki: Journal of the Theoretical Humanities* **4**(3): 221–30.

Žižek, S. 2000a. "*Da Capo senza Fine*". In *Contingency, Hegemony, Universality: Contemporary Dialogues on the Left*, J. Butler, E. Laclau & S. Žižek, 213–63. London: Verso.

Žižek, S. 2000b. *The Art of the Ridiculous Sublime: On David Lynch's Lost Highway*. Seattle, WA: Walter Chapin Simpson Center for the Humanities.

Žižek, S. 2001. *The Fright of Real Tears: Krzystof Kieslowski between Theory and Post-theory*. London: BFI.

Žižek, S. 2002. *Enjoy Your Symptom! Jacques Lacan in Hollywood and Out*, 2nd edn. London & New York: Routledge.

Žižek, S. 2004. *Organs Without Bodies: On Deleuze and Consequences*. London & New York: Routledge.

Žižek, S. 2006a. *The Parallax View*. Cambridge, MA: MIT Press.

Žižek, S. 2006b. *How to Read Lacan*. London: Granta.

Žižek, S. 2008. *Violence: Six Sideways Reflections*. London: Profile.

Zunzunegui, S. 1989. *Pensar la imagen* [Thinking the image]. Madrid: Catedra.

INDEX